PS
310
E8C6
1973

REGULATIONS

FINES ARE CHARGED FOR OVERDUE AND/OR LOST LIBRARY MATERIALS; AND, IN ACCORDANCE WITH BOARD POLICY 8741 "GRADES TRANSCRIPTS, DEGREES, AND REGISTRATION PRIVILEGES SHALL BE WITHHELD UNTIL ALL LIBRARY BOOKS OR OTHER LIBRARY MATERIALS ARE RETURNED (TO THE LIBRARY CIRCULATION DESK)."

Contra Costa College Library
2600 Mission Bell Drive
San Pablo, California 94806

COSMIC OPTIMISM

COSMIC OPTIMISM

A Study of the Interpretation of Evolution by American Poets from Emerson to Robinson

BY

FREDERICK WILLIAM CONNER

OCTAGON BOOKS

A DIVISION OF FARRAR, STRAUS AND GIROUX

New York   1973

Copyright 1949 by the University of Florida Press

Reprinted 1973
by special arrangement with the University of Florida Press

OCTAGON BOOKS
A DIVISION OF FARRAR, STRAUS & GIROUX, INC.
19 Union Square West
New York, N. Y. 10003

Library of Congress Cataloging in Publication Data

Conner, Frederick William, 1909-
    Cosmic optimism.

    Reprint of the ed. published by University of Florida Press, Gainesville.

    Originally presented as the author's thesis, University of Pennsylvania, 1949.

    Bibliography: p.
    1. American poetry—19th century—History and criticism.
    2. American poetry—20th century—History and criticism.
    3. Evolution in literature. I. Title.
PS310.E8C6   1973   811'.009'3   73-4283
ISBN 0-374-91909-7

Manufactured by Braun-Brumfield, Inc.
Ann Arbor, Michigan

Printed in the United States of America

TO
J. B. C.

PREFACE

THIS study had its origin nearly fifteen years ago in curiosity concerning the numerous but usually vague references in histories and critical studies to the influence of the theory of evolution in American literature. Undertaken in a quite virginal state of ignorance and planlessness, it was intended in the beginning to be merely a survey of the treatment of this theory by American poets between the arbitrarily chosen limits of Emerson and Edwin Arlington Robinson. To some extent it remains just that. Though no pretense of completeness is made, probably the bulk of the important references have been noted, and space has been allotted generously to figures who would have been omitted or passed over briefly if the aim had been only critical or philosophical and not historical as well.

Investigation had not proceeded far, however, before a fact began to emerge that was to give the work a more precise unity. That theories of evolution existed to be written about at all was of course almost entirely attributable to the sciences; but in what the poets did with these theories their debt to science appeared to be very slight, limited largely to vocabulary, imagery, and the bare fact that certain evolutions had occurred. The poets showed little interest in the detailed evidence by which the historicity of these evolutions was argued or in the exact mechanisms by which they had taken place. What interested them rather was how the new theories could be related to deeply rooted and persistent convictions concerning the benevolence and efficacy of God and the spiritual nature of man. As might have been predicted, the problem of evolution for the poets was not scientific but philosophical, the facing of certain speculative predicaments, most of them time-honored, that had been raised anew by these theories. For this reason, though scientific influences will not be neglected in what follows, primary emphasis will be placed on the analysis and definition of the philosophic positions of the poets as revealed by their handling of the theories.

In their treatments, moreover, the poets showed a large measure of agreement; and herein was found the unity of the work. It is a commonplace of history that the scientific theories of evolution had a destructive effect in many quarters on just those religious and philosophical convictions about which the poets were so deeply concerned. With very few exceptions, however, the poets' devotion to these beliefs remained quite unshaken. They not only continued to believe in the essentially spiritual nature of man, but they expanded this belief to include the whole cosmos. The entire evolution of the cosmos, most of them held, has been guided by forces somehow akin to this nature, in sympathy with its ends, and working toward its fulfillment. What they were presenting, in short, was not so much the evolutionary theories of science as the old drama of Providence revised to accord with these theories. With revisions suited to the new views and to the current religious humanism, they followed an age-old theological argument which Professor Perry Miller has pointed out as a fundamental principle of their seventeenth-century predecessors: "The Puritans were led to a further deduction: if the creation is ruled by God's will, and His will is itself the norm of justice and equity, the universe must be essentially good. They may be described as cosmic optimists." I must add that though I should have been proud to borrow from Professor Miller, I had used "cosmic optimism" as the title of early drafts of this study some time before I knew of his use of the term.

The theme of the present work may thus be said to be the interpretation of evolution as a progress that is inevitable because in some sense it is divinely motivated. Two consequences of this theme for the proportioning of the work call for a brief further comment. Thus, for one thing, it might be objected that greater attention has been given to the so-called "genteel" poets than is justified by their place in our literature. If it is recalled, however, that this label does not refer merely to politeness or conventionality, but to the attempt on the part of men born in an age of science and business to "find a new status for their inherited theology," the proportioning will be seen to have justification. In this sense, the reflection in American poetry of "the genteel tradition in American philosophy" is very nearly the subject of the work. In the second place, the nearer time limit of the study has proved less arbitrary than it seemed when first chosen. As is pointed out in Part IV, both evolution and optimism have continued to play a part in the writing of poets junior to Robinson, but the interpretation of evolution which constitutes the unity of this study is seldom to be found in that writing. I have no doubt that an interesting essay could be written on the treatment of evolution by these younger poets, but

PREFACE

I also have no doubt that it would tell a different story from that presented here.

In carrying out my study, probably my greatest debt has been to a number of men whom I have known only in their writings, especially, among the living, to Joseph Warren Beach, Arthur O. Lovejoy, Ralph Barton Perry, and George Santayana, and, among the dead, to John Fiske and Josiah Royce. To them, or in their memory, I wish to express deep gratitude and admiration. I also owe much, however, to others with whom my relations have been more personal: to Professor Arthur H. Quinn, for stimulating criticism when it was most needed; to Professor Sculley Bradley, who directed the preparation of the work until its completion as a dissertation in 1944, for unfailing kindness and good advice of many kinds; to many of my colleagues, past and present, who have answered my questions and read portions of my manuscript, especially Professors George G. Fox, C. A. Robertson, Herman E. Spivey, and Harry R. Warfel; to Professor Joe Lee Davis, who read the entire original manuscript and offered many helpful suggestions; to Professor Lewis F. Haines, Editor of the University of Florida Press, and to his staff, for many painstaking and laborious hours spent in making the text presentable; finally, to my wife, whose sympathy and patience have been a resource.

F. W. C.

University of Florida
April 1, 1949

ACKNOWLEDGMENTS

Permission to quote copyrighted material is gratefully acknowledged to publishers as follows: American Book Company: *Major American Poets,* edited by Harry Hayden Clark; *Oliver Wendell Holmes: Representative Selections,* edited by S. I. Hayakawa and Howard Mumford Jones. Columbia University Press: *Leaves of Grass, Reproduced from the First Edition,* edited by Clifton J. Furness; *The Letters of Ralph Waldo Emerson,* edited by Ralph Leslie Rusk; *The Orient in American Transcendentalism,* by Arthur Christy. Dodd, Mead & Company: *Poems,* by W. H. Venable. Doubleday & Company, Inc.: *The Complete Edition of Frank Norris; Leaves of Grass: Inclusive Edition,* edited by Emory Holloway; *The Uncollected Poetry and Prose of Walt Whitman,* edited by Emory Holloway. Didier, Publishers: *Mind at the End of Its Tether,* by H. G. Wells. E. P. Dutton & Company, Inc.: *Cosmic Consciousness,* by R. M. Bucke; *New England: Indian Summer,* by Van Wyck Brooks. Harcourt, Brace & Company, Inc.: *Diedrich Knickerbocker's History of New York,* edited by Stanley Williams and Tremaine MacDowell; *Main Currents in American Thought,* by Vernon L. Parrington; *The Metaphysical Foundations of Modern Physical Science,* by E. A. Burtt; *The Roamer and Other Poems,* by G. E. Woodberry. Harper and Brothers: *A History of the American Drama from the Civil War to the Present Day,* by Arthur Hobson Quinn; *New Letters of James Russell Lowell,* edited by M. A. DeWolfe Howe. Harvard University Press: *The Great Chain of Being,* by Arthur O. Lovejoy; *Walt Whitman's Workshop,* edited by Clifton J. Furness. Henry Holt & Company, Inc.: *Collected Poems* and *A Witness Tree,* by Robert Frost; *Creative Evolution,* by Henri Bergson; *Fire and Ice,* by Lawrence Thompson; *Selected Poems,* by George Sterling. Houghton Mifflin Company: *The Education of Henry Adams; The Heart of Burroughs's Journals,* edited by Clara Barrus; *Introduction to Philosophy,* by G. T. W. Patrick; *John Jay Chapman and His Letters,* by M. A. DeWolfe Howe; *The Making of the Modern Mind,* by J. H. Randall, Jr.; *Selected Poems of William Vaughn Moody,* edited by Robert Morss Lovett. The Johns Hopkins Press: *Primitivism and the Idea of Progress,* by Lois Whitney. Alfred A. Knopf, Inc.: *The*

Works of Stephen Crane, edited by Wilson Follett; *The Collected Poems of Stephen Crane,* edited by Wilson Follett. Little, Brown & Company: *Pedlar's Progress,* by Odell Shepard. Liveright Publishing Corporation: *Robinson Jeffers, the Man and the Artist,* by George Sterling. Longmans, Green & Company, Inc.: *The Present Conflict of Ideals,* by Ralph Barton Perry. The Macmillan Company: *The Cambridge History of American Literature; The New Poetry,* edited by Harriet Monroe and Alice Corbin Henderson; *A Poet's Life,* by Harriet Monroe; *Edwin Arlington Robinson,* by Hermann Hagedorn; *Selected Letters of Edwin Arlington Robinson,* edited by Ridgely Torrence; *The Collected Poems of Edwin Arlington Robinson; Contemporary American Philosophy,* edited by G. P. Adams and W. P. Montague; *The Concept of Nature in Nineteenth-Century English Poetry,* by Joseph Warren Beach; *The Idea of Progress,* by J. B. Bury; *The Phenomenology of Mind,* by G. F. W. Hegel; *Science and the Modern World,* by Alfred North Whitehead; *The Emergency of Modern America,* by Allan Nevins. The New York Public Library: *George Edward Woodberry: An Appreciation,* by John Erskine. W. W. Norton & Company, Inc.: *Mysticism and Logic,* by Bertrand Russell. Oxford University Press: *American Renaissance,* by F. O. Matthiessen. Random House, Inc.: *A Bibliography of the Works of Robinson Jeffers,* compiled by S. S. Alberts; *The Selected Poetry of Robinson Jeffers.* Charles Scribner's Sons: *First Adventures in Philosophy,* by Vergilius Ferm; *From the Greeks to Darwin,* by H. F. Osborn; *History of Philosophy,* by Alfred Weber and R. B. Perry; *The Nature and Destiny of Man,* by Reinhold Niebuhr; *True Humanism,* by Jacques Maritain; *The Last Puritan, Realms of Being, Reason in Art, Some Turns of Thought in Modern Philosophy,* and *Winds of Doctrine,* by George Santayana. The University of North Carolina Press: *The American State University,* by Norman Foerster; *Sidney Lanier,* by Aubrey H. Starke. Vanguard Press, Inc.: *Shall Not Perish from the Earth,* by Ralph Barton Perry. The John C. Winston Company: *Edgar Allan Poe, the Man,* by M. E. Phillips.

I am also indebted to Mr. Edgar Lee Masters, for excerpts taken from *Across Spoon River, Invisible Landscapes, The Open Sea,* and *Toward the Gulf;* and to Professor Perry Miller, for an excerpt taken from *The New England Mind.*

F. W. C.

CONTENTS

Part One

BEFORE DARWIN: THE PATTERN

I.	Introduction	3
II.	Emerson: The Beginnings	37
III.	Poe's *Eureka:* The Problem of Mechanism	67
IV.	Whitman: High Tide	92

Part Two

AFTER DARWIN: QUESTION AND COMPROMISE

V.	The Coming of Darwin	131
VI.	Minor Poets: Straws in the Wind	139
VII.	Bryant, Longfellow, and Lowell: Rejection, Indifference, Discomfort	167
VIII.	Taylor and Lanier: The Romantic Evolutionism Again	191
IX.	Holmes: Evolution Without Transformism?	211

Part Three

THE END OF THE CENTURY: THE "GENTEEL TRADITION"

X.	The Persistence of Teleology	235
XI.	The Influence of Spencer and Darwin: Sill and Certain Minor Poets	247
XII.	The "Genteel Tradition": Stedman, Gilder, and Cawein	275
XIII.	The Paradox of the "Genteel Tradition": Hovey, Lodge, and Moody	294

Part Four

THE TWILIGHT OF COSMIC OPTIMISM

XIV.	Some New Turns of Thought, Less Cosmic and Less Optimistic	331
XV.	Shifting Ground: Some of Robinson's Contemporaries	350
XVI.	Robinson	365

Notes 375
Bibliography 433
Index 443

PART ONE

BEFORE DARWIN: THE PATTERN

I

INTRODUCTION: THE TWO STREAMS OF EVOLUTIONARY THOUGHT

According to Professor G. P. Conger in his instructive little book on evolution in the "Philosophy for the Laymen" series, the general concept of evolution is made up of three subordinate ideas: change in time, serial order, and inherent causes.[1] Technicalities aside, the significance of the first two of these ideas is obvious, and if the third requires any explanation it too becomes clear as soon as it is remembered that evolution is a genetic process; for in such a process each new stage, as the product of the stages preceding, must be said to be in some sense the consequence of causes operating within the series rather than upon it from without. It should be recognized that the rigorous definition of evolution is a highly complex matter much disputed both now and formerly by scientists and philosophers. For the purposes of the present work, however, which will be concerned only with a popular and rather old-fashioned interpretation of the idea, the bare abstraction may be defined simply in Professor Conger's terms as serial change in time brought about by inherent causes. Ralph Barton Perry's definition is not dissimilar:

An evolutionary process is one in which *individualities and novelties may be understood as successive phases of one orderly change.* A thing may be said to have evolved when, having a specific character of its own, it is nevertheless an outgrowth of the past; when it can be understood as produced by the same forces as those which produced its antecedents, and as coming in its own proper turn.[2]

On their own level one can scarcely quarrel with these definitions, which are simply analytical renderings of common usage, and they would suffice here for introductory purposes if it were not that a more extended statement will serve to elicit some of the problems and basic principles of the discussion to follow. In the first place, the definitions present merely the bare bones of the idea and need to be given some more specific content before they can be of much service in such a historical study as this. Of the many possible applications of the general concept, the only one that has had sweeping consequences in the speculations of men has had to do with the universe and its inhabitants, telling how they have come to be what they are and how they shall become what they will be. One may speak of the evolution of a mathematically plotted curve, of the foetus in the womb, of a character in fiction, or of the life of an individual soul, but none of these evolutions has more than a passing interest for the student of the history of ideas in modern times. The area of reference of the term in this historically most important sense has been well marked off by A. S. Packard, the American biographer of Lamarck, in these terms:

The evolution theory, in its broadest aspect, undertakes to explain the origin of the universe, of all created things material and immaterial; and more especially the origin of our own planet, together with the plants and animals living and extinct, including man, his physical and mental nature.[3]

The second, and more important, specification of the definitions has to do with direction of change. The bare concept of evolution presupposes directional change in some sense; otherwise it would be impossible to speak of its serial order. True, in particular cases this direction need not be constant and unvaried, but may be, and indeed is likely to be, interrupted by phases of arrest or reversal. This is notably true in the evolution of life, in which the development is ramifying rather than unilinear and the directional movement "on the whole"[4] rather than in all particulars. Moreover, the direction is not necessarily from worse to better. The theory of evolution per se has nothing to say of values, and this fact, coupled with grave and reasonable doubts concerning the future, if not of values themselves, has caused many recent writers carefully to avoid identifying evolution and progress. Evolution, we are told, is a fact, but progress is a myth.[5] And yet, if we take man as our point of reference and criterion, it is impossible to deny that there has been a progress in the whole evolution of at least this planet, whether there will continue to be or not. Each of the principal steps in this evolution—the formation of the earth, the rise of life, of the vertebrates, of mammals—is in restrospect a step in his direction, and, if he is the standard, this development must be interpreted as a movement from worse to better. This, moreover, and more than this, was the heart of the theory of evolution to most of the

INTRODUCTION 5

American literary men in the nineteenth century who accepted it. They believed not only that there had been such a progress, but that it was necessitated and would continue in the future. The idea of the progress of civilization was already well established when the modern theories of evolution began to make their appearance, and it not only helped to cushion their impact but was readily merged with them. Almost to a man the poets who will be studied here heartily seconded Emerson's dictum, "melioration is the law."[6]

This conviction, moreover, was not simply an inference from the findings of science. The advance from low to high in the geological series offered suggestion and substantiation, but it was neither the logical nor the historical basis of the meliorism of the poets. It showed only what *had* taken place, while to the prophets of this meliorism the advance *had to* take place. This could only mean that something capable of human and moral ends was at work in the cosmic processes guiding them in directions regarded by men as beneficent. True, Herbert Spencer in the nineteenth century and Julian Huxley in the twentieth have attempted to base such a necessitated progress on purely mechanical principles, but Spencer succeeded only by the circular reasoning that anything is good which advances the process of evolution[7] and Huxley by the dubious Darwinian argument that "there will be variations in every direction which will have survival value, and some of these will be progressive; and so the upper level will be once more raised."[8] The belief that a morally superior state *must* grow out of the morally inferior states of present and past can only rest upon what may be called the religious view of the cosmos—that the cosmos is governed by a moral power. This does not mean, of course, that evolution and progress are corollaries of religion; on the contrary, the good end envisaged by most historic faiths has been located in another world, while evolution is concerned exclusively with this. But if one already accepts the fact of evolution on other grounds and at the same time believes that the hand of a benevolent deity is everywhere present in nature, he is likely to find himself in the position of the evolutionary meliorist. These conditions, moreover, were just those which obtained most widely among the intellectual classes in this country during the last third of the nineteenth century, and in a number of cases during the middle third. Not only was the conception of an evolution in nature gaining increasing acceptance during the last two thirds of the century, but the rigorous and otherworldly faith of Calvin had almost entirely given way to the optimistic religion of nature of the Unitarians and others. The benevolent deity was as deeply ingrained in the literature of America in the nineteenth century as the God of wrath had been in that of New England in the seventeenth; and from this it was but a step to this meliorism. If, it came to be reasoned, God is at once all-merciful and all-powerful and the world is imperfect but changing, its change must be for the better.[9] In the words of the Unitarians, its course must be "onward and upward forever."[10] So simple in essence is the central conception with which we shall deal.

We shall oversimplify, however, if we think of this meliorism as merely the result of the impact of the evolutionisms of science on the prevailing religious optimism. Indeed, one of the most frequent sources of misunderstanding in the discussion of popular and literary interpretations of evolution in the nineteenth century lies in the failure to realize that evolution was not exclusively a scientific concept. True, without the compelling evidence of the astronomer, the geologist, the embryologist, and the comparative anatomist, the theory would probably never have been more than a curious speculation. But this means no more than that science convinced men of the fact of evolution; the interpretation of its cause and significance most often came from other sources, particularly, as far as we are concerned, from an older theoretical development that not only contained most of the elements of the concept but was founded on a spiritual rather than a material conception of reality. Its premise was that the material world is a manifestation or effluence of an absolute or divine mind, and its conclusion—here called "cosmic optimism"[11]—that therefore the world must follow the path of orderly progression and must be in some sense good and directed toward good.[12] This conception, first in chronology and in importance in this study, is one of the two streams of evolutionary thought that must be considered in some detail before we can turn to the poets.

1

As is often the case in matters of this kind, the starting point is the Greeks, who, according to the leading student of the subject, Professor Arthur O. Lovejoy, were the originators of the conception

INTRODUCTION

of a great unbroken "chain of being" in which all the possibilities of existence are realized. This conception, Professor Lovejoy states, rested on three metaphysical axioms fathered by Plato and Aristotle, namely, the principles of plenitude, continuity, and gradation. The principle of plenitude, which Professor Lovejoy traces to the *Timaeus* of Plato, is simply the idea that completeness or fullness is an attribute of perfection and that therefore the perfection of the Creator demands that all possible forms of being must exist. The converse of this, that no possible kind of being can be nonexistent, provided the basis of the second principle, which was first enunciated by Aristotle and is formulated by Professor Lovejoy in these words:

If there is between two given natural species a theoretically possible intermediate type, that type must be realized—and so *ad indefinitum;* otherwise, there would be gaps in the universe, the creation would not be as 'full' as it might be, and this would imply the inadmissible consequence that its Source or Author was not 'good' in the sense which that adjective has in the *Timaeus*.[13]

The third of the principles grew out of Aristotle's observation that "everything, except God, has in it some measure of 'privation,'"[14] and is stated in his conclusion that "thus 'all individual things may be graded according to the degree to which they are infected with [mere] potentiality.'"[15] The grand result, the *plenum formarum,* was, in Professor Lovejoy's words,

the conception of the universe as a 'Great Chain of Being,' composed of an immense, or—by the strict but seldom rigorously employed logic of the principle of continuity—of an infinite, number of links ranging in hierarchical order from the meagrest kind of existents, which barely escape non-existence, through 'every possible' grade up to the *ens perfectissimum* . . . every one of them differing from that immediately above and that immediately below it by the 'least possible' degree of difference.[16]

The relation of the principles of continuity and gradation to the idea of evolution, as counterparts of what Professor Conger calls serial order, is clear, but the relation of the principle of plenitude to the particular version of evolution that is being considered here requires a word of comment. When Timaeus said that "the creator was good, and the good can never have any jealousy of anything,"[17] his intention was to justify the existence of evil in a world created by a perfect being. We shall have to do with a similar argument in many later pages, for in a sense the whole conception of evolution with which we shall be dealing was a theodicy. Immediately, however, our interest is rather in its converse, that the perfection of the creator demands the existence of better as well as worse. For it was on this side that the principle of plenitude, when translated into temporal terms, contributed to the later meliorism, making the realization of an increasing perfection a matter of necessity. Emerson and Whitman, for example, would have heartily agreed that the "goodness" at the core of things requires the existence, potentially in the present and actually in the future, of the "best possible" forms of being.

It was a long way from the chain of being to the developmental doctrine, however, for the former was by the very terms of its statement static and unchanging. In the words of Miss Lois Whitney, "it was a logically necessary corollary of the idea of the *plenum formarum* that all the members of the scale should exist simultaneously rather than consecutively."[18] And yet in its notion of an ascending series the conception of the chain possessed one of the elements of the evolutionary idea and needed only to be so modified as to include the notion of change in time to become at least quasi-evolutionary. This it was, moreover, in the eighteenth century, largely as a result of the sharp criticisms of Johnson, Voltaire, and others. "Nature as now observable," it was asserted, "did *not* appear to present even a segment of the chain which was complete and unbroken."[19] Voltaire objected that (1) "some species which once existed have disappeared," (2) "the obvious fact that we can conceive of imaginary species intermediate between the actual ones shows at once that the sequence of forms is broken," (3) "the supposition of the completeness of the chain requires the existence of a vast hierarchy of immaterial beings above man."[20] Plainly, if the chain of being, and along with it the notion of the "fullness" of God, was not to be abandoned, it was necessary to conceive of it as a process of growth; the "full" creation had to be thought of as somehow only potential, and its realization as progressive. And this it was in the writing of a number of men from Leibnitz to Schelling. In the language of Professor Lovejoy, the chain of being was "temporalized": it "came to

INTRODUCTION

be conceived . . . not as the inventory but as the program of nature."[21]

Nor was this simply a shift in philosophical strategy that left the layman untouched. Its most fruitful issue, as will presently be explained, was in the developmental systems of Schelling and Hegel, but its effect was also felt on less technical levels. As has been observed by Miss Whitney, who has been concerned with literature and popular thought rather than with philosophy in the narrow sense:

As the century progressed the tendency in regard to the chain of being was to . . . stress less the beauty of "th' amazing whole" *in statu quo,* and to throw the emphasis on the endless striving of the whole chain toward the perfection next above each member, until in some cases the idea of the chain actually merged into an evolutionary theory.[22]

Two instances of this, studied many years ago by Professor G. R. Potter in an unpublished Harvard dissertation on evolutionary ideas in English poetry before 1850, are particularly instructive. In one of them James Thomson attempted to merge the conception of the chain of being with the Pythagorean idea of the cyclical transmigration of souls, suggesting the following revision of Pythagoras' teaching:

> He taught that life's indissoluble flame,
> From brute to man and man to brute again,
> For ever shifting, runs the eternal round;
> . . . . Delightful truth!
> Had he beheld the living chain ascend,
> And not a circling form, but rising whole.[23]

In the other, Mark Akenside, after describing the creation of the chain by "the Sovereign Spirit of the World," pictured its operation in this fashion:

> Nor content,
> By one exertion of creative power
> His goodness to reveal; through every age,
> Through every moment up the tract of time,
> His parent-hand, with ever-new increase
> Of happiness and virtue, has adorn'd
> The vast harmonious frame: his parent-hand
> From the mute shell-fish gasping on the shore,

> To men, to angels, to celestial minds,
> For ever leads the generations on
> To higher scenes of being; while, supplied
> From day to day with his enlivening breath,
> Inferior orders in succession rise
> To fill the void below.[24]

Neither of these views was evolutionary in any strict sense. Aside from the fact that both envisaged a simple succession rather than a genetic series, Akenside's chain, incomplete at both ends, grew downward as well as upward, and Thomson's was a kind of permanent ladder by means of which souls might climb to higher states. Nevertheless, they are not without significance here. They emphasize the fact that quasi-evolutionary conceptions were to be found in familiar places long before the time of Darwin, or even of Lamarck; they picture evolutionary processes as the working out of the will of an Eternal Goodness; and Thomson, in his conception of the ascent of the soul through a rising series of incarnations, foreshadowed an interpretation of evolution that was to have great appeal for several of our poets. Readers of Emerson and Whitman will be aware that Emerson's "worm striving to be man" mounted through all the spires of form, and that Whitman described evolution as the "long journey" of his own soul.[25]

At about the same period that the concept of the "chain of being" was reaching the height of its influence in modern times another idea arose that cannot be omitted in any attempt to trace the development of evolutionary thought—the much discussed idea of the progress of civilization. More than pleased with the triumphs of the Renaissance, a number of men in the seventeenth century came to feel that the modern age was superior to the ancient, and, becoming embroiled in debate over the issue, sought a rational basis for their position. Their argument, first stated by Fontenelle, was simplicity itself: (1) civilization is based upon learning and skill; (2) learning and skill are cumulative; (3) the modern age possesses the fruits of a longer period of cumulation than the ancient and is therefore more "advanced."[26] This deduction, of course, was only the beginning of the theory, which has had an elaborate history down to our own day. The sensationalist psychology of the following century seemed to show that man was a malleable creature who could be perfected by being subjected to proper influences, and the geometrical rate of advance in the practical arts presented

INTRODUCTION

a palpable kind of evidence that carried conviction where theory was wasted. The influence of progress in this sense on the general development of the idea of evolution was obviously very great. It gave a kind of axiomatic indubitability to the notions of change and melioration and predisposed men to discover these patterns whenever they concerned themselves with temporal phenomena. Its effect on the writers to be considered here, however, was only to predispose, and hence its importance here is no more than incidental. The essence of the evolutionary meliorism with which we are immediately concerned was a universal and necessary spiritual principle, and for this we must turn from the French to the Germans, the "spiritualists" par excellence of modern thought.

The Germany of the *Aufklärung* was not uninfluenced by the French theories, but its own theories of progress tended to be broader in scope, spiritual and cosmic rather than material and social in emphasis, and teleological rather than mechanical in process. Lessing, for example, found progress in the history of religion, but it was a progress caused by God, who was supposed to have been "educating" man through a succession of partial but constantly broadening revelations.[27] And Herder, though he laid as much stress on environmental influences as any *philosophe,* found a benevolent cosmic purpose working itself out even in the destructive processes of nature and the ravages of human conflict.[28] Moreover, the early rise of the Romantic movement in Germany gave a particularly "spiritual" bent to all its speculation which proved fruitful for the evolutionary idea. In their quest for new avenues to truth the Romantic thinkers turned increasingly to the past, and particularly to the past as the parent of the present. According to Josiah Royce, in his chapter on "The Rise of the Doctrine of Evolution" in *The Spirit of Modern Philosophy,* they came to believe that "if the great Spirit is anywhere to be manifest to us, then it should be in the growth of humanity,"[29] and this in turn led to a genetic conception of history that contained the germ of the idea of evolution. Hence Royce was able to assert that evolution "took its rise in . . . an effort of humanity to write its own autobiography"[30] and was "in heart and essence the child of the romantic movement."[31] Furthermore, he meant more by these assertions than he felt called upon to explain in this chapter. This is apparent elsewhere in his book, but is particularly clear in an account given many years later of preparations he had made for writing the chapter.[32] He had compiled a long list of figures influential in the introduction of the genetic approach into scientific study and had found that nearly all had in their early years come under the influence of the *Naturphilosophie* of Schelling. His point, of paramount importance for our purposes, was that the philosophy of Schelling, which summarized and built a metaphysical foundation under the spiritualistic and teleological theories of progress of the Germans, was one of the most important forerunners of what had then come to be called evolution.

To grasp the evolutionary significance of Schelling's thought, we must review at least superficially the principal line of development in German metaphysics, beginning with Kant's proposition that mind moulds the world which it knows out of the raw material supplied in sensation. The next step was Fichte's objection that the external source of sensation postulated in this proposition, since it was not and could not be known, was a pure fiction, and that therefore the only known or knowable source of experience must be consciousness itself—consciousness being understood to mean, not the private or "empirical" consciousness, but a superpersonal consciousness or "subject of knowledge in general."[33] This, as the basic postulate of idealism, is fundamental in the understanding of many of the writers whom we shall consider, but much more important in the development of the idea of evolution was what Fichte did with it. Granted that consciousness was the primary reality, it was still necessary to explain how we come to know a world of objects, a world not ourselves. This explanation Fichte made by an analysis of the process of knowledge that owed something to Kant but was on the whole one of the great original contributions to philosophy. His first two steps were simply a statement of the problem: first, one cannot think without postulating one's own existence as thinker; second, since one also cannot think without an object of thought, something opposed to and limiting oneself must somehow come into existence. However—and this is the heart of the matter—since the self is the source of all existence, this object must have been created by the self; it cannot be an independent entity, but must be an act by which the self has limited or defined itself. To recapitulate briefly, the self in creating an object, or what appears to it as an object, has really only modified its own nature. This is the famous process of dialectic, later so elaborately developed by Hegel, and is itself formally evolutionary: *a* gives rise to *b*, with which it merges to become *c; c* then gives rise to *d*, etc., etc. Perhaps two or three sentences descriptive of the Romantic metaphysic from the pen of the late G. H. Mead will help to clarify the evolutionary significance of the process:

> It is the self which organizes this world; but when it has organized it, it has really organized that which is identical with itself, it has organized its own experiences. . . . The process of experience, according to these idealists, creates its own forms. Now this has a very abstruse sound, of course; but what I want to call your attention to is that it is nothing but an abstract statement of the principle of evolution. These Romantic idealists were undertaking in the field of philosophical speculation what Darwin and Lamarck were undertaking in the field of organic phenomena at the same period. What the Romantic idealists, and Hegel in particular, were saying, was that the world evolves, that reality itself is in a process of evolution.[34]

Fichte, however, was concerned only with mind and the derivation of the categories of knowledge, not with nature, and it was left for Schelling, starting from the Fichtean position, to discover, as Mead said, that "the world evolves." Following Fichte, Schelling reasoned that if mind is the source of its own knowledge, then nature must take its form from mind and be deducible from it. This deduction he proceeded to make, and the result was the system of *Naturphilosophie* of which Royce spoke in his lecture. Reduced to its simplest terms, this system, in its earlier form, may be stated in four propositions, all of which will prove important in the further development of this study. First, since nature is a construction of the mind, it is perfectly correspondent with it, manifesting the same patterns of organization and development. Second, since, as Fichte had shown, the process of mind consists in the union of the opposite forces of self-assertion and self-limitation, nature must likewise represent a union of opposites—of attraction and repulsion, positive and negative, movement and resistance, etc. Third, since mind is characterized by an endless striving to organize itself —that is, to achieve unity amid difference—a similar organic quality must be found in nature, both in individuals and throughout the whole. Lastly and most importantly, since mind produces nature in an effort to realize itself through objectification, and since it proceeds step by step by the process of dialectic, nature must fall into a series of ascending steps moving toward a goal in which mind will be perfectly realized.

Thus the developmental theory of Schelling in so far as it was related to Fichte's theory of knowledge may be summarized as follows: the ultimate ground of existence strives to realize itself through an endless ascending series of forms, which rise one above another through a process of opposition and reconciliation. Schelling, however, because of his greater interest in the "external" world and his less exclusive preoccupation with the problems of mind, could not agree with Fichte that nature was simply a construction of the Ego, and he was led by this disagreement to modify his conception of the ultimate ground in a way that gave a different perspective to his theory. The ultimate ground of existence, he came to believe, was neither nature nor mind, but a mysterious *tertium quid* called the Absolute, of which nature and mind were parallel manifestations. This ambiguous entity, which owed something to Spinoza's conception of a fundamental substance of which matter and mind were different modes, is perhaps most easily grasped through Schelling's metaphor of the magnet, reported as follows in J. B. Stallo's *General Principles of the Philosophy of Nature,* a work which has a particular interest here because it was published in Boston in 1848 and read enthusiastically by Emerson:

The symbol of the Absolute is the magnet: one principle constantly manifesting itself as two poles and still resting in their midst as their identity. Divide the magnet: every part will be a complete system in itself,—two poles and a point of indifference. Just as every part of the magnet is the entire magnet in miniature, so also every individual development in nature is a miniature.[35]

A true *Naturphilosoph,* Stallo began his book with the evolutionary statement that

It is characteristic of true philosophy to study everything in the process of its origination,—to comprehend that which is evolved, by observing the process of its evolution . . . ,[36]

and later showed clearly how Schelling's developmental principle was related to his conception of the Absolute. The activity of the Absolute, he began, consists in "the reproduction of its own being," and since this being is "the identity of the Ideal and the Real," there is everywhere "a tendency to idealize the Real and realize the Ideal."[37] The latter of these tendencies was the subject of

INTRODUCTION

Schelling's philosophy of mind, and the former of his philosophy of nature, which, starting from "the Real," climbed the scale of being toward its "perfect idealization."[38] To comprehend this ascent in terms of the metaphor of the magnet, we must remember that just as every part of the magnet is an entire magnet in miniature, with positive and negative poles, "so also every individual development in nature is a miniature,"[39] with Ideal and Real aspects that constantly seek the perfect balance which is characteristic of the Absolute. This prepares us for Stallo's explanation of the process:

Since the preponderance of the Real, however, is the characteristic of nature, the Ideal, though present, is held, as it were, in the bondage of matter, spellbound in the embrace of reality. But in an ever rising gradation the Ideal effects its disenchantment; the members of that gradation again embody the type, Real, Ideal, and their Identity, where it is to be remembered that in each of the three both principles are present, so that these powers or potentialities (Potenzen), as they are denominated by Schelling, represent but a particular quantitative difference.[40]

Thus by another route we arrive at the "temporalized" chain of being, which we left with a reference to Schelling. Here, as there, an inner compulsion is seen to operate in nature to realize higher and higher forms of existence in a series that is both continuous and graded. Stallo applies it as follows to the evolution of man:

The various animal forms are developments of the primitive animal type on successive stages; a more complete reciprocation, or rather, identification with the universe, occurring on each subsequent one, until all the phases of cosmic life and materialization are incorporated in the perfect animal,—man. . . .

Man, then, is the full realization of the idea of animal life, and the lower forms are only advances towards it. One by one the features of the Universe are produced and incorporated in an individual form, until the perfect ideal expression smiles upon us from the human countenance; one by one the breaths of the Universe are inspired into particular organizations, until the human organism respires the balm of the whole spiritual atmosphere.[41]

"Transcendental method," as Santayana has wryly remarked, "so abused, produced transcendental myth."[42] And myth it certainly was, as the accounts of nature by Schelling, Oken, and Hegel—constructed entirely a priori—testify.[43] And yet its terminal conception was a valuable one and its influence tremendous. Royce showed that it lay behind the genetic theories of such scientists as von Baer, and Professor Lovejoy has argued very acutely that it was both forerunner and source of the creative evolutionism of Bergson.[44]

How far the idea as it stands was compatible with the biological theories of evolution is a question which must be answered before we are finished, but before turning to that problem certain other matters must be attended to. First, with the aid of Stallo, let us review some of the salient points in the nature-philosophy that will reappear in the consideration of the poets. Of these the basic one is the unity of all things: not only a unity amid the diversity of phenomena but between the two great realms of being, the Ideal and the Real; and not simply a unity of sameness, but of interaction and reconciliation, which thus presupposes difference:

the higher identity here spoken of means more than sameness, which is the identity of the understanding. This latter category, the coincidence of two things in quantity and quality in the realm of limited realities, presupposes the ideas of quantity and quality; if, then, *there are higher grounds* than those of quantity and quality, an identity *not excluding,* but *demanding,* simultaneous difference is by no means inconceivable.[45]

The second point, the obverse of this principle of unity, is the presence of opposite or polar forces in all things, which indeed may be said to consist in this opposition:

The vital process of the world (of all existences) is consequently twofold likewise: first, self-extension, self-exterioration, an evolution or rather *eversion* of the identity or unity into multiplicity, and again an introversion of the multiplicity into unity or identity . . . two primitive vital forces: absolute *self-repulsion* and absolute *self-attraction.*[46]

The third is the evolution that results from this opposition, not in a straight line, but by arrested and progressive development that follows a spiral ascent:

All development is, from its nature progressive. . . . Every particular organic form however, appears in a twofold capacity,—that of a self-perpetuating unity, of a whole complete in itself, and that of a mere complementary member, a part of a superior whole, from the connection with which it derives its vital significance. Its development will not, therefore, be absolutely progressive, but characterized by *evolution* and *revolution, advance* and *retrogression;* it will be *self-returning,* as it were, circular. Yet, since a mere retracing of a previous course would preclude all actual advance, and consequently all real development, the term of any evolution will never coincide with its outset, but fall beyond it; the *development of all individual forms will be spiral.*[47]

The fourth is the recognition of conflict as the law of life and the justification of this state of affairs as the eternal self-realizing activity of the Absolute:

There is combat in nature only because infinite activity, infinite life, is the being of the Divine; and activity, life, is combat, because it is endeavor. Or, can you conceive life without combat, and the Divine without life? There is no other method of reconciling the labors, the apparent wars, in existence without absolute enjoyment; activity, labor, is the essence of joy. In many ways we can *palliate* the contradictions of life; in this way only can we *solve* them. *No other theodicea than this.*[48]

It is one thing, however, to show that the *Naturphilosophie* contained the germ of a theory of evolution and another to show that it was available to American readers and influenced our poets. Certainly it did not influence them directly, since Schelling is difficult reading even in English, and since only sparse fragments had been translated in the forties and fifties. Even a superficial survey shows, however, that by way of secondary sources his ideas became increasingly available during these decades and that they entered into the thought of the time by various roundabout routes. To name but a few obvious intermediate sources: of German poets whose writing contained ideas similar to his, Goethe and Novalis were well known in this country; of translations, Oken's *Elements of Physiophilosophy* (*Lehrbuch der Naturphilosophie*) appeared in 1847 and Oersted's *The Soul in Nature* in 1852; and of secondary work, Stallo's book was published in 1848 and Joseph Gost[w]ick's *German Literature* (read by Whitman) in 1854. Probably the most important sources, however, were both more and less direct than these. By countless devious means the natural-philosophical theories, often heavily watered, permeated the thought of the time, and a search of popular publications would certainly reveal many hints in one way or another akin to the German theories. Emerson described Schelling's dictum "all difference is quantitative" as one of a few generalizations that "always circulate in the world,"[49] and in the *Journal* for 1849 he commented on Schelling's teaching that "the form or type became transparent in the actual forms of successive ages as presented in geology" in a way that makes quite clear how that and similar conceptions came to be disseminated:

Schelling's *aperçu* and its statement was a forlorn hope, and all but fell into the pit. Yet just on the eve of ruin, Oken seized and made the most of it; of course, he was ridiculous, and nowhere but in Germany could have survived. Yet Hegel, a still more robust dreamer, clung to this identical piece of nonsense. Then it came rebounding to them in melody from songs of Goethe, and, strange to say, from Geoffroy Saint-Hilaire's *Mémoires* to the Institute in France. Agassiz brought it to America and tried it in popular lectures on the towns. It succeeded to admiration, the lecturer having, of course, the prudence to disown these bad names of his authors.[50]

The most important of the sources as far as the poets were concerned, however, and the most direct, was Coleridge, particularly in the famous twelfth chapter of *Biographia Literaria,* where he borrowed freely from the *Transcendental Idealism* of Schelling.[51] In the most extended of these borrowings Schelling had laid down the basis of the two lines of his philosophy, from Object to Subject and from Subject to Object, and these lines Coleridge promised to follow out in detail "in the third treatise of my Logosophia."[52] For the moment, however, he contented himself with outlining them in a series of theses, in the course of which he represented the aim of philosophy to be the search for an unconditioned basis of thought and being, which, as Schelling had urged, should be neither thought nor being but an identity of the two. This unconditioned ground he then discovered in an absolute self-consciousness, which could be arrived at by following either of Schelling's parallel lines. He said of the philosophy of nature, for example:

... even as natural philosophers we must arrive at the same principle from which as transcendental philosophers we set out; that is, in a self-consciousness in which the *principium essendi* does not stand to the *principium cognoscendi* in the relation of cause to effect, but both the one and the other are coinherent and identical. Thus the true system of natural philosophy places the sole reality of things in an ABSOLUTE, which is at once *causa sui et effectus,* ... in the absolute identity of subject and object, which it calls nature, and which in its highest power is nothing but self-conscious will or intelligence.[53]

INTRODUCTION

From this he proceeded in the next paragraph to the deduction of that principle of reconciliation of opposites which was central in his own thought and, as we have seen, one of the salient points of the *Naturphilosophie:*

> Bearing then this in mind, that intelligence is a self-development, not a quality supervening to a substance, we may abstract from all *degree,* and for the purpose of philosophic construction reduce it to *kind,* under the idea of an indestructible power with two opposite and counteracting forces, which, by a metaphor borrowed from astronomy, we may call the centrifugal and centripetal forces. The intelligence in the one tends to *objectize* itself, and in the other to *know* itself in the object. It will be hereafter my business to construct by a series of intuitions the progressive schemes, that must follow from such a power with such forces, till I arrive at the fullness of the *human* intelligence. For my present purpose, I *assume* such a power. . . .[54]

Moreover, in two passages at the beginning of the next chapter, the relation of this principle to the philosophy of nature was made so clear that even those who had mired in the morasses of the preceding chapter could not escape the hint. The first and briefer is this:

the transcendental philosopher says: grant me a nature having two contrary forces, the one of which tends to expand infinitely, while the other strives to apprehend or *find* itself in this infinity, and I will cause the world of intelligences with the whole system of their representations to rise up before you.[55]

These were only the most obvious and Schellingesque, and probably the most widely read, of the many passages in which Coleridge contributed to the propagation of the Romantic nature-philosophy. They were not, however, the closest to evolution. For though Coleridge never lived up to his threat "to construct by a series of intuitions the progressive schemes" that should lead through nature to the human intelligence, he frequently sketched the dynamic chain of being that would have been the pattern of such a construction. The most extended of these sketches is in the "Hints toward the Formation of a More Comprehensive Theory of Life,"[56] but the most suggestive for our purposes is the following in *Aids to Reflection:*

Every rank of creatures, as it ascends in the scale of creation, leaves death behind it or under it. The metal at its height of being seems a mute prophecy of the coming vegetation, into a mimic semblance of which it crystallizes. The blossom and flower, the acme of vegetable life, divides into correspondent organs with reciprocal functions, and by instinctive motions and approximations seems impatient of that fixture, by which it is differenced in kind from that flower-shaped Psyche, that flutters with free wing above it. And wonderfully in the insect realm doth the Irritability, the proper seat of Instinct . . . typically rehearse the adaptive Understanding, yea, and the moral affections and charities, of man. . . . Thus all lower natures find their highest Good in semblances and seekings of that which is higher and better. All things strive to ascend, and ascend in their striving.[57]

This upward-striving scale, of course, was still not evolution in the true sense—which to Coleridge was "the bestial theory."[58] There was no hint of material connection between the levels, and it is even doubtful whether a temporal succession was intended. There were serial order and continuity, however, and a powerful upward surge toward the realization of the highest possibilities of life, which lent themselves to evolutionary interpretation and provided fruitful hints to younger men who were convinced of the fact of evolution on other grounds. In view of Coleridge's virulent antipathy to the views of Erasmus Darwin, Monboddo, and other early evolutionists, it would be absurd to speak of him as "trembling on the verge" of a true evolutionism, but if this was not true of Coleridge, it was true of many who read and accepted his views. All that was needed to translate the ideal continuities of his nature-philosophy into the physical continuities of evolution was the pressure of a growing accumulation of evidence and inference that such continuities had existed. The growth and significance of this accumulation we must now briefly consider.

2

Through having been repeated in every elementary textbook in geology and biology for many years, the broad outlines of this growth have become so familiar that they would not merit even the brief attention that can be given them here if this were not the most convenient method at the same time of indicating certain outstanding features of the physical theory and of suggesting how by

INTRODUCTION

the mere cumulation of special theories the general theory of evolution became more and more difficult to resist. Disregarding antiquities and eccentricities, the first of the important special theories was the theory that the solar system was not created in its present state but has developed out of a single mass.[59] And of the two aspects of this theory that have a special significance here, the first is that it was thoroughly mechanical. It appealed neither to a supernatural power nor to an inner urge to attain a previsioned goal, but only to the blind and unknowing movements of inert matter; it was an explanation in terms of efficient rather than final causes. According to the classic formulation of Laplace, in the beginning was a fiery nebula rotating on its axis and filling the same space now occupied by the solar system. As the mass cooled, two opposite tendencies came into play: by the laws of heat, the mass tended to condense; and by the laws of dynamics, its speed of rotation and the resulting centrifugal force on its outer parts tended to increase. When at intervals this centrifugal force overcame the contractile tendency, rings were broken off; and these rings in turn, because of the irregularity of their composition, tended to form themselves into planets. Thus the formation of the solar system was exclusively an affair of matter and motion and governed by their inflexible laws. It is true that Kant's principal concern in the book in which he anticipated Laplace was to show that such a mechanistic interpretation was not incompatible with the idea of divine purpose,[60] but that did not mitigate the mechanism of the process itself. What Laplace is supposed to have said to Napoleon when questioned about the absence of the name of God from his *Mécanique Céleste,* he might also have said to Kant: "Sir, I had no need of that hypothesis."[61]

The second point of interest is that this theory set that pattern of evolution by differentiation which reached a climax in Spencer's famous definition of evolution as "an integration of matter . . . during which the matter passes from an indefinite, incoherent homogeneity to a definite, coherent heterogeneity."[62] By processes of aggregation and separation the great original mass was broken up into coherent units which differed among themselves according to the arrangement of their particles. The one became the many, not, as in the ideal theory, by the realization of potentialities, but by a process of rearrangement and configuration—as bricks become a house. The immediate source of Spencer's definition, however, was not Laplace's theory but the second of the special theories in which we are interested, that of "epigenesis" in embryology, advanced by Caspar Friedrich Wolff in 1759 and soundly established by von Baer in the 1820's. According to the account of John Fiske, Spencer, having observed the process of development in society, was in search of an instance of the same process complete from end to end so that he could "follow and exhaustively describe its consecutive phases."[63] And this he found in von Baer's researches. In spite of contrary hints going back to Harvey in the seventeenth century, when Wolff published his conclusions in 1759 the accepted view in embryology was that of "preformation"—that the individual exists fully formed in the ovum and has only to unfold and increase in size. Wolff, however, and later von Baer with the aid of the microscope, showed that no traces of the future individual were to be discovered in the egg and that the development of the egg is a process of differentiation of homogeneous matter. The parallel with the nebular theory, as Spencer later took pains to show, was both significant and inescapable.

Embryology is not a subject to catch the popular imagination, but cosmogony has always had a broad appeal, and by the thirties and forties of the nineteenth century Laplace's theory, even though often held at arm's length as an "hypothesis," had become a commonplace. The most influential of the sciences in winning the general public to an evolutionary view, however, was geology. Shells found at points remote from the sea and fossils embedded deep in rock formations had long puzzled men. Some said that they were simply accidental formations, sports of nature, some that they were relics of the Flood, some even that they were put there by God to try the faith of men. But when late in the eighteenth century the English surveyor William Smith showed that each rock stratum had its characteristic remains and that the chronological order of the strata could be determined by the comparison of these remains, and when a little later the French anatomists Cuvier and Lamarck had systematically compared the extinct with the living forms, three facts became clear. First, the world's immense past was divisible into well-defined epochs; second, all but the earliest of these epochs had been inhabited by living beings cognate to forms of the present; third, new and more elaborate forms of life had appeared in each successive epoch, leading forward to man-

INTRODUCTION

like forms in the most recent. The invitation to a theory of the evolution of species seems obvious now, and it was plain to some even then. Lamarck, who had given his best efforts to the study of the comparative anatomy of invertebrates, found it irresistible, as did Geoffroy Saint-Hilaire and some others. However, two deeply entrenched notions stood in the way: that species are immutable, and that the geological epochs were brought to their respective conclusions by cataclysms which put an end to all life and cleaned the slate for the succeeding age. Neither of these conceptions, obviously, was compatible with evolution.

Smith held to the catastrophic theory, as did Cuvier and a surprising number of others down to the middle of the nineteenth century, but the very principle of principles of modern geology was to involve its contradiction. Because it was a science, geology was devoted to the principle that nature everywhere and always behaves according to uniform laws, and consequently, just as Newton had shown that the movements of heavenly bodies are governed by the same laws that govern the fall of an apple, Charles Lyell in founding modern geology borrowed and developed the principle of "uniformitarianism" of Hutton and Playfair. "Former changes in the earth's surface," he set himself to show in his epochal *Principles of Geology* in 1830, "are referable to causes now in operation."[64] The laying down of the strata had not, he contended, been an affair of extraordinary world-wide cataclysms, but of gradual change, as rock today is worn away by wind and water or metamorphosed by pressure and heat. This meant, of course, that the geological epochs were not isolated from each other and that life in one might be connected with life in another; but quite as important in the development of evolutionary thought was simply its extension of the principle of uniform cause. Newton had explained the far by the near, but it was Kant and Laplace and Hutton and Lyell who established the practice of explaining the past by the present. Since the principal theories of the evolution of species were simply efforts to explain the origin of species in terms of "causes now in operation," one can understand what Darwin meant when he said, "I always feel as if my books came half out of Lyell's brain."[65]

The popular influence of geology can scarcely be overestimated. In differing from the accepted interpretation of *Genesis* it came notoriously into the public gaze and helped to clear the public mind of the Scriptural literalism that stood in the way of evolution. Emerson, for example, wrote that Copernicus' "correction of our superstitions was confirmed by the new science of geology."[66] At first there were attempts to reconcile the two conflicting versions of creation. President Hitchcock of Amherst taught that the seven days of *Genesis* were rather epochs than solar days,[67] and Professor Benjamin Silliman of Yale in editing the second edition of *Bakewell's Geology* provided an elaborate table of the coincidences of *Genesis* and geology, even though he wrote at the same time, "No geologist at the present day erects any system upon the basis of the scripture history."[68] Meanwhile the public discussion continued in a flood of lectures, sermons, articles, and books. Writers like Arnold Guyot and Hugh Miller reached wide audiences, and Silliman's lectures in New Haven and Boston were so successful that he was invited to give a series of twenty-four at the first session of the Lowell Institute in 1839-40.[69] The Union Catalogue of the Library of Congress shows eight American printings of Lyell's *Principles* between 1837 and 1860 and almost as many of his *Elements of Geology* and *A Manual of Elementary Geology*. In July, 1842, a writer in *The Dial* was able to state that "wherever one went he saw a copy of Lyell's *Geology* on the table."[70] Like the astronomy of the Renaissance, the geology of the first half of the nineteenth century opened new vistas to the imagination. It did not prove that one species had evolved out of another, but it showed a progressive succession of organic forms through a period of millions of years with at least a formal connection running through the development.

The crux of the whole problem, however, without some answer to which no evolutionism could be complete, was the question of the mutability of species. Philosophers might postulate an ideal succession of forms and geologists might demonstrate something like this succession in the record of the rocks, but as long as immutability remained a scientific dogma no far-reaching evolutionary conclusions were possible. It cannot be said that this dogma was finally broken until after the appearance of *The Origin of Species,* but as early as the middle of the eighteenth century the progress of thought and investigation had already caused it to be challenged. Thus, though he altered his opinion in subsequent volumes, the engaging and influential Buffon questioned the whole concept of species in volume one of his *Histoire Naturelle* (1749), and to the end

INTRODUCTION

of his days never ceased to urge the importance of homologies between and variation within species.[71] Again, the increasing study of embryology and comparative anatomy gave so much support to the view that species are not air-tight compartments that it became inevitable for bold thinkers to hazard theories of the development of new species by the variation of old.[72] Maupertuis, for example, in his *Système de la nature* (1751) and Diderot in his *Pensées sur la nature* (1754) stated definitely evolutionary conclusions, and Herder in his *Ideen zur Philosophie der Geschichte der Menschheit* (1784-91) came as close to evolution as he could without specifically denying immutability. Again, the eccentric Scotch jurist, Lord Monboddo, was led by his studies in the history of language (*The Origin and Progress of Language*, 1773) to the conclusion that man is a highly developed orangoutang, and in 1794 Erasmus Darwin declared in his *Zoönomia* that "all warm-blooded animals have arisen from a single living filament."[73]

In view of these developments, no greater mistake can be made than to regard the idea of the evolution of species as little known before the second half of the nineteenth century or to credit Tennyson, Emerson, Whitman, and others with a kind of poetic "pre-science" in anticipating it. As early as 1809 Washington Irving paused in the *Knickerbocker History* to poke fun at "the startling conjecture of Buffon, Helvetius, and Darwin, so highly honourable to mankind, and peculiarly complimentary to the French nation, that the whole human species are accidentally descended from a remarkable family of monkies!"[74] And in the same year Lamarck published the second summary of what is still, next to Darwin's, the best known theory of biological evolution. It is true that Lamarck's theory attracted few adherents before its revival in the seventies and eighties, but it became known to many through the refutations that it called forth, most notably Lyell's in *Principles of Geology*.[75] Again, in July, 1830, the elder Geoffroy Saint-Hilaire, professor of zoology at Paris and one of the most eminent of French scientists, defended the continuity of species in a controversy with Cuvier that so impressed Goethe that when his friend, Soret, spoke to him of the July Revolution he thought he was referring to the debate of the scientists.[76] This controversy, however, resulted unfortunately for the evolution-idea in the world of science. Though time seems to have shown that there was truth on both sides, the public victory went to Cuvier, and the evolution of species became a scientific heresy for thirty years to come. Thus, when Robert Chambers revived the idea excitingly and popularly in *Vestiges of the Natural History of Creation* in 1844, his book was reviewed with discredit by those who later espoused Darwinian evolution, and went, as the author himself said, through nine editions without gaining a single uncompromising adherent;[77] and when in the same year Darwin communicated his dawning convictions to Joseph Hooker, he said it was "like confessing a murder."[78] Professor Lovejoy has shown in one of his shrewdest articles that the four principal arguments and the four principal types of evidence later used by Huxley and other champions of evolution "had virtually all been clearly noted and pertinently used in the published evolutionary reasonings of Chambers or Spencer"[79] and "were sufficiently well known to all competent men of science, to require the inference" of evolution.[80] And yet, on the eve of the appearance of *The Origin of Species,* the world of science stood almost as one man for the fixity of species.

Nevertheless, outside the lecture room and the scientific society the evolution-idea retained a good deal of life. Inquiring minds in the lay world continued to hint at it, reach for it, and meditate upon it, and the *Vestiges* alone reached thousands of readers, selling no fewer than ten editions in America from 1845 to 1858.[81] The choice seemed to be between the evolution of species one out of another and special creation by an intervening divine power, and for three hundred years the growing predisposition of the western world had been against supernatural explanations of natural phenomena. One by one, supernatural hypotheses had been displaced, and the sheer momentum of this movement favored the extension of the evolutionary theory. Add to this the cumulative effect of the success of evolutionary hypotheses in cosmogony, geology, embryology, and social theory, and one can understand why many thinking men—Lyell, for example, among scientists and Tennyson among laymen—were sympathetic toward the evolutionary explanation of the origin of species long before what was called a *"vera causa"* had been discovered. It may, in fact, be questioned whether such a cause has yet been established,[82] but such is still the presumption in favor of natural explanations that among intellectuals the general theory of evolution has for a long time gone almost entirely unchallenged.

3

Since, however, the explanation of the universe in terms of physical causes alone was materialism, these same thinking men found themselves in the dilemma that provided the nineteenth century with its most popular philosophical issue. On the one hand, the growing weight of evidence and authority made the evolutionary hypothesis increasingly difficult to reject; on the other, this hypothesis, if accepted without qualification, constituted a threat to the religious view of the cosmos—that the universe owes its existence to and is governed by a Being who is the essence of wisdom and goodness. The importance of adjustment to this view as a condition of the acceptance of evolution in this country in the nineteenth century cannot be overestimated. The religious scepticism of Revolutionary and post-Revolutionary days had long since been absorbed and transmuted and anyhow had not in most cases challenged this general principle. Had not even Thomas Paine said of his own faith that it consisted "in contemplating the power, wisdom, and benignity of the Deity in his works"?[83] Later a new wave of scepticism, much more searching and destructive, was to ensue, and some of its effects will be observed here in later pages. In only a few cases down to the First World War, however, have American poets been willing to accept evolution without somehow harmonizing it with the belief in some kind of moral order in nature, and hence the means by which this could be done are of primary interest here. The details, of course, are matter for the main body of our discussion, but the broad outlines may be indicated at this point, the more particularly because they involve the reconciliation of the two lines of evolutionary thought with which we have been concerned thus far.

In their simplest form these reconciliations took their departure from the natural theology of the preceding century, which they expanded by means of the doctrine of immanence. If the mechanism of hand and eye implied an intelligent Contriver, it was argued, how much more did a continuous development from a primal slime to the great man of the nineteenth century. The Contriver could not, however, be merely an external Artificer in the sense of most of the followers of Paley, for, according to the new view, man had not been created directly and separately by God but had developed out of a nonhuman form of animal life. The creative power of God had to be conceived inwardly rather than outwardly, after the analogy of life to flower, as John Fiske expressed it, rather than of potter to clay; in the coinage of Oliver Wendell Holmes, God had to be conceived as "omni*movent,*" as well as omni*potent.*[84]

Sufficiently elaborated, this argument contained the whole thought of the nineteenth century on the reconciliation of the evolutionary and the religious views of the cosmos, but in this simple form it seemed to many not to get to the heart of the problem. For the larger problem of the teleological and rational character of the cosmos as a whole contained the smaller and no less knotty one of how a world apparently material in substance could give birth to a spiritual being like man. Many years later Josiah Royce put this in the form of a dilemma:

When two objects A and B, say a mass of inorganic matter and an organism with a rational mind, seem to differ as widely as possible, and when, nevertheless, things of the type of A seem pretty obviously to pass by a nearly continuous series of changes into objects of the type of B, that is, when from inorganic matter beings with minds evolve, . . . the first presumption very naturally is that you are dealing with somewhat deceptive appearances. And if you are sure, as the students of evolution are now for their own purposes rightfully sure, that the approximate continuity itself is not the deceptive appearance, . . . then the next natural presumption about A and B is that it is their wide difference which actually constitutes the deceptive appearance, and that A and B are really at heart very much alike.[85]

Either (a) there was no continuous evolution, or (b) mind was "a mere appearance of matter," or (c) matter was "a mere appearance behind which lies Mind." Underlying this dilemma, it must be interpolated, was an assumption which has been widely questioned in our day, but was just as widely accepted in previous times. Royce is assuming, like most of the classical philosophers, that an effect cannot "contain more" than its cause: *e nihilo nihil fit.* If mind is not present in the beginning, it cannot be present at the end, and so with matter.

It is not the place of a study like the present one to judge of such an assumption, but it will be necessary to elaborate it briefly in order to clarify the prevailing interpretation of the poets and to

INTRODUCTION 29

orient this interpretation in relation to contemporary views.[86] Professor Lovejoy provides us with an excellent illustration.[87] In criticizing the developmental theories of Schelling and Oken, Jacobi relied upon this assumption, taking his stand, according to Professor Lovejoy, upon what he regarded "as a self-evident and fundamental axiom of metaphysics: that something cannot 'come from nothing' nor the superior be 'produced by' the inferior." Moreover, Schelling in replying did not deny the "axiom" but only Jacobi's interpretation of it. Those who thought as he did, he explained, did not

maintain that the "more perfect sprang from a less perfect being *independent of* and different from itself," but simply that "the more perfect has risen from its own less perfect condition." Nor, accordingly, did they deny that, in a sense, "the all-perfect being— that which has the perfections of all other things in itself—must be *before* all things." But they did deny that it thus pre-existed as perfect *actu* and not merely *potentia*.

If my reading has not led me astray, this axiom springs from a dialectical conception of nature in which the relation of cause and effect is conceived as not merely physical but logical. The effect is not only produced by the cause but deducible from it, and hence, just as a conclusion is implicit in a premise, the effect is "contained in" the cause. If the real is the rational, then the axiom is sound, for logical derivation does not mean the development of something altogether new but the making explicit of something already implied.

The prominent place of this view in the thought of Aristotle—in his assertion of the priority of actuality to potency[88]—needs no insistence, nor is there any more need in the case of Scholasticism.[89] The important point here, however, is that the idea did not go under in the Renaissance attack on Scholasticism but remained to survive later philosophical wars. Thus, though in a mathematical rather than a teleological sense, Descartes was as much a rationalist as Aristotle and Saint Thomas, and we find him writing:

Now it is manifest by the natural light that there must at least be as much reality in the efficient and total cause as in its effect. For, pray, whence can the effect derive its reality, if not from its cause? And in what way can this cause communicate this reality to it, unless it possessed it in itself? And from this it follows, not only that something cannot proceed from nothing, but likewise that what is more perfect—that is to say, which has more reality within itself—cannot proceed from the less perfect. . . . To take an example, the stone which has not yet existed not only cannot now commence to be unless it has been produced by something which possesses within itself, either formally or eminently, all that enters into the composition of the stone; . . . and so in all other cases.[90]

Locke, too, though he contended against Descartes on many points, was faithful to this principle. The First Cause, he argued, must have been a conscious being, for—as was to be repeated many times in the evolution controversy—"incogitative being cannot produce a cogitative," and "whatsoever is first of all things must necessarily contain in it, and actually have, at least, all the perfections that can ever after exist. . . ."[91]

To be sure, like other aspects of the concept of cause, this suffered from the stringent criticism of Hume; but it did not therefore pass out of currency. For one thing, as we may conclude from the statements of Schelling and Royce, it was resuscitated in the transcendentalisms of the nineteenth century; for another, most academic philosophy in the new century, Anglo-Saxon as well as Teutonic, was devoted to the correction of Hume's heresies. The most important reason, however, is that the old axiom proved indispensable in maintaining the traditional exalted and independent status of the soul against the rising tide of materialism. It was implicit in every one of the hundreds of denials that "mere dead earth, acted on by its chemical and electric forces, should itself originate sense, perception, thought, reason, conscience, heroism,"[92] and in many cases it was made explicit. Thus, as will be illustrated in a later chapter, President McCosh called upon it for this purpose,[93] and in rescuing his Boston lecture audiences from the subversive doctrines of Tyndall's Belfast Address, Joseph Cook appealed to "the axiomatic truth, *that every change must have a sufficient cause.*"[94] What he regarded as a sufficient cause in this instance he described as follows:

Such a cause as makes involution equal to evolution. Sir William Thomson, speaking of the shrewd attempt of materialism to explain living tissues by infinitely complex molecular combinations of merely material particles, says it is forever sure that we cannot get out of the combinations any thing that we do not put into them. . . . The astute attempt of Tyndall is to put into matter what he wishes

INTRODUCTION

to draw out of it. His whole effort is to introduce a new definition of matter. He would have us think of matter as a double-faced somewhat, having a material and spiritual side; and although, in attempting to do so, we necessarily fall into immeasurable self-contradiction, he is forced to undertake the support of even that, because he knows that evolution cannot be greater than involution. He would put into his theory, therefore, on the one side, that power and potency of all life which he wishes to take out on the other. . . . Materialism astounds us by the assertion that physical and chemical forces are enough to explain the formation of living tissues; but no man has shown that in physical and chemical forces there can be an involution equal to the evolution we call organism and life. The evolution in man is intelligence, imagination, emotion, will, or all that we call the soul; and the involution, therefore, must have in it the equivalents of these qualities. Forever and forever it will be true that you can find in living tissue, and take out of it, only what is put into it, visibly or invisibly.[95]

To McCosh and Cook, plainly, as to a host of others, Royce's dilemma was a real one, though the "deceptive appearance" lay in the "approximately continuous" evolution rather than in the "wide difference" between matter and mind.

With some prominent exceptions, the more recent tendency has been to abandon the dilemma altogether. Simply on an empirical basis,[96] it has seemed evident to many that both sides of the dilemma are true: both that the wide difference is a real one and that "beings with minds" have been evolved from "inorganic matter." This is particularly true of "emergent" evolutionists like Morgan and Alexander, who do not attempt to "explain" the derivation but only to describe it as a new form of "relatedness"[97] and to accept it "with natural piety."[98] True novelty in evolution, they point out, is not only possible, but, judging by the common performance of nature, quite to be expected. A knowledge of the properties of hydrogen and oxygen, Morgan argues, going back to suggestions of G. H. Lewes and John Stuart Mill,[99] is of no assistance in predicting the properties of water; hence there is no reason to expect that life and mind should be predictable or deducible from the properties of the chemical components of living tissue. By this reasoning the philosophers of emergence believe that they not only have resolved the dilemma but have refuted nineteenth-century materialism, which they hold to have been as much ridden by the old axiom as theism and idealism had been. To the suggestion that love or thought is "nothing but" chemistry, that *man ist was er isst,* they reply that such a suggestion is based on an entirely false analysis of nature. Thus, where Cook and McCosh charged the materialists with forgetting the old principle, Bergson blamed them, in reducing life to an atomic mechanism, for remembering it too well:

Generally speaking, unorganized bodies, which are what we have need of in order that we may act, and on which we have modelled our fashion of thinking, are regulated by this simple law: *the present contains nothing more than the past, and what is found in the effect was already in the cause.*[100]

It must be pointed out, however, that the new view, while it has gained wide acceptance, has not proved acceptable to all. It is still materialistic, it is contended; for, however novel mind may be as a property of matter, it is still no more than a property, dependent upon its substance, without immortality and probably without freedom in the sense of being able to act on its own initiative upon the world about it. This is quite naturally the view of a modern Scholastic like Jacques Maritain, who requires a much greater novelty than even the emergent evolutionists are able to provide:

Man, in this view, is seen not only as emerging from a long-drawn evolution of animal species (that is a purely historical and, after all, secondary question), but as issuing from this biological evolution *without any metaphysical discontinuity,* without at a given moment, with the coming of human being, anything absolutely new appearing in the series: spiritual subsistence implying that in each generation of a human being an individual soul is created by the Author of all things and cast into existence with an eternal destiny.[101]

On the other hand, Santayana, who observed the importance of novelty in any theory of evolution some time before the announcement of the principle of emergence,[102] frankly avows himself a materialist, even if not in the classical sense of Newton and the nineteenth-century physicists. Quite as much as Morgan and Alexander he denies Royce's dilemma and agrees that the properties of the higher level are not determined by the properties of the lower, but he gives greater emphasis to the fact, not denied by the others,

INTRODUCTION

that the higher nevertheless grows out of the lower and that both are "caused by matter":

> Matter, it is said, cannot explain the origin of life, of consciousness, or of morals. Matter here means the *essence* which some philosopher attributes, or is alleged to attribute, to matter.... Now no essence can be the origin of anything: not even of another essence, much less of any fact.... The incapacity of the materialist to deduce logically from the terms of his theory—such as extension, atoms, electric charges, energy, or what not—the other variegated terms in which our senses or imagination may picture the world, is therefore a matter of course.... But the forms which nature wears could not be successive, or be embodied anywhere, if matter did not assume, connect, and exchange them. Of course this real matter, coming down through the ages, and falling into all these forms, is not anybody's *idea* of matter: its intrinsic essence is unknown, and if we prefer for that reason to call it by another name, we are at liberty to do so, provided we honestly attribute to it, under that sweeter name, all the relations and functions by which the existence of matter has become certain to common sense, and has been assumed by science and the arts, since the beginning of history.[103]

Interesting as these current differences of view may be, however, they are of no concern in this study except for purposes of perspective. For, whatever the situation may now be, in the period of our interest not only was Royce's dilemma a very real one, but, when faced by it, most of the poets whom we shall study found only one choice possible. Accepting evolution and convinced beyond question of the independent reality of the spiritual life known inwardly, they came with Royce to the conclusion that somehow mind is the reality and matter the appearance. However loosely interpreted by the poets, this of course was metaphysical idealism, and was not new even in this use, having since Berkeley been one of the most useful maneuvers for outflanking materialism. The idealism of the nineteenth century, to be sure, differed from that of Berkeley. To Berkeley the "external" world depended upon the perception of individuals, including God, but to idealists after Kant it depended upon an Absolute Mind which was at once the type, sum, and ground of all individual minds—the individual soul universalized. If, as was often the case, this was stated in the less abstruse and more traditional terms of an immanent theism, the consequence for the interpretation of evolution—at least on the nontechnical levels with which we shall be dealing—was substantially the same.

Moreover, as has been shown, this idealism included an evolutionism of its own. To be sure, it differed sharply from the evolutionisms of science, as Hegel and many others were careful to point out. It represented nature as an ascending hierarchy in which each level strove toward the level above, but this striving was ideal rather than actual, logical rather than physical. Thus Hegel dismissed the notion of "the transformation and the transition from one natural form and sphere to a higher as an outward and actual production" as simply "clumsy";[104] and Stallo, writing only eleven years before the appearance of *The Origin of Species,* took especial pains that the theories he was retailing should not be confused with those of Lamarck and Chambers. Referring specifically to these theories, he wrote in one instance:

> The theory of the morphologists, that brute nature will, of her own accord, and by dint of her own forces, percur a series of stages,—that therefore . . . natural forms will, of their own accord, progress to higher stages, is futile. No difference, whether it be said that the craving creates the organ—that when a necessity is felt by an animal, for instance, the organ forms itself to satisfy it (which is the gist of Lamarck's theory),—or whether the addition, greater development, &c., of organs, entire modification of the organism, be made dependent upon a prolonged period of gestation,[105]—the statement of the theory is at the same time the statement of its own insufficiency. Whence the craving? whence the prolongation of the gestative period?—Nature cannot promote herself to superior dignities. The progress is in the Spiritual, which is essentially a progress from and towards itself; this, of course, is simultaneously, then a progress of the Material. . . .[106]

Again, two pages farther on, he says more succinctly:

> But once more be it said, material nature is essentially impotent; the metamorphoses, and thence the variety in the succession and co-arrangement of natural forms, the continuity of the series, is a spiritual, not a material continuity. The coherence is that of logical deduction, not of material propagation.[107]

Plainly, if this transcendental evolutionism was to be of any use to those who accepted the notions of Lamarck and Chambers, Spencer and Darwin, some lively efforts of reconciliation were necessary.

INTRODUCTION 35

It may be that this is possible only through some such manipulation of the concept of time as that of Royce.[108] On the popular level, however, when it was not simply left unexplained, it was done much more loosely and simply. As far as the objections of a Stallo were concerned, it could be replied that there is no necessary incompatability between "logical deduction" and "material propagation." To borrow Professor Riley's rephrasing of the view vigorously upheld by Asa Gray at a later turn in the evolutionary debate, "a material connection between the members of a series of organized beings is not inconsistent with the idea of their being intellectually connected with one another through the deity."[109] What seems to have troubled Stallo, in any case, was not so much the fact of material propagation as the suggestion that it was a sufficient and final explanation in itself. His method of refuting Lamarck and Chambers, it will have been noted, was not to deny the efficacy of the "craving" or the "prolongation of the gestative period," but only to ask whence they came and to suggest that there was more to be said. Might it not be argued that the scientific theories, if demonstrable on their own grounds, were true as far as they went and that the craving or the prolongation was simply the outward manifestation of a deeper cause? This did not settle the matter, of course. It left untouched the question of how the self, the subject of knowledge, could be evolved from nature, its object; but there was an answer to this too in the idea that subject and object are always present and that subject becomes fully aware of itself—becomes its own object—for the first time in man. The important thing here, however, is that the two lines of evolutionary thought were joined and the scientific account was regarded as the "phenomenal outer aspect"[110] of an ultimate spiritual being that was good, true, and beautiful and must therefore operate to good, true, and beautiful ends. In the apt simplification of Oliver Wendell Holmes, physical processes like evolution were "simply God himself in action."[111]

Thus was the theoretical basis of an evolutionary cosmic optimism established. In the words of Professor Randall:

On one point all the romantic and idealistic philosophers agreed: they rejected the traditional dualism of the natural and the supernatural, and united in the monistic belief that the world is the expression of one great principle permeating all its parts and including all events in its cosmic process. Man is one with nature, and man and nature are one with God—not, perhaps, the whole expression of the divine life, but existing as essential parts of it. It was easy for religious souls to see in the whole long story of evolution itself the unfolding of the hand of Providence, and in its goal of a perfected human society "the one far-off divine event to which the whole creation moves."[112]

II

EMERSON: THE BEGINNINGS

IN VIEW of the importance of the idealistic philosophy both in the origin of the idea of evolution in modern times and in the reconciliation of the scientific and religious views of the cosmos, a logical starting point for our discussion of Emerson is the extended passage on that philosophy in his first published work, the 1836 *Nature*.[1] There, after he had set forth the Berkeleian subjectivism at some length as "the uniform effect of culture on the human mind," he criticized it as merely negative, leaving us to wander in the "splendid labyrinth" of our perceptions without an inkling of their cause or significance. It tells us that the material world is a "perpetual effect," "a phenomenon, not a substance," but not how or to what end just this world appears to us and no other. Nevertheless, it is "a useful introductory hypothesis," for, in assuring us that "the mind is a part of the nature of things; the world is a dream," it directs us inward for an answer to these questions. And there we learn:

that the dread universal essence, which is not wisdom, or love, or beauty, or power, but all in one, and each entirely, is that for which all things exist, and that by which they are; that spirit creates; that behind nature, throughout nature, spirit is present; one and not compound it does not act upon us from without, that is, in space and time, but spiritually, or through ourselves: therefore, that spirit, that is, the Supreme Being, does not build up nature around us, but puts it forth through us, as the life of the tree puts forth new branches and leaves through the pores of the old.[2]

More simply, the argument would seem to come down to this. Though the world may be shown to depend upon the mind that perceives it, it is only too obviously indifferent to the wishes of that mind. Hence it must be said to depend upon something within or behind that mind that is deeper, more fundamental, more real. Or, to follow the more usual order of the statement of the Emersonian metaphysic, there is but one reality, the Primal Mind or Over-Soul, which manifests itself in two opposed but perfectly correspondent modes, immediately in the mind of man and phenomenally in nature. This was the absolute idealism or transcendentalism of the nineteenth century—in the vivid, if satirical, words of Professor Perry, "an unseaworthy subjectivism rescued from the shipwreck of solipsism by the miraculous intervention of universalism."[3]

As far as our immediate purposes are concerned, the consequences of this for Emerson's treatment of evolution were two. First, it enabled him to accept the most daring generalizations of science without fear of materialism. During a period when many American men of letters were either uninterested in science or fearful of its materialistic drift, Emerson was persistently curious about it and sprinkled his pages with allusions to it.[4] He valued it because he believed that its exact rendering of nature was one avenue to the truth behind nature, and he was unafraid of it because he was convinced that the laws of nature, no matter how unyielding or ruthless-seeming, were only the sensible expressions of the Primal Mind. "The use of natural history is to give us aid in supernatural history," he wrote in *Nature*,[5] and he added in a later essay:

We may therefore safely study the mind in nature, because we cannot steadily gaze on it in mind; as we explore the face of the sun in a pool, when our eyes cannot brook his direct splendors.[6]

It did not disturb him that the nebular hypothesis, equivocal generation, the conservation of energy, or the evolution of species threatened to reduce the world to formulae of matter and force; matter and force were themselves but symbols of spirit. Thus in his first series of *Essays* he wrote:

Fear not the new generalization. Does the fact look crass and material, threatening to degrade thy theory of spirit? Resist it not; it goes to refine and raise thy theory of matter just as much.[7]

And at the end of his career he commenced his Harvard lectures on *The Natural History of Intellect* with this similar declaration:

I believe in the existence of the material world as the expression of the spiritual or the real, and in the impenetrable mystery which hides (and hides through absolute transparency) the mental nature, I await the insight which our advancing knowledge of material laws shall furnish.[8]

Secondly, Emerson's idealism set him on the road to an evolutionary theory of his own by introducing him to the concept of the chain of being. This was, in fact, an easy and common deduction from his central principle that all created things are but appearances of one fundamental reality. For if this was true, then all things shared to some degree in the essential character of that reality and in that respect bore a resemblance to each other and to the whole. This was his well-known doctrine of identity—that "each particle is a microcosm, and faithfully renders the likeness of the whole."[9] Obviously, however, since objects in nature also differ, they cannot be said to render the likeness of the world with the same degree of faithfulness. Rather, they must all fail in some degree and hence fall into a graded scale according to the degree of their failure. "Self-existence," he said in "Self-Reliance," "is the attribute of the Supreme Cause, and it constitutes the measure of good by the degree in which it enters into all lower forms."[10] One aspect or another of this logic Emerson applied to nature many times, but never more explicitly or completely than in the following two passages, the one written early, the other late. In "Compensation":

These appearances indicate the fact that the universe is represented in every one of its particles. Every thing in nature contains all the powers of nature. Every thing is made of one hidden stuff; as the naturalist sees one type under every metamorphosis, and regards a horse as a running man, a fish as a swimming man, a bird as a flying man, a tree as a rooted man.[11]

And, most explicitly, in *The Natural History of Intellect:*

Well, having accepted this law of identity pervading the universe, we next perceive that whilst every creature represents and obeys it, there is diversity, there is more or less of power; that the lowest only means incipient form, and over it is a higher class in which its rudiments are opened, raised to higher powers; that there is development from less to more, from lower to superior function, steadily ascending to man.
If man has organs for breathing, for sight, for locomotion, for taking food, for digesting, for protection by housebuilding, by attack and defense, for reproduction and love and care of his young, you shall find all the same in the muskrat. There is a perfect correspondence; or 't is only man modified to live in a mud-bank. A fish in like manner is man furnished to live in the sea; a thrush, to

fly in the air; and a mollusk is a cheap edition with a suppression of the costlier illustrations, designed for dingy circulation, for shelving in an oyster-bank or among the seaweed.[12]

It has already been pointed out, however, that the chain of being, even in "temporalized" form, is not necessarily evolutionary.[13] According to the theory of evolution, new forms arise through the modification of old, whereas in the chain of being the relationship between old and new is not one of blood but of idea. Moreover, since it is a logical rather than a genetic sequence, the chain can be read either up or down—a liberty of which, as we shall see, Emerson availed himself. It can be shown that in the end Emerson came to take the evolutionary view in these matters, but the questions remain, when, how, and under what influences? Only after answering these questions can we undertake the analysis of his interpretation of evolution and see its significance in the larger context of his thought.

1

One thing is certain. Emerson did not accept evolution in any form at the beginning of his career in the 1830's. An entry in the Journal of 1834 indicates that he concurred in the general rejection of the teachings of the elder Darwin,[14] and neither of the passages in his early lectures which are sometimes cited to show his early evolutionary sympathies had a truly evolutionary intent. The earlier of these, spoken in 1832, indicated, it is true, an acceptance of the geological account of the past, developing the fact,

the most surprising, I may say the most sublime, that man is no upstart in the creation, but has been prophesied in nature for a thousand thousand ages before he appeared; that, from times incalculably remote, there has been a progressive preparation for him, an effort to produce him; the meaner creatures containing the elements of his structure and pointing at it from every side. . . . His limbs are only a more exquisite organization—say rather the finish—of the rudimental forms that have been already sweeping the sea and creeping in the mud; the brother of his hand is even now cleaving the Arctic Sea in the fin of the whale, and innumerable ages since was pawing the marsh in the flipper of the saurian.[15]

But while this in its clear recognition of the progressive succession of forms marked a distinct advance on a similar passage that he had read in Coleridge's *Aids to Reflection* a few years before,[16] it contains no hint of a genetic relation between the forms. Like Sir Charles Bell, whose Bridgewater Treatise on *The Hand* Professor Beach believes to have been the chief inspiration of the passage, Emerson envisaged a "progressive system" in nature only as the result of an "anticipating or prospective intelligence" in creation.[17] The later of the two passages, moreover, though it refers briefly to the theory of Lamarck, does so only for the purpose of illustrating the "tyrannical instinct" of the mind "to reduce all facts to a few laws, to one law."[18] That Emerson had no intent to approve is indicated by the epithets "imperfect" and "audacious" in the corresponding passages in the Journal.[19]

The strongest evidence, however, of Emerson's disregard of evolution at this stage of his career is its complete absence from the 1836 *Nature,* which was certainly the logical place for the enunciation of any evolutionary view that he might have held. Far from that, the general drift of this essay, with its emphasis on the priority of the perceiving mind to the world that it perceives, is away from rather than toward evolution. No evolutionism is complete in which the mind of man does not somehow emerge out of or grow up through nature, and in this essay that relationship is reversed, nature being presented as dependent upon the mind that knows it. This comes out most strongly, of course, in the chapter on "Idealism," where the Berkeleian subjectivism leads to this specific denial of the evolutionary position:

Idealism . . . beholds the whole circle of persons and things, of actions and events, of country and religion, not as painfully accumulated, atom after atom, act after act, in an aged creeping Past, but as one vast picture which God paints on the instant eternity for the contemplation of the soul.[20]

In the two concluding chapters, as we have seen, this extreme subjectivism was modified, but without approaching closer to the evolutionary conception. Rather, the movement is toward its precise opposite, the theory of emanation, in which nature is regarded as a descending efflux from the All-High. "The Supreme Being," Emerson wrote in a passage already quoted, "does not build up nature around us, but puts it forth through us, as the life of the tree puts forth new branches and leaves through the pores of the old."[21]

With this view of the relation of God, man, and nature, the essay was brought to a close in an extended rhapsody by "my Orphic poet" which contains the following emanational declaration:

"The foundations of man are not in matter, but in spirit. . . . In the cycle of the universal man, from whom the known individuals proceed, centuries are points, and all history is but the epoch of one degradation. . . .
"Man is the dwarf of himself. Once he was permeated and dissolved by spirit. He filled nature with his overflowing currents. Out from him sprang the sun and moon; from man the sun, from woman the moon. The laws of his mind, the periods of his actions externized themselves into day and night, into the years and the seasons. But, having made for himself this huge shell, his waters retired; he no longer fills the veins and veinlets; he is shrunk to a drop."[22]

While it is futile to attempt to identify most such passages in Emerson—the quotation marks being usually simply a means of holding at arm's length a particularly airy flight—there can be no doubt in this case that "my Orphic poet" was Bronson Alcott. The similarity of the emanationism of the passage to Alcott's theory of Genesis and Lapse would make the identification a reasonable conjecture, but we also know that Emerson had Alcott's Journals for 1834 and 1835 before him when he wrote this portion of *Nature*.[23] There he found a radically emanational doctrine, which is summarized by Professor Odell Shepard as follows:

Man, he held, was an emanation from the divine and original Mind. . . . And just as Man had lapsed from Mind, so all Nature, he held, had lapsed from Man. The lower animals he took to be the incarnations of Man's lower self—and that was one reason why he "declined" to eat them. Nature was "Man in ruins," he said. Nature in all its parts and forms and in every atom of its matter was the creation not of the Original Mind but of Man—and of Man, too, in his lower and downward-looking moments.[24]

In many of Emerson's comments on the kinship of man and nature—for example, the sense of an "occult relation between the very scorpions and man"[25] that he experienced at the Jardin des Plantes in 1833 and referred to many times afterward[26]—it is difficult to tell whether he meant that man sprang from nature or nature from man or whether simply both are expressions of the same creative intelligence. Many of these comments, however, in their emphasis on the presence of man's features in nature, are reminiscent of Alcott's view. This was true even in the passage quoted from *The Natural History of Intellect* a few pages back, where the meaning was quite the opposite, and in the earlier passage from "Compensation" in which the horse was described as a running man, the fish as a swimming man, etc.[27]

Though, as we have seen, Emerson stated the ascending view of the order of nature from a public platform as early as 1832,[28] and though he partly neutralized his borrowing from Alcott by placing it in quotation marks and describing it as a mere tradition, he remained strongly attached to the emanational doctrine long after the writing of *Nature*. Plotinus, Proclus, and Plato's *Timaeus* were favorite reading, and at least until 1845 he seems to have been torn between the two alternatives. In 1842, thus, he asked in his Journal:

> Are beasts and plants degradations of man? or are these the prophecies and preparations of Nature practicing herself for her masterpiece in Man? Culminate we do not; but that point of imperfection which we occupy—is it on the way *up* or *down*?[29]

And as late as 1845, a matter of days before he made what has been described as "the most uncompromising declaration Emerson was ever to make that man is a child of earth,"[30] he returned to the question in these words:

> There are always two histories of man in literature contending for our faith.
> One is the scientific or skeptical, and derives his origin from the gradual composition, subsidence, and refining,—from the negro, from the ape, progressive from the animalcule savages of the waterdrop, from *volvox globator,* up to the wise man of the nineteenth century.
> The other is the believer's, the poet's, the faithful history, always testified by the mystic and the devout, the history of the Fall, of a descent from a superior and pure race, attested in actual history by the grand remains of elder ages, of a science of the East unintelligible to the existing population.[31]

Emerson was never, in fact, to forsake the belief that "the foundations of man are not in matter, but in spirit." Powerful forces, however, were at work leading him more and more to doubt that "all history is but the epoch of one degradation."[32] His curiosity about nature, for example, taught him that nature's growth is from simple to complex, from seed to flower and grub to moth; and his sanguine temper, reinforced by the prevailing optimism of the time, led him to favor a progressive view of human events. The most important influence, however, came from the sciences, which taught him that the earth had already had a long history before man appeared. The reading of popular works on astronomy had introduced him to the nebular hypothesis by 1832 at the latest,[33] and he had known something of geology since college days.[34] In 1835, moreover, a renewed interest in geology took him first to the lectures of Benjamin Silliman[35] and then to the reading of Lyell. He criticized Lyell's book as "only a catalogue of facts,"[36] but it was undoubtedly an important influence in leading him to an evolutionary view. It introduced him to the hypothesis of Lamarck through its extended polemic against it, it taught him that past changes in the earth's surface were brought about by causes now in operation, and it showed him again the vastness of the earth's history and the appearance of higher and higher forms of life in successive eras. Some years later he was to pay high tribute to the science of geology, if not to Lyell, in these words:

Geology has initiated us into the secularity of nature and taught us to disuse our dame-school measures, and exchange our Mosaic and Ptolemaic schemes for her large style. We knew nothing rightly, for want of perspective.[37]

These influences began to leave their mark in the Journals and letters in the late 1830's, and they eventuated in a new conception of the history of nature in the following decade. In 1838, for example, he noted in his Journal that "the great-grandfather of all the races, the oldest inhabitant, seems to be the trilobite,"[38] and in 1840 he wrote to Margaret Fuller:

Nothing is to me more welcome nor to my recent speculation more familiar than the Protean energy by which the brute horns of Io become the crescent moon of Isis, and nature lifts itself through everlasting transition to the higher & the highest.[39]

The evolutionary, and even naturalistic, turn that this "recent speculation" had taken is indicated by the following passage entered in the Journal only five days before:

There is no leap—not a shock of violence throughout nature. Man therefore must be predicted in the first chemical relation exhibited by the first atom. If we had eyes to see it, this bit of quartz would certify us of the necessity that man must exist as inevitably as the cities he has actually built.[40]

These private speculations became public utterances in the following year in the address at Waterville College on "The Method of Nature" and in the second part of the poem "Woodnotes," published in *The Dial*. The address began as the 1836 *Nature* had ended, with the assertion that the world about us has had its origin in mind, but it avoided the emanational conclusion of the earlier essay. Though Emerson could still say that "intellect is primary; nature, secondary,"[41] he made it clear that he was speaking of the "divine" order, the order of logic and value, not the natural or temporal order. He could still say in the old vein:

That which once existed in intellect as pure law, has now taken body as Nature. It existed already in the mind in solution; now, it has been precipitated, and the bright sediment is the world.[42]

Yet he could also say, "An individual man is a fruit which it cost all the foregoing ages to form and ripen."[43] He could still say, "Not the cause, but an ever novel effect, nature descends always from above,"[44] but, as he showed in the sentences that followed, his meaning was merely that nature must be explained by a principle higher than itself:

In all animal and vegetable form, the physiologist concedes that no chemistry, no mechanics, can account for the facts, but a mysterious principle of life must be assumed, which not only inhabits the organ but makes the organ.[45]

Here, in fact, was the gist of the essay. Nature is not a mechanism, as many, including the natural theologians of the school of Paley, had held, but the living, growing manifestation of an inner spiritual principle. Nature is truly organic in the sense that the outer depends upon the inner, and hence its "genius or method" is

that it does not exist to any one or to any number of particular ends, but to numberless and endless benefit; that there is in it no private will, no rebel leaf or limb, but the whole is oppressed by one superincumbent tendency, obeys that redundancy or excess of life which in conscious beings we call *ecstasy*.[46]

To all questions of particular ends or purposes nature has one sufficient answer, the answer of development. " 'I grow,' " it says.

All is nascent, infant. . . . We can point nowhere to anything final; but tendency appears on all hands: planet, system, constellation, total nature is growing like a field of maize in July; is becoming somewhat else; is in rapid metamorphosis. The embryo does not more strive to be man, than yonder burr of light we call a nebula tends to be a ring, a comet, a globe, and parent of new stars.[47]

"Woodnotes II," which was being pondered and revised at the same time as the address,[48] was its poetic counterpart. With extensive use of the device of personification and of the transformation-myths of Proteus, Pan, and Bacchus, nature was here again pictured as one living spiritual Being manifesting itself in constantly shifting appearances:

> Onward and on, the eternal Pan,
> Who layeth the world's incessant plan,
> Halteth never in one shape,
> But forever doth escape,
> Like wave or flame, into new forms
> Of gem, and air, of plants, and worms.[49]

Moreover, again as in the address, though he was not yet prepared to render the change in the specific terms of the geological sequence, Emerson showed that he had grasped the essential evolutionary conception of nature as growing by an inner necessity through an immense period of time—the passage in the address beginning " 'I grow' " being clearly paralleled by these famous lines, in which the "old oracle" sings

> Sweet the genesis of things,
> Of tendency through endless ages,
> Of star-dust, and star-pilgrimages,
> Of rounded worlds, of space and time,
> Of the old flood's subsiding slime,
> Of chemic matter, force and form,
> Of poles and powers, cold, wet, and warm.[50]

As far as I have been able to discover, these lines were the first of literary significance in our poetry to deal truly, even though generally, with the theme of evolution.[51]

The very definite question concerning progress and degradation that Emerson asked himself in the following year, 1842,[52] shows the direction that his thought was taking, and two years later, in his second essay on "Nature," he went farther along the road to evolution than in anything he had previously written. Here again he was concerned with the eternal flux of things and with the power that lies behind it, but now he dealt with them in terms more specifically those of science. This statement, for example, not to be taken literally, should have been mechanistic enough to satisfy even Poe:

The astronomers said, "Give us matter and a little motion and we will construct the universe." . . . That famous aboriginal push propagates itself through all the balls of the system, and through every atom of every ball; through all the races of creatures, and through the history and performances of every individual.[53]

The "redundancy or excess of life," the "spiritual principle" or "superincumbent tendency" spoken of in "The Method of Nature" and in this essay given the scholastic name *natura naturans,* now takes definitely evolutionary form. It not only is "the quick cause before which all forms flee as the driven snows," but it "publishes itself in creatures, reaching from particles and spiculae through transformation on transformation to the highest symmetries.[54] Moreover, these changes are described as having taken place gradually and without a shock or leap under the condition of "boundless time" revealed by geology, which has shown

what patient periods must round themselves before the rock is formed; then before the rock is broken, and the first lichen race has disintegrated the thinnest external plate into soil, and opened the door for the remote Flora, Fauna, Ceres, and Pomona to come in. How far off yet is the trilobite! how far the quadruped! how inconceivably remote is man! All duly arrive, and then race after race of men. It is a long way from granite to the oyster; farther yet to Plato and the preaching of the immortality of the soul. Yet all must come, as surely as the first atom has two sides.[55]

Though it must be remembered that Emerson was still to raise the question of degradation once again, there can be no doubt of the evolutionary significance of this passage.

In view of the fact that the *Vestiges of Creation* was published in the same year as this essay and is noted in the reading list of the Journal of that year, one might suspect that the reading of this book lay behind these evolutionary statements. Such, however, was not the case. The geological retrospect just quoted was first written in the Journal in the summer of 1844,[56] and the *Vestiges* was not published until late in the year.[57] Moreover, the passages in the Journal and letters that comment on the *Vestiges* are all dated in the spring of 1845. Nevertheless, it is significant that when Emerson read this book he was highly pleased with it and did not join in the general chorus of denunciation. Though he deplored what he regarded as its timid theology, he declared that otherwise "everything in this *Vestiges of Creation* is good";[58] and though he was aware of its inexactitudes, he wrote a friend that he "found it a good approximation to that book we have wanted so long."[59] Thus it is clear that, though he owed it less than might be expected, Emerson was in fundamental agreement with the only important and well-known pronouncement in favor of the evolutionary origin of species between the Cuvier—Saint Hilaire debate of 1830 and the statements of Darwin and Spencer in the 1850's.

The acid test of the acceptance of evolution, however, is the acceptance of the emergence of man out of nature, and consequently there is particular significance in the following comment, written shortly after the reading of the *Vestiges,* on two lines from the same poem that was quoted at length in the 1836 *Nature*[60] as an instance of emanationism:

> Herbs gladly cure our flesh because that they
> Find their acquaintance there.
>   Herbert, "Man."

This is mystically true. The master can do his great deed, the desire of the world,—say to find his way between azote and oxygen, detect the scene of the new rock superposition, bind the law of the curves,—because he has just come out of Nature, or from being a part of that thing. . . . He knows the laws of azote because just now he was azote. Man is only a piece of the universe made alive.[61]

At this time, in fact, Emerson seems to have been returning to the very Lamarckian conception that he had termed "imperfect" and "audacious" after reading Lyell in 1836.[62] At that time he summarized Lamarck's view in these words:

The system of Lamarck . . . aims to find one monad of organic life which shall be the common element of every animal, and becoming an infusory, a poplar-worm, or a man according to circumstances. It says to the canker-worm, "How dost thou, Brother? Please God you shall yet be a philosopher!"[63]

Now, nine years later, he had not forgotten his worm-philosopher, and, perhaps under the inspiration of the *Vestiges,* returned to him in the first version of two famous lines:

> And, willing to be God, the worm
> Flees through all the spire of form.[64]

Also, six years later, in 1851, he returned in another Journal entry to the "monad of organic life which shall be the common element of every animal" in these words:

I wish I could get the fact about horseshoe nails, which, after being hammered and worn and recast and hammered and worn, are made up into Damascus steel, which is thus a result and simmering down, and last possibility of iron. I believe the tradition is fabulous. But such in Nature are men made up of monads, each of which has held governance of fish or fowl or worm or fly, and is now promoted to be a particle of man.[65]

Of course none of these passages represents Lamarckism as it has continued to have interest for biologists, but only a rather fanciful version of a rejected and forgotten portion of Lamarck's theory.[66] Indeed, they might with equal justification be explained in terms of the theory of transmigration of souls, which also influenced Emerson's conception of evolution. Thus the master who knew the laws of azote because just now he was azote might be said to have re-enacted Pythagoras' legendary assertion, "I was Euphorbus at the siege of Troy." And—to choose only illustrations not already cited—the worm "striving to be man" in the 1849 reissue of *Nature,*[67] the *volvox globator* in the Journal of 1845 that had "got on so far,"[68] and the "poor grass" of the poem "Bacchus" that

> shall plot and plan
> What it will do when it is man,[69]

might be stages in a progressive reincarnation. That such an interpretation, moreover, would have been agreeable to Emerson is evidenced by the fact that he himself wrote in his Journal on the page following his remarks on the *Vestiges:* "The Avatars of Brahma will presently be textbooks of natural history."[70] No matter how the passages are interpreted, however, they leave no doubt that Emerson was thinking of man as growing up through nature.

The fact that all save one of the passages quoted or referred to in the last two paragraphs were written during the forties permits us to conclude that Emerson came to a definitely evolutionary view of the history of nature and the origin of man during that decade.[71] It is true that his thought on the subject was not yet fully developed. He had yet to demonstrate clearly its place in his transcendentalism, and he had yet to present in full that conception of the development of the spiritual essence of things through successive stages of arrest and development that was the core of his view. Both of these steps were taken, however, before the appearance of *The Origin of Species* and without its aid—the first in the essay "Fate," which was in preparation as early as 1853,[72] and the second in "The Song of Nature," which was dispatched to the editor of *The Atlantic Monthly* a month before the English publication of Darwin's book.[73] Thus, with his conception of evolution already fully rounded out, Emerson was no more surprised or alarmed by the advent of Darwin than he had been by the appearance of the *Vestiges.* Indeed, by comparison with the general uproar he seems almost complacent. Darwin's name appears only a few times in the Journals, and the only comment on *The Origin of Species* is patronizing: "Darwin's Origin of Species was published in 1859, but Stallo, in 1849, writes 'animals are but foetal forms of man.' "[74] This silence is not to be construed as lack of interest, however, as two statements in his recently published letters show. A few months after the publication of the book, he wrote eagerly to his wife: "I have not yet been able to obtain Darwin's book which I had depended on as a road book. You must read it,—'Darwin on Species.' It has not arrived in these dark lands."[75] And in 1869 he was sufficiently familiar with Darwin to say: "I am glad you find Huxley interesting. He is an acknowledged master in England. . . . But I have read him less than his compeers, Owen, & Tyndall, & Darwin."[76] Indeed, the discussion precipitated by *The Origin of Species* seems to have stimulated him to write more frequently and with greater assurance on the theme of evolution; for, with the exception of "Fate" and "The Song of Nature," the most extensive and revealing of his evolutionary statements must all be dated after 1859.

2

Such were the steps by which Emerson passed from the conception of nature as a descending scale of being to the theory that it is a continuous evolution in which man is the latest culmination. We have next to consider more exactly what he meant by such an evolution, and to do this it will be necessary to return briefly to the dialectical evolutionism of the post-Kantian idealists discussed in the last chapter. Fichte contended, it will be remembered, first, that the thing known is not something apart from the knower but an act of self-limitation performed by him in an effort to realize or define himself; second, that this act, because it modifies the self, in a sense results in the emergence of a new self; and third, that this modified self performs further acts of self-limitation, which result in still further modifications in what for Fichte was the evolution of the categories of knowledge. It will also be recalled that Schelling, on the assumption basic to idealism that nature is simply thought in a state that can be perceived by the senses, adopted this conception as the fundamental principle of his philosophy of nature. Nature, according to his view, was a tissue of interacting opposites reflecting the basic subject-object relationship in thought. On the one side was a creative effort corresponding to the self-assertion of the subject, and on the other a limiting result corresponding to the object created by the subject, the two sides of the dualism interacting to bring into being an ascending hierarchy of forms.[77] How much or how little Emerson knew of the crabbed and sometimes fantastic writings of Fichte and Schelling is immaterial. Somehow he grasped the evolutionary significance of the dialectical conception and drew out of it a view of the relations of things that had far-reaching consequences in his thinking.

He recognized and made use of this dualism very early, presenting it in the 1844 "Nature" under the scholastic terms *natura naturans* and *natura naturata*. In this essay, however, as in its forerunner, "The Method of Nature," the emphasis was entirely on the active side of the dualism—*natura naturata* standing merely for nature as spectacle.[78] The quick cause before which all forms fled as the driven snows "published itself" in an ascending series of creatures,[79] but there was no explanation of how this took place, no explanation of the relation between the cause and the material it worked in or the result it achieved. Nor was there any explanation in the writings that followed until the essay "Fate" began to take shape more than a decade later.[80] Here, as the title vaguely suggested, he turned to the other side of the dualism: "Once we thought positive power was all. Now we learn that negative power, or circumstance, is half."[81] For by the word "fate" he did not mean simply determinism or predestination, as is sometimes said, but all the limitations that set bounds to the force of life—the unsympathetic environment and all constitutional insufficiencies and incapabilities whatever. Using the more appropriate term "Circumstance," he stated his meaning in one instance as follows:

The Circumstance is Nature. Nature is what you may do. There is much you may not. . . . Nature is . . . the conditions of a tool, like the locomotive, strong enough on its track, but which can do nothing but mischief off of it; or skates, which are wings on the ice but fetters on the ground.[82]

Notwithstanding the fact that this led him to an unflinching recognition of the evil in nature,[83] however, the message of the essay is that "Fate involves the melioration."[84] It will advance our understanding of his conception of evolution to inquire why.

The answer is not difficult or far to seek. As in the ontological proof of the existence of God,[85] it is simply that these limitations presuppose a power greater than themselves. Emerson had used this argument before—as an evidence of the Over-Soul in the first paragraph of the essay of that name,[86] and in "Compensation," where he had argued that everything requires its opposite to make it whole. And here it seems to have provided the original germ of his essay. At any rate among the preliminary jottings preserved by his editors is this reflection: "The very discovery that there is Fate, and that we are thwarted, equally discloses Power. For what is it that is limited? What but Power?"[87] One may well ask, however, why this limitation may not sometime prove insuperable, why Power must always and inevitably overcome Fate. And here the going is more difficult, for it was not simply a matter of faith that the will of God will prevail. The answer, I believe, lies rather in the phenomenal character of the world of the idealist and is suggested in the following passage, usually quoted to more edifying ends:

The secret of the world is the tie between person and event. Person makes event, and event person. . . . He thinks his fate alien, because the copula is hidden. But the soul contains the event that shall befall it; for the event is only the actualization of its thoughts, and what we pray to ourselves for is always granted.[88]

Here Emerson's thought was not only the simple one that man is master of his fate, but, as idealists believe, that the soul is the only reality and the event its visible projection. Moreover, this was true not only of event and person but of the world and its soul, which are synonyms of "Circumstance" and "Power" when applied to nature as a whole. Thus, just as the event is only the "actualization" of the thoughts of the person, so Circumstance is the actualization of Power; it is its creature and therefore subject to its will. As Emerson said again and again, nature, or all that appears to be external and to set limits to the creative essence of existence, is but the "externization"[89] of that essence. One of the difficulties in reading Emerson is that, because he usually does not repeat his epistemological and ontological premises, we are apt to read him as if he took the common-sense, realistic view of the external world. He did not, however, and in considering his theories of external nature it is always necessary to take this into account.

However, the fact that the resisting or limiting side of the dualism was simply the momentary appearance of the active side does not mean that it was merely a chimera without force or function, any more than Fichte's "object" was a nonentity because it was really a self-limitation of the "subject." On the contrary, like the lamentable present state of each of us, it was something to be overcome, and hence a stimulus and guide to the active side of the dualism. The present state of things, by the very fact that it sets limits to the aspiring creative energy, calls forth the effort that shall remove it. The operation of this principle in nature appears in the interaction of organism and environment and is set forth at length in this essay. Thus, on the one hand, the form taken by life is conditioned by the circumstances under which it lives:

A vesicle in new circumstances, a vesicle lodged in darkness, Oken thought, became animal; in light, a plant. Lodged in the parent animal, it suffers changes which end in unsheathing miraculous capability in the unaltered vesicle, and it unlocks itself to fish, bird, or quadruped, head and foot, eye and claw. . . .

Eyes are found in light; ears in auricular air; feet on land; fins in water; wings in air; and each creature where it was meant to be, with a mutual fitness. Every zone has its own *Fauna.* There is adjustment between the animal and its food, its parasite, its enemy. Balances are kept.[90]

On the other hand, the needs created by circumstances stimulate the creative energy of life to produce new forms and adaptations:

The animal cell makes itself;—then, what it wants. Every creature, wren or dragon, shall make its own lair. As soon as there is life, there is self-direction and absorbing and using of material. . . .

When there is something to be done, the world knows how to get it done. The vegetable eye makes leaf, pericarp, root, bark, or thorn, as the need is; the first cell converts itself into stomach, mouth, nose, or nail, according to the want. . . . The ulterior aim, the purpose beyond itself, the correlation by which planets subside and crystalize, then animate beasts and men,—will not stop but will work into finer particulars, and from finer to finest.[91]

It would not be new to point out that there is something of Lamarck in this; Emerson must have been enchanted with the story of the giraffe and his long neck, which he had read in Lyell.[92] Obviously, however, he meant something more than Lamarck. To Lamarck the heart of the evolutionary process was the purely local adaptation of individual and environment, but to Emerson this was but one aspect of a universal relationship fulfilling a universal purpose. Since this purpose was the self-realization of an Absolute Spirit, it followed that the perfect essence of that spirit should become more apparent as each obstacle was overcome in the dialectic of its development. Consequently, the book of Nature, which was the book of Fate, was also a record of continual melioration:

The book of Nature is the book of Fate. She turns the gigantic pages,—leaf after leaf,—never re-turning one. One leaf she lays down, a floor of granite; then a thousand ages, and a bed of slate; a thousand ages, and a measure of coal; a thousand ages, and a layer of marl and mud: vegetable forms appear; her first misshapen animals, zoöphyte, trilobium, fish; then, saurians,—rude forms, in which she has only blocked her future statue, concealing under these unwieldy monsters the fine type of her coming king. The face of the planet cools and dries, the races meliorate, and man is born.[93]

A more poetical way of conceiving this is to say that Emerson's evolutionism was an epic of the growth of the indwelling Soul of the World through a long series of inferior incarnations to self-conscious intelligence and an awakened moral sense in man. And nowhere in his prose is this better expressed than in the following paragraph from "The Sovereignty of Ethics":

> It is in the stomach of plants that development begins, and ends in the circles of the universe. 'T is a long scale from the gorilla to the gentleman—from the gorilla to Plato, Newton, Shakespeare—to the sanctities of religion, the refinements of legislation, the summits of science, art and poetry. The beginnings are slow and infirm, but it is an always-accelerated march. The geologic world is chronicled by the growing ripeness of the strata from lower to higher, as it becomes the abode of more highly-organized plants and animals. The civil history of men might be traced by the successive meliorations as marked in higher moral generalizations;—virtue meaning physical courage, then chastity and temperance, then justice and love;—bargains of kings with peoples of certain rights to certain classes, then of rights to masses,—then at last came the day when, as the historians rightly tell, the nerves of the world were electrified by the proclamation that all men are born free and equal.[94]

In his poems Emerson presented the same conception, but was enabled by the poet's privilege of personification to give greater emphasis to its ideal and volitional character. In "Cosmos," for example, he dramatized its dialectic by picturing the "hid beginnings" of the earth in terms of a titanic struggle between Chaos and Order that has left ineffaceable mementos in our "twisted Hills" and "basalt courses";[95] and in the motto written in 1860 for the essay "Wealth" he presented the active side of the dualism as a "primal pioneer" who

> Knew the strong task to it assigned,
> Patient through Heaven's enormous year
> To build in matter home for mind.[96]

It was characteristic of Emerson, however, that he did not simply tell Nature's story in his own words, but permitted her to speak for herself. In many of his best known nature poems—"The Sphinx," "Earth-Song," "Woodnotes," "Monadnoc," and others—he acted only as interpreter and amanuensis to the voice that he heard so clearly in the world about him, and likewise in two of his best poems of evolution he told its story as a first-hand experience. The lesser of these, "Solution,"[97] was not concerned primarily with evolution, but with the solution of a conundrum propounded by the Muse concerning the five "voices," or poets, who had achieved enduring expression; but the opening lines recount vividly, if briefly, the struggles of the Muse to mould first a living instrument of expression:

> I am the Muse who sung alway
> By Jove, at dawn of the first day.
> Star-crowned, sole-sitting, long I wrought
> To fire the stagnant earth with thought;
> On spawning slime my song prevails,
> Wolves shed their fangs, and dragons scales;
> Flushed in the sky the sweet May-morn,
> Earth smiled with flowers, and man was born.

The other, "The Song of Nature"[98]—written, it will be remembered, before the appearance of *The Origin of Species*[99]—is distinguished as the most extensive of Emerson's evolutionary poems and by the fact that in it man is regarded as only a crude trial effort at the "man-child glorious." The universal dame tells first of her labors in moulding and peopling the earth:

> I wrote the past in characters
> Of rock and fire the scroll,
> The building in the coral sea,
> The planting of the coal.
>
> And thefts from satellites and rings
> And broken stars I drew,
> And out of spent and aged things
> I formed the world anew;
>
> What time the gods kept carnival,
> Tricked out in star and flower,
> And in cramp elf and saurian forms
> They swathed their too much power.
>
> Time and Thought were my surveyors,
> They laid their courses well,
> They boiled the sea, and piled the layers
> Of granite, marl and shell.

EMERSON 57

The stage is set, but "still the man-child is not born, the summit of the whole," and Nature betrays her impatience:

> I tire of globes and races,
> Too long the game is played;
> What without him is summer's pomp,
> Or winter's frozen shade?
> . . .
> I moulded kings and saviors,
> And bards o'er kings to rule;—
> But fell the starry influence short,
> The cup was never full.

Her "oldest force is good as new," however, and she will try again:

> Yet whirl the glowing wheels once more
> And mix the bowl again;
> Seethe, Fate! the ancient elements,
> Heat, cold, wet, dry, and peace, and pain.
>
> Let war and trade and creeds and song
> Blend, ripen race on race,
> The sunburnt world a man shall breed
> Of all the zones and countless days.

In spite, however, of the highly circumstantial character of these sketches and of his repeated assertion that man is the offspring of nature, the question inevitably arises whether Emerson presented a *bona fide* evolutionism. In view of the extensive personification in the poems and the persistent hypostatizing of nature in the essays, it may be asked whether Emerson's position was not similar to that of Coleridge, who, according to Professor Potter,

> refused to accept evolution, and tried to explain the spirit of the very idea he would not accept, by supposing that an abstract "Nature" developed and grew in its production of new and increasingly higher forms of life, but that these forms did not grow or develop from each other.[100]

It must be admitted that Emerson too attributed the development of living forms to an "abstract Nature" in the sense that he traced the causes of all things to a Primal Mind, but I believe that it must also be concluded that he held these forms to "grow and develop from each other." Of the many passages that could be cited in support of this conclusion, all tending to show that the causes of organic development are inherent in nature, the best is the following, occurring in "Fate" in the discussion of the response of the organism to the environment:

> How is this effected? Nature is no spendthrift, but takes the shortest way to her ends. As the general says to his soldiers, "If you want a fort, build a fort," so nature makes every creature do its own work and get its living,—is it planet, animal or tree. The planet makes itself. The animal cell makes itself;—then, what it wants.[101]

The basic reason, however, is that in his idealism there was no gulf between the ultimate cause of things and the things themselves; the things were simply the sensible appearance taken by the cause. Consequently there was no question of whether living forms are attributable to a natural or transcendent cause, for in the Emersonian view there was no such distinction. Since he did not argue about evolution, but assumed it, he did not to my knowledge use this argument in any of his published writings; but, if we may trust the recollection of Moncure Conway, he used it at least once in a private conversation that presents his relation to evolution more clearly than anything he ever wrote:

> I was present at a conversation between Emerson and Agassiz,—in whom, great as he was, the paternal Swiss pastor survived, and who, when the new star appeared, was, like the ancient shepherds, "sore afraid." He regarded this theory of Darwin's as atheistic. Emerson, who loved Agassiz, was greatly disappointed at his rejection of the discovery, and recalled to his mind his (Agassiz's) early lectures, which had made so much of Goethe's Metamorphoses of plants, and Oken's ideas, and the generalization of Buffon, who said: "There is but one animal." Agassiz answered, "Yes, I have always believed in the ideal progression of forms, the gradation from lowest to highest, but to this materialistic development of one into another I cannot agree." Emerson was going on to maintain that the material and the ideal were essentially one, but Agassiz became excited and troubled, and said, "There we must differ." Thereon with his usual tact, Emerson changed the subject.[102]

On the other hand, Emerson's evolutionism was as remote as possible from that of the scientists. Not only was his idealism the polar opposite of their materialism and mechanism, but he was utterly unconcerned about the question of greatest importance to them, the immediate causes of transformation. Never once did he mention natural selection or the inheritance of acquired characteristics, and, as we have seen, he saw no essential advance in Darwin over Stallo.[103] The sciences, Emerson felt, dealt only with surfaces and were to be valued only for the light that, often in spite of themselves, they shed beyond. They were a kind of half-knowledge, not wrong but incomplete. Or, as he most liked to express it, they were "false by being unpoetical."[104] The scientist thought in terms of parts, while the poet and philosopher, taking a broader view, recognized that the parts make up a whole that has a unitary significance superior not only to each of its constituents but to the sum of all. In this view, the parts of nature exhibited an ordered interrelationship that corresponded perfectly with the categories of the individual mind and bodied forth the phases of that Over-Mind which is the ultimate reality. That this supreme One is truly all-encompassing and all-dissolving was Emerson's basic belief, and any interpretation of his thinking that disregarded it would be false to him. Consequently, in the matter of evolution, where empirical thinkers traced the origin of species to the survival of chance variations or the inheritance of acquired characteristics, Emerson saw only the phenomenal manifestation of a Creative Mind. Thus, in "Poetry and Imagination" he wrote that the metaphysician and the poet see "each animal form as an inevitable step in the path of the creative mind,"[105] and probably his truest and most characteristic expressions of his conception of evolution take the form of metaphor, as in the following quatrain:

> Ever the Rock of Ages melts
> Into the mineral air,
> To be the quarry whence to build
> Thought and its mansions fair.[106]

3

That such a view of the cosmos should lead to optimism seems too obvious for statement, and yet because this optimism was so much the final distillation of Emerson's thought on evolution and so great an influence on younger writers, a few words must be said of its two principal phases, the doctrines of the "good of evil" and inevitable progress. We must remember, of course, that though Emerson's sanguine conclusions may follow logically enough from his premises, they owed at least as much to his temperament as to his reasoning. One may question the details of William James' analysis in *The Varieties of Religious Experience,* but certainly he was right in setting Emerson apart among those to whom "happiness is congenital and irreclaimable."[107] From his earliest years there was a quiet and cheerful patience about Emerson that only later ripened into a philosophy, which, as he wrote Carlyle, "teaches acquiescence and optimism."[108]

And yet, for all his optimism, the charge that Emerson's "eyes were thickly bandaged"[109] to the sin and evil of the world is nothing less than absurd. On the contrary, he never flinched or softened the truth in telling of the sloth and wickedness of man or the monstrous indifference of nature. Indeed, the less savory side of the cosmic spectacle called forth some of his most vivid phrases. In the famous opening paragraphs of "Fate," for example:

Nature is no sentimentalist,—does not cosset or pamper us. . . . Without uncovering what does not concern us, or counting how many species of parasites hang on a bombyx, or groping after intestinal parasites or infusory biters, or the obscurities of alternate generation,—the forms of the shark, the *labrus,* the jaw of the sea-wolf paved with crushing teeth, the weapons of the grampus, and other warriors hidden in the sea, are hints of ferocity in the interiors of nature. Let us not deny it up and down. Providence has a wild, rough, incalculable road to its end, and it is of no use to try to whitewash its huge, mixed instrumentalities, or to dress up that terrific benefactor in a clean shirt and white neckcloth of a student in divinity.[110]

"No picture of life can have any veracity," he said elsewhere in the same essay, "that does not admit the odious facts."[111]

However, there is justice in the charge that Emerson treats evil too lightly, is easier on it than the consciences of most men will allow. It misses the point, I believe, to ask "whether 'the wisest American' . . . was unaware of the sin and evil among and within mankind."[112] He was very much aware of it. The question is rather whether he did not acquiesce in it with too great ease—"a trifle jauntily," in the words of Paul Elmer More.[113] A solid case can certainly be made out for this judgment, and in any case such toleration is the corollary of Emerson's whole idealistic position and particularly of the transcendental evolutionism we have been discussing. For though he was more than willing to grant evil its place in the world, he firmly denied it a place in the essential nature of things. Rather he held steadfastly that there is but one reality and that a perfect good, and abided by the consequence that evil must therefore be merely negative, apparent. Thus he said in the bombshell that he tossed into the Harvard Divinity School in 1838:

These facts have always suggested to man the sublime creed that the world is not the product of manifold power, but of one will, of one mind; and that one mind is everywhere active, in each ray of the star, in each wavelet of the pool. . . . Good is positive. Evil is merely privative, not absolute: it is like cold, which is the privation of heat. All evil is so much death or nonentity. Benevolence is absolute and real. So much benevolence as a man hath, so much life hath he. For all things proceed out of this same spirit, which is differently named love, justice, temperance, in its different applications, just as the ocean receives different names on the several shores which it washes.[114]

Furthermore, if, as we have seen, this spirit acts progressively, then the areas of "privation" must continually lessen as good rushes in like heat replacing cold or nature abhorring a vacuum. "There is a force always at work to make the best better and the worst good,"[115] he wrote in one of his numerous testaments of optimism. It is easy to see how from this position it would be difficult to feel a proper hostility to evil: one had only to be patient and it would be gone. I do not know a more startling instance of this than his account of the emancipation of the slaves in the British West Indies. After an unsoftened description of the barbarisms practiced before emancipation, he went on:

The horrid story ran and flew; the winds blew it all over the world. They who heard it asked their rich and great friends if it was true, or only missionary lies. The richest and greatest, the prime minister of England, the king's privy council were obliged to say that it was too true.[116]

Finally, after a considerable passage of time marked by official fumbling and including two years in which Granville Sharpe took up the study of law in order to prove that one man had no right to bash another man's head in, slavery was abolished. Emerson's judgment was: "the crude element of good in human affairs must work and ripen, spite of whips and plantation laws and West Indian interest."[117]

The difficult question concerning Emerson's attitude toward the problem of evil, in fact, is not whether he recognized its existence, but to what extent he relied for its solution on this essentially neo-Platonic view and to what extent on something like the Hegelian conception of evil as necessary. There is no neat or easy answer, for he never chose between them and seems to have leaned on one or the other according to convenience. In general one may perhaps say that he leaned toward the former in his earlier years and toward the latter in his later life. At any rate the strongest statement of the former is in the Divinity School Address and of the latter in "Fate" and the evolutionary conception that took form in that essay. He owed nothing to Hegel in this; indeed he did not recognize it as Hegelian, but rather seems to have drawn it out of the air and out of his speculative ingenuity in handling the dialectical principle. Since in this principle, as we have seen, advance is achieved by overcoming opposition, one may reason that without opposition there can be no advance—or, in so far as evil is interpreted as merely resistance to the force of good, that there can be no advance without evil. This, as has been shown, was the basis of the doctrine of melioration in "Fate" and it was one of the bases of Emerson's tolerant attitude toward evil, the evidence lying in his frequent description of evil as having a use and therefore a good or as being convertible into good. Instances are legion: "Nature knows how to convert evil to good."[118] "Evil . . . is good in the making."[119] "The first lesson of history is the good of evil."[120] Or, with most specific application to evolution:

When we trace from the beginning, that ferocity has uses; only so are the conditions of the then world met, and these monsters are the scavengers, executioners, diggers, pioneers and fertilizers, destroying what is more destructive than they, and making better life possible. We see the steady aim of Benefit in view from the first. Melioration is the law.[121]

Or, again, to choose the most outrageous instance, Emerson was reported by Edward Everett Hale to have made this judgment on a brilliant young student:

I did not know he was so fine a fellow. And now, if something will fall out amiss,—if he should be unpopular with his class, or if his father should fail in business, or if some other misfortune can befall him,—all will be well.[122]

EMERSON

This approaches caricature, to be sure, but the view of evil that it illustrates was not limited to Emerson or to an eccentric few. Rather it was the principal ethical consequence—some would say the *reductio ad absurdum*—of the century's transcendentalism, and its echo will be heard throughout this study. "This is the best possible world," said F. H. Bradley, being witty at his own expense, "and everything in it is a necessary evil."[123] Royce preached it and was rewarded with the ironies of such realists as Perry and Santayana.[124] It is an invitation to wit, and Professor Randall does not miss the opportunity:

Others found the real world a more pleasant and substantial place, somewhat like the last act of a play in which everything is explained and accounted for, the hero and heroine reunited after hardships, and the villain turns out to be no villain at all, but only the hero's father trying to develop his character through opposition.[125]

Under either interpretation of evil it is difficult to contemplate such optimism and doubt that Emerson accepted the idea of progress fully and without reservation. And yet it has been done, and wisely. Miss Mildred Silver,[126] taking her departure from a familiar passage in "Self-Reliance," has shown that this acceptance involved important qualifications. The passage begins:

All men plume themselves on the improvement of society, and no man improves.
Society never advances. It recedes as fast on one side as it gains on the other.

It continues:

There is no more deviation in the moral standard than in the standard of height or bulk. No greater men are now than ever were. A singular equality may be observed between the great men of the first and of the last ages; nor can all the science, art, religion, and philosophy of the nineteenth century avail to educate greater men than Plutarch's heroes, three or four and twenty centuries ago. Not in time is the race progressive. Phocion, Socrates, Anaxagoras, Diogenes, are great men, but they leave no class.[127]

From this point, however, Miss Silver goes on to contend that because Emerson "was not satisfied with such a thoroughgoing denial of his 'seductive faith,'" he "kept picking at the problem for more than fifty years."[128] And in so far as this means that all his life

Emerson was puzzled and undecided about the question of progress I cannot agree. True, he would be a bold man who would deny Emerson his privilege of inconsistency on any question, and, as we have seen, as late as the 1840's he was still asking whether the way was up or down. By the next decade, however, he had become convinced that it was up, and hence the only question remains, in what sense? Definitely—and here is where Miss Silver has done us the greatest service—it was not in the usual sense, the sense, for example, of Charles Sumner's address "The Law of Human Progress," which derived from the French tradition of the seventeenth and eighteenth centuries.[129] For progress in this sense rested on the Lockeian conception of human nature as molded from without, and this was the complete contradiction of Emerson's transcendentalism. It is inconceivable that Emerson should have accepted Sumner's notion that the mind of man is merely the sum of what he has learned and is therefore progressive because as time goes on he learns more and more. This is the most important distinction that Emerson was making in the passage in "Self-Reliance" and in the others quoted by Miss Silver.[130] No amount of advance in mere knowledge and skill, he was contending, will alter the nature of man.

One may well ask, then, whether Emerson intended to exclude man from the progressive movement that he observed in Nature. The answer, I believe, is no, on two counts. In the first place, he did not deny the progress of knowledge and skill; he simply denied that it told the whole story. Secondly and more importantly, he found a kind of progress in the rest of the story, though not in the literal sense of year by year or even century by century advance. In modern terms Emerson's evolutionism would be described as mutational. He did not believe that evolution takes place by the gradual accumulation of minute variations, but by comparatively sudden jumps as the individual fulfills a need, or, in the language of "Fate," as Power accommodates itself to or triumphs over Circumstance. This was the consequence of his dialectic, which dealt with transformations rather than the accumulation of new features, and in Chambers' *Vestiges* he found a phrase for it that he liked well enough to repeat several times.[131] The phrase, in its fullest form, was "arrested and progressive development" and implied that a type may remain for a long time static and then, sporadically, here and there, move on to a higher level. Applying this conception to man, he was enabled to agree that there are no greater men now

EMERSON 65

than in ancient Athens and yet to argue that over the whole sweep of cosmic time melioration is the law. Man, he said, is and has been in a state of arrested development, but here and there and from time to time—in ancient Greece *and* in modern Europe and America—his advance to a higher stage has been heralded by the appearance of superior individuals. This advance has not affected the physical characteristics of the race, but has rather taken the form of enlarged consciousness, the opening up of the spirit through intuition or "inspiration." Thus he wrote in his essay "Inspiration":

> The Hunterian law of *arrested development* is not confined to vegetable and animal structure, but reaches the human intellect also. In the savage man, thought is infantile; and, in the civilized, unequal and ranging up and down a long scale. In the best races it is rare and imperfect. In happy moments it is reinforced, and carries out what were rude suggestions to larger scope and to clear and grand conclusions. . . . In the mind we call this enlarged power Inspiration.[132]

The thought is stated most clearly, however, in *The Natural History of Intellect:*

> Inspiration is the continuation of the divine effort that built the man. The same course continues itself in the mind which we have witnessed in Nature, namely the carrying-on and completion of the metamorphosis from grub to worm, from worm to fly. In human thought this process is often arrested for years and ages. The history of mankind is the history of arrested growth.[133]

An interesting and illuminating analogue of this notion is to be found in one of the unconventional works of Whitman's friend and literary executor, Richard Maurice Bucke. According to Bucke, the evolution of mind through the ages, recapitulated in part in each individual, is divisible into four stages: the perceptual or sensational stage, the stage of simple consciousness, the stage of self-consciousness, and, finally, the stage of "cosmic consciousness," which he describes as follows:

> This consciousness shows the cosmos to consist not of dead matter governed by unconscious, rigid, and unintending law; it shows it on the contrary as entirely immaterial, entirely spiritual and entirely alive; it shows that death is an absurdity, that everyone and everything has eternal life; it shows that the universe is God and

God is the universe, and that no evil ever did or ever will enter into it. . . .[134]

The final stage, in other words, is an illumination, a revelation of the true nature of things. Man has achieved the third stage, Bucke goes on, and there are exact, statistical reasons for believing that he is progressively achieving the fourth:

From Gautama to Dante we count eighteen hundred years, within which period we have five cases [of cosmic consciousness]. Again from Dante to the present day we count six hundred years, in which we have eight cases. That is to say, while in the earlier period there was one case to every three hundred and sixty years, in the later there was a case to each seventy-five years. In other words, cosmic consciousness has been 4.8 times more frequent during the latter period than it was during the former.[135]

Emerson would certainly have been as much amused by the statistics as any one, but there is reason to believe that he would not have found himself far from Bucke in his understanding of the meaning of "melioration" as applied to man.

III

POE'S *EUREKA:* THE PROBLEM OF MECHANISM

THE evolutionism in Edgar Allan Poe's *Eureka*,[1] which is the only one of his works with which we need deal directly, was in an important sense the reverse of Emerson's. Emerson, as we have seen, started from the premises of metaphysical idealism and only gradually, under the influence of the mounting evolutionary suggestions of the day, developed this idealism into a theory of evolution compatible with that of science. Poe, on the other hand, began by accepting the scientific picture of the universe at its face value, and on it as a basis erected a thoroughly mechanistic theory of evolution to which only in the end he attached a "transcendental" interpretation. In the sense in which the term has been used here, the generally transcendental character of this conclusion is indubitable, and yet the same cannot be said of the whole. Not only was Poe deeply scornful of everything that he recognized as transcendental, but he was just as deeply attached to the mathematical physical science of the Newtonian tradition, which led him to take a corporeal view of reality that was in direct contrast to the idealism of the transcendentalists. Thus, on three occasions a little more than three years before the writing of *Eureka*—in "Mesmeric Revelation"[2] and in letters to Chivers[3] and Lowell[4]—he gave the strongest possible statement to the materialistic position. Spirit, mind, and God, he said, are only "infinitely rarefied matter." Consequently, though it is of the utmost importance to observe the resemblance of Poe's theory to the transcendental evolutionism already discussed, it must be done warily and only after its materialistic and mechanistic side has been thoroughly examined.

This can best be done by showing how the cosmogony of *Eureka* was based upon principles derived from three areas of the science of the time.[5] Poe's knowledge of the sciences was perhaps always less than it seemed, but since the days when he had entertained himself with a telescope on the porch of the Allan home in Richmond he had shown a marked interest in astronomy and in time had developed a quite respectable amateur competence in the theory of the field. Like his temperamental and artistic opposite,

Walt Whitman, he drew heavily on periodicals and encyclopedias, and he read with care a number of current works of popular science, the most important of which for our purposes are the following: Sir John Herschel's *Treatise on Astronomy;*[6] various writings by the Scottish parson and amateur of science, Thomas Dick;[7] and, most important of all, a many times reprinted work by another Scottish clergyman, John Nichol, *Views of the Architecture of the Heavens in a Series of Letters to a Lady.*[8] In all of these the most important single principle was Newton's famous law that all bodies attract all other bodies with a force inversely proportional to the squares of their distances. For a hundred and fifty years this law had been as nearly the basis of all physical science as a single law could be, and in consequence Poe gave it a central place in *Eureka*. Newton's law, however, told only how bodies move, not how they have developed, and for this Poe moved on to a second area of theory, that of the nebular hypothesis of Laplace. Finally, since Laplace's theory shed no light on exclusively terrestrial phenomena, he turned to various scraps of the theory of electricity and magnetism which, some believed, were capable of explaining the phenomena of life and thought. Let us consider in more detail how these theories entered into *Eureka*.

1

One of Poe's points of departure in thinking out his cosmogony may have been the following pair of sentences on Newton's law which he quoted from Nichol:

"In truth we have no reason to suppose this great Law, as now revealed, to be the ultimate or simplest, and therefore the universal and all-comprehensive, form of a great Ordinance. The mode in which its intensity diminishes with the element of distance, has not the aspect of an ultimate *principle;* which always assumes the simplicity and self-evidence of those axioms which constitute the basis of Geometry."[9]

Since we cannot know Poe's unrecorded thoughts, this is of course mere conjecture. Whether or not Poe so used the passage, however, it is a most convenient opening wedge in the discussion of his book, enabling us to pass by a single short step from the familiar law of attraction to his novel solution of the basic problem of the cosmogonist, the definition of the beginning of things. Judging by the way in which he worked out his solution, we may conceive him as having asked: If Newton's law is not an "ultimate principle," what is? If it is at present the governing principle of motion, how did it become so? What was its origin? Of what more simple and hence more general principle is it a special instance? His answer, which is not a matter of conjecture, had the simplicity of genius. Since the Newtonian law did not state simply that one body attracts another body, but that *all* bodies attract *all other* bodies, two inferences seemed plain: first, that the dispersed bodies of the universe are drawing together in an endeavor to become one; second, that the oneness toward which they strive is their natural and original state and the ultimate principle which they obey. As he asked at one stage in his argument:

Does not so evident a brotherhood among the atoms point to a common parentage? . . . Does not the entireness of the complex hint at the perfection of the simple? . . . In a word, is it not because the atoms were, at some remote epoch of time, even *more than together*—is it not because originally, and therefore normally, they were *One*—that now, in all circumstances—at all points—in all directions—by all modes of approach—in all relations and through all conditions—they struggle *back* to this absolutely, this irrelatively, this unconditionally *one?*[10]

By this and by a quite different train of thought that will be considered later,[11] Poe deduced the starting point of his history—the creation by God of matter in a state of perfect oneness—and the "great Ordinance" governing it:

Oneness is a principle abundantly sufficient to account for the constitution, the existing phaenomena and the plainly inevitable annihilation of at least the material Universe.[12]

However, if matter had been originally one, it was now obviously many, and the problem remained to account for the transition from the one state to the other. Here again, at least on the surface, the solution was breath-takingly simple: the only possible way for a single original particle to have become the present widely diffused billions of particles was by a process of irradiation. Thus Poe summed up at one point:

I say to myself—"Unity, as I have explained it, is a truth—I feel it.

Diffusion is a truth—I see it. Irradiation, by which alone these two truths are reconciled, is a consequent truth—I perceive it."[13]

Obviously, however, this could not be a perpetual irradiation, since at present matter is drawing together rather than being dispersed; it must rather have been a single determinate act or series of acts, ceasing when the present content of the universe had been emitted and being followed by an immediate reaction or effort to return. In fact, it must have been a series of acts; for a single continuous irradiation like that of light from a candle, giving greater concentration at the center than at the periphery, would have failed to yield that general equality of distribution which, he asserted, even "a very slight inspection of the Heavens" reveals.[14] A series of acts of gradually diminishing intensity, on the other hand, would have yielded just the desired distribution. The first act, lining the outer boundary of what he insisted was a limited, globular universe,[15] must have been followed by a second of slightly diminished intensity, placing a second layer inside the first, and so on until the globe was filled. Moreover, since the aim of the whole process was evidently the greatest possible heterogeneity,[16] the individual particles, while distributed with general equability, must have differed among themselves in size, shape, and distance of separation.

At this point, having described the primal atom and the mode of its dispersion, Poe proceeded to show that the present behavior of matter in accordance with Newton's law was the inevitable result of the withdrawal of the force of irradiation and the consequent impulse to return to unity. He first declared, in words perhaps significantly similar to Nichol's, that the laws of irradiation "belong to the class of *indisputable geometrical properties*"[17] and then showed that the law of attraction was the necessary converse of these laws as applied in his scheme. His first step was to point out that in the irradiation of light, since the degree of diffusion is directly proportional to the square of the distance, the degree of gathering together or "con-centralization" in returning toward the source must be in inverse ratio to the square of the distance, or "*exactly as we know the force of gravitation to proceed.*"[18] However, since the irradiation that he had postulated was not single and continuous like that of light but a series of separate acts, he turned to a more generalized form of the same proof. After show-

POE'S EUREKA

ing that the force of each act of irradiation would be directly proportional to the square of the distance, he proceeded:

> Now, Rëaction, as far as we know any thing of it, is Action conversed. The *general* principle of Gravity being, in the first place, understood as the rëaction of an act—as the expression of a desire on the part of Matter, while existing in a state of diffusion, to return into the Unity whence it was diffused; and, in the second place, the mind being called upon to determine the *character* of the desire—the manner in which it would, naturally, be manifested; in other words, being called upon to conceive a probable law, or *modus operandi,* for the return; could not well help arriving at the conclusion that this law of return would be precisely the converse of the law of departure....
> Matter, then, irradiated into space with a force varying as the squares of the distances, might, *a priori,* be supposed to return towards its centre of irradiation with a force varying inversely as the squares of the distances....[19]

By this means Poe showed that Newton's formula followed as a necessary consequence of the aboriginal irradiation. Though this is the order of chronology, however, and of Poe's exposition, the likelihood, as has been suggested, is that the order of his speculation was the reverse, the irradiation being deduced from gravitation. This would not only be the normal order of reasoning from the known to the unknown, but it is the suggestion of the fantasy "The Power of Words,"[20] in which the "retrograde" analysis made famous by Dupin is applied to the cosmos. Agathos, an old inhabitant of the Beyond who is endeavoring to explain the mysteries of creation to a newcomer, begins by recalling to his pupil's mind the fact familiar in earthly existence that "no action is without infinite result," giving the following illustration, later paralleled in *Eureka:*[21]

> We moved our hands, for example, when we were dwellers on the earth, and, in so doing, we gave vibration to the atmosphere which engirdled it. The vibration was indefinitely extended, till it gave impulse to every particle of the earth's air, which thenceforward, and for ever, was actuated by the one movement of the hand.

By picking their way back through such a chain of cause and effect, he then continues, even earthly mathematicians "found no difficulty, from a given effect, under given conditions, in determining the value of the original impulse." And if this was possible for limited earthly intellects, quite naturally a being "of infinite intelligence" could go much farther, tracing

the remote undulations of the impulse . . . upward and onward for ever in the modifications of old forms—or, in other words, in their *creation of new*—until he found them reflected—unimpressive *at last*—back from the throne of Godhead.

Since this is precisely what Poe achieved in *Eureka*, it is at least plausible that he too "retrograded" in his analysis and that his true moment of illumination was not the discovery that gravitation might be deduced from irradiation but rather the reverse, that irradiation might be the antecedent of gravitation and might therefore be used to bridge the gap between the original unity and the present tendency to return to unity. In either case, however, it is clear that the fundamental formula in his explanation of the universe was, like Newton's, a formula of force acting in the ratio of the square of the distance.

In advancing beyond this point to an account of the development of the sidereal universe, Poe turned to the only existing theory of science that offered any assistance, the nebular hypothesis of Laplace, which he expanded in a way to make that great mathematician shudder. Part of the way he followed Laplace closely. Thus, when the primal nebula in *Eureka* had been filled by the last act of irradiation, its component particles, because of their difference in size and hence in attractive power, began to form themselves into small groups, and these in turn into larger groups, which, because the first atoms that came together approached at an angle, were in rapid rotation. At first, as a result of the force of attraction, the dominant tendency in each group was centripetal, but in time the increased speed of rotation resulting from the expanding diameter of the masses caused this force to be overcome by the centrifugal and led to the breaking off of rings. Still like those of Laplace, these in turn, because of their irregular composition, tended to break up and to form themselves into spherical bodies. Laplace's theory, however, was intended to explain only the solar system, while to Poe the sun and its planets were but a "generic instance" "of the innumerable agglomerations which proceeded to take place throughout the Universal Sphere of atoms on withdrawal of the Divine Volition."[22] The solar system, he pointed out, affirming as fact what even so visionary a writer as Nichol had advanced as no more than a possibility,²³ is but one of a number of similar systems making up what we call the Milky Way, which in turn is but one of the many clusters of systems, all exhibiting unmistakable evidences of the same tendency to aggregation postulated by Laplace. These gigantic clusters, he further held, are not independent of each other, but exert mutual attraction in the same fashion as the original particles; they might, in fact, be regarded as "colossal atoms"²⁴ that would one day merge into a final cluster of clusters and then into "one magnificent sun."²⁵ At first Poe presented this bold prophecy hesitantly, as uncertain because "having to do with the future" (*"mellonta tauta"*),²⁶ but later, in his distressingly equivocal way, he spoke of it as belonging "to the class of the *excessively obvious*"²⁷ and looked forward to the time when

with a thousand-fold electric velocity, commensurate only with their material grandeur and with the spiritual passion of their appetite for oneness, the majestic remnants of the tribe of Stars flash, at length, into a common embrace.²⁸

The mention of electricity brings us to the third and last of the areas of mechanical theory levied upon in *Eureka,* which must be examined briefly before the larger results of Poe's interpretation of the nebular theory can be considered. The sources of Poe's knowledge of electricity are unknown, but certain passages in the *Preliminary Discourse on the Study of Natural Philosophy* by Sir John Herschel, whose *Treatise on Astronomy* Poe is known to have studied, will serve to suggest the basis of his speculations in contemporary science. Herschel touched here and there on four ideas that, from whatever source, entered into *Eureka.* First, that electricity is not limited to a few substances, but is found in all:

This wonderful agent . . . is present, probably in immense abundance, in every form of matter which surrounds us, but becomes sensible only when disturbed by excitements of peculiar kinds.²⁹

Second, that magnetic and electrical phenomena follow the same formula of inverse squares as gravitation:

it has been ascertained that these and all other phenomena exhibited by magnets in their mutual attractions and repulsions are explicable on the supposition of two forces or virtues lodged in the particles of the magnets, the one predominating at one end, the other at the other; and such that each particle shall attract those in which the *opposite* virtue to its own prevails, and repel those in which a *similar* one resides with a force proportional to the inverse square of their mutual distance.[30]

Third, the theory of Volta that electricity is generated by contact of different substances:

It was thus that he arrived at the knowledge of a general fact, that of the disturbance of electrical equilibrium by the mere contact of different bodies.[31]

Fourth, that there is a relation between electrical and nervous phenomena:

it being ascertained, by numerous and decisive experiments, that the transmission of Voltaic electricity along the nerves of even a dead animal is sufficient to produce the most violent muscular action, it became an easy step to refer the origin of muscular motion in the living frame to a similar cause; and to look to the brain, a wonderfully constituted organ, for which no mode of action possessing the least plausibility had ever been devised, as the source of the required electrical power.[32]

Electricity entered into the scheme of *Eureka* through the necessity of some kind of retarding force to prevent immediate collapse after the force of irradiation had been withdrawn. Since there would have been no universe if the resulting tendency to return to unity had not been checked, God, according to Poe, intervened "here, and here only,"[33] to introduce a limited repulsive force sufficient to offset the force of attraction. This was the same force that we know in the phenomenon of electrical repulsion, and was used by Poe quite as freely as the law of Newton or the theory of Laplace. Volta's theory was that electricity is excited by contact, but Poe reasoned that since real contact is prevented by the force of repulsion, this means simply approach or proximity. Again, electricity was supposed by Cavendish and Coulomb to be subject to the law of inverse squares, and thus Poe concluded that the intensity of the electricity generated will increase geometrically with the proximity. Once more, where Volta had said that electricity was generated by the contact of different bodies, meaning specifically different metals, Poe proceeded, on the basis of the general heterogeneity of the atoms as first irradiated, to the conclusion that "electricity . . . is *developed* whenever *any* bodies . . . are brought into approximation," though it is "manifested" only when the bodies are of "appreciable difference" and then "in the ratio of the heterogeneous."[34] Finally, he regarded electricity as but one manifestation of a more fundamental repulsive force, a basic "spiritual" principle that manifested itself not only as electricity but as heat, light, magnetism, and "the more important phaenomena of vitality, consciousness and *Thought*."[35] Indeed, following in a tradition that can be traced by different routes to either Boscovich or Kant,[36] he concluded that attraction and repulsion are the two basic principles of all phenomenal existence, the only principles that we know:

No other principles exist. All phaenomena are referable to one, or to the other, or to both combined. So rigorously is this the case . . . that, for all merely argumentative purposes, we are fully justified in assuming that matter *exists* only as attraction and repulsion— that attraction and repulsion *are* matter:—there being no conceivable case in which we may not employ the term "matter" and the terms "attraction" and "repulsion," taken together, as equivalent, and therefore convertible, expressions in Logic.[37]

Finally, since he had already asserted that repulsion was a basic spiritual principle capable of manifesting itself as thought, he went on to conclude that attraction and repulsion are respectively the body and the soul, the material and the spiritual principles of the universe.

Simply the adoption of the nebular theory joined Poe to the evolutionary tradition, but this development of the theory of electricity took him far beyond Laplace. For if the counter force of repulsion increased in the ratio of the proximity and difference of bodies and was the source of life and thought as well as of the various physical energies, it was inevitable to conclude that as the condensation of the universe proceeded and particles merged into increasingly heterogeneous units, the forms of life and the capacities of mind should increase proportionately. Poe did not develop this line of thought as extensively as he might if he had been more interested in geology and biology,[38] but he definitely recognized it and made it the basis of several interesting inferences. For example, on the basis of the necessity that the sun's heat should have increased as it condensed and decreased temporarily after the whirling off of each of the planets, he suggested that the vestiges of tropical vegetation found in arctic regions might be accounted for as the products of an era of luxuriance brought to an end by the whirling off of the last of the planets, Mercury.[39] He also had some brief but important words to say about the development of "vitalic character." He began by noting the way in which the scope and powers of life "keep pace, very closely, with the heterogeneity, or complexity, of the animal structure," and then laid down the evolutionary principle that *"the importance of the development of the terrestrial vitality proceeds equably with the terrestrial condensation."*[40] This he then illustrated in terms of geology and made the basis of further speculation in a passage that may be quoted entire as his most extended statement on this subject:

> Now this is in precise accordance with what we know of the succession of animals on the Earth. As it has proceeded in its condensation, superior and still superior races have appeared. Is it impossible that the successive geological revolutions which have attended, at least, if not immediately caused, these successive elevations of vitalic character—is it improbable that these revolutions have themselves been produced by the successive planetary discharges from the Sun—in other words, by the successive variations in the solar influence on the Earth? Were this idea tenable, we should not be unwarranted in the fancy that the discharge of yet a new planet, interior to Mercury, may give rise to yet a new modification of the terrestrial surface—a modification from which may spring a race both materially and spiritually superior to Man. These thoughts impress me with all the force of truth—but I throw them out, of course, merely in their obvious character of suggestion.[41]

Since Poe had little interest in either geology or biology, he had little more to say on this subject and returned to it only in such a passing remark as that the stars "grow grey in giving birth and death to unspeakably numerous and complex variations of vitalic development."[42] Nevertheless it is clear, not only from the logic of his principles of attraction and repulsion but also from certain remarks near the end of his book, that the successive emergence of higher forms of life as a result of natural causes was an integral part of his theory. Thus, in discussing the purposes of the cosmic mechanism preparatory to the enunciation of his final conclusions, he pointed out that though throughout most of his book the principle of repulsion had been presented as subserving the interests of matter, enabling it "to exist in that state of diffusion demanded for the fulfillment of its purposes," the complete reciprocity of Divine adaptation made it equally reasonable to say that the subservience had been in reverse order. Since the effect of the condensation of the dispersed particles had been a proportionate increase in the force of repulsion and its vitalic and spiritual manifestations, it might be said that matter had subserved the interests of life and spirit:

With a perfectly legitimate reciprocity, we are now permitted to look at Matter, as created *solely for the sake of this influence*—solely to serve the objects of this spiritual Ether. Through the aid —by the means—through the agency of Matter, and by dint of its heterogeneity—is this Ether manifested—is *Spirit individualized.* It is merely in the development of this Ether, through heterogeneity, that particular masses of Matter become animate—sensitive—and in the ratio of their heterogeneity;—some reaching a degree of sensitiveness involving what we call *Thought,* and thus attaining Conscious Intelligence.[43]

In reading this and the earlier passage it is impossible to avoid the conclusion that Poe envisaged the development of all forms of life, high and low alike, through the operation of the same basic principles by which he explained the formation of the heavenly bodies.

He cast some doubt on this seemingly obvious inference, however, in replying to the criticisms of a "Student of Theology" that had appeared in Charles Fenno Hoffman's *Literary World.* According to Poe's own quotation in his letter to Hoffman,[44] this writer had objected, among other things, to

"Mr. Poe's claim that he can account for the existence of all organized beings, man included, merely from those principles on which the origin and present appearance of suns and worlds are explained. . . ."

Poe's comment was that this was a "perversion" of his meaning, resulting from "a wilfull misapplication of the word 'principles.'" "At page 63," he went on, referring to *Eureka,* "I am *particularly* careful to distinguish between the principles proper, Attraction and Repulsion, and those merely resultant *sub*-principles which control the universe in detail." This distinction can hardly be allowed, however, for the very evident purpose of the passage referred to was not to distinguish the subprinciples from the principles, but rather the reverse—to show that every subprinciple "depends, either more or less immediately, upon these two."[45] As he said elsewhere of the basic principles, *"All* phaenomena are referable to one, or to the other, or to both combined."[46] What evidently troubled Poe was the Student's charge that his book was "'impious'" and he himself "a 'pantheist,' a Pagan, or a God knows what"; and his aim seems to have been to refute these charges by construing his subprinciples anew as "swayed by the immediate spiritual influence of Deity." This, however, was not only inconsistent with his own statement of the relation of the principles and subprinciples, but also flatly contradicted his other statement that in instituting the force of repulsion God intervened "here and here only." As we shall see again, the religious and scientific motives were in conflict in *Eureka;* this is only one of the contradictions that resulted.

Considered simply as an account of the constitution and development of the universe, it is impossible to acquit *Eureka* of materialism and mechanism. If it be argued that Poe did not conceive matter in the brute sense of extended substance but as a synthesis of the divinely instituted forces of attraction and repulsion, it must be replied that by his own account matter had been created and had filled space before either of these forces had begun to manifest itself. Whatever else it may be, *Eureka* is a history of the universe in terms of matter, motion, and force—or, to use the terms in which Professor Whitehead defines "the famous mechanistic theory of nature," of "a succession of instantaneous configurations of matter."[47] Matter is irradiated into a nebula; the particles of the nebula are drawn together by the force of attraction but prevented from immediate collapse by force of repulsion; in drawing together, they are formed into aggregations of steadily increasing magnitude and heterogeneity; finally, the force of repulsion, increasing *pari passu* with the condensation, manifests itself in the form of the various energies, including vitality and thought. Life and consciousness, thus, and all the world that we know, are the result of the rearrangement of particles. The parallel with Herbert Spencer's later formula of evolution as the passing of matter from a state of indefinite, incoherent homogeneity to a state of definite, coherent heterogeneity is as indicative as it is inescapable.

2

Poe, however, had no wish to push this mechanism to atheistic or agnostic conclusions. Quite the contrary. Where a Laplace might declare that he had no need of the "hypothesis" of God, Poe had every need, not only in the obvious instance of the institution of the repulsive force but also in determining the character of the primal particle and the motive of its development. His intellectual connections, in any case, were less with pure science than with the natural theology of the school of Paley and the Bridgewater Treatises, which made a virtue of necessity by arguing that a universal mechanism presupposes a designing and contriving intelligence. To the writers of this school, who had exerted an incalculable influence on the thought of the English-speaking world for more than a hundred years and were Poe's principal tutors in the sciences, science was a species of apologetics, not only proving the existence of God but demonstrating his attributes and purposes. It is sometimes suggested that Poe drew his knowledge directly from Newton, Laplace, and others of their rank, and this may be in some measure true. The writers whom he is known to have read, however, were more usually preachers of the gospel of nature in a vein that may be briefly suggested by the full title of one of their books: *Celestial Scenery: or, the Wonders of the Planetary System Displayed: Illustrating the Perfections of Deity and a Plurality of Worlds.*[48] Indebted as he was to such sources, it is not surprising that Poe was as much concerned in *Eureka* with the relation of nature to God as with simply the mechanism of natural processes.

Though this interest of Poe's reached its fullest fruition only in *Eureka,* there is ample evidence that it had taken root in his thinking much earlier. As early as 1836, three months after he had written a cursory but appreciative review of one of the Bridgewater Treatises,[49] he declared his allegiance to the teleological interpretation of nature in these words:

> To look upwards from any existence, material or immaterial, to its *design,* is, perhaps, the most direct, and the most unerring method of attaining a just notion of the nature of the existence itself. Nor is the principle at fault when we turn our eyes from Nature even to Nature's God. We find certain faculties, implanted within us, and arrive at a more plausible conception of the character and attributes of those faculties, by considering, with what finite judgment we possess, the *intention* of the Deity in so implanting them within us, than by any actual investigation of their powers, or any speculative deductions from their visible and material effects.[50]

Five years later, moreover, after reading Dick[51] and probably

Nichol,[52] he had become thoroughly imbued with the theological usefulness of science and came vigorously to its defense in reply to aspersions cast by Macaulay. In the opening pages of "Ranke's History of the Popes," Macaulay had asserted that knowledge of divinity, natural as well as revealed, is by its nature incapable of increase,[53] and to this Poe took sharp exception, declaring the precise opposite:

That we know no more to-day of the nature of Deity, of its purposes—and thus of man himself—than we did even a dozen years ago, is a proposition disgracefully absurd; and of this any astronomer could assure Mr. Macaulay.[54]

Simply this unsupported statement, with its reference to astronomy, is of great interest in foreshadowing the drift of *Eureka*, but even more significant is the argument supporting it, revealing as it does the theory of truth that underlay *Eureka* and opening the way to what has here been called its transcendentalism. Macaulay erred, Poe believed, by misunderstanding the nature of the proofs involved, treating them as if they were the "direct" proofs by which we reason of "the concerns of earth":

Were the indications we derive from science of the nature and designs of Deity, and thence, by inference, of man's destiny—were these indications proof direct, no advance in science would strengthen them; for, as our author truly observes, "nothing could be added to the force of the argument which the mind finds in every beast, bird, or flower."

Rather, however, the proofs are analogical; and consequently

every step in human knowledge—every astronomical discovery, for instance—throws additional light upon the august subject *by extending the range of analogy*.

On the face of it, this might seem to mean that reasoning from nature to divinity is a mere matter of probability, gaining certainty by mass of evidence, but Poe's further remarks both here and elsewhere show that he had no such mean opinion of analogy. Thus, later in the same paragraph he declared that "analogies deduced from the modern established theory of the nebular cosmogony" were

the *only* irrefutable argument in support of the soul's immortality—

or, rather, the only conclusive proof of man's alternate dissolution and rejuvenescence *ad infinitum.*

Two months later, moreover, he ascribed the highest certainty to analogy in identifying it with the "poetic intellect," which he described as

that intellect which we now feel to have been the most exalted of all—since those truths which to us were of the most enduring importance could only be reached by that *analogy* which speaks in proof-tones to the imagination alone, and to the unaided reason bears no weight. . . .[55]

Analogy meant much more to Poe than a mere indication of probability. As to Emerson and the transcendentalists in general, it was a reflection of a harmony in the constitution of things apprehensible by a faculty higher than the reason; in the case of Poe, the imagination or sense of beauty.[56]

This conception of truth and the method of discovering it had a long history and an important role in Poe's thinking. Its roots, as Professor Stovall has shown, are to be found as early as "Al Aaraaf,"[57] and it was prominent in his mature speculation on the nature of poetry and beauty. Thus in a review of R. H. Horne's "Orion" he described the sense of beauty as "that divine sixth sense . . . which speaks of God through his purest, if not his *sole* attribute—which proves, and which alone proves his existence."[58] Again, in "The Poetic Principle," though he carefully maintained the distinction between beauty and truth that he had made in his early writing, he conceded that when "through the attainment of a truth we are led to perceive a harmony where none was apparent before, we experience at once the true poetic effect," adding by way of qualification that "this effect is referable to the harmony alone, and not in the least degree to the truth which merely served to render the harmony manifest."[59] In *Eureka,* however, though it was published and apparently written before "The Poetic Principle," this distinction was dispensed with and the equivalence of beauty and truth proclaimed without reservation.

We are assisted in understanding the force of this conception of truth in Poe's theory of nature if we remember his great admiration for Kepler, whom he cited in *Eureka* as a supreme exemplar of the place of imagination in science. Science in Poe's day was wholly devoted to the principle of empirical verification, but Kepler and others among the early pioneers of modern science were no less devoted to the Pythagorean conception of the perfect simplicity and harmony of nature and tested their hypotheses as much by this assumption as by appeal to fact.[60] After their example, which he may have come to know through the life of Kepler by John Drinkwater Bethune,[61] Poe not only gave great weight to the function of imagination in the construction of hypotheses but asserted that these hypotheses were to be judged by their inner consistency or harmony or beauty. Thus he described Laplace's theory as "beautifully true" and "far too beautiful, indeed, *not* to possess Truth as its essentiality";[62] and in his dedication he stated that he offered his book "not in its character of Truth-Teller, but for the Beauty that abounds in its Truth; constituting it true."[63] The fullest statement of this view, however, is to be found near the end of the book in a comment on misleading analogies. One must have a care, he stated,

lest, in pursuing too heedlessly the superficial symmetry of forms and motions, he leave out of sight the really essential symmetry of the principles which determine and control them.

If this care is taken, however,

the sense of the symmetrical is an instinct which may be depended upon with an almost blindfold reliance. It is the poetical essence of the Universe—*of the Universe* which, in the supremeness of its symmetry, is but the most sublime of poems. Now symmetry and consistency are convertible terms:—thus Poetry and Truth are one. A thing is consistent in the ratio of its truth—true in the ratio of its consistency. *A perfect consistency, I repeat, can be nothing but an absolute truth.* We may take it for granted, then, that Man cannot long or widely err, if he suffer himself to be guided by his poetical, which I have maintained to be truthful, in being his symmetrical, instinct.[64]

Since this conception rests upon faith in the perfect unity of nature, it takes us back to our starting point in section one, where we found Poe inferring from the present tendency of bodies to draw together that they must once have been "more than together." Here, however, he had established grounds for the direct intuition of the same conclusion. As a cosmogonist, it was incumbent upon him to describe the state of things in the beginning, and, after declaring that only intuition was of assistance, this he did in the following terms:

With this understanding, I now assert—that an intuition altogether irresistible, although inexpressible, forces me to the conclusion that what God originally created—that that Matter which, by dint of his Volition, he first made from his Spirit, or from Nihility, *could* have been nothing but Matter in its utmost conceivable state of— what?—of *Simplicity?*

This will be found the sole absolute *assumption* of my Discourse. . . .

Let us now endeavor to conceive what Matter must be, when, or if, in its absolute extreme of *Simplicity*. Here the Reason flies at once to Imparticularity—to a particle—to *one* particle—a particle of *one* kind—of *one* character—of *one* nature—of *one* size—of *one* form—a particle, therefore, *"without* form and void"—a particle positively a particle at all points—a particle absolutely unique, individual, undivided, and not indivisible only because He who *created* it, by dint of his Will, can by an infinitely less energetic exercise of the same Will, as a matter of course divide it.

Oneness, then, is all that I predicate of the originally created Matter; but I propose to show that this *Oneness is a principle abundantly sufficient to account for the constitution, the existing phaenomena and the plainly inevitable annihilation of at least the material Universe.*[65]

Even Laplace would have agreed that the universe is a unitary system, but he would certainly have accused Poe of mythmaking in respect to his primal particle; for the nebular theory, it should be remembered, begins with a universe that is quantitatively complete, all the matter that is ever to exist having already been created and having only to be rearranged. Moreover, he would certainly have disagreed concerning the explanatory power of "oneness," for here Poe was veering toward transcendentalism, in which the One was hypostatized as an absolute. At this early stage in his book, however, Poe's concept of unity was no more than an abstract principle, and to observe its hypostasis it will be necessary to complete his account of the progressive condensation of the universe, bringing it down to its "plainly inevitable annihilation."[66]

This involved the most extraordinary feat of logical legerdemain in the whole volume and resulted in its best-remembered metaphor. As the condensation continued, the spaces between bodies would naturally grow less and less until finally the bodies would have merged into one unparticled mass, in which attraction and repulsion, since they are possible only between separate particles, would have completely disappeared. However, since matter had previously been defined as the synthesis of attraction and repulsion, this would mean "Matter without Attraction and without Repulsion—in other words, Matter without Matter—in other words, again, *Matter no more.*"[67] Thus would all material existence sink back into that nihility out of which it was created and God remain all in all. This would not necessarily be an ultimate termination, however, for on the basis of "that omniprevalent law of laws, the law of periodicity,"[68] we are justified in entertaining the belief that the whole process might be repeated again and again *ad infinitum.* In the figure that Sidney Lanier singled out for admiration on two occasions, we may look forward to "a novel universe swelling into existence, and then subsiding into nothingness, at every throb of the Heart Divine."[69]

At this point, with that flair for climax that made him the first master of the short-story, Poe revealed for the first time the full meaning of *Eureka.* "And now—this Heart Divine," he asked, "what is it?" and answered dramatically, *"It is our own."*[70] Here his appeal was no longer to the facts and theories of the sciences or to the logic of his basic principles, but to the inner certainties of consciousness. The conventional world tries to tell us, he continued:

"You live and the time was when you lived not. You have been created. An Intelligence exists greater than your own; and it is only through this Intelligence you live at all."[71]

Our own inner experience, however, tells us otherwise. Having in our youth, like Wordsworth, had *"Memories* of a Destiny more vast"[72] that made it impossible to conceive of our own nonexistence, we find it equally impossible in maturity, deep in our hearts, to believe that anything exists greater than our own souls. This, Poe admitted, was an argument based on "spiritual shadows," but to his mind at least was

a species of proof far surpassing what Man terms demonstration, that no one soul *is* inferior to another—that nothing is, or can be, superior to any one soul—that each soul is, in part, its own God—its own Creator:—in a word, that God—the material *and* spiritual God—*now* exists solely in the diffused Matter and Spirit of the Universe; and that the regathering of this diffused Matter and Spirit will be but the re-constitution of the *purely* Spiritual and Individual God.[73]

We are, in Emerson's words, "part or parcel of God," and our intuitions of our own greatness are thus thoroughly justified by the fact that each one of us, like all creatures—"those which you call animate as well as those to whom you deny life for no better reason than that you do not behold it in operation"[74]—is one of many "individualizations of Himself."[75] God is one Being, personal in character if not in form, who "passes his Eternity in perpetual variation of Concentrated Self and almost Infinite Self-Diffusion."[76] Thus that which was presented in the earlier portions of *Eureka* as the irradiation and agglomeration of material particles according to the law of inverse squares appears in the end as the expansion and contraction of the Being of God, who is the totality of all things and selves.

If these opinions had been only a vagary of the moment, Poe's indignation at the charge of "pantheism" in *The Literary World* would be understandable. But they were not. When a friend whose "scientific acquirement" he respected tried to persuade him to soften his pantheistic closing, he was told that *"that* was the dearest part."[77] And among the notes that Poe penciled in his own copy of *Eureka* is one that definitely confirms his pantheistic drift by offering consolation for the loss of individual identity in remergence in all-inclusive Deity.[78] Moreover, though the conclusion of *Eureka* breaks distinctly with the conception of creation expressed in the beginning,[79] it was not a new departure in his thinking. In "Mesmeric Revelation" he had presented God as matter in its rarest form, and much earlier, in "Ligeia," he had described God as "a great will pervading all things."[80] At this early date, in fact, he seems to have been flirting with a kind of hylozoism that eventuated in the pantheism of *Eureka*. Thus, in "The Fall of the House of Usher" the decay of the mansion was joined with the decay of the family by Roderick Usher's theory of the sentience of vegetable and inorganic things,[81] and two years later, in "The Island of the Fay," this conception was expanded in a passage that anticipated *Eureka* in both word and thought. Beginning with a statement on the unity of nature, Poe went on to present a conception of the Universe as one living Being that later became a part of the conclusion of *Eureka:*

I love to regard these as themselves but the colossal members of one vast animate and sentient whole—a whole . . . whose thought is that of a God; whose enjoyment is knowledge; whose destinies are lost in immensity; whose cognizance of ourselves is akin with our own cognizance of the *animalculae* which infest the brain—a being which we, in consequence, regard as purely inanimate and material, much in the same manner as these *animalculae* must thus regard us.

. . . And since we see clearly that the endowment of matter with vitality is a principle—indeed as far as our judgments extend, the *leading* principle in the operations of Deity—it is scarcely logical to imagine it confined to the regions of the minute, where we daily trace it, and not extending to those of the august. As we find cycle within cycle without end—yet all revolving around one far-distant centre which is the Godhead, may we not analogically suppose, in the same manner, *life within life, the less within the greater, and all within the Spirit Divine?*[82] In short, we are madly erring, through self-esteem, in believing man, in either his temporal or future destinies, to be of more moment in the universe than that vast "clod of the valley" which he tills and contemns, and to which he denies a soul *for no more profound reason than that he does not behold it in operation.*[83]

Finally, in the early part of *Eureka* itself, at the very moment of declaring that nature and the God of nature are distinct, he said that "by the former we merely imply the laws of the latter"[84] and went on to describe the initial creative act as

that act by which a God, self-existing and alone existing, became all things at once, through dint of his volition, while all things were thus constituted a portion of God.[85]

3

Thus, far from pushing his mechanism to an atheistic conclusion, Poe pushed it to the conclusion that God is all, and in so doing pushed himself at least part way into the camp of the scorned transcendentalists. For the deity of these glowing final pages was not, like the Christian God, merely universal in spiritual influence, but rather, like the Absolute of the transcendentalists, the sum and substance, the unity and totality of all things. Of the book as a whole, the same thing might be said that was said by the little girl of Emerson's "Brahma": It means "God everywhere." Again, to point another parallel, the egoism of these pages, especially as expressed in the following passage, already quoted in part, could easily be matched in the writings of Emerson, Whitman, and other transcendentalists:

No thinking being lives who, at some luminous point of his life of thought, has not felt himself lost amid the surges of futile efforts at understanding, or believing, that anything exists *greater than his own soul*. The utter impossibility of any one's soul feeling itself inferior to another; the intense, overwhelming dissatisfaction and rebellion at the thought:—these, with the omniprevalent aspirations at perfection, are but the spiritual, coincident with the material, struggles towards the original Unity—are, to my mind at least, a species of proof far surpassing what Man terms demonstration, that no one soul *is* inferior to another—that nothing is, or can be, superior to any one soul—that each soul is, in part, its own God—its own Creator.[86]

Once more, despite contrary earlier pronouncements, God is not described here as having created the universe in the literal sense of having made something not himself out of nothing, but is rather spoken of as having "become" the universe;[87] in the language of the transcendental Stallo, he "realized" himself in the universe. Finally, as was also the case with Stallo and Emerson, this realization took the form of a polarity and interaction of forces and resulted in the serial development of an ascending order of beings from crude inorganic beginnings to higher forms in which life and thought were manifest. So close was Poe to the evolutionism which has been described in the last two chapters as transcendental.[88]

However, if *Eureka* was transcendental, it was certainly transcendental with a difference. Granted all that has been said, the cosmology of Poe was fundamentally different from that of Emerson. There can be no doubt that the closing pages of *Eureka* present a true picture of Poe's belief at this time of his life or that this belief was, in spirit, as fervently religious as Emerson's. The means that he used to establish his position, however, not only were different from Emerson's but, to my reading, fail to support that position. The conclusion, it seems to me, does not follow from the main discussion. The transcendentalist was enabled to establish his religious cosmology by denying that the mechanical categories of science were more than superficially true and by showing that the categories of purpose and value were more fundamental. Down to the last few pages of *Eureka,* however, what Coleridge called the "mechanico-corpuscular"[89] view of the universe remained as predominant as it had been three years before in "Mesmeric Revelation" and the letters to Lowell and Chivers. If one asks what is fundamentally real in the world of *Eureka,* real in the metaphysical sense, the answer must be that it is "atoms and the void" and that the atoms are material in the simple Cartesian sense of "extended substance."

Evident as this must be at this stage of this discussion, however, two objections may be raised against it, which must be met before the discussion can be concluded. One objection is that the particles are not material in the Cartesian sense, but are rather, as Poe insisted, syntheses of the forces of attraction and repulsion[90]—are, in short, energetic rather than substantial. The most damaging reply to this objection, that the particles came into existence before the forces, has already been given; but there are others. In the first place, the account of the final elimination of attraction and repulsion quite contradicts this conception of the particles. Poe's argument, it will be remembered, was that since attraction and repulsion are possible only *between* separate particles, in the final coalescence they will cease to exist. But if attraction and repulsion can exist only *between* particles, it is difficult to see how they can be the *same thing* as the particles. In the second place, the logic by which Poe arrived at this conception really leads to a quite different conclusion. He argued that because "attraction and repulsion are the *sole* properties through which we perceive the universe. . . , we are fully justified in assuming that matter *exists* only as attraction and repulsion."[91] But if we once admit that being has no other nature than the forms of its perception, we can have no rest until we admit that it exists only in perception. Unwittingly and without drawing the appropriate conclusion, Poe had stumbled into Berkeley's argument to prove that only mind is real, and what he had really proved was not that "attraction and repulsion *are* matter" but that all three are mental phenomena.

Moreover, even if he had succeeded in maintaining his energetic theory of matter, he would have been no closer to the spiritualistic cosmology of the transcendentalists; for energy or force is no more "spiritual" than extended substance. The characteristic of a spiritual power is the prevision of and striving toward qualitative ends, while force is merely the exertion of pushes and pulls in space. In short, the principle of explanation that prevails in *Eureka* is mechanical rather than teleological and squares with the classical statements of that principle—that of Professor Burtt, for example:

Its fundamental assumptions are that all causes and effects are

reducible to motions of bodies in time and space and are mathematically equivalent in terms of the forces expressed. From this standpoint the notion of perfection drops out of sight entirely; the task of explanation becomes that of analyzing events into the motions of the elementary mass-units of which they are composed and stating the behaviour of any correlated groups of events in the form of an equation.[92]

To be sure, Poe's explanation of why there is a universe at all is sufficiently teleological. God is seeking to "expand" his pleasures:

It was not and is not in the power of this Being—any more than it is in your own—to extend, by actual increase, the joy of his Existence; but just as it *is* in your power to expand or to concentrate your pleasures (the absolute amount of happiness remaining always the same) so did and does a similar capability appertain to this Divine Being. . . . He now feels his life through an infinity of imperfect pleasures—the partial and pain-intertangled pleasures of those inconceivably numerous things which you designate as his creatures. . . .[93]

But this does not mitigate the fact that the world in which the Divine Being achieves this end is governed by the principles of mechanics. If you ask, for example, why man is as he is, the answer provided by the cosmology of *Eureka* is not that of Plato, Dante, Emerson, that he is an approximation of an ideal, but that he is the consequence of the aggregation of particles obeying fixed mathematical laws of motion and force. In so far as *Eureka* offers any demonstration, there is nothing more spiritual about man than about a spark plug and nothing more spiritual about his world than about the engine of which it is a part.

The second objection to the charge of materialism is like the first in interpreting the particles as but the form taken by something else, but it goes further, contending that this something else is God. It is, moreover, sounder than the first, being consistent with the main body of the work. It is of no more avail in establishing the spiritual character of the universe, however, for in "becoming" the kind of universe that is described in *Eureka* God abdicates for the time just those qualities that make him a spiritual being. Instead of carrying over into his worldly incarnation that spiritual nature in which the governing causes are final causes or motives, he holds this nature in abeyance and submerges himself in a system in which the governing causes are pushes and pulls and the only goal quantitative unity. Thus, though we may grant that the particles are but the form taken by God during the period of the cosmic cycle, if we do, we must also conclude that during that period only the particles exist and that the nature of the world is to be described in terms of their interaction. And here is the essential point of difference between the cosmologies of Poe and Emerson. Emerson too held that God is the sum and substance of things, that nature is "a projection of God in the unconscious";[94] but since, in his idealism, he had reduced things to appearances, his God did not cease to be transcendent and spiritual nor his world of things to be governed by the laws of spirit. What he thought of the conception of spirit as "infinitely rarefied matter" he stated clearly in "Experience":

The physicians say they are not materialists; but they are:—Spirit is matter reduced to an extreme thinness: O *so* thin!—But the definition of *spiritual* should be, *that which is its own evidence*.[95]

The whole epistemological issue was ignored by Poe, however, with the result that instead of sinking the world in God, like the transcendentalists, he sank God in the world.

Granted, however, that this is the meaning to which a close and literal reading of *Eureka* leads us, it is not the meaning that was closest to Poe's heart or that he wished to end with. If it were, his rhapsodical final pages would be simply inconceivable. The ardent, almost frenzied picture that is given there of a divine personality which includes all individual beings and will in time reabsorb them was not envisioned by a man whose only aim was to show that reality consists in the movements of lumps of matter. Rather it was the vision of a man whose private spiritual life was exceptionally vigorous, even if erratic, and who wished to prove to himself and all who would listen that this life was the type and basis of all existence. In short, its aim was the same as that of the transcendentalists, who universalized and apotheosized the spiritual experience of the self. In any full consideration of the place of *Eureka* in Poe's mental life the intent would be as important as the accomplishment, but in dealing with *Eureka* alone and finding its place in the cosmological speculation of its time the latter must be given first place. One cannot but agree with those who insist that *Eureka* is not primarily a work of science or philosophy but a kind of poem—a perfervid mechanical vision projecting one man's sense of the nature of things. But that should not blind one to its basic confusion or to the fact so well stated by Professor Whitehead that "the only way of mitigating mechanism is by the discovery that it is not mechanism."[96]

Unless one provides for the emergence of true novelty in nature—a conception yet undeveloped in Poe's day and certainly not to be found in *Eureka*—there is but one way to reconcile the spiritual life of man with a "mechanico-corpuscular" world, and that is to deny that they are related, to deny that the one has grown out of the other. If, as scientific theists since Newton had maintained, God created the universe as a watchmaker makes a watch and then breathed the spirit into the body of man, the universe might tick merrily along its mechanical way without prejudice to either God or man. Evolution, however, upset this easy solution of the problem, plunging man into nature and making it seem necessary, if any genetic connection between God and man was to be established, to draw God into nature also. In other words, evolution seemed to make some kind of philosophical monism inevitable; and whether Poe thought of it in these terms or not, he was obviously influenced by this necessity. There was a choice of monisms, however. As Royce pointed out,[97] one might contend with the materialists that matter and force were the reality and spirit an illusion, or one might contend with the idealists that spirit was the fundamental reality and the material world in some sense merely an appearance or expression of it and governed by its motives. With more originality than cogency, Poe attempted to build the conclusion of the latter on the foundation of the former. Working with oil and water, he was doomed to failure, but that did not prevent him from writing the most closely worked and profoundly symptomatic document with which we shall deal. In few places is the ambivalence of the nineteenth century in respect to mechanistic science and spiritualistic aspiration more plain than in *Eureka*.

IV

WHITMAN: HIGH TIDE

WITH Walt Whitman we reach the high-water mark of "cosmic optimism." We shall be detained through many pages by other versions of the doctrine, some of them more consistent and defensible, but none more fervid, sweeping, or central in the work of their proponents. Even Emerson, unmitigated optimist that he was, must be placed behind Whitman. For cosmic optimism as it is being discussed here is not simply any optimism concerning the cosmos but an evolutionary optimism; and Emerson did not accept evolution until the forties or fully digest it until the fifties. Emerson's evolutionism was fitted to an optimism already formed, whereas Whitman's evolutionism and optimism grew up together. Whitman is, indeed, the poet of evolution par excellence. To make clear what this means will require considerable elaboration, but for the moment we may simply take him at his word. The "three peerless stars" that he saw rising to be the "natal star" of his country were "Ensemble, Evolution, Freedom."[1] "Haughty this song, its words and scope," he wrote in a poem specifically devoted to the purport of his book,

> To span vast realms of space and time,
> Evolution—the cumulative—growths and generations.[2]

Finally, if further confirmation is needed, consider this note on "Passage to India":

There's more of me, the essential ultimate me, in that than in any of the poems . . . the burden of it is evolution—the one thing escaping the other—the unfolding of cosmic purposes.[3]

1

Placing Whitman in such a position of primacy, however, raises a rather knotty problem. If there is a damaging conflict between materialism and spiritualism in *Eureka*, what are we to say of Whitman, who unblushingly announced, "I believe materialism is true and spiritualism is true, I reject no part"?[4] His final aim was precisely that of Poe—to proclaim that the Heart Divine that throbs in the universe is "our own";[5] but since he was quite as capable of interpreting this Heart in terms of body, he must be at least tentatively confronted with the same charge. "Behold, the body includes and is the meaning, the main concern, and includes and is the soul," he tells us in one place,[6] and elsewhere a long anatomical catalogue ends:

> O I say these are not the parts and poems of the
>   body only, but of the soul,
> O I say now these are the soul![7]

He insisted that he was of the same substance as earth: "I find I incorporate gneiss, coal, long-threaded moss";[8] and that this substance would one day be redistributed: "If you want me again look for me under your boot-soles."[9] "Strange and hard that paradox true I give," he summarized; "objects gross and the unseen soul are one."[10]

Nor can we say, any more than in the case of Poe, that he meant this in the special sense of the older idealism. The Emerson of *Nature* would have found no difficulty in such an identification of soul and nature, but he would have meant that nature has its existence only in the soul's perception, that it is "a phenomenon, not a substance."[11] This, however, was emphatically not Whitman's meaning. Professor Furness may be justified in saying that "the problems of epistemology seem to have fascinated Whitman quite as much as any of the other Transcendentalists,"[12] but it is important to note that though in the passage on which he was commenting Whitman had said of the world, "May-be indeed it is created by us in the winking of an eye," he added immediately, "Or may-be preparing for us."[13] This was Whitman's way: whatever he conceded to subjectivism he as quickly snatched away. When, for example, at the end of *Democratic Vistas*, he asserted that idealism seemed to him to suggest "the course of inquiry and desert of favor for our New World metaphysics," he inserted the qualification, "guarding against extravagance and ever modified even by its opposite."[14] If to be an idealist means to be a phenomenalist, then Whitman was not an idealist. The word "reality" as he used it contained none of the Berkeleian overtones of *Nature*, but, except as qualified by some such adjective as "unseen," always meant stubborn, external, three dimensional *things*—extended substance, to repeat a phrase used in the discussion of Poe. Thus when he declared in the vein of Margaret Fuller, "I accept reality and dare not question it," he added, "materialism first and last imbuing";[15] and the primitive original of this declaration makes clear that he was from the start a realist in respect to the external world:

> I am the poet of reality
> I say the earth is not an echo
> Nor man an apparition;
> But that all the things seen are real,
> The witness and albic dawn of things equally real
> I have split the earth and the hard coal and rocks and the solid bed of the sea
> And went down to reconnoitre there a long time,
> And bring back a report,
> And I understand that those are positive and dense every one
> And what they seem to the child they are.[16]

But if soul is body and body is "positive and dense," what becomes of Whitman's "spiritualism"? By suggesting that the definitive quality of spirit is extension or solidity, did he not reduce it to a state in which it would be capable of no more than the automatism of mechanical action? It may not be the case, but it is at least reasonable, and may be helpful, to ask if he was not a materialist in the same sense as Poe when the latter declared to Lowell and Chivers that spirit is only "infinitely rarefied matter."[17]

2

Of course he was not. Though the passages quoted represent an authentic and important phase of Whitman's thought, to which we shall return, he not only did not draw the inferences suggested but specifically rejected them. He said to Traubel, for example, on this very issue:

after all, there's more to it than that—more to it than these bodies—than the most superb bodies; more than that: and while I cannot argue the matter out, neither can I surrender my profound conviction.[18]

Unlike Poe, moreover, he was quite untouched by the principle of mechanism assumed in science. Indeed, notwithstanding his extravagant and persistent praise of science, its influence upon him was never more than skin deep. To him as to Emerson it was lore rather than principle, inspiration more than instruction. He built a selection of its facts and theories into the mosaic of his thought, but with complete disregard of the purpose for which they were intended. Science, he said truly, was not his dwelling; he but entered by it to an area of his dwelling.[19] Nowhere, furthermore, was this more pointedly the case than in his reaction to the theory of evolution, which in a nonscientific sense was one of the pillars of his thought. His personal admiration for Darwin knew no bounds, but his words for the doctrinaire application of his theory were: "Don't be in such a damn big hurry!"[20] "I have felt from the first that my own works must assume the essential truths of evolution or something like them," he told Traubel, but he had said only a moment before: "When it comes to explaining absolute beginnings and ends, I doubt if evolution clears up the mystery any better than the philosophies that have preceded it."[21] Again, in his essay "Carlyle from American Points of View" he justified the intrusion of a lengthy discussion of Hegel

not only for offsetting the Carlylean letter and spirit . . . but to counterpoise, since the late death and deserv'd apotheosis of Darwin, the tenets of the evolutionists. Unspeakably precious as those are to biology, and henceforth indispensable to a right aim and estimate in study, they neither comprise or explain everything.[22]

Finally, in the little note on Darwinism in *Collect,* after asserting that "the world of erudition, both moral and physical, cannot but be eventually better'd and broaden'd in its speculations, from the advent of Darwinism," he went on:

Nevertheless, the problem of origins, human and other, is not the least whit nearer its solution. In due time the Evolution theory will have to abate its vehemence.[23]

There is more in these criticisms, moreover, than meets the eye. In charging Darwin only with failure to solve the problem of ultimate origins, Whitman gave nothing like an adequate statement of his true objection, as a moment's consideration of the charge in the light of the general drift of his thought will reveal. Let us suppose the impossible, that Darwin's theory had included a true physical first cause—a kind of primitive fountain of matter and energy subject only to mechanical law—would Whitman have been satisfied? His specific objection would have been met, but the answer is quite certainly no, for the reason that like all deeply religious persons he was very little concerned about the mere "firstness" of the first cause and very greatly about its spiritual nature. What he believed in and what he required any theory of the universe to vindicate was the ordering of all things by the same kind of mental and moral nature that he found in himself, and this vindication Darwin not only did not supply but in his role of scientist had no interest in. In briefest statement, Whitman's true objection to the evolutionism of science was that it was not teleological, not "spiritual." The line of attack that he chose, in fact, may be read as only a more naïve and roundabout way of saying this very thing; for when teleology is reduced to simple historical terms attention is inevitably drawn to the beginning of things, where it is supremely dramatized in the act of creation. In the unsophisticated temporal consideration of the universe the "why" of things in general nearly always goes back to the initial "why" of creation—and Whitman was certainly not a sophisticate in matters speculative. Once he put this broader criticism into words. Traubel had attended a discussion of evolution:

You had evolution at the Club last night, did you? What are the limits of evolution as a theory? I assume that Spencer, Huxley, Darwin, the greatest evolutionists everywhere, take the ground that evolution is a process: *do not pretend that it gives a why for existence:* no: only that it expresses a method of nature.[24]

Far from espousing any theory of mechanism, thus, what Whitman was concerned to do—like Emerson, Poe, and nearly all the poets we shall consider—was to pour the old wine of divine purpose into the new bottles of evolutionary "process." The world, he observed, was confronted with two quite contrary theories of the origin of man—the one "those venerable claims to origin from God himself," the other "the theory . . . that we have come on, originated, developt, from monkeys, baboons." He could not agree, however, that the theories were finally incompatible:

far apart as they seem, and angrily as their conflicting advocates to-day oppose each other, are not both theories to be possibly reconciled, and even blended? Can we, indeed, spare either of them? Better still, out of them is not a third theory, the real one, to arise?[25]

Of necessity such a third theory, since it would include both the others, would be radically teleological and anthropocentric, and one could quote almost at random to show that in Whitman's own blending it was. *"For it,"* he said of the soul, in habitual purposive language, "the mystic evolution";[26] *"for it,"* of the body of a slave at auction, "the globe lay preparing quintillions of years";[27] *"for it,"* of his own embryo,

> the nebula cohered to an orb,
> The long slow strata piled to rest it on,
> Vast vegetables gave it sustenance,
> Monstrous sauroids transported it in their mouths and
>   deposited it with care.[28]

"It seems to me," he avowed in a note on the meaning of his poems,

the conception of a divine purpose in the cosmical world and in history . . . is not only the grand antedating background and appropriate entrance to the study of any science but to the fit understanding of the position of one's self in Nature, to the performance of life's duties, to the appreciation and application of sane standards to politics and to the judgment upon and construction of works in any department of art, and that by its realization is provided a basis for religion and theology that can satisfy the modern.[29]

And, again, in "A Backward Glance,"

While I cannot understand it or argue it out, I fully believe in a clue and purpose in Nature, entire and several; and that invisible spiritual results, just as real and definite as the visible, eventuate all concrete life and all materialism, through Time.[30]

The problem of his materialism, however, is still with us. For though we may dismiss the suggestion that he was either a mechanist or a materialist in any usual sense, it must be recognized that he was resolute in his insistence that the nature out of which man has evolved is not a mere "phenomenon" but material in the common sense of the term. "All through writings," he counseled himself in his notes,

preserve the equilibrium of the truth that the material world, and all its laws, are as grand and superb as the spiritual world and all its laws. Most writers have claimed the physical world and they have not over-estimated the other, or soul, but have underestimated the corporeal.[31]

And in his earliest notebook,

When I see where the east is greater than the west,—where the sound man's part of the child is greater than the sound woman's part—or where a father is more needful than a mother to produce me—then I guess I shall see how spirit is greater than matter.[32]

But if the world of matter—of nebulae, "long slow strata," "vast vegetables"—has behaved purposively in its evolution, must not its essential nature have been such as to be capable of such behavior? And if it eventuates in "invisible spiritual results," must not these results have been inherent in it from the beginning? Wasn't Whitman faced by the dilemma borrowed in chapter one from Josiah Royce: either (a) the approximately continuous evolution of beings with minds out of inorganic matter is an illusion or (b) mind is a mere appearance of matter or (c) matter is a mere appearance of mind?[33] What can Whitman have meant by saying in a single breath that he believed both "materialism" and "spiritualism" to be true? If he was to accept the continuity implied in the evolutionary doctrine of his time, was he not forced to choose?

An easy answer to this is that as an untrained and particularly easygoing layman, Whitman was imprecise in both thought and language when he turned to metaphysics. And in a considerable measure this is of course true. One way of stating Whitman's position is to say that he was caught between the monistic necessities of philosophic evolutionism and the ingrained dualism of common sense. I do not believe that this gets to the bottom of the question, however. I do not believe, in other words, that, as a recent writer has said, Whitman merely shuttled "back and forth from materialism to idealism without troubling himself about any inconsistency."[34] Anyone shuttling back and forth between these two positions would not affirm both in the same breath, nor would he write such lines as these, which stand as a kind of preface to the metaphysical drift of the whole of the *Leaves:*

> I will make the poems of materials, for I think they
>   are to be the most spiritual poems,
> And I will make the poems of my body and of mortality,
> For I think I shall then supply myself with the poems
>   of my soul and of immortality.[35]

The man who wrote these lines had, at least to his own satisfaction, effected some kind of synthesis of matter and spirit in which neither was subordinate to or independent of the other but merely its reverse. The preaching of such a gospel, indeed, Whitman regarded as one of his chief missions in *Leaves of Grass:*

> When the full-grown poet came,
> Out spake pleased Nature (the round impassive globe,
>   with all its shows of day and night,) say-
>   ing, *He is mine:*
> But out spake too the Soul of man, proud, jealous and
>   unreconciled, *Nay, he is mine alone;*
> —Then the full-grown poet stood between the two, and
>   took each by the hand;
> And today and ever so stands, as blender, uniter,
>   tightly holding hands,
> Which he will never release until he reconciles the two,
> And wholly and joyously blends them.[36]

Since this problem must be faced by any philosophy of evolution[37] and is particularly pressing on the cosmic optimist, the description of Whitman's synthesis, such as it was, must occupy us for a number of pages before we can return to the more specifically evolutionary aspects of his thinking.

3

Since Whitman was by both temperament and conviction one of his century's most complete anti-intellectualists, we need expect no brilliant rationalization, or indeed any logical approach to the problem at all.[38] He could not argue the matter out, he told Traubel. "What the world calls logic," he said, "is beyond me: . . . what establishes itself in the age, in the heart, is finally the only logic."[39] We can even reverse Traubel's epigram and say that he had *a* philosophy but not *much* philosophy.[40] He had strong and surprisingly coherent convictions about the nature of things, but they were not sharply defined, and it is impossible to think of him arriving at them by the patient analytical methods of the philosopher. His thinking was largely temperamental. He borrowed plentifully from the ideas current in his time, but his borrowings were never closely examined and were for the most part mere garments to clothe intuitions. Surprisingly enough, however, this does not make the solution of the problem more difficult, but easier. For when Whitman is approached with these traits in mind it becomes apparent that he was not so much wrestling with a technical philosophical problem as restating the most primitive of all conceptions of nature, which springs from two simple, quite childlike premises: first, that the material world is as real as it seems; second, that its behavior is very like our own. "What they seem to the child they are," he had said.

The first of these premises, already pointed out in his writing, is the universal intuition of common sense and needs no justification or explanation. In Whitman's case, however, it was reinforced by a number of factors, not the least of which, perhaps, was the unusual sensitivity to touch which Mark Van Doren has discussed at length and given the technical pathological name of "erethism."[41] Phenomenalism is no less consistent with this type of sensitivity than with any other, but it appears to be less congenial to it, as Dr. Johnson illustrated when he kicked the stone to refute Berkeley.[42] The Whitman who wrote, "To touch my person to someone else's is about as much as I can stand,"[43] must have found it hard to believe that the world to which he thrilled was, as Emerson said, but "a vast picture which God paints on the instant eternity for the contemplation of the soul."[44] The second premise also, if we take the whole history of man into consideration, has been only less prevalent, and was quite as strong a conviction of Whitman's. It is after all a great sophistication—greater than Whitman was disposed to—to devise and superimpose upon the universe a mode of action quite foreign to that which men know, not merely by reflection, but by immediate experience. From time immemorial men have accounted for the world in terms of motive and interest, as they feel that they themselves act, and it is not to be supposed that the naïve and intuitive Whitman would do otherwise.

Putting these two simple premises together, we begin to see the resolution of the conflict between Whitman the spiritualist and Whitman the materialist. In one sense he was both, a dualist, insisting on the real existence of both matter and spirit; this, in fact, is the clear primary meaning of his statement that he believed both materialism and spiritualism to be true. His dualism was not of the most common variety, however, in which matter and spirit are opposed; rather he regarded them as inseparable and interdependent, the one permeating the other. Matter is not dead but alive, not dumb but aware. All things, he held, are made of matter, but they are animated by that sensibility and power of autonomous action to which the name spirit is given:

> I swear I think now that every thing without exception
>   has an eternal soul!
> The trees have, rooted in the ground! the weeds of the
>   sea have! the animals![45]

Whitman was a kind of poetic animist—or, as others have called him, a "mystic realist" or "vital materialist."[46] Like the poet in his pathetic fallacies or the cave man fearing and propitiating the spirits within natural objects, he looked upon the world as an aggregation of living entities compounded like himself of body and soul:

> There are in things two elements fused though antagonistic. One is that bodily element, which has in itself the quality of corruption and decease, the other is the element, the Soul, which goes on, I think, in unknown ways, enduring forever and ever.
> The analogy holds in this way—that the Soul of the Universe is the Male and genital master and the impregnating and animating spirit—Physical matter is Female and Mother and waits barren and bloomless, the jets of life from the masculine vigor, the undermost first cause of all that is not what Death is.[47]

With this in mind it is easier to understand what he meant when he said, "Behold, the body includes and is the meaning, and includes and is the soul," or "I will make the poems of materials, for I think they are to be the most spiritual poems." We can see how such a world could behave purposively and eventuate in "invisible spiritual results."

Thus Whitman reaped the cosmological benefits of idealism without accepting the picture world of Chapter VI of *Nature*. He succeeded in reaching the conclusion that, though matter exists, it or its movements are not the governing factor in change. Spirit, rather, is the molding cause and matter merely that which is molded; the world may be constituted of matter, but it is neither governed nor to be explained by mechanical pushes and pulls. Idealism, in any case, does not necessarily presuppose phenomenalism. Plato did not deny the existence of matter, and the world of the Hegelians was not a picture world but a universe of relations. These, and Whitman must in some sense be included among them, were "objective" as opposed to "subjective" idealists. True, as rationalists, they reached their conclusions by the analysis of knowledge, while Whitman reached his intuitively;[48] but the result was the same. So good a judge as Rufus Jones has included Whitman among the mystics,[49] and it is characteristic of the mystic that he knows the essence of things directly rather than by rationalization; in William James' antithesis, his is knowledge by acquaintance rather than knowledge about.[50] For our purposes this is nowhere better illustrated than in the specimen day, "The Oaks and I." One day when caught in the rain after exercising in his natural gymnasium beside Timber Creek, Whitman took refuge under an oak, and there, feeling the oneness between himself and the world with particular force, set this down:

> But now pleasantly imprison'd here under the big oak—the rain dripping, and the sky cover'd with leaden clouds . . . why am I so (almost) happy here and alone? Why would any intrusion, even from people I like, spoil the charm? *But am I alone?* Doubtless there comes a time—perhaps it has come to me—when one feels through his whole being, and pronouncedly the emotional part, that identity between himself subjectively and Nature objectively which Schelling and Fichte are so fond of pressing. How it is I know not, but I often realize a presence here—in clear moods I am certain of it, and neither chemistry nor reasoning nor esthetics will give the least explanation.[51]

It was in such moments and on such a basis that Whitman came to the conclusion that "everything without exception has an eternal soul."

4

Unreasoned as Whitman's conception was, moreover, and crude as it often seems, it is not without parallel in philosophy proper. Fechner, for example, also believed that everything in nature has a soul.[52] The soul, he held, is the inward nature of the thing and body its appearance to other souls. Nature is not a vast picture painted on the instant eternity, but many entities, each with its double aspect: "To others I am a body, to myself I am a consciousness."[53] There is at least a suggestion of this in Whitman's 1847 notebook:

The effusion or corporation of the soul is always under the beautiful laws of physiology—I guess the soul itself can never be anything but great and pure and immortal; but it makes itself visible only through matter. . . .[54]

The most illuminating parallels, however, are with the more famous Germans of the earlier years of the century, particularly Schelling and Hegel, whose "greatest *poetical* representative"[55] Whitman once extravagantly proclaimed himself to be. His knowledge of these thinkers was hazy and superficial in the extreme and may not have been acquired until after the publication of the third or even the fourth edition of *Leaves of Grass*.[56] But to anyone attempting to bring into focus his somewhat vagrant thoughts it is of the greatest interest and use. If it came late, and gave him little that he had not either discovered for himself or learned from Emerson, Carlyle, and others—which is possible—it still provided him, and provides us, with the formulary expression that makes thought more manageable and placed his ideas in a broader and more fully worked-out context that makes easier the detection of their premises and the charting of their direction.

It is instructive, for example, that he admired Schelling and Hegel vastly more than Fichte—maintaining the preference, in fact, in the teeth of the statement of his principal source, Joseph Gostwick's *German Literature,* that the doctrines of his revered Emerson were "simply a reproduction of the ideas of Fichte in a new dress."[57] He made it emphatically clear, moreover, that his choice was based on a preference of Schelling's "objectivity" to Fichte's "subjectivity." "*Subjectiveness* is his principle, explaining all," he said of Fichte, and then of Schelling, "The difference between him and Fichte is that Schelling's philosophy is more largely objective."[58] Something of what this meant to him is well stated by another source to which there is an indication that he turned. "Fichte had neglected the outer world," this source asserted, and even Kant had "held that the laws and order found in nature were not its own, but imparted to it by the investigating mind"; but Schelling said, "Nature is life, a living organism, replete with formative powers; there is an ideal in the real, a subject in the object, reason in matter."[59] Whether Whitman knew this source or not, he went on in his notes to define Schelling's position in these similar terms:

The chief forte of it [Schelling's philosophy]—seeking to counterbalance and restrain Fichte's all-devouring egoism—is *the essential identity of the subjective and objective worlds*, or, in terms [sic], that what exists as mentality, intelligence, consciousness in man, exists in equal strength and absoluteness in concrete forms, shows and practical laws in material nature—making the latter one with man's sane intuitions. The same universal spirit manifests itself in the individual Man, in aggregates, in concrete Nature, and in Historic progress.[60]

In other words, though the world of things is not "put forth through us," as was said in *Nature*,[61] it is still not "foreign" to us, but matches us like an image in a mirror. "Objects gross and the unseen soul are one," not because either is the product of or an appearance to the other, but because both are manifestations of the same fundamental reality. Further consideration of Whitman's relation to these thinkers will contribute to clearing up his conception of the relation of this fundamental reality to the things and soul in which it manifests itself.

For the apple of Whitman's philosophic eye was not Schelling but Hegel. "Without depreciating poets, patriots, saints, statesmen, inventors and the like," he said, "I rate (Hegel) as Humanity's chiefest teacher and the choicest loved physician of my mind and soul."[62] He discussed him first, last, and most fully in the elaborate notes on philosophy that his editors have preserved, and he regarded him as the culmination of German idealism: "These idealists fit into each other like a nest of boxes—and Hegel encloses them all."[63] The line between this largest box and that of Schelling next inside, however, is very difficult to discover in his commentary, if it exists at all. Following Gostwick, he said in his essay on Carlyle that Hegel had substantially adopted the system of Schelling, merely carrying it out and fortifying it; and both here and elsewhere his summaries of the philosophies of the two men bear out the assertion. Compare these versions of Hegel, for example, with that of Schelling just quoted:

Metaphysics . . . is . . . that which considers the whole concrete show of things, the world, man himself, either individually or aggregated in History, as resting on a spiritual, invisible basis, continually shifting, yet the real substance, and the only immutable one. This was the doctrine of Hegel.[64]

As a face in a mirror we see the world of materials, nature with all its objects, processes, shows, reflecting the human spirit and by such formulation, identifying, developing and proving it. Body and mind are one; an inexplicable paradox, yet no truth truer.⁶⁵

Nevertheless, apparently without his knowing it, there was one respect in which Whitman clove to Hegel as against Schelling, parting company with Emerson in much the same way that Hegel had departed from Schelling. Hegel's departure, which is a commonplace of textbooks, is described by one historian of philosophy as follows:

According to Hegel, the common source of the ego and of nature does not transcend reality; it is immanent in it. Mind and nature are not aspects of the absolute, or a kind of screen, behind which an indifferent and lifeless God lies concealed, but its successive modes. The absolute is not immovable, but active; it is not the principle of nature and of mind, but is itself successively nature and mind. This succession, this process, this perpetual generation of things, is the absolute itself. In Schelling, things *proceed from the absolute,* which, for that very reason, remains outside them. In Hegel, the *absolute is the process itself;* it does not produce movement and life, it *is* movement and life.⁶⁶

Is this not essentially the same divergence that Professor Howard has pointed out between Whitman and Emerson?

In this conception of the supreme self resulting from the proper union of material and ideal, then, Whitman is at variance with the Transcendental conception of enlarged being growing out of the union of the individual soul with the over-soul.⁶⁷

In the final issues of his thought, as we have seen, Emerson was also an "objective" idealist, just as Schelling was, but his treatment of the locus of reality as transcendent marks him off from Whitman. Constantly he speaks of man and nature as, not realities in themselves, but façades which reality lies behind.⁶⁸ Whitman, on the other hand, though he occasionally falls into similar language,⁶⁹ insists that no other reality exists than that which is to be found in objects gross and the unseen soul. With Whitman, in other words, the world-soul has ceased to be an *over*-soul. Like Hegel as against Schelling, he entertained a more thoroughgoing conception of immanence than Emerson, a matter of no little significance in a philosophy of evolution, which, if it is to be theistic at all, always enforces some form of this doctrine.

In speaking of Hegelian elements in Whitman one must of course keep a sense of proportion. The only known source of his knowledge of Hegel is a few pages by a literary hack, and there is evidence, if it be needed, that closer acquaintance would have produced only revulsion. On one of Traubel's visits Whitman greeted him with a copy of the most thoroughly Hegelian publication in the country at the time, W. T. Harris' *Journal of Speculative Philosophy*. "I shall ask you to take that away and never bring it back," he said laughing. "Mind you, I don't say read it—I only say, take it away."[70] Two more unlike minds than those of Whitman and Hegel could scarcely be imagined. The one, unswervingly rationalistic, held that the heart of things can be discovered by logical analysis because that heart is reason itself, whereas the other, just as unswervingly the opposite, felt that this heart is something more like passion or impulse and to be known only by acquaintance. Moreover, when Hegel said that the Absolute does not transcend reality but is immanent in it, he meant something rather different from Whitman's crude animism or pantheism. He did not mean that it is "in" things as water is in a pail or even as electricity is in a wire or life in a mosquito, but rather as roundness and redness are in the wire and the species in the individual insect. To Hegel as to Plato the real world was a world of logical universals and the world of things merely the particular forms in which they were alone perceivable. The Absolute was not a thing or a force to be sensed, but an idea to be thought; it was—and here we leave Plato—the whole train of thought of a Mind, though that Mind was not to be considered as existing apart from its thoughts. It was in this sense—that the Mind, its thoughts, and the objects of its thoughts are one—that the Absolute of Hegel was "immanent." Such subtleties, obviously, were not for Whitman.[71]

And yet the analogy still holds. In the crude pictoral thought of the unsophisticated or in the imagery of the poet, such an idealism inevitably appears as a kind of pantheism. Thus Whitman went on in the essay on Carlyle, again following Gostwick, to picture Creative Thought as moving literally and spatially in nature and the affairs of men:

According to Hegel, the whole earth, . . . with its infinite variety, the past, the surroundings of to-day, or what may happen in the future, the contrarieties of material with spiritual, and of natural with artificial, are all, to the eye of the *ensemblist,* but necessary sides and unfoldings, different steps or links, in the endless process of Creative thought.[72]

If he did not realize the true and full significance of the words "endless process of Creative thought" as applied to Hegel, he was not alone; and if this misunderstanding occasionally took a materialistic guise, he was again not alone, as is illustrated by the materialism of the "Hegelians of the left." His metaphysic, if such it may be called, was merely the older transcendentalism modified to square with the veneration of material reality inspired in him by his peculiar temperament and experience and by science; but his third-hand Hegelianism gave him terms in which to define it. The combination was particularly well adapted to a philosophy of evolution.

Before we leave these parallels, there is one other that must be briefly explored. The egotism of Whitman is popularly regarded as an eccentricity, if not a mania; but even the little that has been said in this and the last three chapters should make it clear that, disregarding its vociferous expression, it was not in the least unusual. Emerson's Over-Soul was but a deeper and universal self, and it will be remembered that Poe proceeded from "the utter impossibility of any one's soul feeling itself inferior to any other" to the conclusion that the Heart Divine that throbs in the universe is "our own."[73] This, moreover, was not simply a vagary of overwrought literary imagination but a common denominator of modern idealisms, going back to Descartes' doubt of everything except his own thought and constituting the principal distinction between them and their ancient counterparts. Thus, where the Idea of Plato was an abstraction, a static perfection or essence, that of Hegel was a procession of relations which has just been likened to the train of thought of a "subject." "In my view," he said, " . . . everything depends on expressing the ultimate Truth not as Substance but as Subject as well."[74] It is in the dynamism of this conception that its significance for evolution lies, but for the moment we are less concerned with the consequences of the conception than with the conception itself, with the simple fact that selfhood was the fundamental category of the philosophic tradition of which Whitman was a part.

In one important respect, however, Whitman's version of this conception must be at least partly differentiated from that of the principal exponents of the tradition, who had in mind, not empirical selves, yours and mine, but an absolute self, deeper and all-inclusive. This, in fact, has been one of the gravest sources of dissatisfaction with the whole tradition, which has seemed to many to drown the individual in the whole, sacrificing at once his freedom and his immortality. Even Emerson, for all his "self-reliance," could say, "From within or from behind, a light shines through us upon things, and makes us aware that we are nothing, but the light is all";[75] and Poe, as well perhaps as Emerson, acquiesced in the loss of identity in death.[76] Emerson was commendably cautious in most of his statements on this subject, but we find him saying in his essay "Immortality":

I confess that everything connected with our personality fails. Nature never spares the individual; we are always balked of a complete success: no prosperity is promised to our self-esteem. We have our indemnity only in the moral and intellectual reality to which we aspire. That is immortal, and we only through that. The soul stipulates for no private good. That which is private I see not to be good.[77]

The things connected with personality, however, were just what Whitman would not give up. "Nothing endures," he said, "but personal qualities."[78] "I believe in immortality, and by that I mean *identity*," he told Traubel on one occasion,[79] and again not long afterward, "When I say immortality I say identity—the survival of the personal soul, your survival, my survival."[80]

Nor, whatever may have been the case during most of his years, was he to remain alone among American Hegelians in this defense of the person. A number of the subtle and learned troop who brought about the substitution of the German for the Scottish philosophy in American colleges at the end of the century exercised themselves to the point of contortion to reconcile Hegelian absolutism with American individualism, and some simply abandoned orthodox Hegelianism for idealisms of their own. They were, says Professor Perry, "bad Hegelians."[81] Such, for example, was G. H. Howison of the University of California, who in a famous symposium with Professors Royce, Mezes, and Le Conte attacked Royce's notion of an "Infinite Inclusive Self" as inconsistent with and destructive of personality. Since selfhood is essentially a moral consciousness, he argued, it implies the existence of other selves.[82] Another independent Hegelian was Borden P. Bowne of Boston University, whose philosophy of "Personalism" presents, besides the same general likeness to Whitman's, an interesting verbal parallel.[83] "This second principle [on which democracy rests]," said Whitman in *Democratic Vistas* in 1871, "is individuality, the pride and centripetal isolation of a human being in himself—identity—personalism."[84] Whitman, in fact, seems to have started this term on the way to its wide currency, through Bronson Alcott, who borrowed it and took it to the Concord School of Philosophy.[85] In any case, it was very little used in any similar sense before the appearance of the *Vistas*,[86] but had become, by the first decade of the new century, a well-worn philosophical tag.

The word, however, is less important than the thought, which constitutes so great a departure from Hegel's universalism that it must be questioned whether Whitman had not contradicted himself more seriously than usual. Consider his own versions of the thought of this choicest loved physician of his mind and soul. All things, individuals included, are but "necessary sides and unfoldings . . . in the endless process of Creative Thought." "The whole concrete show of things, man himself, individually or aggregated in History" rests "on a spiritual, invisible basis, continually shifting, yet the real substance, and the only immutable." Does it not seem from Whitman's assent to such views that he too found the individual but secondary, but a temporary manifestation of a single all-inclusive spirit? Remember also that if Evolution and Freedom were two of the "three peerless stars" in his heaven, Ensemble was the third. Note that in the strongest expression of the meaning of Ensemble, "Crossing Brooklyn Ferry," Whitman presents himself as a part of a unitary whole and at least suggests that the whole is the reality and the individual but a fleeting "disintegration," like a drop in Niagara:

> I too had been struck from the float forever held in solution,
> I too had receiv'd identity by my body. . . .[87]

Was Whitman inconsistent? No doubt there is copious laughter among the leaves of grass on Whitman's grave that such a question should even be asked. Since on the whole it can be answered in the negative, however, no harm is done. Again we may levy on Howison for a side light. Like Whitman, Howison believed that the fundamental reality is persons. He did not look upon them, however, as simply atomic, with no unity tying them together: "There is one *nature*," he pointed out, "in manifold *persons*."[88] They are not united in totalitarian fashion, by the loss of individuality, but as in a republic, by being of the same kind and having interacting ties of responsibility and antagonism. To use a word that Howison liked, reality is a "league" of persons. This parallel, of course, can easily be overworked, for there are points of decided difference between the two men. Handled with restraint, however, it sheds light on Whitman's conception of "ensemble," in which, philosophically as well as politically, individuals are tied together by their common nature and the "adhesiveness" inherent in that nature rather than by sacrifice of autonomy. In this way was Whitman's universe thoroughly individualistic and yet a true cosmos—"one *nature* in manifold persons."

5

The only excuse under the present circumstances for an analysis of the kind and length of that just concluded is that the "personalism" which it has yielded supplies the key to Whitman's conception of evolution. Not that his evolutionism was simply a deduction from a metaphysic, as was the case with Fichte, Schelling, and Hegel. On the contrary, Whitman not only was incapable of such a deduction but had no need of it to arrive at the evolutionary idea. The evolutionary fruits of the idealists' analyses were plentifully available in simplified secondary accounts and in the rhapsodies of Emerson, and the air was fairly bursting with the scientific theory as foreshadowed by historical geology—in which, as we know from the notes and clippings he left behind him, Whitman took a keen interest from an early date. The metaphysic implicit in his writings does not explain *why* Whitman was an evolutionist, but *how*—what the theory meant to him and why he set such store by it.

The first of the two most important phases of this explanation is most conveniently approached by considering his treatment of the theme of universal flux, which was not only one of his most characteristic themes but has been a point of frequent attack by one school of his critics. Thus Paul Elmer More deplored "the sense of indiscriminate motion"[89] that he found in his writing, and H. B. Reed has charged him with a "Heracleitan obsession."[90] Looked at more closely, however, Whitman turns out to be less Heracleitan than he gives the impression of being—in part, it seems likely, because the Heracleitan view that the only unchanging thing is change is a very difficult one to maintain. Common sense always conceives of change in terms of a *thing* that changes, that is, in terms of something that persists through change so that we can say, " 'This is the thing which yesterday was so-and-so and is to-day something else.' "[91] In the same way was Whitman's "Heracleitan obsession" limited; always in the midst of the flowing of which he sang so appreciatively he found something that retained its identity. This difficulty of common sense statement was not the only factor involved, however, for the same qualification is to be found at the very fountainhead of the Romantic philosophy, where the inconsistencies were seldom those of common sense. Professor Lovejoy has traced Bergson's philosophy of change to the *Naturphilosophie* of Schelling, but in so doing has felt it necessary to warn that the "Romantic pantheism" had "two gods"—not only the *"ewiges, lebendiges Tun"* from which Bergsonism is descended but "the Eternal Changelessness of Neo-Platonism or of the Vedanta."[92] In the considerable degree in which Whitman shared in this tradition a similar qualification was to be expected from him.

By all odds the most important deterrent upon his Heracleitanism, however, was his unwavering faith in personal survival. He was not simply caught in a logical trap or held in the grip of a historical tradition; he did not simply concede that *something* persists. Rather he knew with all the certainty of intuition precisely what persists—personal identity. The unequivocal way in which he held to this belief has already been insisted upon, and it will be recalled that he distinguished between body and soul on the ground that the former has in it "the quality of corruption and decease," while the latter "goes on, I think, in unknown ways, enduring forever and ever." Only in his "downcast hours" did he even reckon with the possibility that "matter is conqueror."[93] Curiously, in a note to the 1876 Preface he stated that because *Leaves of Grass* was primarily concerned with "the Body and Existence" it had originally been his intention to "compose a further, equally needed Volume, based on those convictions of perpetuity and conservation which, enveloping all precedents, make the unseen Soul govern absolutely at last."[94] No thorough reader of the existing volume, however, would ever admit that a second was needed. How his convictions of perpetuity and conservation could ever have been more firmly or fully stated it is difficult to imagine. The very heart of the book, they were also the weightiest meaning of the symbolism of its title. As early as 1847 he had set down a note concerning "different objects which decay, and by the chemistry of nature, their bodies are [transformed] into spears of grass."[95] Eight years later this observation in the chemistry of life—owed almost certainly to Liebig's great work on organic chemistry, which he had reviewed in the *Eagle*[96]—had become a definite intimation of immortality. "The smallest sprout shows there is really no death," he wrote in a well known passage of his initial poem,

> And if ever there was it led forward life, and does
>   not wait at the end to arrest it,
> And ceased the moment life appeared.
>
> All goes onward and outward . . . and nothing collapses,
> And to die is different from what any one supposed,
>   and luckier.[97]

As root and branch of the "personalism" just analyzed, this conviction was the inevitable and inexorable condition of Whitman's acceptance of evolution. If evolution meant that nature was truly careless of the single life, then it was not for him. Apparently it might be interpreted otherwise, however. Had not Emerson said that the worm striving to be man mounted through all the spires of form? In all probability Whitman had not seen these famous phrases when he began to put together his own notions of evolution in the early fifties,[98] just as he could not have seen the comment in the Journal that the avatars of Brahma were becoming textbooks of natural history. But that he had reached an almost identical conclusion will presently be obvious. There is also a difference, however, that must be equally insisted upon. In view of his caution on the subject of personal immortality, it seems unlikely that Emerson wished to be taken as literally as we may be sure that Whitman did. It is a matter of no small significance that though both men told the evolutionary story in the first person, Emerson's "I" was that of a personified Nature or World-Soul, while Whitman's was his own.

It may be that there is a touch of drama—of hesitation and sudden illumination—in our record of Whitman's arrival at this interpretation of evolution. In his second notebook, at any rate, appears this passage, in which the brackets indicate words crossed out:

Amelioration is the blood that runs through the body of the universe.—I do not lag—I do not hasten—[it appears to say] I bide my hour over billions of billions of years—I exist in the void that takes uncounted time and coheres to a nebula, and in further time cohering to an orb, marches gladly round, a beautiful tangible creature, in his place in the processions of God, where new comers have been falling in the ranks for ever, and will be so always. . . .[99]

Originally, it would seem, Whitman meant by the first personal pronoun merely the universe, as Emerson did; whether he changed his mind later and dramatically or whether in the usual vagrant way of his note writing he merely caught himself shifting from one subject to another is anybody's guess. Shift he did, however, and there is no doubt as to the meaning of the "I" in the passage as it reappears in the "Song of Myself." As Whitman's fullest statement of his conception of evolution, this must be quoted at length:

> I am an acme of things accomplish'd, and I an encloser
>   of things to be.
> My feet strike an apex of the apices of the stairs,
> On every step bunches of ages, and larger bunches between
>   the steps,
> All below duly travel'd, and still I mount and mount.
>
> Rise after rise bow the phantoms behind me,
> Afar down I see the huge first Nothing, I know I was even
>   there,
> I waited unseen and always, and slept through the
>   lethargic mist,
> And took my time, and took no hurt from the fetid carbon.
>
> Long I was hugg'd close—long and long.
>
> Immense have been the preparations for me,
> Faithful and friendly the arms that have help'd me.
>
> Cycles ferried my cradle, rowing and rowing like cheerful
>   boatmen,

> For room to me stars kept aside in their own rings,
> They sent influences to look after what was to hold me.
>
> Before I was born out of my mother generations guided me,
> My embryo has never been torpid, nothing could overlay it.
>
> For it the nebula cohered to an orb,
> The long slow strata piled to rest it on,
> Vast vegetables gave it sustenance,
> Monstrous sauroids transported it in their mouths and
>   deposited it with care.
>
> All forces have been steadily employ'd to complete and
>   delight me,
> Now on this spot I stand with my robust soul.[100]

"Of the progress of the souls of men and women along the grand roads of the universe," he reaffirmed in the "Song of the Open Road," "all other progress is the needed emblem and sustenance."[101]

Evolution being construed in such a fashion, there is no mystery as to Whitman's devotion to it. It was the rationalization of his dearest belief. It taught, as he wrote in a notebook,

> that our immortality is *located* here upon earth—that we *are immortal*—that the processes of the refinement and perfection of the earth are in steps, the least part of which involves trillions of years—that in due time the earth beautiful as it is now will be as proportionately different from what it is now, as it now is proportionately different from what it was in its earlier gaseous or marine period, uncounted cycles before man and woman grew. That we also shall be here, proportionately different from now and beautiful. That the Egyptian idea of the return of the soul after a certain period of time involved a beautiful . . . nature . . . mystery. . . .[102]

The theme of Whitman's that is probably most puzzling to the inexperienced reader is his celebration of death. In love with life as he was, he insisted again and again that he was no less in love with death. "For not life's joys alone I sing," he proclaimed, but "the joy of death."[103] Nor, though he called it "soothing" in a famous passage,[104] did he welcome it merely as surcease; its joy was positive. No doubt there is a psychological explanation of this, and a mystical;[105] but its rational explanation certainly lies in this conception of the persistence of the soul through evolutionary change. Whitman chants the praise of death for a very good reason: it is not an end but a beginning; like birth, which he praises for the same reason, it is "the outlet again."[106] He "estimates" it

not at all as the cessation, but as somehow what I feel it must be, the entrance upon by far the greatest part of existence, and something that Life is at least as much for, as it is for itself.[107]

Consequently he has no fear of its approach, but cries:

> welcome, ineffable grace of dying days!
>
> Every condition promulges not only itself, it promulges
>   what grows after and out of itself,
> And the dark hush promulges as much as any.[108]

This was his "whisper of heavenly death":

> I see, just see skyward, great cloud-masses,
> Mournfully slowly they roll, silently swelling and
>   mixing,
> With at times a half-dimm'd sadden'd far-off star,
> Appearing and disappearing.
>
> (Some parturition rather, some solemn immortal birth;
> On the frontiers to eyes impenetrable,
> Some soul is passing over.)[109]

Such a conception is of course open to grave objections, seeming inevitably quite chimerical to the matter of fact mind and running into certain logical difficulties. Professor Perry, for example, has objected strenuously to the similar view of Howison:

The trouble with this view is that the immortal soul is as effectually prevented from living as from dying. The bodily and mental life which it cognizes, which belongs to the phenomena of nature and history, has all the adventures, and *it* dies.[110]

Whitman did not reason of such matters, however, and it is vain to hold him too closely to the tests of reason when he is writing about them. "These are not reasons," he once told Traubel when discussing the subject; ". . . they are impressions, visions."[111] Like the other cosmic optimists, including even such a logician as Poe, he was fundamentally a man of imagination, and his reflections on the cosmos are in large measure myth. Nor is this intended as a condemnation. His reflections were, like all the best of myths, the embodiment of an aspiration—not a copy of the world of fact but a construction to express the author, and through him all men. That Whitman's belief in personal survival was the criterion of his acceptance of evolution, however, and was justified by his interpretation of it, is plain. The latter half of a sentence in a note to "Good-by My Fancy" reads: "to me Development, Continuity, Immortality, Transformation, are the chiefest life-meanings of Nature and Humanity, and are the *sine qua non* of all facts, and each fact"—the first half: "Behind a Good-bye there lurks much of the salutation of another beginning."[112]

6

Whitman's representation of the universal life, then, was of a procession of souls. "All is a procession," he said, "the universe is a procession with measured and perfect motion."[113] Nor did he value the movement of this procession less than the identity of its constituents. Indeed, the reappearance of life in the new forms of growth seemed to him a principal evidence of that identity:

> But the soul is also real, it too is positive and direct,
> No reasoning, no proof has establish'd it,
> Undeniable growth has establish'd it.[114]

If the charge of "Heracleitan obsession" against Whitman must be qualified in the manner suggested earlier, within the limits of this qualification the charge must be admitted. From beginning to end *Leaves of Grass* is on the move. "I tramp a perpetual journey," Whitman proclaimed in bringing his longest poem to a climax,[115] and the mere names of a few of the others are sufficient to demonstrate the prevalence of the theme in the whole—"Starting from Paumonok," "Song of the Open Road," "Song of the Rolling Earth," "Pioneers! O Pioneers!" "Passage to India." "Allons!" was peculiarly his word, and the call that it sounded expressed a central fact in his conception of the nature of things:

> Allons! whoever you are come travel with me!
>   . . .
> To know the universe itself as a road, as many roads,
>   as roads for traveling souls.
>
> All parts away for the progress of souls,

> All religions, all solid things, arts, governments—all that was or is apparent upon this globe, or any globe, falls into niches and corners before the procession of souls along the grand roads of the universe.[116]

That this journey, moreover, was no aimless meander but a true progress is so familiar a fact about Whitman that it needs no demonstration. The word "amelioration" came as often and emphatically from his pen as from Emerson's.[117] As the ultimate fruit of his cosmic optimism, however, it deserves careful explication and examination. This, in fact, is the other reason for the metaphysical discussion to which the first half of this chapter was devoted.

For Whitman's doctrine of progress, like that of all who are here called cosmic optimists, was no mere calculation from past events but a profound conviction that the universe is so constituted that it *must* progress. At bottom, of course, and particularly in Whitman's case, this was sheer faith. He stood for the "sunny point of view," he told Traubel, not because he merely guessed but "because my faith seems to belong to the nature of things, is imposed, cannot be escaped."[118] In elaborating this faith, however, he followed the same highway of reason that we have already trodden several times and shall tread again—followed it, indeed, more boldly and a greater distance than any other poet we shall consider. He set, as was said, the high-water mark of cosmic optimism. The absurdities in his claim that he was the greatest poetical representative of the German philosophy are obvious, but if technicalities and special Teutonisms are stripped away the claim has much to recommend it. With this qualification, in fact, he is probably its most dauntless representative in our literature, following it at times quite to the point of caricature. With the aid of Santayana, Professor Perry has ridiculed its cosmological pretensions in these terms:

> So there springs from idealism . . . the pride that claims the world in the name of those spiritual powers which are man's prerogative. It is a short step from believing that you are like the Absolute, or a part of the Absolute, to believing that you *are* the Absolute. Then looking upon nature and history as yours, you may be raised to a new level of faith and a new ecstasy of inspiration. Contemplating your work you may say, to use the words which Santayana has put into the mouth of the romantic hero: "What a

genius I am! Who would have thought there was such stuff in me?"[119]

Said Whitman after surveying the amplitude of nature:

> I am larger, better than I thought,
> I did not know I held so much goodness.[120]

The major premise of cosmic optimism was that the universe is not alien to man but the embodiment or reflection or prototype of his own deepest self; because this is the case, the conclusion then follows, the universe *must* aspire toward the same ends as man. That Whitman accepted this premise has been the burden of most that has been said here; and the conclusion as well, following so obviously, has necessarily been hinted many times. It may be finally clinched, however, by continuing one passage from the place where it was broken off in earlier quotation and adding another. "As a face in a mirror we see the world of materials," the former began, and continued after the interruption:

> The human soul stands in the centre, and all the universes minister to it, and serve and revolve round it. They are one side of the whole and it is the other side. . . .
> The varieties, contradictions and paradoxes of the world and of life, and even good and evil, so baffling to the superficial observer, and so often leading to despair, sullenness or infidelity, become a series of infinite radiations and waves of the one sea-like universe of divine action and progress, never stopping, never hasting. "The heavens and the earth" to use the summing up of Joseph Gostick whose brief I endorse: "The heavens and the earth and all things within their compass—all the events of history—the facts of the present and the development of the future (such is the doctrine of Hegel) all form a complication, a succession of steps in the one eternal process of creative thought."[121]

If it is objected that Whitman was here merely expounding Hegel, it must be replied that his endorsement was so strong that Hegel became for all practical purposes just another name for Whitman. The last sentence, as we have seen, became a part of the essay on Carlyle;[122] the last but one is closely paralleled in one of his most explicit confessions of faith, that near the end of *Democratic Vistas*;[123] and the doctrine of the whole is embodied in the second most important evolutionary declaration in *Leaves of Grass*—the "Song of the Universal":

> In this broad earth of ours,
> Amid the measureless grossness and the slag,
> Enclosed and safe within its central heart,
> Nestles the seed perfection.
>   . . .
>
> Lo! keen-eyed towering science,
> As from tall peaks the modern overlooking,
> Successive absolute fiats issuing.
>
> Yet again, lo! the soul, above all science,
> For it has history gather'd like husks around the
>   globe,
> For it the entire star-myriads roll through the sky.
>
> In spiral routes by long detours,
> (As a much-tacking ship upon the sea,)
> For it the partial to the permanent flowing,
> For it the real to the ideal tends.
>
> For it the mystic evolution,
> Not the right only justified, what we call evil also
>   justified.
>
> Forth from their masks no matter what,
> From the huge festering trunk, from craft and guile
>   and tears,
> Health to emerge and joy, joy universal.
>
> Out of the bulk, the morbid and the shallow,
> Out of the bad majority, the varied countless frauds
>   of men and states,
> Electric, antiseptic yet, cleaving, suffusing all,
> Only the good is universal.[124]

Of Whitman's acceptance of this central deduction of cosmic optimism we were already at least partly aware, and in itself it requires no further comment. Our understanding of its significance in his writing will not be complete, however, without following out at least briefly certain of its implications, the first of which in order of convenient exposition is a distinctive attitude toward the past. All events in time, according to this philosophy, are organically interrelated: the past is summed up in the present, and the present was implicit in the past, going back, if one pleases, to an initial "seed perfection." Thus Whitman not only proclaimed himself "an encloser of things to be"[125] but stated in a note apparently prepared for a friend to use in expounding the *Leaves:* "His notion explicitly is that there is nothing actually new only an accumulation or fruitage or carrying out these new occasions and requirements."[126] It is not difficult to see how such a conception would lead to a peculiarly tolerant and deferential attitude toward the past, every event in which had made its contribution to the present. Hegel, for example, never criticized a past philosophy as simply false but only as incomplete, contributing one or another element to the true philosophy which the fullness of the historical dialectic had left to him to synthesize.[127] Likewise Whitman seldom mentioned the past without pious gestures of respect. "America does not repel the past" were the first words of his first book,[128] and the opening lines of "Passage to India" are but one of many paeans in its celebration which could be culled from his writing:

> Singing my days,
> Singing the great achievements of the present,
>   . . .
> Yet first to sound, and ever sound, the cry with thee
>   O soul,
> The Past! the Past! the Past![129]

Since this esteem was based less on recognition of intrinsic merit, however, than on a kind of filial piety, it is not surprising that it was mightily diluted by condescension. Hegel always found it necessary to look down from his Teutonic pinnacle, and Whitman's mingling of something bordering on contempt with his praise is almost too familiar to be pointed out. Thus, though he took the trouble to say that America does not repel the past, he compared it in the same paragraph to a corpse and dismissed it as "fittest for its days." "Placard 'Removed' and 'To Let' on the rocks of your snowy Parnassus," he crowed in the brash "Song of the Exposition," and then, feeling the need of dressing the balance ("hold—don't I forget my manners?"), offered this gem of patronage:

> We do not blame thee elder World, nor really separate
>   ourselves from thee,
> (Would the son separate himself from the father?)[130]

Like any thorough devotee of the doctrine of progress, Whitman had little real regard for the past. When he said that his feet rested on an apex of the apices of the stairs,[131] he meant literally what he said, and though he always retained a sentimental respect for those he had climbed, his eyes were on the flight rising ahead. His position is well stated in a sentence in *Democratic Vistas:*

> America, filling the present with greatest deeds and problems, cheerfully accepting the past, including feudalism (as, indeed, the present is but the legitimate birth of the past, including feudalism), counts, as I reckon, for her justification and success, (for who, as yet, dare claim success?) almost entirely on the future.[132]

But, turning to another facet of the philosophy, where did these stairs lead? A partially true answer is, nowhere in particular. The procession of time was destined never to arrive at a final resting place but to be forever on the march, finding a new goal beyond each one attained. Thus, though Whitman said that "the goal that was named cannot be countermanded," he added immediately:

> Now understand me well—it is provided in the essence
> of things that from any fruition of success, no
> matter what, shall come forth something to make
> a greater struggle necessary.[133]

Here he touched one of the deepest motives in the Romantic spirit and the heart of its evolutionism, that Faust-spirit in which Lovejoy found the germ of the philosophy of Bergson.[134] It was, moreover, not a deduction but a premise, a fundamental reading of life. The Romantic experience was preeminently one of yearning, whether of simple creature hunger or ideal aspiration, and in turning itself inside out and calling the result the world, it quite naturally made this experience fundamental. Striving was not merely an aspect of life or one of its means, but its essence, simply another name for it, the cessation of which would be death. Hence the procession had either to move on or, as was unthinkable, cease to be. In his 1847 notebook Whitman wrote in words later incorporated in modified form in "Song of Myself":

> I think the soul will never stop or attain to any growth beyond which it shall not go.—When I walked at night by the sea shore and looked up at the countless stars, I asked of my soul whether it would be filled and satisfied when it should become god enfolding all these, and open to the life and delight and knowledge of everything in them or of them; and the answer was plain to me at the

breaking water on the sands at my feet: and the answer was, No, when I reach there, I shall want to go further still.[135]

Whitman did not mean by such statements, however, that the cosmic procession is merely aimless, but rather that its goal is ideal, never to be finally won and having even in approximation to be constantly re-won. The goal is an activity rather than a final resting place, and, in the paradox of the Romantic dialectic, is to be achieved only by the continual pursuit of something ever out of reach. How important this was to Whitman, furthermore, and how central it was in his interpretation of evolution is clearly indicated by its place in "Passage to India," of which it will be remembered that he said not only that it contained more of him than any of his poems but that its burden was evolution.[136] For though the point of departure in the poem is the geographical "passage" made possible by the newly completed Suez Canal and Union Pacific Railroad, it is evident from the beginning that the fourth dimension of time is to count more than the other three—that the journey in space is but a symbol for the journey of history, past and to come.[137] Thus India is not merely the land of spices and tea, the objective of circumnavigators, but, as the ancient seed-ground of religions, a symbol of the full spiritual life which has been "God's purpose from the first."[138] The "passage" is thus, as is said at the climax, a "Passage to more than India,"[139] a passage to the new illumination and beatitude that are the next stage in evolution. Like Emerson, Whitman concluded in respect to evolution that "the continuation of the divine effort that built the man" is "inspiration"[140]—though with this difference, that it is less a passive transformation than a new adventure. This thought is probably best expressed in the following passage, in which the retention of the imagery of the journey is significant:

> O we can wait no longer,
> We too take ship O soul,
> Joyous we too launch out on trackless seas,
> Fearless for unknown shores on waves of ecstasy to sail,
>   . . .
> O soul . . . .
> Bear me indeed as through the regions infinite,
> Whose air I breathe, whose ripples hear, lave me all over,
> Bathe me O God in thee, mounting to thee,
> I and my soul to range in range of thee.

> O Thou transcendent,
> Nameless, the fibre and the breath,
> Light of the light, shedding forth universes, thou centre
>   of them,
> Thou mightier centre of the true, the good, the loving,
> Thou moral, spiritual fountain—affection's source—
>   thou reservoir,
> (O pensive soul of me—O thirst unsatisfied—waitest
>   not there?
> Waitest not haply for us somewhere there the Comrade
>   perfect?)
> Thou pulse—thou motive of the stars, suns, systems,
> That, circling, move in order, safe, harmonious,
> Athwart the shapeless vastnesses of space,
> How should I think, how breathe a single breath, how
>   speak, if, out of myself,
> I could not launch, to those, superior universes?[141]

Faced by such mysticism, the expositor can go no further—nor, since this was the goal of Whitman's evolutionism, need much more be said. There is one touch in this poem of a more definite nature, however, that merits brief consideration because it relates Whitman's evolutionary speculation to one of his most frequently reiterated convictions and links him once again to the philosophical tradition that he so much admired. Thus, after picturing the wandering progeny of Adam with their sad refrain, "Whither O mocking life?" he asks, "Ah, who shall soothe these feverish children?" His answer is this:

> After the great captains and engineers have accomplish'd
>   their work,
>   . . .
> Finally shall come the poet worthy that name,
> The true son of God shall come singing his songs.
>
> Then not your deeds only O voyagers, O scientists and in-
>   ventors, shall be justified,
> All these hearts as of fretted children shall be sooth'd,
> All affection shall be fully responded to, the secret
>   shall be told,
> All these separations and gaps shall be taken up and
>   hook'd and link'd together,
> The whole earth, this cold, impassive, voiceless earth,
>   shall be completely justified,
> Trinitas divine shall be gloriously accomplish'd and
>   compacted by the true son of God, the poet.[142]

Thus we know at least one definite thing of the future: the poet, as Whitman had been saying since the 1855 Preface, is to be the instrument of deliveration. Not only a sayer but a seer, he shall see and say the truth that shall make men free and blessed—or, better, that shall make them aware of the freedom and blessedness that is already theirs for the taking. Hegel had no such exalted conception of the poet (though Schelling did), but it is of interest that he too found the culmination of his evolutionary series in the revelation and apprehension of the divinity in all things. We know that Whitman used Dana and Ripley's *New American Cyclopedia*[143]—that he even reviewed some of its earlier volumes[144]—but we can only wonder whether he noticed this summary of the conclusion of the *Phenomenology of Mind* in its article on Hegel:

Arrived at this stage of knowledge, the spirit knows itself to be identical with universal reason; the finite self-consciousness and the absolute self-consciousness are one; the infinite is no longer foreign to and outside the finite. . . . Man knows the absolute reason; the absolute knows itself in man. To this all history, all thought have been tending; the history of thought is this very process; the completion of thought is found in the science of the absolute.

Whether he did or did not, if the word "reason" is interpreted as liberally as he would have been likely to interpret it, it is a serviceable approximation of his conception of the goal of evolution.

7

One could scarcely ask for a more sweeping doctrine of progress than this quasi-Hegelianism of Whitman's. "Roaming in thought over the Universe," he wrote "after reading Hegel,"

> I saw the little that is Good steadily
> hastening towards immortality,
> And the vast all that is call'd Evil I saw hastening
> to merge itself and become lost and dead.[145]

Hence it may seem hypercritical, if not ungrateful, to point out that he sometimes maintained the opposite, denying progress and the whole conception of better and worse on which any theory of progress must rest. It is a fact, however, and must be faced. "There . . . will never be any more perfection than there is now," he asserted flatly early in the "Song of Myself,"[146] and in the very passage in which he told the evolutionary story:

> I do not call one greater and one smaller,
> That which fills its period and place is equal to any.[147]

The same idea is presented more metaphorically in "Song of the Open Road":

> The earth, that is sufficient,
> I do not want the constellations any nearer,
> I know they are very well where they are,
> I know they suffice for those who belong to them.[148]

There is not only no likelihood of improvement, these passages suggest, but no need of it; everything is perfect here and now. Nor was this a mere vagary to be dismissed as the privilege of one who was large and contained multitudes. Rather it was a judgment that ran deep and far in what Whitman had to say. Thus, a writer in a recent number of *Ethics* has made out a strong case for the view that Whitman maintained an absolute equalitarianism in value, the basis of his valuation lying, not in the "specific quality" of a thing, its difference from other things, but "purely in its own being."[149] Whitman's answer, for example, to the question "What good amid these, O me, O life?" was

> That you are here—that life exists and identity,
> That the powerful play goes on, and you may contribute
>   a verse.[150]

This is not the place to elaborate on this contention, but it may be pointed out that it is strongly supported by Whitman's extreme tolerance of evil, amounting practically to a denial of it. "I reject none, accept all," he says.[151] But if one thing is as good as another, how can there be change for the better?

This was not simply the philosophical illiteracy of an unlearned man, moreover, but a prevailing idiosyncrasy of the tradition of cosmic optimism, the result of grafting the evolutionary conception on the optimisms of Plato and Leibnitz. Thus it was suggested without comment in Chapter I, but with this in mind, that the logic of cosmic optimism leads from the premise that the world is the expression of an absolute perfection to the conclusion that it is not only directed toward good but good in itself;[152] and it is this among other things that underlay Emerson's denial of progress in "Self-Reliance."[153] Moreover, within the limits of the assumptions of this tradition, it admits of explanation as a paradox rather than a contradiction. There are two planes of valuation, it was here assumed, time and eternity (or, in the terms of a later advocate, a world of "description" and a world of "appreciation"),[154] and though there is a definite progress and a definite differentiation of good and evil on the former plane, they disappear under the aspect of eternity, where things are seen to be in both a literal and slangy sense "all one." Even on the plane of time, for that matter, all things are seen to be necessary parts of a totality which in its wholeness is perfect. The key word here is "necessary." Professor Perry puts it this way:

Idealism does not, it is true, attribute *equal* significance to all things; but it does attribute *necessary* significance to all things. It is essentially the all-saving philosophy, as opposed to the philosophy of extermination. It encourages the supposition that a profounder insight would reinstate what ordinary discrimination rejects out of hand.[155]

This closely approximates Whitman's position. Compare it, for example, with this statement in "Starting from Paumonok":

> Omnes! omnes! let others ignore what they may,
> I make the poem of evil also, I commemorate that part also,
> I am myself just as much evil as good, and my nation is
>   —and I say there is in fact no evil,
> (Or if there is I say it is just as important to you to the land or to me, as anything else.) [156]

Whitman was very probably ignorant of this distinction as such; certainly he shifted from one plane to the other without warning. The distinction exists, however, it is implicit in his writing, and it may be used to reconcile his apparent contradictions, as it has been by his philosophical betters to reconcile theirs.

Even when this reconciliation has been admitted, however, the sceptic is still moved to ask, with the whole school of modern philosophical realism, whether this philosophy is truly as optimistic and progressive as it prides itself in being. Since it would certainly hold the view of eternity to be the final view, are not its claims of progress merely incidental, even nugatory? As a problem of evaluation this falls outside the scope of this study, but no consideration of Whitman's cosmology would be complete if it were not raised. Professor Perry states the objection more largely as follows:

> It needs no philosophical subtlety to see that this view of history contradicts the common man's conception of progress. It is half of progress, according to the common view, to be able to leave something behind and get rid of it altogether. Progress is inspired both to achieve a better and escape a worse. But according to idealism nothing is lost, nothing has been in vain. The future is not to wipe out the past, but to round it out....[157]

> ... the ideal which this philosophy glorifies is not the gradual amelioration of life through the human conquest of nature; but rather the perfection that was from the beginning and is forever more.... Idealism does, it is true, emphasize historical development, but of the sort in which the value attaches to the progress itself rather than to the result; and in which the merit of historical achievement is apparent rather than real.[158]

True as this may be of the philosophical position in question, however, it cannot be allowed to be the last word in a discussion of Whitman's evolutionism. Quite apart from what has already been said, *Democratic Vistas,* one of the most trenchant criticisms of the Gilded Age, is sufficient witness that Whitman could take the "common view" of progress as well as Professor Perry and lay about him with a mighty vigor.

PART TWO

AFTER DARWIN:
QUESTION AND COMPROMISE

V

THE COMING OF DARWIN

Though both returned to the theme of evolution many times after the appearance of *The Origin of Species*, Emerson and Whitman may be described as pre-Darwinian evolutionists with nearly as much justice as Poe, whose claim is of course incontestable. Neither owed anything of consequence to Darwin. Both had arrived at matured evolutionary conceptions quite unlike his some years before 1859 and despite warm words of praise looked upon his celebrity with a somewhat patronizing air.[1] In this they were almost alone among American poets, however. Though the evolutionary hypothesis was well enough known by the fourth decade of the century for Barnum to exhibit "the missing link,"[2] the poets almost to a man either remained silent on the subject, or, if they spoke out, echoed the prevailing indignation and derision.[3] George Henry Boker, for example, could find in the *Vestiges of Creation* only material for comic relief. In the first scene of his tragedy *Calaynos* (1848), Martina replies sharply to her master's secretary:

> Why talk you thus, you demi-atheist?
> . . .
> They say you have no faith in good men's prayers;
> And talk not of salvation, but progression.[4]

Again, in the first scene of the third act the secretary enlarges upon the antiquity of his master's family in these disrespectful terms:

> O, they were fishes then, and swam unchoked.
> They were advancing from their primal slime—
> Hatched by the sun on some wide river's bank—
> Through worms, fish, frogs, and beasts, upward to men.
> They lived here monkeys, till their tails wore off,
> Then became Moors, and last you find them thus.[5]

The evidence of fossil remains convinced even Agassiz, later the arch-foe of Darwin, of a "parallelism between the geological succession of plants and animals and their present relative standing,"[6] but leading naturalists everywhere were immitigably opposed to the theory of transmutation and either ignored the question of origins or like Agassiz accepted a theory of multiple creation. After 1859, however—at first gradually, then with a rush—all was changed: even if rejected or accepted only with qualifications, evolution became an issue that had to be faced.

Largely because of the distraction of war, immediate attention to Darwin's book in this country was limited to the leading special students. Their reaction, however, was more sympathetic than is sometimes realized, and within two decades amounted to practically unanimous approval. "The controversy about Darwin's book," wrote Charles Eliot Norton in 1860,

has been carried on with great activity and animation among our men of science. The best among them seem to be ready to admit that his theory though not proved, and not likely to be proved and accepted in all its parts, is one of those theories which help science by weakening some long-established false notions, and by suggestions leading toward truth if not actually embracing it.[7]

Even Darwin was of the opinion that the two "most striking" reviews of his book appeared in the New York *Times* and *The American Journal of Science*,[8] the one in the latter being by Asa Gray, who defended Darwin on many occasions with vigor and success. Many, to be sure, led by Agassiz, were opposed to him, and as late as 1873 the president of the American Association for the Advancement of Science characterized him as "one of those philosophers whose great knowledge of animal and vegetable life is only transcended by his imagination."[9] Three years later, however, A. S. Packard denominated the period of American zoological study after 1859 "the epoch of evolution,"[10] and by 1888 E. S. Morse was able to proclaim summarily in his presidential address to the American Association that "American biological science stands as a unit for evolution."[11]

Moreover, after war and its aftermath had ceased to dominate public attention, a wider audience became interested. No fewer than ten editions of *The Origin of Species,* nine of *The Descent of Man,* and fourteen of Spencer's *First Principles* appeared in this country between their dates of first publication and 1880.[12] Indeed, interest seems to have been more widespread here than in England. Twenty thousand copies of Spencer were sold in the United States while the first small edition was being gone through in England, and in 1865 E. L. Youmans was able to raise seven thousand dollars to aid Spencer in his work.[13] At the beginning of the seventies Emerson expressed the opinion that Tyndall had "a larger public of readers" in America than in England;[14] and in that decade and the next, Tyndall, Huxley, and Spencer made lecture tours in this country that were modest triumphs, Huxley's lectures being popular enough to be published in an extra edition of the New York *Tribune*.[15] Liberal members of the clergy and such advanced thinkers as the members of the Boston Radical Club[16] and the New York Nineteenth Century Club[17] welcomed the theory, which worked down through the intellectual levels until it came to be a kind of test of being up to date. The "salient feature" in the intellectual history of this period, says Professor Nevins, "may be summarized in the statement that during these years the evolution theory, with all that it implied in science, philosophy, and religion, dawned upon the United States."[18]

But if the theory gained wide currency during these two decades, it also encountered stubborn opposition. Dr. Loewenberg, in his dissertation on the impact of evolution on American thought, names the period from the death of Agassiz in 1873 to the end of the century the period of "the Great Debate,"[19] and the stormy record of polemics in press and pulpit and of trials for heresy and dismissals from educational institutions bears witness to the accuracy of his phrase. The challenge to the historicity of Scripture was the most obvious issue and drew first fire in blasts like the following:

If this hypothesis be true, then is the Bible an unbearable fiction; . . . then have Christians for nearly two thousand years been duped by a monstrous lie. . . . Darwin requires us to disbelieve the authoritative word of the Creator.[20]

More important both then and for our purposes, however, was the supposed assault of the new theory upon the argument from design, which had long been the stoutest bulwark in Protestant apologetics. This rational basis of faith as expounded in the eighteenth century from Locke to Paley had long before taken a strong hold on American religious thought, and nearly all works of popular science as well as of theology contained one version or another of Paley's inference that "there is precisely the same proof that the eye was made for vision, as there is that the telescope was made for assisting it."[21] In *The Origin of Species,* however, Darwin went out of his way to suggest that this inference was "presumptuous,"[22] and there were many who regarded his theory of natural selection as the death sentence of the design argument. Natural adaptations, according to his theory, are not the result of prevision but of a gradual and random process of variation governed by ability to survive in a ruthlessly competitive environment. Of all the innovations of science in the nineteenth century, writes one historian of philosophy,

the Darwinian theory is the one which materialism appropriated most readily, and to which it is most indebted. This theory answers the following cardinal question, which had remained unsolved until the days of Darwin: How can the purposiveness which is revealed in the structure and arrangement of our organs be produced without the intervention of an intelligent creative cause, and through the purely mechanical action of unconscious forces? or, rather: How can we explain finality without final causes? Darwinism provides materialism with a satisfactory answer to the main objection of theistic spiritualism, and thereby becomes its indispensable ally.[23]

How keenly the opponents of Darwin were aware of this is well illustrated by the following declaration from the pen of the Reverend Charles Hodge, a Princeton theologian, in his book *What Is Darwinism?* (1874):

The conclusion of the whole matter is that the denial of design in nature is virtually the denial of God. Mr. Darwin's theory does deny all design in nature, therefore, his theory is virtually atheistical.[24]

We are well aware from earlier discussion, of course, that the horns of this dilemma could be evaded. Though natural selection or any other theory of evolution might make the concept of design unnecessary, it could not disprove it, and the apologists for evolution made full use of this fact. It will be remembered that Gray, who accepted both evolution and natural selection, affirmed against Agassiz that a material connection between the members of a series is not inconsistent with their intellectual connection in the mind of God;[25] and in announcing his conversion to Darwin's general position Lyell suggested:

The whole course of nature may be the material embodiment of a preconcerted arrangement; and if the succession of events be explained by transmutation, the perpetual adaptation of the organic world to new conditions leaves the argument in favour of design, and therefore of a designer, as valid as ever.[26]

Indeed, many supporters of evolution not only denied this charge but asserted in rebuttal that the progressive development of matter from a fiery nebula to the brain of man presupposed a plan and purpose vaster and more marvellous by far than the petty contrivances of Paley. "Design by wholesale is grander than design by retail," said Henry Ward Beecher,[27] and John Fiske, the sworn enemy of teleological explanation in science, was equally convinced that

The Darwinian theory, properly understood, replaces as much teleology as it destroys. From the first dawning of life we see all things working together toward one mighty goal, the evolution of the most exalted spiritual qualities which characterize Humanity.[28]

As these remarks make clear, however, the evolutionists' conception of design differed from that of Paley and his school. Instead of Paley's piecemeal contrivance, they believed in one increasing purpose that informs and molds the whole of existence;[29] and instead of Paley's absentee Creator, they believed in a God whose influence, if not his existence, is suffused through all things—who is, as Holmes said, "omni*movent*"[30] as well as omnipotent. The *"status quaestionis,"* said James McCosh, who made bold to declare his acceptance of evolution[31] only a week after taking his chair as president of Princeton in 1868, "is here not between God and not-God, but between God working without means and by means, the means being created by God and working for him."[32]

This brings us back to the main theme of our study—the explanation of past development in terms of the action of an immanent God and the deduction of hope for the future from the benevolence and wisdom of that God. Most of the poets to be considered in the remaining chapters of this section were enabled to clear the hurdle of teleology by the aid of this interpretation, and to this extent will appear as genuine cosmic optimists. As we are aware, however, there was another, higher hurdle, and at this many of them balked, with the result that they were evolutionists—and hence, in our sense, cosmic optimists—only within certain definite limits. If evolution was wholly true, it was argued, then was man's free soul reduced to the automatism of nature; then were vice and virtue not defeat and victory but, as Taine said, "products, like vitriol and sugar."[33] Since this was inadmissible, however, the conclusion seemed obvious that evolution was not wholly true, the soul at least being excluded from its operations. This, in fact, was the position of McCosh, who, though he made a considerable stir about his acceptance of evolution, actually limited it severely, eliminating from its province of explanation light, life, sensation, instinct, intelligence, and the moral sense.[34] Of man he wrote:

If any one ask me if I believed man's body to have come from a brute, I answer that I know not. I believe in revelation, I believe in science, but neither has revealed this to me; and I restrain the weak curiosity which would tempt me to inquire into what cannot be known. Meanwhile I am sure, and I assert, that man's soul is of a higher origin and of a nobler type.[35]

The reasoning followed by McCosh in arriving at these limitations, furthermore, is of the greatest interest here, because it takes us back to that dilemma of Royce's which we have found to be central in the cosmological speculation of the nineteenth century.[36] On the assumption that an effect cannot "contain more" than its cause, Royce argued, it will be remembered, that there must be something wrong with the proposition that matter evolves into mind: one of the three terms, matter, evolution, or mind, must stand for something other than it appears to. To Royce it was matter that was the "deceptive appearance," but to McCosh and most of the poets who will presently be considered it was evolution. A cause, says McCosh,

cannot create anything new; it cannot give what it has not within itself. There is nothing in the effect which was not potentially in the cause; that is, in the agents which constitute the cause. There is no proof that any of the agents just named, say sensation or intelligence, were in the atoms, or in the mechanical or chemical powers. . . . Whence came they? . . . As evolution by physical causes cannot [produce them], we infer that God does it by an immediate fiat, even as he created matter and the forces which act in matter.[37]

Here was a fundamental difference of view for which we must pause.

It is scarcely news to point out that many of Emerson's compatriots rejected much of what he taught. Andrews Norton, as is well known, branded his Divinity School Address of 1838 "the latest form of infidelity," and he remained *persona non grata* at Harvard for several decades thereafter. A principal cause of this, moreover, was just the present point. It was widely held that his all-encompassing idealism plunged man back into nature as surely as if he were a materialist. True, his "nature" was but the "externization of soul," but this did not mitigate his apparent obliteration of the distinction between kinds of being that is presupposed in man's freedom and responsibility. Thus Horace Bushnell, a few pages after disposing of the author of the *Vestiges* on this point, attacked Emerson on the same ground:

Intoxicated by his brilliant creations, the reader thinks, for the time, that he is getting inspired. And yet, when he has closed the essay or the volume, he is surprised to find—who has ever failed to note it?—that he is disabled instead, disempowered, reduced in tone. . . . Surely, it is a wonderfully clear atmosphere that he is in, and yet it is somehow mephitic! How could it be otherwise? As it is a first principle that water will not rise above its own level, what better reason is there to expect that a creed which disowns duty and turns achievement into a conceit of destiny, will bring to man those great thoughts, and breathe upon him in those gales of impulse, which are necessary to the empowered state, whether of thought or action. Grazing in the field of nature is not enough for a being whose deepest affinities lay hold of the supernatural, and reach after God. Airy and beautiful the field may be, shown by so great a master; full of goodly prospects and fascinating images; but, without a living God, and objects of faith, and terms of duty, it is a pasture only—nothing more. Hence the unreadiness, the almost aching incapacity felt to undertake any thing or become any thing, by one who has taken lessons at his school. Nature is the all, and nature will do every thing, whether we will or no.[38]

Not only did ordinary morality depend for its existence on the reality of choice but Christian theology required that sin be possible if redemption was to have any meaning. On the other hand, however, science and common sense, philosophical[39] and otherwise, required that the world of matter be rigidly subject to the law of causation. The inevitable consequence was that the soul of man, somehow and in some degree, had to be excepted from evolution.

No doubt there are ways out of this difficulty. Emerson seems to have held that since the individual is the Absolute writ small he possesses in some degree all the attributes of the Absolute, including freedom; and Whitman veered toward a highly individual combination of primitive animism and spiritual pluralism. Since poets are not philosophers, moreover, the problem was sometimes ignored or resolved by fiat. Among those who touched on evolution in their verses between 1859 and about 1890, however, it was very strongly felt. Largely because of its force, Bryant rejected evolution, Longfellow avoided it, Lowell was troubled by it, Lanier criticized it, and Holmes developed a theory of his own which got round the problem. These men will be our principal concern in the pages to follow, but first it will perhaps be helpful to gather together some scraps from minor writers to illustrate which way the wind blew.

VI

MINOR POETS: STRAWS IN THE WIND

IT IS significant of the uncertain status of the theory of evolution during the first decade after *The Origin of Species* that of the few poems touching upon it in any considerable way four treated it comically.[1] In 1866 a fossil skull that had been found in a mine shaft in Calaveras County was adjudged by the California Geological Survey to have belonged to "the oldest human being,"[2] and Bret Harte at once turned the incident into a typical Western joke. In a poem loaded with every paleontological polysyllable that his rime and metre would support, he addressed the venerable memento in hushed and reverent tones, only to have it complain hollowly through teeth stained suspiciously brown:

> "Which my name is Bowers, and my crust was busted
> Falling down a shaft in Calaveras County;
> But I'd take it kindly if you'd send the pieces
>   Home to old Missouri!"[3]

As Mark Twain showed in the incident of the petrified man, such rifling of man's antiquities was well fitted to the West's love of hoax and burlesque, and Harte turned to it twice more: once in the well-known "Society upon the Stanislaus,"[4] whose tale of a row in a frontier scientific society has reminded one historian of American biology of the intense rivalries among the men of science of the day;[5] and once in a mock-sentimental "Geological Madrigal,"[6] in which the poet begins with Shenstone's familiar line "I have found out a gift for my fair"[7] and goes on to promise his beloved:

> I will show thee the sinuous track
>   By the slow-moving Annelid made,
> Or the Trilobite that, farther back,
>   In the old Potsdam sandstone was laid;
>
>   . . .
>
> And though the Darwinian plan
>   Your sensitive feelings may shock,
> We'll find the beginnings of man,
>   Our fossil ancestors in rock!

The fourth of the poems, Herman Melville's "The New Ancient

of Days,"[8] is of a different character, satirical rather than farcical. Lyell's *Geological Evidences of the Antiquity of Man* and the rigorous *Syllabus of Errors* of Pope Pius IX had appeared respectively in 1863 and 1864, and Melville appears to have taken a kind of unholy glee in their incongruity. "Yea, the spook of the cave of Engihoul," he chortled, referring to Lyell's discussion of the fossil skulls of the caves of Engis in Belgium,[9] "from Moses knocks under the stool . . . he flogs us and sends us to school":

> Hyena of love! Ah, beat him down,
>   Great Pope, with Peter's key,
> Ere the Grand Pan-Jam be overthrown
> With Joe and Jos and great Mahone,
>   And the firmament mix with the sea;
>   And then, my masters, where should we be?
> But the ogre of bone he snickers alone,
> And grins for his godless glee.
> "I have flung my stone, my fossil stone,
> And your gods, they scamper," saith he.

However, though the obvious object of Melville's satire was the discord between science and priestcraft, his poem cannot be regarded as an attack on faith in the name of evolution, for it ends, as the Epilogue of *Clarel* was to begin, with an apprehensive question concerning the consequences of the philosophy suggested by the new-found skulls:

> Imp of the cave of Engihoul
> Shall he grin like the Gorgon and rule?

The particular significance of these poems lies in the middle-of-the-road attitude that they imply. All four find something absurd or suspicious or ominous in the idea of man's development from a subhuman ancestry, and yet not one specifically denies or attacks the general concept of evolution. As we are aware, moreover, in this they foreshadowed a growing sentiment among the poets of the seventies and eighties. No doubt there were many whose disapproval was concealed by silence, but the growing consensus of published verse was that evolution, though not proved and greatly in need of interpretation and limitation, was probably correct in general outline and certainly to be preferred to the Calvinists' scheme of arbitrary creation and damnation. Thomas Wentworth

Higginson expressed the point clearly and concisely at a meeting of the Boston Radical Club:

> So far as personal feeling is concerned, the Darwinian theory is far nobler than any other ever formed. After the ignoble scheme of the theologians, it is like opening the windows to sunlight and heaven, and in its light the great march of humanity becomes superb. The theologian is defunct as a power in the world; but I fear the despotism of science more than the despotism of theology. . . . Poets who patronize science assume faith and love and reverence, but science does not. We may hope and expect that Darwinism is correct, but cannot affirm it is; and much less may we construct the whole theory of the universe on it.[10]

Here was the gist of the attitude of most of the literary men of the time toward the new theory. Insofar as it exemplified the confidence of the age in its present excellence and greater prospects, and insofar as it could be made to body forth the kindly God in which the age believed, it was deserving of all praise and encouragement. Insofar, however, as it denied or ignored this destiny, the human capabilities that made it possible, or the God who guaranteed it, it was suspect and in need of qualification. In the miscellany that follows, both sides of this issue will be illustrated.

1

As the discussion in the last chapter was intended to indicate, the leading objection to the evolutionism of science was that it seemed to issue in materialism, obviating the principle of design and thrusting man back into the mechanism of nature. True, since the scientists and their philosophical allies were not speaking metaphysically but only of that narrow world of phenomena which they believed constituted the limit of man's power to know, they were able to reply that this charge somewhat overstated their meaning. To those whose cherished beliefs were threatened by the new theory, however, this qualification offered little comfort, since the noumenal realm had been set aside by the scientific philosophers as "unknowable" and hence ineligible for consideration in man's evaluation of his estate. Had not Spencer, despite his discourse on this realm, described the world that can be known as a mere mechanical rearrangement of matter? Had not Huxley declared that life—and, by inference, all supramaterial qualities—is a mere property of matter in certain combinations, as "aquosity" is a property of hydrogen and oxygen in the proportion of two to one?[11] Had not Tyndall asserted in his notorious Belfast Address that in matter was to be found "the promise and potency of all terrestrial life"?[12] To such contentions it was rejoined on every hand that evolution might be true as far as it went, but that if this was its meaning it went something less than the whole way. Another speaker at the Radical Club, for example, stated that while "he himself had been a Darwinian in theory before Darwin ever wrote," "he believed these Darwinian theories must be supplemented with something else; something, perhaps, corresponding to Swedenborg's doctrine of influx,—the breathing in of spiritual life."[13] Some, of course—a decreasing number—went much further, rejecting the notion of evolution altogether; and one of these, J. G. Holland, must be adduced for the sake of his argument as well as of his conclusion. "A stream can rise no higher than its source," he asserted by way of premise, and then concluded: it is therefore "repugnant to human reason that a low form of life, uninformed by a higher life, has the power to evolve a form of life higher than itself."[14] This objection, it will be recognized, rested upon the acceptance of that dilemma of Josiah Royce's which has so often been referred to in these pages.

We are aware, of course, that this objection could be avoided—that the higher life could be regarded as latent in the lower and the stream hence as never really rising higher than its source. Thus, J. T. Trowbridge reasoned from the same analogy:

> Of nothing comes nothing: springs rise not above
>   Their source in the far-hidden heart of the mountains:
> Whence then have descended the Wisdom and Love
>   That in man leap to light in intelligent fountains?[15]

But Trowbridge was, as we shall see, an enthusiastic evolutionist of the transcendental stamp.[16] To the Huxleys he replied: "The Creator is not the blind physical force you believe him"; and to the Hollands: no form of life, high or low, is "uninformed by a higher life"—

> Though in their beginning all things be one essence,
>   Through all, over all, flows the formative Soul:
> In each particle thrills the Divine Omnipresence,
>   As gravity binds and embraces the whole.[17]

Much the same position was also taken by Christopher Pearse Cranch, who had been active in the Transcendental movement in his youth. He too scorned the "cold philosophers"—

> Drawing forth from matter raw
> Protoplasmic threads, to fashion
> What Creation never saw—
> Mind apart from faith or passion

—and retorted:

> Not from matter crude and coarse
> comes this delicate creation.

Like Trowbridge, however, he took the idealistic tack between the Scylla of materialism and the Charybdis of creationism, adding:

> Twinned with it a finer force
> Rules it to its destination.[18]

However, though this maneuver permitted Trowbridge and Cranch to be evolutionists of a kind, their evolutionism was decidedly not that of Huxley, Spencer, and Tyndall, which they criticized severely. This not only is clear from the lines quoted but will be illustrated further in a moment. First, however, it will be instructive to consider a slightly different version of their maneuver. Jones Very, the "God-intoxicated" one among the Transcendentalists, was far from unwilling to accept the evolutionary narrative, but he resolutely denied that it in any way accounted for the origin or nature of the soul. "Man has forgot his origin," he wrote in the first of a pair of sonnets on the subject;

>   in vain
> He searches for the record of his race
> In ancient books, or seeks with toil to gain
> From the deep cave, or rocks, some primal trace.
>   . . .
> With mind bewildered, weak, how should he know
> The Source Divine from which his being springs?
> The darkened spirit does its shadow throw
> On written record and on outward things,
> That else might plainly to his thought reveal
> The wondrous truths which now they but conceal.[19]

Very did not agree, however, that the failure of the causal sequence to provide such an explanation can be corrected by merely postulating some immanent power such as the "finer force" of Cranch or the Swedenborgian "influx" of the speaker at the Radical Club. Like the thorough mystic that he was, he remembered rather—what was so often forgotten—that if God is truly all, time and the evolutionary sequence must be merely appearances. The beginning and the end of all is God, he proclaimed; and though some men may doubt and others fail to understand, they do so only because of the darkness of the human intellect. As he wrote in a poem depicting the geological succession as well as other events in the past:

> In God alone my wandering mind can rest;
> In Him the Present, Past, and Future meet,
> . . .
>
> Though, to our narrow view, succession marks
> The history of man and all we see,
> And e'en our language echoes with the past,
> Yet this is but the weakness of our thought,
> That sees not from beginning to the end.[20]

In Very, thus, we come again to the mystical proposition that there is but one reality, a Soul of All, known intuitively in the individual spiritual life, and to the two consequences of this proposition for evolutionary thinking: (1) that since the soul is eternal, not created, the evolutionary history, so far as it goes, may be accepted without fear, but (2) that insofar as evolution presupposes a philosophy of mechanism or materialism, it is mistaken and must be rejected.

Beneath these charges and counter-charges one of the nicer ironies of the history of ideas in the nineteenth century may be seen. For Very and his kind were, in a broad sense, quite as agnostic as Huxley and Spencer, holding with equal vigor that sense and reason are inadequate to the solution of the fundamental problems of the nature of things. Agreed as the two parties were in this limitation of the power of the understanding, however, they were in violent disagreement concerning what ought to be done about it. The Huxleys accused the Verys of sentimentality and self-delusion in proclaiming their religious solutions, and the Verys retorted that the physical explanations of the Huxleys were in fact materialism, however they might be hedged about with qualifications. The Huxleys, again, urged that in view of the limitations of his intellect, man ought to confine himself to the practical management of his phenomenal world, in which he stands some chance of success; and to this the Verys replied that life is such that the questions of God, freedom, and immortality cannot be ignored and that if reason is inadequate to answer them some other, "higher" faculty must be called upon. Such was the fundamental limitation of the intellect by both science and trancendentalism.

These arguments will be heard again in these pages, notably in the case of Lowell, but immediately they are of interest as the means by which Trowbridge and Cranch carried further their attack on the scientific evolutionists. The title of Trowbridge's poem, "The Missing Leaf," refers to a search for one page to redeem the "portentous verbosity" of

> a stout volume, entitled the Origin
> And End of Creation (a sort of review
> Of the works of the Lord, by a confident critic).[21]

The volume, redolent of Spencer, discourses blandly of all things, uncovering no mysteries in man or nature too great for its logic, and in the end causes the poet, exasperated, to fling it aside and take refuge in his garden, where he finds,

> The snail with his pack on his back, taught me more
> Than all the pedantic sad stuff I'd been reading.[22]

With living nature before him he cries out against what he regards as the monumental conceit of all such volumes:

> "Who can say how this life has its being;
> How landscape and sky with delight overfill me;
> Why sound should enchant; how these eyes have their seeing;
> How passion and rapture enkindle and thrill me?
>   . . .
> And you—did you fancy that you could infold it,
> And label it fast in your tissue of fallacies?
>   . . .
> There's something that will not be measured and weighed,
> And brought to the test of your last sublimation;
> And this is the little mistake that you made,
> That you left it quite out of your grand calculation."[23]

"Larger vision you must find," said Cranch in the poem already referred to,

> Ere your evolution-plummets
> Sound the abysses of the mind,
>   Or your measure reach its summits.
>
>   . . .
>
> Vain your biologic strife,
>   Your asserting, your denying;
> Ygdrasil the Tree of Life
> Flouts your narrow classifying.[24]

Something of the same point of view is to be found in Herman Melville's *Clarel*. This vast, difficult, and uneven poem, having as its theme the failing faith of the day, is an important document in the soul-searching of the age of Arnold and Clough, and yet, surprisingly enough, it contains almost no direct comment on the theory of evolution. Darwin's name is mentioned only three times, twice insignificantly,[25] and the few references to the general idea of evolution are for the most part merely tangential and so closely identified with individual characters that it is difficult to tell when they express Melville's own views.[26] And yet, not only does the whole poem revolve around questions brought to a head by *The Origin of Species,* but in the Epilogue[27] Darwin's name is used to symbolize these questions. "If Luther's day expand to Darwin's year," the poet asks, "shall that exclude the hope—foreclose the fear?" The conclusion is that oscillation between hope and fear, faith and despair, is too deeply ingrained in human nature to be greatly affected by such a mere novelty in speculation as evolution. This is expressed in a vivid parable:

>   Unmoved by all the claims our times avow,
> The ancient Sphinx still keeps the porch of shade;
> And comes Despair, whom not her calm may cow,
> And coldly on that adamantine brow
> Scrawls undeterred his bitter pasquinade.
> But Faith (who from the scrawl indignant turns),
> With blood warm oozing from her wounded trust,
> Inscribes even on her shards of broken urns
> The sign o' the cross—*the spirit above the dust!*

Science, it is added, has not only failed to dissolve the mystery but has deepened it:

>   Yea, ape and angel, strife and old debate—
> The harps of heaven and dreary gongs of hell;
> Science the feud can only aggravate—

> . . .
> Degrees we know, unknown in days before;
> The light is greater, hence the shadow more.

Thus, the final statement is not one of doubt but of faith based on the fact that even though the new science has shed no light on the eternal mysteries, neither has it extinguished the light of hope. The appeal is to the heart. "Then keep thy heart, though yet but ill resigned—Clarel, thy heart, the issues there but mind," the poet advises, and even suggests the possibility of immortal life:

> Emerge thou mayst from the last whelming sea,
> And prove that death but routs life into victory.

Admittedly, these comments are but straws in the wind and present the greatest variation in interpretation, from the complete rejection of a Holland to the qualified acceptance of a Trowbridge. Even such straws may serve a purpose, however, and these help to show the apprehension that was widely felt concerning the scientists' cosmology. Lowell, I believe, felt the danger more keenly and articulately than any other of our poets; the "mush" of protoplasm, he said, is "a poor substitute for the Rock of Ages."[28] But a few others may be mentioned. Julia Ward Howe, for example, felt it necessary to attack the "sons of science," who "have spread their nets for the Godhead";[29] the position of atheistic mechanism she stated and refuted as follows:

> "We need no God," the Atheist said;
> "The world is wound and set to go;
> How it was wound we do not know;
> But go it will when we are dead."
>
> . . .
>
> And what the need, both old and new,
> The eternal need of human-kind?
> Not that we keep a fable blind:
> It is that thou, dear God, be true.[30]

Similarly, Cranch expressed the repugnance of morality to the predatory world pictured by Darwin,[31] and Helen Gray Cone pointed out that if the Darwinian hypothesis is true, then "that Perfect Man, to whom we tend, the great Inheritor," will possess a heavy heritage of grief for those who suffered to make his advance possible.[32] Probably the most forceful protest, however, was a sonnet by Thomas William Parsons, a translator of Dante, telling of the relief with which he turned from Darwin to Thomas Aquinas. Parsons' poem, in fact, concludes with a figure that is certainly not surpassed in any of the poems cited thus far in this chapter and may well stand as the perfect expression of the reaction of many devout minds to the theory that man is but a more finished brute:

> Are we but apes? Oh! give me, God, to know
> I am death's master; not a scaffolding,
> But a true temple where Christ's word could grow.[33]

2

In turning to the other side of the picture, we find, as we are prepared to expect, the most glowing optimism resulting from the immanental reinterpretation of the evolutionary theories. John Fiske has been quoted as saying that evolution replaced as much teleology as it removed,[34] and the typical poetic presentation of evolution at this time followed the broadly teleological pattern described in the last chapter. "Around one infinite intent," wrote Julia Ward Howe in one of the first poems to be written on evolution in this country after the appearance of *The Origin of Species,*

> All power and inspiration move,
> Thrilling with light the firmament,
> Lifting the heart of man with love.[35]

The word "love" here, furthermore, is worth pausing for. For teleology by itself is not a sufficient guarantee of man's earthly desires, the cosmology of Calvin, for example, being sufficiently teleological, but not progressive in any worldly sense. The nineteenth century, however, tended to minimize the stern justice of Calvin's God and to give correspondingly greater emphasis to God's love, to the end that he could be conceived as using his omnipotence to bring to pass those things by which men set store. Love, said Trowbridge characteristically, is "the sweet band that binds the world,"[36] and the never-resting heartstrings of Ella Wheeler Wilcox vibrated to a whole sentimental cosmogony:

> The impulse of all love is to create.
>   God was so full of love, in His embrace
>   He clasped the empty nothingness of space,
> And lo! the solar system! High in state

MINOR POETS

> The mighty sun sat, so supreme and great
>   With this same essence, one smile of its face
>   Brought myriad forms of life forth; race on race
> From insects up to men.[37]

The poems of Trowbridge and Mrs. Wilcox are lush with the sentimentality of their times and their authors, but they convey vividly the fact that the poets continued to believe that the world owes its existence to a benevolent divine power, even though evolution had stretched out the creation from seven days to as many aeons and had made it necessary to conceive of the act of creation as continuous and immanent. Wrote Trowbridge:

> Thou alone art everlasting, O thou inmost Soul of all!
> Through all height, all depth, all distance,
>   All duration, all existence
> Moves one universal nature, flows one vast Intelligence,
>   Out of chaos and gray ruin
>   Still the shining heavens renewing,
> Flashing into light and beauty, flowering into form and
>   sense.[38]

This interpretation, in fact, not only established a *modus vivendi* between evolution and theistic faith but formed the foundation of a new natural theology in which what Fiske called the "dramatic tendency"[39] in evolution took the place of Paley's contrivances. One participant in the theological wars, for example, declared that just when science had pushed the Deists' God further and further back, making him an absentee and forgotten First Cause, "Darwin appeared and under the guise of a foe did the work of a friend."[40] A leading aim of much of the verse written about evolution during this period was, thus, the celebration of God's handiwork. Trowbridge's "Hymn of the Air," for example, in which the Air tells of the part it has played in the evolution of life, ends with this affirmation:

> Enfolder and disposer of all life
> Am I; and yet not I. Oh! faithless man,
> How canst thou feel my power and mystery,
> And know the invisible force that clasps thee round,
> And have in me thy being, and yet doubt
> The Spirit whose similitude I am,
> The Power that framed the world, and me, and thee?[41]

Again, W. H. Venable, an Ohio poet who appropriately named his son Emerson, wrote as part of his "Triune Creed":

> The spreading circle of the known,
>   That Science strives to bound with laws,
> Is but a glowing sparkle thrown
>   From God, the radiant central cause.
>
> His mystery is vaster far
>   Than knowledge is or e'er can be;
> The wheel of Evolution's car
>   Rolls onward through eternity.[42]

Finally, this was the theme of the most widely quoted of all poems on evolution, W. H. Carruth's "Each in His Own Tongue."[43] Carruth, who was professor of German in the University of Kansas and an active worker in the American Unitarian Association, has few claims as a poet even in this one instance, but he did succeed in saying simply and pointedly what many had thought:

> A fire-mist and a planet,—
> A crystal and a cell,—
> A jelly-fish and a saurian,
>   And caves where the cave-men dwell;
> Then a sense of law and beauty
>   And a face turned from the clod,—
> Some call it Evolution
>   And others call it God.

This was a far cry from Spencer and Darwin, who, though they made allowances for deity, did so only to satisfy the demands of logic.[44] It is the very point of this study, however, that the poets reversed this argument. To them the primary fact was that God is good and wise and that evolution is only a revelation of the way in which He works. They reasoned much as did a utopian writer in *The Harbinger:* "The universal Association of Humanity *must* some day take place, for Humanity is a child of God, and as such, *must* fulfill the Laws of its Author."[45] This aspect of the poets' interpretation of evolution can scarcely be overemphasized, for it was not only everywhere evident in their writing but the basis of their unwavering optimism, which, as we shall now see, interpreted the reddest tooth or claw as the agency of a glorious consummation.

3

It would be false, however, to conclude that the poets owed their evolutionary optimism only to this faith in divine benevolence. The meliorism of the nineteenth century had as many roots as ramifications. The eighteenth-century theories of social and intellectual progress had found fertile ground in America, material progress had been spectacular and was highly appreciated, and the Romantic movement had shown principally its brighter side here. Moreover, Darwin and Spencer themselves were as optimistic as the most trusting evolutionary theist could wish. In time Huxley was to dampen this optimism by pointing out that "retrogressive is as practicable as progressive metamorphosis";[46] but in the conclusion of *The Origin of Species* Darwin declared that since "natural selection works solely by and for the good of each being, all corporeal and mental endowments will tend to progress toward perfection,"[47] and Spencer's whole philosophy was a rationale of progress. At the end of his career he had only minor reservations to make concerning such sanguine declarations in his first book as that "the ultimate development of the ideal man is logically certain—as certain as any conclusion in which we place the most implicit faith; for instance, that all men will die."[48]

The bulk of the theory of progress, however, so largely a social concept, falls outside the scope of this study, the interest of which lies in the broader, cosmic aspects of the theme. Hence the numerous proud rhapsodies on the triumphs of freedom, democracy, and science that reached a crescendo in the centennial year must be passed by in favor of such more general statements as this from another part of Venable's "Triune Creed":

> From good to better and to best,
>   From myth of dawn to fact of day,
> The world progresses, hath progressed,
>   And surely shall progress for aye.[49]

And this, dealing more obviously with the theory of evolution in nature, from the pen of an obscure upcountry versifier, George McKnight:

> 'T was needful that with life of low degree
>   But slowly rising, long the earth should teem

> Ere man was born, and still the guiding scheme
> Seemed not to rest in full maturity.
> For Nature since has so assiduously
> > Cherished his growth in spirit, it would seem
> > That lofty human souls, in her esteem,
> Are the best trophies of her husbandry.[50]

Since nearly all of the poems that touched upon evolution at all also expressed faith in progress, only a few typical examples need be presented here to show the way in which the theme was handled and to illustrate its later fortunes. One obvious variation of the theme was a reply to the charge that evolution is a libel on human dignity. Thus in a sonnet entitled "The Rise of Man"[51] John White Chadwick urged that man—"thou for whose birth the whole creation yearned"—should be proud rather than ashamed of his ascent through "fiery vapors," "senseless crystal," and "the plant which grew to something more"; for

> in thyself art thou not deified
> That from such depths thou couldst such summits win?
> While the long way behind is prophecy
> Of those perfections which are yet to be.

The most usual treatment, however, involved some kind of apocalyptic vision of freedom and goodness. C. P. Cranch, for example, in one of the lyrics in the second part of his drama *Satan,* proclaimed in the strain of Shelley:

> From out the chaos and the slime,
>   From out the whirling winds of fire,
> From years of ignorance and crime,
>   From centuries of wild desire,
> The shaping laws of truth and love
>   Shall lift the savage from the clod;
>
>   . . .
>
> Shall hurl all despots from the throne,
>   And lift the saviors of the race:
> And law and liberty alone
>   From sea to sea the lands embrace.[52]

One of the most interesting of these poems is Trowbridge's "Ancestors," in which the speaker is inspired by reading a family history to reflect on the "innumerable streams" that "meet to blend their mystic forces in the torrent of my heart." His reflections call up a vision of primitive origins:

> I was moulded in that far-off time of ignorance and wrong,
> When the world was to the crafty, to the ravenous and strong.[53]

These reflections lead him, however, to the conclusion that since the best is yet to be, the faults of today should be viewed tolerantly:

> Scarcely gleams as yet the crescent of the full-orbed golden age,
>
> . . .
>
> Half our virtues will seem vices by your broader, higher right,
> And the brightness of the present will be shadow in the light;
> For, behold, our boasted culture is a morning cloud, unfurled
> In the dawning of the ages and the twilight of the world![54]

At the end of the century a strong counter-tendency set in against such easy optimism, but by that time the theme had become conventionalized and was a part of the stock in trade of the popular versifier. In her 1901 volume Ella Wheeler Wilcox doggerelized it in such lines as these:

> Ever on the world is moving and all human life is proving
> It is reaching toward the purpose that the great God meant it for.[55]

And

> Forth from little motes in Chaos,
> We have come to what we are,
> And no evil force can stay us,
> We shall mount from star to star,
> We shall break each bond and fetter
> That has bound us heretofore,
> And the earth is surely better,
> Than it ever was before.[56]

Another magazine writer of sounder talent, Jane Dransfield Stone, put it this way:

> Alone in eons of uncounted years
> Has God unrolled the splendor of the world;
> The All came not by single action hurled,
> But slowly, mid the sound of strife and tears.
> Nought yesterday existed as appears;
> Unseen the change, but each dawn's light, unfurled,
> Means upward step, with beauty rarer pearled.
> God's ways are slow; he hastens not, nor fears.[57]

4

It was inevitable that this optimism should have led the poets to the lesson that Emerson said was taught by all history: the good of evil.[58] For certainly if the course of the world's history is a continuous development toward perfection, the evils of past and present must play a part in bringing about the good of the future. In the minds of the evolutionary optimists, evils, both natural and moral, were simply impediments to be overcome, and the acts of overcoming them resulted in progress just as surely as overcoming the resistance of a flight of steps results in ascent. This corollary, as has been pointed out in the writing of Stallo and Emerson, had already been drawn by the transcendental evolutionists, and was thus familiar to the poets, who knew their Emerson well, before they found something like it in the writing of Darwin and Spencer, both of whom emphasized "struggle for existence" as a factor in a general progress. Darwin, for example, found "grandeur" in the fact that "from the war of nature, from famine and death, the most exalted object which we are capable of conceiving, namely, the production of the higher animals, directly follows."[59] And Spencer wrote that "even in evils the student learns to recognize only a struggling benevolence."[60] Thus the evolutionary optimists did not deny that evil exists but only that it is entirely a curse; rather, on occasion they wallowed in the brutalities of the past in order to heighten the contrast of present and future and to show that what we adjudge evil has been an agency in bringing forth good. Their aim was to justify the goodness of the scheme of things by showing that life meliorates, overcoming a hostile environment and converting native weakness into strength. This was certainly the moral that Darwin drew, just as it had earlier been equally implicit in the transcendental evolutionism of Emerson.

If this conception was not new in the time of Darwin and Spencer, neither did it rest entirely on an evolutionary cosmogony. It might, for example, be deduced from the mere conjunction of an awareness of nature's asperities with a firm faith in the infinite goodness of God—as in Alfred B. Street's sonnet, "The Sympathy of Nature":

Her brightest mirth says, "Cease

> Thy thoughtless rapture! Flowers must suffer blight,
> Change is my law of order!" Then a voice
> Swells from her deep and solemn heart, "Rejoice . . . !
>
> . . .
>
> In this swift changeful life, whate'er befall,—
> Blest truth,—a loving God is guardian over all."[61]

And it had often been derived from the observation of the emergence of life from death in the rotation of the seasons and of the more perfect from the less perfect in the artist's creation of beauty. Thus William Cullen Bryant had sung repeatedly of death as the destroyer of evil and of birth as the bringer of good; and George Henry Boker, in a poem celebrating the creativeness of the artist, caused the chief of three Spirits to answer the complaints of his brothers concerning the persistence of sin by saying,

> Patience, dear brothers: ye who ask
> Quick, sweeping changes, set a task
> Beyond earth's power. She slowly draws,
> By due procession of her laws,
> Good out of evil.[62]

This conception always involved some kind of principle of change, however, as the passages quoted illustrate, and it attained its greatest influence only after Darwin and Spencer had spread the doctrine of evolutionary change broadcast. Darwinism accentuated rather than minimized the suffering and death that had gone into the world's development, but the optimists were undaunted. Trowbridge, for example, wrote that "The shapes of ill and error . . . the forms of death and terror" are "but light-obstructing phantoms, which shall vanish late or soon,"[63] and he hailed and acknowledged his debt to man's brutish ancestors in these terms:

Wild forefathers, I salute You! Though your times were fierce and rude,
From their rugged husk of evil comes the kernel of our good.

. . .

'T was the roughness of the thistle that insured the future flower.[64]

To so extreme a meliorist as Trowbridge the very destructiveness of the evolutionary process was something to ask thanks for and to urge onward, and in another poem he personified this scheme of things as a "mighty-statured Phantom" standing, fan in hand, on "the threshing-floor of Time." Nothing, he observed, could endure the flailing of this "Dread Conserver that must yet destroy":

> Empires, beliefs, the things of art and fame,
>   The broad-based pyramids, the poet's page;
> To his eternal patience, 't is the same,
>   A moment or an age.
>
> Before this fan the mountains form and flee,
>   Continents pass; and in its rhythmic beat
> The flying stars and whirling nebulae
>   Are but as chaff and wheat.

But this he could not regard as cause for grief, for

> There's naught so true in science and in creeds,
>   And naught so good in governments and states,
> But something truer evermore succeeds,
>   And better still awaits.[65]

By all odds the most considerable expression of this theme, however, was a lyric drama by C. P. Cranch first called *Satan: A Libretto* and later revised under the more significant title of "Ormuzd and Ahriman."[66] It is one of many attempts to build a new Divine Comedy on the basis of nineteenth-century science, and as the play opens the eight Planetary Spirits are discussing the various bodies which they control, from the "small and sparkling starworld," Mercury, to those most distant from the sun, "cold, cold, and dark." The Earth appears to them "half-drowned and thunder-rifted," and Mars, interestingly, in a state of paleozoic luxuriance, with "Saurian growths" and "giant ferns." Later, after an interval of singing, the Spirits approach the Earth and are so touched by the plight of the Eden pair, beset by "yon shadow that creeps," that they call upon the angels for an explanation. Raphael answers their call, and, after reminding them that "to spirits time and space may be condensed into a throb of feeling or thought," goes on to tell them of the evolution that has taken place while they were talking and singing idly in the interstellar spaces:

> While ye were singing as ye watched your worlds,
> They grew and grew from incandescent globes
> Girdled with thunder, wreathed with sulphurous steam—
> Or from the slime where rude gigantic forms
> Of crocodile or bat plunged through the dense

> And flowerless wilds of cane, or flapped like dreams
> Of darkness through the foul mephitic air.
> These shapes gave way to forests, rocks, and seas,
> And shapely forms of beast and bird and man—
> Man—the tall crowning flower and fruit of all—
> And the vast complex tissues he hath wrought
> Of life and laws and government and arts.[67]

Raphael also tells them that the Eden drama did not actually occur, but was only a poet's dream, "a truth half-typed in legend," though he adds that this does not impair its significance, for

> men and Angels can conceive
> Through symbols only, the eternal truths.[68]

Thus reassured, the Spirits go on with their effort to "guess the meaning of the mythic tale," and call up Satan, who introduces both himself and the main theme of the play by saying, "I am not what I seem." This he proceeds to amplify as follows in terms of the transcendental conception of evil:

> I am not what I seem to finite minds;—
> No fallen Angel—for I never fell,
> Though priest and poet feign me exiled and doomed;
> But ever was and ever shall be thus—
> Nor worse nor better than the Eternal planned.
> I am the Retribution, not the Curse.
> I am the shadow and reverse of God;
> The type of mixed and interrupted good;
> The clod of sense without whose earthly base
> You spirit-flowers can never grow and bloom.[69]

Here it becomes apparent why Cranch changed the title of his poem. He wished to present that conception of life as a conflict of opposites which has been presented here as notably adaptable to an evolutionary theology. He wished to express a correlative relationship between Good and Evil in which the latter is not a separate and eternal power but a kind of inertia that continually resists but also continually gives way before the inevitable progress of the former: "the type of mixed and interrupted good." Thus he had written in the concluding lines of the opening Overture:

> Ah, what are all the discords of all time
>   But stumbling steps of one persistent life
> That struggles up through mists to heights sublime.[70]

In the dialogue between Satan and the Planetary Spirits, Satan further expands this view in reply to the Spirits' anxious inquiry, "Shall we then doubt the sacred books—the faith that Satan was of old the foe of God?" He says:

> Nations have planned their demons as they planned
> Their gods. Say, rather, God and Satan mixed,—
> A hybrid of perplexed theology,—
> Stood at the centre of the universe;
> Ormuzd and Ahriman, in ceaseless war—
> A double spirit through whose nerves and veins
> Throbbed the vast pulse of his feverish moods
> Of blight and benediction.[71]

In the second part of the drama, which consists almost wholly of a series of songs, this interpretation of evil is given many applications, but none is more pertinent here than one called "Song of an Evolutionist," which is as thoroughgoing a statement of evolutionary optimism as is to be found in our poetry. The first stanza begins and ends with the unequivocal statement, "All in its turn is good," and the second reads:

> Up from the centre striving
>   Through countless change on change,
>   Through shapes uncouth and strange—
> The weakest doomed to perish—
>   The strongest still surviving;
>   Purpose divine in all.
>   Whether they rise or fall
> Pledged to maintain and cherish
>   Types higher and still higher,
>   To struggle and aspire.
> One vast divine endeavor
> Upward and onward ever—
> Through fish and bird and beast—
> Power that hath never ceased—
> Through darkness and through light—
> Through ape and troglodyte,
> Till best with best unite;
> Through melancholy wastes
>   Of unknown time and space—
> A power that never hastes,
>   And never slackens pace
>   Until the human face,
>   Until the human form
>   Beautiful, and swift and warm,

> Awaits the crowning hour,
> And blooms—a spirit flower—
> Upward and onward ever
> One primal plan pursued.
> All in its turn is good.[72]

5

Just as the crowning point in Cranch's song is the suggestion of immortality in the line "And blooms—a spirit flower," there can be no doubt that cosmic optimism went its greatest length in attempting to bring together the old doctrine of eternal life and the new theory of organic evolution. Evolutionists have usually regarded immortality with scepticism, but during the closing decades of the last century a number of them sought not only to reconcile the two doctrines but to establish the truth of the former upon the basis of the latter. Cautious and orthodox thinkers—like Father Tabb in his trenchant and deservedly famous epigram entitled "Evolution"[73] —ascribed no more than a metaphorical relationship to the two views, but there was a widespread feeling that the principle of development was as applicable to the soul as to the body and that evolution was therefore at least a prophecy of immortality. The radical Unitarian, John Albee, wrote, for example:

> If once but dust or ape or worm,
> A growing brain and then a soul,
> Sure these are but prophetic germ
> Of that which makes our circle whole.[74]

and a poet only recently dead, Richard Burton, expressed the same thought in these lines:

> Good, probing friend, I accept your view:
>   We are apes, time-mellowed, you and I;
> But you stop half-way,—for if such be true,
>   We both may be angels, by and by.[75]

Some were willing to go even further. Darwin had hinted vaguely that somewhere in the gradually ascending organic scale man may have become an "immortal being,"[76] and a number of those who had an equal affection for the old faith and the new science took up this suggestion and theorized that immortality, like the power of conceptual thought, is an attribute of superior beings developed at a late stage in evolution. For example, the well-known University of California geologist, Joseph Le Conte, wrote in his book on *Evolution in Its Relation to Religious Thought:*

I believe that the spirit of man *was* developed out of the *anima* or conscious principle of animals, and that this again was developed out of the lower forms of life-force, and this in turn out of the chemical and physical forces of nature. And that at a certain stage in its gradual development, viz., with man, it acquired the property of immortality precisely as it now, in the individual history of each man at a certain stage, acquired the capacity of abstract thought.[77]

Again, John Fiske ended his popular lectures at the Concord School of Philosophy on *The Destiny of Man Viewed in the Light of His Origin* on the same reassuring note:

According to Mr. Spencer, the divine energy which is manifested throughout the knowable universe is the same energy that wells up in us as consciousness. Speaking for myself, I can see no insuperable difficulty in the notion that at some period in the evolution of Humanity this divine spark may have acquired sufficient concentration and steadiness to survive the wreck of material forms and endure forever.[78]

Such a theory was too tentative and conjectural, however, to elicit much enthusiasm on the part of the poets, who preferred daring certainties to vague possibilities. Though it was suggested by McKnight in a sonnet that drew the inference from evolution that Nature's "crowning joy" is "to transmute time's results into soul-fruit,"[79] most of the poets who considered the theme at all turned back to the ancient theory that the soul is not only immortal but eternal and hence has pre-existed through all time. This view had already been expressed by Emerson in his poem on the worm striving to be man and by Whitman in his various accounts of the evolutionary career of his ego, but it gained new impetus in the eighties and nineties from a wave of enthusiasm for the scientific investigation of psychic phenomena. However, in spite of the novelty of the scientific paraphernalia, this theory owed more to the age-old conceptions of reincarnation and the chain of being than to science, which merely provided new illustrations. Ever since the "Ode on Intimations of Immortality" the idea of pre-existence had made frequent appearance in English and American poetry, but toward the end of the century, sentiments, serious and otherwise, like Henley's "when I was a king in Babylon and you were a Christian slave," became epidemic. Lafcadio Hearn attempted to mediate between the oriental theory of transmigration and the occidental theory of evolution,[80] Paul Hamilton Hayne wrote on "Pre-existence,"[81] and Thomas Bailey Aldrich on "Metempsychosis."[82] Aldrich's poem made no direct appeal to the theory of evolution, but it described the advance of the soul from low to high estate and well illustrates the adaptability of the idea of reincarnation to a progressive interpretation:

> I brood on all the shapes I must attain
> Before I reach the perfect, which is God
> . . .
> I was a spirit on the mountain tops,
> . . .
> I was ere Nineveh and Babylon;
> I was, and am, and evermore shall be,
> Progressing, never reaching the end.

Moreover, as James Thomson had made clear a hundred and fifty years before[83] and as Aldrich's poem shows, this conception came to the same end as the "temporalized" chain of being, which supposed a continuous scale of ascent from the infinitely humble to the infinitely great. As Alfred B. Street wrote in his *Poems* of 1867,

> Is not this life a link of that vast chain,
>   Commencing in the past eternity
>   And stretching o'er this being's transient sea,
> To reach, far, far beyond, God, its grand source again?[84]

The nineteenth century saw the waning of the chain of being idea, with its subordinate concepts of plentitude, continuity, and gradation; but, as was shown in the discussion of Emerson, this concept was in some cases merged with the idea of evolution, and it was implied in the writing of some younger poets. It played an important part, as will be shown, in Bayard Taylor's *Prince Deukalion,* which dealt with both immortality and evolution, and it appeared in Epes Sargent's narrative poem *The Woman Who Dared.* There Sargent described the "Love Divine" that emerges after the passing of youth's fervor as

> A love that sees the good beyond the evil,

> The serial life beyond the eclipsing death,—
> That tracks the spirit through eternities,
> Backward and forward, and in every germ
> Beholds its past, its present, and its future,
> At every stage beholds it gravitate
> Where it belongs, and thence new-born emerge
> Into new life and opportunity,
> An outcast never from the assiduous Mercy,
> Providing for His teeming universe,
> Divinely perfect not because complete,
> But because incomplete, advancing ever,
> Beneath the care Supreme.[85]

Many were convinced that this serial life beyond the eclipsing death, this universe divinely perfect because incomplete and advancing ever, was the final lesson of evolution.

This conception was handled by the poets with varying degrees of audacity. Cranch treated it with caution and reserve in a pair of sonnets whose title, "The Human Flower,"[86] recalls the "spirit flower" of the concluding lines of the "Song of an Evolutionist." The first of the two tells how "in the old void of unrecorded time" "a seed from out the weltering fire-mist cast" "took root," "grew, changing form and issue," and finally

> burst in bloom beyond compare
> The world's consumate, peerless human flower.

The second then asks humbly, though with little doubt concerning the answer, "Shall that bright flower . . . by death be foiled?" . . .

> Shall that Celestial Love . . . .
> . . .
> Leave it to perish when the summons harsh
> Of Death is rung,—or, ere its leaves are shed,
> Transplant it to his realm of Paradise?

In a bizarre piece of social verse by one Langdon Smith,[87] however, the treatment is extravagant in the extreme. Like Harte's "Geological Madrigal," the poem is a mock-sentimental address to a lady, and proceeds from a farcical opening:

> When you were a tadpole and I was a fish
> In the Paleozoic time . . . [88]

to a farcical climax:

> And that was a million years ago,
>   In a time that no man knows;
> Yet here tonight in the mellow light
>   We sit at Delmonico's. . . . [89]

However, though the poem is eminently unserious, not to say absurd, and may for that reason seem out of place here, it admirably illustrates the concept under discussion. Beginning in the "Cambrian fen," it tells with voluminous evolutionary lore a story of many lives, loves, deaths, and rebirths through which the gallantry that was to culminate at Delmonico's persisted, and in the end it provides as concise and instructive a summary of this latter-day metempsychosis as one could wish for:

> We have left our bones in the Bagshot stones,
>   And deep in the Coraline crags;
> Our love is old, our lives are old,
>   And death shall come amain;
> Should it come today, what man may say
>   We shall not live again?
>
> God wrought our souls from the Tremadoc beds
>   And furnished them wings to fly;
> He sowed our spawn in the world's dim dawn,
>   And I know that it shall not die. . . . [90]

The other poems in which evolution and immortality were brought together were sufficiently dignified, but their basic conception, which had been suggested by Emerson and fully developed by Whitman, was the same as Smith's—that of evolution as the recollected experience of a soul that has known many changes but has not lost and will not lose its identity. Thus, when John White Chadwick, who was a follower of Emerson and Whitman, applied himself to the question that God put to Job, "Where wast thou when I laid the foundations of earth?" he related this series of events:

> Then I was where now I am,—
>   In thy bosom; . . . .
>
> Strange my fortunes since have been,—
>   Bathed in fire, in floods congealed,
> In the nebulous mass aglow,
>   In the ardent planet wheeled;
> From the shapeless, slow but sure,

>   Taking shapes with beauty rife;
> From the senseless clod at length
>   Plucking out the heart of life.
>
> Upward, onward, striving still
>   Through the elemental forms;
> Cradled in the monster trees,
>   Rocked by earthquakes, nursed by storms;
> Out of weakness growing strong
>   Working still the heavenly plan,
> Learning what the beast must do,
>   Ere he find himself a man.[91]

Again, Edith M. Thomas told the same story in a poem that repeated Chadwick's point of departure in its opening lines—"I dwelt with God, ere he fashioned the worlds with their heart of fire"—and then went on:

> Part had I not in the scheme till He sent me to work on the reef.
> . . .
> Strength had I not till chiefdom supreme of the waters He gave;
> . . .
> Lightness I had not till, decked with light plumes, He endued me with speed—
> . . .
> I trod not the earth till on plains unmeasured He sent me to rove,
> . . .
> Foresight I had not, nor memory, nor vision that sweeps in the skies,
> Till He made me man, and bade me uplift my marvelling eyes![92]

Finally, in Ina Coolbrith's posthumous volume, *Wings of Sunset*, the theme was once again repeated:

>   An Atom, formless, in the void of space,
>   Wherein but the One presence, All in All,
>   That drew me, drew me, until like a cry,
>   Was felt at Last the pulse of my desire—
>   "Life! Life! O Thou that Art, give me to be!"
>   Aeon on aeon, change evolving change,
>   Time, time, almost that seemed eternity,
>   And then the Being I! the answered prayer![93]

Plainly the authors of these poems and of the others that have been considered in this chapter were little troubled by the gloom that is sometimes supposed to have darkened the skies of the Western world as soon after November, 1859 as *The Origin of Species* became generally known. There is nothing here of agnosticism, of the ethic of tooth and claw, or of the somber self-questioning of Arnold and Clough. Of course the number of poets touched upon has been much too small to be thoroughly representative, but the following chapters, dealing with the more prominent poets of the time, will bear out the general implication of the present chapter, that, with only a few exceptions, evolution caused our poets little spiritual discomfort. In the absence of an influential school of naturalistic and positivistic thought like that which included Huxley, Tyndall, Spencer, Harrison, and Lewes in England, it was easy to reject evolution in whole or in part, as Bryant and Lanier did, or to ignore it like Longfellow, or, under the prompting of Fiske, Drummond, the Beechers, and others, to accept it in a modified form compatible with the theistic view. Moreover, certain other factors served to cushion the impact of evolution on our men of letters. The Unitarian and Transcendental movements, which had been felt by most New Englanders and by many others, had already liberalized theology and the interpretation of Scripture, and the Romantic natural philosophy as rendered by Emerson and others had already popularized a true though not a naturalistic evolutionism. It is important to note that of the poets mentioned in this chapter, Cranch, Trowbridge, Chadwick, and Venable were all followers of Emerson, and others doubtless felt his influence. Many probably could have said with the speaker at the Radical Club that they were evolutionists before Darwin, though they would have meant only that they accepted the progression of forms presented by geology and interpreted it as the manifestations of an immanent creative principle without a demonstrated physical connection. From this stage, however, it was but a step to the theistic modification of Darwinism. In fact, the differences between this evolutionism and that developed by Emerson in the forties and fifties are negligible. The younger poets minimized Emerson's Romantic metaphysics and avoided some of his scientific extravagances, but they agreed on the central thesis that evolution, whether accomplished by natural selection of some other means, is the unfolding of an indwelling and all-encompassing Power whose divine nature is a guarantee that all is for the best. They had little to say of the theories of identity and correspondence and of the dualism of *natura naturans* and *natura naturata,* but their optimism was not less unspotted—though certainly less moving, less infectious—than Emerson's, because in the last analysis it was cut from the same cloth.

VII

BRYANT, LONGFELLOW, AND LOWELL: REJECTION, INDIFFERENCE, DISCOMFORT

IN THE light of the older Christian tradition, the majority of American poets of the mid-century were theological radicals. A strict constructionist like Augustus H. Strong at first refused to write a book on their theology on the ground that they had none, and even when he later undertook the task he found more or less defection from his evangelical Calvinism in all the nine he considered.[1] There are degrees of radicalism, however, and alongside Emerson, Poe, and Whitman, the poets who will be considered in this chapter seem staunch conservatives. As laymen and Unitarians they were not much inclined to give precise definition to their theological opinions, but they retained enough of the traditional Christian dualism to render them inimical to the evolutionary view. Each in his own way believed in and preached a kind of cosmic optimism, but with an antagonism varying from outright rejection to grudging tolerance toward the theory that the world and man have come to be what they are solely through the action of forces inherent in nature. Not merely as against Huxley and Spencer, in short, but as against Emerson and Whitman, they were on the side of Bushnell and McCosh.

1

Bryant mentioned the name of Charles Darwin only twice in all his published writing, but he left no doubt about his opinion of Darwin's theory. On the earlier and more revealing occasion, speaking facetiously but earnestly in addressing an appeal for funds to the alumni of Williams College, he turned the theory quite around. "Allowing all that Darwin says of the consanguinity of man and the inferior animals," he argued,

> ... where does he find his proof that we are improving instead of degenerating? He claims that man is an improved monkey; how does he know that the monkey is not a degenerated man, a decayed

branch of the human family, fallen away from the high rank he once held, and haunted by a dim sentiment of his lost dignity, as we may infer from his melancholy aspect? Improvement, Mr. President, and gentlemen, implies effort; it is uphill work; degeneracy is easy; it asks only neglect, indolence, inaction.... How, then can Mr. Darwin insist that we admit the near kindred of man to the inferior? Is not the contrary the more probable? Is it not more likely that the more easy downward road has been taken, that the lower animals are derived from some degenerate branch of the human race, and that, if we do not labor to keep the rank we hold our race may be frittered away into the meaner tribes of animals, and finally into animalcules.... If we hold to Darwin's theory—as I do not—how are we to know that the vast multitudes of men and women on the earth are not ruins, so to speak, of some nobler species, with more elevated and perfect faculties, mental, physical, and moral, but now extinct?

Let me say, then, to those who believe in the relationship of the animal tribes that it behooves them to avoid the danger which I have pointed out by giving a generous support to those institutions of wholesome learning, like Williams College....[2]

That this is not to be taken quite literally does not mean that it should not be taken seriously; Bryant's animus against Darwinism was nonetheless real for being couched in terms of burlesque. Nor can it be regarded as obscurantism founded upon ignorance and lack of sympathy with the sciences. On the contrary, Bryant had a much more lively interest in the sciences than he has often been credited with. In his youth he studied chemistry and botany in his father's library and laboratory;[3] in later life he numbered many scientists among his friends and admirers;[4] and, as we shall see, he gave praise and encouragement to the popular dissemination of scientific knowledge. He had utterly no sympathy, however, with the materialistic or agnostic drifts that the sciences had set in motion, and on several occasions he spoke out stingingly against what seemed to him the conceit and impiety of the leaders of this movement. In his eightieth year, for example, a few months after Tyndall's notorious Belfast address, he wrote as follows to a female correspondent:

Well, in spite of all that the scientists say, there *is* a morning beyond the night of Death.... The "International Review" is now on my table, in which Dr. McCosh does battle with Tyndall in an able article on "Ideas in Nature overlooked by Dr. Tyndall." One great characteristic of these scientists is their conceit.[5]

The fact that Bryant was strongly opposed to all that Darwin stood for did not prevent him, however, from being profoundly impressed by the universal phenomenon of change or from developing themes implicit in that phenomenon which have a relevance to the general notion of evolution and an even closer relation to what has here been called cosmic optimism. Except for Whitman and Emerson, in fact, probably no other American poet of his time was so sensitive to the flux of existence as Bryant. Because he resolutely maintained the dualism of man and nature and the transcendence of God, he was never the victim of the "Heracleitan obsession" with which Whitman has been taxed, but two of the most familiar themes in his verse—the impermanence of human life and the perpetual renewal of life in the cycle of the seasons—are themes of change. A mortuary poet from the very beginning, he never tired of repeating that life is a march to the grave, and he often observed the contrast between human mortality and the relative permanence of the natural scene. He wrote, for example, of a familiar rivulet:

> And I shall sleep—and on thy side,
> As ages after ages glide,
> Children their early sports shall try,
> And pass to hoary age and die.
> But thou, unchanged from year to year,
> Gayly shalt play and glitter here;
> Amid young flowers and tender grass
> Thy endless infancy shall pass;
> And, singing down thy narrow glen,
> Shalt mock the fading race of men.[6]

Sensitive as he was to the somber fact of death, however, he was too much of an optimist to conclude that it was wholly without good. If death brought an end to life, it also arrested pain and evil, and at more than one time in his life he was willing to call it "Deliverer!" and address it in words of praise:

> God hath anointed thee to free the oppressed
> And crush the oppressor . . . .
> . . . from the first of time, hast thou been found
> On virtue's side; the wicked, but for thee,
> Had been too strong for good.[7]

After the death of his father in 1820, it is true, he repudiated these lines as the "record of an idle memory";[8] but the sentiment was apparently too strong to be so easily dismissed, for he frequently repeated it, writing, for example, in "The Ages" a few months later:

> Lo! the same shaft by which the righteous dies
> Strikes through the wretch that scoffed at mercy's law
> And trode his brethren down, and felt no awe
> Of Him who will avenge them.[9]

As a phase of the doctrine of the "good of evil" this sentiment has a familiar ring, but it occupies a relatively minor place in Bryant's optimism, which was more positive. The process of change that he observed all about him was not merely an executioner but a builder and preserver. The individual might be doomed to the grave,[10] and whole races, like the Indian,[11] might fall into subjection or even extinction; but the life of the species flowed on as steadily as that of nature, and—what is more important—it flowed progressively. Thus, when invited to deliver the Phi Beta Kappa poem at Harvard in 1821,[12] he called the roll of the past ages that had culminated in the formation of the American Union as the land of hope and freedom, and a few years later he expressed his view of the future in terms of the quiet and purity of atmosphere that follow a storm. This seemed to him

> An emblem of the peace that yet shall be,
> When o'er earth's continents, and isles between,
> The noise of war shall cease from sea to sea,
> And married nations dwell in harmony;
> When millions, crouching in the dust to one,
> No more shall beg their lives on bended knee,
> Nor the black stake be dressed, nor in the sun
> The o'erlabored captive toil, and wish his life were done.[13]

As his editorial career witnesses, he had a keen eye for abuses, but like all liberals of his time he was convinced that time, effort, and good will would ultimately bring about the triumph of good and right. Like scores of others he was moved to gratulatory verses by the spread of political liberty and the advance of the arts,[14] and he not only joined sincerely in the idealism that accompanied the Civil War[15] but even in the dark days of Reconstruction was able to look forward to "a nobler age than ours."[16] "Truth, crushed to earth," he said in a well-remembered phrase, "shall rise again."[17]

Nor was this faith merely the result of a calculating observation of events or merely applicable to man's earthly lot. As with all cosmic optimism, it rested at bottom on trust in a power at the heart of things that works for good, and, like the faith of many others, it held out a promise of life beyond death. In "An Evening Revery," for example, he proceeded from observation of the daily and seasonal resurgence of life in nature to such a cosmic promise:

> O thou great Movement of the Universe,
> Or Change, or Flight of Time—for ye are one!
> . . .
> . . . . . . whither art thou bearing me?
> . .
> . . . do the portals of another life
> Even now, while I am glorying in my strength
> Impend around me? Oh! beyond that bourne,
> In the vast cycle of being which begins
> At that dread threshhold, with what fairer forms
> Shall the great law of change and progress clothe
> Its working? Gently—so have good men taught—
> Gently, and without grief, the old shall glide
> Into the new; the eternal flow of things,
> Like a bright river of the fields of heaven,
> Shall journey onward in perpetual peace.[18]

Like the Unitarians, with whom he was always sympathetic even though he did not join them until he was sixty-four, Bryant's was a God of love rather than of wrath—an "Eternal Love" that

> doth keep
> In his complacent arms the earth, the air, the deep.[19]

From this it was but a step to the Unitarian tenet of "the progress of mankind onward and upward forever." In "The Ages," for example, from which the lines above are quoted, he went on confidently, after pointing out that nature does not falter with old age but continues with ever renewed vitality:

> Will then the merciful One, who stamped our race
> With his own image . . . .
> . . .
> Forget the ancient care that taught and nursed
> His latest offspring? . . . .[20]
>
> Oh, no! a thousand cheerful omens give
> Hope of yet happier days, whose dawn is nigh.

> He who has tamed the elements, shall not live
> The slave of his own passions; he whose eye
> Unwinds the eternal dances of the sky,
> And in the abyss of brightness dares to span
> The sun's broad circle, rising yet more high,
> In God's magnificent works his will shall scan—
> And love and peace shall make their paradise with man.[21]

If Bryant's religious belief facilitated his acceptance of this much of the doctrine of cosmic optimism, however, it was equally obstructive of his acceptance of the rest. He might generalize his conception of deity in such statements as the following:

The poet who wrote atheist after his name knew not of what manner of spirit he was. He, too, paid a willing and undissembled homage to the Divinity. He called it Nature, but it was the Great First Cause whom we all worship, whatever its essence, and whatever its name.[22]

He could never bring himself, however, to accept the principle of divine immanence in the pantheistic fashion in which it was interpreted by most evolutionists. One way of saying this is that he found God's influence, but never God, in nature. Thus, though in "A Forest Hymn" he wrote of the "presence" of God in nature, it is clear from his creational language that he did not mean to represent God and nature as in any way one. To quote W. A. Bradley, his English biographer, he worshiped God, "not in the forest, but through the forest."[23] The following lines, adapted freely from Boethius and entitled "The Order of Nature," leave us in no doubt concerning his understanding of the relation between nature and its Creator:

> the Great Founder, he who gave these laws,
> Holds firm reins and sits amid his skies
> Monarch and Master, Origin and Cause,
> And Arbiter supremely just and wise.
>
> He guides the force he gave; his hand restrains
> And curbs it to the circle it must trace:
> Else the fair fabric which his power sustains
> Would fall to fragments in the void of space.[24]

God, one may infer from these lines, is not limited by the laws of nature, but, just as he made and maintains them, so may he alter or break them for purposes of destruction or further creation.

Such a transcendent conception of God may of course be adapted to a kind of evolutionism, as it was by McCosh; but it is much more congenial to creationism, for which, as we have seen, McCosh made a generous allowance.[25] For under such a conception the establishment of a new level of being is not merely a manifestation of the will of God (a view that Emerson would not have disagreed with) but a radical departure from those established ways of God that constitute the "order of nature." In other words, though in the daily round of nature God merely "guides the force he gave," in those innovations that constitute the stages of evolution he *intervenes;* the world changes, yes, but the *kinds* of being have been determined in the original act or acts of creation and cannot be augmented in the ordinary course of nature. Bryant gives us regrettably little to go on in arriving at this interpretation, but it not only is implicit in his general treatment of the relation of God and nature and his flat rejection of Darwinism but is strongly hinted in two more particular instances. In "A Forest Hymn," for example, he described nature as "finished, yet renewed,"[26] and long afterward, six years after the appearance of *The Origin of Species,* he gave evidence that he looked upon natural history with the eyes of Agassiz rather than Darwin. In a letter expressing approval of a course in natural history for teachers, he indicated that his conception of the province of this study, like Agassiz's, centered in description and classification rather than in the study of origins:

Man is necessarily a naturalist. It is a remarkable passage in sacred history which relates that all the beasts of the field and the fowls of the air were made to pass before the father of the human race, who distinguished them from each other, and gave to each species the name it was afterward to bear.[27]

Admittedly this is the slightest kind of evidence, but when read against the background of its author's more general reflections, it supplies significant corroboration.

It is apparent, however, that Bryant's strongest objection to evolution was that it deprived the soul of its independent, supernatural character. On this point he was as firm as Horace Bushnell.[28] Thus in a satirical reference to Darwinism at the Goethe Club in 1877[29] it was the difference between man and monkey that he stressed, and he many times went out of his way to assert his inflexible adherence to this conception of man—in an address at a testimonial dinner for Samuel F. B. Morse, for example:

Mr. President, I see in the circumstances which I have enumerated a new proof of the superiority of mind to matter, of the independent existence of that part of our nature which we call the spirit, when it can thus subdue, enslave, and educate the subtilest, the most active, and in certain of its manifestations the most intractable and terrible, of the elements. . . . I infer the capacity of the spirit for a separate state of being, its indestructible essence and its noble destiny, and I thank the great discoverer whom we have assembled to honor for this confirmation of my faith.[30]

To be sure, as the circumstances of this statement make clear, Bryant did not believe that there was any incompatibility between his belief and *true* science. He did hold, however, that any scientific theory which contradicted the belief was *ipso facto* false and ought therefore to be combated not only by denial but by a more careful search for the truth. Less than a month before his death he wrote:

There is an attempt to make science, or a knowledge of the laws of the material universe an ally of the school which denies a separate spiritual existence and a future life; in short, to borrow of science weapons to be used against Christianity. The friends of religion, therefore, confident that one truth never contradicts another, are doing wisely when they seek to accustom the people at large to think and to weigh evidence, as well as to believe.[31]

Coming as it did in 1878, this statement leaves no doubt about Bryant's position.

2

For one of his learning Longfellow had remarkably little interest in speculative questions. The dominating motives of his character being sympathy and artistic sensibility, love and beauty meant more to him than doctrinal differences; the burden of his message, from his youthful inaugural address at Bowdoin to his *magnum opus, Christus,* was "the deed, and not the creed."[32] Sermons or a lecture by Emerson, for example, are judged in his journal on the basis of rhetorical excellence rather than ideas, and such interest in the sciences as he displayed was exclusively poetic. After a lecture on botany by Asa Gray he wrote, "What a wide sweep the subject has; and how poetical!"[33] and after reading Nichol's *Architecture of the Heavens:* it "wafts one away into infinite depths of space."[34]

The extremes of thought left him cold: Emerson was "all *dreamery*, after all,"[35] and Voltaire an "arch-scoffer"[36] whom he could view only with distaste. Books that opened up new avenues of speculation he noted only laconically, and none more so than those that led toward evolution. Of a lecture by Agassiz on "The Races of Men" he said simply, "He thinks there were several Adams and Eves";[37] an essay by Kant on the supposed origin of man, read in the year of the appearance of *The Descent of Man*, was "an interesting interpretation of Genesis";[38] Büchner's *Origin of Man*, of which he read parts during the following year, he dismissed curtly as "a Darwinian book."[39] In the light of this tendency it is not surprising that Longfellow has little to contribute to this study— that he ignored rather than accepted or rejected evolution. His whole attitude is perhaps best revealed in a story told of him and Agassiz by Moncure Conway. Agassiz once half jokingly urged Longfellow to write the epic of geological history, outlining the project in glowing rhetoric. Longfellow replied simply but conclusively that he had no doubt there ought to be such a poem but that he was not the man to write it.[40] If Bryant had been a younger man—he was sixty-five when *The Origin of Species* appeared— it is conceivable that he might have made the compromise with evolution that was made by so many others. Longfellow, wholly indifferent to such speculative questions, would perhaps not have troubled; or, if he had accepted evolution as a historical fact, would perhaps, like Edward Rowland Sill at a later time,[41] have dismissed it as of little importance in daily spiritual and ethical life.

In spite of this lack of interest, however, it must be recorded that on two occasions Longfellow dallied with some of the quasi-evolutionary speculations of German Romanticism and merged some phases of those speculations into his thinking on the life of the soul. Thus in *Hyperion* he borrowed the ruminations of a minor follower of Schelling, Gotthilf Heinrich Schubert, for his "cloud-land" Professor.[42] Starting from the premises of the unity, gradation, flux, and aspiration of life, the Professor rhapsodizes:

And this is the fate of the soul, that it should die continually. No sooner here on earth does it awake to its peculiar being, than it struggles to behold and comprehend the Spirit of Life. In the first dim twilight of its existence, it beholds this spirit, is pervaded by its energies, is quick and creative like the spirit itself, and yet slumbers away into death after having seen it. But the image it has seen remains; in the eternal procreation, as a homogeneal existence, it is again renewed, and the seeming death, from moment to moment, becomes the source of kind after kind of existences in ever-ascending series. The soul aspires ever onward to love and behold.

... And thus death is neither an end nor a beginning. It is a transition, not from one existence to another, but from one state of existence to another. No link is broken in the chain of being, any more than in passing from infancy to manhood, from manhood to old age.

... The feeling of our dignity and our power grows strong, when we say to ourselves: My being is not objectless and in vain; I am a necessary link in the great chain, which, from the full development of consciousness in the first man, reaches forward into eternity. All the great and wise and good among mankind ... have labored for me. I have entered into their harvest.[43]

True, Longfellow intended this partly as a parody of the German philosophy and caused his hero to dismiss it as "day-dreams only." He repeated it once again, however, in the Prelude to Part Three of *Tales of a Wayside Inn,* where the Spanish Jew replies as follows to a question concerning the silent grace he said before breaking bread:

> I said the Manichaean's prayer.
> It was his faith,—perhaps is mine,—
> That life in all its forms is one,
> And that its secret conduits run
> Unseen, but in unbroken line,
> From the great fountain-head divine
> Through man and beast, through grain and grass.
> Howe'er we struggle, strive, and cry,
> From death there can be no escape,
> And no escape from life, alas!
> Because we cannot die, but pass
> From one into another shape:
> It is but into life we die.[44]

This again he disclaimed by giving the speech to the Jew and having the Poet offer objections. However, though he did not choose to accept the doctrine outright, much less to develop its evolutionary possibilities, he neither forgot it nor rejected it entirely. In general he was distrustful of all transcendentalism and, according to Felton, had neither much knowledge of nor interest in the German brands;[45] but we find that wherever the transcendental doctrines could be assimilated to his conservative Unitarian Christianity he accepted them and molded them to his needs. It is instructive, for example, to find him writing in his journal after reading Fichte:

And this is a German philosopher! Why, there is more of the soul of Christianity in these lectures than in the sermons of all the rebel crew of narrow-minded, dyspeptic, so-called *orthodox* preachers who rail against German philosophy, should they preach from one end of the year to the other.[46]

His treatment of Schubert's conception is similar. The conception of life as a perpetual round of aspiring change appears elsewhere in his writing, but certainly not with the implications developed by Whitman and Emerson:

>   the Seer
> With vision clear,
> Sees forms appear and disappear,
> In the perpetual round of strange,
> Mysterious change
> From birth to death, from death to birth,
> From earth to heaven, from heaven to earth;
> Till glimpses more sublime
> Of things unseen before,
> Unto his wondering eyes reveal
> The Universe, as an immeasurable wheel
> Turning forevermore
> In the rapid and rushing river of Time.[47]

"From earth to heaven"—this was the evolution in which Longfellow was most interested and the transition that he seized out of Schubert's ruminations. "There is no Death! What seems so is transition," he wrote in Schubert's terms on the occasion of the death of his daughter; but the change that he had in mind was transition to a Christian heaven:

>   This life of mortal breath
> Is but a suburb of the life elysian,
>   Whose portal we call Death.
>
>   She is not dead,—the child of our affection,—
>   But gone unto that school
>   Where she no longer needs our poor protection,
>   And Christ himself doth rule.[48]

There was little of the speculative philosopher about Longfellow.

As it had been to St. Paul, the attempt to delve into the ends and means of creation was to him as if the jar should question the potter:

>   This earthen jar
> A touch can make, a touch can mar;
>   And shall it to the Potter say,
> What makest thou? Thou hast no hand?
> As men who think to understand
> A world by their Creator planned,
>   Who wiser is than they.[49]

Hence his conception of the progress of the soul to a better life is of all things not to be taken as a hint of a cosmology. It is present and even prominent in Longfellow's writing, however, and deserves to be mentioned in a study like this. It was the theme of "Excelsior," of which he said that the voice heard in the air in the last stanza was "the promise of immortality and progress upward,"[50] and it was stated interestingly in the Bowdoin inaugural, delivered at the age of twenty-three. There, in characterizing modern literature, he not only revealed his own literary ideal but the place that this theme was to hold in his later work:

It is this *religious feeling,*—this changing of the finite for the infinite, this constant grasping after the invisible things of another and higher world,—which marks the spirit of modern literature. The ancients, it is true, dreamed of an immortality; but their heaven was an earthly heaven, and the eye could take in at a glance the sensuous paradise of the Elysian Fields, where the prerogative of the soul is not that it should grow better, but that it should merely live longer.[51]

Here, to be sure, was the *ewiges, lebendiges Tun*[52] that underlay all the Romantic evolutionisms, but no more than that.

3

Longfellow's bland indifference to the issues raised by evolution was nicely balanced by the lively perturbation of James Russell Lowell, who felt probably more keenly than any other American poet the horns of the Victorian dilemma of doubt and faith. As no one knew better than he, there was an undertone of indecision and self-distrust running through much of his work that was due in part to the troubled spirit of the times and in part to a mixed and impressionable temperament that was acutely sensitive to that spirit. "One half of me is clear mystic and enthusiast, and the other humorist," he wrote to his friend Briggs,[53] and a similar judgment, applied in this case to all men, is to be found in the most deeply thoughtful of his poems, "The Cathedral,"[54] inspired by a visit to Chartres. "We men," he wrote in one place, "too conscious of earth's comedy, . . . see two sides, with our posed selves debate," and in another place he added, speaking more personally:

> I thank benignant nature most for this,—
> A force of sympathy, or call it lack
> Of character firm-planted, loosing me
> From the pent chamber of habitual self
> To dwell enlarged in alien modes of thought.

The whole poem is an elaboration of this judgment in respect to both himself and his times. "The born disciple of an elder time," he was filled with the keenest kind of nostalgia for the untroubled faith symbolized by the noble structure of the cathedral and was able through his sympathy to render its artistic and spiritual character unforgettably. Even at the height of his rapture, however, he was unable to detach himself from the questioning spirit of his own age, with the result that the poem is less a song of praise for what the structure stood for than a lament for its passing. "Was it not mere sympathy of brain?" he asked of his momentary persuasion,

> A sweetness intellectually conceived
> In simpler creeds to me impossible?
> A juggle of that pity for ourselves
> In others, which puts on such pretty masks
> And snares self-love with bait of charity?
> Something of all it might be, or of none:
> Yet for a moment I was snatched away
> And had the evidence of things not seen;
> For one rapt moment; then it all came back,
> This age that blots out life with question-marks,
> This nineteenth century with its knife and glass
> That make thought physical, and thrust far off
> The Heaven, so neighborly with man of old,
> To voids sparse-sown with alienated stars.

Naturally this profound dichotomy of scepticism and faith, head and heart, strongly colored his reaction to evolution and to the religious and philosophical issues which it raised. True, his position on these issues was more stable than on some others, and he never wavered in his opposition to the school of Huxley. As we shall see, however, he found it necessary to make concessions. While his basic faith held firm, the relativism of the philosophy of change crept insidiously into his thinking, he came to accept many of the facts on which the evolutionists based their theories, and in the end he gave grudging assent to a modified version of the theory itself. Each of these concessions must be examined in turn.

As had been the case with many before him, Lowell's religious conviction was predicated on a basis of philosophical scepticism. He could almost have said with Kant that he "found it necessary to deny *knowledge* of *God, freedom,* and *immortality,* in order to find a place for *faith.*"[55] His inner conviction was never shaken, but again and again he asked, What can we *know?* In the early pages of "The Cathedral," for example, he dwelt on the subjectivity of knowledge:

> What we call Nature, all outside ourselves,
> Is but our own conceit of what we see,
> Our own reaction upon what we feel;
> . . .
>
> And therefore we the more persuade ourselves
> To make all things our thought's confederates,
> Conniving with us in whate'er we dream.

And in the closing years of his life he returned forcefully to the same theme. Thus, "How I Consulted the Oracle of the Goldfishes,"[56] which conceals deep seriousness behind a façade of whimsy, opens with the question,

> What know we of the world immense
> Beyond the narrow ring of sense?

and then goes on to liken the limitations of sensory knowledge to the glass bowl in which the fish swim aimlessly round and round. To be sure, the poem ends with an affirmation of a world beyond sense, but along the way the poet asks of such a life,

> Is it illusion? Dream-stuff? Show
> Made of the wish to have it so?

and draws an unflattering parallel between his own life and that of the captive fish:

> With a half-humorous smile I see
> In this their aimless industry,
> These errands nowhere and returns
> Grave as a pair of funeral urns,
> This ever-seek and never-find,
> A mocking image of my mind.

His most outspoken expression of the theme, however, striking at the very basis of theological knowledge, is a little fable of a fire-fly, "The Lesson." Having seen a bolt of lightning, the fire-fly reasons that it must have been made by a superior kind of fly. The poet then concludes:

> And is man wiser? Man who takes
> His consciousness the law to be
> Of all beyond his ken, and makes
> God but a bigger kind of Me?[57]

In this subjectivism lay the germ of a historical relativism; for if all truths are man-made they will change with man and the conditions to which he is subject. Thus, again in "The Cathedral," after he had concluded that the ancient faith was irrecoverable, he went on:

> Each age must worship its own thought of God,
> . . .
> Nor saint nor sage could fix immutably
> The fluent image of the unstable Best,
> Still changing in their very hands that wrought:
> To-day's eternal truth To-morrow proved
> Frail as frost-landscapes on a window-pane.

He reckoned immediately with the possibility that this might be "drift" rather than "progress," but in the end took refuge in the Tennysonian hope that

> Perhaps the deeper faith that is to come
> Will see God rather in the strenuous doubt,
> Than in the creed held as an infant's hand
> Holds purposeless whatso is placed therein.

What Lowell was expressing here was in large measure merely the familiar Unitarian and Romantic notion that religious truths are mysteries that cannot be captured in theological formulae and that men advance spiritually as they come to realize this. Whatever its background, however, the thought was pregnant with the subtlest and gravest of the consequences of evolution, that Darwinian conception of truth as contingent upon circumstances which has culminated in the pragmatisms and instrumentalisms of the twentieth century.[58]

Side by side with this philosophy of change, Lowell's omnivorous appetite for learning was storing his mind with scraps of the body of fact on which the scientific theory of evolution was based. His passion for recondite allusion was great, and geology and anthropology often served his purpose as well as literary history or the folkways of old New England. In one essay, for example, he compared snow tracks to the fossilized prints of giant birds on "preadamite sea-margins,"[59] and in another, dated 1854, he spoke as follows of the inconvenience of getting up at half past three in the morning:

The primary geological formations contain no traces of man, and it seems to me that these eocene periods of the day are not fitted for sustaining the human forms of life.[60]

These references of course are simply rhetorical, but their growing frequency makes clear that Lowell was becoming increasingly cognizant of the new science. There are too many to examine them in detail, but a few may be cited for purposes of illustration. Thus two sonnets dated 1877 involve the assumption that man's early life on this planet was quite as primitive as the anthropologists claimed,[61] and one of the questions concerning the validity of spiritual intimations in "How I Consulted the Oracle of the Goldfishes" is expressed in the terms of a familiar anthropological theory:

> Are these . . . rude heirlooms
> From grovellers in the cavern-glooms,
> Who in unhuman Nature saw
> Misshapen foes with tusk and claw,
> And with those night-fears brute and blind
> Peopled the chaos of their mind,
> Which, in ungovernable hours,
> Still make their bestial lair in ours?

Lowell had a deeply ingrained antipathy for such theories, and yet he had a lively interest in them and a considerable respect for them as honest efforts to solve difficult problems. In this connection it is interesting to note that he once undertook the translation of a sketch of the life of Darwin into Spanish and offered the following explanation to the daughter of Charles Eliot Norton, who was also the daughter-in-law of his subject:

Not that I like science any better than I ever did. I hate it as a savage does writing, because he fears it will hurt him somehow; but I have a great respect for Mr. Darwin, as almost the only perfectly disinterested lover of truth I ever encountered.[62]

It was this point of view that led Lowell in the decade of the eighties at once to make considerable concessions to evolution and then to deplore and in part reject them. In 1886 he was offered a thousand dollars by the Boston publishing firm of Gately and O'Gorman to write a preface for a compendium of popular knowledge to be called *The World's Progress,* and somewhat against his better judgment he accepted. As he wrote to Henry James while he was considering the offer:

I fear this may be a temptation of the Devil who knows I care so little about money as to be always more or less in want of it. I know very little of the P. of the W., and what little I know doesn't altogether please me, as being plainly toward the Pit. However, I am to see the book before I decide.[63]

He began with mild strictures on the whole notion of progress, but was presently conceding, in the vein of the sonnets of 1877, that life in the modern world "is better than a life of caves," and even giving hesitant and partial assent to the theory of organic evolution. His retelling of the evolutionary story is a little gem of irony as well as of fancy, which carefully avoids the question of the origin of life and the soul but concurs in the general proposition in these terms:

slowly, slowly, it [the earth] became capable of sustaining living organisms, rising by long and infinitesimal gradations, symbolically rehearsed again, it is said, by the child in embryo, from the simplest to the more complex, from merely animated matter to matter informed with Soul, and, in man, sometimes controlled by reason.[64]

Moreover, he was able to find reasons not only to accept but to welcome this theory. In the first place, he agreed that it was not, as some thought, degrading:

> Though these memories of the rocks and mountains and ocean-beds seem to belittle and abbreviate man, yet it is nothing so; . . . If Science have made men seem ephemeral as midges, she has conferred a great benefit on humanity by endowing collective Man with something of that longaeval dignity which she has compelled the individual to renounce. He is no longer the creature of yesterday, but the crowning product and heir of ages so countless as to make Time a sharer in the grandeur of that immensity to which Astronomy has dilated the bounds of Space.[65]

In the second place, it seemed to him to offer a basis for hope:

> To me it seems not unreasonable to find a reinforcement of optimism, a renewal of courage and hope in the modern theory that man has mounted to what he is from the lowest step of potentiality, through toilsome grades of ever-expanding existence, even though it have been by a spiral stairway, mainly dark or dusty, with loopholes at long intervals only, and these granting but a narrow and one-sided view. The protoplasmic germ to which it was incalculable promotion to become a stomach, has it not, out of the resources with which God had endowed it, been able to develop the brain of Darwin, who should write its biography? Even Theology is showing signs that she is getting ready to exchange a man who fell in Adam for a man risen out of nonentity and still rising through that aspiring virtue in his veins which is spurred onwards and upwards by the very inaccessibility of what he sees above him.[66]

Moreover, that these sentiments were not simply gotten up for the occasion is indicated by the presence of similar passages in "Credidimus Jovem Regnare,"[67] which, while it was first published in the following year, went back in its first draft to the early seventies.[68] This was a vigorous satire on the naturalism and agnosticism of the school of Huxley, but it acceded to the evolutionists to the extent of saying:

> I don't object, not I, to know
> My sires were monkeys, if 't was so;
> I touch my ear's collusive tip
> And own the poor-relationship.
> That apes of various shapes and sizes
> Contained their germs that all the prizes
> Of senate, pulpit, camp, and bar win
> May give us hopes that sweeten Darwin.

> Who knows but from our loins may spring
> (Long hence) some winged sweet-throated thing
> As much superior to us
> As we to Cynocephalus?

Lowell was only nibbling at the theory of evolution, however, not swallowing it whole, and the general tenor and particular comments in this poem make it clear that what he left unsaid in *The World's Progress* was quite as important as what he said. One may even go so far as to say that he was more tactful than forthright in that essay. For example, in an address delivered at very nearly the same time he took a quite different view of the "longaeval dignity" conferred upon man by science, saying:

this imputed and vicarious longevity, though it may be obscurely operative in our lives and fortunes, is no valid offset for the shortness of our days, nor widens by a hair's breadth the horizon of our memories.[69]

In addition, in "Credidimus" he followed up his remarks on sweetening Darwin with the judgment:

> This is consoling, but, alas,
> It wipes no dimness from the glass. . . .

Though Lowell absorbed something of the evolutionary outlook and accepted in part the theories of cosmic and organic evolution, his animus in the controversy that raged in the seventies and eighties was definitely *contra* rather than *pro*. He differed sharply with the exponents of the new theory on many incidental points, and he was wholly opposed to their general philosophy of life.

Specifically, he criticized them on two points. Their physico-chemical theories, he said, were not capable of explaining life and the soul, and, even granting that they were, they still left unsolved the problem of ultimate origins. Thus in both "The Cathedral" and "Credidimus" he pointed out in sharp language the limits of scientific explanation in physiology. In the former:

> The armëd eye that with a glance discerns
> In a dry blood-speck between ox and man
> Stares helpless at this miracle called life,
> This shaping potency behind the egg, . . .

and in the latter:

> Our dear and admirable Huxley
> Cannot explain to me why ducks lay,
> Or, rather, how into their eggs
> Blunder potential wings and legs
> With will to move them and decide
> Whether in air or lymph to glide.

In Germany at the time of Lowell's visit in 1855 a dogmatic materialism had succeeded the earlier idealism and seems to have made a strong though unfavorable impression on his mind. At any rate, he sent a photograph to Jeffries Wyman, the Harvard biologist, showing the skeleton of a lion standing above the skull of a man and inscribed with these original German verses:

> Mäste dein Vieh in geigenter Art mit erleuchtenden
>   Phosphor—
> Weiser als Moleschott wirds, triffst du das richtige
>   Mass.
> Giebst du zu wenig, so folgst der Fluch entsetzlicher
>   Dummheit.
> Aber ein Gran zu viel—! Siehe dies Löwenscelett!![70]

The reference was to Moleschott's dictum, "Ohne Phosphor, kein Gedanke," which Lowell later recalled parenthetically in "Credidimus" in the following passage:

> My soul—I mean the bit of phosphorous
> That fills the place of what that was for us—
> Can't bid its inward bores defiance
> With the new nursery-tales of science.

Much more important than these specific strictures on the doctrine of materialism, however, was his belief that the whole effort to solve the problem of origins by the examination of the external world was futile and misguided. In "Credidimus" he asked:

> Who gets a hair's breadth on by showing
> That Something Else set all agoing?
> Farther and farther back we push
> From Moses and his burning bush;
> Cry, "Art Thou there?" Above, below,
> All Nature mutters *yes* and *no!*
> 'T is the old answer: We're agreed
> Being from Being must proceed,
> Life be Life's source.

Lowell's scepticism told him that the truth that gives certainty and peace was not to be found outside but inside man; "faith was never found in the bottom of a crucible, nor peace arrived at by analysis or synthesis."[71]

For all his intellectual accomplishments, Lowell was more a man of faith than of reason. He had his wars of heart and head, but in the end the heart was always the victor. Even his sweeping doubts—like Kant's, as was said before—were a preface to an affirmation of hope and trust that went deeper than reason. In a poem dated 1863 he told humorously of the disillusionments of middle age, but added,

> Ah, Fate, should I live to be nonagenarian
> Let me still take Hope's frail I. O. U.'s upon trust,[72]

and in one of the first of his poems of doubt and faith in the late sixties he said of the question of a future life,

> I know not, and will never pry,
> But trust our human heart for all.[73]

Lowell was by nature both sanguine and mystical. His mother was said to possess second sight, and an experience of his own of "the presence of Something I knew not what" was recorded by William James in *The Varieties of Religious Experience.*[74] Thus, "How I Consulted the Oracle of the Goldfishes," in spite of its scepticism, was in the end an expression of faith in the validity of inner spiritual intimations. Considering his fish behind their wall of glass, he wrote:

> The things ye see as shadows I
> Know to be substance; tell me why
> My visions, like those haunting you,
> May not be as substantial too.
> Alas, who ever answer heard
> From fish, and dream-fish too? Absurd!
> Your consciousness I half divine,
> But you are wholly deaf to mine.
> Go, I dismiss you; ye have done
> All that ye could; our silk is spun:
> Dive back into the deep of dreams,
> Where what is real is what seems!
> Yet I shall fancy till my grave
> Your lives to mine a lesson gave;

> If lesson none, an image, then,
> Impeaching self-conceit in men
> Who put their confidence alone
> In what they call the Seen and Known.
> How seen? How known? As through your glass
> Our wavering apparitions pass
> Perplexingly, then subtly wrought
> To some quite other thing by thought.
> Here shall my resolution be:
> The shadow of the mystery
> Is haply wholesomer for eyes
> That cheat us to be overwise,
> And I am happy in my right
> To love God's darkness as His light.

This will-to-believe comes out strongly in Lowell's correspondence with Leslie Stephen. Since Stephen was a utilitarian who had modified the older doctrines of that school to fit the evolutionism of Darwin and Spencer, there was inevitably an element of disagreement in the very real admiration and affection of the two men. Stephen was a thoroughgoing agnostic who had renounced clerical orders, and as his books appeared, though Lowell greeted them as "full of wit and trained muscle," he was always under necessity of entering a demurrer. This was the case first with "Are We Christians?" and especially with the whole of *Essays in Free Thinking and Plain Speaking,* which appeared in 1873 and probably had no small influence in spurring the examination of his beliefs that Lowell had begun in the late sixties. Characteristically, he did not meet Stephen's arguments, but rested in the position that, since the unaided reason may lead one astray, the court of highest appeal is intuition. His insistent repetition of this view in almost identical phrasing in several letters is of great help in defining his whole attitude toward the war of doubt and faith. Thus he wrote to Stephen on May 16, 1874:

My only objection to any part of your book is, that I think our beliefs more a matter of choice (natural selection, perhaps, but not logical) than you would admit, and that I find no fault with a judicious shutting of the eyes.[75]

And again some ten days later:

My objection was a purely personal one. I shut my eyes resolutely

(I confess) when I turn them in certain directions, and trust my instincts or my longings or whatever you choose to call them.[76]

At about the same time he wrote with somewhat more animus concerning Stephen's book to their mutual friend Charles Eliot Norton:

I emancipated myself long ago, and any friendly attempt to knock off my shackles is apt to result in barking my shins, don't you see? Science has scuttled the old Ship of Faith, and now they would fain persuade me that there is something dishonest as well as undignified in drifting about on the hencoop that I had contrived to secure in the confusion. They undertake to demonstrate to me that it's a hencoop and an unworthy perch for a philosopher. But I shall cling fast. 'T is as good as a line-of-battle ship if it only keep my head above water.[77]

Two years later he returned to the same theme after reading *English Thought in the Eighteenth Century,* writing in May:

I don't think a view of the universe from the stocks of any creed a very satisfactory one. But I continue to shut my eyes resolutely in certain speculative directions, and am willing to find solace in certain intimations that seem to me from a region higher than my reason.[78]

And again in December:

I am very much in the state of mind of the Bretons who revolted against the Revolutionary Government and wrote upon their banners, "Give us back our God!" I suppose I am an intuitionalist, and there I mean to stick. I accept the challenge of common-sense and claim to have another faculty, as I should insist that a peony was red, though twenty color-blind men denied it.[79]

Few men better illustrate Mill's characterization of the age as one "in which people feel sure, not so much that their opinions are true, as that they should not know what to do without them."[80]

Knowledge based on sense and reason is uncertain, said Lowell the sceptic; but the man of faith added, where we cannot know we may believe. "When they tell me that I can't *know* certain things," he wrote in one of the letters to Stephen, "I am apt to wonder how *they* can be sure of that, and whether there may not be things which they can't know."[81] And again, in a letter to Grace Norton:

I don't care where the notion of immortality came from. . . . It is there, and I mean to hold it fast. Suppose we don't know. How much *do* we know, after all?[82]

Lowell wrote a moving elegy on the death of Agassiz, which, like all good elegies, tells more about its author than its subject. There, in touching on the question of immortality, he admitted some comfort in leaving this "shifting life of tents" and simply being "mingled with the elements," as the naturalists believed; he added, however,

> such was not his faith,
> Nor mine: it may be he had trod
> Outside the plain old path of *God thus spake,*
> But God to him was very God.[83]

"God to him was very God"—this was the perfect epitaph for Agassiz, and it would have done nearly as well for Lowell. No compromise could satisfy him. Notwithstanding his concessions to the geological record and his recognition of the attractive aspects of the new evolutionary faith, he uttered the simple truth of his own stand when he wrote on Christmas day, 1886: "I am a conservative (warranted to wash) and keep on the safe side—with God as against evolution."[84] He had never admitted the material origin of man, and the evolution of animal species might or might not be true—it was quite irrelevant to his central faith in the good and the holy.

VIII

TAYLOR AND LANIER: THE ROMANTIC EVOLUTIONISM AGAIN

1

EVEN in jest, neither Bayard Taylor nor Sidney Lanier would ever have said, as Lowell did, that he feared science as a savage does writing, for fear it would hurt him somehow. Lanier was as thorough and serious a student of the sciences as his many interests and limited span of life permitted, and though it is impossible to say as much of Taylor, he too was uniformly curious and respectful toward them.[1] He gave the muse Urania a prominent place in his drama of universal history, *Prince Deukalion,* and his journalist's keenness for the up to date kept him always in touch with the more popular scientific developments. As a young man in the 1840's, he passed through a wave of enthusiasm for phrenology and animal magnetism;[2] later Alexander von Humboldt became, next to Goethe, his chief admiration;[3] when he visited Tennyson in 1857, they talked geology as well as poetry, religion, and politics;[4] and three years before Taine developed the point in his *History of English Literature,* he lectured on the influence of climate on man's development.[5] Thus it is not surprising that when the controversy over evolution began to wax warm in the late sixties and early seventies, he turned to that. In a column of literary news that he conducted in *Putnam's Magazine* in 1869-70 he noticed several evolutionary volumes,[6] and in the extensive reading that ushered in what one of his biographers has termed his third and most thoughtful period, Darwin held a place. He wrote a friend in March, 1871:

I have been reading "Ecce Homo" and Darwin lately, and am full of all sorts of prohibited doubts, for which God be thanked!—since doubt is always the first step toward knowledge.[7]

A few months later he wrote *The Masque of the Gods,* a philosophic drama, which, along with *Prince Deukalion,* was his principal contribution to the literature of evolution.

power of entering into the feelings of the animals. This is an element which science will not accept; hence I doubt whether her deductions may not fall as far short of the truth as a vivid imagination may go beyond it. To me, it is very clear that there is at least a rudimentary moral sense in animals.[10]

Taylor had no intention of defining a theory of evolution in this article, but his preoccupation with a "moral sense" gives us a valuable hint. He was less concerned with the physical than with the moral and spiritual sides of life. A zealous moral idealist, he was not so much interested in the mechanics of evolution as in a principle of betterment that he believed to be at the very heart of things and that might be seen working itself out not only in nature but in the history of man.

If we look for traces of an evolutionary outlook in Taylor's earlier work, we find hints of this principle. "The Continents" (1848), for example, sounds once again the inevitable glories of America's future,[11] and "Metempsychosis of the Pine" (1851) tells of the poet's sense of a past existence going back to primeval chaos and progressing through his incarnation as a pine, when his first music was made by the rustling of the wind in his boughs.[12] The theme was not fully developed, however, until the writing of the philosophic dramas in the seventies. There was much of the utopianism of Shelley in these plays and an equal measure of the generally diffused Victorian hope that somehow good will be the final goal of ill; but the chief influence seems to have come from Taylor's studies in German literature. He had begun these studies early, but they culminated at the beginning of this last period of his development in his translation of *Faust,* which is today his best-remembered work. As we have seen, German literature and philosophy during Goethe's later years were rife with the idea of the progressive realization of spiritual values. In France, the idea of progress was concerned only with the attainment of personal liberty, social happiness, and material comfort and security; but in Germany it was directed toward the fulfillment of a World-Soul or universal spirit. As we shall see, there was something of this philosophy in *Prince Deukalion,* though it was derived less from the philosophers than from the men of letters. Taylor learned rather from Lessing, Herder, and Goethe than from Schelling and Hegel. The two dramas, in fact, bear a striking resemblance to progressive conceptions advanced by the first two of these writers.

Lessing's *Education of the Human Race* (1780) has been described as "an account of how the world received and is still receiving revelation that is to prepare man for the attainment of the best that is in him";[13] and this might stand as a statement of the theme of *The Masque of the Gods,* which Taylor himself explained as follows to Thomas Bailey Aldrich:

I'll tell you what I chiefly meant. The gradual development of man's conception of God: first a colossal reflection of human powers and passions, mixed with the dread inspired by the unknown forces of nature; then, the idea of Law (Elohim), or Order and Beauty and Achievement (love and Apollo), and of the principles of Good and Evil (Persian), and of the Divine Love (Christ).

But now over all is the ONE supreme Spirit, yet unnamed, and whom men only now begin to conceive of,—the God of whom all previous gods gave only faint and various reflections,—to whom Christ is still nearest, but who was also felt, more or less dimly, in all creeds. The poem is not *un*christian at all, but, in its relation to the conventional orthodox ideas, *over*christian.[14]

But if Taylor owed anything to Lessing in the conception of *The Masque,* he was able, with increased knowledge of anthropology and the history of religion, to enlarge considerably upon his original. Lessing limited himself almost entirely to the history of the Old and New Testaments, but Taylor began with Perun, Baal, Manito, and Odin, and allowed most of the principal deities of human history to speak during the course of the three scenes of the play. The last and most significant scene begins with a song in which the theme of the play is stated: "The Deities die when their work is done";[15] and ends with the appearance of Immanuel, who addresses the unnamed One in a speech ending, "Thou art Love!" To this a Voice from Space replies:

> Thou art my one begotten Son, in whom
> I am well pleased.[16]

E. C. Stedman objected justifiably that this was inconsistent with the theme of the play and not only jarred upon the artistic and rationalistic senses, but did not suit the Philistines either;[17] but it is clear from the letter to Aldrich that in spite of his phrasing Taylor meant no more than that Christ was nearest to the Supreme Being.

During the whole pageant, Man has stood by, listening and only now and then interpolating a comment, but he is allowed the privilege of the last full speech, summing up his position in this newer "Education of the Human Race." Far from making merely "a twice-told tale of God," his growing knowledge of nature has, he believes, rendered his conception of God more exalted and sublime:

>   All we learn
> From delving in the marrow of the Earth,
> From scattering thought among the timeless stars,
> From slow-deciphered hieroglyphs of power
> In chemic forces, planetary paths,
> Or primal cells whence all Thy worlds are born,
> But lifts Thee higher, seats Thee more august,
> Till Thou art grown so vast and wonderful,
> We dare not name Thee, scarce dare pray to Thee.

Moreover, time will bring a more perfect revelation. Man begs:

> Chide us not: be patient; we
> Are children still, we were mistaken oft,
> Yet we believe that in some riper time
> Thy perfect Truth shall come.

A Voice from Space replies: "Wait! Ye shall know."[18]

If *The Masque* resembles Lessing's tractate, *Prince Deukalion* is more like Herder's larger work, *Ideas toward a Philosophy of the History of Mankind*, which, in Taylor's own words,

> traces the upward tendency, the preparation for a higher spiritual life, through all the varied forms of civilization, and infers the existence of a sublime progressive destiny, of which all our past history is a part.[19]

In choosing to present this upward struggle in terms of the Prometheus legend, Taylor joined a large company of the poets of his time,[20] but he departed from the usual handling of the theme by centering interest around Prometheus' two protégés, Deukalion and Pyrrha. These two symbolize Man and Woman and are taken on a journey through time from 300 A. D. to an indeterminate date in the future, in the course of which the poet is enabled to play the part of critic of past and present and prophet of the future. The first act, which serves rather as a point of departure than a stage in the historical thesis, has as its principal event the visit of Deukalion and Pyrrha to Hades in search of Prometheus. Deukalion is troubled by doubts, and asks Prometheus, ". . . shall thy meditated plans . . . prevail at last?"[21] Prometheus' reply is that, by virtue of the will that he has implanted in man and the love that the mother of Pyrrha has implanted in woman, they shall. Before sending them on their journey, however, he provides them with two guides, Epimetheus (afterthought, knowledge) and Eos (hope, vision); and in the last scene of the act, as the little group looks eastward from the highest verge of the tableland of Hades, Eos tells the two wanderers that "thou and she, inheritors of holy destiny"[22] shall earn the distant glory, but only by unfailing aspiration amid unremitting disappointment.

The next two acts present the medieval and modern stages in this troubled progress, and shed light on Taylor's attitude toward the sciences through the fortunes of the Muse Urania. Medusa, or the Church, is the villainess of the medieval scenes, and though she is warned by a Voice, "Growth is the law,—or death!"[23] she refuses Urania the freedom she allows the other Muses and orders her to be seized. Urania makes her escape, however, and in the next and last scene counsels Epimetheus: "Learn what to ask, I give."[24] Deukalion is much pleased with Urania, and foreshadows later developments when he orders Epimetheus:

> Go, Epimetheus, sunward,
> And seek thy childhood in the dust of ages!
> Burrow in buried fanes: wash clean the altars,
> And spell forgotten words on mouldering marble.
> Perchance thy limbs shall fail, thy lids be weary,
> And thou shalt sleep; fear not, I will awaken!
> Thy brother's words fulfil: "Take one new comfort,
> Still Epimetheus lives!" and now the morning
> Shall not withhold the unseen eyes of Eos![25]

This passage foreshadows more than just the scientific developments of later times, however; for Epimetheus is more than the servant of Urania, and at the end of the next act, laid in the nineteenth century, he turns against her. The significance of Epimetheus is not immediately apparent in all its aspects, but Mrs. Hansen-Taylor's note on the first appearance of the line quoted by Deukalion, "Take one new comfort, still Epimetheus lives!"[26] gives valuable assistance. It reads:

For those who have been following the wonderful progress of human knowledge, the lighting up of dark ages, in our own days, it ought not to be difficult to see what is meant in Epimetheus. A long vista into the Past has been opened before our amazed eyes by discoveries and researches, until we see our race almost young again. But Epimetheus is not merely an intellectual force: he is also an ethical power. If Prometheus—will, aspiration, genius—leads us onward and upward, Epimetheus, through perception of and insight into all that is past without us and within us, gives us self-knowledge, which is the awakening of the soul—its rejuvenescence.[27]

Since, then, Epimetheus represents a humanistic knowledge of self that is attained through the study of the past, it is quite understandable that he should turn on Urania when, taking a handful of dust, she proclaims, "I have found in this the secret of all worlds";[28] and that he should then force her to acknowledge the limits of her powers. Beset by his charges, she cries,

> Cease!—thy words renew the chill
> That seizes me at each new victory.
> The cry of old affections shakes my hand;
> The gush of human heart's-blood comes to dim
> My crystal eyesight; and a something lost,
> Because unsought, perchance unsearchable,—
> Unknown, because unknowable to sense,
> Assails my right.[29]

Urania's position in the play remains an honored one, but she is thus brought to admit the presumption of her claim to the whole truth. Epimetheus has discovered a deeper truth than the truth of the dust—an "equal truth revealed to them that seek"[30]—the announcement of which heralds the enlightenment of the future, which is depicted in the last act.

The central personage in this act is Agathon, a child, who may be said to represent Taylor's ideal of human development in being equally at peace with the physical and spiritual sides of life.[31] In token of his double enlightenment, Agathon counters the arrogance of Urania by an appeal to Love, and, in a manner reminiscent of *The Masque,* dismisses the older teachers of men—Buddha, Medusa, Calchas—in favor of a higher wisdom. In scene two, with great significance, Deukalion removes from the altar all except the Cross, the symbol of self-sacrifice, and causes to be placed above and below it a star and a sphere, the symbols of knowledge. Love and wisdom—these were the twin goals endlessly sought in the progress that Taylor envisaged: "endlessly," because this last act is not to be regarded as a blueprint of man's final stage, but as a vision of the direction in which the principle of perfection that is at the heart of things is leading him. This is the message of Prometheus' last speech, the following six lines of which were engraved on the reverse of the medallion on Taylor's grave:

> For Life, whose source not here began,
> Must fill the utmost sphere of Man,
> And, so expanding, lifted be
> Along the line of God's decree,
> To find in endless growth all good,—
> In endless toil, beatitude.[32]

These lines not only contain the heart of the play, but in their appeal to the "temporalized" principle of "plenitude," serve to place Taylor in the sequence of ideas being traced in this study. The logic of this principle, it will be recalled, was as follows: the perfection of the Creator demands that all conceivable kinds of being should exist; but there is a great gap between the most perfect conceivable beings and those which now exist; therefore, the creation must be regarded as continuing in the direction of the perfection that will bring about the final fullness. Plainly, this was not the evolutionism of Darwin, but rather a version of that transcendental evolutionism that was discussed in the chapters on Emerson, Poe, and Whitman and that had its origin in the idealisms of the Germans.

Moreover, since he regarded the principle of development as universal, Taylor applied it to man as an individual as well as to man collectively. In the discussion here of the two dramas the emphasis has been on the progress of the species, but *Prince Deukalion* was devoted equally to the progress of the individual soul, both in this life and after death. It was, in fact, the opinion of Taylor's biographer, A. H. Smyth, that immortality was the "central fire"[33] burning in this play, and the pertinence to the theme of a future life of the lines just quoted from Prometheus' last speech is plain from their presence on Taylor's grave. Like others who have been discussed in earlier chapters, Taylor believed that the scientific conception of the universe, with its principles of conservation and evolution, at least gave support to the doctrine of the undying continuance and development of the soul. In the last act of *Prince Deukalion,* thus, when Urania demanded of Agathon, "Why, to flatter life, wilt thou repeat the unproven solace?" 'Agathon replied not only by advancing the arguments of "justice" and the "promises of love," but by an appeal to the science of Urania herself:

> Yea, by thy law!—since every being holds
> Its final purpose in the primal cell,
> And here the radiant destiny o'erflows
> Its visible bounds, enlarges what it took
> From sources past discovery, and predicts
> No end, or, if an end, the end of all![34]

These lines may be glossed by a passage referring to them in a letter to Paul Hamilton Hayne:

The very wisdom and wonder of the universe and its laws prove conclusively to me that the intuitions of power and knowledge in ourselves, which we cannot fulfill here, *assure us* of continued being. . . . I can conceive the Infinite much more easily than I can the Finite; I *know* (but I cannot demonstrate) that my being cannot be annihilated. This feeling is in accordance with all that science teaches me; if I depended on theology alone I should have little comfort. If the Divine Law manifest in matter be good, we shall live on,—*we must:* if there is no future for me, a Devil, and not a God, governs the universe. *Dixi!*[35]

This was the furthest reach of that evolutionary faith which, compounded of the theory of progress of the Enlightenment, transcendental meliorism, and the evolutionary views of science, was one of the bonds between Taylor and Lanier. Lanier gave it the name "etherealization" and developed it much more elaborately on the theoretical side than Taylor. It is significant, as well as curious, that Lanier devoted seven pages to *Prince Deukalion* in his work on *The English Novel* and represented it as an advance, philosophically, on the handling of the Prometheus theme by Aeschylus and Shelley.

2

Lanier was much closer to the sciences than Taylor. Taylor, after all, knew science only casually and was less concerned with evolution in nature than with historical progress. Lanier, however, in his feverish zeal to take all knowledge for his province, applied himself strenuously to scientific study whenever opportunity offered, and attempted to absorb the methods and results of science into his critical and creative work. We are told that in Baltimore he conducted experiments in sound, did "good hard work" with a borrowed microscope,[36] and appealed ambitiously to President Gilman of Johns Hopkins for a fellowship to study not only French and German literature but the physics of musical tone and "a thoroughly scientific *general* view of Mineralogy, Botany, and Comparative Anatomy."[37] Also, with more precise pertinence to the interests of this study, Professor Mims has testified to having seen "a copy of the 'Origin of Species' owned by Lanier—the marks and annotations indicating the most careful and thoughtful reading thereof."[38] Lanier had been introduced to the sciences by Professor James Woodrow during his student days at Oglethorpe and had imbibed much of this fine teacher's enthusiasm for learning and his conviction that there was no essential conflict between science and the humanistic disciplines.[39] As early as *Tiger-Lilies* (1867) Lanier ridiculed the notion, associated with the name of Macaulay, that poetry must decline as science flourishes,[40] and one of the most emphatically stated themes of his later writing was that science and poetry are complementary rather than antagonistic. All existence is a "congeries of forms," and science but "the knowledge of these forms," art "the creation of beautiful forms," and religion "the faith in the infinite Form-giver and in that infinity of forms which many things lead us to believe as existing, but existing beyond any present correlative capacities of our senses."[41] This was the basis of Lanier's critical principle that there is a science as well as an art of painting, music, and verse, and of his belief—more important for our purposes—that science, as the eyes and ears by which we know nature, is "quartermaster and commissary"[42] to poetry and indispensable to the poet who would write meaningfully for a sophisticated age. Science, he contended, was only ordinary sensory knowledge carried into areas hidden to the unaided senses, and in a time when these regions had become a part of the common country of the mind, they could not safely be disregarded by the poet. This he stated flatly in *The English Novel:*

And here I cannot help adding to what was said on this subject in the last lecture, by declaring to every young man who may entertain the hope of poethood, that at this stage of the world you need not dream of winning the attention of sober people with your poetry unless that poetry, and your soul behind it, are informed and saturated at least with the largest final conception of current science.⁴³

Lanier erected the same defense against the materialism and positivism of science, however, as was erected by all the nineteenth-century transcendentalists. Like Whitman he uttered hurrahs for positive science, but added that, excellent as it was, science was not his dwelling but only an entrance to an area of his dwelling. According to his definition, science did not encompass the "infinite Form-giver," or—at least yet—that "infinity of forms" lying beyond the present capacities of our senses. Moreover, in other statements, he was even more firm about the limits of scientific knowledge, stating, like Spencer and other phenomenalists back to Kant, that in all inquiry there is always an unknowable residuum. "What we call explanation in science," he said, "is at bottom only a reduction of unfamiliar mysteries to terms of familiar mysteries."⁴⁴ Spencer recognized this realm of mystery only in order to dismiss it, but to Lanier, as to transcendentalists in general, it was all-important. Despite all his praise of science and his veneration of nature, Lanier remained a religious poet in the sense that his ultimate appeal was always to a Power beyond phenomena, and he never hesitated to point out the shortcomings of science as a revelation of truth. In "Acknowledgment," for example, he arraigned the times as

> Blinking at o'er-bright Science, smit with desire
> To see and not to see,⁴⁵

and in his poem on the death of Taylor he spoke of "the shame of science that cannot prove proof is."⁴⁶ His favorite device, however, was to ask the questions that science cannot answer. Thus, because he held that life remains a mystery, he asked concerning the mocking-bird:

> Sweet Science, this large riddle read me plain:
> How may the death of that dull insect be
> The life of yon trim Shakspere on the tree?⁴⁷

And because, even more, he believed that the soul of man defies analysis, he asked in "The Symphony":

> For I, e'en I,
> As here I lie,
> A petal on a harmony,

> Demand of Science whence and why
> Man's tender pain, man's inward cry
> When he doth gaze on earth and sky?[48]

Lanier believed that the naturalistic evolutionisms of Darwin and Spencer were mistaken and presumptuous efforts to answer just such questions as these; for, as he understood them, the essence of these theories was that all phenomena are inexorably determined by "precedent conditions." This conception he rejected vigorously, of course, and he took the opportunity of making his point in commenting in *The English Novel* on the statement of a critic that the novels of George Eliot were merely an application of the principles of Spencer to the portrayal of character:

> This seems to me so far from being true that many of George Eliot's characters appear like living objections to the theory of evolution. How could you, according to this theory, evolve the moral stoutness and sobriety of Adam Bede, for example, from *his* precedent conditions, to wit, his drunken father and querulous mother? How could you evolve the intensity and intellectual alertness of Maggie Tulliver from *her* precedent conditions, to wit, a flaccid mother, and a father wooden by nature and sodden by misfortune? Though surely influenced by circumstances her characters everywhere seem to flout evolution in the face.[49]

That he should have insisted on this point in this work was to be expected, for his subject was only nominally the novel and really the principle of autonomous selfhood as it had been expressed in literature with increasing explicitness from Aeschylus to George Eliot. The subtitle of the work is "A Study in the Development of Personality," and its governing principle is laid down in the beginning in these words: "I shall insist with the utmost reverence that between every human being and every other human being exists a radical, unaccountable, inevitable difference from birth."[50] It is a matter of some curiosity, however, that he then illustrated this criticism of evolution by an article on "Sociology and Hero-Worship" by John Fiske,[51] in which it was stated that under the Darwinian theory a genius is a "spontaneous variation" in the same sense as a moth born with a proboscis of twice the average length. One would think that such an appeal by a bona fide evolutionist to an element of chance would have caused Lanier to reconsider his rigidly deterministic understanding of the theory. It appears, however, that he preferred to persist in his interpretation and to regard this appeal as an evidence of failure. Not only does the comment on George Eliot and Spencer come at the end of his book, long after he had taken Fiske's views into account, but the terms in which he paraphrases Fiske in the earlier passage are practically identical with those which he represents in the later passage as "living objections to the theory of evolution": " . . . there [are] absolutely no precedent conditions by which the most ardent evolutionist could evolve William Shakspere, for example, from old John Shakspere and his wife."[52] It is clear that Lanier understood Darwin and Spencer to be determinists and that he rejected them on that ground.

In this jealous guardianship of personal identity and autonomy, moreover, Lanier did not address himself to the scientific evolutionists alone, but also challenged the pantheists and absolute idealists. In "The Crystal,"[53] for example, he criticized his revered Emerson as

> Most wise that yet, in finding Wisdom, lost
> Thy Self, sometimes,

and elsewhere he was specific in his avoidance of Emerson's error. Thus, in "A Florida Sunday"[54] he told

> How All's in each, yet every one of all
> Maintains his Self complete and several,

and in "Individuality"[55] he summarized his position succinctly in these words:

> My Lord is large, my Lord is strong:
> Giving, he gave: my me is mine.

This poem, in fact, is not only one of Lanier's strongest statements of the independence of the individual, but, when read in the light of a letter to J. F. Kirk, demonstrates the part played by this conviction in his opposition to evolution. In the poem, after the writer has belabored a cloud for visiting its lightning on those who deserve better, the cloud retorts:

> *What the cloud doeth*
> *The Lord knoweth,*
> *The cloud knoweth not.*
> *What the artist doeth*

The Lord knoweth:
Knoweth the artist not?

To this the poet then rejoins:

Well answered!—O dear artists, ye
—Whether in forms of curve or hue
Or tone your gospels be—
Say wrong This work is not of me,
But God: it is not true, it is not true.

In the letter to Kirk, Lanier told of his studies in biology, chemistry, and evolution, and of the dreams with which the "enormous modern generalizations" had filled him, but then went on to point out the error into which the evolutionists had fallen through their neglect of the idiocratic character of living beings:

But it is precisely at the beginning of that phenomenon which is the underlying subject of this poem, "Individuality," that the largest of such generalizations must begin, and the doctrine of evolution when pushed beyond this point appears to me, after the most careful examination of the evidence to fail. It is pushed beyond this point in its current application to the genesis of species, and I think Mr. Huxley's last sweeping declaration is clearly parallel to that of an enthusiastic dissector, who, forgetting that his observations are upon dead bodies, should build a physiological conclusion upon purely anatomical facts.[56]

He conceded that "for whatever can be proved to have been evolved," evolution was "a noble and beautiful and true theory," but added that he knew of no case of species differentiation supported by evidence that would stand "the first shot of a boy lawyer in a moot court." He concluded, in explication of his poem: "A cloud (see the poem) *may* be evolved; but not an artist; and I find, in looking over my poem, that it has made itself into a passionate reaffirmation of the artist's autonomy, threatened alike from the direction of the scientific fanatic and the pantheistic devotee."

Plainly, Lanier was stoutly opposed to any theory of evolution that seemed to imply that living beings are wholly explicable in terms of "precedent conditions," whether those conditions are of heredity, environment, or the immanent action of God. He may be shown, however, to have accepted evolution in a less exacting sense. Thus, on one page of *The English Novel* he followed

Spencer in defining evolution as "a process from the uniform and indefinite to the multiform and definite,"[57] and on another he agreed that "all accounts, the scientific, the religious, the historical, agree that the progress of things is from chaos or formlessness to form,—and, as we saw in the case of verse and prose,—afterwards from the one-formed to the many-formed."[58] Evolution in this sense, in fact, was the theme of this whole work, in which Lanier sought to show that cultural history since the time of the Greeks, and especially since the Renaissance, has consisted in the liberation and differentiation of individual personality. "My first line," he wrote in one of his opening pages,

will concern itself with the enormous growth in . . . this sacred difference between man and man, by virtue of which I am I and you are you, this marvellous separation which we express by the terms "personal identity," "self-hood," "me,"—it is the unfolding of this, I shall insist, which since the time of Aeschylus (say) has wrought all those stupendous changes in the relation of man to God, to physical nature, and to his fellow, which have culminated in the modern culture.[59]

In earlier times, according to this theory, men had feared God, physical nature, and their fellows, and had shrunk away from them; but as time went on they gained confidence and sought to repair the disunion. In the Renaissance and afterward, a new yearning for the Unknown found expression in the development of music, a new curiosity about nature found expression in the advance of natural science, and a new sympathy among men found expression in the rise of the novel—whence the title and subject of the work. All this was the result of an expansion of the soul, an extension of the "scope and sovereignty" of the ego; and this in turn was a special case of the process of "etherealization," which Lanier found in all things.

The principle of "etherealization" was not new to Lanier when he lectured on the novel in 1881, but had been outlined as early as 1867 in the essay "Retrospects and Prospects." There he took his departure from the old problem of how long it would take to go a given distance if every three steps forward were followed by two backward; for that, he added, is the way of the world. Soul and sense are the two basic antagonistic forces in the world, and though soul is the more powerful it is continually restrained by sense, which it overcomes and transmutes only slowly and fitfully. This, in brief, was the doctrine of etherealization, which he defined as follows:

> As time flows on, the sense-kingdom continually decreases, and the soul-kingdom continually increases, and this not by the destruction of sense's subjects, but by a system of promotions in which sensuous things . . . constantly acquire the dignity of spiritual things, and so diminish their own number and increase the other.[60]

Such a thesis, like all radical theories of progress, was difficult to substantiate in detail, and in his enthusiasm Lanier allowed himself to fall into the absurdity of praising photography and the sculptural groups of Rogers at the expense of the painting and sculpture of an older day. Nevertheless, he carried his scheme boldly into many fields and applied it briefly to religion, politics, and all of the major arts. Most interesting for our purposes, however, was its application to the history of nature, in which Lanier drew about equally on the Romantic poets and the evolutionary geologists:

> Nature, in that fine ramble of hers along the shore of the great deep (a ramble which we call Time), has been good enough to write and strew along the sand at intervals short monographs of autobiography which remain for our reading. These quaint epistles of Nature . . . all breathe one tone in respect of the constant etherealizing process which she has been undergoing. He who collates her earliest letters with her latest will discover that whereas she was a stormy virago of sixty, she has now been magically rejuvenated and is become marvellously like a gentle and dainty-fingered maiden of sixteen. What Frederic von Hardenberg has called the "old Titanic times" of Nature, "in which all objects lay strewn about the earth like the remains of a terrific repast;" times in which . . . land, air, and water were horrible with megatherium and pterodactyl and ichthyosaurus,—these times are gone: things are less hideous, and behave more gently.[61]

This, moreover, was not just a random illustration, but an expression of the writer's profound conviction that the principle of etherealization is universal and therefore to be found alike in the history of man and nature. Thus, it is repeated in *The English Novel:*

> Even from out the ancient Titanic times of geological convulsion . . . , times when nature as if in a nightmare swarms with the great

Saurians and grotesque forms that make terrible the air and the oozy earth— . . . even from out these times a vast cone of shadow seems to project itself and to extend far beyond the time when nature's mood itself has become more gentle, when instead of the pterodactyl she gives us the antelope, and instead of tree-fern and club-moss she gives us the lily and the rose.[62]

And, again, in *Shakspere and His Forerunners:*

Go back to the old Devonian and Jurassic times. What gigantic and monstrous forms of lizards and winged reptiles loom over the land! . . .
But recalling your thoughts down again along the path of geologic time to the modern period, all is changed. The mood of nature has become finer and sweeter. . . .[63]

Pursuing this visionary hypothesis, Lanier came to the conclusion that parallel lines of etherealization in man and nature had met and reached a point of culmination in the nature-love of the nineteenth century:

. . . this veneration for Nature has within the last century come to be the most prominent Fact, to my mind, in the history of the modern man, and to-day it has two sides, or phases.
Here are thousands upon thousands of acute and patient men to-day who are devoutly gazing into the great mysteries of Nature and faithfully reporting what they see. . . .
But, beside the phase of Nature-communion which we call physical science, there is the other artistic phase. . . .[64]

These two phases, moreover, reinforced each other. "The hearer of the Seventh Symphony last night," he wrote elsewhere, " . . . will find himself at the verge of a whole new field of appreciation . . . if he will remember that the same era which produced Maillet, Darwin, Spencer, Huxley, and Tyndall has produced also Beethoven in music and the landscape school in painting."[65] Love and harmony were the basis of Lanier's philosophy and the goal of "etherealization," and this new brotherly relationship between man and nature was one of their manifestations. Just as nature had become more gentle through the passage of aeons, man had grown more trusting and sensitive with the passing of centuries, with the result that "the modern personality can love nature directly as a man loves his friend; when this love formulates itself in observing the facts of nature, classifying them, we have a Newton, a Darwin."[66]

This was undiluted romanticism, and further examination reveals that just as there was more of Lessing and Herder than Darwin in Taylor, so there was less of Darwin in Lanier than of Emerson and a second-hand *Naturphilosophie*. The struggle of soul and sense, for example, recalls Emerson's opposition of Power and Circumstance, and the problem of the three steps forward and two backward suggests Schelling's conception of nature as "self-activity . . . in two directions, one forward or positive, the other backward or negative."[67] Everywhere Lanier found conflicting opposites merging, as in music, into the rhythm and harmony that he believed to be the essence and ideal of all existence. "Music," a character in *Tiger-Lilies* said, "means harmony, harmony means love, and love means God."[68] Lanier seems to have owed something of this idea to Poe, whose striking comparison of "the outsending and inbringing of the worlds" to the beating of the heart of God he singled out for praise on two occasions;[69] and to Spencer, in whose analysis of the place of antagonism and rhythm in nature he was greatly interested.[70] It went deeper than this, however, to the persistent effort of many of the great Romantic thinkers to interpret life in terms of art. Like theirs, Lanier's philosophy was largely esthetic in inspiration. Briefly, he perceived the conflict and harmonizing of opposite impulses to be the essence of the arts he knew best, music and verse, and he expanded this observation into a universal antagonism of soul and sense culminating in a perfect harmony of life.[71]

This conception also takes us back to the Schellingesque and Emersonian conception of evil as a necessary condition of the good. Many times in past pages it has been pointed out how intimately this idea was bound up with the Romantic theory of evolution, and in Lanier's handling of the problem the relation was no less close. It is perhaps simple logic that without evil good could not be known, but the adherents of the Romantic theory went further and asserted that evil plays an active part in the production of any moral progress. Progress, they contended, is like climbing a flight of steps: it is impossible without the resistance of the steps, and it is achieved only by constantly contending against and overcoming that resistance. As was evident in his illustration of the three steps forward and two backward, Lanier likewise believed that the resistance between soul and sense, and their harmonizing, constituted not only the rhythm and beauty of life but the process of its progress or "etherealization" as well.

This may be seen partly in the most Emersonian of his poems, "Opposition,"[72] containing the lines,

> Of fret, of dark, of thorn, of chill,
>   Complain no more; for these, O heart,
> Direct the random of the will
>   As rhymes direct the rage of art.

It is most fully apparent, however, in "Clover,"[73] which is concerned primarily with the place of death in the scheme of things. Lying idly in a field of clover on a summer's day, the poet asks:

> Tell me, dear Clover . . . .
>   . . .
>
> Of what avail, this color and this grace?
> Wert thou but squat of stem and brindle-brown,
> Still careless herds would feed.

Shortly afterward, the prospect widens and becomes a vision in which the clover blooms appear as the heads of the artists of the past; but then:

>   Lo, what bulk is here?
> Now comes the Course-of-things, shaped like an Ox,
> Slow-browsing, o'er my hillside, ponderously—
> The huge-brawned, tame, and workful Course-of-things,
> That hath his grass, if earth be round or flat,
> And hath his grass, if empires plunge in pain
> Or faiths flash out. This cool, unasking Ox
> Comes browsing o'er my hills and vales of Time,
> And thrusts me out his tongue, and curls it, sharp,
> And sicklewise, about my poets' heads,
> And twists them in, all—Dante, Keats, Chopin,
> Raphael, Lucretius, Omar, Angelo,
> Beethoven, Chaucer, Schubert, Shakespeare, Bach,
> And Buddha, in one sheaf—and champs and chews,
> With slantly-churning jaws, and swallows down;
> Then slowly plants a mighty forefoot out,
> And makes advance to futureward, one inch.
> So: they have played their part.

But, the poet pleads, can the end of things be only the feeding of this brute? "This was all? This Ox?"

> "Nay," quoth a sum of voices in mine ear,
> "God's clover, we, and feed his Course-of-things;
> The pasture is God's pasture; systems strange
> Of food and fibrement He hath, whereby
> The general brawn is built for plans of His
> To quality precise. . . ."

This was Lanier's parable of progress: the living clover had to perish in order that God's Course-of-things might put one foot forward.

Thus the tragic plodding of events was not truly tragic, for one might look forward to that distant moment in progress when the perfect balance, the perfect harmony, would be struck, and evil would disappear. In a faithful rendering of the theory this would perhaps be a kind of Nirvana, involving the disappearance of life as well as of evil,[74] but Lanier, as a son of his age, was on occasion inclined to give it a temporal setting. Thus in his paean of American greatness, "Psalm of the West," he sang:

> Freedom, thy Wife, hath uplifted thy life and clean
>   shriven thee!
>   . . .
> For Weakness, in freedom, grows stronger than Strength
>   with a chain;
> And Error, in freedom will come to lamenting his stain,
>   . . .
> And Science be known as the sense making love to the All,
> And Art be known as the soul making love to the All,
> And Love be known as the marriage of man with the All—
>   Till Science to knowing the Highest shall lovingly turn,
>   Till Art to loving the Highest shall consciously burn,
>   Till Science to Art as a man to a woman shall yearn,
>   —Then morn!
> When Faith from the wedding of Knowing and Loving shall
>   purely be born,
> And the Child shall smile in the West, and the West to the
>   East give morn,
> And the Time in that ultimate Prime shall forget old regretting
>   and scorn,
> Yea, the stream of the light shall give off in a shimmer the
>   dream of the night forlorn.[75]

IX

HOLMES: EVOLUTION WITHOUT TRANSFORMISM?

SEVERAL circumstances conspire to give more than usual interest to the contributions of Oliver Wendell Holmes to the discussion of evolution. Not only did he speak with the knowledge of a professional scientist and the deep concern of a fervent amateur in theology, but there is sufficient ambiguity in his statements to give rise to a question of interpretation. Some readers, impressed by the sympathetic comments in his later writings, have identified him more or less closely with the followers of Darwin. Parrington, if I read a difficult sentence aright, says that he "followed Darwin,"[1] and Professor Harry Hayden Clark that he was "taught by Darwinian evolution."[2] Others, detecting a certain vagueness in his remarks, have treated the whole question with prudent inconclusiveness. The truth seems to be that, while he was undoubtedly an evolutionist, he was extremely chary of Darwinism. For one thing, even in the sympathetic comments referred to above he carefully avoided committing himself concerning the peculiarly Darwinian aspects of evolution. For another, he had been an evolutionist before *The Origin of Species,* and in quite un-Darwinian fashion. He early accepted the geological record at its face value, and in 1857, two years before the appearance of Darwin's epoch-making work, he set forth in some detail a theory of the origin of species of his own that differed radically from Darwin's. Since the purpose here is to define his views on evolution and to investigate their backgrounds, a sensible procedure will be to examine these pre-Darwinian speculations first, and then to consider the later comments with a view to discovering what modifications, if any, they introduced.

1

In reviewing four books on physics and biology in the July, 1857, issue of the *North American Review,*[3] Holmes took the opportunity to set forth his views on the whole question of the nature of life and vital action. As an anatomist and physiologist, he was primarily interested in structure and process, but the consideration of these matters led him in the end to the problem of origins, which presented itself to him in the following way. The fossil record seemed to show that in the remote past the development of new forms of life had been a part of the regular order of things, but since there was no authentic evidence that living beings had ever arisen except from other living beings of the same kind, it was difficult to see how this could have occurred. Earlier evolutionists from Lamarck to Chambers had advanced the theory that variations in offspring had accumulated until a new species was produced, but Holmes was thoroughly convinced of the fixity of species and therefore could not accept this solution of the problem. He had observed, however, not only that the chemical constituents of living and nonliving matter are the same but also that we daily witness "the combination of pre-existing elements, and the development of new properties in the resulting compounds,"[4] and on this as a basis he concluded that new species might have arisen directly out of nonliving elements by a process of spontaneous generation. This process he described as the "evolution of life by means of the existing forces of nature, setting in different degree or intensity from the present ordinary mode of operation."[5]

This hypothesis he then elaborated, first in the vegetable[6] and then in the animal kingdom, by a series of presumptions. He began by observing that within the experience of man vast quantities of carbon have been extracted from the atmosphere and stored in solid form in the bodies of plants, and from this observation he inferred that in the time before the existence of plants the soil and atmosphere must have constituted "a saturated solution of the elements of vegetable organisms." If in this state, he then supposed, some "natural, but exceptional" change of condition had occurred—a violent change of temperature, for example—it might have brought about the precipitation of "living crystals" in the form of some such simple vegetation as grass. With the original solution reduced by this first precipitation, later precipitations would necessarily take different forms and would probably be "more slowly formed, more complex, a higher vegetable growth." This hypothesis, however, requiring plants to spring full-grown from the brow of Nature, was extremely implausible, and Holmes immediately modified it by the introduction of an intermediate stage. Instead of the finished organism emerging directly from its elements, the first step was now but the production of an "indifferent germ," itself unformed, but endowed with a "general organizing principle" and subject to a "local determining one" that should work with the other to determine the ultimate form of the plant. It was much easier to conceive of the spontaneous generation of the seed of a plant than of the plant itself.

In accounting for the origin of animal life[7] Holmes was much more cautious, omitting all details concerning the process of precipitation and presenting only two sketchy possibilities. Since plant life is necessary for the support of animal life and must therefore have originated first, he leaned toward the theory that animal life evolved out of plant life, but he did not at the same time exclude the possibility of the direct generation of animal life out of its elements. It is conceivable, he stated—reasonable men have thought so, though they have failed to verify their hypotheses—that an "infusorial seed or ovum" might be formed "by the 'concourse of atoms,' guided by the Infinite Wisdom which we see every day grouping the same atoms about their living nuclei." If that be Lucretian, he added in effect, make the most of it.[8]

The first and most obvious comment to make on this theory is that it is not evolution in the usual and historically important sense. Evolution in this sense is the theory that later complex types have come into being through the modification and transformation of earlier and simpler types, but in Holmes's theory each species was separately generated out of nonliving matter. A good illustration of this is his explanation of the appearance of oak forests where only pine had grown before.[9] Since the acorn was too heavy to have been transported any distance by the wind, he reasoned that the seed of the new forest must have been formed directly by chemical combination in the soil. The oak, in other words, did not evolve out of other forms of arboreal life, but out of the earth itself. Holmes was well aware that such a theory presented difficulties, and he emphasized the fact that he was speaking only hypothetically. Still, however, he preferred it to the transformation theory, or "progressive development" as it was then called. Not once but twice he took special care that his theory should not be confused with the latter:

This hypothesis is by no means identical with that of progressive development. It supposes the existence of permanent types. . . . [10]

So difficult has the problem of the evolution of the higher animal forms appeared to speculative philosophers, that they have invented the theory of progressive development of the superior from the lower types. The sharp lines which separate species, as shown by observation of every organic form extinct as well as living, have caused this famous and seductive hypothesis to be very generally rejected as untenable.[11]

Plainly, in 1857 Holmes was not, as the author of *The Vestiges of Creation* had been a decade before, a rebel against the principle of immutability. As has been pointed out before in these pages, this principle was something like a dogma between the Cuvier-St. Hilaire controversy of 1830 and the acceptance of Darwin's work in the sixties, and it needed either great recklessness or strong conviction to defy it. Lacking either on this issue and yet strongly tempted by the geological record, Holmes attempted a compromise, which may be loosely described as midway between the positions of Chambers and Agassiz.

Another way in which Holmes's theory differed from the Darwinian was in its firm exclusion of the soul of man from the evolutionary series. At the very beginning of his essay, many pages before the question of origins made its appearance, he set himself the following limitation:

what we have to say must be considered as applying solely to the living body, and not to the divine emanation which, in the human form, seems but only seems, to identify itself for a while with the shape it uses.[12]

This is an important point, for it sets Holmes's views apart from the various monisms—idealistic, materialistic, neutral—toward which evolutionary theory tended. At least at this stage of his thinking, Holmes was a dualist in two related senses. In the first place, like the Critical Philosophers, he was well aware of the subject-object relationship in knowledge and of the difficulty of accounting for mind in terms of the world which it knows. We have "two ranges of mental vision," he said, which "should not be confused for good or bad":[13] our knowledge of the external world, which is knowledge of appearance only;[14] and our intuitions concerning our own moral and spiritual nature which are irresistibly compelling without being objectively verifiable.¹⁵ In the second place, Holmes distinguished "two, and only two,"¹⁶ great divisions in Creation, according to their relation to Deity. With the first, the world of general nature, God sustains only "active" relations, while with the second, man, he sustains "passive" as well as active relations. That is, the elemental forces and forms of nature are but manifestations of God's will and consequently wholly subject to his control, whereas man is endowed with the "prerogative of self-determination." This sets off the soul of man from the world of nature and makes it impossible to account for it in terms of any process of naturalistic evolution. In Holmes's words:

if our previous view of matter and of elemental force as continuous Divine manifestations is correct, they could not in the nature of things become self-determining existences. The creation of independent centres of will and action involves a change in the character of the formative agencies hitherto at work in the portion of the universe with which we are acquainted. . . . There is nothing in light or heat, or electricity, or chemical or mechanical force, that can give any account of spiritual existence. When the first human soul was introduced to earthly being, if not before the date of this last birth of creation, there was a new force put forth which was not any one of these. And so, whenever a new soul takes mortal shape, we recognize it as an emanation from its Maker by some other channel than through the elemental substances or influences that wait upon its secondary and simply organic necessities.¹⁷

This in itself is sufficient demarcation of Holmes's views at this time from those that were presently to be identified with the names of Darwin, Huxley, and Spencer, but in pursuing his distinction Holmes moved even further from the Darwinian position. He found that if he started with the soul—the "spiritual apex" of creation—and reasoned downward, he could come as easily to a theory of Creation as he had come to spontaneous generation by starting with inorganic nature and reasoning upward. "We could not think it strange," he wrote, that at the time of the emanation of the soul from its Maker,

a force running parallel with it in the material world—a force not identical with any of the ordinary physical agencies,—should combine the elements of the bodily form, and shape it to the wants of the immaterial principle. . . . But this conclusion would oblige us to argue backward from it to the lower animals, whose material frames and food-needing existence are essentially identical in their composition and mode of being with our own. And conceding that a special change of character in the forces of Nature marks the appearance of animal life, there would be strong reason for extending the same supposition to the vegetable kingdom.[18]

This concession need not be taken too seriously, however. Holmes wished to explore all of the logical possibilities, but there is ample reason to believe that he did not favor this one. In the first place, it was itself not very logical: it scarcely follows that, because intervention is necessary to account for the free spirit of man, it must also be called in to account for beings that resemble man only in "material forms and food-needing existence." In the second place, Holmes had never insisted upon this possibility before and he never did again. In the third place, it was inconsistent with the mechanistic theory of life that was the main argument of his essay. In the absence of verification, Holmes was willing to entertain any reasonable doubt of his hypothesis, scientific or philosophic, and he was adamant on the exclusion of the spirit of man; but he seems to have been thoroughly convinced that life not only could be explained in terms of physical and chemical forces but had probably originated spontaneously in inorganic matter.

2

Because of the close dependence of Holmes's theory of origins upon his theory of the nature of life, it will be illuminating to investigate further the meaning and sources of the latter. First, however, in order to view it in proper perspective, it will be necessary to bear in mind the state of medical science during the early years of Holmes's professional career. All of the biological sciences were in revolt against the "hollow theories and empty phraseology"[19] of the preceding half-century, and in this movement medicine led rather than followed. According to the eminent German physicist and physiologist, Helmholtz, medical men were in a state of despair in the opening decades of the century and turned to such empirical systems as homeopathy in sheer bewilderment. Their salvation, he believed, came only through the adoption in the middle decades of the century of the exact methods and mechanistic principles of the inorganic sciences.[20] Holmes's medical education came at the very beginning of this movement, and he was considerably influenced by it. In Paris he acquired from his revered teacher, Pierre Louis,[21] a respect for precise observation and a scorn of "apriorism" that he preached all his life long. Louis may even have provided the groundwork for his mechanistic views through his opposition to the theories of the elder and more famous Broussais, whose *"chimie vivante"* Holmes referred to disparagingly in the essay of 1857.[22] Louis and the Paris hospitals were only a starting point, however, and Holmes was more indebted on the theoretical side to later developments in the sciences, most of which issued from Germany, where the medical reforms begun in France were carried out on a large scale. Several times during his career Holmes reviewed and interpreted these developments, but never more interestingly to the student of his mental development than the first time, in an address before the Boylston Society at Harvard in 1844.[23] Here in his comments on the development of organic chemistry may be found the beginning of his theory of the mechanism of life, and in his comments on the cell-formation theory of Schleiden and Schwann the beginning of his theory of the spontaneous generation of species.

Friedrich Wöhler may be said to have founded organic chemistry in 1828 by synthesizing the first organic compound, but the work of his colleague, Justus von Liebig, was more widely influential. In 1840 an epoch-making volume on the chemistry of plant life by Liebig was published in English[24] and this was followed up two years later by an equally important work on the chemistry of animal life,[25] dealing especially with the analysis of foods in relation to body products and teaching that body heat is caused by internal oxidation. The influence on Holmes of the results contained in this work can scarcely be overestimated. He not only paid them glowing tribute in the address of 1844 but returned to them again and again in his later writing. To take an amusing example, all that remained of the hapless De Sauty at the end of the "electro-chemical eclogue" in *The Professor at the Breakfast-Table* was

> a cloud of elements organic,
> C. O. H. N. Ferrum, Chlor. Flu. Sil. Potassa,
> Calx. Sod. Phosph. Mag. Sulphur, Mang. (?) Alumin. (?)
>   Cuprum (?)
>   Such as man is made of.[26]

In the address he praised the work of the organic chemist in these words:

> Look again at the progress of chemistry in its application to the phenomena of life. The attempt has been made to show, not merely that certain combinations and decompositions take place in living bodies, by which new products are evolved, and life kept active in the midst of the shifting organization, but the analyst has taken his balance, his measuring jar, his pound of food, and his *man,* and traced the material of support through the organs of the recipient, with all its successive changes, to its resolution into the elements of the earth or atmosphere, calling every organ to account for its share in exact decimals, as a manufacturer might trace the progress of a bale of cotton through the hands of his various operatives.[27]

The body, it seemed, was composed of the same elements as the inorganic world and obeyed the same forces and the same laws. From this it was but a step to the mechanistic theory of the essay of 1857, which, in fact, opened with a fanciful sketch of the chemical changes in the body that is simply an elaboration of the above statement.

The argument from organic chemistry remained basic in Holmes's mechanistic theory, but in the essay of 1857 he was able to add other arguments and illustrations too numerous and complex to be more than suggested here. Thus he pointed out that just as the same substances are found in the living and nonliving realms, so ordinary physical forces such as gravity, cohesion, capillary attraction, hydraulics, light, sound, and mechanics "are manifested in the organism in the same way as in ordinary matter."[28] Again, he was able to develop many parallels between vital and nonvital processes: in the flame, for example, which, like life, grows, is fed by incessant waste and supply, and dies at length "exhausted, clogged, or suddenly quenched";[29] and in the crystal, which, like a living organism, is limited in size and duration of existence, is constant in form, and is able to assimilate just the right materials to build its own substance.[30] Further, he even sought to show that the process of reproduction combines "several modes of action, no one of which is without inorganic parallel,"[31] and he replied to the objection that life had never been successfully imitated in the laboratory by pointing out that neither had precious stones.[32] The arguments, however, are less important here than the conclusion, which Holmes stated as follows:

Life is a necessary attribute, then, of a perfect organism exposed to the proper external influences, just as much as gravity belongs to a metal, or hardness to a diamond.[33]

It is easy to see how this conclusion, simply by being stated, suggested a theory of evolution in Holmes's sense of spontaneous generation. If life is defined as a property of certain substances in certain combinations under certain conditions, it is natural to infer that life will arise whenever those combinations and circumstances concur. This was the basis of Holmes's theory of origins, and at this point in his essay he turned to the elaboration of the theory.

Such views inevitably brought him into conflict with his good friend Louis Agassiz, who condemned all mechanistic theories and was later the ablest opponent of Darwinism in America. The difference was not personal and is of little importance in itself, but it is of considerable help in defining the relation of Holmes's mechanism to his religious beliefs. In his *Contributions to the Natural History of the United States* Agassiz had contended that the world of life

has not grown out of the necessary action of physical laws, but was the free conception of the Almighty Intellect, matured in his thought before it was manifested in tangible, external form.[34]

When Holmes came to review this work in the *Atlantic Monthly* in 1858[35] he felt it necessary to criticize Agassiz's stand. In the sense of the "customary definitions" of physical laws he professed complete agreement, but added that these definitions left something to be desired and that in a more judicious interpretation he found no incompatibility between the necessary action of these laws and the free exercise of the Almighty Intellect:

The forces which act according to these laws, and the various forms of the so-called *matter*, or concrete forces, are often spoken of as if they were blind agencies and existences, acting by an inherent fate-like power of their own. But if everything outside our consciousness resolves itself, in the last analysis, into force, or something capable of producing change, and if force existing by the will of an omniscient and omnipresent Being, to whom time has no absolute significance, is simply God himself in action, then we shall find it impossible to limit the causal agency of the physical forces.[36]

This was the doctrine of God's "active relation" with the world of nature that has already been mentioned in connection with the essay of 1857. There Holmes wished to prevent the confusion of his mechanistic views with materialism and atheism, and to this end developed a doctrine of the immanence of divine action. "Every action, or series of actions," he began, "is referred by the mind to a force, and this again to a power";[37] and this finally, he continued, leads to a Prime Mover unmoved. God is not merely a prime mover, however, for, since "we cannot allow forces to be self-sustaining any more than self-originating,"[38] we must assume that the power of the Prime Mover is continuously manifested in nature. In Leibnitz's Latin, which he quoted, *"Actualia dependent a Deo tum in existendo, tum in agendo."*[39] Thus there emerges a "Transcendental Physiology" which is in complete agreement with the doctrine of the hymn-book,

> His Spirit moves our heaving lungs,
> Or they would breathe no more,[40]

and which rids us of many difficulties in the way of speculative inquiry into the origin and nature of things. "If the student of nature and the student of divinity," he concluded,

can once agree that all the forces of the universe, as well as all its power, are immediately dependent upon its Creator,—that He is not only omni*potent*, but omni*movent*—we have no longer any fear of nebular theories, or doctrines of equivocal generation, or of progressive development. If we saw a new planet actually formed in the field of the telescope, or the imaginary "Acarus Crosii" put together "de toutes pièces" under the microscope, true to its alleged pedigree,—out of Silex, by Galvanism,—it would no more turn us into atheists, than a sight of the mint would make us doubt the national credit.[41]

If, however, Holmes's mechanism, and consequently his theory of origins, owed a great deal to the chemistry of Liebig, the latter theory owed an independent debt to the cell-theory of Schleiden and Schwann.[42] This theory had two parts, one of which, that the cell is the structural unit of life, was a lasting contribution to science, while the other, a theory of cell-formation, was shorter-lived but of greater importance in the development of Holmes's evolutionary views. Schleiden first, and after him Schwann, held that cells are formed out of their elements by a process of aggregation, the nucleolus being formed first by the accumulation of granulate particles, then the rest of the nucleus by stratification around the nucleolus as a center, and finally the cell wall, which they regarded as the essential and distinguishing feature of the cell. Both Schleiden and Schwann specifically denied spontaneous generation in the sense of the evolution of living organisms out of non-living matter, but it is easy to see how their theory of the formation of the cell within the organism directly out of its constituents might suggest that doctrine to others, as it seems to have to Holmes.

Schwann's *Mikroskopische Untersuchungen*, the most important publication of either of the men, appeared in 1839, and, although it was not translated until 1847,[43] its results immediately became widely known, and, judging by parallels between it and the essay of 1857, exerted a considerable influence on Holmes. Like Holmes's essay, the work was thoroughly theistic, and yet it insisted on the mechanistic interpretation of life and made extensive use of parallels between the phenomena of crystallization and of life. In any case, Holmes, already a good microscopist in 1844, greeted the theory with almost rhapsodic enthusiasm in his address. "But how can we speak in terms of sufficient delight and wonder," he said,

> of that discovery which has lifted the veil between the mortal eye and the life-giving energy, at the moment when the flowing atoms of matter are uniting into the mysterious harmony of organized structure! The recent microscopic discoveries concerning the development of living tissues, animal and vegetable, are among the most remarkable truths ever yet reached by observation.[44]

Continuing in this fervid vein, which is sufficient evidence of the unusual impression that the theory had made upon him, he then drew a parallel with the nebular theory in cosmogony, the evolutionary significance of which is obvious:

> The most sublime vision that ever dawned upon the eye of discovery is that which reveals the evolution of new worlds from the luminous ether of the nebulae, commencing by the condensation of their particles in a solid nucleus at the centre of gravitation.
>
> This telescopic phenomenon has at length found its counterpart in the microscopic history of the primitive organization of the living tissues. It is now received as an established truth, that every organized structure is developed from a cell, itself evolved from a nucleus, which again is constituted by the spontaneous aggregation of granules in the midst of a fluid. Thus the tube of the astronomer has carried his vision into illimitable space, and shown him the

hand of creative power, as it shapes worlds and systems out of chaos; while the lens of the microscopic observer has lifted the invisible up to the level of his senses, to display the same eternal agency as it fashions a living creature from the elements of a formless fluid.[45]

It must be noted that, like Schwann, Holmes was here speaking only of the "evolution" of the cell within the body, but still it can be seen that when the bars to speculation were let down it was but a step from "spontaneous aggregation" within the body to spontaneous generation without.

Unfortunately for Holmes's evolutionary speculation, however, this "grossly mechanical precipitation-theory"[46] of Schleiden and Schwann was viewed with suspicion by later cytologists, who, having observed that division is the normal method of cell reproduction, admitted free cell-formation only within the narrowest limits. This certainly is the reason why the theory was not developed in the essay of 1857, where it would have been most useful. Holmes was not ready to give the theory up entirely, however. Even in 1861, after he had digested Virchow's evidence that cells are evolved only out of other cells,[47] he seemed inclined to hold the question open:

It seems at present necessary to abandon the original idea of Schwann, that we can observe the building up of a cell from the simple granules of a blastema, or formative fluid. The evidence points rather towards the axiom, *Omnis cellula e cellula;* that is, the germ of a new cell is always derived from a preëxisting cell. The doctrine of Schwann, as I remarked long ago (1844), runs parallel with the nebular theory in astronomy, and they may yet stand or fall together.[48]

Of course the nebular theory was itself highly speculative, but since at the time it had not been seriously rivaled or challenged, we may conclude that Holmes still held out hope for Schwann's theory. As we shall presently see, he held out the same hope as late as 1872.

We may conclude our survey of this pre-Darwinian phase of Holmes's thinking by stating the positions to which his speculation had led him. These were: (1) that the various forms of life have emerged successively and progressively over a vast period of time, but that this succession has not been accomplished by the transformation of species; (2) that life is a property of certain elements existing in certain combinations under certain conditions, and that therefore it may conceivably have arisen directly out of nonliving matter under "natural, but exceptional" conditions; (3) that all the known species of life may have been thus derived—probably by some such process as Schwann's theory of cell-formation—out of their constituent substances, vegetable out of nonliving matter and animal out of vegetable, but that this does not deny the efficacy of the divine creative will, because this will operates immanently; (4) that the free spirit of man cannot be accounted for by any such natural process but only by the direct intervention of its Creator, with whom its relations are different from those of nature. Several of these positions were presently challenged by the development of evolutionary theory. Two years after the essay of 1857, *The Origin of Species,* at least as far as most scientists were concerned, demolished the conception of species as absolute and immutable. Seven years afterward, Pasteur conducted the experiments that were widely regarded as putting an end to the theory of spontaneous generation. Five years afterward, Spencer published the complete version of his plans for a mechanistic explanation not only of organic and inorganic nature but of the mental and social life of man as well. Six years afterward, Huxley published the available evidence for man's descent from a prehistoric ape. And before many years, Haeckel was to begin the propagation of the pugnacious materialism that he called "monism of the cosmos." The question thus arises: What, in the face of these developments, became of Holmes's theories? Did he abandon those that were inconsistent with the new developments, or modify them, or oppose the new developments, or simply suspend judgment? Did he "accept Darwinism" in the sense of the evolution of man from the higher animals and the transformation of species by the natural selection of random variations, or did he reject it or attempt to establish some kind of compromise with it? We may now turn to the consideration of these questions.

3

In the first place, by way of clearing ground, we may observe that he continued to declare the necessity of accepting the geological account of the antiquity and successive emergence of the forms of life. In the "Autobiographical Notes" published in the *Life and*

Letters, he tells us that ever since he paid ten cents for a peep through the telescope on the Common his whole idea of the creation had been "singularly changed,"[49] and certainly in his mature years his conception of the creation was decidedly un-Biblical. True, in *The Poet at the Breakfast-Table,* when the Master was asked whether he accepted "Mr. Darwin's notions about the origin of the human race," he replied:

—Better stick to Blair's Chronology; that settles it. Adam and Eve, created Friday, October 28th, b. c. 4004. You've been in a ship for a good while, and here comes Mr. Darwin on deck with an armful of sticks and says, "Let's build a raft, and trust ourselves to that."[50]

But even without the ridicule of the identical chronology of Ussher in the earlier *Professor at the Breakfast-Table,*[51] there would be no reason to take this seriously. Holmes was too firmly convinced of the truth of the geological record for that. Thus he was particularly severe on that last extremity of the fundamentalist, the argument that fossils were especially planted in the strata to try the faith of men. He dealt out an appropriate measure of scorn to this theory in *The Poet at the Breakfast-Table,*[52] and in 1860 he replied to an epistolary critic in these sharp words:

If you choose to accept that hypothesis I mentioned, and which seems to have struck you, viz., that the world was created with mock skeletons of almost innumerable mock genera and species, many of them holding the remains of mock food in their mock interiors, and with their teeth ground down as if by long use; in other words, if you choose to believe the Creator the prototype of charlatans and jugglers, I shall have to say again, always with perfect respect and courtesy: "Good morning, Mr. Kimball."[53]

The book of Genesis, he continued more drastically to his critic, is a "collection of beliefs and traditions, most of which God hath in these last days flatly contradicted out of his own authentic bibles of the firmament and the planetary strata."[54] Finally, in *Elsie Venner* (1861), the physician, who in most cases presents Holmes's own views, leaves no doubt of his own position by stating flatly that "Geology *proves* a certain succession of events, and the best Christian in the world must make the earth's history square with it."[55]

It will be noted, however, that these statements do not in any way modify Holmes's position as stated in the essay of 1857. They continue to assert the successive emergence of the forms of life, but have nothing at all to say of the transformation of species. Nor did Holmes ever, to my knowledge, specifically declare his acceptance of the transformation theory. True, one may infer from his later friendly statements about Darwinism, and his failure to controvert it, that he was not as firm as before on this point; but, for all that he says, the succession of species might still be explained by successive acts of spontaneous generation. And down at least until 1872 he still showed a preference for this explanation. The whole question of spontaneous generation had been reopened by the sensational experiments of Pouchet in 1859, and though Pasteur thoroughly discredited these experiments five years later, the idea would not down. Many scientists turned to speculation and experiment on the subject,[56] and in the early seventies, just before the publication of *The Poet at the Breakfast-Table,* a highly articulate English physiologist, H. C. Bastian, began an energetic campaign to establish the theory. These developments, and particularly the experiments of his good friend and colleague Jeffries Wyman,[57] undoubtedly encouraged Holmes and kept alive some faint confidence in his theory of 1857, which otherwise was hard pressed by the almost universal acceptance of transformism.

Wyman conducted his experiments between 1862 and 1867, and in the latter year published his results in *The American Journal of Science.*[58] In one phase of his investigation he first boiled various organic solutions for varying lengths of time, then sealed them hermetically, and finally, after the lapse of from a few days to more than two months, examined their contents microscopically for signs of life. If life had appeared in every case, he believed that he would have established a supposition in favor of spontaneous generation; but as it turned out, though life did appear in solutions boiled as long as four hours, there were no signs of it in those boiled for six. This experiment Holmes caused the Master to perform in abbreviated form in *The Poet at the Breakfast-Table.* One time when the narrator in this work came to the room of the Master, he found him holding a small hermetically sealed flask up to the light. The liquid was turbid, and when they broke the seal and examined a drop of it under the microscope they found it wriggling with life. This had been boiled for three hours, but another, boiled for six, showing under the microscope only a clear circle of lifeless light. It was "one more negative result," the Master had to admit, but he was not daunted, since, as he said later, "a hundred negative results don't settle such a question."[59] With full faith in the possibility of a positive result, he then went on to exclaim as follows, first alone to the narrator and then to the assembled group at the breakfast-table, on the significance such a result would have had:

Sir, if that liquid had held life in it the Vatican would have trembled to hear it, and there would have been anxious questionings and ominous whisperings in the halls of Lambeth palace! . . . If it should prove that dead things come to life of themselves, it would be awkward, you know, because then somebody will get up and say if one dead thing made itself alive another might, and so perhaps the earth peopled itself without any help. Possibly the difficulty wouldn't be so great as many people suppose. We might perhaps find room for a Creator, after all, as we do now, though we see a little brown seed grow till it sucks up the juices of half an acre of ground, apparently all by its own inherent power. That does not stagger us; I am not sure that it would if Mr. Crosse's or Mr. Weekes's *acarus* should show himself all of a sudden, as they say he did, in certain mineral mixtures acted on by electricity.[60]

This, even to the citation of the *acarus*,[61] was the essay of 1857 over again, and presently the young Astronomer interrupted to provide us with reminiscences of the address of 1844:

—You and I are at work on the same problem,—said the young Astronomer to the Master. —I have looked into a microscope now and then, and I have seen that perpetual dancing about of minute atoms in a fluid, which you call molecular motion. Just so, when I look through my telescope I see the star-dust whirling about in the infinite expanse of ether; or if I do not see its motion, I know that it is only on account of its immeasurable distance. Matter and motion everywhere; void and rest nowhere. You ask why your restless microscopic atoms may not come together and become self-conscious and self-moving organisms. I ask why my telescopic star-dust may not come together and grow and organize into habitable worlds,—the ripened fruit on the branches of the tree Yggdrasil, if I may borrow from our friend the Poet's province.[62]

Of course these statements must be taken with caution. Holmes was writing fiction, not science, and in any case neither the Master nor the Young Astronomer urged the spontaneous generation of specific species, as their author had done fifteen years before. Even Huxley admitted (indeed, he was under the necessity of admitting) that life had probably arisen out of inorganic matter in some remote time ("archebiosis"), but this also was not the same thing as the spontaneous generation of individual species. Holmes felt the weight of Darwin's evidence and was fully aware of the tenuous character of his earlier theory, but still there is more than a little significance in the fact that in 1872, thirteen years after *The Origin of Species*, he was still wondering why "restless microscopic atoms may not come together and become self-conscious and self-moving organisms." If he had wished, he had ample opportunity to deny his earlier theory or affirm transformation. But he did neither. It seems not unreasonable to conclude that he remained unconvinced both of the truth of Darwin's theory and the error of his own.

Granted that Holmes made no visible modification of his conception of the origin of species, what about his exclusion of man's free spirit from nature? Did he modify this conception, subordinating the soul to the determinism of natural law, or did he maintain the dualism of his original position? Here appearances would seem to indicate more of a change than elsewhere, for from the time of writing *Elsie Venner* in 1860 he was even more taken with the mechanism of thought and morals than he had formerly been with the mechanism of vital actions. All three of his novels centered about the conditioning of moral character by external circumstances, and in two formal essays, "Mechanism in Thought and Morals" (1870) and "Crime and Automatism" (1875), he examined at length the physiological and sociological factors that affect moral action and limit moral responsibility. The question is, did Holmes, in following out this line of thought, put man entirely back into nature and deprive him of the freedom that he had so carefully preserved in the essay of 1857?

At times he certainly seemed to. Again and again he came down to the principle of no psychosis without neurosis, and he could find no evidence of freedom except the subjective "sense of effort in willing; the sense of responsibility in view of the future; and the verdict of conscience in review of the past."[63] Freedom, it sometimes seems in these discussions, is no more than a useful illusion. This turn in his thought led Holmes to such a statement as the fol-

Taylor was less concerned, however, with the theory of the evolution of species than with a broader conception that this theory seemed to him to verify. Organic evolution, in fact, makes its appearance in the dramas only twice, and then only in passing. Thus, early in *The Masque of the Gods* the primitive god Baal proclaims:

> None older is than I. When Man came forth,
> The final effort, wrung from monstrous forms,
> And Earth's outwearied forces could no more,
> I warmed the ignorant bantling on my breast.[8]

And at the beginning of *Prince Deukalion*, Gaea, the earth-mother, describes the gestation of the man-child in these terms:

> Ere he was born I dreamed that he might be,
> And through long ages of imperfect life
> Waited for him. Then, vexed with monstrous shapes
> That spawned and wallowed in primeval ooze,
> I lay supine and slept, or seemed to sleep;
> And dreamed, or waking felt as in a dream
> Some touch of hands, some soft, delivering help,—
> And he was there![9]

Since neither of these passages was essential to the action of the drama in which it appeared, it is clear that Taylor introduced them in order to pay his respects to the theory of evolution; but it is equally clear that his understanding of that theory was not Darwinian. There is no hint of the Darwinian pattern of survival of chance variations, and even when allowance is made for poetic personification, the teleological factor occupies a position of primary importance. Taylor was, in fact, in no sense a Darwinian. This will become abundantly clear when we examine the dramas in greater detail, but it may be illustrated beforehand by an article, "Studies of Animal Nature," that he published in the *Atlantic* in February, 1877. There he conceded that Darwin's theory is "not degrading to man; it simply raises the animal world in dignity"; but in advancing the claim that animals possess "a faculty allied to the moral sense in man," he found it necessary to part company with the Darwinians in both method and conclusion. He said of Darwin and the scientific method:

Darwin, as I understand him, is still doubtful whether there is a moral sense in animals. We can judge only from acts, of course, but our interpretation of those acts depends upon our sympathetic lowing, which seems to remove man from his independent, "passive" relation to Deity and subject him to the active determination of the "omnimovent" Will:

> Do we not all *hope,* at least, that the doctrine of man's being a blighted abortion, a miserable disappointment to his Creator, and hostile and hateful to Him from his birth, may give way to the belief that he is the latest terrestrial manifestation of an ever upward-striving movement of divine power?[64]

If this hope is justified, does not Holmes's choice of words raise the suspicion that man is now one with nature and as little free as the other terrestrial manifestations of divine power?

Holmes has been accused of ambiguity on this question. Professors Jones and Hayakawa, for example, in the splendid introduction to their volume of selections, quote an affirmation of mental independence from "Mechanism in Thought and Morals" to the effect that Hamlet and Faust cannot be found by "testing for albumen or examining fibres in microscopes," and then comment as follows:

> If, of course, these "spiritual" attainments of man are not to be found in the material condition where they have their birth, where are they to be sought? This is a question never quite answered by Holmes, so that the complaints about the ambiguity of his position made by some of his contemporaries were not without justification.[65]

One wonders, however, if this ambiguity is not more apparent than real. Aside from a certain lack of cogency in the criticism just quoted—it being equally difficult to trace the properties of water to its chemical constituents—it does not follow that because men's actions are influenced by inner and outer circumstances they are completely determined by them. That the will is both limited and free is, rightly or wrongly, the view of common sense, and was, I believe, Holmes's. Moreover, it followed consistently from the theory of knowledge advanced in the essay of 1857. There, it will be remembered, he distinguished between empirical knowledge of the external world and intuitive knowledge of the self, and ascribed superior certainty to the latter. If that position is accepted, then it follows that the subjective "sense of responsibility" is adequate testimony to the freedom of the will no matter what may be revealed by empirical investigation.

This dualism is implied or stated again and again in Holmes's writing on this subject. At the beginning of "Mechanism in Thought and Morals," for example, he clearly warned that though he would treat only of the generally observable aspects of mental action, he did not deny the existence of others:

> It is a well ascertained fact, for instance, that certain sulphates and phosphates are separated from the blood that goes to the brain in increased quantity after severe mental labor. But this chemical change may be only one of the factors of intellectual action. So, also, it *may* be true that the brain is inscribed with material records of thought; but what that is which reads any such records, remains an open question. I have meant to leave absolutely untouched the endless discussion as to the distinctions between "mind" and "matter" and confine myself chiefly to some results of observation in the sphere of thought, and some suggestions as to the mental confusion which seems to me a common fact in the sphere of morals.[66]

It should be remembered that one of Holmes's principal objections to Calvinism was its iron determinism, and he was not anxious to fall into another equally binding and less dignified. Consequently, like nearly all of the academic philosophers in this country down to his later years—adherents of the Scottish philosophy descended from Reid—he placed his ultimate reliance on intuition and on its assurance affirmed man's freedom. Nothing could be clearer than this statement later in the same essay:

> I reject, therefore, the mechanical doctrine which makes me the slave of outside influences, whether it work with the logic of Edwards, or the averages of Buckle; whether it come in the shape of the Greek's destiny, or the Mahometan's fatalism; or in that other aspect, dear to the band of believers, whom Beesly of Everton, speaking in the character of John Wesley, characterized as "The crocodile crew that believe in election."[67]

In the face of such a categorical assertion as this, we must conclude that, soundly or not, Holmes once again failed visibly to depart from his position in the essay of 1857.[68] This does not mean, however, that he looked with disfavor on the theories of evolution that differed from that essay on the points discussed. On the contrary, though he made pointed reservations, his attitude was more than friendly. In *The Poet at the Breakfast-Table,* for example, the following enthusiastic, though conditional, statement is quoted from "the book of the Master":

> What is the secret of the profound interest which "Darwinism" has excited in the minds and hearts of more persons than dare to confess their doubts and hopes? It is because it restores "Nature" to its place as a true divine manifestation. It is that it removes the traditional curse from that helpless infant lying in its mother's bosom. It is that it lifts from the shoulders of man the responsibility for the fact of death. . . . If development upward is the general law of the race; if we have grown by natural evolution out of the caveman, and even less human forms of life, we have everything to hope from the future.[69]

The same sentiment was repeated in his last work, *Over the Teacups,* published in 1891:

> The doctrine of evolution, so far as it is accepted, changes the whole relation of man to the creative power. It substitutes infinite hope in the place of infinite despair for the vast majority of mankind.[70]

Plainly Holmes was well disposed toward even Darwinism in so far as it was a support to his hope of progress, and if he felt constrained to speak only obliquely he was sufficiently convinced of the general notion of evolution to refrain from pressing his objections. By way of conclusion, let us look more carefully into the basis of this amiable disposition, for there we shall find the central spring of his attitude.

Basically it was theological. If there was any one motive in Holmes's life that was stronger than any other, it was resistance to the theology of his fathers. Long after the intelligentsia of New England had left the doctrines of predestination and depravity behind them, Holmes attacked them with all the zeal of the newly emancipated. He was turned against Calvinism, he tells us,[71] almost in his infancy, and the passage just quoted, which was part of a general arraignment of the old theology, was written at the age of eighty-one. There were two sides to Holmes's theology, however, one destructive and the other constructive. On the destructive side, he attacked the doctrine of transmission of sin through his investigation of the mechanism of thought and morals, and sapped the revealed foundations of the belief by the acceptance of the higher—or "honest"[72]—criticism of Scripture. On the constructive side, which is of greater importance here, he found a progressive view—"the progress of mankind onward and upward forever"—the only one that would answer the problem of evil without demeaning the character of Deity. If the evils of nature and human sinfulness had the purpose of developing character through opposition and were temporary and meliorable, then was the Creator merciful and just; but if man was held strictly accountable for an original transgression in which he had no part and for others that were beyond his poor human strength to prevent, then was God a trickster and a tyrant. Your God, he liked to say to the Calvinist, in a borrowed phrase, is my Devil. Thus he reached the conclusion that "it is more consonant with our ideas of what is best, to suppose that suffering, which is often obviously disciplinary and benevolent in its aim, is to be temporary rather than eternal."[73] This was the central article in Holmes's faith; in his own words, there is but one theory that will

"justify the ways of God to man," namely, that this colony of the universe is an educational institution so far as the human race is concerned. On this theory I base my hope for myself and my fellow-creatures. If, in the face of all so-called evil to which I cannot close my eyes, I have managed to retain a cheerful optimism, it is because this educational theory is the basis of my working creed.[74]

Secure in this optimism, which went back to his earliest years and had other bases than the theological, Holmes had early felt that evolution ought to be true. Moreover, the geological record had convinced him that it was true. And if he was uncertain of the means by which it had been accomplished and believed that in the development of man as a "subcreative center" something more than the forces of nature had to be taken into account, it was nonetheless true for that. For evolution in the general sense meant simply the advance in the forms of life from simple to complex by natural means, and Holmes had proclaimed this doctrine in 1857. Of more specific commitments he was wary. Perhaps the following sentence, written originally about Jeffries Wyman, is equally applicable to his friend:

No one can help seeing that he inclined toward belief in the general doctrine, but he neither indorses "Darwinism" nor denounces those who find themselves unable to accept "derivation" in any sense.[75]

PART THREE

THE END OF THE CENTURY:
THE "GENTEEL TRADITION"

X

THE PERSISTENCE OF TELEOLOGY

For a decade and more after the appearance of *The Origin of Species* even scientists were sceptical of evolution, but by the end of the century this was no longer the case. "Evolution—once an Hypothesis, now the Established Doctrine of the scientific world" was the toast proposed as early as 1882 at a banquet attended by many leaders of American science,[1] and a few years later Joseph Le Conte, the eminent geologist of the University of California, was no less positive in saying: "Among scientific men there is no longer any discussion of the truth of this law, but only of the theories of the causes of the law."[2] Moreover, the scientists were followed by a growing number of laymen. Where Bryant had scoffed and Lowell had stood "with God as against evolution,"[3] such a nature-lover of the succeeding generation as John Burroughs wrote in his journal after reading *The Descent of Man:* "The book convinces like Nature herself. I have no more doubt of its main conclusions than I have of my own existence."[4] Not many, to be sure, were as zealous in their espousal of evolution as Burroughs, who went on from Darwin to the radical evolutionism of Bergson, but by the beginning of the new century few men in the world of literature and learning were willing to deny that an evolution of some kind had really occurred. Evolution had become a fact to be reckoned with rather than an issue to be debated and the burning question not so much whether it was compatible with established beliefs as the reverse. Where Holmes, for example, had conceded in his essay of 1857 that "progressive development" might be accepted without fear of atheism if it were interpreted in terms of the doctrine of immanence,[5] thirty-odd years later Madison Cawein reversed the argument and spoke of

> Some purpose, some divine development—
> That protoplasmic evolution proves.[6]

It is scarcely necessary to point out that this widespread acceptance of evolution served to intensify the tendency of the age toward materialism and mechanism in its philosophy. The fact is a commonplace of history, and it has already been reported in these pages that the principle of natural selection was widely regarded as having administered the coup de grâce to all teleological cosmologies.[7] Plainly, it was held, if the forms of life owed their origin merely to the interaction of teeming productivity and pressure of environment, there was no need to postulate "an intelligent creative cause" and hence no necessity, except as comfortable fictions, for the transcendental and theistic evolutionisms with which we have been concerned. In the chapters that follow, however, little will be heard of this objection. Granted that the transcendental postulate was unnecessary in accounting for the forms of life, it was not therefore proved untrue, and there were many to object to the Occamite parsimony of denying it. For a number of reasons that it will be the purpose of this chapter to review, most of the poets in this country at the turn of the century rejected the rising naturalism and insisted on some kind of rational and moral element in their interpretation of evolution.

One reason that cannot be left out of account, even though it is difficult to estimate, lay simply in the fact that they were poets. Given the fact of evolution, the very nature of their calling at least started them in the direction of a teleological interpretation. Poetry is rooted in the same traits that caused primitive men to make myths, and has always tended to treat nature animistically. The peculiar work of the poet is to render the world as it seems to immediate experience rather than as it appears to analysis, and since the most immediate and inescapable element in experience is the sense of personal will and identity, he has always tended to read this element into his subject. The poet, as Mr. Santayana has observed, "is incorrigibly transcendental":[8] the world is his mirror. Hence, for reasons of art if for no other, when confronted with the fact of energy he has tended to set it apart as something with a self-sufficient existence like his own, and in dealing with the manifestation of that energy in evolution has found a similar persistent and purposeful will. Of course in many cases this has been simply an accident of metaphor. Great names from Lucretius to the twentieth century are sufficient evidence that one may be both a materialist and a poet, and this factor by itself would not be enough to account for the flourishing of teleological cosmologies in the poetry of this time. There were others, however. The closing decades of the old century saw a decided reaction against the mechanisms that had accompanied the expansion of science and a vigorous resurgence of the idealisms of several decades before.

A part of this development had its origin within science itself, or at least among those who wished to base their beliefs on the findings of science. Thus, to mention an important movement which we cannot pause to consider, the whole conception of the nature and basis of science underwent sweeping revision at the hands of Peirce, Mach, Poincaré, Bergson, and others; and, to turn to one that we cannot omit, the peculiarly Darwinian aspects of evolution were subjected to a thorough re-examination by many critics. The former random fire of these critics was now concentrated on the principle of natural selection, which, as was just stated, was its great gift to the mechanistic philosophy. Some, echoing the old charge of Joseph Cook that evolution explains much but not itself,[9] complained that natural selection was not a true cause but only a restraint; that, in the words of a recent writer, it was "not an agency of any kind, . . . merely the name of a certain sifting process in nature which checks the insurgency of life."[10] Others, from John Burroughs to Hans Driesch, not only joined in this objection, but, taking the positive side of the argument, insisted that some kind of vital principle or organizing influence was as necessary in the explanation of the universe as it ever was. Still others—Germans like Wilhelm Roux and Theodor Eimer, Englishmen like Samuel Butler and Bernard Shaw, and Americans like E. D. Cope, Alpheus Hyatt, and A. S. Packard—attempted with at least temporary success to resuscitate some of the factors enumerated by Lamarck three-quarters of a century before. The present opinion is that they failed as far as the crucial and peculiarly Lamarckian factor of use and disuse is concerned, the experiments of Weismann in the late eighties seeming to have proved that acquired characteristics are not inherited. These experiments, however, were not immediately accepted by all concerned, and the Lamarckists in any case, by casting doubts on the sufficiency of natural selection, had already paved the way for newer and broader hypotheses—among many, "creative evolution," "orthogenesis," "emergent evolution."

Moreover, this was not merely a quibble over biological details. As the Bohemian historian of biology, Emanuel Radl, has sagely observed, its underlying motive was philosophic:

Most of modern Neo-Lamarckism arises, not from a conviction that Lamarck was right, but from the feeling that Darwin was, in part at least, wrong. Many of this school simply opposed the idea of the will to the Darwinian idea of chance, soul to matter, understanding to mechanism, form to structure.[11]

Thus E. D. Cope attempted to work his way from the Lamarckian factor of use and disuse to a kind of idealism by reasoning as follows:

If then, we grant these propositions, first, that effort and use modify structure; and, second, that effort and use are determined by mind in direct ratio to its development, we are led to the conclusion that evolution is an outgrowth of mind, and that mind is the parent of the forms of living nature.[12]

Again, some others believed that they could reach a similar conclusion even if they started from the Darwinian factor of struggle. This possibility has been outlined as follows by Professor Perry in reviewing the reasoning of those who sought to reconcile "the materialistic monism of the evolutionary type of Spencer and Haeckel and the idealistic monisms of Fichte, Schelling and Hegel":

Does not the Darwinian principle, which materialism invokes with such absolute confidence, corroborate, rather than overturn, the hypothesis of immanent teleology? Is it really true that the *struggle for existence* is a *first* cause and exclusively mechanical? Does not the struggle for life, in turn, presuppose Schopenhauer's *will-to-live, will* or *effort,* without which, according to the profound remark of Leibniz, *there can be no substance?* Does it not, therefore, presuppose an anterior, superior, and immaterial cause? What can the formula: struggle *for* existence, mean, except: struggle *in order* to exist? But this carries us directly into teleology. Besides, the entire Darwinian terminology is derived from the teleological theory: the terms, *selection, choice,* seem to introduce an intellectual element into nature. These are mere images, it is said, or figures of speech. But does not the very impossibility of avoiding them prove the impossibility of explaining nature by pure mechanism?

Thus the biological form of materialism suggested the transition, through a vitalistic or voluntaristic conception of life, to spiritualism, its philosophical opposite.[13]

The old debate between mechanism and vitalism in biology and mechanism and teleology in cosmology, in fact, is never a purely scientific affair. It is never simply a question of facts, but of their interpretation—whether, in short, they should be interpreted in the relatively simple, quantitatively definite terms of causal sequence or in the more immediately realizable logical and psychological terms of the mind that knows them.

The teleological view thus has a powerful drive behind it that is denied to mechanism: the profound human passion for a world that shall not be alien to it but of essentially the same stuff. It is at bottom a religious drive, and the philosophies that express it have not only been uniformly friendly to religion but, below the level of philosophy in the narrow sense, have tended to blend into it. This was to some extent true of the earlier Transcendental movement, and it was eminently true of a number of movements very much in the ascendant in this country at the turn of the century. The dissipation of orthodoxy and the failure of positivism and social reform to provide spiritual satisfaction had left a vacuum that was filled with a rush by all manner of sublimated idealisms: Christian Science, Mental Science, Theosophy, New Thought, Spiritualism, Delsartism, and others. Mary Baker Eddy declared that matter and evil were illusory and hence subject to the control of mind; Ralph Waldo Trine, of the school of New Thought, that matter is but an inferior form of mind; and Madame Blavatsky, the founder of the Theosophical Society, that it is "the manifested God" "voluntarily circumscribing the range of His own Being."[14] Excepting Delsartism,[15] none of these movements directly affected any of the writers whom we shall consider, but they are revealing symptoms of their times. A time in which such doctrines could flourish would offer no discouragement to the expression of similar ideas in poetry.

On the plane of philosophy proper the movement corresponding to these vagaries was the resurgence of post-Kantian idealism, which reached high tide in the nineties. "Philosophical idealism had more devoted followers toward the end of the nineteenth century than did any of its opponents," write Professors Anderson and Fisch.[16] This philosophy of course has a continuous history throughout the century, but it was imported into Anglo-Saxon countries in two distinct waves, the earlier literary, in the writing of Coleridge, Carlyle, and Emerson, and the later philosophical, in the studies of Green, Bradley, Royce, Howison, and a score of others.[17] The birthplace of the latter phase in this country was St. Louis, where in the late sixties H. C. Brokmeyer and W. T. Harris undertook the translation of Hegel's "larger Logic," inaugurated what is said to have been the world's first philosophical journal, and led an enthusiastic group in ransacking Kant, Fichte, Schelling, and Hegel. The movement drew strength from many impulses, but the one that was probably most easily understood by the uninitiated was the desire to show that there were more things in heaven and earth than were dreamt of in the philosophies of Spencer and Comte. At one time or another all of the leaders of the movement turned their guns on the negations of these thinkers and their followers, Harris stating for his part in the Preface of the first volume of his journal:

We, as a people, buy immense editions of John Stuart Mill, Herbert Spencer, Comte, Hamilton, Cousin, and others; one can trace the appropriation and digestion of their thoughts in all the leading articles of our Reviews. . . . If this is American philosophy, the editor thinks that it may be very much elevated by absorbing and digesting more refined aliment.[18]

It is difficult to assay the influence of this movement on the literary men of the time, but at least on those with academic connections it seems to have been considerable. By the eighties it had displaced Scottish realism as the reigning philosophy of the colleges, and its teachers—as vigorous and articulate a group of academic philosophers as this country has seen—carried weight without as well as within the walls of their institutions. Their influence was great, not only on the younger men who came under them, but on older men like Gilder and Stedman who maintained collegiate associations—on any, for that matter, who concerned themselves about current philosophical tendencies. And even if their direct influence is discounted, it must be remembered that they were merely elaborating principles that had domesticated themselves in this country long before. The older and newer transcendentalisms were joined in the Concord School of Philosophy in the persons of Alcott and Harris, and just as the person of Emerson circulated quietly but forcefully in the background of that school, so did his words in the whole movement. Van Wyck Brooks quotes Dean Stanley to the effect that having heard the great American preachers he had come to the conclusion that the sermon was always by Emerson no matter who delivered it,[19] and the same might be said both of a number of these philosophers and of many of the poets to be studied in the chapters that follow. Since this is the case, the philosophy involved must be briefly enlarged upon.

George Santayana, who grew to his philosophical majority during the flourishing of the movement, had hard words for it: "the genteel tradition in American philosophy."[20] It did not, he believed, faithfully reflect American life and was therefore a bloodless orthodoxy. In view of the moral level of American public life at the time this might be regarded as a merit, but that of course is not our concern. Immediately the important thing is the light Santayana shed on its meaning. Its heart, he said, is the "Calvinistic principle," which "asserts three things: that sin exists, that sin is punished, and that it is beautiful that sin should exist to be punished."[21] Having an almost physical loathing for this philosophy, Santayana is perhaps not wholly to be trusted as its expositor, but his sharpness in analysis is always to be reckoned with and his very antipathy enabled him to see some aspects of it with a particular clearness of outline. Moreover, that in this case he had singled out one of its most dearly held doctrines might be illustrated many times out of Royce—in the final, climactic chapter of *The Spirit of Modern Philosophy*, for example:

Two principles must be propounded at the start. . . . They are . . . in sharp apparent conflict with each other. Yet they must both be true, for they are both demonstrable.

One of them is the principle that there must be some sort of evil present wherever there is a finite will. . . .

The other . . . is the thought that, notwithstanding all this, the Logos in his wholeness must find his choice of this universe rational, and so, in and through all this imperfection, must find a total perfection.[22]

Santayana's antipathy to this doctrine lay partly in an exaggeration of Royce's position—which was not that the punishment of sin is in itself good, but that virtue is achieved only through overcoming sin—and partly in his inhospitality to religious motives in metaphysics. Thus, though he adjudges this principle "fantastic and even unintelligible," he also points out that it is to be found not only in thinkers like Carlyle and Royce but in the Koran, Spinoza, and Cardinal Newman.[23] It is in fact one of the commonest propositions in religious thought and is scarcely avoidable if one believes both that God is all-good and all-powerful and that evil exists. In any case it is thoroughly familiar in this study, where in its evolutionary aspects it has been something like a central theme.

Farther on in the same essay Santayana throws into relief still another conception familiar here. "In order to see just what part Calvinism plays in current idealism," he writes, "it will be necessary to distinguish the other chief element in that complex system, namely, transcendentalism."[24] Transcendentalism he defines as "systematic subjectivism" and then goes on to summarize the Germanic development that was paralleled in this country. He concludes:

And full as they were of their romantic isolation and romantic liberty, it occurred to them to imagine that all reality might be a transcendental self and a romantic dreamer like themselves; nay, that it might be just their own transcendental self and their own romantic dreams extended indefinitely. *Transcendental logic, the method of discovery for the mind, was to become also the method of evolution in nature and history.* Transcendental method, so abused, produced transcendental myth.[25]

Clearly, though the particular fancies of Schelling and Oken had disappeared, the transcendental interpretation of evolution had not yet been wholly supplanted by the Darwinian or Spencerian. Indeed, and here we leave Santayana, in the thinking of the exponents of the "genteel tradition" the latter had been absorbed by the former. These thinkers might, like Howison in his best-known essay, set "limits"[26] to the evolutionary theories of science, but they "interpreted" rather than denied them. Indeed, Royce acclaimed them as a chief evidence of an intelligence at the heart of things: "If there is anything true in a philosophy of evolution, then there is something *more* than mere physical causation, mere mechanism in the world."[27] To Royce, as has been pointed out before in these pages, the physical sequence of evolution was but the "phenomenal outer aspect" of the Logos.

Granted, however, that this conception of evolution and the philosophy underlying it were very much in the air at the turn of the century, they were not without rivals. The evolutionists proper, Spencer, Huxley, Fiske, and their followers, wrote in the English empirical tradition and were for the most part agnostics; of the "Logos" and that in the world which is "*more* than mere physical causation" they contended that nothing could be known. Fiske, for example, had this to say of the major premise of all spiritualistic philosophy:

THE PERSISTENCE OF TELEOLOGY 243

In the mint of nature, the coin Mind has been stamped; and theology, perceiving the likeness of the die to its impression, has unwittingly inverted the causal relation of the two, making Mind, archetypal and self-existent, to be the die.[28]

One of the main themes of Fiske's *Outlines of Cosmic Philosophy*, in fact, was that the whole history of man's thinking has been a progressive "deanthropomorphization," culminating in the righting of this inversion. Primitive persons, according to his account, first explained natural events in terms of the only cause they knew, human volition, and then, as they observed that the phenomena of nature were more uniform in behavior than human beings, inferred that there must be a single will for each of the great classes of phenomena rather than for each object. This was an advance from "fetishism" to polytheism and was followed by an advance first to monotheism and then, by the elimination of the element of caprice, to the "abstract embodiment of reason and volition"[29] of the metaphysician. Even here, however, "it is still the human personality, however refined and etherealized, which is appealed to alike as the source and as the explanation of all phenomena."[30] The true nature of things, he concluded, can only be understood by the complete "deanthropomorphizing" of our conception of the universe, a consummation which he described as follows:

further progress in deanthropomorphization involves the extrusion of the notion of a volitional Cause altogether, and leaves us with the conception of a Cause manifested throughout the entire world of phenomena, which is an indestructible element of consciousness, and which, equally with the anthropomorphic conceptions which have preceded it, is the proper object of religious feeling, but concerning the nature of which—in itself, and apart from its phenomenal manifestations—the human mind can frame no verifiable hypothesis.[31]

It is but a step from this position to the view, of which we shall see two rather striking instances in the next chapter, that, since the ultimate cause of things is unknowable, it might just as well be ignored. Significantly, however, this was not the course of Fiske himself, who seems to have regarded it as his special mission to uncover the neglected religious import of the philosophy of Spencer. In *Outlines of Cosmic Philosophy*, for example, he gave climactic position to his development of the religious possibilities of the "Unknowable," which Spencer had stated and dismissed at the beginning of *First Principles* merely to forestall criticism.[32] Spencer himself seems to have looked somewhat coldly on this aim, but Fiske was independent enough and sufficiently a man of his time and place not only to carry it through in his *Cosmic Philosophy* but to enlarge upon it in later lectures. Thus in a series on *The Destiny of Man* at the Concord School of Philosophy in 1884 he described evolution in terms of a "dramatic tendency" in which "the creation and the perfection of Man is the goal toward which Nature has all the while been tending";[33] and in the following year in the Preface to *The Idea of God as Affected by Modern Knowledge* he not only defended the teleological drift of these remarks but went so far as to affirm the "psychical" character of the Moving Cause. The delineation of the delicately outlined middle ground that he marked out in this place cannot safely be entrusted to any but his own words:

> I do not wish to take back a single word of all that I have said in my chapter on "Anthropomorphic Theism" [in *Outlines of Cosmic Philosophy*] in condemnation of the teleological method and the peculiar theistic doctrines upon which it rests. As a means of investigation it is absolutely worthless. Nay, it is worse than worthless; it is treacherous, it is debauching to the intellect. But that is no reason why, when a distinct dramatic tendency in the events of the universe appears as the *result* of purely scientific investigation, we should refuse to recognize it. It is the object of the "Destiny of Man" to prove that there is such a dramatic tendency; and while such a tendency cannot be regarded as indicative of purpose in the limited anthropomorphic sense, it is still, as I said before, the objective aspect of that which, when regarded on its subjective side, we call Purpose. There is a reasonableness in the universe such as to indicate that the Infinite Power of which it is the multiform manifestation is psychical, though it is impossible to ascribe to Him any of the limited psychical attributes which we know, or to argue from the ways of Man to the ways of God.[34]

In spite of this carefully thought out apology, however, and of the many footnoted references to earlier writings in the printed versions of both lectures, there can be no doubt that the agnosticism of the *Outlines of Cosmic Philosophy* was undergoing revision and that in these later writings Fiske was moving as far in the direction of teleology and spiritualism as he could without losing contact with his original position. How he could conceive of "purpose" in terms other than anthropomorphic and how a cause that is unknowable might be described as "psychical" it is difficult to understand. What Fiske seems to have been saying in his Preface is that while the cosmic evolution has all the appearance of a teleological process, man has no right to say so.[35] Josiah Royce, in the long introduction that he wrote for the 1903 reissue of the *Outlines of Cosmic Philosophy,* came to the conclusion that Fiske's thought was in a state of transition. After referring to Fiske's well-known theory of the significance of infancy in evolution, he concluded as follows:

This thought, and that other thought regarding the priority of mind over matter in our conception of the universe, combined to lead him to a teleological interpretation of the process of evolution. By perfectly natural steps he was hereupon led to an interpretation of the Idea of God and to a conception of the Destiny of Man which brought him to the threshold of Constructive Idealism. This threshold he indeed never crossed, partly because he had no time for technical philosophy in his later years, and partly because he retained to the end his profound respect for the Spencerian arguments against our right to define in precise theoretical terms the actual and inner nature of reality.[36]

The importance of this for our purposes is that here again an American evolutionist, and in this case an arch-evolutionist, appealed in the end to a spiritual, or at least immaterial, principle. For such an appeal, notwithstanding the general drift of the Western world toward philosophic naturalism, is what we shall find in most cases in the pages that follow. The tendency, ultimately religious in character, to interpret the cosmos in moral and psychological terms was too deeply ingrained in the American religious tradition, in the idealistic philosophy of the Romantic movement, and perhaps also in the psychology of the poet, to be easily uprooted. Fiske was following scientific thinkers since Galileo in contending that it is presumptuous and misleading to ask "why?" concerning events in nature, but the poets, and even Fiske himself in veiled terms, persisted in asking it. Moreover, in being asked it was answered, for it presupposed that events in nature occur for reasons and hence that nature is governed by a power capable of having reasons and of acting on them. To those inclined to entertain it, furthermore, this presupposition seemed the firmest possible basis for optimism; for, since such a power must be God, its acts must be good. To restate the simple argument of cosmic optimism once more, if one accepted the fact of evolution and believed that God was both benevolent and omnipotent, one could not escape the conclusion that the evolutionary process must also be good.

XI

THE INFLUENCE OF SPENCER AND DARWIN: SILL AND CERTAIN MINOR POETS

THOUGH the remainder of this study will be mainly devoted to poetry written after 1890, it must include a few poets who began their work before that time. Thus, though both had been well known since the seventies, E. C. Stedman and Richard Watson Gilder will be discussed in the next chapter, and the present chapter will treat, besides Edward Rowland Sill, who died in 1887, several deservedly little-known writers who nevertheless made extended contributions to the literature of evolution between 1878 and 1883. They belong here rather than in Part II, however, not only because in most cases they continued their work into the new century but because of their thorough and unquestioning acceptance of the fact of evolution, however they might interpret it. Gone are the enmity of Bryant, the suspicions and regrets of Lowell, and the objections of Lanier. The writers in this chapter, in fact, were closer to what is usually regarded as the main line of evolutionary thought than any others we shall consider, being the only ones who followed at all closely in the steps of Darwin, Spencer, and their schools. Sill, to be sure, was not truly a Spencerian, but he owed Spencer a greater debt and paid him fuller homage than any other American poet of equal rank, and the others, except as they detoured into something like Fiske's cosmic theism, followed him unflinchingly in his agnosticism, mechanism, and utilitarianism.

1

The chronological misplacement of Sill is emphasized by the fact that, young as he was at the time, he was one of the first Americans to put the evolutionary story into verse after the appearance of *The Origin of Species*. Except for Melville's "New Ancient of Days" and some poems and passages by Emerson and Whitman, I have found no specifically evolutionary verse between 1859 and the publication of Julia Ward Howe's "Kosmos" in 1866[1] except these opening lines of Sill's "Man, the Spirit," almost certainly written in 1865:

> A small, swift planet, glimmering round a star,—
> A molten drop with thinnest crusted shell
> Of lime and flint, roofed-in with azure air,—
> A winding stair of life, from Trilobite
> And Saurian up to one who walks their king,
> Drawing the lime and flint up through themselves
> And kindling them to spirit, till on him,
> Whose limbs are clay, there flames a lambent crown
> Of fire from heaven,—these make our world.[2]

Notwithstanding his priority, however, Sill represented a new dispensation, as a comparison of his lines with those of Mrs. Howe will reveal. Mrs. Howe's poem, like most of those that we have seen and many that we shall see, began with certain assumptions concerning the nature of things, which it used evolution to illustrate; it took cognizance of the scientific theory, but only as an "emblem" of an immanent spiritual evolution known intuitively. Sill, in contrast, had no other purpose than to place man in proper perspective by stating the facts concerning his lineage. After stating the facts, moreover, he dismissed them and went on to the ethical questions that he then and later regarded as more important.

In this acceptance and dismissal of the particular facts of evolution, furthermore, Sill's whole relation to the theory is foreshadowed. Written in his early twenties, the passage leaves no doubt of his early acceptance of the main outlines of the theory, and yet one looks in vain beyond this poem for further sketches of the geological and biological story. Evolution was not an issue to Sill and consequently lay in the background rather than the foreground of his thought. Its influence on him, however, was none the less real and important. In fact, notwithstanding certain differences that were greater than he realized, the ethical thought of Herbert Spencer was perhaps the greatest single influence in all his intellectual life. Curiously also, this influence did not weaken the fervor of his moral convictions, as it did in the case of some of his juniors, but rather reinforced it. Theodore Dreiser has said that *First Principles* and *The Data of Ethics* plunged him into depths from which he was never sure that he had emerged,[3] but these same works had precisely the opposite effect on Sill. He had been searching fruitlessly for a basis of value long before he read Spencer, and the latter's doctrine of "complete living" came to him somewhat as a deliverance. Something of the part that Spencer played in his mental history is indicated by the following comment of a classmate on a wave of scepticism that swept the undergraduate body during their attendance at Yale between 1857 and 1861:

Spencer had not yet put within general reach his point of crystallization for faith and hope, and thinking young men were in the dark and anxious atmosphere that pervaded Sill's and Shearer's early letters, and Sill's early poems.[4]

Let us briefly review this quest to which Spencer brought an end. Sill had been thoroughly out of sympathy with the threadbare piety that he found at Yale. His favorite mentors, Carlyle, Emerson, and Tennyson, had taught him that it was the duty of man to doubt and to find truth for himself, and most of his undergraduate poems expressed either dissatisfaction with the dull routine of the college or earnest questioning concerning the nature of things. In "Morning,"[5] for example, he attacked the empty drill of all uninspired worship, including compulsory chapel, and in "The Polar Sea"[6] he set down the darker thought that life itself is an aimless drift from the unknown to the unknown. Again and again he asked in these poems, "Is it not time to tell us why we live?" and on at least one occasion he answered, "Time gives back no answer."[7] Nor did such questions cease with graduation. A year later he wrote from California, where he had gone in search of physical and intellectual health:

We are . . . planted down in the midst of a great snarl and tangle of interrogation points. We want to find—we *must* find—some fixed truth. . . . As Kingsley puts it, we are set down before that greatest world-problem—"Given self, to find God."[8]

Behind this fervent doubt there was, of course, a strong will to believe, and this led him by 1864 and 1865 to an earnest, if tentative, Christian belief. For the moment he accepted the doctrine of immortality on the ground of "the implanted certainty . . . that God is Perfect,"[9] and wrote categorically to a friend:

Either Christ was God or He was not. And if He was, we must take what He said as actual truth, not to be twisted or turned aside. . . . Through his name, his sacrifice, and his intercession, and *thus alone,* can we inherit eternal life.[10]

Though he could not keep himself from asking, "What is there in man worth perpetuation?"[11] by 1866 he had sufficient hope of conviction to depart with his friend Shearer for the Harvard Divinity School. According to the surmise of an acquaintance, they chose Harvard only because "they would not be required there to believe so much as in other American schools," but even at that "the beliefs were too much" for Sill. "It was the same old whine in new bottles,"[12] he said, and did not return after the summer holiday.

Moreover, these doubts increased rather than diminished as he grew older, perhaps partly under the influence of Spencer himself. In the words of his biographer, his doubtful hope deepened into hopeful doubt.[13] The "Christian Church," he wrote, was "a nuisance and a fraud,"[14] and "the Christian mythology and the Church grip on society . . . very hurtful things."[15] He hoped that the president chosen to succeed Porter at Yale would be "no 'Doctor' of an exploded 'Divinity.' "[16] And yet his scepticism was far from complete. His belief in some kind of a Supreme Being was as fervent as ever, even if much less definite, and the most vivid recollection of his students during his later years at the Oakland High School and the University of California was of his ethical idealism. Millicent Shinn, for example, later the editor of *The Overland Monthly*, remembered of his teaching that "it was as if he carried into the schoolroom the same ideals that would have taken him into the pulpit."[17] In this his position was not unusual. One's way of life is likely to be more deeply rooted than one's doctrine, and like many others in the nineteenth century Sill found his zeal for righteousness not only undiminished but even stimulated by the dissolution of its supernatural foundations. He was not one to let it go at that, however; his very thoughtful mind demanded a rational as well as a temperamental basis for good.

Thus was the ground prepared for his reading of Spencer. Of course he must have known very early who Spencer was and something of what he stood for, but he does not appear to have studied him until later. In a letter of 1864 or 1865 he said explicitly that he had not read him,[18] and in another of the latter year he expressed strong disapproval of the "Spencer chaps"[19] for their separation of religion from life. Three years later, however, after he had left Harvard and begun to teach in Ohio, he had relented sufficiently to include Spencer along with Shakespeare, Shelley, Mill, and Browning as one of the "companions" who were "one compensation in living in a heathen country."[20] Apparently he had begun to read Spencer and to admire him, but the fact that there are no further references until 1879, after which there are many, suggests that more careful study was not undertaken at least until after he returned to California to teach in 1871, and perhaps not until he began to grapple with advanced studies on the faculty of the University of California in 1874. These later comments, however, are not only intensely enthusiastic, but certain proof that he had read Spencer widely and thoughtfully over a considerable period of time. Because they document his debt to Spencer so explicitly, three are worth quoting.[21] In 1880 he wrote to Henry Holt:

I knew about the Social Science Association, but my point was that they don't get to the bottom-difficulty, viz., what end are we after? And secondly, is it the end we had *better* be after? My notion is that Spencer is the only man that has begun to answer that question —namely in the "Data"—and in previous hints which he that didn't run too fast might read. . . .[22]

Again, in a prefatory note to the essay "What Do We Mean by 'Right' and 'Ought'?" he stated:

While the substance of this essay was written, and propounded to a limited circle, before the publication of Herbert Spencer's "Data of Ethics," it comes—from a different point of view—to results in harmony with that work. Nor is this strange, since the writer had been familiar with Mr. Spencer's previous writings, and had no doubt been greatly indebted to him in all his later thinking on the subject.[23]

He added, finally, in 1883 in a criticism of Spencer's theories of education:

the writer begs leave to say that he feels the greatest obligation to Mr. Spencer for intellectual help in many directions; and that in several years of college teaching . . . he has aimed to bring students to the thorough comprehension of Mr. Spencer's works as a part of our modern English literature, and has considered this to be one of the highest services he could render them.[24]

Sill differed from Spencer more than he knew, but it is evident that Spencer gave him something that he valued most highly.

What this something was is not difficult to discover. Sill was thoroughly dissatisfied with the reigning metaphysical and theological bases of morals, and Spencer purported to offer an ethic grounded on positive fact. He professed to have demonstrated that the course of the universe was an evolution from indefinite, incoherent homogeneity to definite, coherent heterogeneity, and his ethical theory was a corollary of this basic proposition. Good actions, he deduced, are those which advance the evolutionary process, elaborating and fulfilling the possibilities of life, the product of evolution. Conduct is a matter of the adjustment of means to ends, and is good when that adjustment tends toward the greatest length, breadth, and fullness of life. He did not develop the theory fully until *The Data of Ethics* in 1879, but it was implicit in all that he had written before and had been stated in a special application in *Education* in 1861:

To prepare us for complete living is the function which education has to discharge; and the only rational mode of judging of any educational course is, to judge in what degree it discharges such function.[25]

Sill severely criticized Spencer's deductions from this premise, but was in thorough agreement with the premise itself. And since, in view of his serious attitude toward his profession, this is the one of Spencer's books in which Sill must have had the most immediate interest, it is not unlikely that this definition was the germ of the ethic of "complete living" that he elaborated in several essays in the eighties and exemplified in many poems.

Spencer's theory was not its only ingredient, however. In its simplest terms it was a call to action, a Yea to Life, and as such was present in much that he wrote before he knew Spencer. If we recall his early devotion to Carlyle,[26] we can see how he was prepared for it. "The Hermitage,"[27] for example, reflecting the storm and stress of his early years in California, was a kind of sentimental *Sartor Resartus*. Disappointed in love, the hero of this poem sought a far-off refuge to live out his life in solitude. A convinced egoist and fatalist, he doubted man's ability to alter the course of things, and in the depths of his scepticism derided the whole idea of man's freedom. This was his Everlasting No. Something like an Everlasting Yea followed as the result of a nearly fatal illness which "burned away some lies." He reasserted man's freedom—"fate is fate through man's free will alone"—and in an embarrassingly bathetic denouement was reunited with his beloved and brought back to the world and a life of struggle and accomplishment. Not that Sill, any more than Carlyle, found good only in extraverted action. On the contrary, he never ceased to urge the rewards of a wise passiveness, which he regarded as one of the means of achieving the fullness of conscious life which is man's distinction and highest achievement. His ideal was an almost Emersonian ideal of self-realization and was well expressed in the lines entitled "Life" in his volume of 1868:

> Forenoon and afternoon and night,—Forenoon,
> And afternoon, and night,—Forenoon, and—what!
> The empty song repeats itself. No more?
> Yea, that is Life: make this forenoon sublime,
> This afternoon a psalm, this night a prayer,
> And Time is conquered, and thy crown is won.[28]

But if we must allow for other influences than Spencer's in accounting for Sill's outlook, we must in the end recognize that Spencer contributed more than any other to its formulation. This is made clear in various of his essays. Thus in "Principles of Criticism," after crediting Spencer with having come closest to the central truth of the nature of beauty, he built an aesthetic on the ideal of "complete living." Spencer had graded aesthetic pleasure according to the number and quality of powers called into activity, the lowest being simply the pleasure of sense, the next adding the pleasure of perception, and the highest including also, according to Sill's summary, "the pleasure of the aesthetic sentiments proper, composed of multitudinous emotions excited in the mind by associations, some of them reaching far back in the race experience of man."[29] This was tantamount to saying that the highest aesthetic pleasure involves the most complete activity of mental and emotional life, and this Sill developed into a basic critical canon that has a particularly modern sound:

> The secret of all art is . . . within the reach of our hand when we have realized one single fact concerning man. As we look out upon life we see its myriad activities all springing from certain desires. But there is one desire among them which is permanent, and paramount to all. It is not the desire for mere pleasure, for it often overrides that; it is not the desire for mere happiness, for it often overrides that. It is the desire for life: not the poor negative desire to escape death and cling to existence, merely, but the aspiration for full and abounding life. To be alive in every faculty; to have the greatest possible total of conscious being, in physical impression

and effect, in intellectual force and grasp, in emotional glow, in the out-stream of the active will; in short, completely to be and live, this is the one paramount human desire. . . .

And now where is there to be found a perpetual source of this power and activity that we perpetually desire? Nowhere but in the expressed power and activity of other human spirits,—and that is art. . . .

The test, then, for all art is that, expressing much life, it shall give much life.[30]

At this point it can be seen that Sill was parting company with Spencer. If art was a "perpetual source" of the highest life, it was one of the most important of human activities—which it certainly was not to Spencer. When Spencer said that art was the play of the mind,[31] he meant literally what he said; it was a purely incidental activity, pleasurable, but of no use in the struggle for existence. In that part of the *Principles of Ethics* that was published after Sill's death, the arts were dismissed with sports in a single chapter entitled "Amusements."[32] Sill does not seem to have known how far he had departed from Spencer, but that he was aware of a difference is clear from his article written in 1883 on Spencer's twenty-two-year-old essays on education. There, after stating the definition that has been quoted, Spencer had classified in order of importance "the leading kinds of activity which constitute human life":

1. those activities which directly minister to self-preservation; 2. those activities which, by securing the necessaries of life, indirectly minister to self-preservation; 3. those activities which have for their end the rearing and discipline of offspring; 4. those activities which are involved in the maintenance of proper social and political relations; 5. those miscellaneous activities which fill up the leisure part of life, devoted to the gratification of the tastes and feelings.[33]

Sill contended that this was both a perversion and an inversion of the principle of "complete living." He quite agreed that activities directed to self-preservation were essential, but argued that "complete living" implied the realization of the potentialities of life rather than simply its preservation. In ramming this point home he was able to take Spencer up neatly on a questionable analogy that helps to define their difference. In making the point that the primary motive in human life is self-preservation, Spencer had used the example of the horticulturist, whose primary interest, he said, must of necessity be seed and soil. Sill replied that the primary interest of the horticulturist is not seed and soil but flowers and that he busies himself with the former only in order to produce the latter.[34] Here was a vital disagreement, Spencer the philosopher of science standing for means, Sill the artist and humanist standing for ends.

In this connection it is significant that Sill evolved his principle by a method quite different from Spencer's. Reasoning directly from biological evolution, Spencer argued that those acts must be regarded as good which make for biological success, that is, which make for survival in the struggle for existence.[35] Sill, however, approached the problem psychologically and semantically, asking what we mean when we use the words "right" and "ought." In other words, Spencer found the locus of good in the relation between organism and environment, while Sill found it in conscious experience. This might be demonstrated at length out of the essay "What Do We Mean by 'Right' and 'Ought'?" but a single passage in which Sill stated what he understood by the Spencerian term "human welfare" will suffice:

If the stone's condition is, least of all, "welfare," if that of the mollusk is but little better, and so on, what is this increasing element, as we go higher in the grade of existence, that approaches more and more our ideal of real "good," real "welfare"? It is nothing less than *Being—conscious existence, completeness of life.* Why does intellectual pleasure seem higher to us than animal pleasure? Because it involves more of the man....[36]

This was worlds away from Spencer's statement in *The Data of Ethics* that

evolution, tending ever towards self-preservation, reaches its limit when individual life is the greatest both in length and breadth; and ... that, leaving other ends aside, we regard as good the conduct furthering self-preservation, and as bad the conduct tending to self-destruction.[37]

Sill was certainly unaware of the profundity of this difference. Even in the review of the essays on education he suggested that the error of the master might be rectified in a new edition; and in connection with the passage just quoted he said, "this brings us, from a different standpoint, to Spencer's conclusion in the 'Data of Ethics,' "[38] just as he had announced at the beginning of the essay:

We shall find that "right," as a quality of actions, has reference to their consequences; that when we say a thing is "right" we mean that it conduces to human welfare; that the highest welfare is conceived to be that which Herbert Spencer describes in his "Data of Ethics" as "complete living."[39]

However, the difference was real and deep, for when Sill and Spencer spoke of acts and consequences, means and ends, they meant different things. Spencer was thinking in terms of quantity and had reference to the duration and complexity of life, while Sill was thinking in terms of quality and had reference to the realization of the powers peculiar to a particular kind of organism, the rational animal man. Though he himself used quantitative language in this instance, this was plainly his meaning in "Principles of Criticism" when he spoke of "the greatest possible total of conscious being, in physical impression and effect, in intellectual force and grasp, in emotional glow, in the out-stream of the active will."[40] In short, Spencer and Sill differed by so much as a utilitarian ethic differs from an ethic of self-realization. And this is a great deal, for an ethic of self-realization implies a discontinuity that was quite foreign to the Spencerian evolutionism. Such an ethic judges a man according to his development of those faculties in which he differs from an animal, while the Spencerian ethic, which is concerned with the relation between organism and environment, finds the ethical situation essentially the same on all levels of existence. This does not mean that Sill was on the way to a denial of evolution in the sense of a genetic connection of species, but only that he chose to ground his ethic on those aspects of man's nature that are novelties in the evolutionary series.

Moreover, it does not gainsay Spencer's influence on Sill so much as define it. Spencer stimulated rather than indoctrinated him. He came upon Spencer at a time when the metaphysical and theological bottom had dropped out of his world, and Spencer suggested to him, first, that a bottom of "positive" experience was sufficient, and, second, that such a bottom might support an affirmative code of values. If he did not follow Spencer to the bitter end, it was partly because, bred in the ethical idealism of Carlyle and Emerson, he did not wholly understand him and partly because he wished to develop the "positive" point of view in a direction that he felt had been neglected by the devotees of science. This is apparent in a review of the works of Emerson in *The Overland Monthly* in

1884, in which he misinterpreted Emerson as badly as he had Spencer but was again quite clear about his own views. Attacking philosophy at length as "a vast system of words concerning what we cannot know,"[41] he found approvingly that "the essential quality of Emerson is that, while possessing the point of view, the predilection, the mental temperament of the scientist, while having the positive spirit, he had the human instead of the material interests."[42] This was false as a statement about Emerson, but true of Sill, at least in intention. Elsewhere in the essay he stated that when modern civilization emerged from the Dark Ages, two great fields of inquiry opened up, metaphysics and natural science, and then added that "now there has opened a third field, between the two— humanics, or matters concerning that which is on the earth, but not of it—man and human life."[43] This was the field which Sill wished to cultivate and which he believed Emerson had cultivated with particular success. "Who, then, will read and enjoy these volumes of the prose and verse of Emerson?" he asked at the end. His answer was:

Not he who is still looking for a system of philosophy, woven out of the cob-webs of logic, that shall pretend to expound "the riddle of the painful earth"; nor he who cares only for the processes of brute nature; but rather those fewer persons who are already disposed to believe that we shall never get wisdom from gazing up into the fog, or down into the sand, but from looking around us on human life, trying with cheerful courage to see what is the precise fact of our condition, and what is the nearest duty to be done.[44]

Even those who know Sill only through the anthologies will observe that the negative side of this position is that of "Five Lives" and the positive that of "Opportunity."

Admitting, however, that Sill was indebted to Spencer in his ethical thought, the question inevitably arises, why was he not closer to Spencer in his philosophy of nature?—or, more specifically, why did he have so little to say on the subject? As has been pointed out, after "Man the Spirit" his references to evolution were few and oblique and never had the purpose of judging or presenting the conception as a whole. Take "Infirmity," for example, which comes nearest to contradicting this statement:

> Free of the doubting mind,
> Full of the olden power,

> Are the tree, and the bee, and the wind,
>   And the wren, and the brave may-flower.
>
> Man was the last to appear,
>   A glow at the close of day;
> Slow clambering now in fear
>   He gropes his slackened way.
>
> All the up-thrust is gone,
>   Force that came from of old,
> Up through the fish, and the swan,
>   And the sea-king's mighty mould.
>
> The youth of the world is fled,
>   There are omens in the sky,
> Spheres that are chilled and dead,
>   And the close of an age is nigh.
>
> The time is too short to grieve,
>   Or to choose, for the end is one:
> And what is the truth to believe,
>   And what is the right to be done?[45]

The evolutionary drift of these lines is obvious, but it is equally evident that Sill's purpose was not to define or support any cosmological thesis. He exceeded his usual reticence, to be sure, in asserting that "the close of an age is nigh," but the plain final meaning of the poem is that the cosmic situation is irrelevant to the ethical life. Since time is short, it is idle to speculate on causes and ends; only moral conviction and action matter. As in the Emerson review, his point is that wisdom lies in "trying with cheerful courage to see what is the precise fact of our condition, and what is the nearest duty to be done." Most emphatically, Sill did not wish, here or elsewhere, to contribute to the vexed questions of first and final cause. Indeed, he was convinced that nothing could be contributed to these questions; that they, like all metaphysical problems, were beyond human powers. Berkeley, he approvingly quoted G. H. Lewes as saying, "failed as the greatest Philosophers of all times have failed, not because he was weak, but because Philosophy was impossible."[46]

Paradoxical as it may seem, Sill had learned the Spencerian scepticism too well to concern himself much with the Spencerian cosmology. Spencer held that since knowledge of ultimate reality is impossible, the positive knowledge and mechanistic hypotheses of the sciences are sufficient; but this deduction Sill vigorously denied. He seems to have detected that Spencer's philosophy of nature came down in practice to a dogmatic mechanism, and on this he was as unsparing as on dogmatic rationalism or idealism. In naming those who would continue to read and enjoy Emerson, it will be remembered, he eliminated not only those who were "still looking for a system of Philosophy" but those who cared "only for the processes of brute nature"; and in both poetry and prose he was no less hard on the exponents of a narrow scientism than on the metaphysicians. "Five Lives"[47] contains one of the nicest satires of positivism extant, and the Emersonian article balanced its anti-metaphysical polemic with this statement:

In the reaction in favor of material studies, most of the loud voices have naturally been on the side of the reactionists. They have almost persuaded us that, while a fact, set down with care and carried to a number of decimal places, concerning the length of a beetle's wing, is scientific and of great value, a truth about human feeling, thought, passion, motive, is nothing but literature; perhaps, even, nothing but poetry; and therefore of no value but to entertain a leisure hour. We need to recover our recognition of the greater value of the truth concerning man, and of the greater value of writings that throw light on human life.[48]

The fact is that in a sense important for the later development of this study, Sill was a man ahead of his time. For the history of cosmic optimism in the sense here intended will come to a close when the great majority of poets begin, tacitly or explicitly, to emulate Sill's position, turning back, along with James and Dewey, to Hume, and dismissing the nineteenth-century "philosophies of evolution" as mere metaphysical creeds.[49] Sill could be devoted to Spencer and yet fail to celebrate his evolutionism because he had learned Spencer's critical philosophy well enough to have acquired an aversion for any total or ultimate formulation of the universe. Man, his scepticism told him, is not to be accounted for—much less, to be morally enlightened—by any cosmic system, mechanical or metaphysical. He heartily accepted evolution as a historical fact, but he also knew well that no theory of origins can alter by one iota the present facts of his spiritual and moral life.[50] In view of the influence upon him of such thinkers as Spencer and Lewes, this is, for our purposes, probably the most important orientation of

Sill's thought; but it should not be forgotten that another, more backward-looking parallel is also possible. Sill frequently blended with his scepticism the quite consistent romantic principle that "the heart can apprehend a deeper purport than the brain may know,"[51] and he would certainly have subscribed to Longfellow's preference for "the deed and not the creed."[52] But then so would James and Dewey and many of the later writers who were to abandon the "quest for certainty." In either case, he was quite indifferent to the cosmic thesis which is the subject of this study.

2

Others who came within the Spencerian orbit were less rigorous in their repression of cosmological speculation than Sill. Like the master himself they were more than willing to generalize about the cosmos, even tending to exceed his limits in one or the other of two directions. Thus to some his denial of knowledge of anything beyond phenomena had the effect merely of a denial of anything non-material beyond phenomena. He had said that the universe is a machine in so far as we can know it, and this was not infrequently received as meaning that the universe is nothing but a machine. On the other hand, in admitting an unknowable cause beyond phenomena, Spencer had left an x-quantity which he himself said might be the proper object of religious feeling and which others were inclined to refurbish as a god of nature. Fiske, it will be remembered,[53] reasoned from a "dramatic tendency" in evolution to intimations of the "psychical character" of this cause. With the exception of Charles De Kay, who was nearly independent of both tendencies, all of the five minor writers who will occupy the remainder of this chapter violated the agnostic limitations in one or the other direction. The first two to be considered, H. H. Boyesen and William Leighton, moved in the direction of Fiske, finding adumbrations of purpose in the cosmos and seeking to develop the religious significance of evolution; the last two, Edgar Fawcett and Starr Hoyt Nichols, turned toward dogmatic materialism and mechanism.

Boyesen (1848-95), who published a series of five sonnets entitled "Evolution" in *The Atlantic Monthly* in 1878,[54] even seems at first glance to hark back beyond Fiske to Whitman and Emerson. Like them he used an exclamatory formula to evoke a sense of the vastness of evolutionary time ("What dizzying aeons passed ere yet a lichen patch the bare rock flecked!"); he told the story of evolution in the first person ("My lullaby by hoarse Silurian storms was chanted."), and his theme was the oneness of man and nature. Closer inspection, however, shows that the resemblance is no more than superficial. When Whitman and Emerson wrote of evolution in the first person and proclaimed the unity of man and nature, they meant that nature is the outward appearance or changing incarnation of a World-Soul of which the soul of man is a microcosm, while Boyesen meant the reverse, that the soul of man is a superior manifestation of the physical force of nature. This difference is of course difficult to demonstrate in detail because both views may be expressed in the same terms, but if we consider those lines in the poem that deal most specifically with the nature and cause of evolution the difference becomes apparent. Thus, like Lucretius, Boyesen began with the statement that "a mighty will" swayed the primeval atoms, and followed this up with a thoroughly mechanistic description of the sequel as "vast, resounding undulations of effect." Moreover, in denying all knowledge of the nature of this "will," as in the following passage, he definitely allied himself with the school of Spencer. The word "life," as the context indicates, must be interpreted in a broader sense than the biological:

> What life is in its essence, who doth know?
> The iron chain that all creation girds,
> Encompassing myself and beasts and birds,
> Forges its bond unceasing from below,—
> From water, stone, and plant, e'en unto man.

However, it is a matter of importance that Boyesen used the word "will," which has anthropomorphic connotations not present in the Spencerian "force," and that he elsewhere spoke of "a potent mystery" that "thrills the mean clay into refulgence grand." No doubt this was in part merely poetic diction, but it also reveals the tendency to isolate and celebrate a moving cause that was pointed out in the later writings of Fiske. This is the more evident because Boyesen did not present evolution as blind and directionless, but as having had man as its goal in the past and untold wonders in the future. "The toiling ages wrought to fashion me," he said in the second sonnet, which is strongly reminiscent of Whitman, and the fifth concludes with this glowing vision:

> gazing down the misty aisles of space
> And time, upon my sight vast visions throng
> Of the imperial destiny of man.
> The life that throbbed in plant and beast ere long
> Will break still wider orbits in its van,—
> A race of peace-robed conquerors and kings,
> Achieving evermore diviner things.

There is no mention of God in any of the sonnets, but the author says this of the spectacle of the geological record:

> Oh, what wide vistas thronged with mighty deed
> And mightier thought have here mine eyes descried!

"Mightier thought" as used here may be taken to have an import similar to Fiske's use of the word "psychical" in the Preface to *The Idea of God*.

The fullest poem on evolution written in this country was *Change: The Whisper of the Sphinx* (1879; rev. ed., 1906)[55] by William Leighton (1833-1911), a Wheeling glass manufacturer and amateur of poetry and science. In something over a hundred pages Leighton sought to expound and interpret the science of his time on the basis of its assumption that

> Seeking to know the origin of all,
>   . . .
> [Man] finds philosophy of no avail;
> In Nature's elements his utmost reach,[56]

and in the light of the principle of flux embodied in its theories of evolution:

> Looking abroad for Nature's moving powers
> He only grasps results as atoms fly;
> Finds Change the ruler of created things,
> The doom of every wandering molecule,
> The history of planets and of suns,
> The ripple under which there stirs a law.[57]

In his development of the latter principle, moreover, Leighton was more radical than any other writer we have studied, recognizing that evolutionary change involves not only development but passing away. The complement of Spencer's theory of evolution was a theory of dissolution, but this Spencer himself and most of his followers, dazzled by the notion of progress, tended to neglect. Leighton too made much of the evolutionary ascent, but it is to his credit that he gave equal weight to the evanescent character of all things under the law of evolution, whether solar systems or men. Of the earth he observed that "the fires of friction burn up force"[58] and predicted that in time it would be drawn back into the sun whence it had been discharged. True, he allowed himself the comfort of a vision of cosmic rebirth reminiscent of Poe's in *Eureka*,[59] but he found no consolation in this for men, who could not survive the ordeal and whose civilizations meanwhile obeyed the iron laws of decay. After speaking of the displacement of the red man by the white, he added that "a hundred causes could be found" why "we . . . have no more security of life than they,"[60] and though he admitted the wonders of modern material progress he questioned whether it was necessarily enduring or beneficent. In answer to the question, "How will the years roll over men? Will such progression make them wiser, happier?"[61] he stated in his earlier and less sanguine edition that we cannot say, and in both editions he concluded his discussion of the modern world with ominous passages on the vigorous arming of nations. Finally, he even questioned the identity of the individual soul. A section on "Force" ends:

> Force into consciousness—there still is Change:
> The human mind is not a steadfast thing;
> If immaterial its substance be,
> It hath so much analogy with Earth
> To feel the active tyranny of Force,
> And dance with atoms in their frenzied whirl.[62]

And the following section, devoted wholly to the subject of identity, adds, "I dare not hug the thought that I, myself, am constant to myself. . . . How false to deem that I alone am stable!"[63]

To point out only these things would be to misrepresent the poem, however, which in its main drift is anything but pessimistic. Even in the earlier edition Leighton did not minimize the implications of the over-all progress from the cohering of the nebula to the rise of Western man, and in the later edition he tempered nearly all of his more severe statements. Thus he inserted these lines on the geological record:

> Throughout the paths of earth
> Are found life's foot-prints and their changing
>   shapes,

> Showing slow growth from crude, inferior being
> Upward to man. From the first dawn of life,
> Each in its wonderful diversity,
> Mollusk, worm, insect, reptile, fish, bird, beast,
> And all the myriad forms of vegetation,
> Have joined one universal prophecy.[64]

And these on the immediate future:

> in the ferment of this strenuous age
> Who fails to see that large results are brewing?
> That in the menstruum of the present moment,
> Are greater transmutations being wrought
> Than wildest dream of olden alchemist?[65]

He even, in defiance of his statement on the mutability of the soul, argued from universal progress to a life after death. In both editions he had said, "Yet am I not content to sleep in dust forever,"[66] but only in the second did he add:

> We yet may work life's problem so far out,
> To recognize the movement everywhere,
> Eternal progress through the universe,
> The constant march of life-thrilled atomies,
> Unnumbered forms endued with vital force
> That drives them onward—on to death?
>
> . . .
>
> No atom of the Earth is lost in death;
> How can I then be lost? Are human souls
> So valueless that Nature casts them out
> From the vast kingdom of immortal things,
> And falsifying all her promises,
> Plunges them only into nothingness?
> So we were less than all the world of matter,
> The only food for death, while meaner things—
> Things that have been subservient to our uses—
> Go on immortal in unending progress.[67]

Finally, both editions are in the end theistic. Indeed, the expression of an evolutionary theism may be accurately said to be the governing purpose of the poem, whether consistently with the denial of philosophy at the beginning or not. Like Fiske, Leighton was deeply concerned to salvage the broader tenets of religion, and to this end he devoted the entire final third of his poem to the inferences that might be drawn from nature concerning God and the

SILL AND CERTAIN MINOR POETS 265

spiritual life of man. Thus, far from denying the truth of any particular faith, he found truth in all:

> A keen perception of th' unresting force
> That drives its chariot wheels round the Earth,
> And flashes change from every star of heaven,
> Combined with consciousness of impotence
> To stay one atom or delay one change,
> Compels the worshiper, on bended knees
> To lift his prayer to some symbolic god. . . .[68]

And like Fiske he turned back to the argument from design. Earlier in the poem he had hinted reservedly at a teleological interpretation of nature:

> If 'tis too much to hope to know the whole,
> Then we may learn a little; lift ourselves
> Toward the light whose glimmering intimates
> A wise intent hath drawn the myriad lines
> Of tangled web. . . .[69]

But later, throwing caution to the winds, he quite outdid the modest concessions of Fiske. Fiske would certainly have agreed that "all the showings of the nice powers of sense . . . are little parts of a well-ordered whole"[70] and would probably have passed the statement that nature is "a positive showing of the Infinite Will,"[71] but he would certainly have wished to qualify the broader claim that the facts of nature are

> Letters engraven broadly on the world,
> Telling of power, beneficence, and love,[72]

and would have flatly rejected the argument that

> That which can comprehend must be of kind
> With that which hath contrived. . . .[73]

"Change," Leighton concluded in fulsome peroration,

> is the movement of the Master's hand,
> And constant purpose is divinely whispered
> Beneath its touch.[74]

If all the thought of Charles De Kay (1848-1935) were available to us, we should probably associate him with Boyesen and Leighton rather than with Fawcett and Nichols. This, at any rate, is the suggestion of his dedication to Emerson as well as Darwin of *The Vision of Esther* (1882), the second of a proposed series of three epics dealing with modern themes against an oriental background:

Dedicated to Darwin, the great student of nature without us, and to Emerson, the believer in the ideal and supernatural within, the second volume proceeds on the assumption of the first, that always the study of nature coexisted beside the study of God and never did the one really invalidate the other. Only it needs to-day more width of mind to bridge the gap made inevitably by the progress of ideas in separate directions.[75]

However, in that part of the first of the epics, *The Vision of Nimrod* (1881), in which evolution is the main theme, the cosmological questions on which such an alignment would be made are completely passed over. For once, the evolutionary story is told exclusively for its narrative interest. At the beginning of the poem we find the hero and heroine, modern figures, resting in a barren land near the site of ancient Babylon. The ghost of the ancient warrior-leader Nimrod appears to them in the form of a lion, and, after transforming himself into a man, tells first his own story and then the adventure of his friend and vizier, Ahram, in the Tarn of Kaf. This, comprising all of Book IV of the poem,[76] is the story of evolution, and is worth summarizing in some detail both for its own sake and for certain of its implications.

Long before he met Nimrod, Ahram found himself in a steeply cliffed valley, and there, crouched in hiding beside the glassy surface of the tarn, waited and watched and saw a mysterious growth of one being in succession to another until finally man arrived. First "fine crystals 'gan to form," then "shapes that are not shapes" that "join and disjoin" and "break in twain." Life increased and teemed, and in time there came a monster, "sans feet, sans wings," succeeded by a fish "with triple strength," which

> if the former shape it quite devoured,
> Or by some change grew out of it who knows?

The fish ruled for a time, and then a reptilian beast with tail and gills that presently "shrank, being useless," crawled from the edge of the water, bellowed its triumph, and began immediately to transform. "For wings it longed and wings it won," and it became the first bird. In due course the reptile-bird was killed by a bulk so vast that "mere living things her life could not sustain," but scarcely had the victory been won before "a smaller beast, forth crept whose sabre teeth of grass had never tasted," and "with hoofs, teeth, horns, began a conflict dire." "But soon arose a tyrant in the forest in shape like man, yet not man at all." "Working his ends by thought which force deceives," this newcomer overcame the sabre-toothed feline and ruled for a time in his stead. But even so, "short was his reign," and "soon, on the apelike plan, issued a man." "Till now the broods of fish and beast and bird lived planless," but "now had a king of all of them with forethought armed." This new ruler was not succeeded by new forms but only by improved versions of himself. He learned the power of deceit, he learned to "imitate and read the intention behind an act," he acquired "ordered speech," he learned to "defend the forest he ranges," he "began the luxuries to gather, the useless arts that good and evil shape in equal measure," and finally he learned to perform specialized tasks and to trade for what he desired. Not that all stopped there, however, for the last that Ahram saw before he fled in fright was that

> some grew wise beyond all human bounds
> And at their death, or violent, or peaceful,
> Out of the mouths of such, with moaning sounds,
> A something fluttering, took shape, or graceful
> Or else as bestial as those monsters grim
> That went before.

This in brief abstract is the story that De Kay put into the mouth of the ancient Persian. It is a lively story, swiftly and vividly told and heightened and distinguished from the general run by the only slightly absurd fantasy in which it is framed. Moreover, though no direct comment is given by the author, enough is implied to add materially to the history of the idea we have been following. Here, in fact, for the first time in American poetry the note of Darwinism is heard unmodified by any systematic preconceptions, whether transcendental or Spencerian. For the emphasis of Darwin was not on any universal cosmic order, mechanical or otherwise, but rather on a profuse, unplanned abundance and the ruthless elimination of the beings less well adapted to their environment. And of this one is made keenly aware in De Kay's poem. It is true that the exact details of the process of evolution are left in doubt and that the language is sometimes more Lamarckian than Darwinian, but the memories that linger in the mind of the reader are of the bloody battles that followed the advent of each new creature.

It does not tell all about Edgar Fawcett (1847-1904) to point out that he was the author of a volume entitled *Agnosticism and Other Essays*[77] with a Prologue by Robert Ingersoll, but it makes a substantial beginning. In the title essay of this collection he contended against the middle ground of Unitarianism through a criticism of Mrs. Humphry Ward's *Robert Elsmere* and sought in general to justify the agnostic suspension of judgment on ultimate questions. He had not always been of this mind, however. Though he was the son of an Englishman of Spencerian leanings and had been a member of the free-thinking Nineteenth Century Club of New York since its founding in 1880, among his early poems there are several that evince a decided distaste for the comfortlessness of the new doctrines. In his earliest volume, for example, even though there is a poem that praises Herbert Spencer as the "archenemy of lies,"[78] there is another that quotes and rejects with disdain John Stuart Mill's asseveration that the long life of the race is sufficient response to "any reasonable demand for grandeur of aspiration" without personal immortality.[79] This theme is repeated in an elegy on the death of Albert F. Webster,[80] and still another poem is devoted to the refutation of the quoted statement of Herbert Spencer that "in its essence nothing can be known."[81]

These objections were contrary, however, to the main and mature drift of Fawcett, who came in time to accept the new scepticism and to regard its asperities with stoicism. In the intervening volumes one finds a mingling of views, but in the last, *Songs of Doubt and Dream* (1891), the transformation is complete. Here, in fact, in an elegy on the death of Courtland Palmer,[82] the founder of the Nineteenth Century Club, is a perfect foil for the elegy on Webster. This time, twelve years after Webster's death, the poet consoles himself with the fact that death treats all alike, and devotes his verses to the gifts that the dead leave the living. The most complete rejection, however, of the comforts of a life after death is to be found in the last poem in the volume, which, as its title, "Courage!"[83] indicates, takes a stoical and disillusioned position; and the most intimate joining of the theme with evolution is to be found in the seventeenth of a series of "Intermezzos."[84] The subject of the latter is a dream in which the poet sees "a system of dead worlds, rolling, huge cinders, round a mightier sun, itself a cinder."[85] A voice says to the dreamer:

> "Each world . . . .
> Was once, when millions of slow years had passed,
> Glorious for beauty nature dowered it with,
> But still more glorious for the habitants
> That rose from ape to angel on its orb.
> Then came, when millions of more years were spent,
> Gradual extinction of the vast sun's fires."[86]

To the question, " 'Will our sun fade like this?' " the voice replies,

> "Yes . . . .
> With worlds in space to evolve is to dissolve,
> And even with us being born is but to die.
> An individual immortality
> Haunts with its hollow myth men's trusting hearts.
> Forsake that shadow, and live thy human life
> Nobly and adequately till the end."[87]

Such comfort as there is, the voice concludes, lies in the painlessness of oblivion.

In spite of these dour views of the future of the individual, however, Fawcett was blithely confident of the future of the race. Thus "Courage!" ends:

> Ah, courage, courage, faltering souls!
> Perchance to paradisiac goals
> The race moves; and if this be true,
> Each individual deed ye do
> Fraternity's diviner way,
> Will speed that large millennial day
> When men shall walk, bright-browed and grand,
> Our beauteous planet's wrong-cursed land![88]

It was of course a progress based on the new dispensation in human knowledge rather than on a divine plan or an immanent spirit of goodness, as the poet indicated as early as 1880 in an ode read to the Harvard Phi Beta Kappa.[89] In the last section of this poem, after having reviewed the ills and advances of America, he pictured the freedom of the republic walking with the light of science toward a new and brighter world. Again, in the 1886 volume, the poet looked forward in a poem called "The Future"[90] to "a race unutterably grand," and in another poem[91] a dying archangel who had been banished for sin chose as a place of retirement a planet, obviously the earth, which had always been a favorite of his because of its persistent melioration. "O star," he said, addressing his new home,

> I knew thee in thy luminous prime,
> And loved thee not alone that thou wert fair,
> But for the attainments and the victories
> Wrought of thy peoples till they rose like gods!
> For slowly did they climb, while aeons passed,
> From brutish aims to deeds of golden worth.[92]

The most significant of Fawcett's many poems on this theme, however, is a long one, "In the Year Ten Thousand," in the 1891 volume.[93] Here two citizens "meet in a square of the vast city, Manattia, ages ago called New York."[94] They talk about the past of their city and contrast its former hideousness and vice with its present beauty, peace, and contentment. The men of the time have come to realize that beauty is the proper and natural environment of man rather than merely a vain ornament, and their recognition of the "idiocy of sin"[95] has driven away church and prison alike. They know that their blessed state has been a slow growth out of an inferior past, for one of them says, "from grosser types we have risen by grades of change to what we are; this incontestably we clutch as truth";[96] but they are quite satisfied with their present state, which has put to work the "etheric force" and reduced the barriers of language. One of them says, in fact, of the etheric force,

> Nay, more, if chronicles
> Err not, they worshipped it and named it God.
> We name it Nature and it worships us.[97]

This poem, in short, is a Utopia, like the better-known *Looking Backward,* which followed it by only a few years. It is a kind of positivist's paradise, in which what Comte called the "theological" and "metaphysical" modes of thinking have been banished and the knowledge of things placed completely at man's service.

The poet who removed himself furthest from the transcendental tradition, however, and who produced the fourth of the lengthy poems on evolution that appeared between 1878 and 1883 was

SILL AND CERTAIN MINOR POETS 271

Starr Hoyt Nichols (1834-1909), a onetime Unitarian minister and later co-editor of the radical *Social Economist*. His poem was *Monte Rosa: The Epic of an Alp*,[98] a long, discursive work in which attention is about equally divided between the exhilaration of mountain scenery and the philosophical significance of nature. The theme of evolution is introduced quite naturally in telling the story of the mountain's growth and leads to such passages as the following, in which events occurring elsewhere in nature are related. "Time," the poet says, using an innocent personification, saw

> tropic climes invade the polar rings,
> Then polar cold lay waste the tropic marge;
> Saw monster beasts emerge in ooze and air,
> And run their race and stow their bones in clay;
> Saw the bright gold bedew the elder rocks,
> And all the gems grow crystal in their caves;
> Saw plant wax quick, and stir to moving worm,
> And worm move upward reaching towards the brute;
> Saw brute by habit fit himself with brain
> And startle earth with wondrous progeny;
> Saw all of these and still saw no true man.
> For man was not, or still so rawly was,
> That as a little child his thoughts were weak,
> Weak and forgetful and of nothing worth,
> And Nature stormed along her changeful ways
> Unheeded, undescribed, and while man slept
> Infolded in his germ, or with fierce brutes,
> Himself but brutal, wages a pigmy war,
> Unclad as they, and with them housed in caves.
> Nor knew that sea retired or mountain rose.[99]

More interesting for our purposes, however, are the philosophical reflections inspired by the prospect from the peak of Monte Rosa.[100] Though the grandeur of the scene spread out before him fills the poet with a sense of a "divine World-Spirit," he hastens to add that he does not mean this literally. There are no "gods" present; rather,

> A goodly world unhaunted lies serene
> In its sufficing loveliness; no more![101]

It is true that a "charm remains," that "still bound our nerves with exultations, hopes," but this must not be regarded as supernatural inspiration. Nature, he urges, is enough; for, as he says in apostrophe to the world about him, to

> him that takes
> Thy meaning thou dost fill with gracious gifts,
> And such rare transport, that the vanished gods
> Seem re-disclosed to him, and daedal earth
> Enough without a better heaven.[102]

With this, as explicit a rejection of supernaturalism as we have yet met with, we may dismiss *Monte Rosa;* but not Nichols, who had much more to say on the same theme, at first in prose and later in verse. Thus, six years afterward in a lecture on "The Philosophy of Evolution" before the Brooklyn Ethical Association[103] he dismissed contemptuously the attempt to marry the theory of evolution "into the fine old family of spiritualism" and attacked Emerson in particular and transcendentalism in general on the naturalistic ground that since thought is the product of a physical organ, inner experience must always be subordinated to outer. These tendencies he developed at greater length in a volume, *The Breath of the World* (1908), which may be described as an enchiridion in the sonnet form of materialism, positivism, utilitarianism, and Manchester economics. Suggestive of the tenor of the whole is the contrast between two sonnets, one on Plato and the other on Bacon, which appear on adjacent pages.[104] Here truly was what Lowell called "Poor Richard elbowing Plato out," for while the latter praises without stint, the former merely patronizes—which was only natural for a man who wrote elsewhere,

> Ages men spent upon their vaporous souls,
> Making poor progress in a human way.[105]

The most significant for this study, however, are thirteen of the sonnets grouped together under the general heading "Evolution." They do not comprise such an orderly sequence as Boyesen's, but they are unified by their subject and certain pervading tendencies in interpretation. For one thing, one finds running through them something of the same mingling of the doctrines of Darwin and Lamarck that was present in De Kay's poem. Thus, in the true spirit of Darwin, nature is pictured as chaotic, fumbling, and completely devoid of anything like benevolence. The first of the poems, bearing the interestingly ironical title "Natura Naturans,"[106] compares "the undying tree of evolution" to "some huge banyan of far Indian lands," which with magnificent indifference produces fruit only to drop it into death. Likewise the second,[107] though it indicates an order in the whole by comparing the whole process to an orchestra, hears as much cacophony as harmony in earth's "gigantic quires," where

> restless fickleness of theme and phrase
> Express the vast caprice of her desires. . . .

On the other hand, Nichols, who followed Spencer in so many things, followed him also in his Lamarckism. The sonnet entitled "The Making of Man,"[108] for example, tells that the silent years have introduced innovations "as each fresh need bade," and the last sonnet in the group, as its title, "Habits as Fate,"[109] suggests, ascribes the origin of species to the accumulation of acquired characteristics.

Again, as a sonnet depicting the evolution of mind emphasizes,[110] the understanding of evolution being presented is a thoroughly materialistic one. Twelve of the fourteen lines in this poem are devoted to telling how

> That artful matter which we count as dead
> Steals forward hour by hour to higher form,

and the last two come to the characteristic conclusion that in man

> the atom scans the universe
> And its deep secrets doth for tales rehearse.

In the last chapter it was pointed out that at least one thinker developed the theory of Lamarck into a kind of idealism, but this was not the case with Nichols, whose emphasis was rather on the determinism of outer circumstances and inner drives. Thus one of his sonnets is significantly entitled "Man the Animal,"[111] and two others, "Rising and Risen"[112] and "Ancestors,"[113] elaborate the implications contained in this title. "Rising and Risen" points out that man "risen" is wont to "call the dove his emblem and sing hymns," but that when his rights are touched, "then tooth and claw are bared." "Ancestors" lays bare the less benign aspects of man's nature in the following apt figures:

> A pirate crew deep in his tissues hid,

> Armed to the teeth with primitive passions strong,
> Ready for mischiefs though his soul forbid,
> Deaf to all reason, fond of old-time wrong.

This unflattering picture of man was thoroughly at odds with the evolutionisms of most of the earlier writers we have studied, but on one particular point, the inevitability of progress, Nichols was quite in agreement with them. Nature, he wrote,[114] is not "conservative," looking upon "all past gain as the last gain gainable," but "radical," eternally changing, and characterized by a "prodigious, forward urgency." This, in fact, he believed to be the very point of the "tale of years":[115]

> What lazy ages hath the beadsman Time
> Taled on his rosary of years wherein were coached
> Earth's forms from low to higher—a mounting rhyme—
> Till the grave monkey's cousin had approached
> To laughing man!

And a fair augury of progress in the future:

> On him time further waits
> To give his wrangling clans from jars release,
> Of blood-stained warriors make friendly states
> Where goodliness and gain may thrive in peace.
> Years hale him forward through sharp agonies
> To ampler dignities and waxing powers
> That show his past as reek of miseries
> Matched with the mercies of arriving hours;
> The weedy wilderness a garden grows,
> Where brambles throve, abounds the gorgeous rose.

This optimism is not that which has prevailed in this study, however, any more than is Spencer's or Comte's.

XII

STEDMAN, GILDER, AND CAWEIN: THE "GENTEEL TRADITION"

FAWCETT'S AND NICHOLS' interpretation of evolutionary progress differed from that which has prevailed in these pages in two principal respects. First, turning their backs on the spiritualistic metaphysic, they based their hopes for the future, not on any indwelling "seed perfection," but on the empirical inference that since the world had progressed in the past, it was likely to continue to do so in the future. Second, they interpreted progress to mean, not the spiritual enlargement envisaged by the transcendentally-minded, but what Bacon called "fruit," the amelioration of man's "condition." Both of these differences are instructive in approaching the three poets to be considered in this chapter, all of whom were of the "genteel tradition" in more than one sense and hence sworn enemies of such materialism and utilitarianism. In turning first to E. C. Stedman, however, the second takes precedence, for as a historian of poetry and spokesman of its interests Stedman was deeply agitated by just this standard of value, with its corollary that poetry and the life of the spirit generally were on the way to being displaced by science. Macaulay's impudent assertion that "as civilization advances, poetry almost necessarily declines"[1]— made fifty years before but at this time more widely accepted— echoed offensively in his ears and was given careful and frequent consideration in his critical writing. The distinctive feature of his contribution to the literature of evolution and progress, in fact, was a retort to Macaulay. Far from being left behind, he insisted, poetry marches in the van of civilization, being itself progressive and the herald of advance in other fields.

1

In finding ultimate justification for his contention, Stedman turned back in the end to the metaphysic from which Fawcett and Nichols turned away, but for the most part his arguments were more immediate. Science and poetry, he preached continually, are not enemies but allies. Poetry not only is necessary as a supplement to science but is necessary in it. Like Poe he pointed out that since every discovery is first an act of the imagination, every scientist who is not a mere grubber after facts must also be in some sense a poet. "The investigator," he wrote in *The Nature and Elements of Poetry,* "if he would leap to greater discoveries, must have the poetic insight and imagination."[2] He did not pause here, moreover, but went on to the rasher inference that because the poet is preeminent in imagination he always precedes and forestalls the scientist. This, it must be interpolated, is contrary to the experience of this study, in which such apparent anticipations have most often turned out to have had some more sober source than a flight of fancy. Stedman's talk about Emerson's intuitive anticipation of Darwin, for example, is sheer nonsense;[3] anyone in Emerson's day who had to discover the notion of evolution by an act of divination simply did not read much. To Stedman, however, such anticipation was not simply an occasional historical accident but literally the law of the progress of the intellect, which he stated most baldly as follows in *Victorian Poets:* "As in chemical physics, first sublimation, then crystallization, then the sure and firm-set earth beneath our feet; so in human progress, first the ethereal fantasy of the poet, then discovery by experience and induction, bringing us to what is deemed scientific, prosaic knowledge of objects and their laws."[4] The poet, hence, is not merely a follower, an adorner of the world that science creates, but a pioneer without whose trail-breaking science itself would be at a standstill.

To do Stedman justice, he meant not only that the poet goes beyond the scientist in his own field but that he goes deeper, revealing the human or eternal significance of what the scientist has established. And in this sense he was on firmer ground in declaring that the poetry of his time found "science offering it fresh discovery as the terrace from which to essay new flights."[5] In either case, however, he was defending the thesis that poetry is not dying but advancing. Of course he did not mean anything so absurd as that poetry is continuously progressive, each new poet being an improvement on the last, but his faith was unshakable that the poetic lull that he deplored in his own time would be followed by an outburst superior in at least one respect to the great creative epochs of the past. Thus, counting the Elizabethan and Romantic periods as the two great ages of English poetry, he twice predicted in *Nature and Elements* "a third imaginative lustre . . . enkindled, perchance, by the flame of a more splendid order of discovery, even now so exalting."[6] This might or might not surpass the previous ages in merely aesthetic aspects, but it would inevitably express a broader, deeper, and truer vision of life—as he described it in words to which we shall return, "a higher knowledge and reverence than we have yet experienced."[7] Nor were these predictions indiscretions penned in the heat of a moment. The words just quoted were written late in life, *Nature and Elements* was published midway in his career, and he wrote as follows in his first assault upon the question in 1873:

that the years of transition are near an end, and that, in England and America, a creative poetic literature, adapted to the new order of thought and the new aspirations of humanity, will speedily grow into form, I believe to be evident wherever our common tongue is the language of imaginative expression. . . . Ere long, some new Lucretius may come to reinterpret the nature of things, confirming many of the ancient prophecies, and substituting for the wonder of the remainder the still more wondrous testimony of the lens, the laboratory, and the millennial rocks. The old men of the Jewish captivity wept with a loud voice when they saw the foundations of the new temple, because its glory in their eyes, in comparison of that builded by Solomon was as nothing; but the prophet assured them that the Desire of all nations should come, and that the glory of the latter house should be greater than the former. But I do not endeavor to anticipate the future of English song. It may be lowlier or loftier than now, but certainly it will show a change, and my faith in the reality of progress is broad enough to include the field of poetic art.[8]

As the concluding words of this statement clearly suggest, moreover, Stedman's optimism was not limited to the possibilities of poetry but was part of a larger progressive faith. The wave of the future was rolling, he held, and was not to be stemmed. As he wrote to H. C. Robinson, apropos of the errors of traditionalism:

The glory of civilization is that its law (not its laws) *is* elastic, progressive, and that its lawyers—though solemnly pretending to believe in their rules and traditions—smash them utterly when progress, policy, the spirit of the time are against them.[9]

Nor was there any doubt in his mind as to the direction of the wave. "Nature herself," he wrote in a poem read at the Yale Bicentennial,

> ... knows grandly to await
> The masterful estate
> Which from her secret germ Time conjureth.[10]

He was even willing, in fact, to extend his trust in progress to the life of the soul itself, and was led on two occasions—prompted perhaps by the widely heralded discussions of the Society for Psychical Research—to hazard the speculation that immortality might be deducible from evolution. "Theology, teaching immortality," he pointed out in illustration of the new flights for which science was preparing the imagination, "now finds science deducing the progressive existence of the soul as an inference from the law of evolution."[11] And in a letter he expressed a similar view as a personal belief:

> As for this question of continued personality, I have somewhat changed my views as modern experiment and knowledge have increased. Revelation has been a myth, and no traveller has returned; but it *may* be that our human race, *through the advances of science,* will yet discover that its differentiations are enduring beyond its corporal dissolution. It may be that every planet, revolving around whatever sun, is to learn at *some stage of its evolution,*—when ripe enough to be fitted for the discovery,—the secrets of spiritual existence, of personal endurance after bodily death.[12]

Like many others of his generation, Stedman appears to have been confident that the law of progress was large enough to include, not only the poetical art, but any desirable end.

Granted, however, his conviction that in the course of the cosmic evolution the soul and its characteristic life must inevitably prosper, what were his grounds? To one who has followed these pages they scarcely need to be stated. To begin with, he interpreted evolution in terms of a divine immanence. "The deity whom we know and adore in our day," he wrote in *Nature and Elements,* echoing President McCosh, "has taken us into his workshop. We see that he creates, as we construct, slowly and patiently, through ages and by evolution, one step leading to the next."[13] This divine immanence, moreover, he interpreted after the transcendental fashion as the private soul universalized. This is made clear in "Fin de Siècle," a poem of moderate length in which most of the issues we have been discussing are brought together, the point of departure being the issue of science versus poetry:

> Dark Science broods in Fancy's hermitage,
>   The rainbow fades,—and hushed, they say, is Song
> With those high bards who lingering charmed the age
>   Ere one by one they joined the statued throng.
>
> I hear the dirge for beauty sped, and faith
>   Astray in space and time's far archways lost,
> Till Life itself becomes a tenuous wraith,
>   A wandering shadow whom wandering shades accost.[14]

As we have seen, Stedman was unwilling to join in this dirge, and the remaining stanzas give his reasons in broader terms than those already presented—in terms of what he sometimes called the "new revelation."[15]

The heart of this revelation is contained in two stanzas that are a bit puzzling at first reading. "I hear," he wrote of the dirge for beauty sped,

>   yet have no will to falter so.
>   We seek out matter's alchemy, and tame
> Force to our needs, but what shall make us know
>   Whether the twain are parted, or the same?
>
> The same! then conscious substance, fetterless
>   The more when most subdued to Will's control,
> Free though in bonds, foredestined to progress,—
>   Ever, and ever still—the soul, the soul:
>
> The unvexed spirit, to whose sure intent
>   All else is relative.[16]

The puzzle here lies in the meaning of the word "twain" in the last line of the first stanza, which at first glance seems to refer to "matter" and "force," but which, if the second stanza is to be relevant, must refer to "we" on the one hand and "matter" and "force" on the other. Such an identification of subject and object, "I" and "it," soul and nature, is of course the hallmark of the transcendental metaphysic and identifies Stedman with the main line of the tradition that has dominated these pages. This interpretation, moreover, is verified by the concluding lines of the poem, which reverse the order of the early stanzas, taking their departure from the metaphysic in question and concluding with an affirmation of the higher activities of man's conscious life, including, of course, poetry:

> We time the ray, we pulsate with the fling

>   Of ether—feel the sure magnetic thrill
> Make answer to each sombre vortex ring
>   Whirled with the whirling sun that binds us still;
>
> That binds us, bound itself from girth to pole
>   By some unconquerable deathless force
> *Akin to this which thinks, acts, feels,*—the soul
>   Of man, forever eddying like its source.
>
> Passion and jest, the laugh and wail of earth,
>   High thought and speech, the rare considerings
> Of beauty that of fairer art gives birth,
>   The winnowing of poesy's swift wings,—
>
> These—though the hoary century inurn
>   Our great—no gathering mould of time shall clod:
> They bide their hour, they pass but to return
>   With men, as now, the progeny of God.[17]

To paraphrase: since poetry is the expression of an all-pervading spiritual force foredestined to progress, it has nothing to fear from the future. This Stedman put more simply in the passage to which it was said that we should return and with which we may conclude; indeed, this is probably as direct and uncompromising a statement of a divinely motivated progress as we are likely to find:

> throughout my writings I am constantly saying that the want of some sort of *Faith* is killing to modern art and poetry. Yet I have no fear that things will not come out right in the end. I believe in a Supreme Power that works for Righteousness, and all this is in the order of His law of progress to some higher knowledge and reverence than we have yet experienced.[18]

2

That Richard Watson Gilder shared Stedman's premise in this matter and that both harked back to Emerson and the earlier transcendentalism is well illustrated in a comment of Stedman's on a speech delivered by Gilder at Cornell in 1906:

> Well, I see you are an avowed Parsee, as I have been from the youth in which I found Emerson's avowal that everything is of "one stuff" confirmed by those discoveries of the "Correlation of Forces."[19]

Having much the more speculative turn of mind, however, Gilder elaborated the premise more extensively than Stedman and in a somewhat different direction. Though he was far from averse to the idea of progress,[20] the "good" that lay closest to his heart was not a future good to be slowly realized but that other good of the transcendentalist which is total and eternal and includes evil as a necessary ingredient. On the transcendental assumptions, as was pointed out at the end of the chapter on Whitman, these two goods were not necessarily incompatible, the one being true from the standpoint of time and the other from that of eternity. The latter, however, as Santayana insisted, was more central in the "genteel tradition" and will for that reason require greater attention here and in the next chapter than hitherto. It is only with Gilder, in fact, that we come fully to grips with this tradition, Stedman standing philosophically rather on its fringes. I am not aware that Gilder was acquainted with the work of Josiah Royce, the leading philosophical exponent of the tradition in this country; but, as will be shown, there are illuminating parallels in what the two men had to say. Let us consider, first, Gilder's actual descriptions of the process of evolution; second, the idealistic implications and underpinnings of his treatment of the theme; and, third, his resultant position in respect to the problem of evil.

In view of this difference in interest between Stedman and Gilder it is not surprising that all of the three instances in which the latter dealt at greatest length with evolution were devoted to the permanence rather than the melioration of the soul and that two of the three emphasized the ultimate dissolution rather than the progress of our physical system. In "Mors Triumphalis," for example, the dying bard is caused to sing

> Of the day when the sun shall be withered, and shrunken, and cold;
> When the stars, and the moon, and the sun,—all their glory o'erpast,—
> Like apples that shrivel and rot, shall drop into the Vast.[21]

And in the sonnet "Destiny" the process is pictured in these doleful terms:

> I see it all; my soul the dregs hath drunk
> Of man's last, helpless, hopeless destiny;

> Born of the primal ooze, where slow light sunk,
> And climbing to the secrets of the sky;
> Through countless million years the spiral mounts
> Till nature, a companionable slave,
> Bows to man's bidding; lo, then, the deep founts
> Run gradual dry, earth turns its own chill grave;
> The insatiate desert marches on the sown,
> The sea exhales, the very air is gone,
> And, gasping in the silent void, the race
> Dies with the planet.[22]

The other poem also, "Recognition,"[23] is less concerned with evolution as melioration than with the relation of the whole process to God and of both to the soul of man. True, because it is a straightforward retelling of the story, most of its fifty-three lines are devoted to the ascent from nebula to man, but the poet's obvious purpose was not merely to chronicle this ascent but to provide a connecting link between God at the beginning and man at the end. The whole thing is seen by the poet in a vision, and begins, Poe-like, with the issuing forth from God of material substance in a cloudlike nebula, which then coheres and differentiates after the scheme of Laplace. Significantly, however, these events are not explained in terms of mechanical action but of a primal volitional urge:

> One mighty cloud it seemed, nor star, nor earth,
> Or like a nameless growth of the under-seas;
> Creation dumb, unconscious, yet alive
> With some deep, inward passion unexprest,
> And Swift, concentric, never-ceasing urge.

The inward passion, moreover, did not go long unexpressed, and as the swiftly moving mass swept nearer to the poet in his vision, he

> beheld crawl forth
> Upon the earth's cool crust most wondrous forms
> Wherein were hid, in transmutation strange,
> Sparks of the ancient, never-ending fire;
> Shapes moved not solely by exterior law
> But having will and motion of their own—
> First sluggish and minute, then by degrees
> Monstrous, enorm.

These forms, finally, were followed by others "more fine" until at last,

> Rising and turning its slow gaze about
> Across the abysmal void, the mighty child
> Of the supreme, divine Omnipotence—
> Creation, born of God, by Him begot,
> Conscious in MAN, no longer blind and dumb,
> Beheld and knew its father and its God.

Particularly when read in the light of the title of the poem, these final and climactic lines leave no doubt as to the center of Gilder's interest in evolution. If further evidence were needed, however, the confident concluding lines of "Destiny," balancing the gloom of the first part, would suffice:

> But not this the doom
> Of man's outlooking soul; that hath no tomb,
> Being quenchless as the law and lord of space.

These poems raise an old problem, however. Like Royce in the passage quoted at the end of Chapter I and referred to several times since, we must ask how a being "born of the primal ooze" can evolve by a continuous development into a being "quenchless as the law and lord of space"; how, if creation is "dumb, unconscious" matter at the beginning, it becomes a conscious, immortal soul at the end. The shorter of the two poems, of course, since it depends for its effect upon sharpness of contrast, sheds little light on this question, but the answer given by "Recognition" is also something less than final. Not that it contributes nothing; on the contrary, Gilder was careful to plant seeds in the earlier portions of the poem that he believed might flower as conscious man at the end. Thus he said of his nebula that, while dumb and unconscious, it was "yet alive with some deep, inward passion unexprest," and that hidden in his creatures "monstrous, enorm" were "sparks of the ancient never-ending fire." Gilder was apparently well aware that if spirit is to emerge at the end it must be prepared for in the beginning; and, when viewed in the light of other poems, his recognition of this necessity will take on a larger significance. However, if the preparations made in the earlier portion of this poem are considered in isolation, the sceptic may object that they say little more than was said by many naturalists, who were equally aware of the problem and answered it by the manipulation of the concept of force. Ernst Haeckel, for example, regarded the energies of matter as sense and will in their lowest form and was thus able to say in an oft-quoted passage:

> The irresistible passion that draws Edward to the sympathetic Ottilia, or Paris to Helen, and leaps over all bounds of reason and morality, is the same powerful "unconscious" attractive force which impels the living spermatozoon to force an entrance into the ovum in the fertilization of the egg of the animal or plant—the same impetuous movement which unites two atoms of hydrogen to one atom of oxygen for the formation of a molecule of water.[24]

What more than this Gilder may have meant we must inquire.

The major part of the answer is clear enough. To begin with, because he started with God he was able to endow matter with more than its minimum of physical properties. An absolute spiritual being was the center of his cosmological speculation, and hence the material substance of his cosmos, as an expression of this being, was possessed with the potentiality of spiritual life. This, rather than Haeckel's, was the meaning of the "inward passion unexprest." In his statement of it, however, Gilder's language often resembles that of Poe in *Eureka* and is consequently open to the same charge of unintentional materialism. Thus when he speaks of a God "that made all, and is all that was made"[25] and "that made the whole and lives in all He made,"[26] it must again be asked whether a God that becomes matter does not cease to be God. I do not believe, however, that Gilder's words mean the same thing as Poe's. Poe's account of the cosmos seems to signify a literal transformation of God into matter in the simple sense of extended substance; but Gilder seems rather to have thought of the material universe after the transcendental fashion as simply an expression or manifestation of God. In the paradox of that doctrine, his God both was and was not the universe, was transcendent as well as immanent.

There is a hint of this at the beginning of "Recognition," where he speaks of

> God who in dual nature doth abide—
> Love, and the Loved One, Power and Beauty's
>   self,

and his scores of religious poems leave no doubt of his belief that God is not only one with all he made but "distinct."[27] How he squared this with his conviction of the deathlessness of the soul, however, is made most nearly explicit in "The Invisible,"[28] which begins with the familiar story by the "nebulous spiral told" and expresses in much the same terms the same undaunted faith in the soul as "Destiny":

> Such new sense
> Of magnitudes that make our world an atom
> Might crush the soul, did not this saving thought
> Leap to the mind and lift it to clear heights:—
> " 'Tis but the unseen that grows not old nor dies,
> Suffers not change, nor waning, nor decay. . . ."

Here the logic of "Recognition" is carried a step further, the familiar transcendental reconciliation of the "outlooking soul" with the unconscious material universe being once again performed. Thus, though it is said that the heavens are "naught but matter"—

> we who gaze forth fearless on the sight
> Find not one equal, facing from the vast
> Our sentient selves

—the concluding lines make it clear that this dualism is not the final truth, but that we who gaze forth are one with what we gaze upon. Though "not one, sole, lonely star . . . can make one conscious movement," all the material universe is nevertheless a manifestation of conscious thought and will. The stars are "slaves to law material," but this very law is or represents a

> Power immense, mysterious, intense,
> Unseen as our own souls, but which must be
> Like them the home of thought, with will and might
> To stamp on mindless matter the soul's will.

"Like them the home of thought"—this was the same thing that Stedman had said in "Fin de Siècle." Gilder carried it further, however, making it the basis of a direct inference of immortality. The kinship that Stedman observed between the unconquerable deathless force that binds the universe and "this which thinks, acts, feels" was to Gilder proof that the soul of man is also unconquerable and deathless. Man, the product of evolution, is creation returned to consciousness. In the words of "Recognition": "creation, born of God, . . . conscious in MAN, . . . beheld and knew its father and its God." Thus man, one in his conscious soul with the essence of existence, rises superior to its flux and change: "quenchless" is his soul "as the law and lord of space."

There is no difficulty up to this point; Gilder's position was clear and has needed only to be disentangled. Going deeper, however, will involve some speculation. Superficially, of course, his reasoning echoed that of natural theology, in which it was argued that the rational order of nature indicates an identity in kind between the Creator of the universe and man its end and aim. There is some evidence, however, that Gilder also had in mind the epistemological argument, presumed by most transcendentalists, which proceeds from the conditions of knowledge to the subordination of matter to mind. This at any rate is the suggestion of "A Midsummer Meditation,"[29] which Stedman singled out for comment in *The Nature and Elements of Poetry*.[30] The subject of the poem is immortality, and it begins with the gloomy assertion that "thy spirit that looks forth . . . shall cease, but not the things that pleasure thee." The second stanza, however, presents a refutation of this that seems to rest on the idealistic conception of the material world as the phenomenal construction of a mind:

> All that thou seest, thou art, and without thee
> Were nothing. Thou, a god, dost recreate
> The whole; breathing thy soul in all, till all
> Is one wide world made perfect at thy touch.
> And know that thou, who darest a world create,
> Art one with the Almighty, son to sire—
> Of His eternity a quenchless spark.

Stedman was of the opinion that Gilder had in mind the similarity between the creative power of the artist and of God, and this is certainly true as far as it goes; it was unquestionably the experience of being an artist that prompted Gilder to write the poem. It seems unlikely, however, in view of his other poems on immortality, that he would have singled out the artist alone to be "one with the Almighty." Rather more likely seems the interpretation that the creative thought of the artist is the pattern and ideal of the conscious life of all men; that Gilder means, like the idealists, that each being creates his world in knowing it, just as God does the whole. One becomes more convinced of this, moreover, when he observes the emphasis here, as in "The Invisible" and "Recognition," on that vis-à-vis of spectator and spectacle which underlay Emerson's idealism and has been termed by a critic of the philosophy "the egocentric predicament." At all events, Gilder's point of departure, like that of the Transcendentalist in Emerson's essay of that name, was consciousness rather than matter.

To what extent Gilder would have blessed this interpretation must remain uncertain, but that he regarded mind or spirit as primary and matter as secondary is clear enough. In his poetry, however, and no doubt in his private speculation as well, this most often took the form of the mystic's intuition of union rather than any argument from epistemology. Of man he said in poems already referred to, "thou . . . art one with the Almighty"[31] and "one are we with the ever-living One";[32] and he had much the same thing to say of nature. In "Mors Triumphalis," to choose one of many suitable examples:

> One thought, and one law, and one awful and infinite
>   power;
> In atom, and world; in the bursting of fruit and of
>   flower;
> The laughter of children, and roar of the lion untamed;
> And the stars in their course—one name that can
>   never be named.[33]

There is no danger of confusing this with Haeckel's "monism of substance." It was rather the resurgent transcendentalism of the closing years of the century, in which evolution was, as we have many times seen, "the phenomenal outer aspect" of the Logos.

But what we are most interested in is the conclusions Gilder drew from this cosmology concerning the status of good and evil. Here it is instructive to consider one respect in which the "genteel" philosophy was opposed to mysticism, at least of the traditional sort. Ethically, mysticism is a doctrine of renunciation, while the "genteel tradition" was one of acceptance. More fully, the position of the mystic is that since the world is evil it should be renounced in favor of contemplation of the Perfect Good,[34] while the position of the transcendentalist is that, since the world is evil in particulars but good in totality and essence, evil must be in some sense necessary to the existence of good and ought to be accepted and understood rather than simply renounced. The standing criticism of transcendentalism back to Emerson is not that it ignored evil but that it justified it. Thus, to introduce the parallel suggested at the beginning of this discussion, Royce held that temporal evil is necessary to the existence of a moral world and hence to the existence of moral good:

> If I find in myself an evil impulse, I find what in itself considered is, indeed, something hateful, lamentable, possibly horrible, something which regarded for itself can apparently form no part of a good order. If I tolerate the impulse, if I declare it to be just the nettle of sin, if I call its evil illusory, then my moral optimism is indeed open to the condemnation of Amos, who cries woe upon all such vindications of the divine order. But suppose I resist the evil impulse, hate it, hold it down, overcome it, then, in this moment of hating and condemning it, *I make it a part of my larger moral goodness.* The justification of the existence of my evil impulse comes *just at the instant when I hate and condemn it.* Condemning and conquering the evil will make it part of a good will. . . . There are elements in a good world which, individually regarded, ought not to be there, which are in themselves hateful, regrettable, the just object of wrath. Yet they become part of the world of the good will just in so far as they are in fact hated, condemned, subdued, overcome. The good world is not innocent. It does not ignore evil; it possesses and still conquers evil.[35]

This was also Gilder's view; for, though there is no reason to believe that there was any indebtedness one way or the other, Gilder was probably closer to the philosophy of Royce than any other American poet. He left unconsidered many details that Royce, as a technical philosopher, elaborated minutely, but the upshot was the same. Thus in "Mors Triumphalis," following the description of the ancient bard's song of "the day when the sun shall be withered," we read that even such an evil is as much a part of the blessed whole as any good:

> still he sings
> One theme, that o'er all and through all his wild music
>   outrings—
> This one theme: that whate'er be the fate that has
>   hurt us or joyed;
> Whatever the face that is turned to us out of the void;
> Be it cursing or blessing; or night, or the light of
>   the sun;
> Be it ill, be it good; be it life, be it death, it is
>   ONE.[36]

This is a different optimism from that of Stedman, resting not on the promise of good things in the future but on faith in an essential goodness of which all things, even the most painful, degrading, and destructive, are the manifestation. It is not simply that the world-process leads to good, but that with all its apparent faults it is good. Like Royce, too, Gilder did not limit suffering to man and nature, but found it in God as well; for it is only in painful strife with evil that good, divine or otherwise, can make itself manifest.

> If He lives on, serene and unafraid,
> Through all His light, His love, His living thought,
> One with the sufferer, be it soul or star;
> If He escape not pain, what beings that are
> Can e'er escape while Life leads on and up the
>   unseen way and far?
> If He escape not, by whom all was wrought,
> Then shall not we,—
> Whate'er of godlike solace still may be,—
> For in all worlds there is no Life without a pang,
>   and can be naught.
> *No Life without a pang! It were not Life,*
> *If ended were the strife—*
> *Man were not man, nor God were truly God!*[37]

Royce wrote:

If we have the true insight of deeper idealism, we can turn from our chaos to him, who is our own true and divine self, and can hear from him with absolute assurance this one word: "Oh ye who despair, I grieve with you. Yes, it is I who grieve in you. Your sorrow is mine. No pang of your finitude but is mine too. I suffer it all, for all things are mine; I bear it, and *yet* I triumph." . . . it is this thought, I say, that traditional Christianity has in its deep symbolism first taught the world, but that, in its fullness, only an idealistic interpretation can really and rationally express.[38]

It is not for nothing that Gilder wrote many poems on the Passion: "Cost," for example:

> Because Heaven's cost is Hell, and perfect joy
>   Hurts as hurts sorrow; and because we win
>   Some boon of grace with the dread cost of sin,
>   Or suffering born of sin; because the alloy
> Of blood but makes the bliss of victory brighter;
>   Because true worth hath surest proof herein,
>   That it should be reproached, and called akin
>   To evil things—black making white the whiter;

> Because no cost seems great near this—that He
>   Should pay the ransom wherewith we were priced;
> And none could name a darker infamy
> Than that a god was spit upon,—enticed
>   By those he came to save, to the accursèd tree,—
> For this I know that Christ indeed is Christ.[39]

3

Madison Cawein is of less consequence both intrinsically and for the purposes of this study than either Stedman or Gilder, but a few of his verses will prove useful in giving added emphasis to the idealistic bent of the poetry of the *fin de siècle* and in illustrating further the adaptation of this idealism to the theory of evolution and its application to the problem of what the future holds in store. For his philosophy Cawein went to the very fountain-head of idealism, Plato. The name of Plato is never pronounced in his writings except in the hushed tones of the disciple, and a number of Platonic and Neoplatonic doctrines are repeated, the most interesting for us being that of emanation. Thus, in one of the sections of "Intimations of the Beautiful," a long meditative poem that has the most of all Cawein's writings to contribute to this history, the "pure thought-creations of the mind" are described as emanations and then this analogy is drawn:

> So Nature pours her thoughts in forms;
>   . . .
>
> The sensuous substance of her thought
> From immaterial matter wrought—
> Matter, which death can not annul,
> That constitutes the Beautiful,
> And, dead, repeats itself from naught.[40]

Earlier in the same poem, moreover, is a stanza which leaves no doubt that the author wished to preserve as much of the Platonistic cosmogony as contemporary knowledge would permit:

> Idea, god of Plato! one
> With beauty, justice, truth and love:
> Who, type by type, the world begun
> From an ideal world above!
> Reason, who into Nature wrought
> Your real entities,—which are

> Ideas,—giving to our star
> Their beauty through reflected thought. . . .[41]

Cawein's Platonism was as hybridized as Emerson's, however, and his emanationism bore a closer resemblance to Emerson's than to that of the *Enneads*. That is, it is not to be taken as a statement of the historical order of events, but of the "divine order"—the order of logic and value.[42] When Cawein says that the world began from an ideal world above, he must be understood to mean, not, as was held by Plotinus and Bronson Alcott, that the development of the forms of being has followed a descending order, but, like Emerson, merely that the ultimate cause and origin of the material world is spirit.

For mingled with these emanational declarations are many that assert not only that the world has made itself but that the order of the making has been ascendant. "God leaves progression in her care," Cawein wrote of Nature; "through her it must materialize."[43] Nor, he urged, did this demean either creation or Creator. Since God permitted Magi and Aztecs to worship him in the material form of fire,

> should man,—
> All ignorant of heavenly ends,—
> Despise the means, since Earth began,
> God works by to perfect His plan,
> Which through immediate forms ascends
> Of nature, lifting, race by race,
> Man to the beauty of His face?[44]

It was not degrading because Cawein's God, like the God of Gilder and so many others studied here, was immanent as well as transcendent. Evolving material nature is but the sensuous embodiment of the thought which is God and which is known to us only through this embodiment. Many pages back Cawein was quoted as referring to "some purpose, some divine development, that protoplasmic evolution proves,"[45] and elsewhere in "Intimations of the Beautiful" he wrote:

> Through Nature only we arrive
> At God: identical with truth,
> By periods of repeated youth,
> Through Nature must the Ages strive. . . .[46]

Again, in the sestet of a sonnet on a theme familiar in nineteenth century poetry he included these lines:

> the sunset and the dawn
> Preach sermons more inspired even than
> The tongues of Pentecost; as, distant heard
> In forms of change, through Nature upward drawn,
> God doth address th' immortal part of man.[47]

The most interesting aspect of Cawein's handling of evolution, however, and the most definitive of his optimism, is suggested by the last of these lines and the following passage in "Intimations of the Beautiful":

> Nature in herself resolves
> All parts of beauty to one whole,
> And from the perfect whole evolves
> The high ideas that control
> Advancement, till the time be ripe
> To doff disguise and type by type,
> Reveal the emanated soul. . . .[48]

Quite plainly, in Cawein's interpretation, evolution down to the present has been a progressive realization, a making manifest, of the indwelling soul of all existence, and it can be shown that his fondest belief was that by the continued operation of the same law of this manifestation will one day be carried to completion. Like Stedman, Cawein found "science deducing the progressive existence of the soul as an inference from the law of evolution." Thus the "purpose" proved by protoplasmic evolution was that man, the fruit of past growth, shall be lifted up,

> heart and soul and mind,
> From matter to ideal potencies,
> Up to the source and fountain of all mind,
> To be resumed and re-absorbed in them—
> One more expression of eternity.[49]

Elsewhere in the same poem he spoke of the time

> when the soul, refined
> Through love and wisdom through a thousand years,
> Shall mount as pure intelligence and pierce
> The separate cycles singing under God,—

. . .

>   (Through God-propinquity become a God).

And in "Intimations of the Beautiful" he described the ages in these terms:

> The Epochs, that must purify
> Themselves through her experience,
> Her knowledge, which each Age lays by
> To clothe it better for the sky
> In robes of new intelligence
> Befitting life, that upwardly
> Approaches ends, which none can see.[50]

Like James Thomson, Cawein regarded the scale of being as a ladder for souls;[51] like Emerson, he found "the avatars of Brahma . . . text books of natural history.[52]

XIII

HOVEY, LODGE, AND MOODY: THE PARADOX OF THE "GENTEEL TRADITION"

STEDMAN, GILDER, AND CAWEIN were of the "genteel tradition" in more than one sense—in the special sense of the transcendental optimism that Santayana had in mind when he coined the phrase and in the looser popular sense of preoccupation with the conventionally more noble sides of life. The soul and its immortality, love, art, worship, and patriotism—these were their major themes; the less dignified and more unruly aspects of man's nature they touched only exceptionally and with reserve. The three younger poets to whom we must now turn, however, had grown restive under this devotion to propriety and instituted a genuine, if still quite mannerly, rebellion against it. Still a long way from the Dreisers and Sandburgs and quite as concerned as their predecessors about the life of the spirit, they nevertheless made a special point of giving the insurgencies of flesh and will their due. In the swing of the historical pendulum between restraint and release, the *fin de siècle* took the latter turn, reacting against the prohibitions of the age of Victoria and moving in the direction of the moral position that it matters less what you do than how sincerely and passionately you do it. Intensity was the prime value of the day, whether it took the form of the "hard and gem-like flame" of the esthete, the "strenuous life" of Roosevelt, or the Nietzschean will-to-power. "Vitality is the thing, after all," wrote Frank Norris,[1] one of the brasher among the new voices. "Give us men, strong, brutal men, with red-hot blood in 'em, with unleashed passions rampant in 'em, blood and bones and viscera in 'em, and women, too, that move and have their being."[2] The red-hot blood in the poetry of Richard Hovey, George Cabot Lodge, and William Vaughn Moody may be less tangible, more metaphorical, but it is most un-genteely there.

It is the strange and interesting fact, furthermore, that in taking this turn these writers were not rejecting the philosophy of the genteel tradition but carrying it to a further extreme. The principle of this philosophy, as we have many times seen, is the paradox that evil is good. If all things are of God, then all things are good and our naming some of them evil is mere local prejudice; or if, as Royce held, virtue is not simply a state of innocence but the successful wrestling with evil, then evil is necessary to its achievement; or if, again, as has been held by our cosmic optimists, the world is a progressive realization of the divine spirit, then all things, including those called evil, are potentially excellent. This philosophy, as has been observed here before, was essentially a theodicy, and like many theodicies it had the effect not only of justifying the ways of God to man but of man and nature to God. The novelty of Hovey, Lodge, and Moody is that they were, excepting Whitman, the first of our poets to develop this implication with any degree of literalness. It is no small irony that a philosophy usually blamed for being overnice should plead the cause of violence, of egoism, of "the lewd spirit [that] stings the core of nature." We have seen that this philosophy leaned toward the tolerance of evil; here we shall find it leading on occasion to positive delight in it.

1

A quite startling illustration of this paradox is Hovey, who could scarcely have leveled the barriers of convention, even in a sense of morals, with greater enthusiasm if he had been a thorough cynic. His most popular verses urge us to exchange the restraints and discriminations of gentility for the liberties of Vagabondia—

> Off with the fetters
> That chafe and restrain,
> Off with the chain![3]

—and in his imperialistic outbursts at the time of the Spanish war, the language is quite that of a neo-Darwinian apostle of blood and iron. "By strife as well as loving," he intoned to a G.A.R. Post on Memorial Day, 1898,

> —strife,
> The Law of Life,—
> In brute and man the climbing has been done
> And shall be done hereafter. Since man was,
> No upward-climbing cause
> Without the sword has ever yet been won.[4]

The Craven peace of Philistia, he added in another poem, is far worse than war;[5] and in still another:

> We come to birth in battle; when we pass,
> It shall be to the thunder of drums.[6]

For a "genteel" philosopher the rattle of the sabre sounded extraordinarily sweet in the ears of Hovey.

And yet, far from being a cynic, Hovey was exceedingly devout. He was a year at the General Theological Seminary of the Episcopal Church, served for a time as lay assistant at the Church of St. Mary the Virgin, and gave up the idea of taking orders for other reasons than loss of faith. To the end of his days he saw the hand of God in all things, and the religious note was as constant in his verses as in those of any other American of his time. Even the accidents of art, he believed, unmask

> the likeness of Intent
> And ever in blind Chance's darkest crypt
> The shrine-lamp of God's purposing is found,[7]

and in a poem originally intended to be the dedication of his unfinished cycle of verse-dramas, *Launcelot and Guenevere,* he proclaimed worship the highest mode of art:

> God, in whose being only we become
>   And in whose wisdom only we grow wise,
> Eternal Love! first unto Thee I come,
>   First unto Thee I lift adoring eyes.
> Before Thy face the prophet's speech is air,
>   In songs of praise the only music lies,
> The only wisdom in the lips of prayer.[8]

Even in the war poems he called upon God again and again; battle, he wished to say, is one of the means, in a sense the only means, by which God's will is realized:

> We know not to what Goal God's purpose tends:
> We know He works through battle to his ends.[9]

Franklin's saw about there never being a good war or a bad peace is quite reversed—in the well-known "Unmanifest Destiny," for example:

> There is a Hand that bends our deeds
> To mightier issues than we planned,

> Each son that triumphs, each that bleeds,
> My country, serves Its dark command.[10]

Or, more pertinently to the subject of evolution, in the Memorial Day poem:

> Great is war—great and fair!
> The terrors of his face are grand and sweet,
> And to the wise the calm of God is there.
> God clothes himself in darkness as in light,
> —The God of love, but still the God of might.
> Nor love they least
> Who strike with right good will
> To vanquish ill
> And fight God's battle upward from the beast.

On the face of it, this is shocking doctrine. That Godhead should achieve characteristic expression in slaughter is a bitter pill to swallow even if true, and Professor Boynton probably expressed the usual reaction to it in writing of "Unmanifest Destiny":

> in the light of this poem, in which he acknowledges that "God moves in a mysterious way His wonders to perform," it seems extraordinary that he could not conceive of God's ever fostering "an upward climbing cause without the sword."[11]

Though it may still shock, it ceases to surprise, however, when Hovey's intellectual ancestry is examined. For behind these poems lay not only American transcendentalism, with its tendency to the tolerance of evil, but Hegelianism, with what Royce called its "logic of passion." Though Hovey was not, of course, an Hegelian in any exact sense, his wife assures us of his active interest in that philosophy through his friendship with W. T. Harris and "his somewhat close association with Dr. Momerie, the great English Hegelian."[12] In any case, the "logic of passion" occupied an important place in his thinking. By this excellent phrase Royce meant to suggest the dynamic, contentious, developmental character of the Hegelian universe, which evolved from pure abstraction to rich and varied concreteness through a logic of struggle. "Spirituality," he says in his chapter on Hegel,

> lives by self-differentiation into mutually opposing forces, and by victory in and over these oppositions. This law it is that Hegel singles out and makes the basis of his system. This is the logic of passion. . . .[13]

In the formula of the textbooks, thesis breeds antithesis, which it contends against, overcomes, and absorbs to make a new synthesis. This formula, moreover, is not simply a description of the process of thought or the way of the world, but of the nature of God, who contains all struggle within himself, is its cause and its resolution. Continuing with Royce:

The absolute self with which I am seeking to raise my soul, and which erelong I find to be a genuine self, yes, the only self, exists by the very might of its control over all these contradictions, whose infinite variety furnishes the very heart and content of its life.[14]

Strife, as Gilder had said, without drawing Hovey's noisy corollaries, is the law of life; without it, "man were not man, nor God were truly God."[15] With this Hovey agreed literally, employing the symbols of Ormuzd and Ahriman. "Angro-mainyus," as he spelled it, speaks:

I am the Most High God;

. . .

Ahura-mazda is God too,
The beneficent one, the savior!
He dwelleth in the Sun,
But I in the terror of tempests.
There are two thrones, but one God.

. . .

There is no war between our legions,
But in us peace.
Behold, he knoweth my thoughts and I his,
And there is no discord in us.
He worketh in light
And I in darkness;
His ways and my ways are asunder.
But blaspheme not, calling me 'Devil,'
Neither saying, 'There are two Gods';
I am the Most High God,
And I and Ahura-mazda are one.[16]

"The God of love," as he had said in the Memorial Day poem, "but still the God of might."

As had been the case with Hegel, there was no crude lust for the spoils of conquest in Hovey's celebration of this bloody dialectic, but a vision of it as part of a larger total good and, on the plane of time, as the preparation of greater good to come. Hegel's

Philosophy of History, which Hovey like most readers probably knew better than his more difficult works, was both a theodicy and a sermon on spiritual progress. "The insight then to which . . . philosophy is to lead us," Hegel wrote in the introduction of the work,

is, that the real world is as it ought to be—that the truly good—the universal divine reason—is not a mere abstraction, but a vital principle capable of realizing itself. This *good,* this *Reason,* in its most concrete form, is God. God governs the world; the actual working of his government—the carrying out of his plan—is the History of the World.[17]

On one side this is a justification of things as they are, and in this sense its like is to be seen in Hovey's insistence, reflected throughout the Vagabondia poems, that life be accepted on its own terms, without flinching or pretense or regret:

> Life as it is! Accept it; it is thine!
> The God that gave it, gave it for thy good.
> The God that made it had not been divine
> Could he have set thee poison for thy food.[18]

On the other side, however, it is a philosophy of evolution based on a particular conception of the relation of God and the world;[19] and this is the meaning that seems to have affected Hovey most deeply. God and the world, he joined other transcendentalists in contending, are both one and not one. In the sense of the epistemological contention that has been called their "cardinal principle," God and the world are as thought and thinker, identical and yet opposed. Or, leaving epistomology, God is the universal soul, of which the world is the precipitation and the individual soul the immediate awareness. As expressed in the titles of two of Hovey's quatrains that take us to the heart of his philosophy, God is both an "Immanence" and a "Transcendence."

> Enthroned above the world although he sit,
> Still is the world in him and he in it;
>   The selfsame power in yonder sunset glows
> That kindled in the words of Holy Writ.
>
> Though one with all that sense or soul can see,
> Not prisoned in his own creations he,

>   His life is more than stars or winds or angels—
> The sun doth not contain him nor the sea.[20]

This thought—for the two poems present the same thought from different sides—lay behind all Hovey's serious writing and is well expressed in "The Laurel," his ode to Mary Day Lanier. "I see," he wrote in the final epode, "beneath what comes and goes . . . the perfect act of God that changeth not . . .

>   Behold, He is other than earth and transcendeth
>   its seeming;
>   Behold, He is one with the earth and the earth is
>   His dreaming.[21]

However, if the perfect act of God "changeth not," still on earth, in time, change is the law. "Thou art, but our being is yearning," he added in a following line, and the poem as a whole leaves no doubt that this yearning is meliorative. As stated in the execrable opening lines of this section of the poem,

>   surely from the childing night
>   That labors in a God's birth-throes,
>   Shall come at last dawn's baby-rose
>   The potency of perfect light.

It was no mere accident of acquaintance that led Hovey to write an ode to Mrs. Lanier, but a deep admiration of her husband and sense of kinship with him. The abundance of praise of the older poet in the poem, and particularly the assault upon the "Trade-snake" in the third antistrophe, place this beyond question, but it is also implicit in the similarity between Hovey's conception of cosmic progress and Lanier's doctrine of "etherealization."[22] This doctrine, as has been explained, was based upon an essentially aesthetic conception of the nature of things and expressed a gospel of melioration in which "soul" and "sense" interact rhythmically and issue in a harmonious development of personality expressable alike in terms of love and beauty. Now listen to Hovey as he addresses Apollo, the god of measure:

>   Spirit of beauty, born of the divine breath
>   With its first issuance into Time and Space!
>   Shaping the whole creation into grace
>   Through intimate interflux of life and death!

> Lifting the transient, as it anguisheth,
> To the serene wherein change hath no place![23]

This, of course, was only generally transcendental rather than specifically Hegelian, but further aspects of the Hegelian influence are to be seen in the verse-dramas, and particularly in the "unitrinianism" which they embody and which Hovey had first learned from his wife and then developed and shared with Bliss Carman, his collaborator in the Vagabondia series.[24] In France before her marriage Mrs. Hovey had been a pupil of François Delsarte, who taught an esoteric system of self-culture based on a radically "Trinitarian" principle. In his own words:

The principle of my system lies in the statement that there is in the world a universal formula which can be applied to all sciences, to all things possible—the trinity—our being is life, mind, soul—man feels, thinks, loves.[25]

As Delsarte taught his system, it was primarily a therapeutic discipline, beginning with "dynamic breathing, the pivot of all culture,"[26] but Hovey and Carman, whose interests were broader, merged it with the other transcendentalisms, native and foreign, in which they had been soaked, and developed it into a philosophy, including a cosmology, to which Carman gave the name "unitrinianism." Like Lanier's "etherealization," this doctrine rested on belief in a harmony at the core of things and envisaged the unfolding of perfect and beautiful personality as the goal of evolution. Thus Carman wrote in the prefatory poem of a prose treatise on the subject:

> He who espouses perfection
> Must follow the threefold plan
> Of soul and mind and body,
> To compass the stature of man.
>
> For deep in the primal substance
> With power and purposes and poise,—
> An order under the chaos,
> A music beneath the noise,—
>
> The urge of a secret patience
> Throbbed into rhythm and form
> Till instinct attained to vision
> And the sentient clay grew warm.

> For sense was a smouldering fire
> And spirit a breath of air
> Blowing out of the darkness,
> Fostering reason's flare.
>
> . . .
>
> Wherefore the triune dominion,—
> Religion, science, and art,—
> We may not disrupt nor divide
> Setting its kingdoms apart,
>
> But ever with glowing ardour
> After the ancient plan,
> Build the lore and the rapture
> Into the life of man.[27]

The novelty of Hovey lay in his development of this triplicity, this "threefold plan," even beyond Carman and certainly beyond Lanier; and here, as Mrs. Hovey has made clear, we must reckon with an Hegelian influence. Thus, after speaking of her husband's indebtedness to Harris and Momerie, she continued:

> These together with a deep study of the Trinity, as asserted, though not explained, by the Church and as taught as a part of psychology by Delsarte, who first applied the scientific method to psychic phenomena, turned his thoughts strongly to go on from duality to trinity, as all philosophers must inevitably do in time. A synthesis, or inter-action of two, reacts, of course, on each, and in all evolution causes the existence of a third.[28]

Influence or no, this is plainly the same dialectical principle that has recurred in these pages from the beginning, and it was not simply a conception that Hovey was willing to admit but the very backbone of his most ambitious literary undertaking, the series of nine dramas on the Launcelot-Guenevere theme that he was working on at the time of his death. He completed only the first four, and hence his plan does not emerge in its fullness; but from his notebooks and her own knowledge of his intentions, Mrs. Hovey has been able to reconstruct the drift of the whole. There were to have been three groups of a masque and two plays each, the whole expressing, in the words of a "Schema and Commentary" prepared by the poet, this dialectical interpretation of the legend:

> Launcelot and Guenevere are placed in a position where they

must either sacrifice the existing order of things to themselves or themselves to the existing order of things.
Part I.—They attempt to set their relation to each other above their relation to the world. Tragic issue. (Thesis)
Part II.—They attempt to set their relation to the world above their relation to each other. Equally tragic issue. (Antithesis)
Part III.—The reconciliation. (Synthesis)[29]

This relationship, furthermore, not only provided the framework of the narrative, but it seems to have been Hovey's intention to embody a parallel progression of ideas in the three masques. This is in part Mrs. Hovey's observation and in part her speculation:

The masque of Merlin begins with the Norns and ends with the angels and final star prophesies. Taliesin again begins with the magic of the wood, of physical nature and our own nature, and ends with Taliesin's human song going on even terms with the angelic choirs....
Whether this progression from primitive chaos to the holiest flights of human inspiration was to be repeated in "Morgana," we do not find indicated in the notebooks; but there is no doubt that in its own variation this was what it was to be, and that a like progression was to pass through the masques themselves, each rising to a different height, so that in the end the last, "Avalon," should be supreme.[30]

Avalon, it seems, was to have embodied some such conception as the following, the Hegelian character of which is plain:

Somewhere in eternity, not regarding place, all stages of the human race must coexist, regardless of their place in time, and their relation or absence of relation of their experiences. This condition he uses as a place, and calls Avalon.[31]

We must turn to the texts of the masques themselves, however, to discover reflections of the theme with which this discussion began— the justification of earth, of struggle, of passion, of evil, in the name of Him who works through them. The first, which foreshadows the action of the whole series, prophesies the doom that will result from the marriage of Arthur and Guenevere, but in keeping with the transcendental principle that "evil is good in the making" not only looks beyond the evil to the good that will ensue, but makes clear that only through this evil can the good arrive. Thus Argent philosophizes in the very act of spelling the doom of the lovers:

> Ai, ai!
> It is not all a good to see the things
> That shall be. He that will soar to topmost
>   heaven,
> Must plunge, too, down to the voiceless lowest
>   of hell,
> Ye shall not know the good without the evil,
> Saith the Lord God.[32]

Again, at the end of *Taliesin,* the second of the masques, Perceval is denied the vision of the Graal because, ironically, he has not learned to love evil:

> Thy heart is yet too full of anger, and the hate
>   of evil clots thy soul;
> Too far from hell to hate it must he be whom God
>   shall breathe on as a coal
> Until the pure light of perfection burns about
>   him like an aureole.[33]

And when Taliesin objects that if Perceval is unworthy no less is he, Uriel tells him:

> Better the rose of love out of the dung-hill of
>   the world's adulteries
> Than the maid icicle that keeps itself from stain
>   of earth where no life is
> In the aloof of splendors boreal.[34]

As Moody was to repeat, it follows from the fact that God "is one with the earth and the earth is His dreaming" that all the life of the earth, better and worse alike, is to be, not shunned or confined, but loved and liberated.

As was pointed out in the discussion of the bloody dialectic of the war poems, however, acceptance was not Hovey's last word on the "dung-hill of the world's adulteries." Evil was not to be loved and liberated for its own sake but for its potential good as a part of a whole which on the plane of time unfolds progressively. This was clear enough in the war poems, but nowhere in Hovey's writing is the full scope of the idea better expressed than in a speech of Taliesin's uttered a few moments later in this masque when the glories of the Graal are shown reflected in a diamond sphere held aloft by Uriel. Here certainly is cosmic optimism:

> Stir in the dark of the stars unborn that desire

Only the thrill of a wild, dumb force set free,
Yearn of the burning heart of the world on fire
  For life and birth and battle and wind and sea,
Groping of life after love till the spirit aspire
  Into Divinity ever transmuting the clod,
Higher and higher and higher and higher and higher
  Out of the Nothingness world without end into God.[35]

2

The most visible strand in the slender and somewhat faded reputation of George Cabot Lodge seems to be pessimism. Ferris Greenslet, writing in the *Dictionary of American Biography,* observes that in his early years (which he did not long outlive) Lodge developed "a poetic pessimism which sat oddly on his perfect health and joyous vitality"; and Van Wyck Brooks, who is the only historian of American literature who has paid him more than the scantiest attention, includes him in *New England: Indian Summer* as one of "the epigoni, the successors, in whom the nineteenth century went to seed."[36] With Henry Adams, G. E. Woodberry, and Barrett Wendell, he was, according to Brooks, one of the "prophets of doom and destruction" who reflected a time and place "full of the sense of last things, as if it hoped for no resuscitation."[37] Nor is this without justification. From end to end Lodge's rather ornate verse is heavy with world-weariness and a sense of the tragedy of life and of the sham and timidity of those who live it. One may quote almost at random:

> We have seen that the progress they praise is
>   of tears and enslavement and blood.[38]

> But at least I have learned thro' the ages all
>   the lies of the world and of God.[39]

>   I discern across the shadow of years
> The self-same tragic life and death of men,
> The passion and the pathos and the tears,
>   The love and labor of humanity....[40]

This tells only half about Lodge, however, whose discontent was less with life itself than with the way it has been lived. His discontent was a rebellion, beneath which was an idealism deep, fervid, and carefully thought out.

Another facet of his work that is even more startling when seen against the background of the genteel tradition is its outspoken egoism. "And vast beyond all and inclusive of all things, my God is Myself" ends a poem in his second published volume,[41] and the heroes of his two verse-dramas, *Cain* (1904) and *Herakles* (1908), seem on first acquaintance quite Nietzchean in self-assertion. Both were rebels and murderers in whose own eyes their actions were entirely justified. Cain is presented as having slain Abel with the conscientious purpose of preventing him from bringing to birth others as craven as himself and only after pleading with him to renounce his timid dependence upon God. For self-righteous independence of any god not himself was the prime article of Cain's creed. Earlier in the play, when Adam had pleaded his submissiveness to God ("Grant me, O God, to say, 'Thy will be done'."),[42] Cain had observed, "His will and mine are twain. . . . The truth is mine and yours in measure of our will."[43] Cain is his own god, and when in the end he goes forth to endless wandering he prophesies that men shall

> press the hemlock to my shrinking lips
> Or nail my scourged flesh naked to the cross![44]

Herakles, who is the same messianic superman more fully developed, murders his own children, in madness to be sure and with remorse, but with no disturbance of his faith in his own divinity: "I am the madman," he says afterward to their mother,

> and the murderer
> I am; and I am Herakles; and I,
> I am the Resurrection and the Life;
>   . . .
> I am the Life of Life; I am the Soul;
> I am the strength, the flux, the growth, the trend;
> I am the future and the hope of man![45]

In this study, where benevolence and faith have been cornerstones, such megalomania, if that is what it is, is strange doctrine.

And yet it is perhaps not as strange as it seems. Whitman's egoism, while gentler, is legendary; Poe based the conclusion of *Eureka* on "the utter impossibility of any one's soul feeling inferior to another"; and Emerson took occasion to say, "Empedocles undoubtedly spoke a truth of thought, when he said, 'I am God.' "[46] Transcendentalism, to repeat what has been said here many times, is "radical subjectivism," resting on the belief that the "I" is the only immediately experienced reality and that the objects of knowledge are known only as the contents of consciousness. From this the transcendentalist proceeds, by the questionable inference that therefore the "external" world must be somehow dependent on the "I," to an interpretation of nature in terms of an evolution that reflects the spiritual aspiration or logical progression that he regards as the essential activity of the "I." Logically, even God enters into his philosophy only because the world about him is not amenable to his conscious wishes and thus forces him to postulate a deeper or more inclusive Self below the level of everyday consciousness. Thus, no matter how he may palliate the fact by the use of traditional theological terminology or how much it may be actually extenuated by the persistence of traditional religious attitudes, the god of the transcendentalist is simply himself writ large. Lodge, I believe, simply made this plainer than the others, deliberately rejecting the palliations to which many clung.

That this philosophy underlay Lodge's thought is clearly implicit in his poems, but it might have been inferred from some of the major influences on his intellectual life. A number of his early poems read like Whitman regularized;[47] he was at Harvard when Royce delivered his immensely popular lectures on *The Spirit of Modern Philosophy*;[48] he was devoted to the *Upanishads*;[49] and in the winter of 1896-97 he attended lectures on philosophy at the University of Berlin and continued the study of Schopenhauer which he had begun at Harvard. His most important debt to Schopenhauer was his conception of the place of tragedy in life, but he also owed him another notion that is of especial interest in these pages, the idea that nature is not inert or mechanical but active and striving, an "objectification of the Will." Thus his poem "The Will"[50] is headed by a quotation from Schopenhauer—*"Was jeder im innersten WILL, das muss er sein und was jeder ist, das WILL er eben"*—and, picturing nature in these terms, follows a kind of evolutionary sequence from inorganic nature to man. These are the opening stanzas:

> It sprang from the brows of a star
> And it lives with the life of the world,

> It appeared like the lightning of God
>   Through the dust of eternity hurled.
>
> And much as a luminous thought
>   May shine through the dusk of a dream,
> It awoke in the childhood of light
>   And crimsoned the twilight with gleam.
>
> It arose in the first blade of grass
>   That brake the stone mountains apart,
> And it budded and blossomed and bloomed
>   Till it stirred in the human heart.

Regardless of whether one made an absolute of the Will, as Schopenhauer did, the element of striving that he made central in his account of nature was essential in the transcendental evolutionism and is embodied in one form or another in all of Lodge's specifically evolutionary poems. In one sonnet, for example, he apostrophizes "Life" in these terms in the octave:

> Pride, power and substance of created things,
>   Gross, vital element of all that is,
>   Womb of interminable pregnancies,
>   Perennial source of earth's resurgent Springs....

and goes on to infer in the sestet:

> When, as my peers before me, I shall fall
>   Shattered with light, and, lost beyond recall,
>   Mix and resolve in thy creative slime,—
> Thence shall I rise in endless avatars,
>   And still once more, for Truth's eternal stars,
> Leap from the cloud-capped battlements of Time.[51]

Another example is these lines from his Harvard Phi Beta Kappa poem of 1906:

> from granite, schist and shard,
> From senseless jellies and brute envelopes,
> We mark our stages of deliverance,
> The age-long, upward levels of our flight,—
> And feel the restless, resolute, firm soul,
> Conscious and lord of life after so long,
> Still by the insatiable impulse driven,
> Transgress the forms and infidelities,
> The calculations and economies,
> That prove our insufficiency.[52]

Lodge's attachment to Schopenhauer was not, however, as close as the common linking of their names would seem to suggest. Greenslet joins mention of his study of Schopenhauer with the observation of his poetic pessimism, Brooks makes the same suggestion,[53] and Henry Adams wrote in his life of Lodge,

Lodge's dramatic motive was always the same, whether in "Cain," or in "Herakles," or in the minor poems. It was that of Schopenhauer, of Buddhism, of Oriental thought everywhere,—the idea of Will making the universe, but existing only as subject. The Will is God; it is nature; it is all that is; but it is knowable only as ourself.[54]

It is just the point, however, that Lodge did not follow Schopenhauer in his pessimistic interpretation of the will.[55] To Schopenhauer the will meant an eternal yearning that was stimulated rather than satisfied by fulfillment, and his conclusion was that therefore serenity could be achieved only by the abnegation of the will in religious asceticism. Lodge contended, on the contrary, that the will ought not to be suppressed but liberated. He did not mean this, it is true, in the simple sense of giving free rein to impulse or in the sense that the liberation of will would yield private pleasure. Rather, his two chief exponents of the will, Cain and Herakles, were pre-eminently sufferers. Looking forward to hemlock and cross, Cain said to Eve at the start of his homeless pilgrimage:

> Mother, it must be as the soul demands:
> Justice shall not refrain nor truth relent:
> What is shall be endured. For life's sole sake
> Wast thou creative. Ask no more of life
> Than life, for life has nothing more to give—
> . . .
> Beauty and happiness are casual gifts
> . . .
> The fruit is of thy labour and pain and peril.[56]

Herakles too expected no private satisfaction, but looked upon his labors and his crimes as the killing of the man that the over-man might be free. After recovering from the madness in which he had committed his murders, he mourned:

> O verily, verily the human thing
> I was—the man who once was Herakles—
> After this wild, irreparable wrong,

> This cruel, senseless, irremediable
> Accident of my own infirmities—
> Is dead, is damned, is shattered, is destroyed. . . .
> Know me at last, Megara, Megara!
> Behold me naked and ruined as I am!—
> All that makes human life desirable;
> All that sustains and comforts and consoles;
> All that the years can give from birth to death
> Of perishable, profound, pure happiness,
> And honour, and the clear, sweet, tranquil sense
> Of innocence, and sane, beneficent deeds;—
> All, all is lost![57]

Lodge's relation to Schopenhauer, in fact, is like that of Royce—acceptance of his tragic interpretation of life, but without pessimism. Royce's statement is long but instructive:

> . . . finite life is tragic, very nearly as much so as Schopenhauer represented, and tragic for the very reason that Schopenhauer and all the counsellors of resignation are never weary of expressing, in so far, namely, as it is at once deep and restless. This is its paradox, that it is always unfinished, that it never attains, that it throbs as the heart does, and ends one pulsation only to begin another. . . . For the individual the lesson of this tragedy is always hard; and he learns it first in a religious form in the mood of pure resignation. "I cannot be happy; I must resign happiness." . . . Schopenhauer's special reason for this view is, however, the deep and philosophical one that at the heart of the world there seems to be an element of capricious conflict. . . . But is this the whole story? No; if we ever get our spiritual freedom, we shall, I think, not neglecting this caprice which Schopenhauer found at the heart of things, still see that the world is divine and spiritual, not so much in spite of its capriciousness, as just because of it. . . . The spirit exists by accepting and by triumphing over the tragedy of the world. Restlessness, longing, grief,—these are evils, fatal evils, and they are everywhere in the world; but the spirit must be strong enough to endure them. In this strength is the solution. And, after all, it is just endurance that is the essence of spirituality. Resignation, then, is indeed part of the truth,—resignation, that is, of any hope of a final and private happiness. We resign in order to be ready to endure. But courage is the rest of the truth,—a hearty defiance of the whole hateful pang and agony of the will, a binding of the strong man by being stronger than he, a making of life once for all our divine game, where the passions are the mere chessmen that we move in carrying out our plan, and where the plan is a spiritual victory over Satan. Let us thank Schopenhauer, then, for at least this, that in his pessimism he gives us an universal expression for the whole negative side of life.[58]

Beside this, particularly the last sentence but one, we may place these words of Herakles, uttered in the same scene as the mournful speech quoted in the last paragraph:

> I am the Soul, whose inmost virtue is
> Thus to outlive destruction and return,
> Valid with Truth's perennial victory!—
>
> . . .
>
> And thus, in power and splendour and dominion,
> To rise from man's wild weakness calm and strong;
> To sing in man's disconsolate heart; to find
> Faith in man's abject infidelities;
> To make of man's infirmities the means
> Of victory; to be imperishable;
> To realize God in self and strength; to save
> And serve and strive—till man is overcome!—
> Till the immortal energy of Life,
> Transfigured with its own divine intent,
> Evolves still further to its perfect end![59]

Royce's position, as we know, was near that of Hegel, who recognized the same restless, eternally seeking quality at the base of reality, but made it a basis of optimism rather than pessimism. This is a point eminently worth observing, moreover, for the evolutionism of Lodge comes even more within the Hegelian orbit than did that of Whitman, Gilder, or Hovey. This is apparent in the best statement of it, in Herakles' last long speech to Prometheus in the final scene of the play:

> Knowledge alone is victory! When all
> Is understood, all is subdued, received,
> Possessed and perfect . . . .
> O then, at last, when all is lived and learned,
> Loved and received in its eternal kind—
>
> . . .
>
> When the long life of all man's endless lives,
> Its gradual pregnancies, its pangs and throes,
> Its countless multitudes of perished Gods
> And outworn forms and spent humanities,—
> When all the cosmic process of the past
> Stands in the immediate compass of our minds—
> When all is present to us and all is known,
> Even to the least, even to the uttermost,
> Even to the first and last—. . . . . .
> Then, tenoned in our foothold on the still,

> Supernal, central pinnacle of being,
> Shall we not look abroad and look within,
> Over the total Universe, the vast,
> Complex and vital sum of force and form,
> And say, in one, sufficient utterance,
> The single, whole, transcendent Truth—"I am!"[60]

The first thing to observe about this passage is that it gives a preeminent position to knowledge; the second is that this knowledge is not of any one thing, but of all things; the third is that only through this knowledge can the fullest *self*-realization be achieved.

Now compare Royce's summary of Hegel's *Phenomenology of Spirit:*

> Here he seeks to show how, in case you start just with yourself alone, and ask who you are and what you know, you are led on, step by step, through a process of active self-enlargement that cannot stop short of the recognition of the Absolute Spirit himself as the very heart and soul of your own life. This process consists everywhere in a repetition of the fundamental paradox of consciousness; in order to realize what I am I must, as I find, become more than I am or than I know myself to be. I must enlarge myself, conceive myself as in external relationships, go beyond my private self, presuppose the social life, enter into conflict, and, winning the conflict, come nearer to realizing my unity with my deeper self. But the real understanding of this process only comes, according to Hegel, when you observe that in trying thus to enlarge yourself for the very purpose of self-comprehension you repeat ideally the evolution of human civilization in your own person. This process of self-enlargement is the process which is writ large in the history of mankind. The "Phenomenology" is thus a sort of freely told philosophy of history. It begins with the Spirit on a crude and sensual stage; it follows his paradoxes, his social enlargement, his perplexities, his rebellions, his skepticism, all his wanderings, until he learns, through toils and anguish and courage, such as represent the whole travail of humanity, that he is, after all, in his very essence the absolute and divine spirit himself....[61]

This is not to say that Lodge knew or was indebted to Hegel's book, though this could easily have been the case, or even to Royce's summary, though this he had probably read or heard. There is nothing in the details of the organization of the *Phenomenology* that suggests Lodge, and a student of philosophy in Berlin would have seen or heard a dozen similar summaries. The point is merely that this all-important culminating stage of Lodge's evolutionism is strikingly Hegelian in pattern—closer indeed to Hegel than anything we have seen—and that therefore, with all its savage egoism, well within the structures of premise and inference that has been called here by Santayana's satirical phrase, the genteel tradition.

It is not to say either that Lodge's evolutionism was merely Hegelian. Hegel's evolutionism was rather logical than genetic, while Lodge's was outward and actual and included a link with the prehuman history which is "evolution" in the narrow sense. One passage illustrating this has already been quoted,[62] but another is a sonnet in which the effort "to find perfection in all things, and in ourselves perfection" is presented as

> The secret aim
> Of life's dim aspiration, from the sod
> Through countless forms, thro' beast and man and God![63]

Its most important aspect, however, is the Hegelian, in which the Absolute Self comes to self-realization through a brutal but progressive dialectic at the end of which it knows itself in all-inclusive knowledge. It was no doubt because Lodge conceived evolution, in Schelling's words, as such an "Odyssey of the spirit" that he stated it so often in terms of reincarnation. One instance of this has already been cited, but there are a number of others in *Cain*, of which one is the following:

> Yea, even when flesh dissolves in final change
> Still may it feel the growth of flowers and still
> Serve the insatiable desire of life!
> While soul with passionless and immortal eyes,
> Sleepless and strained to glimpse eternity,
> Thro' endless time, ascending avatars,
> Keeps way and vista to the throne of God
> And thence beyond to new infinities![64]

It was also because of this that in so many poems he sought, like Whitman, to "tally" the past and that he urged the Harvard Phi Beta Kappa, in order "to retrieve the soul's inheritance,"

> To find at last, beyond to-day, in all
> The innumerable yesterdays of time,
> The onward, latent, long millenniums,
> A rumor of us and a recollection![65]

It was, finally, because of this that he found the ego, not something to be suppressed or hidden, but to be celebrated and liberated; that he found it, not the root of evil, but a god in the making. Thus Cain says of God to Abel:

> He is what I shall be,
> I am what he has been! Hours, days, years,
> Centuries, cycles, aeons,—I shall pass
> To where he waits and longs for me![66]

And Herakles exults, in the scene following the murders:

> I know I am invulnerable—I know
> Life shall endure, life shall evolve in me!—
> In me essential metamorphoses,
> Phases and transformations of the soul!
> In me new strengths and new validities!
> In me conceptions, pangs, and pregnancies,
> Labours and parturitions, throes of change.[67]

3

Though Moody seems to have been quite innocent of direct influence by the band of transcendental philosophers whose names have appeared so frequently in these pages, his views in the matters with which we are concerned not only were cut to much the same pattern as Hovey's and Lodge's but provide us with a most convenient résumé of the whole pattern of cosmic optimism at a time when our history of that conception is drawing to a close. Governed by the same motive and faced by the same problems as its leading exponents since Emerson, he came to the same conclusions, which he was enabled by the shrewd use of myth and the choice of a broad canvas to present with a completeness and coherence seldom equaled in verse. One of the deepest motives in his verse, as it is scarcely necessary to point out, was the religious: like the others since Emerson, he believed to the depths of his being that the world and man were not, in the much-quoted words of Bertrand Russell, "the product of causes which had no prevision of the end they were achieving,"[68] but somehow the manifestation of a Being supreme not only in power but in wisdom and goodness. On the other hand, however, again like the others, he also found it impossible to reject the view of science that the world contains within itself all the principles and causes of its own development. The problem, once again, was the reconciliation of these apparently contrary views, the solution an identification of God and the universe, and the consequence a vindication of "the lewd spirit [that] stings the core of nature."

Thus it is not surprising to find the unity of Creator and created the major premise of Moody's *magnum opus,* his unfinished trilogy of verse dramas. Indeed, in a sense it is their theme, for though the theme proper is the unity of God and man only, as an evolutionist Moody perforce regarded man as, in Emerson's words, "a piece of the universe made alive." The part played by this broader conception is less important in *The Fire-Bringer* and in what can be conjectured concerning the unfinished *Death of Eve* than in *The Masque of Judgment,* but of its centrality in this play, the first to be written, Moody has left us in no doubt. It is not only the plain sense of the play but was hinted beyond mistake by the author when he referred two disturbed feminine readers to "Raphael's humanistic attitude and Uriel's philosophy, especially his 'confession of faith' in Act III, Scene II" for "the kernel of the thing."[69] Turning to this scene, we find Raphael and Uriel discussing God's resolution to destroy his creation and hear Uriel predict that God's vengeance will result in his own extinction. The basis of this prediction, and the only thing in the scene that can be called a "confession of faith," is that God and the world, including its tenantry, are one:

> The worlds and all their tenantry are Him,
>
> . . .
>
> Are effluence of the life that moves in Him,
> Thought of his brain, wish of his working blood:
>
> . .
>
> Oh, not a sparrow falleth to the ground
> But He regardeth it! Since ere it fell
> A little gladness died away in Him.
> And not a creature sinneth but He weeps
> His own sin with his creature's—fourfold pain,
> Since God and creature, false each to itself,
> Was false each to the other. Not a heart
> O'ercometh evil and mounts up to good,
> But He o'ercometh and is lifted too.[70]

Moody's Uriel, apparently, was quite as much a transcendentalist as Emerson's.

As we are prepared to recognize, however, such a view leads to a thorny problem. If the world is the "effluence" of God, why is it a place of evil? In terms of evolutionary theory, why have the worlds and their tenantry been condemned to develop through aeons of chaos and degradation toward a goal still incalculably remote? So far as the God of the play is concerned, this was simply a caprice, though a profound and uncontrollably powerful one. Wearied with the torpor of his Nirvana, God came to crave the greater stimulation of finite life. Thus Uriel recounts to the less well-informed Raphael the story of the two creations, first of heaven, then of earth:

> Of old the mind of God, coiled on itself
> In contemplation single and eterne,
> Felt suddenly a stealing wistfulness
> Sully the essence of his old content
> With pangs of dim division. Long He strove
> Against his bosom's deep necessity,
> Then, groping for surcease, put forth the orbs
> Of Paradise, with all their imagery,
> And the ordered hierarchies where we stand;
>
> . . .
>
> Demand of joy, hardly to be gainsaid,
> And vast necessity of grief, still worked
> Compulsive in his breast: our essence calm,
> Those lucid orbs accordant, could not bring
> Nepenthe long. His hand He still withheld
> Ages of ages, fearing the event,
> Till, bathed in brighter urge and wistfulness
> He put forth suddenly this vine of Time
> And hung the hollow dark with passionate change.[71]

This preference, moreover, was not only that of the God of the play but Moody's own. Moody too, zestful to a fault, preferred the refracted light of the many-colored glass to the white radiance of eternity. Like the good romantic that he was he preferred striving to arriving:

> God, who gives the bird its anguish, maketh
> nothing manifest,
> But upon our lifted foreheads pours the boon
> of endless quest.[72]

Like a good pagan he loved life for its own sake. The lines spoken by a doomed youth in the catastrophe of *The Masque* might have been a personal lyric:

> Oh, for a voice
> Here in the doors of death
> To speak the praise of life, existence mere,
> The simple come and go of natural breath,
> And habitation of the body's house with its
> Five windows clear![73]

Of the two sides of his nature that Moody constantly sought to balance and reconcile in his work, one was, in the words of one of his closest friends, "a great joy in nature and life, a natural paganism to which the visible and tangible world made instant and constant appeal."[74] Professors Manly and Lovett have both told of his devotion to Euripides' *Bacchae,* and his preoccupation with the Dionysus theme must be evident to anyone who reads his poems. Dionysian symbols are everywhere in *The Masque* and *The Fire-Bringer* and are not even excluded from a poem on Christ:

> "Yes, I have loved thee—loved thee, yes;
>   But also—hear'st thou?—also him
> Who out of Ida's wilderness
>   Over the bright sea-rim,
>
> "With shaken cones and mystic dance,
>   To Dirce and her seven waters
> Led on the raving Corybants,
>   And lured the Theban daughters."[75]

The account of creation in *The Masque,* we may conclude, was no idle fancy, but the projection in myth of a motive deep in Moody's personality, and, as we shall see, in his philosophy.

Its principal spokesman in the play, however, is not God but Raphael, whose "humanism," it will be remembered, was the other half of the "kernel of the thing." By the time the action of the play begins, God's new joys have turned bitter, and even Uriel regards creation as a mistake, telling its story to Raphael, not in praise, but to warn him away from the leavings of God's misery. Raphael is not to be dissuaded from his love of the lowly creatures of God's act, however, and when Uriel reaches the point in his narrative where God "hung the hollow dark with passionate change," he can contain himself no longer. "I think for me Heaven seemed not Heaven till then," he bursts forth,

> When from our seats of peace we could behold
> The strife of ripening suns and withering moons,
> Marching of ice-floes, and the nameless wars
> Of monster races laboring to be man;
> When we could hear the wrestle of hoarse sound
> Hurl gust on gust obscurely toward the time
> Of disinvolvéd music. . . .[76]

Even earlier, for that matter, he had made clear his love of earth and its "lewd spirit of rebellion." The first line of the play comes from his lips and expresses it, and later when he encounters the disapproval of Uriel, he puts sharply the central issue of the play in these words:

> My heart makes question which were worthier state
> For a free soul to choose,—angelic calm,
> Angelic vision, ebbless, increscent,
> Or earth-life with its reachings and recoils,
> Its lewd harsh blood so swift to change and flower
> At the least touch of love, its shell of sense
> So subtly made to minister them delight,
> So frail, so piteously contrived for pain.[77]

The "contemplation single and eterne" that had been God's life before Creation is hollow and meaningless to Raphael, as it was to Moody, and he repeats his distaste for it many times, most notably in the crucial second scene of the third act. "Why did He quench their passion?" he asks of God's vengeance.

> All things declare
> Struggle hath deeper peace than sleep can bring;
> The restlessness that put creation forth
> Impure and violent, held holier calm
> Than that Nirvana whence it wakened Him.[78]

There is a more philosophic justification of evil in the play than this, however, for which we must turn to the play as a whole and to the interpretation of it put into the mouth of Uriel. The destruction of the world and man, it will be recalled, entailed the death of God; and in this lies the point of the play. The plain implication is that the world with all its evil is not only an affair to evoke the sympathies of a humanitarian like Raphael but somehow essential to the existence of the good as symbolized by God—or rather by what God failed to be. Thus the main question at the end of the play, put by Raphael, "For what end should we love an evil thing?" receives this uncompromising answer from Uriel: "When evil dies, as soon good languisheth."[79] It should be noted that Moody's argument here is not that of St. Augustine, that "there can be no evil where there is no good,"[80] but the reverse. Evil, in other words, is not merely privative, negative, the absence of good, but a positive force that is the condition though not the cause of good, as oxygen is the condition but not the cause of animal life. Moody, in other words, has come to the same conception of evil as opposition that was first discussed here in connection with Emerson and that has been restated many times in this chapter and Chapter XII in quotations from Royce. Royce uses the illustration of holiness.[81] Holiness in the sense of mere innocence, he contends, is nugatory; we can set no store by the purity of an infant, who may be an infant Attila or Hitler. It is only when temptation has been striven with and overcome that purity becomes holiness, becomes a virtue rather than merely a quality. No other conception of evil is compatible with the particularly vivid figure in which the central situation of the play is twice summarized, in the final scene by Raphael[82] and in Act III, scene 2, by Uriel:

> The Shining Wrestler, tired of strife, hath
>   slain
> The dark antagonist whose enmity
> Gave Him rejoicing sinews; but of Him
> His foe was flesh of flesh and bone of bone;
> With suicidal hand He smote him down:
> Soon we shall feel His lethal pangs begin.[83]

There is, I believe, quite as much significance as meets the eye in the parallel between this and Professor Perry's sharply satirical description of the theories of evil of Royce, Bradley, and Bosanquet:

The good life is a wrestling with evil, not a killing of it. Without an adversary one cannot wrestle, so one must not be too rough with one's opponent.[84]

If there is to be positive good, then, if there is to be anything but the nothingness of Nirvana, there must be positive evil; in the language of the philosopher, finite existence implies limitation. In order to understand this fully, however, we must return to a paradox which we have met many times before and which is clearly included in Moody's treatment of evil. Though evil is the bitter opponent of good, it is also one with it; in Uriel's expression, it is flesh of its flesh and bone of its bone. "I am the Most High God, and I and Ahura-mazda are one," said Hovey's Angri-mainyus, and there is a closer parallel between the catastrophes in Moody's play and Poe's *Eureka* than one might expect. In *Eureka* too, finite existence was dependent upon an opposition of forces and ceased the moment that opposition was ended. The most illuminating parallel that we have examined, however, is Emerson's dualism of Power and Fate and the German dialectic that anticipated it. Fate in Emerson's essay was simply the finite aspect of things, whatever set limits and gave body to the infinity of Power. As a limit upon Power—which, as the activity of the Absolute, was to be construed as good—Fate had to be accounted evil; but it was only through this limitation that Power became "real," and only through overcoming that limitation and reaching out to another that advance was achieved. Or, to return once again to the epistemology of Fichte, the self achieves awareness only by limiting itself, positing itself as its own object. Evil is thus not "other than" good but merely its present limited state; take it away and good ceases to exist.

Thus closely was Moody bound up with the tradition whose history he is here helping to bring to a conclusion. In this history, however, we have been no less interested in the protagonist than in the antagonist in this eternal combat, and likewise with Moody we must turn from his statement of the place of evil in the scheme of things to what that statement implies concerning the nature and prospects of the good.

The most obvious implication of the statement is that goodness in living does not consist in renunciation but in giving the fullest and freest possible expression to the positive vital forces that well up from deep within man's nature. It is Emerson's "self-reliance" over again: self-assertion may lead to sin, but without it virtue is impossible. This is the obvious moral of *The Masque,* in which the heroic martyrdom of men consists in their refusal "to render up their clamorous will to Him";[85] and it is repeated in *The Fire-Bringer,* which in some ways reads like the sequel of the earlier play, even though it stood first in Moody's conception of his trilogy. Here the situation that was central in *The Masque* has already occurred. Man has already been punished for his pride,[86] and the subject of the play is rather the restoration of the power of will that made that pride possible than the chastening of it. The fire that Prometheus brings is not merely a tool of the will but the will itself. "To light the passion of the world again" is Prometheus' avowed purpose,[87] and when he has brought the lost element back in the fennel stalk provided by Pandora he gives it with these words:

> Unto this twain, man-child and woman-child,
> I give the passion of this element;
> This seed of longing, substance of this love;
> This power, this purity, this annihilation.[88]

So wedded was Moody to the noble necessity of self-will, in fact, that he even considered making it the condition of the reconciliation of God and man in the person of Eve in the third member of the trilogy. He later modified his conception, but in the epical trial version it was anything but a humble Eve—"the one rebel unsubduable by God," said Paul Shorey[89]—who stole back to the Garden to sing this song to God:

> Look where Eve lifts her storied soul on high,
> And turns it as a ball, she knows not why,
> Save that she could not die
> Till she had shown Thee all the secret sphere—
> The bright rays and the dim, and these that run
> Bright-darkling, making Thee to doubt and fear,—
> Oh, love them every one!
> Eve pardons Thee not one, not one, Lord; dost
>   Thou hear?[90]

Whatever else it may have been, Moody's was not a philosophy of submission.

But is passion to be so trusted? Blasphemy aside, would not such an emancipation lead to anarchy and naked abandonment to the will-to-power? The twentieth century, more disillusioned than its predecessor, has been increasingly inclined to believe that it would. Moody, however, was of the romantic nineteenth and like Rousseau and Emerson subscribed unquestioningly to the faith that all the deepest yearnings of men are good. This is particularly apparent in *The Masque,* where it was necessary on the one hand to paint man's sins dark enough to justify God's vengeance, but on the other to make it clear that this vengeance was mistaken. Thus Uriel in reproving Raphael for his visits to earth tells of man's

> Perfidies, hungers, dreams, idolatries,
> Pain, laughter, wonder, anger, sex, and song![91]

Even here it will be noticed that the good is mingled with the evil, and later, in more philosophical vein, Uriel comes round to the view that

> Man's violence was earnest of his strength,
> His sin a heady overflow, dynamic
> Unto all lovely uses. . . .[92]

Raphael, whose faith in man is never doubted, knows that man's yearning, crude and misguided though it may be, is always for something better than he knows. "Why live," he despairs at the time of the catastrophe,

> Why live, when all these wills that searched
>   the earth—
> Until they found their one and inward love,
> Refusing to be still—have ceased to search,
> Though quite unsatisfied?[93]

Another way of saying this is that the force of self-assertion that Moody extolled and wished to emancipate was not an end in itself but a means to an end—however obscure that end might be. It was the steam that drove the vessel but not the rudder that steered or the port that was its goal. The will that God took back in *The Masque* and that was restored in *The Fire-Bringer* was a will *for* something, never a mere blind yearning. Note, for example, the teleological language in Raphael's famous "hymn to man":

> O struggler in the mesh
> Of spirit and of flesh
> Some subtle hand hath tied to make thee Man,
>   . . .
> Though now the Master sad
> With vehemence shall break thee,
> Not lightly did He make thee,
> That morning when his heart was music-mad:
> Lovely importings then his looks and gestures had.

> . . .
> Darkly, but oh, for good, for good,
> The spirit infinite
> Was throned upon the perishable blood;
> . . .
> Not in vain, not in vain,
> The spirit hath its sanguine stain,
> And from its senses five doth peer
> As a fawn from the green windows of a wood.[94]

The spirit so tragically to be quenched, quite plainly, was not merely an energy but an aspiration—a fact which becomes even more explicit in the second play in Prometheus' parting message as he goes to pay the inevitable penalty. His gift, he tells the revitalized men and women, was not merely the assurance of continued existence, but

> The sun whose rising and whose going down
> Are joy and grief and wonder in the heart;
> The moon whose tides are passion, thought, and
>   will;
> The signs and portents of the spirit year. . . .[95]

True, to win and keep these gifts will require continual struggle, but the gift includes both means and end. The words that Prometheus addresses to the clod-people are a clear promise:

> O rude and dazéd spirits! Ye shall grope
> And wonder toward a knowledge and a grace
> That now we dream not of; then loneliness
> Shall flee away, and enmity no more
> Be spectral in the houses and the streets
> Where walk your primal hearts in the large light
> That floods the after-earth.[96]

Though Moody was both modest enough and poet enough not to formulate this ideal end, it is, if a single word can encompass it, "love"—love in a sense broad enough to include personal affection, sexual passion, motherhood, humanitarian sympathy, and the love of God. The evidence for this is so widely distributed and it is so universally the assumption of Moody's writing that it is difficult to single out individual passages that make it explicit. It is everywhere hinted. Prometheus' prophecy in the passage just quoted is one of brotherhood. What touches Raphael in the earth-life is "its lewd harsh blood so swift to change and flower at the least touch of love,"[97] "the notes of querulous love from pool and clod," "the dreamy underhum of hived hearts swarming."[98] Pandora is mother of the clod-people, the beloved of Prometheus, and, in her most famous lyric, the lover of God.[99] Without doubt, however, the culminating expression of this was to have been the dramatic *Death of Eve*. Indeed, the most logical reason for Moody's rejection of the epical version is that it merely repeated the self-assertive motif instead of rounding it out by bringing to the fore the more positive aspects of the ideal that were merely latent in the earlier plays. What was to have taken place after the first act, in which Eve persuades Cain to accompany her on her return to the Garden, we know only in the scantiest outline, but what we know assures us that the theme of love was to have been dominant. Professor Quinn, writing on the authority of Mrs. Moody, has summarized the remainder as follows: "Adam in his broken age was to have followed her, and Eve, relieved of her long-borne burden, was to have seen in the love story of her descendants the solution of the eternal problem of the human race."[100]

We also know, of course, that this play was to have locked the whole by healing the breach between God and man which was the catastrophe of *The Masque*. Though this is true, however, and is repeated in even the briefest treatments of Moody, it is easily misunderstood. For there never was a real breach. The breach in *The Masque* was only a dramatic way of saying that God and man are inseparable, of denying the Calvinistic doctrine of man's alienation. Hence it seems reasonable to conclude that the "healing" would have been achieved, not by contrition and penitence, but by reasserting this unbreakable unity and pointing to the coming fruits of the passion that was its legacy. The Eve who appears in the dramatic fragment is less assertive than the Eve of the epical version, but she is not markedly contrite; and, in any case, for her to have admitted sin in eating of the Tree of the Knowledge of Good and Evil would have unlocked rather than locked the whole. The best reason for this interpretation, however, does not lie in the trilogy itself but in the prose plays, which were written at the time that Moody was pondering his Eve problem and return to the theme of "salvation by passion" which was aired for the first time in *The Masque*. Passion, as need hardly be said concerning this play, is not to be reprobated or repressed, but directed into loving channels, where it will find its own metamorphosis. "Passion is power, and, kindly tempered, saves," said Raphael;[101] and Moody, who set great store by the phrase, wrote to Mrs. Toy, "To me the whole meaning and value of the poem lies in the humanistic attitude of Raphael, the philosophic outlook of Uriel, and *the plea for passion as a means of salvation latent everywhere*."[102] Turning to the two prose plays, we find that both are concerned with passion and its power to elevate through love. In *The Faith-Healer* Michaelis learns that his love for Rhoda is not only not incompatible with his mission but a support to it; the play, Moody said, in words that recall his comment on Raphael, sets up the "human" against the "ascetic" ideal.[103] And in *The Great Divide* Stephen Ghent, after starting out in the dregs of drunkenness and lust, not only achieves a "Second Birth" through the love that he finds in his passion for Ruth Jordan but earns for her emancipation from the Puritan tradition of renunciation in which she had lived. A connection with *The Masque* is established and much light is shed on what *The Death of Eve* might have been by final speeches in both plays. Says Michaelis:

I tasted your struggle, went down with you into the depths of your anguish, and in those depths,—the miracle! . . . Out of those depths arose new-born happiness and new-risen hope. For in those star-lit depths of pain and grief, I had found at last true love.[104]

In *The Great Divide* Ruth Jordan announces her *Umwertung des Wertes* in these words:

you found me, a woman in whose ears rang night and day the cry of an angry Heaven to us both—"Cleanse yourselves." . . . You have taken the good of life and grown strong. I have taken the evil and grown weak, weak unto death. Teach me to live as you do.[105]

Here, at the very least, was a way of rising and something to be risen to.

Though this may seem a long way from the theory of evolution, distances are sometimes deceiving. For if these sentiments, already given a cosmological association in *The Masque,* are taken out of their personal context and applied to the rising of the forms of life in nature, they lead to the same interpretation of evolution as cosmic aspiration that has been the theme of this study. And this application is warranted by the author. In turning to "The Menagerie," probably the best-known poem on evolution in American literature, this interpretation is precisely what we find. The most obvious thing about this poem is that it does not present the Darwinian or any other of the mechanical theories of evolution:[106]

> Survival of the fittest, adaptation,
> And all their other evolution terms,
> Seem to omit one small consideration,
> To wit, that tumblebugs and angleworms
> Have souls: there's soul in everything that squirms.[107]

The most important thing, however, is that it presents in biological terms the same notion of the capability of passion freely exercised to rise above itself that was pointed out in *The Masque, The Fire-Bringer,* and the prose plays. Let the "little man in trousers," shocked into vision by alcohol, the storm, and the complaints of the beasts, speak for himself:

> And souls are restless, plagued, impatient things,
> All dream and unaccountable desire;
> Crawling, but pestered with the thought of wings;
> Spreading through every inch of earth's old mire,
> Mystical hanker after something higher.
>
> Wishes *are* horses, as I understand.
> I guess a wistful polyp that has strokes
> Of feeling faint to gallivant on land
> Will come to be a scandal to his folks;
> Legs he will sprout, in spite of threats and jokes.
>
> And at the core of every life that crawls
> Or runs or flies or swims or vegetates—
> Churning the mammoth's heart-blood, in the galls
> Of shark and tiger planting gorgeous hates,
> Lighting the love of eagles for their mates;
>
> Yes, in the dim brain of the jellied fish
> That is and is not living—moved and stirred
> From the beginning a mysterious wish,
> A vision, a command, a fatal Word:
> The name of Man was uttered, and they heard.
>
> Upward along the aeons of old war
> They sought him: wing and shank-bone, claw and bill
> Were fashioned and rejected; wide and far
> They roamed the twilight jungles of their will;
> But still they sought him, and desired him still.[108]

If, as is obvious, Moody's wistful polyp was a blood brother of Emerson's "worm striving to be man," he was also akin to Stephen Ghent, who was no less a scandal to his folks.

The advance of Moody's polyp was not as easy or certain, however, as that of Emerson's worm or the favored embryo of Walt Whitman. For the point of the poem lies in the scorn of the beasts over the fact that the addled interloper before them does not measure up to the mystical hanker they have been obeying. Doubt is cast on the regularity, if not on the inevitability, of progress:

> Man they desired, but mind you, Perfect Man,
> The radiant and the loving, yet to be!
> I hardly wonder, when they came to scan
> The upshot of their strenuosity,
> They gazed with mixed emotions upon *me*.[109]

And it is true that Moody was neither a smug nor a naïve devotee of progress as it was commonly interpreted in the nineteenth century. On the contrary, his keenness to social injustice and his sense of the mounting chaos of his time caused him many times to question the direction events were taking. In "Road-Hymn for the Start," for example:

> What we are no tongue has told us: Errand-
>   goers who forget?
> Soldiers heedless of their harry? Pilgrim
>   people gone astray?[110]

And, of the ship of society, in "Gloucester Moors":

> God, dear God! Does she know her port,
> Though she goes so far about?
> Or blind astray, does she make her sport
> To brazen and chance it out?[111]

In "The Brute," moreover, he made especially clear his complete rejection of the monumental blindness that equated betterment with technological advance. Says the monster, who stands for the industrial machine but could include all mere techniques of control:

> "On the strong and cunning few
> Cynic favors I will strew;
> I will stuff their maw with overplus until
>   their spirit dies;

> From the patient and the low
> I will take the joys they know;
> They shall hunger after vanities and still
>   an-hungered go.
> Madness shall be on the people, ghastly
>   jealousies arise;
> Brother's blood shall cry on brother up
>   the dead and empty skies."[112]

The powerful muscles of the Brute were emphatically not the object of the polyp's "mystical hanker after something higher." The Perfect Man after whom the beasts had striven, it will be remembered, was "the radiant and the loving, yet to be." However, if he was "yet to be" in the sense that he had not yet arrived, the words also contained the meaning that he was inevitably coming. Even the Brute "must bring the good time on; he has no other choice."[113] The defects of his times never caused the cosmic optimist to despair, but only to turn his eyes to the future. As Raphael insisted,

> the soul utters, as she must,
> Her meanings with a loose and carnal lip;
> But deep in her ambiguous eyes
> Forever shine and slip
> Quenchless expectancies,
> And in a far-off day she seems to put her trust.[114]

Said Moody in a lyric:

> How long, old builder Time, wilt bide
> Till at thy thrilling word
> Life's crimson pride shall have to bride
> The spirit's white accord,
> Within that gate of good estate
> Which thou must build us soon or late,
> Hoar workman of the Lord?[115]

PART FOUR

THE TWILIGHT OF COSMIC OPTIMISM

XIV

SOME NEW TURNS OF THOUGHT, LESS COSMIC AND LESS OPTIMISTIC

WILLIAM VAUGHN MOODY is the last important figure in American poetry who can be called, in the sense of this study, a bona fide "cosmic optimist." True, the two chapters following this will be devoted to instances of the doctrine in the writing of some of Moody's contemporaries, but with a single minor exception these instances will prove no more than vestiges, so attenuated or so modified as to make clear that the venerable gospel had passed from full blaze into twilight and that the time has come to bring its history to a close. To be sure, if one accepted its premises, its argument was as sound as ever. If evolution explained as much as was claimed by its more extreme interpreters and was the work of an omnipotent and benevolent God, it was certainly a subject for rejoicing. Both of these premises had come under vigorous attack from many quarters, however, with the result that the doctrine at first dwindled and has now all but subsided into history. It is beyond the scope of this study to attempt anything like a complete account of these attacks, but if the fate of cosmic optimism is to be understood, some brief explanation must be offered. Hence, in the discussion that follows in the present chapter, three movements that ran counter to the doctrine will be briefly identified and illustrated in the work of poets on or just over our chronological borderline. These movements are the naturalists' denial of the principle of benevolence, the humanists' denial of the relevance of evolution to the problems of man, and the pragmatists' denial of the whole sphere of speculation in which any discussion of cosmic optimism must be carried on.

1

The most obvious source of opposition to cosmic optimism was evolutionary science itself, which, as has been pointed out here before, neither required nor continued very strongly to suggest the happy and idealistic interpretation. Beginning in the nineties, the theme of a "mystical hanker after something higher" began to fade from the story of evolution, and since that time even poets have tended increasingly to take their science unsweetened, remembering, among other things, that it has offered theories of dissolution and decline as well as of evolution and progress. To choose a recent example, Robinson Jeffers, in looking west from California's shores, has revised Whitman and seen a gloomy end to the old journey from the East,[1] just as elsewhere he has pictured the course of the world's tragic history as bounded at beginning and end by blank lifelessness:

> the column of ice that was
> before on one side flanks it,
> The column of ice to come closes it up on the
> other; audience nor author
> I have never seen yet. . . .[2]

Again, turning back within the time limits of this study, we find the delightful Oliver Herford, always quick to make capital of current fashions in thought, achieving a quite stoical whimsy on a variation of the same theme:

> If this little world to-night
> Suddenly should fall through space
> In a hissing, headlong flight,
> Shrivelling from off its face,
> As it falls into the sun,
> In an instant every trace
> Of the little crawling things—
> Ants, philosophers, and lice,
> Cattle, cockroaches, and kings,
> Beggars, millionaires, and mice,
> Men and maggots all as one
> As it falls into the sun . . .
> Who can say but at the same
> Instant from some planet far
> A child may watch us and exclaim:
> "See the pretty shooting star!"[3]

We have seen this theme before, in Poe, Trowbridge, Gilder, and others, but never without saving clauses. In our own day it has become a commonplace and no special mark of pessimism. "We are all doomed to broken-off careers," writes Robert Frost, who can scarcely be called a pessimist,

> And so's the nation, so's the total race.
> The earth itself is liable to the fate
> Of meaninglessly being broken off.[4]

Evolutionary science carried to the bitter end, it seemed, was not altogether a subject for jubilation. This was true, moreover, not only because it envisaged a catastrophic end of the world but because it embodied the methodological assumption of science that the universe is a soulless machine. This view did not have as much influence on poetry as on prose fiction at the turn of the century, but there are two instances before the end of the century that are suggestive straws in the wind. One, "Disenchantment: Soliloquy of Victor Fauvel, Naturalist," by William Roscoe Thayer,[5] is the callowest kind of youthful verse but a useful illustration of the point. A year before the opening of the poem the title character had been rapturously in love, but in the interval science had taught him that love is only a biological phenomenon. This year he and his former mistress meet "without tremor, and wonder how either could e'er have been stirred." "Farewell to the rapture of kisses," he sighs,

> Farewell to the hope in the bud,
>   If we guess that our holiest bliss is
> But a trick of the ripening blood!

He upbraids Nature on two counts: first, for having cozened man into the belief that the world exists for his special benefit; secondly, for not having kept up the imposture. Nature has "flatter'd, as flatters a woman" in telling man what has so often been heard in these pages:

> "I have dower'd thee, darling, tho' human,
>   With gifts of the gods above:
> When the Earth was at its beginning
>   I foresaw thy glory a-wing.
> And I patiently waited, spinning
>   Robes meet for creation's king."

As he ponders Nature's duplicity, it crosses Fauvel's mind that she may only have grown "suddenly spiteful tow'rds the innocents she created," but he quickly turns to the less flattering and more soundly naturalistic conclusion that she is quite indifferent—that "she neither loves us nor hates." Such is the new view, the polar opposite of cosmic optimism, the view of a

>Science
>That neither desponds nor exults
>But measures its dungeon coldly,
>And dares to cross-question its doom.

The sharpest sounding of this note in that early time came from Stephen Crane, in some of the trenchant free verse epigrams that now seem more alive than all but the best of his fiction. Like a number of his contemporaries, Crane was violently in revolt against the bland optimism of most of his elders, and, falling into the opposite romanticism of the cynic, he concluded sarcastically that the so-called higher aspirations are a benighted pursuit of the impossible:

>I saw a man pursuing the horizon;
>Round and round they sped.
>I was disturbed at this;
>I accosted the man.
>"It is futile," I said,
>"You can never—"
>
>"You lie," he cried,
>And ran on.[6]

Not only was this the truth of life, moreover, but nature was utterly indifferent to it; nature was neither cruel nor beneficent nor treacherous nor wise, but "indifferent, flatly indifferent."[7] "God," if there is one, "is cold."[8] Down to recent times I know of no lines in American literature more inimical to the tradition of cosmic optimism than these, perhaps Crane's best known:

>A man said to the universe:
>"Sir, I exist!"
>"However," replied the universe,
>"The fact has not created in me
>A sense of obligation."[9]

Gone in these lines is the basic premise of cosmic optimism that nature is somehow the mirror of man's aspirations. Crane felt as Henry Adams did after witnessing the cruel death of his sister: "God might be, as the Church said, a Substance, but He could not be a Person."[10]

SOME NEW TURNS OF THOUGHT

The fullest transvaluation of the values of cosmic optimism was not achieved within the time limits of this study, however, but only later, by Jeffers, who not only recognized the indifference, the insensibility, of the cosmos, but made of this indifference a kind of Nirvana. Cosmic optimism was essentially a projection of human values into a theory of the universe, but what Jeffers prizes in nature is precisely that it is not human, that it is

> Unmeasured power, incredible passion, enormous craft:
> no thought apparent but burns darkly
> Smothered with its own smoke in the human brain-vault:
> no thought outside. . . .[11]

Conversely, what he despises in man is that he falls short of both this thoughtless violence and the rock-like impassibility which Jeffers admires equally. Far from being the highest stage in an evolutionary advance, mankind to him is an excrescence upon nature, "the mould to break away from."[12] Man's vaunted sensibility, his heart, is not his virtue but his vice, undermining his independence and embroiling him in desires and revulsions that are at best contemptible and at worst calamitous. His salvation, hence, is not to be achieved by the fulfillment of what has most commonly been regarded as his humanity, but by abandoning it, by imitating the granite imperturbability of inorganic nature, by "falling in love outward"[13] and climbing "the tower beyond time."[14] In view of these sentiments, it is not surprising that Jeffers has no news of progress but much of the *Untergang;* nor is it surprising that he is not saddened by this news. Catastrophe will be a deliverance:

> Oh distant future children going down to the foot of the
> mountain, the new barbarism, the night of time,
> Mourn your own dead if you remember them, but not for
> civilization, not for our scuttled futilities.
>
> You are saved from being little entrails feeding large
> brains, you are saved from being little empty bundles
> of enjoyment,
> You are not to be fractional supported people but complete
> men; you will guard your own heads, you will have
> proud eyes.[15]

Jeffers is exceptional, to be sure, even in his own age. But that he should have written in this vein at all, and been read on any wide scale, is a sign of the waning optimism of the time—of a time in which the leading apostle of progress concluded before his death that mind is "at the end of its tether."[16] The optimism of the nineteenth century, cosmic or otherwise, has come to have curiously archaic sound, even the theologians having become—or having again become—pessimists concerning this world.[17] The "escalator" theory of history retains a place in current thought almost alone in Marxist propaganda, and is there chiefly criticized as sharing the romanticism of a past age.[18] The twilight of cosmic optimism in our poetry is not simply a shift in literary fashion, but a decisive step in history.

2

It was possible, however, to abandon the doctrine of cosmic optimism completely and to accept the worst that science had to say without falling into Crane's or Jeffers' contemptuous estimate of the lot of man. This escape was possible in a number of ways, but one which has been influential enough to deserve comment here is well illustrated in the eminently humanistic poetry of George Edward Woodberry. Woodberry devoted his whole life to the celebration of the spiritual triumphs of man in the world of art and letters and yet was outspoken in his belief that science had deprived nature of its religious significance:

> For deity in things we do not look;
> Now closed to all the gods is nature's book.[19]

> Nature will not cast for thee
> The starry robe of deity.[20]

Woodberry's conception of nature was not that of Emerson, as can be seen by reading his life of that great optimist; but that of science, as is shown by the first book of his thinly veiled spiritual autobiography, "The Roamer," written in the eighties though not published until 1920.[21] Here the title character, apparently typifying Woodberry's own experience in that era of the warfare of science and religion, holds "the skull of nature in his hand," and, "versed . . . to read what there is found," follows "the cosmic tale that vaunts its ignorance":

SOME NEW TURNS OF THOUGHT

> No chaos, no catastrophe, no more
> But definite order in indefinite time,
> Events, successions, processes, fixed change.

Nor is man exempt from the ravages of this ordered mutability. All things pass away, and man's works have no more durability than the earth he treads:

> Then, startled, he remembered what man is,
> Hidden in his dark corner of chilled space,
> His history with all its circumstance,
> Races, religions, policies, archives
> Of scriptured wisdom, monumental war,
> The passing of a grain of that gray sand
> That measures Nature's period,—a drop
> That falls within the glacier's blue crevasse,
> While the slow frozen motion creeps along
> Through ages, and the sun expires in frost.

Granting all this, however, Woodberry does not conclude that man's life is *only* the shifting of a grain of nature's sand. Man and his works will pass away as certainly as his body will turn to mould, but that does not mean that they are idle or worthless. Values are still values even if not everlasting or cosmic in scope. Indeed, according to Woodberry, the only values that exist are those that take their rise in man's consciousness, which is differentiated from its material basis precisely by that capability. Nature can feed and fight and reproduce, but only man can understand, can worship, can know love and beauty:

> "The light? the light?"
> The Roamer said; "the light divine?" "The light?"
> Came the answer, "from thyself it flows."[22]

"Nature is great," Woodberry once said, "and her science marvellous; but it is man who knows it."[23] It is true, as the evolutionists contend, that man has risen from nature:

> Oh, foul and bloody strife, since time began,
>   Up from the beast to man's imperial mold!
> Oh, long his empire-toil, since he was man,
>   The soul's confederation to unfold!
> And many heavens he scaled, ere Bethlehem's star
>   Hymned human love above all gods that are![24]

But by this very fact he is now on a higher level. Man has "transcended nature," the poet affirms; for

> There is no truth save what to him is known;
> There is no beauty save within his eye;
> There is no love but what in his has grown,
> And only in his mandate right doth lie;
> Justice and mercy his, and good and ill,
> And virtue throneless save within his will.[25]

Or, most forthrightly stated, in one of the sonnets of *Ideal Passion:*

> I know not what in other men may sleep
> Of lower forms, which nature knew to shape
> To higher, and from her primal slime escape
> To sea, and land, and heaven's aerial deep;
> Nor with what stirring their thick blood may leap
> Of ante-natal slaughter, brutish rape;
> I own no kinship with the obscene ape;
> No beast within my flesh his lair doth keep.
>
> The memory of the rose-tree runs not back
> Through the dim transmutations of the rose;
> Sphere over sphere, above the solar track,
> The round of heaven greatens as it goes;
> So am I changed; though the last change I lack,
> When over love itself oblivion flows.[26]

Woodberry's view looks both forward and back. One cannot, for example, miss in it the note of the jealously guarded Christian dualism of Lowell or of the equally dualistic humanism of Matthew Arnold. As was pointed out in Chapter I,[27] however, something approaching this dualism survived the monistic drift of the later nineteenth century and reappeared in evolutionary form in the twentieth-century concept of "emergence." A new level of existence, the advocates of this concept contend, is really new, having its being on a quite different plane from its antecedent. True, the theory was not developed in these terms until late in Woodberry's life, and the terms in any case were not those with which, as a poet and literary critic, he was most concerned. The closer analogue to his thought in the matter is no doubt the empirical dualism of such a neo-Humanist as Norman Foerster. Humanism, says Professor Foerster,

does not seek to show how life came from non-life or consciousness from unconsciousness, or perhaps why consciousness is not a fact at all. . . . Ungoaded by the *Einheitstrieb* of any such monism, humanism is content to accept, without explanation, the "doubleness" of human experience, experience shared with nature and experience not shared with nature. It is willing to acknowledge two realities, the reality of nature and the reality of human spirit, without subsuming either under the other.[28]

In either case, however, the point is that the characteristics specific to man are not to be found on lower levels and are not determined by the characteristics of those levels; and this has an important consequence for this study. For if evolution thus loses its explanatory power in respect to man's peculiar nature, it loses much of its interest for the poet, or indeed for any nonspecialist. Woodberry, of course, had the interest of emancipating himself on the one hand from the myths of the transcendentalists and on the other from the materialism of the Darwinians; but, once his view is accepted, evolution ceases to have relevance to those aspects of man's life in which the poet is traditionally most interested. As many more recent writers seem to have concluded—and at least Sill among older writers[29]—man is what he is regardless of his descent.

3

Probably the most important single factor in the passing of cosmic optimism, however, has been the widespread abandonment of the whole universe of discourse to which it belonged, a development resulting in part from Darwinism itself. For the most potent single influence of Darwinian theory on the world of speculation has been a subtler and more inclusive one than any that has yet been discussed in these pages. The heart of Darwin's contention was that new forms of life are established by their ability to survive in the struggle for existence: nature produces them abundantly and at random, but only those that are able to meet the needs of specific life-situations survive to multiply their kind. At first the significance of this conception outside the realm of biology seemed to lie in the blessing it conferred on philosophical mechanism and the ethics of self-interest, but later, when seized upon by students of logic, it yielded more sweeping inferences. If the exaggerated toe of the horse was to be explained and judged by its survival value, why not man's thoughts as well? Were they not also "tools for living," particularly delicate weapons by which men achieved essentially the same end as the sabre-toothed tiger? Did not their "truth" really reside in the success with which they helped to achieve this end, rather than, as had been traditionally believed, in any correspondence or consistency or intuitive certainty? There is no such thing as truth, it was concluded; there is only belief that works.

This conception, pragmatism or instrumentalism, of course also had other roots than the Darwinian; but, from whatever roots, it was the utter negation of the classical philosophy of which cosmic optimism was a part, which had sought truths that were eternal and ultimate. "Pragmatism is really less a philosophy than a method of doing without one," said the Italian pragmatist Papini,[30] and John Dewey has written as follows of his own instrumentalism and of "the influence of Darwin on philosophy":

Philosophy forswears inquiry after absolute origins and absolute finalities in order to explore specific values and the specific conditions that generate them. . . . Interest shifts from the wholesale essence back of special changes to the question of how special changes serve and defeat concrete purposes; shifts from an intelligence that shaped things once for all to the particular intelligences which things are even now shaping; shifts from an ultimate goal of good to the direct increments of justice and happiness that intelligent administration of existent conditions may beget and that present carelessness or stupidity will destroy or forego.[31]

The consequences of this for the premises of cosmic optimism are as obvious as they were drastic. Baldly, these premises were reduced to the status of useful—or useless—hypotheses. Evolution was to have nothing to do with "absolute origins and absolute finalities"; it was not a universally coherent and necessary system but a number of special theories for the interpretation of specific astronomical, geological, biological, and social facts; at best it was merely something that had happened, not the embodiment of any cosmic intent. Nor did the Cosmic Being who might have had such intent suffer a gentler fate. True, William James insisted that we retain the "right to believe,"[32] but the belief that he had in mind was purely private and accepted only because it "tempts our will";[33] the right to make it the basis of public inferences concerning the nature of things was remorselessly sacrificed. "The plain truth," James said elsewhere, "is that the 'philosophy' of evolution . . . is a metaphysical creed, and nothing else."[34] He was speaking of

SOME NEW TURNS OF THOUGHT 341

Spencer, but his remark applies, *a fortiori,* to the transcendental conception that has been presented in this study.

The pervasiveness of this turn of thought in the new century and its destructiveness in respect to all metaphysical speculation must be clearly seen if the fate of cosmic optimism is to be understood.[35] The kind of knowledge of the inner nature and motive of the universe necessary to any cosmic optimism had come to be regarded—in the word that Sill borrowed from Lewes[36]—as "impossible." The experience of John Jay Chapman is typical, even symbolic. At Harvard he had heard George Herbert Palmer expound Berkeley's paradox of knowledge, and he at once concluded: "Very well; until one can get past this barrier, I do not intend to burden my mind with philosophy."[37] "There is no such thing as philosophy," he wrote apropos of Royce,

but there are such things as philosophers. A philosopher is a man who believes there is such a thing as philosophy, and who devotes himself to proving it. He believes that behind the multifarious, contradictory, and often very unpleasant appearances of the world there is a unity which he can put into typewriting. Probably there is, but certainly he can't.[38]

The whole conception of knowledge was changing. By an increasing number it was no longer regarded as "a transcript of reality," but as "conceptual shorthand," "plans of operations," "the good in the way of belief," "faith mediated by symbols." Far from knowing God's plan, the younger Oliver Wendell Holmes argued, man can not even tell what brute matter is:

If we believe that we came out of the universe, not it out of us, we must admit that we do not know what we are talking about when we speak of brute matter. We do know that a certain complex of energies can wag its tail and another can make syllogisms. These are among the powers of the unknown, and if, as may be, it has still greater powers that we cannot understand . . . why should we not be content? . . . That the universe has in it more than we understand, that the private soldiers have not been told the plan of campaign, or even that there is one . . . has no bearing on our conduct.[39]

Conceptions such as those which have been discussed in these pages were now commonly believed to be rationalizations, myths, which, if they had any relation to truth at all, were true to the men who uttered them rather than to the world they pretended to describe. Cosmic optimism was one more "moral fable," a model illustration of what Dewey calls "*the* philosophic fallacy":

For reflection the eventual is always better or worse than the given. But since it would also be better if the eventual good were now given, the philosopher, belonging by status to a leisure class relieved from the more urgent necessity of dealing with conditions, converts the eventual into some kind of Being, something which *is,* even if it does not *exist.* Permanence, real essence, totality, order, unity, rationality, the *unum, verum, et bonum* of the classic tradition, are obviously eulogistic predicates. . . . Reflection determining preference for an eventual good had dialectically wrought a miracle of transsubstantiation . . . conversion of eventual functions into antecedent existence: a conversion that may be said to be *the* philosophic fallacy, whether it be performed in behalf of mathematical subsistences, esthetic essences, the purely physical order of nature, or God.[40]

Not all of those involved in this critical movement, to be sure, have been as scornful of the inventiveness of philosophy as Dewey and Holmes. Santayana, for example, regards man's moral fables as in many respects more important than his more verifiable notions,[41] and such a conservative theologian as Reinhold Niebuhr holds that myth is the only form in which man's predicament in creation can be adequately rendered.[42] No matter how faithfully myth may prefigure the experience and problems of man, however, it is still not "true" in the matter of fact sense of the correspondence of thought and thing; as was said above, it is true to the man who conceives it, or perhaps to man in general, rather than to what it describes. Nor do Santayana and Niebuhr ask for more; rather they agree with Dewey that sense and reason are incapable of detecting and defining fundamental reality. The attempt to arrive at such a fundamental definition leads inevitably to paradox, according to Niebuhr, and though Santayana calls himself a materialist, he insists, like Holmes, that neither he nor anyone else can tell what matter is. Vastly at odds as they are on most points, it is still not surprising that Santayana, Niebuhr, and Dewey are in general agreement on this delimitation of knowledge, for they are merely articulating a fundamental and nearly universal assumption of their time. Today suspicion of assertions concerning ultimate matters is as prevalent as was the opposite in the day of *Nature* and *Eureka.* Yesterday this suspicion began to make itself felt in the world of poetry, where it produced an atmosphere in which such a "metaphysical creed" as cosmic optimism could not survive.

4

One consequence of this development for many poets was simply the avoidance of metaphysical and cosmological themes. One may be sure, for example, that scepticism played a part along with esthetics in the Imagists' taboo against the philosophical mode of nineteenth-century poetry; in any case, they condemned that mode vigorously:

We are not a school of painters, but we believe that poetry should render particulars exactly and not deal in vague generalities, however magnificent and sonorous. It is for this reason that we oppose the cosmic poet, who seems to us to shirk the real difficulties of art.[43]

Moreover, even when "nature" was dealt with as such, it was seldom treated transcendentally. In the poetry of the present century nature has been presented less and less as the embodiment of reason or benevolence and more and more as merely the setting or matrix of man's life, governed perhaps by regular laws but quite devoid of "purpose." Affection aplenty has been lavished by modern poets on "earth" (the substitution for the older "nature" is significant), but rather because of its intimate associations than because of any evolutionary destiny. These are but vague and general drifts, however, and for more specific illustration we must turn to the work of a single poet, the most celebrated of the poets immediately junior to Robinson, Robert Frost. Though Frost falls outside our time limits, his position in this matter deserves consideration for the excellent illustration that it offers of the passing of the cosmic theory with which we have been concerned.

From reading a poem like "The Bear," with its satirical picture of philosophic man as "swaying between two metaphysical extremes,"

> At one extreme agreeing with one Greek,
> At the other agreeing with another Greek,[44]

one might conclude that Frost is as unsympathetic toward metaphysical pursuits as John Jay Chapman claimed to be. Such, however, is not the case. He has confessed "a great leaning for the philosophy department,"[45] and in a very illuminating essay has not only defined philosophy in the highly metaphysical sense of an attempt to make a final unity of matter and spirit[46] but has called this attempt "the height of all thinking."[47] If he is sympathetic, however, it is with the sympathy of a Santayana rather than with the blanket approval of one who believes that firm metaphysical truth can be achieved. Thus, in the same breath with his statement that philosophy is the height of all thinking, he called it "the height of poetry," and but a moment before had spoken of it, in terms reminiscent of Sill and Lewes, as "the greatest attempt that ever failed." It fails, furthermore, not because of any peculiar difficulty in its problem but because all thought must fail in its attempt to state the nature of a thing. Such statements, Frost believes, are always metaphors, and metaphors are never literally true. "All thinking, except mathematical thinking," he says, "is metaphorical,"[48] "just saying one thing in terms of another";[49] and "all metaphor breaks down somewhere."[50] "A thing, they say, is an event. Do you believe it? Not quite. I believe it is almost an event. But I like the comparison of a thing with an event."[51]

Let me ask you to watch a metaphor breaking down here before you.

Somebody said to me a little while ago, "It is easy enough for me to think of the universe as a machine, as a mechanism."

I said, "You mean the universe is like a machine?"

He said, "No. I think it is one . . . well, it is like . . ."

"I think you mean the universe is like a machine."

"All right. Let it go at that."

I asked him, "Did you ever see a machine without a pedal for the foot, or a lever for the hand, or a button for the finger?"

He said, "No—no."

I said, "All right. Is the universe like that?"

And he said, "No. I mean it is like a machine, only. . . ."

" . . . it is different from a machine," I said.[52]

While this last illustration excludes Frost from the school of thought that was most sharply opposed to cosmic optimism, that of philosophic mechanism, the point that it illustrates just as effectively eliminates him from the company of the cosmic optimists. For if there was any one conviction that was shared by all the latter, it was that they were stating real truths concerning the cosmos, and not merely telling what it is like. The implication of Frost's position, however, especially when read in the light of the numerous sceptical passages in his poems,[53] is that no such ultimate truths can be stated—that statements about such matters are not descriptive but expressive, are statements that the matter may be so viewed rather than that something is the case. Even the most casual reader of Frost must be aware that he is certain of his way only in the realms of particular fact and of moral preference and that when he turns to the realm of speculation he is not merely uncertain but conscientiously so, being convinced that he has reached the limits of knowledge:

> Some may know what they seek in school and church
> And why they seek it there; for what I search
> I must go measuring stone walls, perch on perch;
>
> . . .
>
> Such as it is it promises the prize
> Of the one world complete in any size
> That I am like to compass, fool or wise.[54]

In this Frost resembles Santayana, and no doubt many another modern realist and naturalist like him; for Santayana also regards the realm of fact as the only realm of truth, also believes that the basis of thought is similitude, and also finds greatness in speculation going beyond the realm of truth.[55] The aim here, however, is not so much to define Frost's intellectual position as to contrast it with that of cosmic optimism, and this can be done by a brief comparison with Emerson. Emerson would have agreed heartily that metaphor is basic in thinking—"man is an analogist, and studies relations in all objects"[56]—but with a rather different meaning:

Parts of speech are metaphors, because the whole of nature is a metaphor of the human mind. The laws of moral nature answer to those of matter as face to face in a glass. . . . This relation between the mind and matter is not fancied by some poet, but stands in the will of God, and so is free to be known by all men.[57]

To Emerson the similitude in metaphor did not express a merely apparent likeness but pointed to a real identity bodying forth that "final unity" which Frost regards as a will-o'-the-wisp, even if a glorious one. It is difficult to imagine Frost telling what "stands in the will of God."

Quite naturally, if philosophy and science are, as Frost says, "simply made of metaphor," evolution is no exception:

Another metaphor that has interested us in our time and has done all our thinking for us is the metaphor of evolution. Never mind going into the Latin word. The metaphor is simply the metaphor of the growing plant or of the growing thing. And somebody very brilliantly, quite a while ago, said that the whole universe, the whole of everything was like unto a growing thing. That is all. I know the metaphor will break down at some point, but it has not failed everywhere. It is a very brilliant metaphor, I acknowledge, though I myself get too tired of the kind of essay that talks about the evolution of candy, we will say, or the evolution of elevators— the evolution of this, that, and the other. Everything is evolution. I emancipate myself by simply saying that I didn't get up the metaphor and so am not much interested in it.[58]

Though the frequent evolutionary allusions in Frost's poetry[59] suggest that he has been more interested in evolution than his last sentence would indicate, his remark is a just one in the sense that evolution is with him no longer the touchstone that it has been throughout most of this study. The allusions are in almost every case no more than allusions and are often enough ironical or satirical to indicate that he has been impressed at least as much by the comic possibilities of the theory as by the prophetic. A good example is to be found in "Wild Grapes," but the best is in "The Literate Farmer and the Planet Venus," where the lunatic fringe of evolutionary optimism is treated as it deserves:

> "What's a star doing as big as a baseball?
> Between us two it's not a star at all.
> It's a new patented electric light,
> Put up on trial by that Jerseyite
> So much is being now expected of,
> To give development the final shove
> And turn us into the next specie folks
> Are going to be, unless these monkey jokes
> Of the last fifty years are a libel,
> And Darwin's proved mistaken, not the Bible.
> I s'pose you have your notions on the vexed
> Question of what we're turning into next."[60]

Of the evolutionism of the "mystical hanker after something higher" I find no trace in Frost's writings, though an advocate might make the following points concerning "West-Running Brook."[61] First, it deals with origins: the eddying wave which is the object of comment

> is from that in water we were from
> Long, long before we were from any creature.

Second, it presents existence as a continuous stream or flow:

> Here we, in our impatience of the steps,
> Get back to the beginning of beginnings,
> The stream of everything that runs away
> . . .
>
> It flows between us, over us, and *with* us.
> And it is time, strength, tone, light, life and love—
> And even substance lapsing unsubstantial. . . .

Third, it speaks of a movement "up":

> the fall of most of it is always
> Raising a little, sending up a little.

Finally, though it presents this movement upward as especially characteristic of man, it refers it back to the "source" of all existence:

> It is this backward motion toward the source,
> Against the stream, that most we see ourselves in,
> The tribute of the current to the source.
> It is from this in nature we are from.
> It is most us.

To leave the poem at this, however, would be the rankest special pleading. For one thing, the movement "up," being the rise of the eddy, is not pictured as being followed by something that rises a little higher, and so on in progression. For another, the rise of the eddy is in opposition to the flow of the stream, which is described as down or "away." In contrast to the usual view of the cosmic optimist, the achievement celebrated by the poem is not the result of going with the current but of resisting it:

> It seriously, sadly, runs away
> To fill the abyss' void with emptiness.
> The universal cataract of death
> That spends to nothingness—and unresisted,
> Save by some strange resistance in itself,
> Not just a swerving, but a throwing back,
> As if regret were in it and were sacred.
> It has this throwing backward on itself

>So that the fall of most of it is always
>Raising a little, sending up a little.

Such an opposition of movement and resistance is susceptible of evolutionary interpretation, as was first shown here in the case of Emerson, but it is not so interpreted in this case. Frost has paid his respects to the Hegelian dialectic, praising its doctrine of the conflict of opposites; its rational evolutionism, however, he is unwilling to accept. "A time succession," he has said, "is the fallacy."[62] The theme of "West-Running Brook" is not progress but that persistent theme of Frost's that virtue consists in bucking the tide rather than in going with it, in having one's "sticking-points." The principle of life that he is celebrating is not the flow but resistance to the flow.

But is there no sense in which Frost may be called a cosmic optimist? Of course there is. If the words as here used carried no other sense than their simple meaning of facing the cosmos with courage and hope, they would have to be applied to Frost. Lawrance Thompson is thoroughly justified in claiming for him an "optimistic acceptance of a world which may seem too evil, too confused, too hopeless for some people."[63] As Thompson suggests, however, this optimism is not based on any illusions concerning the benevolence of the cosmic process[64] or on such a belief as Emerson's that "the laws of moral nature answer to those of matter as face to face in a glass." We saw earlier that he reckoned with the fact that we are all faced with the doom of broken off careers, and in "West-Running Brook" he described the prevailing flow of existence as "the universal cataract of death." As with such "naturalistic humanists" as Dewey and Santayana, however, it is perhaps just because he is unable to regard an Emersonian philosophy as more than a glorious fancy that he can face so untoward a universe with composure. If the universe cannot be regarded as embodying intent, it cannot be regarded as benevolent, but neither can it be regarded as malicious. Perhaps it is only difficult, the rather recalcitrant raw material out of which something can be made. As Thompson says, "there is a difference between the passive acceptance of 'whatever is' and the active doing with 'whatever is.'"[65] Frost's view is not that of cosmic optimism, that the universe is in reality better than it seems, but simply that man can make a life in it. "I never tire," he has written, "of being shown how the limited can make snug in the limitless."[66] How a man may be an optimist in facing the universe without being a "cosmic optimist" he showed clearly in a letter to the Amherst *Student*.[67] First he pictured a "background in hugeness and confusion shading from where we stand into black and utter chaos," and "against the background any small man-made figure of order and concentration." He then asked:

What pleasanter than that this should be so? Unless we are novelists or economists we don't worry about this confusion; we look out with an instrument or tackle to reduce it. . . . We like it, we were born to it and have practical reasons for wanting it there. To me any little form I assert upon it is velvet, as the saying is, and to be considered for how much more it is than nothing. If I were a Platonist I should have to consider it, I suppose, for how much less it is than everything.

This may be a better or worse philosophy than that which has been studied here, but it is not the same.

XV

SOME OF ROBINSON'S CONTEMPORARIES: SHIFTING GROUND

THE last leaf upon the tree of unqualified cosmic optimism was the prolific and earnest Kentucky poet, Cale Young Rice. Rice was not only without peer among the poets of his time in his faith in the "Upward Urge of Being,"[1] but he founded this faith firmly and frankly on belief in a divine Immanence. The Galileo of his poem of that name he caused to mutter in denial of the charge of blasphemy that "motion and force are God's";[2] an Atheist, the title character of another poem, laments that he has

>   missed
> Something that only they who tryst,
> Not with the sequence of events
> But with their viewless Immanence,
> Find and acclaim with spirit-sense;[3]

in a third poem, concerned with the "devil-wrought" life of the undersea world, the poet reflects:

> Too strange it is, too terrible! And yet
>   It matters not how we were wrought or whence
>   Life came to us with all its throb intense
> If in it is a Godly Immanence.
> It matters not,—if haply we are more
>   Than creatures half-conceived by a blind force
>   That sweeps the universe in a chance course;
> For only in Unmeaning Might is met
> The intolerable thought none can ignore.[4]

The optimistic inference from this premise, moreover, is specifically drawn. Thus, in "The Strong Man to His Sires,"[5] after paying his respects to "all shapes whom birth and nature could affine unto me"—"they who had been me"—the title character addresses them finally:

> I say, Immortal do I hold your will!
>   Its gathered might ascending

> Is sacred with the unconquerable might
>   Of God—who sees its ending;
>
> Of God—on whose strong Vine, Heredity,
>   Rooted in voids primeval,
> The world climbs ever to some great To-Be
>   Of passion or reprieval.

This would stand as Rice's best statement of the theme, in fact, if it were not for the following passage in a poem appropriately entitled "Cosmism":[6]

> As if I knew with a deeper sense
>   That good alone is ultimate;
> That never an evil wrought of God
>   Or man came truly out of hate.
> That Better springs from the heart of worse,
>   As calm from the heaving elements;
> That all things born to the Universe
>   May suffer and perish utterly hence,
>   But never refute its innocence.

We shall find nothing more so unshadowed as this. Rather, in the poems of the three of Robinson's contemporaries who remain to be considered, Edgar Lee Masters, Harriet Monroe, and George Sterling, we shall find an increasing defection from the old doctrine, a shifting of ground in which some touch will be maintained with the old view, but with increasing tenuosity, until a flat denial is reached in one of the poems of Sterling. There is irony in the fact that of the three, Masters is closest to the old belief; for his best-known work has associated him rather with the pessimistic naturalists. This association has considerable justification, furthermore, as might be illustrated at length out of his verse and is illuminated by the following neo-Darwinian reminiscence in his autobiography, referring to the year 1911 or thereabouts:

I was reading science all the time. DeVries and others, books on botany and biology; and I saw but one story, which was that Nature pours forth creatures and lets them live or perish, according to chance.[7]

Masters has objected strenuously to being lumped uncritically with the naturalists, however. Elsewhere in his autobiography he insists many times on a mystical element in his make-up that balances his hard-eyed realism and causes his poems to fall into two distinct categories:

All through my poems there run the two strains of realism and mysticism. I wrote with my cyclopean eye many of the portraits of Spoon River, and with my dreaming eyes I wrote "The Star" and "The Loom."[8]

There is little evidence of the dreaming eyes in the relevant poems in his earliest work, much of it published under pseudonyms,[9] but beginning with *Songs and Satires* and *The Great Valley* in 1916 there are numerous instances, some presenting evolution with an optimism quite the equal of any we have seen. In "The Conversation,"[10] for example, the cosmic "Voice" that is heard in so many of these poems speaks to the author concerning the evolutionary story and tells him that, though it is impossible for a mortal to visualize forms of being that do not yet exist, "your soul may be the germinal cell of vaster evolution." Again, in "Neanderthal," the same Presence, appearing to the poet in the night, carries him across land and sea to the anthropologically famous village named in the title, and there, after recounting the story of life before man, puts the meaning of the story into these words of praise and hope:

> *Change and progression from the glazed slough,*
> *Where life creeps and is blind, ascending up*
> *The jungled slopes for prey till spirits bow*
> *On Calvaries with crosses, take the cup*
> *Of martyrdom for truth's sake.*[11]

To man's impatience with his failure in historic times to achieve anything like the advance of the prehistoric and prehuman ages, the mystical visitor responds that "the test is not five thousand years,"[12] and adds that sufficient promise can be drawn from the fact that investigators of the past have found no "skulls of greater races . . . to shame us for our day" but only the remains of lower beings.[13] "I see the things which balk, retard, divert," he admits,

> But who beholds the stream turned back to mock,
> Not just itself, but make equivocal
> A Universal Reason, Vision? No.
> You find no proof of this, but prodigal
> Proof of ascending life![14]

"So life shall flow here on this globe," he promises, "until the final fruit and harvest."[15]

The fullest fruition of this theme did not appear in Masters' work, however, until his 1935 volume, *Invisible Landscapes*, in which he made specific the immaterialist ontology—only hinted in the "Universal Reason" of "Neanderthal"—that was necessary to raise this trust in progress above an empiricist's gamble. "We may not say that matter is all," he wrote in this volume, in the first stanza of "Ultimate Selection,"

>   nor even
> That energy is all, save by the meaning
> That energy is mind, and mind is all;
> And being mind is life and labor for life,
> Selecting what is best to lift the living.[16]

In another poem in the same volume, "Hymn to the Earth," he ascribed various views to "the ancients" which are as certainly his own as they were certainly not theirs, and in so doing indicated two familiar reasons for adopting this metaphysic. Thus, for one, "they dreamed of a Life that worked these miracles."[17] In other words, they and the poet adopted the teleological argument that where there is organization there must in some sense be an Organizer—"Mind" in Masters' case, both here and in "Ultimate Selection," where the point is made that though protoplasm is nothing but chemical elements in particular combinations,

>   in these is an invisible element
> Which toils within, and chose those chemicals,
> And with them made blue algae, ferns at first;
>   . . .
> Then fashioned man at last, kin to them all.[18]

Secondly, he and they returned to Royce's contention that "if from inorganic matter beings with minds evolve," inorganic matter must be somewhat less exclusively material than is supposed. Thus, the "ancients" questioned

>   how will and vision were in the mind
> Of man if the Earth was blind and moved without will
> And whence were will and thought if not from Earth?[19]

Their conclusion, and Masters', was this conception of material nature:

> Earth! The veil of the intelligence of Nature,
> Which owes nothing to any external essence,
> But contains within itself from the All the chlorophyll
> Which extracts life from the universe.
> Earth! Whose seeming lifelessness is deeper life,
> Whose seeming unconsciousness is profounder thought,
> Being at the basis of thought.[20]

Quite naturally, the optimism of "The Conversation" and "Neanderthal" burned no less brightly in these poems, particularly in "Ultimate Selection," the theme of which is that mind works in evolution to select, in the words already quoted, "what is best to lift the living." It "uplifts" the primal elements "along the ascending slope of perfecter life." "The cells of man and sponges are alike," and

> Both toil as germinal cells to change, advance,
> To vary, select the best of preformed good
> Whereby to rise in the scale, and make the past
> Serve best for safer paths, the fuller life.[21]

In the climax of the poem, moreover, there emerges in man what would appear an entirely new realm of being were Masters not so insistent in his monism. For mind in this new development is not merely intelligent behavior—"testing, choosing and rejecting"—but inner experience, esthetic, logical, and moral:

> And as the seed springs into stems and blossoms,
> Which fill the garden with color and with scent
> As a realm above that world of flaming life,
> So man by music, wisdom and by verse
> Has lifted above his body and mortal days
> Of labor and aspiration a higher sphere
> Of being than that of sleeping and of waking.[22]

A stratosphere has been reached in the evolutionary climb, in which mind is freed from the weakness of the flesh which supports it, and, in some sense not quite clear, lives on beyond the flesh:

> This stratosphere created by verse and music,
> And made another existence and a world,
> Lives calm and deathless, and is to flesh and days
> The fragrance of the garden; it is the soul
> Which lives through ages, selected to survive.
> This is that higher mind which after wandering
> In flesh ways joins the Mind and lives therewith.[23]

Anyone searching for cosmic optimism could scarcely ask for more than this, and to quarrel with the place of it or its author in this study without further evidence would be the merest quibbling. When, however, others of Masters' poems, in which the cyclopean eye is more in evidence than the dreaming, are placed beside these, deep shadows develop and a basic difficulty appears which, while not new here, is considerably more obvious and unpalliated than in earlier cases. For cosmic optimism always threatens to run afoul of the problem of evil. It draws its optimism from belief in the essential goodness of a power capable of producing the ascent from star-mist to man, but in recounting this ascent it cannot blink the fact that the power has been, to say the least, careless of the single life. The usual reply, either in simple logic or elaborate dialectic, is that present evil is necessary for future (or larger) good. But to say that an evil is necessary does not make it a good, and hence the Power in question is always in danger of seeming a monster. As has been contended against the God of St. Augustine and John Calvin, it seems a contradiction to call him just "when he is unjust in the only sense in which the word justice has a meaning among men."[24]

In the face of what Emerson called the odious facts, indeed, it sometimes seems that the best that can be said of this Power is that it is beyond good and evil, that it is not malicious but only indifferent, going its cosmic way in complete disregard of the local prejudices that men call by these terms of praise and blame. Since it is all, by what standard is it to be judged? Thus Masters asks in a poem entitled "Nature," "Is life evil, good?" He answers the question by abandoning the distinction, at least on the cosmic plane:

> Is life not of you? Is there aught without
> By which to judge this restless brotherhood
> Of will and water, and to quiet doubt
> That life is good? . . . .
> . . . . You are all!
> And man who moves within you may imbrue
> His hands in war, or famine on him fall
> Out of your eyeless genius, yet what wrong
> Is wrought to your creating, magical
> Renewal, scheme? What arbiter more strong
> Than you are judges discord for the strife
> That stirs upon our earth, wherever throng
> Thoughts, forces, fires? What is evil? Life!

> Even as life is struggle, whether it smite,
> Or lift, as waves to waves in will are rife
> With enmity.   Whatever is, is right.[25]

When in another poem Masters questions his mystical companion concerning the shocking fact that all things in nature "are fierce for place and garner life from weaker things," the only answer he gets is that "that is life";[26] and even in the midst of the optimism of the 1935 volume we are told that one of the things to be praised in Nature is that "she will snatch the hood of morality from your eyes," will show you

> that what comes to man amid his own laws,
> And what comes to him as famine, plague and war,
> As storm, earthquake and the cruel elements,
> And from demonic powers,
> Are all her work,
> And are part of the Universal Power
> Of which she is a part:
> For she is not Pity, or Love,
> Save as she is vastness.
> She is inexorable, just in her injustice,
> Giving life and taking it,
> And visiting upon innocence
> Pain and uninterrupted consequence.[27]

But if this is the character of the Moving Cause, or God, of Masters' evolutionism, what becomes of his optimism? Is his position really so far from the neo-Darwinism of his reaction to his scientific studies in 1911? Is it possible that when he saw with his dreaming eyes he was really dreaming? The easiest and perhaps the best answer is that he was, and that in employing his two sets of eyes he was a kind of philosophical Jekyll and Hyde. Another that has much to recommend it, however, is that his inconsistency was not the result of any personal infirmity but simply the emergence into clear light of a difficulty latent in all cosmic optimisms of the kind we have been considering. It may be that he merely illustrates the bad end against which the archenemy of these optimisms, Santayana, has repeatedly warned: "if we . . . insist on assigning to spirit the functions proper to matter, *spirit, before we know it, has become but another name for matter in our philosophy and in our lives.*"[28] If we identify God with the evolutionary process, Santayana holds, then we must not only credit him with the good but blame him for the evil; and if after this we continue to insist on his perfect goodness, we shall find that we really have abandoned the distinction between good and evil and can only say, "it is all one." We have met this issue before, particularly in Whitman, but in Masters it appears in such sharply contradictory terms that his two visions, cyclopean and dreaming, have much the effect of cancelling each other out. In this nullification, however it may be explained, is another shadow in the twilight of cosmic optimism.

A similar ambivalence is to be seen in the work of Harriet Monroe, several of whose poems, viewed in isolation, seem to present as authentic a cosmic optimism as that of Rice and Moody. Though her "Columbian Ode," from which much might have been expected as an expression of the millennial fever of the end of the century, is a disappointment in this respect,[29] two poems of more recent vintage which she valued highly enough to include in her anthology of "new poetry" are not. Both present the kind of rapid, impressionistic sketch of the story of evolution with which we are familiar, and both suggest that there is a controlling force running through this story making certain that all will be well. In "Mother Earth," for example, after she has carried the story from the lifting of the land out of the sea to the rise of animal life, she goes on:

> There are wings and songs in her trees,
> There are gleaming fish in her seas;
> The brute beasts brave her;
> And gnaw her and crave her;
> And out of the heart of these
> She wrests a dream, a hope,
> An arrogant plan
> Of life that shall meet her,
> Shall know and complete her,
> That through ages shall climb and grope,
> And at last be man.[30]

"Dream," "hope," "plan," the personification of Nature, the determinate form of the future tense—these are of the tradition. Nor does the promise end here. The historical record demands that when man appears he must be buffeted about rather severely, but he too is given hope, which we are to suppose is as well founded as that of his predecessors:

> Through her ages of years,

> Through his toil and his tears,
> At her wayward pleasure
> She yields of her treasure
> A gleam—yes, a hope,
> Even a day of days,
> When the wide heavens ope
> And he loves and prays;
> Then she laughs in wonder
> To see him rise
> Her leash from under
> And brave the skies!³¹

"Supernal Dialogue," which recalls *The Masque of Judgment* in presenting the comments of two angelic beings as they view the course of evolution from a point of vantage "on the edge of things," is even more conclusive. In contrast to "Mother Earth," which was limited to the history of the earth, it is also more inclusive—beginning like *Eureka* with the first outpouring of worlds by God—and more directly concerned with the goal of this outpouring and the likelihood of its attainment. "Will he get what he wants—the perfect flower?" one of the speakers asks concerning God. Apparently he will not, on earth, which is allowed to meet the fate forecast in the second law of thermodynamics, but it is not denied that he will in the end:

> II Has he lost again? Can he fail?
>
> I Who are we to question? Though he fail again and again—
>
> II Yes, who are we?
>
> I He must go on—he must get the flower.³²

The word "must" in such a statement, as we are prepared to recognize, is significant.

Taken alone, there can be no doubt that these poems approximate to the theme with which we are concerned. When viewed against the background of the strong agnostic current that runs through Miss Monroe's work, however, it becomes equally clear that they must be read rather as expressions of mood than of conviction. This current might be illustrated by a number of her poems—"At the Prado,"³³ "The Quest,"³⁴ "The Man of Science Speaks"³⁵ — but it is stated more directly and succinctly in a passage in her autobiography in which she declares in so many words that she has been unable to accept any theory of the universe and regards all as myths:

> No system of beliefs that I have ever examined seems to me in the least adequate as an explanation or interpretation of the universe .... The imagination of a little earthbound creature cannot scale the heights or sound the depths of that power's prodigious energies; man's efforts to do so result in myth, and myths too often lose their fluid and changeable beauty and harden into dogma.[36]

It would not, of course, detract from the optimistic purity of "Mother Earth" and "Supernal Dialogue" to say that they are myths; so are "Woodnotes" and Moody's *Masque*. But the point is that Moody and Emerson regarded their myths as essentially true to the facts of nature, while Miss Monroe thought of hers as true only to herself. Hers expressed an attitude rather than a belief and took the form of cosmic optimism only to give this attitude dramatic concreteness. One is reminded of the pragmatical German work, *The Philosophy of "As If,"* when she tells of the visions yielded by the "golden moments" of imagination:

> At such times the beauty of life seems too keen to be borne.... It is as if one watched this earthly episode from some far planet of larger spaces and years, and saw its crisscross of lines, its blots and splashes of color, merge into a noble pattern set for the delight of gods. *From that vantage ground* ... all [becomes] an act of the eternal passion, a daring flight of the universal spirit.[37]

This, which recalls "Supernal Dialogue," is what the universe seemed to Miss Monroe in moments of enthusiasm; what she had found it to be in more sober moments she had stated a few pages earlier:

> I gained also a realization of the heroic audacity of the "thousand creeds" in imposing a name and a more or less human personality upon the Creative Force animating the universe, an audacity which amazes but does not persuade me. Call the Force God and worship it at a million shrines, and it is no less sublime; call it Nature, and worship it in scientific gropings and discoveries, and it is no less divine. It goes its own way, asking no homage, answering no questions. Reluctantly it makes a place for life, on one little planet in ten trillion, through the labor of ages too vast for reckoning. And when life's tremors are over and our lovely little earth grows cold,

that mysterious Force will still swing the starry nebulae and perhaps light other living worlds here and there among them.³⁸

Miss Monroe is the poorer representative of the cosmic optimism that has been described in these pages just because she is the better representative of another optimism about the cosmos that departs from the older so sharply as to make its history another story. This optimism is that of Bergson and Dewey, in which evolution is regarded as good, not because it is divinely caused or because it is approaching a goal held to be good, but for its own sake. Growth is regarded as relative only to more growth, as *being* rather than *having* an end;³⁹ God "has nothing of the already made; He is unceasing life, action, freedom."⁴⁰ The philosophers would perhaps wish to refine the point, but Miss Monroe, like many other celebrants of the life-force back to Goethe, seems to value life and growth not for their fruits but for their sheer wonder and excitement. If the following lines approach burlesque, they make the point no less clearly:

> How wild, how witch-like weird that life should be!
> That the insensate rock dared dream of me,
> And take to bursting out and burgeoning—
>   Oh, long ago—yo ho!—
> And wearing green! How stark and strange a thing
>   That life should be!
>
> Oh mystic mad, a rigadoon of glee,
> That dust should rise, and leap alive, and flee
> Afoot, awing, and shake the deep with cries—
>   Oh, far away—yo hay!—
> What moony masque, what arrogant disguise
>   That life should be!⁴¹

This view of life and evolution is of course not altogether new here. Professor Lovejoy holds that it had its philosophical origin in Schelling,⁴² Santayana believes that it is the heart of Romanticism and expresses a latent restlessness and protestantism in North European peoples going back to primitive times,⁴³ and we have seen a forcible illustration of it in the writing of Walt Whitman.⁴⁴ Even in these cases, however, there is a difference. As Lovejoy pointed out in the case of Schelling, the *"ewiges, lebendiges Tun"* was balanced by an eternal perfection that was before all created things and set the standard by which the evolutionary pattern might be said to be progressive.⁴⁵ So in Whitman,⁴⁶ and so even more with the others we have considered; but not so in the case of the Creative Force of Miss Monroe and many of her juniors.

Three poems published by George Sterling in 1915 and 1916 make clear that he too had at least a few drops of millennial blood in his veins. "The Builders"⁴⁷ makes the point that regret for the past is idle in view of the fact that "a world reborn awaits us," and *Yosemite* contains a fine paean to "the glad unrisen Day," "the vaster Dawn" of "morning! morning! morning! on the world!"⁴⁸ True, in the "Ode on the Opening of the Panama-Pacific International Exposition" some salutary warnings are offered. "Can it be we build upon the sands?" the poet asks,⁴⁹ and points out:

> except Love build the House of Man,
> In vain we labor and in vain we guard!⁵⁰

His confidence that "what we dream, a wiser Age shall do"⁵¹ was unimpaired, however, and the poem concludes with the kind of fulsome peroration on this theme that his rhetorical bent made inevitable.

The millennial drops were few, however, were often mixed with others less shining, and were sometimes completely swamped. Thus "The Midges"⁵² is a sarcastic apologue satirizing "progress" as mere increase in tempo, and Sterling's most detailed retelling of the evolutionary story ends by picturing man as "the last monster."⁵³ Moreover, a faint hint of cosmic optimism that is to be found in the Exposition ode is belied elsewhere. In the ode it is asked concerning man's ascent "from the slime of old abysses,"

> What seed of what Design was in that soul
>   And what its destined goal,
>   That he, once halt and blind,
> Hath won the peaks above the brutish years . . . ?⁵⁴

This is a question, however, not an answer, and elsewhere it becomes clear that Sterling, like Miss Monroe, regarded such speculation as a greater credit to man's imagination than to his judgment—in this sonnet in his 1914 volume, for example, which, while it deals primarily with immortality, has broader implications also:

> Lo! this audacious vision of the dust—
>   This dream that it has dreamt! Unresting wings,

> Too strong for Time, too frail for timeless things!
> Whence all thy thirst for God, thy piteous lust
> For life to be when matter's chain shall rust?
> What pact hast thou with the undying kings,
> Silence and Death? What sibyl's counsellings
> Assure thee that the eternal laws are just?
> Nay! all thy hopes are nothing to the Night,
> And justice but a figment of thy dream!
> Upon the waste what wide mirages glow,
> With hills that shift, and palms that mock the sight,
> And cities of the desert's far extreme—
> Those veils we name, and dare to think we know![55]

The poem of Sterling's that has most to contribute to this discussion, moreover, presents, not cosmic optimism, but cosmic pessimism. As its title, "The Testimony of the Suns,"[56] makes clear, it is concerned with the light that astronomy has to shed on just these aspirations, and its conclusion is that it does not substantiate them. "What tidings of the heavenly fray?" it asks at the outset, and answers:

> These, as our sages nightward turn
> To gaze within the gulfs where burn
> The helms of that sublime array:
>
> Splendors of elemental strife;
> Smit suns that startle back the gloom;
> New light whose tale of stellar doom
> Fares to uncomprehending life.[57]

This conflict, moreover, is not a means to an end but is itself the only end there is, a meaningless round:

> How haste the unresting feet of Change,
> On life's stupendous orbit set!
> She walks a way her blood has wet,
> Yet thinks her path untrodden, strange.
>
> By night's immeasurable dome
> She dreams her hopes in surety held—
> Lo! from insurgent deeps impelled
> The fleeting systems lapse like foam.[58]

In the course of these rounds, universes quite pointlessly spring into being, wax magnificent, grow old, and die:

> Vague on the night the mist we mark
>   That tells where met the random suns:
>   In changeless molds of law it runs
> To orbs that roam anew the dark,
>
> And unto which the worlds are born,
>   Where Life awakes to know again
>   The light of stars, caress of rain,
> And winds of the forgotten morn.
>
> Lift up, ye everlasting gates
>   Whence fare her feet to wars unknown,
>   To heights august of Reason's throne,
> And heritage of ampler Fates!
>
> When she, the mindless clay no more
>   In Lust's or Fear's potential hands,
>   Shall range her uncontested lands
> Or sister world's befriending shore.[59]
>
> Till lapse her beatific years
>   In emperies of art untold,
>   The music of her age of gold
> Requiting for unnumbered tears;
>
> Till she behold—the visual boon
>   Surviving elemental risk—
>   The nearing sun's enormous disc,
> Blood-red at dusk of sullen noon;
>
> Till her appointed course be run;
>   Till on the darkness faint her breath,
>   Flown to the silent void, and Death
> Sit crowned upon the ashen sun.[60]

Here was a cosmogony to please Henry Adams rather than Walt Whitman. For cosmic optimism is not only refuted by the facts, the testimony of the suns; it is presented as on its face absurd. It is a contradiction in terms, Sterling retorts to the pantheistic blender of naturalism and religion, to suppose that a Being already perfect should labor painfully up the ladder of evolution:

> Shall Godhead dream a transient thing?
> Strives He for that which now He lacks?[61]

What stronger denial of the claims of the cosmic optimist could there be than this?

O dream not all the worlds fulfill!
   Unblest, unbidden, save of hope.
   Not for finality the scope
And strength of that unaltered will.

The eternal Night has writ in stars
   Denial of the ends ye name;
   Ye stand rebuked by suns who claim
The consummation of her wars.[62]

XVI

ROBINSON

THE fate of cosmic optimism among the poets of this generation was less often a cataclysmic revulsion like that of Sterling in "The Testimony of the Suns" than a quiet deliquescence, the spirit remaining but the substance being gone. The hope was there, the feeling that somehow and in the long run things are for the best; but the structure of premise and inference in which this hope had been articulated as a necessary progress was fading with a rapidity that foreboded ultimate disappearance. This dissolution was variously observable in the poems of Masters, Monroe, and even Sterling himself, but it is particularly evident in the work of Edwin Arlington Robinson, who has been chosen as the concluding figure in this study for this reason and not merely because of his poetic eminence or familiarity as a literary landmark.

It must be granted that Robinson retained traces of the underlying philosophy of the cosmic doctrine and, as a kind of lining to his cloud, a notable tinge of its fundamental hopefulness. He was, he said, "an insane optimist,"[1] "the damnedest optimist that ever lived."[2] He was even in a sense a "cosmic" optimist, for his belief was not simply that things would turn out well for himself or his group but that somehow justice was inherent in the nature of things and would one day, here or hereafter, right the scandalously overset balances of the present. Tenaciously held as this optimism was, however, it is of the greatest importance to note that it never appeared in Robinson's writing without the closest qualification. He did not call himself an "insane optimist" because he believed that good was actually in the process of coming to prevail, but only because he recognized the potentiality of good in men, "the possibilities of good in thwarted lives that seemed wholly evil."[3] He felt the "coming glory of the Light," but he avoided saying that he could tell what it is or show it to another or demonstrate its necessity.[4] He believed that the flame of life "must burn somehow for the best," but he regarded man as a "bewildered insect" plunging at it haphazard.[5] An optimism of a kind must certainly be granted to Robinson, but he was too painfully aware of the ills of the world to accept the easy rationalizations of the evolutionary faith. He was an optimist in spite of what the world had to show, or promised to show, not because of it.

Much the same thing is true of his relation to the spiritualistic metaphysic characteristic of this doctrine, to which he adhered truly but only in very general terms and without drawing the melioristic inference. His exhortation in the rejected poem "Children of the Night"[6]—"So let us in ourselves revere the Self which is the Universe"—is quite in the transcendental tradition, and the same thought reappears in somewhat less bald terms in other poems which he retained. Thus, in "Octaves" he tells us that we shrink too sadly from

> the larger self
> Which for its own completeness agitates
> And undetermines us,[7]

and speaks of

> God's parallel completeness in the vague
> And incommensurable excellence
> That equitably uncreates itself
> And makes a whirlwind of the Universe.[8]

Again, twenty years later, he permitted Merlin to make use of the same conception to find hope in the downfall of Camelot:

> When I began with Arthur I could see
> In each bewildered man who dots the earth
> A moment with his days a groping thought
> Of an eternal will, strangely endowed
> With merciful illusions whereby self
> Becomes the will itself and each man swells
> In fond accordance with his agency.
> Now Arthur, Modred, Lancelot, and Gawaine
> Are swollen thoughts of this eternal will
> Which have no other way to find the way
> That leads them on to their inheritance
> Than by the time-infuriating flame
> Of a wrecked empire, lighted by the torch
> Of women, who, together with the light
> That Galahad found, is yet to light the world.[9]

If this means, as it could, that the world is the manifestation of a Self whose light will one day shine clearly and without distortion through the world, it is very close indeed to what has here been called "cosmic optimism."

However, though it is but a step from this implication to the sanguine conclusion that the obstacles obscuring this light are gradually and steadily falling away, I see no evidence that Robinson took this step. Possibly the nearest that he came to it was in this other passage in "Octaves":

> Tumultuously void of a clean scheme
> Whereon to build, whereof to formulate,
> The legion life that riots in mankind
> Goes ever plunging upward, up and down,
> Most like some crazy regiment at arms,
> Undisciplined of aught but Ignorance,
> And ever led resourcelessly along
> To brainless carnage by drunk trumpeters.[10]

The words "ever . . . upward" cannot, of course, be gainsaid, but so strong is the qualification that follows that they must be taken as referring merely to aspiration or rare and purely accidental advance rather than to a regular course of development. And elsewhere we find no more, if as much. I can, for example, find no trace of the "faith in . . . evolutionary progress" that Professor Waggoner ascribes to "Children of the Night,"[11] and Professor Stovall's speculation that the Arthurian poems present a conception of historical progress looking forward from the breakup of the Middle Ages to the development of modern individualism[12] has been contradicted by passages in the *Selected Letters* which indicate that in so far as these poems have any historical reference at all it is modern rather than medieval.[13] To be sure, as in the passage just quoted from *Merlin,* Robinson several times predicted that the world would one day be better than it is now. At the end of "Demos and Dionysus," as Professor Stovall points out,[14] Dionysus, representing the spirit of life and art, says to Demos, who stands for the spirit of leveling and utilitarianism:

> I may go somewhere for a while,
> But I am one of those who have perforce
> To live and to return.[15]

This is something less, however, than the evolutionary millennialism of which we have seen so much. For Dionysus to say that he will "return" is not the same thing as saying, as Professor Stovall does, that he will "rule," and there is no assurance in the poem that his new advent will be more brilliant than his great past appearances— in the fifth century B.C., for example, or the thirteenth or sixteenth A.D. For Robinson to say that the world would one day be better than it was during his lifetime was assuredly something, but, in view of his low opinion of that world, not much. Moreover, he did not hold even this hope unquestioningly, as may be illustrated by another poem in the same volume with "Demos and Dionysus":

> And when we are all gone, shall mightier seeds
> And scions of a warmer spring put forth
> A bloom and fruitage of a larger worth
> Than ours? God save the garden, if by chance,
> Or by approved short sight, more numerous weeds
> And weevils be the next inheritance![16]

Robinson, indeed, seems to have pinned his hopes less on the perfection and worldly bliss of a remote posterity than on some kind of personal immortality. A less happy man living in less happy times than most of the men who have been discussed here, he was acutely aware of the Achilles heel of all evolutionary optimisms —that they offer little consolation to the individual. This was the point of the early "Amaryllis":

> Far out beyond the forest I could hear
> The calling of loud progress, and the bold
> Incessant scream of commerce ringing clear;
> But though the trumpets of the world were glad,
> It made me lonely and it made me sad
> To think that Amaryllis had grown old.[17]

The point was repeated as late as 1931 in a letter to Will Durant:

But if life is only what it appears to be, no amount of improvement or enlightenment will ever compensate or atone for what it has inflicted and endured in all ages past, or for what it is inflicting and enduring today.[18]

Moreover, since the sentence preceding this was devoted to the statement that he had no fear of annihilation, the antithesis in this makes clear that Robinson's meaning was that only immortality can atone for life's injuries. Nor is this view isolated or exceptional in

Robinson's writing. He never, to my knowledge, stated that immortality is or must be a fact, but he repeatedly argued that nothing else will justify the belief in an essential justice which alone makes life supportable. He so argues, for example, in "Children of the Night":

>   And if there be no other life,
>   And if there be no other chance
>   To weigh there sorrow and there strife
>   Than in the scales of circumstance,
>
>   'T were better, ere the sun go down
>   Upon the first day we embark,
>   In life's imbittered sea to drown,
>   Than toil forever in the dark.[19]

And in "The Man Against the Sky":

>   No planetary trap where souls are wrought
>   For nothing but the sake of being caught
>   And sent again to nothing will attune
>   Itself to any key of reason
>   Why man should hunger through another season
>   To find out why 't were better late than soon
>   To go away and let the sun and moon
>   And all the silly stars illuminate
>   A place for creeping things....[20]

The argument reappears even as late as *King Jasper* in a passage which might be taken as a declaration of earthly progress if it were not that it is a comment on some remarks by the elder Jasper concerning the "last freedom" of death. Zoë is speaking:

>   "No God,
>   No Law, no Purpose, could have hatched for sport
>   Out of warm water and slime, a war for life
>   That was unnecessary, and far better
>   Never had been—if man, as we behold him,
>   Is all it means."[21]

This is not to say, of course, that Robinson turned away from the world in contempt or disgust, fixing his gaze on eternity. As we have seen, he looked for a better day on earth, and on the very next page Zoë repeats the sentiment:

>   Today the devil is more than God. Tomorrow

> He will be more, and more. Out of it all
> He'll come with crutches, and not the devil he was.
> Father, don't ask me when, for I don't know.

At best this is remote and minimal, however, and not the justification of the will-to-live that was the heart of Robinson's belief.

One thing is certain: Robinson derived little comfort from the evolutionary theories of science. To be sure, he speaks broadly of "our bleeding progress upward from the mud,"[22] but he does even this only rarely, incidentally, unemphatically, and without the intention of starting any inferences. The aspect of these theories that has made the greatest stir in these pages left him quite unmoved. He had quite as strong a sense of a "mystical hanker after something higher" as Moody, but not in the same meaning, regarding it as the exception rather than the rule in nature, of the benevolence of which he had a low opinion:

I'm afraid, on the whole, that there isn't much comfort in nature as a visible evidence of God's infinite love. It appears to be a shambles and a torture-chamber from the insects up—or should we say down? The insects will have the world some day, and maybe they'll eat everything that's in it, and then eat each other.[23]

There is, in fact, no reason to believe that Robinson thought any more highly of nature per se than did the Shakespeare of his poem,[24] and there is good reason to believe that he looked upon such science-founded optimisms as Fiske's as ludicrously presumptuous. Such, at any rate, is the suggestion of these satirical lines in "The Man Against the Sky":

> Or maybe there, like many another one
> Who might have stood aloft and looked ahead,
> Black-drawn against wild red,
> He may have built, unawed by fiery gules
> That in him no commotion stirred,
> A living reason out of molecules
> Why molecules occurred,
> And one for smiling when he might have sighed
> Had he seen far enough,
> And in the same inevitable stuff
> Discovered an odd reason too for pride
> In being what he must have been by laws
> Infrangible and for no kind of cause.[25]

The inference from the biological theories of evolution that most interested Robinson, in fact, was not optimistic but pessimistic—that of materialism. He did not accept the inference, regarding it rather as the cardinal philosophical error of his time, but he gave it a great deal of attention. Thus in *Matthias at the Door* it is identified with the suicide of Garth, and the books in which Matthias mistakenly tries to find light are described in these terms:

> The best of them were moonshine without light,
> Or news of an ingenious mechanism
> That must have built itself mysteriously
> And infinitely out of infinite nothing.[26]

Its language is used to describe the abyss out of which Matthias is striving to climb in the last third of the poem:

> A life without a scheme and to no purpose—
> An accident of nameless energies;[27]

and it is condemned by Timberlake in terms of the characteristically Robinsonian argument that if it is true life is not worth living:

> There's a malignance in the distribution
> Of our effects and faculties. It is nature,
> And our faith makes it more. If it's no more,
> Garth waited longer than was logical
> For a good atheist who believed himself
> And life a riot of cells and chemistry—
> If he believed it.[28]

It may not help much merely to point out what Robinson did *not* believe—either scientific mechanism or cosmic optimism—but it is very nearly the best that can be done, since his thought, like his style, was distinguished by an unusually high proportion of negatives. Even in respect to immortality, it will have been noted, he did not argue that it was true but only that he could not believe that it was not true. Like many others, Robinson found it easier to define what he rejected than what he accepted. Witness these statements of his "philosophy" written for two thesis-writing young ladies:

I am naturally gratified to learn that you are writing a thesis on my poetry, but I am rather sorry to learn that you are writing about my "philosophy"—which is mostly a statement of my inability to accept a mechanistic interpretation of the universe and of life.[29]

There is no "philosophy" in my poetry beyond an implication of an ordered universe and a sort of deterministic negation of the general futility that appears to be the basis of "rational" thought. So I suppose you will put me down as a mystic, if that means a man who cannot prove all his convictions to be true.[30]

"As I do not know that such a tragic absurdity is not a fact," he wrote in characteristic language and logic to Will Durant, apropos of the futility of materialism, "I can only know my native inability to believe that it is one."[31] If there is any one constant that stands out more than another in Robinson's reflections, it is not merely that things are somehow for the best but that this best cannot be demonstrated and had better not be formulated. It is a matter of personal faith, which, though essential and inevitable ("There's not a man who lives and believes nothing."[32]), can be taught "no more than may the color of our eyes."[33] Long before, he had warned off his formulators in these words:

> The prophet of dead words defeats himself:
> Whoever would acknowledge and include
> The foregleam and the glory of the real,
> Must work with something else than pen and ink.[34]

Whitman, of course, had said as much and then gone on to formulate by the page, but Robinson wore a tighter intellectual rein and practiced what he preached. It cannot be repeated too often or too forcibly that he believed literally that his optimism could not be argued, least of all in terms of the theory of evolution. Consider, for example, in addition to the evidence already presented, the following turn in the debate between Matthias and the returned soul of Garth. Hot for certainties, Matthias throws down the challenge:

> "Why do you laugh,
> When you had better tell me," said Matthias,
> "If these untold progressions and expansions
> Of yours, or Timberlake's, begin with us,
> Or if worms, armadillos, and hyenas
> Have them as well. Where may the soul begin?
> And why not grass? There's a mystery living in grass
> As dark as any in me."

Garth replies:

> "Language, Matthias.
> With a few finite and unfinished words
> That are the chips of brief experience,
> You restless and precipitate world-infants
> Would build a skiff to circumnavigate
> Infinity, and would find it, if you could,
> No more sufficient or more commodious
> Or comprehensive in its means and habit
> Than a confused, confined phenomenon
> Prisoned within a skull, with knowledge in it."[35]

It is a materialistic evolutionism that Garth is refuting here, to be sure, and his reply to Matthias' ironic question about the grass and armadillos is, Why not? His meaning, however—that "nothing of an infinite nature can be proven or disproven in finite terms"[36]— is as applicable to Hegel as to Haeckel. Robinson once said that his "transcendentalism" was to be seen in "The Man Against the Sky" and *Matthias at the Door*.[37] Perhaps it is best expressed, with all its firmness of conviction, all its indefiniteness, all its appeal to intuition, in this speech of Timberlake's:

> "Why are we as we are? Don't ask, Matthias.
> Why do we come to nothing who have more,
> We'll say than most? What is our value here
> Unless we fit? To make a mould that fits us,
> You'd like to say, Matthias, but aren't going to.
> Read a few years of history, and you'll see
> The stuff is not so pliable as all that.
> If it were so, we should all be each other—
> So great that nature would be on her knees,
> Which is not nature's natural attitude.
> Why are we as we are? We do not know.
> Why do we pay so heavily for so little?
> Or for so much? Or for whatever it is?
> We do not know. We only pay, and die.
> To a short-sighted and earth-hindered vision
> It would seem rather a waste, but not to mine.
> I have found gold, Matthias, where you found gravel,
> And I can't give it to you. I feel and see it,
> But you must find it for yourself."[38]

So sinks the sun of cosmic optimism. Robinson was a transcendentalist, as has been said, to the extent of denying the mechanistic determinism of the naturalists and of believing that somehow the opposite was true; and he was an optimist to the extent of believing that somehow and sometime the injustice of men's lives would be corrected. Beyond this, however, to the beguiling theory that has been considered in these pages, he would not go. When he was a young man foregathering with cronies over a dry goods store in Gardiner, one of the number was "caught in the gears of the mechanistic system on the rebound from a theology that his intelligence would not let him accept." Robinson, ever the spiritual physician, came to his rescue. " 'Idealize yourself!' " he said; " 'take your mind off the material and focus it on the real existence.' "[39] It is characteristic that he did not tell him that evolution is any better than it appears, but only to look inward and not out.

NOTES

CHAPTER I

INTRODUCTION

[1] *New Views of Evolution* (New York: The Macmillan Co., 1929), p. 24.

[2] *The Present Conflict of Ideals* (New York: Longmans, Green & Co., 1918), p. 118.

[3] "Evolution," *New International Encyclopedia* (2nd ed.; New York: Dodd, Mead & Co., 1923), VIII, 221.

[4] Joseph Le Conte, *Evolution and Its Relation to Religious Thought* (New York: D. Appleton & Co., 1888), pp. 13-16.

[5] See especially W. R. Inge, "The Idea of Progress," *Outspoken Essays*, 2nd series (New York: Longmans, Green & Co., 1922), pp. 158-83.

[6] See below, p. 62.

[7] See especially the early essay, "Progress, Its Law and Cause" (1857). For further developments see below, pp. 151, 251-52, and 254-56.

[8] "Progress, Biological and Other," *Essays of a Biologist* (Harmondsworth, England: Penguin Books, 1939), p. 39. Another instance of the mechanistic concept of progress that should not be forgotten is that of Karl Marx. On his "escalator" theory of history see Max Eastman, *Marxism: Is It Science?* (New York: W. W. Norton & Co., 1940), p. 15 and *passim*.

[9] Evolutionary meliorism may be said to have taken the place of the doctrine of the Fall in nineteenth-century liberal theology. After the latter doctrine had been rejected, some explanation had still to be given of the disparity between the actual world and the perfect world of which benevolent Omnipotence is capable. The new explanation was that this perfect world is in the making. The approach of such an explanation can be seen in Channing's "The Moral Argument against Calvinism," where he argues from nature to the justice and goodness of God, but then is forced by the fact of evil to add that the complete manifestation of this justice and goodness is not "immediate." (*The Works of William E. Channing, D. D.* [17th ed.; Boston: American Unitarian Association, 1867], I, 231.)

[10] Attributed to James Freeman Clarke in the article on "Unitarianism," in the *New International Encyclopedia* (2nd ed.), XXII, 259.

[11] Readers of Professor Perry Miller's *The New England Mind: The Seventeenth Century* (New York: The Macmillan Co., 1939) will note in this phrase a similarity to a doctrine of the Puritans. I have not developed this parallel because it seemed more pertinent to consider those phases of the broad and ancient tradition in question that were more directly related to the development of the evolutionary conception. The Puritan version of the tradition has importance here, however, not merely as an interesting native analogue but because the Puritans, in contrast to the general drift of eighteenth-century deism, deduced the goodness of the creation from the goodness of God rather than the reverse. Many of the nineteenth-century writers to be examined below will be found to be in either explicit or implicit agreement with this position. Compare Professor Miller's analysis in this respect with the view of such a later figure as Theodore Parker. Professor Miller writes: "Also in the interests of consistency, the Puritans were led to a further deduction: if the creation is ruled by God's will, and His will is itself the norm of justice and equity, the universe must be essentially good. They may be described as cosmic optimists." (*Op.*

cit., p. 18; see also pp. 34, 168, and 208). Parker wrote: "This conclusion of the perfection of the universe is a transcendent truth, not dependent on your observation or mine, not to be disturbed by any facts which seem to contradict it; but it is deduced straightway from the idea of the infinite perfection of God which is given in our consciousness." (*The World of Matter and the Spirit of Man* [Boston: American Unitarian Association, 1907], p. 288). Parker then goes on (pp. 330-40) to show that the evolving universe does in fact manifest such perfection.

[12] Here is the standing paradox of transcendentalism in its evolutionary form: that the world is perfect but is getting better. See below, pp. 125-26.

[13] *The Great Chain of Being* (Cambridge: Harvard University Press, 1936), p. 58.

[14] *Ibid.,* p. 59.

[15] *Ibid.* Inner quotation from W. D. Ross, *Aristotle* (2nd ed.; London: Methuen & Co., 1930), p. 178.

[16] *Ibid.*

[17] *Dialogues of Plato,* trans. Jowett (3rd ed.; New York: Charles Scribner's Sons, 1924), III, 450.

[18] *Primitivism and the Idea of Progress* (Baltimore: The Johns Hopkins University Press, 1934), p. 144.

[19] Lovejoy, *op. cit.,* p. 251.

[20] *Ibid.,* p. 252.

[21] *Ibid.,* p. 244.

[22] Whitney, *op. cit.,* p. 145.

[23] *Liberty,* III, ll. 63-70. See Potter, "James Thomson and the Evolution of Spirits," *Englische Studien,* LXI, No. 1 (1926), 57-65.

[24] *Pleasures of the Imagination,* II, ll. 337-50. See Potter, "Mark Akenside, Prophet of Evolution," *Modern Philology,* XXIV (August, 1926), 55-64.

[25] See below, pp. 49, 111 ff.

[26] See J. B. Bury, *The Idea of Progress* (New York: The Macmillan Co., 1932), chap. v and *passim.*

[27] See J. D. Haney, *Lessing's Education of the Human Race,* Columbia University Contributions to Education, Teachers College Series, No. 20, New York: Teachers College, 1908.

[28] See H. E. Barnes, *A History of Historical Writing* (Norman: University of Oklahoma Press, 1938), p. 193.

[29] *The Spirit of Modern Philosophy* (5th ed.; Boston: Houghton, Mifflin & Co., 1892), p. 273.

[30] *Ibid.,* p. 282.

[31] *Ibid.,* p. 291.

[32] "Relations between Philosophy and Science in the First Half of the Nineteenth Century in Germany," *Science,* n. s., XXXVIII (October 24, 1913), 567-84.

[33] R. B. Perry, *Present Philosophical Tendencies* (New York: Longmans, Green & Co., 1912), p. 135. For my exposition of Fichte and Schelling I am indebted to many sources, but especially to John Watson, *Schelling's Transcendental Idealism* (2nd ed.; Chicago: S. C. Griggs & Co., 1892), Albert Schwegler, *A History of Philosophy,* trans. Seelye (New York: D. Appleton & Co., 1903), and J. B. Stallo, mentioned below, pp. 14 ff.

[34] *Movements of Thought in the Nineteenth Century* (Chicago: University of Chicago Press, 1936), pp. 125, 154.

³⁵ J. B. Stallo, *General Principles of the Philosophy of Nature* (Boston: Crosby & Nichols, 1848), pp. 223-24.
³⁶ *Ibid.*, p. x.
³⁷ *Ibid.*, p. 222.
³⁸ *Ibid.*
³⁹ *Ibid.*, p. 224.
⁴⁰ *Ibid.*
⁴¹ *Ibid.*, pp. 107-8.
⁴² "The Genteel Tradition in American Philosophy," *Winds of Doctrine* (New York: Charles Scribner's Sons, 1940), p. 195.
⁴³ See the account of Agassiz, who studied under Schelling and Oken and was himself an idealist in science, in *Louis Agassiz: His Life and Correspondence*, ed. Elizabeth Cary Agassiz (7th ed.; Boston: Houghton, Mifflin & Co., 1887), I, 151-54.
⁴⁴ "Bergson and Romantic Evolutionism," *University of California Chronicle*, XV (October, 1913), 429-87. Compare, however, the criticism of Lovejoy's interpretation by Woodbridge Riley in *American Thought* (New York: Peter Smith, 1941), pp. 413 ff.
⁴⁵ Stallo, *General Principles of the Philosophy of Nature*, p. 54.
⁴⁶ *Ibid.*, p. 29.
⁴⁷ *Ibid.*, p. 15. Cf. Emerson, below, p. 49.
⁴⁸ *Ibid.*, p. 47. I have supplied the italics in the last sentence.
⁴⁹ *Complete Works of Ralph Waldo Emerson* (Centenary Edition; Boston: Houghton Mifflin Co., 1903-4), V, 242.
⁵⁰ *Journals of Ralph Waldo Emerson* (Boston: Houghton Mifflin Co., 1909-14), VIII, 76-77.
⁵¹ Comparison can be made easily without recourse to the German since the parts of Schelling's book on which Coleridge levied most heavily have been translated by Benjamin Rand and included in his anthology *Modern Classical Philosophers* (2nd ed.; Boston: Houghton Mifflin Co., 1936), pp. 535-68. See also the notes in Shedd's edition of Coleridge (New York: Harper & Bros., 1884), Vol. III.
⁵² *Complete Works*, ed. Shedd, III, 341-42.
⁵³ *Ibid.*, p. 349.
⁵⁴ *Ibid.*, p. 350.
⁵⁵ *Ibid.*, p. 357. The other passage will be found on pp. 359-60.
⁵⁶ *Ibid.*, I, 373-416.
⁵⁷ *Ibid.*, pp. 180-81. See also J. W. Beach, *The Concept of Nature in Nineteenth-Century English Poetry* (New York: The Macmillan Co., 1936), pp. 330-36.
⁵⁸ *Works*, ed. Shedd, VI, 463.
⁵⁹ Anticipated by Descartes and Leibnitz in the seventeenth century, advanced seriously and in detail by Kant in 1755, and rigorously worked out by Laplace in the last decade of the eighteenth century.
⁶⁰ See Ueberweg, *History of Philosophy* (New York: Charles Scribner's Sons, 1884), II, 143, and Höffding, *History of Modern Philosophy* (London: Macmillan & Co., 1936), II, 34-35, 42-43.
⁶¹ Sir William Dampier, *A History of Science* (New York: The Macmillan Co., 1932), p. 193.
⁶² *First Principles* (New York: D. Appleton & Co., 1875), p. 396.
⁶³ "The Scope and Purport of Evolution," *A Century of Science and Other Essays* (Boston: Houghton, Mifflin & Co., 1899), p. 43.
⁶⁴ The subtitle of the third edition: *Principles of Geology: Being an In-*

quiry How Far the Former Changes of the Earth's Surface are Referable to Causes Now in Operation (London: John Murray, 1834). The subtitle of the first edition is slightly different in wording.

[65] *More Letters of Charles Darwin,* ed. Francis Darwin and A. C. Seward (New York: D. Appleton & Co., 1903), II, 117.

[66] *Complete Works,* X, 336.

[67] Riley, *American Thought,* p. 177.

[68] Quoted by R. T. Young in *Biology in America* (Boston: Richard G. Badger, The Gorham Press, 1922), p. 45. The table is reprinted by G. P. Merrill in *The First Hundred Years of American Geology* (New Haven: Yale University Press, 1924), pp. 155-56.

[69] "Silliman, Benjamin," *Dictionary of American Biography,* XVII, 161.

[70] Quoted by Alice L. Cook in "Whitman's Indebtedness to the Scientific Thought of His Day," *University of Texas Studies in English,* XIV (July, 1934), 101.

[71] See A. O. Lovejoy, "Buffon and the Problem of Species," *Popular Science Monthly,* LXXXIX (November, December, 1911), 464-73, 554-67.

[72] See A. O. Lovejoy, "Eighteenth Century Evolutionists," *Popular Science Monthly,* LXV (July, August, 1904), 238-51, 323-40.

[73] Quoted by H. F. Osborn in *From the Greeks to Darwin* (2nd ed.; New York: Charles Scribner's Sons, 1929), p. 210.

[74] *Diedrich Knickerbocker's History of New York,* edited from the 1st ed. by S. T. Williams and T. McDowell (New York: Harcourt, Brace & Co., 1927), p. 46.

[75] In the 3rd ed., see Book I, chap. ix, and Book III, chaps. i-iii.

[76] *Conversations with Eckermann and Soret,* trans. J. Oxenford (London: G. Bell & Sons, 1883), pp. 477-78.

[77] In the Preface to the 10th ed. Cited by Julius Drachman, *Studies in the Literature of Natural Science* (New York: The Macmillan Co., 1930), p. 126.

[78] *Life and Letters of Charles Darwin,* ed. Francis Darwin (New York: D. Appleton & Co., 1896), I, 384.

[79] "The Argument for Evolution before 'The Origin of Species,'" *Popular Science Monthly,* LXXV (November, December, 1909), p. 502.

[80] *Ibid.,* p. 499.

[81] According to a check of the Union Catalog of the Library of Congress.

[82] Cf. T. H. Morgan: "The causes of the mutations that give rise to new characters we do not know, although we have no reason for supposing that they are due to other than natural processes." (Quoted by J. H. Randall in *The Making of the Modern Mind* [rev. ed.; Boston: Houghton Mifflin Co., 1940], p. 489.)

[83] *Life and Works* (Patriots' Edition; New Rochelle, N. Y.: Thomas Paine Historical Association, 1925), VIII, 73.

[84] See below, p. 220. Cf. Parker: "Science wants a God that is a constant force and a constant intelligence, immanent in every particle of matter. The old theological idea of God is as worthless for science as it is for religion." (Letter to Edward Desor, dated Rome, February 24, 1860; *The World of Matter and the Spirit of Man,* p. 420.)

[85] *The World and the Individual* (New York: The Macmillan Co., 1923), II, 210-11.

[86] A good brief statement of the point, with adverse criticism, will be found in Randall and Buchler's *Philosophy: An Introduction* (New York: Barnes & Noble, Inc., 1942), pp. 231-34. More detailed and inclusive is the

article, "Cause, Causality," by F. R. Tennant, in *Hastings' Encyclopedia of Religion and Ethics,* III, 261-66.

[87] *The Great Chain of Being,* pp. 321-22.

[88] See *Metaphysics,* 1049b, 1050a, and 1050b, and *De Partibus Animalium,* 639b.

[89] A good example, with pertinent comment, is given by William James (*Principles of Psychology* [New York: Henry Holt & Co., 1918], II, 670n): "Consider, e. g., the use of the axioms *'nemo potest supra seipsum,'* and *'nemo dat quod non habet,'* in this refutation of 'Darwinism,' which I take from the much-used scholastic compendium of Logic and Metaphysics of Liberatore, 3d ed. (Rome, 1880): 'Haec hypothesis . . . aperte contradicit principiis Metaphysicae, quae docent essentias rerum esse immutabiles, et effectum non posse superare causam. Et sane, quando, juxta Darwin, species inferior se evolvit in superiorem, unde trahit maiorem illam nobilitatem? Ex ejus carentia. At nihil dat quod non habet; et minus gignere nequit plus, aut negatio positionem. . . .' It is merely a question of fact whether these ideally proper relations do or do not obtain between animal and vegetable ancestors and descendants. If they do not, what happens? Simply this, that we cannot continue to class animal and vegetal facts under the *kinds* between which those ideal relations obtain. Thus, we can no longer call animal breeds by the name of 'species'; cannot call generating a kind of 'giving,' or treat a descendant as an 'effect' of his ancestor. . . ." Cf. Aquinas, *Summa Theologica,* I, Q.4, a.2.

[90] *Meditations on First Philosophy,* Meditation III. *Descartes: Selections,* ed. Eaton (New York: Charles Scribner's Sons, 1927), pp. 113-14.

[91] *Essay Concerning Human Understanding* (London: Routledge, n. d.), Book IV, chap. x, p. 532. The American Samuel Johnson, a student of Locke, writes: "It is moreover manifest, that no cause can give what it hath not, or, which is the same thing, produce an effect more noble, or of greater powers or perfections than itself; for then again, there would be an effect without a cause, or something produced by nothing, which is impossible." (*Ethics: Or Moral Philosophy,* Part I, chap. ii; in W. G. Muelder and L. Sears, eds., *The Development of American Philosophy* [Boston: Houghton Mifflin Co., 1940], p. 49). It is interesting to note that Thomas Cooper, a materialist, rejected this principle. See P. R. Anderson and M. H. Fisch, *Philosophy in America* (New York: D. Appleton-Century Co., 1939), pp. 253 ff.

[92] Horace Bushnell, *Nature and the Supernatural* (New York: Charles Scribner's Sons, 1870), p. 82.

[93] See below, p. 136.

[94] *Boston Monday Lectures: Biology* (Boston: James R. Osgood & Co., 1877), p. 99.

[95] *Ibid.,* pp. 309-10.

[96] Note, for example, Santayana's comment on Locke's version of the causal problem: "He seriously invoked the Scholastic maxim that nothing can produce that which it does not contain. For this reason the unconscious, after all, could never have given rise to consciousness. Observation and experiment could not be allowed to decide this point. . . ." (*Some Turns of Thought in Modern Philosophy* [New York: Charles Scribner's Sons, 1933], pp. 15-16.)

[97] C. Lloyd Morgan, *Emergent Evolution* (New York: Henry Holt & Co., 1923), p. 19 and *passim.* Just as the rejection of evolution on the ground that mind could not come from matter implied the old maxim, so the evolutionists' claim that mind had been so produced made inevitable an attack

upon it. This Santayana observed long before the word "emergence" began to make a stir in the world: "The point of evolution, as selection produces it, is that new species may arise. The very title of Darwin's book, 'The Origin of Species', is a denial of Aristotelianism and, in the pregnant [i. e., the etymological] sense, of evolution." (*Reason in Science* [New York: Charles Scribner's Sons, 1905], p. 106). The beginnings of the new interpretation can often be seen. Cf., for example, John Fiske, *Outlines of Cosmic Philosophy* (Boston: Houghton, Mifflin & Co., 1889), II, 368 ff. For a later interpretation by John Dewey, see below, chap. xiv, note 41.

[98] *Emergent Evolution*, p. 4. The phrase, however, is Alexander's.

[99] His references are to Lewes, *Problems of Life and Mind*, Vol. II, prob. v., chap. iii, p. 412; and to Mill, *Logic*, Book III, chap. vi, sect. 2.

[100] *Creative Evolution* (New York: Henry Holt & Co., 1911), p. 14.

[101] *True Humanism* (New York: Charles Scribner's Sons, 1938), pp. 20-21.

[102] See above, note 97.

[103] *The Realm of Matter*, in *Realms of Being* (New York: Charles Scribner's Sons, 1942), pp. 140-41. The last two passages have been reversed in order.

[104] Quoted by H. Höffding in "The Influence of the Conception of Evolution on Modern Philosophy," *Darwin and Modern Science*, ed. Seward (New York: G. P. Putman's Sons, 1909), p. 449.

[105] See below, Chapter II, note 131. This is Chambers' theory.

[106] *General Principles of the Philosophy of Nature*, p. 41.

[107] *Ibid.*, p. 43.

[108] *The World and the Individual*, II, Lectures III, IV, V, but especially pp. 227-33. See also *The Spirit of Modern Philosophy*, pp. 424 ff.

[109] Riley, *American Thought*, p. 189. See Gray's *Darwiniana* (New York: D. Appleton & Co., 1878), pp. 22, 156.

[110] Royce, *The Spirit of Modern Philosophy*, p. 423.

[111] See below, p. 219.

[112] *The Making of the Modern Mind*, p. 555.

CHAPTER II

EMERSON

[1] Chapters VI and VII. *The Complete Works of Ralph Waldo Emerson*, ed. E. W. Emerson (Centenary Edition; Boston: Houghton Mifflin Co., 1903-4), I, 47-65.

[2] *Ibid.*, pp. 63-64.

[3] Ralph Barton Perry, "Realism in Restrospect," in *Contemporary American Philosophy*, ed. G. P. Adams and W. P. Montague (New York: The Macmillan Co., 1930), II, 190. Professor Perry was, of course, speaking of a later idealism than Emerson's, but his remark is equally applicable here.

[4] The fullest, best documented study of Emerson's interest in science is H. H. Clark's "Emerson and Science," *Philological Quarterly*, X (July, 1931), 225-60.

[5] *Complete Works*, I, 25.

[6] "The Method of Nature" (1841), *ibid.*, p. 197.

[7] "Circles," *ibid.*, II, 306.

[8] *Ibid.*, XII, 5. The same statement will be found in "Perpetual Forces," *ibid.*, X, 72.

⁹ "Nature" (1836), *ibid.*, I, 43.
¹⁰ *Ibid.*, II, 70.
¹¹ *Ibid.*, p. 101.
¹² *Ibid.*, XII, 21-22.
¹³ See above, pp. 8-10.
¹⁴ *Emerson's Journals*, ed. E. W. Emerson and W. E. Forbes (Boston: Houghton Mifflin Co., 1909-14), III, 299-300.
¹⁵ Lecture, "On the Relation of Man to the Globe," quoted by J. E. Cabot in *A Memoir of Ralph Waldo Emerson* (Boston: Houghton, Mifflin & Co., 1888), I, 223-24.
¹⁶ See above, p. 20.
¹⁷ J. W. Beach, *The Concept of Nature in Nineteenth-Century English Poetry* (New York: The Macmillan Co., 1936), p. 337. On Emerson's reading of Bell, see *Journals*, II, 330.
¹⁸ In the first of twelve lectures on "The Philosophy of History," December 8, 1836; Cabot, *op. cit.*, II, 724-25.
¹⁹ *Journals*, IV, 116-17.
²⁰ *Complete Works*, I, 60.
²¹ See above, p. 37.
²² *Complete Works*, I, 70.
²³ *Journals of Bronson Alcott*, ed. Odell Shepard (Boston: Little, Brown & Co., 1938), p. 78. See also Shepard, *Pedlar's Progress: The Life of Bronson Alcott* (Boston: Little, Brown & Co., 1937), p. 200.
²⁴ *Pedlar's Progress*, p. 454.
²⁵ *Journals*, III, 163.
²⁶ See Cabot, *op. cit.*, II, 710 and *Complete Works*, I, 10, 67 and XII, 23.
²⁷ See above, p. 39.
²⁸ See above, p. 40.
²⁹ *Journals*, VI, 435.
³⁰ Beach, *op. cit.*, p. 339. For Emerson's declaration see below, p. 48.
³¹ *Journals*, VII, 80-81.
³² See above, p. 42.
³³ In February, 1832, he was awaiting with interest the appearance of the younger Herschel's *Discourse on the Heavens* (*Journals*, II, 461); and Mary Somerville's *Mechanism of the Heavens*, a digest of Laplace's *Mécanique Céleste*, appears in the reading list for this year (*ibid.*, p. 542).
³⁴ A subject of the Pythologian Club during his undergraduate membership was the existence of fossils on mountains (Cabot, *op. cit.*, I, 66).
³⁵ *Correspondence of Thomas Carlyle and Ralph Waldo Emerson*, ed. C. E. Norton (Boston: Houghton, Mifflin & Co., 1888), I, 54.
³⁶ Letter to Margaret Fuller, October 20, 1836; *Letters of Ralph Waldo Emerson*, ed. R. L. Rusk (New York: Columbia University Press, 1939), II, 41.
³⁷ "Nature" (1844), *Complete Works*, III, 179-80. See also above, p. 24.
³⁸ *Journals*, V, 59.
³⁹ *Letters*, ed. Rusk, II, 37.
⁴⁰ *Journals*, V, 464.
⁴¹ *Complete Works*, I, 197.
⁴² *Ibid.*
⁴³ *Ibid.*, p. 206.
⁴⁴ *Ibid.*, p. 199.

⁴⁵ *Ibid.*
⁴⁶ *Ibid.*, p. 204.
⁴⁷ *Ibid.*, pp. 202-3.
⁴⁸ See *Letters*, ed. Rusk, II, 407, 413.
⁴⁹ *Complete Works*, IX, 58.
⁵⁰ *Ibid.*, p. 52.
⁵¹ He was not the first simply to put the theme in verse, however. Constantine Rafinesque, a Franco-American naturalist to whom Darwin gave credit in the historical introduction of *The Origin of Species*, devoted a portion of his didactic poem *The World; or Instability* (Philadelphia: J. Dobson, 1836) to theories of evolution.
⁵² See above, p. 43.
⁵³ *Complete Works*, III, 184. As far as Emerson is concerned, this is of course metaphorical, emblematic of a deeper motive of an ideal nature. See below, p. 90.
⁵⁴ *Ibid.*, p. 179.
⁵⁵ *Ibid.*, p. 180.
⁵⁶ Along with another of evolutionary import that later became a part of the address "Emancipation in the British West Indies," delivered in August, 1844. See *Journals*, VI, 532.
⁵⁷ "The book was published in October, 1844," said Alexander Ireland, who was Chambers' go-between in the original anonymous publication of the work. See Introduction to 12th edition, Edinburgh, 1884.
⁵⁸ *Journals*, VII, 52.
⁵⁹ April 30, 1845; *Letters*, ed. Rusk, III, 283.
⁶⁰ *Complete Works*, I, 68-69.
⁶¹ *Journals*, VII, 104.
⁶² See above, p. 41.
⁶³ *Journals*, IV, 116-17. See also summary of the lecture "The Humanity of Science" in Cabot, *op. cit.*, II, 725.
⁶⁴ *Journals*, March, 1845, VII, 17. For an intermediate version, see *ibid.*, p. 58. Since Stallo's book was not printed until 1848, this proves conclusively that these lines owe nothing to his similar words (quoted above, p. 17), with which they are often associated—by Professor Beach, for example (*op. cit.*, p. 340).
⁶⁵ *Journals*, summer, 1851, VIII, 248.
⁶⁶ The following appears to be Emerson's source in Lyell (*Principles of Geology* [3rd ed.; London: John Murray, 1834], II, 338-40): "Nature . . . is always beginning anew, day by day, the work of creation, by forming monads, or 'rough drafts' (ébauches), which are the only living things she gives birth to *directly*.

". . . These are gradually developed into the higher and more perfect classes by the slow but unceasing agency of two influential principles: first, the *tendency to progressive advancement* in organization, accompanied by greater dignity in instinct, intelligence, &c.; secondly, *the force of external circumstances*. . . .

"Now, if the first of these principles, *the tendency to progressive development*, were left to exert itself with perfect freedom, it would give rise, says Lamarck, in the course of ages, to a graduated scale of being, where the most insensible transition might be traced from the simplest to the most compound structure, from the humblest to the most exalted degree of intelligence. But in consequence of the perpetual interference of the *external causes* before mentioned, this regular order is greatly interfered with, and an approximation only to such a state of things is exhibited by the animate creation, the progress of some races being retarded by unfavourable, and that of others accelerated by favourable, combinations of circumstances. . . .

"I have only space for exhibiting a small part of the entire process by which a complete metamorphosis is achieved, and shall, therefore, omit the mode whereby, after a countless succession of generations, a small gelatinous body is transformed into an oak or an ape; passing on at once to the last grand step in the progressive scheme, by which the orang-outang, having been already evolved out of a monad, is made slowly to attain the attributes and dignity of man."

[67] *Complete Works*, I, 1.
[68] *Journals*, VII, 67. See also *Complete Works*, IV, 290.
[69] *Complete Works*, IX, 126. A passage in the *Letters*, ed. Rusk, III, 341, indicates that this was written as early as July, 1846.
[70] *Journals*, VII, 53.
[71] Besides the references already cited, see *Journals*, VII, 436 and VIII, 66, 76-77, and the comments on Owen's rejection of the hypothesis of transmutation of species, *ibid.*, VII, 421, 480-81.
[72] See note in *Complete Works*, VI, 337, and letter to C. S. Tappan in *Letters*, ed. Rusk, IV, 376-77.
[73] *Letters*, ed. Rusk, V, 178.
[74] *Journals*, 1873, X, 423. The only other references to Darwin are in the reading lists, *ibid.*, IX, 581; X, 344, 425.
[75] Lafayette, Indiana, February 5, 1860; *Letters*, ed. Rusk, V, 195.
[76] *Ibid.*, VI, 63.
[77] On this transfer of the epistemological dualism to the world of nature, see above, pp. 12 ff., and below, Chapter III, notes 67 and 90.
[78] *Complete Works*, III, 169-79, 330-31.
[79] See above, p. 47.
[80] See above, p. 50.
[81] *Complete Works*, VI, 15.
[82] *Ibid.*, pp. 14-15.
[83] See below, p. 60.
[84] *Complete Works*, VI, 35.
[85] "The argument may be stated in modern terms as follows: I have an idea of perfection. If I had not, I should not know, as I certainly do know in regard to various imperfect things that they are in fact imperfect, since I should not have any standard by reference to which to convict them of imperfection. But perfection which does not exist is not really perfect, since, lacking existence, it would lack an element whose presence would, it is obvious, enhance and improve it. Therefore the idea of perfection implies the existence of the perfect thing or being which the idea postulates. Therefore perfection exists. Therefore God exists." (C. E. M. Joad, *Guide to Philosophy* [New York: Random House, n. d.], p. 117.)
[86] *Complete Works*, II, 267-68.
[87] *Ibid.*, VI, 350.
[88] *Ibid.*, p. 40.
[89] "The Poet," *ibid.*, III, 14.
[90] *Ibid.*, VI, 14, 37.
[91] *Ibid.*, pp. 38-39. Compare with these two passages the following statement by G. H. Mead (*Movements of Thought in the Nineteenth Century* [Chicago: University of Chicago Press, 1936], pp. 139-40) of a biolog-

ical analogy of the Hegelian dialectic: "The world, then, is a creation of thought; it arises out of the process of thinking. . . . It is a relationship in which the self finds conflicts in its world and then reconstructs this world through a synthesis, through a hypothesis, and finally advances to a new conflict. This is a statement of what goes on in science, in the process of the evolution of thought. It parallels the process of organic evolution. In the latter we have forms, animals, and plants that have certain habits, certain ways of living in the world. And then something happens, some geologic change occurs so that the animal can no longer get hold of the object that it eats as food. It meets a problem in obtaining nourishment; it meets a new enemy, a parasite, a microörganism. Something happens in its world which makes it run counter to the world in which it has been living. If we can conceive of a sufficiently successful mutation, we can perhaps find the solution of this problem within a single generation. What seems most often actually to take place are gradual changes, but the result of these changes is that there arises a new type of animal or plant which is adjusted to these changed surroundings. But with this arises a new world, for the animal or plant determines its world, its environment, in terms of its life-process. If an animal has eyes, it has an environment that has color; if it has ears, it lives in a world of sounds; if it has taste, its environment is sapid; if nostrils, its world is odorous."

[92] *Op. cit.*, II, 334. For Lamarck's use of the factors of Power and Circumstance, see above, note 66.

[93] *Complete Works*, VI, 15.

[94] *Ibid.*, X, 186-87.

[95] *Ibid.*, IX, 366-67. Published posthumously, the verses are described by the editor as "trials for a 'Song of Nature' " (*ibid.*, p. 513).

[96] *Ibid.*, pp. 285-86.

[97] *Ibid.*, pp. 220-23. "The Test," to which this poem supplied the answer, was published in the *Atlantic Monthly*, June, 1861.

[98] *Ibid.*, pp. 244-47.

[99] See above, p. 50.

[100] G. R. Potter, "Coleridge and Evolution," *Publications of the Modern Language Association*, XL (June, 1928), 394.

[101] *Complete Works*, VI, 38.

[102] "The Evolution of Evolution," *Open Court*, XI (August, 1897), 501-2.

[103] See above, p. 50.

[104] *Complete Works*, VIII, 10.

[105] *Ibid.*

[106] *Ibid.*, IX, 355.

[107] *The Varieties of Religious Experience* (New York: Longmans, Green & Co., 1929), p. 79.

[108] *Correspondence of Thomas Carlyle and Ralph Waldo Emerson*, I, 367.

[109] Henry James, *Partial Portraits*, 1905, p. 31. Quoted by C. E. Jorgensen in "Emerson's Paradise under the Shadow of Swords," *Philological Quarterly*, XI (July 1932), 274.

[110] *Complete Works*, VI, 6-8.

[111] *Ibid.*, p. 19.

[112] Jorgensen, *loc. cit.* Since the error has persisted, however, Professor Jorgensen must be said to have done a service to the cause of understand-

ing Emerson. Also his comparison of Emerson's views with Milton's is highly suggestive and not inconsistent with what follows here.

[113] "Emerson," *Cambridge History of American Literature* (New York: The Macmillan Co., 1933), I, 361.

[114] *Ibid.*, I, 123-24.

[115] *Ibid.*, XI, 486.

[116] *Ibid.*, XI, 104-5.

[117] *Ibid.*, XI, 103.

[118] "Success," *ibid.*, VII, 289-90.

[119] "Swedenborg," *ibid.*, IV, 138

[120] "Considerations by the Way," *ibid.*, VI, 253.

[121] "The Sovereignty of Ethics," *ibid.*, X, 188.

[122] Quoted by H. D. Gray in *Emerson: A Statement of New England Transcendentalism as Expressed in the Philosophy of Its Chief Exponent*, Leland Stanford Junior University Publications, University Series (Stanford: Stanford University Press, 1917), p. 77.

[123] Quoted by J. H. Randall and J. Buchler in *Philosophy: An Introduction* (New York: Barnes & Noble, Inc., 1942) p. 244.

[124] See below, pp. 241, 319.

[125] *The Making of the Modern Mind* (Boston: Houghton Mifflin Co., 1940), p. 600.

[126] "Emerson and the Idea of Progress," *American Literature*, XII (March, 1940), 1-19.

[127] *Complete Works*, II, 84-86.

[128] *Op. cit.*, p. 4.

[129] *Complete Works*, ed. G. F. Hoar (Boston: Lee and Shepard, 1900), II, 243-90.

[130] The other difficulty, contained in Emerson's statement that society "recedes as fast on one side as it gains on the other," is I believe, a rather literal instance of a paradox common in nineteenth-century idealism—that the world is at once perfect and getting better. See below, pp. 125-26.

[131] In his published statements Emerson assigned the phrase to John Hunter (see below, p. 65, and *Complete Works*, VIII, 7), and, since a careful search of Hunter's works did not turn it up, Emerson's editors believed that it had been mentioned to him by Owen as having appeared in Hunter's manuscripts (see *Journals*, VII, 69, and *Complete Works*, I, xxix). In the *Journals*, however, Emerson assigned it to Chambers: "We owe to every book that interests us one or two words. Thus to *Vestiges of Creation* we owe 'arrested development.'" (VII, 69). As a matter of fact, Chambers does not use this precise phrase, at least in the edition I have examined, but he comes close enough to it to justify the avowal of indebtedness, and in any case it is an excellent statement of his general thesis. Like later evolutionists, he was struck by the parallel between the embryological and evolutionary series, but, unlike them, he went on to the conclusion that the latter is the result of the former (*op. cit.*, p. 170): "Thus, the production of new forms, as shown in the pages of the geological record, has never been anything more than a new stage in the process of gestation." Hence any species may be said to be in a state of arrested development, which it will one day transcend by prolonging its period of gestation. Thus, after pointing out that the gestatory period of the queen bee is sixteen days, that of the neuter twenty, and that of the male twenty-four, he went on to comment, using the words apparently seized upon by Emerson: "Development may be said to be thus arrested at a particular stage—that early one at

which the female sex is complete. In the other circumstances, it is allowed to go on four days longer, and a stage is then reached between the two sexes. . . . Four days more make it a perfect male." (P. 163). For a dualism of power and circumstance similar to Emerson's see Lyell's account of Lamarck, above, note 66; note also in that place Lyell's use of the term "progressive development."

[132] *Complete Works,* VIII, 270-71.
[133] *Ibid.,* XII, 59-60.
[134] *Cosmic Consciousness* (New York: E. P. Dutton & Co., 1923), p. 17.
[135] *Ibid.,* p. 67.

CHAPTER III

POE'S EUREKA

[1] *Eureka: A Prose Poem* (New York: G. P. Putnam, 1848). Elaborated from a lecture, "The Cosmogony of the Universe" delivered at the Society Library, New York on February 3, 1848. *The Complete Works of Edgar Allan Poe,* ed. J. A. Harrison (New York: The University Society, 1902), XVI, 179-354. Unless otherwise noted, all references will be to this edition.
[2] *Columbian Magazine,* August, 1844; *Complete Works,* IV, 247.
[3] In a letter dated July 10, 1844, now in the Huntington Library. See Arthur Hobson Quinn, *Edgar Allan Poe: A Critical Biography* (New York: D. Appleton-Century Co., 1941), p. 430. See also Chivers' reply, dated August 6, 1844, in *Complete Works,* XVII, 184-86.
[4] July 2, 1844. George Edward Woodberry, *The Life of Edgar Allan Poe* (Boston: Houghton Mifflin Co., 1909), II, 92.
[5] The sources of Poe's scientific knowledge are voluminously, if indiscriminately, studied by Margaret Alterton in "The Origins of Poe's Critical Theory," *University of Iowa Humanistic Studies,* Vol. II, No. 3, 1925. See also F. D. Bond, "Poe as an Evolutionist," *Popular Science Monthly,* LXXI (September, 1907), 267-74. Since I am not concerned with Poe's entire relation to the sciences, I have not entered into the question of his anticipation of recent physical theory. On this question see G. Nordstedt, "Poe and Einstein," *Open Court,* XLIV (March, 1930), 173-80; Clayton Hoagland, "The University of Eureka," *Southern Literary Messenger,* I (May, 1939), 307-13; and especially Quinn, *op. cit.,* chap. xvii.
[6] Edition used here: *Treatise on Astronomy* (London: Longman *et al.,* 1833).
[7] The author of the following works that appeared before *Eureka: The Christian Philosopher* (1823 *et seq.*); *Celestial Scenery* (London, 1837; New York, 1845); *The Sidereal Heavens* (London, 1840; New York, 1844). On the evidences of Poe's indebtedness to Dick see Alterton, *op. cit.,* chaps. iv and v *passim.* Edition used here: *The Complete Works of Thomas Dick* (Cincinnati: Applegate, 1853), 2 Vols.
[8] First published in 1838, this work went through seven editions in seven years and several more later. Since it seems to have been of the utmost importance in the development of *Eureka,* I have indicated some of the more important parallels in the notes that follow, using the edition issued in New York in 1840 by Chapin, though I do not know that that is the edition Poe used. Nichol was also the author of these other astronomical works before 1848: *Phenomena of the Solar System,* 1838, 1844, 1847; *The System of the World,* 1846.

⁹ *Complete Works,* XVI, 222. This does not appear in the 1840 edition of *The Architecture of the Heavens.*
¹⁰ *Ibid.,* p. 219.
¹¹ See below, pp. 82-83.
¹² *Complete Works,* XVI, 207.
¹³ *Ibid.,* p. 228.
¹⁴ *Ibid.,* p. 227. It should be pointed out that in the marginal notes in his copy of *Eureka* Poe expressed the intention of revising his description of the process of irradiation so as to present it as "one continuous flash" (*ibid.,* p. 326). Since, however, this contradicts his whole exposition of irradiation and its relation to equability of diffusion, without further explanation it is simply puzzling. See especially p. 229 where he says explicitly of irradiation of the type of light: "But I have assumed *no* such irradiation *as this.* I assumed no *continuous* irradiation."

In the matter of equability of diffusion it is interesting to note that though Poe disagreed with Nichol he was in agreement with Nichol's account of the views of the elder (Sir William) Herschel. Nichol writes (*op. cit.,* p. 17): "There is obviously one source of error in Herschel's sketch, which we may be able to eliminate and thus approach still nearer the truth. Throughout the whole speculation you find the latent assumption, *that the stars are distributed equably . . . generally,* in all directions, on a principle approaching to indifference." It is perhaps significant, however, that Nichol does not raise this issue in his ninth edition (London: Bailliere, 1851).

¹⁵ *Complete Works,* XVI, 200-204. Cf. Nichol, p. 9: "The usual inference from the aspects of the sky is, I believe, that *our* skies are infinite, or that stars, as we see them, stretch through all space; which, critically examined, appears only a repetition of the old fallacy, that what is great to us, must be great absolutely. . . . The firmament, with its countless and glorious orbs, is doubtless vast,—perhaps inconceivably so; but calmly placing the utmost sphere within our possible sight, beside the idea of what is really infinite,—or comparing the vision of man with the reach of an Almighty eye—it flashes instantly upon us that we neither have nor can have positive ground for the assertion that our stars are diffused through all existence. Herschel proceeded to refute systematically this common delusion, and to unfold the true scheme of the universe."

¹⁶ *Complete Works,* XVI, 208. Cf. Nichol, p. 32: "Not improbably it is one aim of the stupendous System of Evolution, of which creation as it exists is only one phase, to develop all possible variety, to exhibit how, without infraction of steadfast law, Being may be infinitely diversified, and room found for unfolding the whole riches of the Almighty."

¹⁷ *Complete Works,* XVI, 225.
¹⁸ *Ibid.,* p. 227.
¹⁹ *Ibid.,* pp. 232-33.
²⁰ *Democratic Review,* June, 1845; *Complete Works,* VI, 139-44.
²¹ *Ibid.,* XVI, 218.
²² *Ibid.,* pp. 267-68.
²³ Cf. Nichol, p. 68: "Of the relations of these subordinate groups, or of the binding or compacting principle of our singular firmament—considering it as a *whole,*—I can inform you nothing. The more capricious class of external clusters equally mocks our imagining, although the application of the principle of probabilities fully assures us that these masses are not grouped together by chance or at random, but that through every such un-

ion of stars, law and system must prevail, as clearly as in binary or ternary aggregations. The only light we find among these spaces is a welcome gleam of evidence that Nature, there also, is uniform, since the simpler firmaments manifest by their shapes the prevalence of an *internal attractive power*—like that whose effective presence bestows a consistency on our subordinate clusters."

[24] *Complete Works,* XVI, 269. Cf. Nichol, p. 111: "How immense is the field of contemplation opened by these very simple considerations! Even the larger forms of the Heavens are not stable! Those globular masses at least, appear, in process of growth, of *ripening*—they are congregating towards that nucleus, around which the new order of things is slowly upgrowing, and where the mighty orb, foretold by their progressing aggregation, is preparing to be born. I cannot avoid reverting to the notion of Mr. Coleridge; what is this after all, save a prolongation of the condensation of a Nebula? Already some few of its particles have come together and formed its secondary stage; and now, that secondary stage, which we term a firmament, is passing into a third, where all the dispersed atoms will be gathered together, and lodged at the centre of the mass!

"We may venture even one step higher. If the suns of each firmament, which are but the congress of multitudes of atoms originally distinct, are related in this wise—may not some similar system and similar destiny characterize Systems of Firmaments?"

[25] *Complete Works,* XVI, 269.
[26] *Ibid.*
[27] *Ibid.,* p. 302.
[28] *Ibid.,* p. 308.
[29] Sir John Herschel, *Preliminary Discourse on the Study of Natural Philosophy* (London: Longman et al., 1830).
[30] *Ibid.,* p. 327.
[31] *Ibid.,* p. 337.
[32] *Ibid.,* pp. 342-43. It should be noted that W. H. Weekes' claims to have produced living organisms in inorganic solutions by means of charges of electricity were first published in 1842 and constituted one of the sensations of popular science in the ensuing decade. See below, pp. 220, 226.
[33] *Complete Works,* XVI, 212.
[34] *Ibid.,* p. 213.
[35] *Ibid.*
[36] On Boscovich see the remarks of Professor Irving Stringham in *The Works of Edgar Allan Poe,* ed. E. C. Stedman and G. E. Woodberry (New York: The Colonial Co., 1903), X, 309. On Kant see Ueberweg, *History of Philosophy* (New York: Charles Scribner's Sons, 1884), II, 179, and Höffding, *History of Modern Philosophy* (London: Macmillan & Co., 1935), II, 69-70. On the place of the principle in the transcendental cosmology, see above, pp. 13, 16, 51-52, and below, note 90; cf. also Holmes, below, Chapter IX, note 14.
[37] *Complete Works,* XVI, 214.
[38] The *Complete Works* contain only one perfunctory reference to Lyell (XVI, 3), and Poe was under the necessity of inquiring of a friend if *Eureka* resembled Chambers' *Vestiges* (*ibid.,* I, 277).
[39] *Complete Works,* XVI, 257-58.
[40] *Ibid.,* p. 259.
[41] *Ibid.,* 259-60. Cf. Nichol, pp. 75-76: "What is the intention of such a

mass [that is, a nebula]? Is it to abide for ever in that chaotic condition—void, formless, and diffuse in the midst of order and organization,—or is it the germ of more exalted Being—the rudiments of something only yet being arranged? . . . nay, who can tell—who that has looked on those monuments of bygone worlds, the fossil relics which mark the early progress of our own planet—but, this amorphous substance may bear within it, laid up in its dark bosom the germs, the producing powers of that LIFE, which in coming ages will bud and blossom, and effloresce, into manifold and growing forms, until it becomes fit harborage and nourishment to every degree of intelligence, and every shade of moral sensibility and greatness?" See also Appendix E of Nichol's book.

[42] *Complete Works,* XVI, 291.
[43] *Ibid.,* p. 309.
[44] *Ibid.,* XVII, 300-303.
[45] *Ibid.,* XVI, 238. P. 63 in the first edition is almost exactly coextensive with p. 238 in *Complete Works,* XVI.
[46] *Ibid.,* p. 214.
[47] *Science and the Modern World* (New York: The Macmillan Co., 1925), pp. 73-74. For other definitions see below, pp. 88-89 and note 92. What Poe had done was to universalize the conceptions of mechanics. For a similar speculative experiment see the discussion of W. K. Clifford's essay "The First and Last Catastrophe" in Josiah Royce's *The Spirit of Modern Philosophy* (Boston: Houghton, Mifflin & Co., 1893), pp. 314-36.
[48] By Thomas Dick. Though both devoted their lives to science, Dick and Nichol were ordained clergymen. Nichol formally resigned from the ministry and later became Professor of Astronomy at the University of Glasgow. The clerical stamp remained indelibly upon him, however, as any who read his books will be aware.
[49] Roget's *Animal and Vegetable Physiology,* in *Southern Literary Messenger,* February, 1836; *Complete Works,* VIII, 206-11.
[50] Review of Drake's *Culprit Fay* and Halleck's *Alnwick Castle* in *Southern Literary Messenger,* April, 1836; *Complete Works,* VIII, 281.
[51] Since Poe seems to have gotten the idea for the catastrophe in "The Conversation of Eiros and Charmion" from *The Christian Philosopher* (*Complete Works of Thomas Dick,* II, 32, 135), he may be supposed to have read this work by 1839. See Alterton, *op. cit.,* p. 141.
[52] Since a "Dr. Nichols" is identified with the nebular cosmogony in "Murders in the Rue Morgue," there is some likelihood that Poe had read Nichol by 1841. This supposition receives some support from the interpretation of the nebular theory in the Macaulay review of the same year.
[53] *Critical and Historical Essays* (Everyman's Library edition; New York: E. P. Dutton & Co., 1909), II, 40 ff.
[54] *Graham's Magazine,* June, 1841; *Complete Works,* X, 159.
[55] "The Colloquy of Monos and Una," *Graham's Magazine,* August, 1841; *Complete Works,* IV, 202.
[56] I do not attempt to give a complete account of the meaning of "analogy" to Poe. Any such account would have to consider the place of the conception in the empirical tradition, particularly as modified by the Scottish philosophy, in which Poe took a great interest. Nichol, for example (*op. cit.,* pp. 8, 36), praises Sir William Herschel for his intelligent use of the analogical method, and Francis Wayland, the American philosopher and college president, had written on "The Philosophy of Analogy" as early as 1832 (see Joseph Blau, ed., *American Philosophic Addresses* [New York:

Columbia University Press, 1946], pp. 344-63). Wayland's point, which would not have been uncongenial to Poe, was that science does not advance merely by induction and deduction but by the ability of the individual scientist to guess, on the analogy of the known, what the unknown is probably like.

[57] See "An Interpretation of Poe's 'Al Aaraaf,' " *University of Texas Studies in English,* IX (1929), 106-33.

[58] *Graham's Magazine,* March, 1844; *Complete Works,* XI, 256.

[59] *Sartain's Union Magazine,* October, 1850; *Complete Works,* XIV, 290.

[60] See E. A. Burtt, *The Metaphysical Foundations of Modern Physical Science* (rev. ed.; New York: Harcourt, Brace & Co., 1932), chap. ii.

[61] In *Lives of Eminent Persons,* published by the Society for the Diffusion of Knowledge. Though the only copy I have seen lacks a title page, its owners (the University of North Carolina) date it c. 1837. The evidence that Poe read this book is inconclusive. On the ground of the brief quotation from Kepler in *Eureka* (*Complete Works,* XVI, 198) Miss Alterton ("The Origins of Poe's Critical Theory," pp. 142-43) believed that he did, but the quotation could easily have come from another source. An inspiration of Poe's admiration of Kepler could have been the following passage in Coleridge's *Table-Talk* (note the tell-tale word "guesses"): "Galileo was a great genius, and so was Newton; but it would take two or three Galileos and Newtons to make one Kepler. . . . There is not a more glorious achievement of scientific genius upon record, than Kepler's guesses, prophecies, and ultimate apprehension of the law of the mean distances of the planets as connected with the periods of their revolutions round the sun." (*Complete Works,* ed. Shedd [New York: Harper & Bros., 1884], VI, 350). If Poe read the Bethune book, he would have found two items of interest: (1) Kepler's comparison of the world to an enormous living animal (p. 40); (2) the author's introductory dispraise of his subject for just those characteristics that Poe chose to admire: "This extraordinary man pursued, almost invariably, the hypothetical method. His life was passed in speculating on the results of a few principles assumed by him, from very precarious analogies, as the causes of the phenomena actually observed in Nature. We nevertheless find that he did, in spite of this unphilosophical method, arrive at discoveries which have served as guides to some of the most valuable truths of modern sciences." (P. 1.)

[62] *Complete Works,* XVI, 252.

[63] *Ibid.,* p. 183.

[64] *Ibid.,* p. 302.

[65] *Ibid.,* pp. 206-7.

[66] Cf. Nichol, *op. cit.,* p. 105: "Still farther;—the system, though strong, is not framed to be EVERLASTING; and our Hypothesis also develops the mode of the certain decay and final dissolution of its arrangement. . . . And mark the nature of this decay. It comes, not as Newton thought, by accident, derangement or disease, but through the midst of harmony; it is an easy consequence of the venerable power which first evolved us, infused our scheme with the spirit of life, and gave it structure and strength. . . . So dies Nature's unblemished child—the simple flower! It bursts its seed, buds and blooms; and then, in unpained obedience, draws in its leaves and sinks into the lap of its Mother Earth."

[67] *Complete Works,* XVI, 310-11. An interesting parallel with the transcendental philosophy of nature may be noted here. W. T. Harris

quotes Hegel as follows: " 'Spirit,' says Hegel, 'is self-contained being. But matter, which is spirit outside of itself [turned inside out], continually manifests this, its inadequacy, through gravity—attraction to a central point beyond each particle. (If it could get at this central point, it would have no extension, and hence would be annihilated).'" (*Journal of Speculative Philosophy*, Vol. I, No. 1; quoted in W. G. Muelder and L. Sears, *The Development of American Philosophy* [Boston: Houghton Mifflin Co., 1940], p. 230). Cf. note 90, below.

[68] *Complete Works*, XVI, 311. Cf. Nichol, *op. cit.*, p. 106: "The idea of the ultimate dissolution of the solar system, has usually been felt as painful, and forcibly resisted by philosophers. . . . The phenomenon referred to would simply point to the close of one mighty cycle in the history of the solar orb; . . . Thus is the periodic death of a plant perhaps the essential to its prolonged life. . . . The broken bowl will yet be healed and beautified by the potter, and a Voice of joyful note will awaken, one day, even the silence of the Urn!"

Cf. also Herbert Spencer, *First Principles*, 2nd ed., Sect. 182, abridged as follows by F. Howard Collins in *An Epitome of the Synthetic Philosophy* (London: Williams & Norgate, 1889), p. 60: "If, pushing to its extreme the argument that Evolution must come to a close in complete equilibrium or rest, the reader suggests that for aught which appears to the contrary, the Universal Death thus implied will continue indefinitely, it is legitimate to point out how, on carrying the argument still further, we are led to infer a subsequent Universal Life. Motion as well as Matter being fixed in quantity, it would seem that the change in the distribution of Matter which Motion effects, coming to a limit in whichever direction it is carried, the indestructible Motion thereupon necessitates a reverse distribution. Apparently, the universally coexistent forces of attraction and repulsion, which, as we have seen, necessitate rhythm in all minor changes throughout the Universe, also necessitate in the totality of its changes—produce now an immeasurable period during which the attractive forces predominating, cause universal concentration, and then an immeasurable period during which the repulsive forces predominating, cause universal diffusion—alternate eras of Evolution and Dissolution. And thus there is suggested the conception of a past during which there have been successive Evolutions analogous to that which is now going on; and a future during which successive other such Evolutions may go on—ever the same in principle but never the same in concrete result."

[69] *Complete Works*, XVI, 311. For the Lanier references see below, p. 208.

[70] *Ibid.*

[71] *Ibid.*, p. 312.

[72] *Ibid.*

[73] *Ibid.*, p. 313.

[74] *Ibid.*, p. 314.

[75] *Ibid.*

[76] *Ibid.*

[77] Mary E. Phillips, *Edgar Allan Poe, the Man* (Chicago: The John C. Winston Co., 1926), p. 1265.

[78] *Complete Works*, XVI, 336.

[79] See below, note 87.

[80] In what is represented as a quotation from Joseph Glanvill. *The American Museum*, September, 1838; *Complete Works*, II, 248.

[81] *Burton's Gentleman's Magazine,* September, 1839; *Complete Works,* III, 286.

[82] Cf. *Complete Works,* XVI, 315. Italics supplied.

[83] *Graham's Magazine,* June, 1841; *Complete Works,* III, 194-95. For the parallel of the last italicized passage see above, p. 85. For an interesting parallel to the whole passage in the thought of Kepler, see above, note 61.

[84] *Complete Works,* XVI, 254.

[85] *Ibid.,* p. 255.

[86] *Ibid.,* pp. 312-13. See below, pp. 107-8.

[87] Poe is not altogether consistent in this matter. There is no doubt about his meaning in his final statement, but elsewhere he clearly assumed a dualistic relation between God and nature. Thus in the beginning he spoke of "that Matter which, by dint of his Volition, he [God] made from his Spirit, or from Nihility" (see above, p. 83), and later he said that God "intervened" to introduce the force of repulsion (see above, p. 74). Again, in one of his most extended considerations of the subject he began by stating that "Nature and the God of Nature are distinct" and yet ended by describing the creation as "that act by which a God, self-existing and alone existing, became all things at once, through dint of his volition, while all things were thus constituted a portion of God." (See above, p. 86). Poe seems to have reconciled the contradiction in his own mind by the reasoning that "by the former [nature] we imply merely the laws of the latter [the God of nature]." But this presupposes an idealism that he does not maintain.

[88] In addition, Poe found a justification of evil that parallels the optimism of the transcendentalists. The source of evil is the diffusion of God's existence in the universe of particles (*Complete Works,* XVI, 233), but "just as it is in your power to expand or to concentrate your pleasures (the absolute amount of happiness remaining always the same) so did and does a similar capability appertain to this Divine Being. . . . He now feels his life through an infinity of imperfect pleasures—the partial and pain-entangled pleasures of those inconceivably numerous things which you designate as his creatures, but which are really but infinite individualizations of Himself." (*Ibid.,* p. 313). "In this view, and in this view alone," he had said on the preceding page, "we comprehend the riddles of Divine Injustice—or Inexorable Fate. In this view alone the existence of Evil becomes intelligible; but in this view it becomes more—it becomes endurable. Our souls no longer rebel at a Sorrow which we ourselves have imposed upon ourselves, in furtherance of our own purposes—with a view—if even with a futile view—to the extension of our own *Joy.*"

[89] *Aids to Reflection. Complete Works,* ed. Shedd, I, 363.

[90] It has already been pointed out that this conception was paralleled in the transcendental nature-philosophy (see above, p. 16 and Chapter III, note 67). Another illustration would be Watson's statement concerning Schelling (*Schelling's Transcendental Idealism* [Chicago: S. C. Griggs & Co., 1892], p. 93): "Matter is therefore definable as the product of the two forces of attraction and repulsion, and as in space and time." This is as appropriate a place as any to point out the difference of the transcendental conception from Poe's. To Poe, attraction and repulsion were fundamental "principles" explaining all created things. To the transcendentalist, however, they were merely one among many manifestations of a more fundamental opposition, that of knowledge. Thus Watson, expounding Schelling's

Ideas for a Philosophy of Nature (1797), offers this explanation of the definition given above: "In a purely analytical way Kant had shown that matter implies the presence of two opposite forces. Schelling's aim is to derive those forces from the nature of perception, and to explain the various phenomena of nature by the same method. . . . All reality or objectivity implies the presence in consciousness of something, the primary origin of which must be sought in an unconscious or unreflective act of production. Intelligence, which in its own nature is infinite, limits its productivity and presents to itself that which has the appearance of an independent object. At first this object is simply the purely abstract 'something we-know-not-what,' and hence it calls for more definite characterization. This further definition of reality is the task of the philosophy of nature. . . . The first and fundamental determination of matter is given in the conception of force, as specifying itself in attraction and repulsion, which correspond respectively to the objective and subjective activities implied in perception." (*Ibid.,* pp. 92-93.)

⁹¹ *Complete Works,* XVI, 214.

⁹² *The Metaphysical Foundations of Modern Physical Science,* p. 306. Cf. Whitehead, above, p. 78, and the following definition from the pen of Professor Lovejoy: "The essence of mechanism . . . [consists] in the assertion that all physical processes, including those of organisms, consist in the redistribution of a fixed sum of matter and energy in accordance with fixed laws of relative motion." ("Bergson and Romantic Evolutionism," *University of California Chronicle,* XV [October, 1913], 449.)

⁹³ *Complete Works,* XVI, 314.

⁹⁴ *Complete Works of Ralph Waldo Emerson* (Centenary Edition; Boston: Houghton Mifflin Co., 1903-4), I, 64-65.

⁹⁵ *Ibid.,* III, 53.

⁹⁶ Whitehead, *Science and the Modern World,* p. 111.

⁹⁷ See above, p. 28.

CHAPTER IV

WHITMAN

¹ "Thou Mother with Thy Equal Brood," *Leaves of Grass,* ed. Emory Holloway (Inclusive Edition; Garden City: Doubleday, Doran & Co., 1931), p. 383. Further references to this edition will be to *"Leaves."*

² "L. of G.'s Purport," *ibid.,* p. 456.

³ Horace Traubel, *With Walt Whitman in Camden* (New York: M. Kennerley, 1905-12), I, 156-57. Further references to this work will be to "Traubel."

⁴ "With Antecedents," *Leaves,* p. 204.

⁵ See above, p. 84. There appears to have been even a verbal resemblance. Rufus Jones quotes from R. M. Bucke (*Cosmic Consciousness,* pp. 188-90) a reference by Whitman to "the eternal beats, eternal systole and diastole of life in things." (*Some Exponents of Mystical Religion* [New York: Abingdon Press, 1930], p. 188). In this form, of course, the metaphor was too well worn to indicate indebtedness.

⁶ "Starting from Paumonok," *Leaves,* p. 19.

⁷ "I Sing the Body Electric," *ibid.,* p. 86.

⁸ "Song of Myself," *ibid.,* p. 50.

⁹ *Ibid.,* p. 76.

¹⁰ "A Song for Occupations," *ibid.*, p. 183.
¹¹ See above, p. 37.
¹² *Walt Whitman's Workshop,* ed. Clifton J. Furness (Cambridge: Harvard University Press, 1928), p. 236.
¹³ *Ibid.*, p. 132.
¹⁴ *Prose Works* (Philadelphia: David McKay, n. d.), p. 250.
¹⁵ "Song of Myself," *Leaves,* p. 43.
¹⁶ *Uncollected Poetry and Prose of Walt Whitman,* ed. Emory Holloway (Garden City: Doubleday, Page & Co., 1921), II, 69-70. Further reference to this collection will be to *"Uncollected."*
¹⁷ See above, p. 67.
¹⁸ Traubel, II, 169.
¹⁹ "Song of Myself," *Leaves,* p. 43. Probably the best statement of Whitman's attitude toward science is in the Preface to the 1876 edition of *Leaves of Grass (Leaves,* p. 520). See also Alice L. Cook, "Whitman's Indebtedness to the Scientific Thought of His Day," *University of Texas Studies in English,* XVI (June, 1934), 89-115.
²⁰ Traubel, III, 97.
²¹ *Ibid.,* III, 94.
²² *Prose Works,* p. 177.
²³ *Ibid.,* p. 326.
²⁴ Traubel, III, 94. Italics mine. It should be noted that this was said almost in the same breath with the objection to evolution just quoted from the same source.
²⁵ "Darwinism," *Prose Works,* p. 326. Cf. Emerson, above, p. 43.
²⁶ "Song of the Universal," *Leaves,* p. 192. The italics in this and the two following quotations are supplied.
²⁷ "I Sing the Body Electric," *ibid.,* p. 84.
²⁸ "Song of Myself," *ibid.,* p. 69.
²⁹ *The Complete Writings of Walt Whitman,* ed. Bucke, Traubel, and Harned (New York: G. P. Putnam's Sons, 1902), IX, 183.
³⁰ *Leaves,* p. 534.
³¹ *Complete Writings,* IX, 5.
³² *Uncollected,* II, 66.
³³ See above, p. 28.
³⁴ F. O. Matthiessen, *American Renaissance* (New York: Oxford University Press, 1941), p. 521.
³⁵ "Starting from Paumonok," *Leaves,* p. 14.
³⁶ "When the Full Grown Poet Came," *ibid.,* pp. 451-52.
³⁷ Positivists, of course, sweep it aside as unanswerable or illegitimate.
³⁸ This is as good a point as any to meet the objection that since Whitman was not a metaphysician this whole discussion is irrelevant. Such a declaration as the following is sufficient reply: "The culmination and fruit of literary artistic expression, and its final fields of pleasure for the human soul, are in metaphysics, including the mysteries of the spiritual world, the soul itself, and the question of the immortal continuation of our identity." ("Democratic Vistas," *Prose Works,* p. 250n.)
³⁹ Traubel, I, 149. See also *Leaves,* p. 127, and *Complete Writings,* IX, 38, 142. This attitude was common in the Romantic movement and is well stated in the article "Romanticism" in D. D. Runes' *Dictionary of Philosophy* (New York: Philosophical Library, 1942):
"Hence, the epistemology of romanticism is exclusively emotional and intuitive, stressing the necessity for fullness of experience and depth of feel-

ing if reality is to be understood. Reason, being artificial and analytical, is inadequate to the task of comprehending the Absolute; knowing is living, and the philosopher must approach nature through inspiration, longing, and sympathy."

[40] Traubel, I, 156. Traubel said "plenty of" rather than "much."

[41] "Walt Whitman, Stranger," *The Private Reader* (New York: Henry Holt & Co., 1942), pp. 80-81.

[42] Boswell, *Life of Johnson* (London: Macmillan & Co., 1900), I, 347-48. Cf. the opening paragraphs of Jonathan Edwards' "Notes on the Mind," in which he finds it most necessary to demonstrate the ideality of things known through touch.

[43] "Song of Myself," *Leaves,* p. 48. Cf. 1847 Notebook: "A touch now reads me a library of knowledge in an instant." (*Uncollected,* II, 72.)

[44] See above, p. 41.

[45] "To Think of Time," 1872, *Leaves,* p. 368.

[46] The first expression, used by an admirer writing on the stationery of the *Dublin University Magazine,* pleased Whitman very much (Traubel, II, 219). The second appears in Newton Arvin's *Whitman* (New York: The Macmillan Co., 1938), p. 161.

[47] Furness, *op. cit.,* p. 49.

[48] Whitman, thus, did not so much ignore epistemology as give an intuitive answer to it. On his estimate of its importance note the following: "The most profound theme that can occupy the mind of man . . . is doubtless involved in the query: What is the fusing explanation and tie—what the relation between the (radical, democratic) Me, the human identity of understanding, emotions, spirit, &c., on the one side, of and with the (conservative) Not Me, the whole of the material objective universe and laws, with what is behind them in time and space, on the other side?" ("Carlyle from American Points of View," *Prose Works,* p. 175). See above, note 39.

[49] *Some Exponents of Mystical Religion,* p. 218.

[50] *Ibid.,* p. 14.

[51] *Prose Works,* p. 105. Italics supplied.

[52] See Höffding, *A History of Modern Philosophy* (London: Macmillan & Co., 1935), II, ix, 524-32.

[53] R. B. Perry, *The Present Conflict of Ideals* (New York: Longmans, Green & Co., 1918), p. 193.

[54] *Uncollected,* II, 65.

[55] Furness, *op. cit.,* p. 236.

[56] When Whitman began to acquire his knowledge of German Philosophy is unknown, but the earliest reasonable date is 1854, the publication date of his principal source (Joseph Gost[w]ick's *German Literature,* [Philadelphia: Lippincott, Grambo & Co.]), and the latest date is the late sixties or early seventies, the date assigned by his editors to the philosophical notes in which the use of Gostwick is evident (*Complete Writings,* IX, 166n). Professor Arvin's opinion, which has not been attacked, is that the acquisition probably took place "after two editions of *Leaves of Grass* had appeared and perhaps mainly during the sixties" (*op. cit.,* p. 191). A tenuous suggestion that it took place before the fourth edition (1866) is the following parallel. In his notes on Hegel, Whitman wrote, "Body and mind are one; an inexplicable paradox, yet no truth truer." (For the full quotation, see below, p. 105). In the fourth edition he inserted these lines in "A Song for Occupations" (*Leaves,* p. 183):

> Strange and hard that paradox true I give,
> Objects gross and the unseen soul are one.

Whitman's debt to Gostwick was first demonstrated by Mody C. Boatright in "Whitman and Hegel," *University of Texas Studies in English,* IX (July 8, 1929), 134-50, and it has been studied in greater detail by W. B. Fulghum, Jr., in "Whitman's Debt to Joseph Gostwick," *American Literature,* XII (January, 1941), 491-96. A more general study is Robert P. Falk's article, "Walt Whitman and German Thought," *Journal of English and Germanic Philology,* XL (July, 1941), 315-30. Boatright was inclined to venture the earliest dating, and Falk accepts the latest. The argument for the latest date is that in the notes on the philosophers, Whitman refers to "my Vistas," which, if the reference is to *Democratic Vistas,* appeared in preliminary form in *The Galaxy* in 1867 and 1868 and in final form in 1871. Regardless of the date of these notes, however, Fulghum has shown that Whitman used Gostwick in some notes on Schlegel as early as 1857.

[57] *Op. cit.,* p. 273.
[58] *Complete Writings,* IX, 180.
[59] "Schelling," *New American Cyclopedia* (1858-63), XIV, 396. According to Professor Arvin (*op. cit.,* p. 308), Whitman refers to this article in a manuscript note.
[60] *Complete Writings,* IX, 180-81. This is an enlargement of Gostwick, *op. cit.,* p. 269.
[61] See above, p. 37.
[62] *Complete Writings,* IX, 172. Whitman's praise of Hegel approaches the fulsome. See *ibid.,* pp. 170, 182-83, and *Prose Works,* p. 177n.
[63] *Complete Writings,* IX, 181.
[64] *Ibid.,* p. 168.
[65] *Ibid.,* p. 171.
[66] Alfred Weber and R. B. Perry, *History of Philosophy* (New York: Charles Scribner's Sons, 1925), p. 406.
[67] "For a Critique of Whitman's Transcendentalism," *Modern Language Notes,* XLVII (February, 1932), 84.
[68] See below, p. 108.
[69] For example: "there is something that underlies me, of whom I am a part and instrument" (*Uncollected,* II, 80); "there is a phase of the Real, lurking behind the Real, which it is all for." (*Leaves,* p. 250.)
[70] Traubel, I, 191.
[71] One characteristic misunderstanding of Hegel by Whitman may be pointed out. "Nor does the Hegelian system," he said (*Complete Writings,* IX, 196), "strictly speaking, explain the universe either in the aggregate or detail." If there is anything that the Hegelian system does in considerable degree and should logically do to a much greater degree, however, it is just this. See W. T. Stace, *The Philosophy of Hegel* (London: Macmillan & Co., 1924), pp. 307-11. Though it expresses his own native bent, Whitman may have gotten this idea from the article on Hegel in the *New American Cyclopedia* (IX, 56), where it is said, "Neither its principle nor its method has been proved to be sufficient to explain the universe." This, however, was the opinion of the author of the article, not Hegel's. For a vigorous delimitation of Whitman's Hegelianism see Olive Wrenchel Parsons, "Whitman the Non-Hegelian," *Publications of the Modern Language Association,* LVIII (December, 1943), 1073-93.
[72] *Prose Works,* pp. 175-76. See below, p. 118, and Gostwick, *op. cit.,*

p. 269.

[73] See above, p. 84.

[74] *Phenomenology of Mind*, trans. J. B. Baillie (New York: The Macmillan Co., 1931), p. 80. Cf. Whitman: *"Leaves of Grass* must be called not objective, but altogether subjective—'I know' runs through them as a perpetual refrain." (*Complete Writings*, IX, 43). Neither of these declarations contradicts the statement in the text that their authors were "objective" idealists. The principle of all these thinkers was that there is a "subject in the object."

[75] "The Over-Soul," *Complete Works* (Centenary Edition; Boston: Houghton Mifflin Co., 1903-4), II, 270. See Lanier's criticism of Emerson on this point, below, p. 203.

[76] See above, p. 85.

[77] *Op. cit.*, VIII, 342-43.

[78] "Song of the Broad-Axe," *Leaves*, p. 159.

[79] Traubel, I, 110.

[80] *Ibid.*, p. 149.

[81] *Shall Not Perish from the Earth* (New York: The Vanguard Press, 1940), p. 53.

[82] "The City of God, and the True God as Its Head: Comments by Professor Howison," in Josiah Royce, G. H. Howison, Joseph Le Conte, and S. E. Mezes, *The Conception of God* (New York: The Macmillan Co., 1909), pp. 81-132 *passim*, but especially pp. 112-13.

[83] See especially *Personalism* (Boston: Houghton Mifflin Co., 1908).

[84] *Prose Works*, p. 228. A portion of *Democratic Vistas* had appeared under the title of "Personalism" in the *Galaxy* for May, 1868.

[85] A good summary of the evidence on this point will be found in Gay W. Allen, *Walt Whitman Handbook* (Chicago: Packard & Co., 1946), p. 302 ff.

[86] The *N. E. D.* indicates that Grote used the term in 1865 as a rough equivalent of idealism.

[87] *Leaves*, p. 136.

[88] *The Conception of God*, p. 93.

[89] "Walt Whitman," *Shelburne Essays*, fourth series (Boston: Houghton Mifflin Co., 1906), p. 203.

[90] "The Heracleitan Obsession of Walt Whitman," *Personalist*, XV (Spring, 1934), 125-38.

[91] C. E. M. Joad, *Guide to Philosophy* (New York: Random House, n. d.), p. 170.

[92] "Bergson and Romantic Evolutionism," *University of California Chronicle*, XV (October, 1913), 458.

[93] "Yet, Yet, Ye Downcast Hours," *Leaves*, p. 372.

[94] *Ibid.*, p. 513.

[95] *Uncollected*, II, 64. The word in brackets is supplied by me, not by the editor.

[96] Whitman reviewed Liebig's *Chemistry in Its Application to Agriculture and Physiology* in the *Eagle* of June 28, 1847 (Arvin, *op. cit.*, pp. 158-59, 306).

[97] *Leaves of Grass, Reproduced from the First Edition (1855)*, ed. Clifton J. Furness (New York: Published for the Facsimile Text Society by the Columbia University Press, 1939), p. 17.

[98] Emerson's poem appeared for the first time in 1849 at the head of the reprint of "Nature." Whether Whitman wrote the prose passage quot-

ed in the next paragraph before or after this date is problematical. The second notebook, from which the passage is quoted, is undated. On its probable date see *Uncollected,* II, 79, note 1.

[99] *Uncollected,* II, 79-80.
[100] *Leaves,* pp. 68-69.
[101] *Ibid.,* p. 131.
[102] *Complete Writings,* IX, 150-51.
[103] "A Song of Joys," *Leaves,* p. 154.
[104] "When Lilacs Last in the Dooryard Bloom'd," *ibid.,* p. 281.
[105] For a profound and suggestive interpretation see Santayana, *Reason in Common Sense* (2nd ed.; New York: Charles Scribner's Sons, 1922), pp. 57-58.
[106] "I Sing the Body Electric," *Leaves,* p. 82. Cf. "Fancies at Navesink" (*ibid.,* p. 426):
Weaving from you, from Sleep, Night, Death itself,
The rhythmus of Birth eternal.
[107] Preface to 1876 edition, *ibid.,* p. 513n.
[108] "Song of Myself," *ibid.,* p. 69.
[109] "Whispers of Heavenly Death," *ibid.,* pp. 369-70.
[110] *The Present Conflict of Ideals,* p. 213. Professor Perry states Howison's view as follows: "Our personal self . . . [is] possessed of a being that by its essence transcends all the vicissitudes of the merely natural world, surviving all its possible catastrophes and supplying the ground for its continuance in new modes under new conditions."
[111] Traubel, I, 149.
[112] *Leaves,* p. 444n.
[113] "I Sing the Body Electric," *bid.,* p. 83. For an excellent account of the procession motif in Whitman from a somewhat different point of view from that of the following, see G. W. Allen "Walt Whitman's 'Long Journey' Motif," *Journal of English and Germanic Philology,* XXXVIII (1939), 79-95.
[114] "A Song of the Rolling Earth," *Leaves,* p. 190.
[115] "Song of Myself," *ibid.,* p. 70.
[116] "Song of the Open Road," *ibid.,* pp. 128-31.
[117] See, for example: above, p. 113; *Complete Writings,* IX, 150; "A Song of the Rolling Earth," *Leaves,* p. 187. Emerson usually left off the prefix. See above, pp. 52, 62.
[118] Traubel, II, 430. See also *ibid.,* II, 71.
[119] *The Present Conflict of Ideals,* pp. 233-34. The quotation is from Santayana's "Genteel Tradition in American Philosophy," *Winds of Doctrine* (New York: Charles Scribner's Sons, 1940), p. 199.
[120] "Song of the Open Road," *Leaves,* p. 126.
[121] *Complete Writings,* IX, 171-72.
[122] See above, pp. 106-7.
[123] "Above the doors of teaching the inscription is to appear, Though little or nothing can be absolutely known, perceiv'd, except from a point of view which is evanescent, yet we know at least one permanency, that Time and Space, in the will of God, furnish successive chains, completions of material births and beginnings, solve all discrepancies, fears and doubts, and eventually fulfil happiness—and that the prophecy of those births, namely spiritual results, throws the true arch over all teaching, all science." *Prose Works,* p. 250n.
[124] *Leaves,* pp. 192-93.

[125] See above, p. 113.

[126] *Complete Writings*, IX, 12. Cf.: "Earth's résumé floats on thy keel O ship" ("Thou Mother with Thy Equal Brood," *Leaves*, p. 381); "The earth . . . has all attributes, growths, effects, latent in itself from the jump" ("A Song of the Rolling Earth," *ibid.*, p. 187); "The American poets are to enclose old and new for America is the race of races" (1855 Preface, *ibid.*, p. 489).

[127] This point is developed at some length by Gostwick (*op. cit.*, p. 272).

[128] 1855 edition, p. iii.

[129] *Leaves*, p. 343.

[130] *Ibid.*, pp. 166-68.

[131] See above, p. 113.

[132] *Prose Works*, p. 203. Among innumerable illustrations see especially "Song of the Redwood Tree."

[133] "Song of the Open Road," *Leaves*, p. 132.

[134] "Bergson and Romantic Evolutionism," *loc. cit.* For an excellent analysis of this spirit in one of its great sources, see Santayana's essay on Goethe's *Faust* in *Three Philosophical Poets* (Cambridge: Harvard University Press, 1935). Santayana's most amusing and most vivid statement of the principle, however, which he abominated, is given to Irma in *The Last Puritan* (New York: Charles Scribner's Sons, 1936, p. 111): "I can no longer cry with Goethe, *Verweile doch*. No: such loitering is unworthy of the German spirit! We must not cling to anything achieved, but stretch out our eager hands for ever to the Beyond. And I won't say, towards 'Something Higher.' I won't climb up any ladder set up for me beforehand, with rungs all numbered higher and higher, like degrees in the thermometer! What is that but a remnant of mediaeval metaphysics? The free, bold, pure German genius cannot be confined to such a single narrow path. It will forge its way out of Itself in any direction, in all directions, into the infinite, scorning all law save that which It imposes on Itself at each moment by living, molested by no facts, recognising no conditions, but creating always the next step by Its untrammelled sudden inspiration. Nature is a prison. As for me, give me Chaos."

[135] *Uncollected*, II, 66. The passage in "Song of Myself" is in *Leaves*, p. 71. See also "Who Learns My Lesson Complete?" *ibid.*, pp. 329-30; *Complete Writings*, IX, 70; "Going Somewhere," *Leaves*, p. 433; and reference in Traubel, III, 165-66.

[136] See above, p. 92.

[137] The interweaving of these dimensions is common in the *Leaves* and productive of some of its most striking effects. Probably the best illustration is "Crossing Brooklyn Ferry."

[138] *Leaves*, p. 344.

[139] *Ibid.*, p. 350.

[140] See above, p. 65.

[141] *Leaves*, p. 349. For parallels to the pattern of this poem see "Facing West from California's Shores," "O Star of France," "A Broadway Pageant," "Prayer of Columbus," and "A Thought of Columbus."

[142] *Ibid.*, pp. 346-47.

[143] See above, note 59.

[144] *I Sit and Look Out*, ed. Emory Holloway and Vernolian Schwarz (New York: Columbia University Press, 1932), p. 198.

[145] *Leaves*, p. 233.

[146] *Ibid.*, p. 25.

[147] *Ibid.*, p. 68.
[148] *Ibid.*, p. 124.
[149] Maximilian Beck, "Walt Whitman's Intuition of Reality," *Ethics*, LIII (October, 1942), 14. The conclusion, making a questionable but common use of the word "democratic," reads as follows: "The absolute equality of the value of every real existing thing is self-evident if the principle of its value lies in its very reality rather than in anything by which things are differentiated. It is the intuition of a democratic metaphysics which Whitman is trying to communicate indirectly by emphasizing the worth of all being, even the lowest." (*Ibid.*, p. 24). A sharp criticism of this element in Whitman's thought is contained in Yvor Winters' essay "The Significance of *The Bridge,* by Hart Crane, or What Are We to Think of Professor X?" in his volume *In Defense of Reason* (New York: The Swallow Press, 1947), pp. 577-603.
[150] "O Me! O Life!" *Leaves,* p. 231.
[151] "By Blue Ontario's Shore," *ibid.,* p. 286.
[152] See above, p. 6.
[153] See above, Chapter II, note 129.
[154] Josiah Royce, *The Spirit of Modern Philosophy* (Boston: Houghton Mifflin & Co., 1893), Lecture XII.
[155] *Present Philosophical Tendencies* (New York: Longmans, Green & Co., 1912), p. 190.
[156] *Leaves,* pp. 15-16.
[157] *The Present Conflict of Ideals,* p. 279.
[158] *Present Philosophical Tendencies,* pp. 188-89. See also Santayana, *Reason in Science* (New York: Charles Scribner's Sons, 1932), pp. 112-14.

CHAPTER V

THE COMING OF DARWIN

[1] See above, pp. 50, 95.
[2] M. R. Werner, *Barnum* (New York: Harcourt, Brace & Co., 1923), pp. 56 ff.
[3] A notable exception is Oliver Wendell Holmes, who hazarded an evolutionary theory of his own in 1857. See below, Chapter X. He is included in this section, however, because of the interest attaching to his attitude toward post-Darwinian evolution and because of his reflection of the predicament described at the end of this chapter.
[4] *Plays and Poems* (Boston: Ticknor & Fields, 1856), I, 13-14.
[5] *Ibid.*, I, 47-48.
[6] *Contributions to the Natural History of the United States* (Boston: Little, Brown & Co., 1857), I, 107.
[7] *Letters of Charles Eliot Norton,* ed. Sara Norton and M. A. De Wolfe Howe (Boston: Houghton Mifflin Co., 1913), I, 210-11.
[8] *Life and Letters of Charles Darwin,* ed. Francis Darwin (New York: D. Appleton & Co., 1896), II, 99.
[9] "Science in America and Modern Methods of Science," *American Naturalist,* VII (October, 1873), 577.
[10] "A Century's Progress in American Zoology," *American Naturalist,* X (October, 1876), 591-98.
[11] "What American Zoologists Have Done for Evolution," *Popular Science Monthly,* XXXII (February, 1888), 503.
[12] In the Union Catalogue of the Library of Congress I find the follow-

ing entries by American publishers:
  Spencer, *First Principles* (first complete edition, 1862): 1860 (part I), 1864, 1865, 1866, 1868, 1869, 1870, 1873, 1876, 1877, 1879, 1880 (entries by three publishers).
  Darwin, *The Origin of Species* (first edition, 1859): 1860, 1868, 1870, 1871, 1872, 1873, 1877, 1878, 1880.
  Darwin, *The Descent of Man* (first edition, 1871): 1872, 1873, 1874 (entries by four publishers), 1875, 1879.

[13] Allan Nevins, *The Emergence of Modern America* (New York: The Macmillan Co., 1927), pp. 286-89.

[14] Harriet C. B. Alexander, "Tyndall and Emerson," *Atlantic Monthly*, LXXV (February, 1889), 281.

[15] Nevins, *loc. cit.*

[16] See Mrs. John T. Sargent, *Sketches and Reminiscences of the Radical Club of Chestnut Street, Boston* (Boston: J. R. Osgood & Co., 1880), especially pp. 184-87, 243-50, 259-70, 285-92, 316-28, and 329-33.

[17] See Courtland Palmer, *The Nineteenth Century Club of New York, Shall Similar Associations Become General?* (London: W. Reeves, 1887); Courtland Palmer, *Tributes Offered by Members of the Nineteenth Century Club* (New York: F. W. Christenson, 1889); and the yearly bulletins of the club.

[18] Nevins, *op. cit.*, p. 286.

[19] *Harvard University Summaries of Theses*, 1934 (Cambridge: Harvard University Press, 1935), pp. 165-68.

[20] Quoted by Andrew D. White in *A History of the Warfare of Science with Theology in Christendom* (New York: D. Appleton & Co., 1896), I, 72.

[21] *Natural Theology* (Boston: Lincoln & Edmands, 1829), p. 14.

[22] "It is scarcely possible to avoid comparing the eye with a telescope. We know that this instrument has been perfected by the long-continued efforts of the highest human intellects; and we naturally infer that the eye has been formed by a somewhat analogous process. But may not this inference be presumptuous? Have we any right to assume that the Creator works by intellectual powers like those of man?" (*The Origin of Species* [6th ed.; New York: P. F. Collier & Son, 1901], p. 254.)

[23] Alfred Weber in Weber and Perry, *History of Philosophy* (New York: Charles Scribner's Sons, 1925), p. 473.

[24] Quoted by Ambrose Vernon White in "Later Theology," *Cambridge History of American Literature* (New York: The Macmillan Co., 1933), III, 209.

[25] See above, p. 35.

[26] *The Geological Evidence of the Antiquity of Man* (1863) (Everyman's Library edition; New York: E. P. Dutton & Co., n. d.), p. 393.

[27] Quoted by D. D. Addison in *The Clergy in American Life and Letters* (New York: The Macmillan Co., 1900), p. 317.

[28] *The Destiny of Man* (Boston: Houghton, Mifflin & Co., 1885), pp. 113-14.

[29] Paley's comments on Erasmus Darwin's theory of the development of organisms out of undifferentiated matter through the operation of implanted "Appetencies" illustrate this point. Such a theory, Paley held, was not wholly atheistic, since the appetencies themselves might be referred to a Creator. But he added: "In one important respect, however, the theory before us coincides with atheistic systems, viz. in that, in the formation of

plants and animals, in the structure and use of their parts, it does away final causes. Instead of the parts of a plant or animal, or the particular structure of the parts, having been intended for the action or use to which we see them applied, according to this theory they have themselves grown out of that action, sprung from that use. The theory, therefore, dispenses with that which we insist upon, the necessity in each particular case, of an intelligent, designing mind, for the contriving and determining of the forms which organized bodies bear." (*Natural Theology*, p. 245.)

[30] See below, p. 220.

[31] *The Religious Aspect of Evolution* (2nd ed.; New York: Charles Scribner's Sons, 1890), pp. viii-ix.

[32] *Ibid.*, pp. 7-8.

[33] *History of English Literature*, trans. Van Laun (New York: Henry Holt & Co., 1879), p. 6.

[34] *Op. cit.*, chap. iii.

[35] *Ibid.*, pp. 103-4.

[36] See above, pp. 28, 91, and 98.

[37] *Op. cit.*, pp. 52-54.

[38] *Nature and the Supernatural as Together Constituting the One System of God* (2nd ed.; New York: Charles Scribner & Co., 1870), p. 69. On Chambers, see pp. 60-61. For further consideration of evolution, taking Agassiz's position, see pp. 76-90.

[39] Here I wish to refer to the Scottish philosophy, the effect of which on American writers was very great and is, as yet, unmeasured. For its predominance at Harvard down to about 1860, see Benjamin Rand, "Philosophical Instruction in Harvard University from 1636 to 1906," *Harvard Graduates' Magazine*, XXXVII (1928-29), 29-47, 188-200, and 296-311. The gist of this philosophy was that certain judgments concerning reality are presupposed in knowledge and necessary to it. Among these are the law of causation and the reality of freedom and personal identity. The clearest exposition of the philosophy that I have seen is Henry Laurie, *The Scottish Philosophy in Its National Development* (Glasgow: Maclehose, 1902). But see also McCosh, *Realistic Philosophy Defended in a Philosophic Series* (New York: Charles Scribner's Sons, 1887), 2 Vols.

CHAPTER VI

MINOR POETS

[1] Another instance not discussed in the text is an absurd verse play by Henry Peterson entitled *The Modern Job* (Philadelphia: H. Peterson & Co., 1869).

[2] Bret Harte, *Poetical Works* (Household Edition; Boston: Houghton, Mifflin & Co., n. d.), p. 315.

[3] "To the Pliocene Skull (A Geological Address)," *The Californian*, July 28, 1866; *Poetical Works*, pp. 268-69.

[4] San Francisco *News Letter*, September 26, 1868; *Poetical Works*, pp. 132-34.

[5] R. T. Young, *Biology in America* (Boston: Richard G. Badger, 1922), p. 43.

[6] San Francisco *News Letter*, April 27, 1867; *Poetical Works*, pp. 279-80.

[7] "A Pastoral Ballad." *The Works of the English Poets, from Chaucer to Cowper*, ed. Alexander Chalmers (London: J. Johnson *et al.*, 1810), XIII, 299.

⁸ *Standard Edition of the Works of Herman Melville* (London: Constable & Co., 1924), XVI, 408-10.
⁹ The full title of the poem is "The New Ancient of Days. The Man of the Cave of Engihoul. (See Lyell's *The Antiquity of Man* and Darwin's *The Descent of Species*)." The misnaming of Darwin's book suggests that the immediate reference is to Lyell, an inference which is supported by the fact that Lyell has a chapter on the Engis caves while Darwin makes no mention of them in either *The Origin of Species* or *The Descent of Man*.
¹⁰ Mrs. John T. Sargent, *Sketches and Reminiscences of the Radical Club of Chestnut Street, Boston* (Boston: J. R. Osgood & Co., 1880), p. 268.
¹¹ 1868. *Collected Essays* (New York: D. Appleton & Co., 1893-94), I, 153. On the basis of his agnosticism Huxley of course rejected the materialism implied. See *ibid.*, pp. 155 ff.
¹² 1874. *Fragments of Science* (New York: D. Appleton & Co., 1896), II, 191.
¹³ Sargent, *op. cit.*, p. 264.
¹⁴ "Mr. Huxley's Visit," *Every-Day Topics*, 2nd series (New York: Charles Scribner & Co., 1882), p. 42.
¹⁵ "The Missing Leaf," *The Emigrant's Story and Other Poems* (Boston: J. R. Osgood & Co., 1875), p. 103; *The Poetical Works of John Townsend Trowbridge* (Boston: Houghton Mifflin Co., 1903), p. 110.
¹⁶ "Of all writers ancient or modern, poets, philosophers, prophets, the one to whom my spiritual indebtedness was first and last the greatest, was Emerson." (*My Own Story* [Boston: Houghton Mifflin Co., 1903], p. 336.)
¹⁷ "The Missing Leaf," *The Emigrant's Story and Other Poems*, p. 103. This stanza is omitted in *Poetical Works*.
¹⁸ "A Word to Philosophers," *Ariel and Caliban* (Boston: Houghton, Mifflin & Co., 1887), pp. 97-98.
¹⁹ "The Origin of Man," *Poems and Essays* (Boston: Houghton, Mifflin & Co., 1886), p. 276. Cf. "The Soul's Questioning of the Universe, and Its Beginning," *ibid.*, pp. 332-33, and "Evolution," *ibid.*, p. 516.
²⁰ "The Past," *ibid.*, pp. 292-93. Cf. Royce on time and evolution, above, p. 35.
²¹ Trowbridge, *Poetical Works*, p. 107.
²² *Ibid.*, p. 108.
²³ *Ibid.*, p. 109.
²⁴ "A Word to Philosophers," *Ariel and Caliban*, pp. 98-99.
²⁵ *Standard Edition*, XIV, 215, a mystifying statement, certainly figurative, that "Darwin quotes from Shelley, that forever floats over all desert places known, mysterious doubt"; XV, 253, an aside in a discussion of science, "own Darwin is but his grandsire's son."
²⁶ For example, another statement of the Royce dilemma, spoken by Rolfe: "What novel thing may be, no germ being new?" (*Ibid.*, XV, 222). It is set off against evolution and a pessimistic conclusion is drawn.
²⁷ *Ibid.*, XV, 297-98.
²⁸ *Letters of James Russell Lowell*, ed. C. E. Norton (New York: Harper & Bros., 1894), II, 245.
²⁹ "Without and Within," *Later Lyrics* (Boston: J. E. Tilton & Co., 1866), pp. 216-18.
³⁰ "First Causes," *ibid.*, pp. 133-34.
³¹ "Survival of the Fittest," *Ariel and Caliban*, pp. 95-96.
³² "The Inheritance," *Oberon and Puck* (New York: Cassell & Co.,

1885), pp. 64-65.
³³ *Poems* (Boston: Houghton, Mifflin & Co., 1893), p. 222.
³⁴ See above, p. 135.
³⁵ "Kosmos," *Later Lyrics*, p. 132.
³⁶ "Love," *The Emigrant's Story and Other Poems*, 1875, p. 113; *Poetical Works*, p. 114.
³⁷ "Creation," *Poems of Passion* (Chicago: W. B. Conkey, 1883), p. 120.
³⁸ "Under Moon and Stars," *A Home Idyl and Other Poems* (Boston: Houghton, Mifflin & Co., 1881), pp. 106-7; *Poetical Works*, p. 238.
³⁹ See below, p. 244.
⁴⁰ Aubrey Moore, "The Christian Idea of God," *Lux Mundi*, 1889; quoted by A. C. McGiffert, *The Rise of Modern Religious Ideas* (New York: The Macmillan Co., 1915), pp. 181-82. The passage continues: "Either God is everywhere present in nature, or He is nowhere. . . . He cannot delegate His powers to demigods, called 'second causes.' In nature everything must be His work, or nothing. We must frankly return to the Christian view of direct divine agency, the immanence of divine power in nature from end to end, the belief in a God in whom not only we but all things have their being, or we must banish Him altogether."
⁴¹ *The Lost Earl and Other Poems* (Boston: D. Lothrop Co., 1888), p. 93; *Poetical Works*, p. 308.
⁴² "Faith," the first of the three parts of "A Triune Creed," *Melodies of the Heart, Songs of Freedom and Other Poems* (Cincinnati: R. Clarke & Co., 1885), p. 45; *The Poems of William Henry Venable*, ed. Emerson Venable (New York: Dodd, Mead & Co., 1925), p. 86.
⁴³ Originally published in *New England Magazine*, XIII, n. s. (November, 1895), 322. Frequently republished. See, for example, *Journal of Education*, LXX (September 16, 1909), 264; *Each in His Own Tongue and Other Poems* (New York: G. P. Putnam's Sons, 1908), pp. 2-4.
⁴⁴ Spencer in the discussion of the Unknowable in *First Principles* (see below, chap. x, note 31); Darwin in the last chapter of *The Origin of Species*. Darwin speaks, for example, of life as having been "breathed by the Creator into a few forms or into one" (*op. cit.* [6th ed.; New York: P. F. Collier & Sons, 1901], II, 316).
⁴⁵ Quoted in *The American Mind*, ed. H. R. Warfel, R. H. Gabriel, and S. T. Williams (New York: American Book Co., 1937), I, 398. Italics supplied.
⁴⁶ "The Struggle for Existence in Human Society," 1888, *Evolution and Ethics and Other Essays* (New York: D. Appleton & Co., 1898), p. 199.
⁴⁷ *Op. cit.*, II, 315.
⁴⁸ In *Social Statics*. Quoted by J. B. Bury in *The Idea of Progress* (New York: The Macmillan Co., 1932), p. 338. For the reservations see the revised edition of *Social Statics* (New York: D. Appleton & Co., 1892), p. 32.
⁴⁹ Venable, *Poems*, p. 86.
⁵⁰ *Firm Ground: Thoughts on Life and Faith* (Sterling, N. Y.: published by the author, 1877), p. 107; *Life and Faith: Sonnets* (New York: Henry Holt & Co., 1878), p. 105.
⁵¹ *In Nazareth Town and Other Poems* (Boston: Roberts Bros., 1883), p. 77.
⁵² "Song of a Wise Spirit," *Satan: A Libretto* (Boston: Roberts Bros., 1874), p. 31; text used is that in the later revision, "Ormuzd and Ahriman: A Cantata," *Ariel and Caliban*, pp. 221-22.
⁵³ *A Home Idyl*, p. 151; *Poetical Works*, p. 261.

[54] *A Home Idyl,* pp. 152-57; *Poetical Works,* pp. 261-63.
[55] "Progress," *Poems of Power* (Chicago: W. B. Conkey, 1901), p. 56.
[56] "The World Grows Better," *ibid.,* p. 45.
[57] "Evolution," *Independent,* LV (February 19, 1903), 445.
[58] See above, p. 62.
[59] *The Origin of Species,* II, 316.
[60] Quoted by Bury, *The Idea of Progress,* p. 340.
[61] *The Poems of Alfred B. Street* (New York: Hurd & Houghton, 1867), II, 205.
[62] Prologue to "The Ivory Carver," *Plays and Poems* (Boston: Ticknor & Fields, 1856), II, 256.
[63] "Under Moon and Stars," *A Home Idyl,* p. 110; *Poetical Works,* p. 239.
[64] "Ancestors," *A Home Idyl,* pp. 151-53; *Poetical Works,* pp. 261-62.
[65] "The Winnower," *Atlantic Monthly,* LXXXIV (1899), 431; *Poetical Works,* pp. 353-54.
[66] "Ormuzd and Ahriman: A Cantata," *Ariel and Caliban,* pp. 189-229.
[67] *Ibid.,* p. 204.
[68] *Ibid.,* p. 205.
[69] *Ibid.,* p. 209.
[70] *Ibid.,* p. 193.
[71] *Ibid.,* p. 212.
[72] *Ibid.,* pp. 224-25.
[73] *The Poetry of John Bannister Tabb,* ed. F. A. Litz (New York: Dodd, Mead & Co., 1928), pp. 157-58.
[74] "Evolution," *Independent,* LV (February 26, 1903), 494.
[75] "To an Evolutionist," *From the Book of Life* (Boston: Little, Brown & Co., 1909), p. 74; *The Collected Poems of Richard Burton* (Indianapolis: Bobbs-Merrill Co., 1931), p. 225.
[76] *The Descent of Man* (2nd ed.; New York: D. Appleton & Co., 1917), p. 627.
[77] *Evolution in Its Relation to Religious Thought* (2nd ed.; New York: D. Appleton & Co., 1891), p. 313. This passage is not in the first edition, 1888.
[78] *The Destiny of Man* (Boston: Houghton, Mifflin & Co., 1885), pp. 117-18.
[79] "Consummation," *Life and Faith,* p. 55.
[80] See "Hearn as a Mediator between Buddhism and Modern Science," *Current Literature,* XLI (August, 1906), 204-5.
[81] *Poems of Paul Hamilton Hayne* (Boston: Lothrop, 1882), pp. 204-5.
[82] *The Writings of Thomas Bailey Aldrich* (Boston: Houghton Mifflin Co., 1907), I, 30.
[83] See above, pp. 9-10.
[84] "Pre-existence," *Poems,* I, 243.
[85] *The Woman Who Dared* (Boston: Roberts Bros., 1870), pp. 4-5.
[86] Sonnets LI and LII, *Ariel and Caliban,* pp. 182-83.
[87] Originally published as "A Toast to a Lady" in *The Scrap Book,* April, 1906. Reprinted several times: *Evolution, a Fantasy* (Boston: J. W. Luce, 1909); *Evolution, a Fantasy* (Boston and Chicago: W. A. Wilde, 1911); *Evolution,* with correlative poems selected and edited by Laurens Maynard (Boston: J. W. Luce, 1915). The 1909 edition has been used here. Though the description given in the text seems accurate to the present writer, the poem was apparently taken more seriously by some readers.

Lewis Allen Browne speaks in the Introduction of the 1909 edition of Smith's effort "to weld the theory of soul-transmigration to the reality of evolution" (p. i) and states that "he reduced immortality to a science and science to immortality." (P. iii.)

[88] *Evolution, a Fantasy* (1909), p. 1.
[89] *Ibid.,* p. 33.
[90] *Ibid.,* pp. 35-37.
[91] "The New Science," *Later Poems* (Boston: Houghton Mifflin Co., 1905), pp. 103-4.
[92] "Palingenesis," *The Dancers and Other Legends and Lyrics* (Boston: Richard G. Badger, 1903), pp. 90-92.
[93] "Atom," *Wings of Sunset* (Boston: Houghton Mifflin Co., 1929), p. 157.

CHAPTER VII

BRYANT, LONGFELLOW, AND LOWELL

[1] *American Poets and Their Theology* (Philadelphia: The Griffith & Rowland Press, 1916), p. v.

[2] *Prose Works,* ed. Parke Godwin (New York: D. Appleton & Co., 1884), pp. 291-93. Since the address was delivered December 28, 1871, the Darwinian point was probably suggested by *The Descent of Man,* which was first published in that year. The other reference to Darwin was briefer but equally satirical and was made at a reception tendered Bryant by the Goethe Club in November, 1877 (John Bigelow, *William Cullen Bryant,* [Boston: Houghton, Mifflin & Co., 1890], p. 254). With the query whether men and women are not "ruins," compare Alcott and Emerson, above, p. 42.

[3] In the summer of 1811, after his resignation from Williams College, he studied the chemistry of Lavoisier and the Linnaean system of botanical classification. (Godwin, *A Biography of William Cullen Bryant* [New York: D. Appleton & Co., 1883], I, 36.)

[4] Bryant not only knew many scientists in this country, but in 1845 he attended a meeting of the British Association at which he met Whewell, Buckland, Lyell, Hutton, and others. (*Ibid.,* II, 6-7.)

[5] December 22, 1874 (*ibid.,* II, 351).

[6] "The Rivulet" (1823), *Poetical Works,* ed. Parke Godwin (New York: D. Appleton & Co., 1883), I, 32. See also "The Stream of Life" (1845), *ibid.,* II, 11.

[7] "Hymn to Death" (1820), *Poetical Works,* I, 46.

[8] In thirty-five lines added to the poem.

[9] *Poetical Works,* I, 55. See also "The Massacre at Scio" (1824), *ibid.,* I, 73, and "The Hymn of the Waldenses" (1824), *ibid.,* I, 100.

[10] The description of the earth as "the great tomb of man" occurs as early as the first printing of "Thanatopsis" in the *North American Review* in 1817, and therefore doubtless goes back to the first draft of 1811. The same sentiment reappears again and again. See "The Journey of Life" (1826), *Poetical Works,* I, 169; "The Past" (1828), *ibid.,* I, 199; "The Prairies" (1832), *ibid.,* I, 228; "Life" (1835), *ibid.,* I, 262.

[11] "An Indian at the Burial Place of His Fathers" (1824), *ibid.,* I, 97. See also "The Ages" and "The Prairies."

[12] "The Ages," *ibid.,* I, 53-68.

[13] "After a Tempest," *ibid.*, I, 109-10.
[14] See "The Antiquity of Freedom" (1842), *ibid.*, I, 305, and "Fifty Years" (1863), *ibid.*, II, 327.
[15] See "Fifty Years" and "The Better Age" (1862), *ibid.*, II, 310.
[16] "Among the Trees" (1868), *ibid.*, II, 112.
[17] "The Battle-Field," *ibid.*, I, 276.
[18] (1840), *ibid.*, I, 297. See also the concluding lines of "The Flood of Years" (1876), *ibid.*, II, 188.
[19] *Poetical Works*, I, 55.
[20] *Ibid.*, I, 55-56.
[21] *Ibid.*, I, 56.
[22] The second of his lectures on poetry in 1825. *Prose Works*, I, 18.
[23] W. A. Bradley, *William Cullen Bryant* (New York: The Macmillan Co., 1905), p. 85.
[24] First printed in edition of 1871. *Poetical Works*, II, 288.
[25] See above, p. 136.
[26] *Poetical Works*, I, 132.
[27] Godwin, *Biography*, II, 226.
[28] See above, p. 137.
[29] See above, note 2.
[30] Bigelow, *William Cullen Bryant*, p. 206.
[31] Godwin, *Biography*, II, 395.
[32] Spoken by the Theologian in the Prelude to Part I of *Tales of a Wayside Inn*. *Complete Poetical Works*, ed. H. E. Scudder (Boston: Houghton Mifflin Co., n. d.), p. 206.
[33] February 21, 1846. Samuel Longfellow, *Life of Henry Wadsworth Longfellow* (Boston: Houghton, Mifflin & Co., 1891), II, 34.
[34] December 16, 1847, *ibid.*, II, 103.
[35] Letter to George Washington Greene, October 22, 1838, *ibid.*, I, 313.
[36] *Ibid.*, I, 241.
[37] June 13, 1850, *ibid.*, II, 182. On another occasion he went so far as to state the theme of one of Agassiz's lectures: "the theory that all animals can be traced back to an original form in the egg,—as Goethe traced the plant back to an original *phyton*." (February 6, 1849, *ibid.*, II, 144). He made no comment, however.
[38] August 8, 1871, *ibid.*, III, 182. The essay was read in Hedge's *Prose Writers of Germany*.
[39] September 8, 1872, *ibid.*, III, 206.
[40] *Ibid.*, III, 396.
[41] See below, pp. 247-60, but especially p. 260.
[42] According to J. T. Hatfield (*New Light on Longfellow* [Boston: Houghton Mifflin Co., 1933], p. 40), Longfellow read Schubert's *Die Geschichte der Seele* (1830) when he was in Heidelberg in 1836. Schubert became known in this country through W. H. Furness's translation of another of his books, *The Mirror of Nature* (Philadelphia, 1849).
[43] *Prose Works* (Boston: Houghton, Mifflin & Co., 1886), II, 102-5.
[44] *Complete Poetical Works*, p. 263.
[45] Felton scotched the attempt of a reviewer to identify Longfellow with the Transcendentalists after the appearance of *Hyperion*. See Lawrence Thompson, *Young Longfellow* (New York: The Macmillan Co., 1938), pp. 292-93.
[46] *Life*, II, 35-36.

⁴⁷ "Rain in Summer" (1844), *Complete Poetical Works*, p. 60.
⁴⁸ "By the Fireside," *ibid.*, p. 107.
⁴⁹ "Keramos," *ibid.*, p. 330.
⁵⁰ In a letter to C. K. Tuckerman, quoted by Scudder in a headnote to the poem, *ibid.*, p. 19.
⁵¹ *Life*, I, 186.
⁵² See above, p. 111.
⁵³ *The Complete Writings of James Russell Lowell* (Cambridge: The Riverside Press, 1904), XIV, 164.
⁵⁴ *The Complete Poetical Works of James Russell Lowell*, ed. H. E. Scudder (Boston: Houghton Mifflin Co., n. d.), pp. 350-60.
⁵⁵ Quoted from the *Critique of Pure Reason* by J. H. Randall in *The Making of the Modern Mind* (rev. ed.; Boston: Houghton Mifflin Co., 1940), p. 413.
⁵⁶ *Complete Poetical Works*, pp. 433-35.
⁵⁷ *Ibid.*, p. 410 (1888).
⁵⁸ See below, pp. 339 ff.
⁵⁹ "A Good Word for Winter," *Complete Writings*, I, 361.
⁶⁰ "A Moosehead Journal," *ibid.*, p. 79.
⁶¹ "The Brakes" and "Pessimoptimism," *Complete Poetical Works*, pp. 406-7.
⁶² To Mrs. W. E. Darwin, September 1, 1878; *Complete Writings*, XVI, 55.
⁶³ *New Letters of James Russell Lowell*, ed. M. A. DeW. Howe (New York: Harper & Bros., 1932), p. 296.
⁶⁴ *Complete Writings*, VIII, 143.
⁶⁵ *Ibid.*, pp. 145-46.
⁶⁶ *Ibid.*, pp. 146-47.
⁶⁷ *Complete Poetical Works*, pp. 423-25.
⁶⁸ Letter to Mrs. Owen J. Wistar, Christmas, 1886 (*New Letters*, p. 301): "I have furbished up for the February *Atlantic* a longish piece of octosyllabic verses, halfhumorous halfsentimental, a kind of lamentation of Jeremiah, written fifteen years ago."
⁶⁹ "Harvard Anniversary," *Complete Writings*, VII, 169.
⁷⁰ F. T. Lewis, "Unpublished Metrical Epigram," *Science*, n. s., LX (October 10, 1924), 333-34. Lewis supplies the following translation: "Fodder your beasts in a suitable way with light-giving Phosphorous—Wiser than Moleschott, they,—granted the dose be correct. Feed them too little, you blight them, and make of them stupidest asses. Give but a grain too much—! See them all burnt to a bone!!"
⁷¹ "The Function of the Poet," *The Function of the Poet and Other Essays*, ed. Albert Mordell (Boston: Houghton Mifflin Co., 1920), pp. 19-20.
⁷² "In the Half-Way House," *Complete Poetical Works*, pp. 426-27.
⁷³ "The Footpath" (1868), *ibid.*, p. 333.
⁷⁴ *Varieties of Religious Experience* (New York: Longmans, Green & Co., 1929), pp. 65-66. See letter to G. B. Loring, September 20, 1842, *Complete Writings*, XIV, 95-97.
⁷⁵ *Complete Writings*, XV, 335-36.
⁷⁶ *Ibid.*, p. 338.
⁷⁷ Quoted in H. E. Scudder, *James Russell Lowell: A Biography* (Boston: Houghton Mifflin Co., 1901), II, 175-76.
⁷⁸ *Complete Writings*, XV, 388.
⁷⁹ *Ibid.*, p. 408.

⁸⁰ "On Liberty," *Utilitarianism, Liberty, and Representative Government* (Everyman's Library edition; New York: E. P. Dutton & Co., n. d.), p. 83.
⁸¹ May 15, 1876, *Complete Writings,* XV, 388.
⁸² September 12, 1879. Quoted in E. E. Hale, Jr., *James Russell Lowell and His Friends* (Boston: Houghton, Mifflin & Co., 1890), pp. 281-82. This letter contains the famous passage on protoplasm quoted above, p. 147.
⁸³ *Complete Poetical Works,* p. 381 (1874).
⁸⁴ *Complete Writings,* XVI, 172.

CHAPTER VIII

TAYLOR AND LANIER

¹ Taylor contrasted favorably Goethe's attitude toward science with that of Poe as expressed in the "Sonnet—To Science." Goethe, he believed, would have replied as follows to the charge that science is the enemy of poetry: " 'Science is truth and Poetry is truth: both are infinite and inexhaustible: both are kindred fields through which the human approaches the Divine Mind, and they can never be antagonistic in a healthy nature.' " (*Studies in German Literature* [New York: G. P. Putnam's Sons, 1907], p. 327.)
² Marie Hansen-Taylor and H. E. Scudder, *Life and Letters of Bayard Taylor* (Boston: Houghton, Mifflin & Co., 1884), I, 18-19.
³ Taylor admired Humboldt as an even greater traveler than himself, and was much moved when he met him on his Northern journey in 1856. Three years later he wrote an introduction for R. H. Stoddard's *Life of Humboldt,* and his biographers have this to say of Humboldt's influence on his later work, particularly *Prince Deukalion:* "There is little doubt that his acquaintance with Humboldt at this time deepened the reflections which had been occupying his mind. . . . It also stimulated him to a profounder conception of the use to which he might put the material he was gathering. Might there not be such a work as a human Cosmos?" (*Life and Letters,* I, 327.)
⁴ Letter to G. H. Boker, *ibid.,* I, 334.
⁵ November 9, 1860. See R. C. Beatty, *Bayard Taylor: Laureate of the Gilded Age* (Norman: University of Oklahoma Press, 1936), p. 152. Beatty points out the anticipation of Taine, but it should be noted that the idea was not new, having been developed by Buckle, Humboldt, Herder, and no doubt others.
⁶ "Literature, Art, and Science Abroad." In June, 1870, he mentioned with varying degrees of brevity A. R. Wallace's *Contributions to the Theory of Natural Selection* and Büchner's *Position of Man in Nature, Six Lectures on Darwin's Theory,* and *Force and Matter.*
⁷ A. H. Smyth, *Bayard Taylor* (Boston: Houghton, Mifflin & Co., 1896), p. 231.
⁸ *The Dramatic Works of Bayard Taylor,* ed. Marie Hansen-Taylor (Boston: Houghton, Mifflin & Co., 1880), p. 170.
⁹ *Ibid.,* p. 203.
¹⁰ *Atlantic Monthly,* XXXIX (February, 1877), 197. For Darwin's discussion see *Descent of Man* (2nd ed.; New York: D. Appleton & Co., 1917), chap. iv.
¹¹ *The Poetical Works of Bayard Taylor* (Household Edition; Boston: Houghton Mifflin Co., n. d.), pp. 17-18. Apparently similar to this was

his unpublished Harvard Phi Beta Kappa poem, "The American Legend." See *Life and Letters*, I, 173.

[12] *Poetical Works*, pp. 39-42. Pertinent also are "The Pine Forest of Monterey," dated 1849 (*ibid.*, pp. 21-23), with its sense of vast, slow changes in nature, and "The Summer Camp," dated 1851 (*ibid.*, p. 25), with its sense of the stream of time.

[13] J. D. Haney, *Lessing's Education of the Human Race*, Columbia University Contributions to Education, Teacher's College Series, No. 20 (New York: Teachers College, 1908), p. 3.

[14] March 5, 1872. *Life and Letters*, II, 575.

[15] *Dramatic Works*, p. 183.

[16] *Ibid.*, p. 188.

[17] *Life and Letters of E. C. Stedman*, ed. Stedman and Gould (New York: Moffat, Yard & Co., 1910), I, 458-59.

[18] *Dramatic Works*, pp. 188-89.

[19] *Studies in German Literature*, p. 261.

[20] Down to Moody's *The Fire-Bringer* (1904), which will be considered in a later chapter, the following writers dealt with the Prometheus theme in some way: Bridges, Browning, Byron, Hartley Coleridge, Goethe, Herder, Home, Hugo, Keats, Landor, Longfellow, Lowell, Monti, Percival, Quinet, Ruskin, Schlegel, Shelley, Simcox, Stickney, Thoreau. (See G. E. Woodberry, "The Titan Myth," *The Torch* [New York: Harcourt, Brace & Howe, 1920], pp. 57-109), and J. C. Bailey, "Prometheus in Poetry" (*The Continuity of Letters* [Oxford: The Clarendon Press, 1923], pp. 103-38).

[21] *Dramatic Works*, p. 219.

[22] *Ibid.*, p. 224.

[23] *Ibid.*, p. 233.

[24] *Ibid.*, p. 254.

[25] *Ibid.*, p. 259.

[26] *Ibid.*, p. 220.

[27] *Ibid.*, p. 338.

[28] *Ibid.*, p. 286.

[29] *Ibid.*, p. 287.

[30] *Ibid.*, p. 293.

[31] Taylor often expressed the opinion that spirit had been over-emphasized at the expense of the body. See the lecture, "The Animal Man" (Beatty, p. 149; *Life and Letters*, I, 197).

[32] *Dramatic Works*, p. 321. On the inscription see *Life and Letters*, II, 717.

[33] *Bayard Taylor*, p. 256.

[34] *Dramatic Works*, p. 299.

[35] *Life and Letters*, II, 717.

[36] Edwin Mims, *Sidney Lanier* (Boston: Houghton Mifflin Co., 1905), pp. 314-15.

[37] Aubrey H. Starke, *Sidney Lanier: A Biographical and Critical Study* (Chapel Hill: University of North Carolina Press, 1933), p. 301.

[38] Mims, *op. cit.*, p. 313. There are many amiable references to Darwin in Lanier's writing; e. g., "our own grave and patient Charles Darwin." (*The English Novel* [New York: Charles Scribner's Sons, 1903], p. 191.)

[39] Starke (*op. cit.*, p. 39) expresses the belief that Lanier's early ambition was, like Woodrow, to study in Germany and teach natural science. Lanier told an acquaintance in the closing weeks of his life: "I am more indebted to Dr. Woodrow than to any living man for shaping my mental attitude towards nature and life." (See Marion W. Woodrow, *Dr. James Woodrow*

[Columbia, S. C.: R. L. Bryan Co., 1909], p. 12.)

[40] Quoted by Starke, *op. cit.*, pp. 97-98.
[41] *The English Novel*, p. 30.
[42] *Ibid.*, p. 45.
[43] *Ibid.*, p. 49. An excellent brief survey of Lanier's relation to science is Philip Graham's "Lanier and Science," *American Literature*, IV (November, 1932), 288-92.
[44] *The English Novel*, p. 49.
[45] *The Poems of Sidney Lanier*, ed. Mary Day Lanier (New York: Charles Scribner's Sons, 1912), p. 77.
[46] *Ibid.*, p. 41.
[47] *Ibid.*, p. 27.
[48] *Ibid.*, p. 63.
[49] *The English Novel*, p. 299.
[50] *Ibid.*, p. 5.
[51] *Atlantic Monthly*, LVII (January, 1881), 75-84.
[52] *The English Novel*, p. 6.
[53] *Poems*, pp. 31-32.
[54] *Ibid.*, p. 145.
[55] *Ibid.*, p. 12.
[56] June 15, 1880, in Starke, *op. cit.*, pp. 397-98.
[57] *The English Novel*, p. 73.
[58] *Ibid.*, p. 30.
[59] *Ibid.*, p. 5.
[60] *Retrospects and Prospects* (2nd ed.; New York: Charles Scribner's Sons, 1899), p. 6. For a vigorous arraignment of this conception and all that it implies, see R. P. Warren, "The Blind Poet: Sidney Lanier," *American Review*, II (November, 1933), 27-45.
[61] *Retrospects and Prospects*, pp. 7-8.
[62] *The English Novel*, pp. 139-40.
[63] *Shakspere and His Forerunners* (New York: Doubleday, Page & Co., 1902), I, 54.
[64] *Ibid.*, p. 72.
[65] *Music and Poetry* (New York: Charles Scribner's Sons, 1898), pp. 70-71.
[66] *The English Novel*, p. 141.
[67] John Watson, *Schelling's Transcendental Idealism* (2nd ed.; Chicago: S. C. Griggs & Co., 1892), p. 96. As in earlier reference, I do not assert a direct influence of Schelling but use him only as a developed type and fountain-head of philosophical ideas common in this study. Besides Emerson and Coleridge, Lanier could have felt the indirect influence of Schelling through Novalis, in whom he displayed an interest as early as *Tiger-Lilies*. See Starke, *op. cit., passim,* and Philip Graham, "Lanier's Reading," *University of Texas Studies in English*, No. 11 (September 1, 1931), pp. 63-89.
[68] Quoted by Starke, *op. cit.*, p. 209.
[69] *Shakspere and His Forerunners*, II, 328; *The Science of English Verse* (New York: Charles Scribner's Sons, 1880), p. 249.
[70] *Ibid.*, pp. 248-50.
[71] It was in this aesthetic interpretation that the cosmic optimism of Lanier differed most pronouncedly from that of Whitman, to which it otherwise bore a general family resemblance. Whitman could only have been revolted by Lanier's conception of evolution as a process of gentling, a progressive displacement of sense by soul, particularly when the latter was

thought of in terms of a "dainty-fingered maiden of sixteen."
⁷² *Poems,* p. 51.
⁷³ *Ibid.,* pp. 19-22.
⁷⁴ Cf. Poe, above, and Moody, below.
⁷⁵ *Poems,* pp. 114-15.

CHAPTER IX

HOLMES

¹ *Main Currents in American Thought* (New York: Harcourt, Brace & Co., 1927), II, 455.
² *Major American Poets* (New York: American Book Co., 1936), p. 888. Clark also states that Holmes "appeals to logical science and to Darwinism," p. 889.
³ "The Mechanism of Vital Actions," *North American Review,* LXXXV (July, 1857), 39-77.
⁴ *Ibid.,* p. 67.
⁵ *Ibid.*
⁶ *Ibid.,* pp. 68-72. Compare with Holmes's conception that of Lamarck as presented by Lyell, above, Chapter II, note 66.
⁷ *Ibid.,* pp. 72-74.
⁸ *Ibid.,* p. 71.
⁹ *Ibid.,* p. 72.
¹⁰ *Ibid.,* p. 71.
¹¹ *Ibid.,* p. 73.
¹² *Ibid.,* p. 44.
¹³ *Ibid.,* p. 43.
¹⁴ "We know nothing of matter itself except as a collection of localized forces, points of attraction and repulsion. . . ." (*Ibid.,* p. 50). See also "Mechanism in Thought and Morals," *Works of Oliver Wendell Holmes* (Riverside Edition; Boston: Houghton Mifflin & Co., 1891), VIII, 264a; and see above, pp. 16, 75.
¹⁵ "Our convictions, even without special divine illumination, reveal us to ourselves, not as machines, but as sub-creative centres of intelligence and power." ("The Mechanism of Vital Actions," *op. cit.,* p. 43.)
¹⁶ *Ibid.,* p. 74.
¹⁷ *Ibid.,* pp. 75-76.
¹⁸ *Ibid.,* p. 76.
¹⁹ J. T. Merz, *A History of European Thought in the Nineteenth Century* (London: W. Blackwood & Sons, 1907-12), I, 209.
²⁰ *Ibid.,* pp. 209-10.
²¹ Mentioned many times, but see especially "Some of My Early Teachers," *Works,* IX, 431 ff. On Louis, see Sir William Osler, "The Influence of Louis on American Medicine," *An Alabama Student* (London: Oxford University Press, H. Milford, 1908), pp. 189-210.
²² "The Mechanism of Vital Actions," *op. cit.,* p. 57.
²³ *The Position and Prospects of the Medical Student* (Boston: John Putnam, 1844). References here are to the reprint of the address in *Currents and Counter-Currents in Medical Science, with Other Essays* (Boston: Ticknor & Fields, 1861). The surveys included in the collected works are "Currents and Counter-Currents in Medical Science" (1860), IX, 173-208, and "Border Lines of Knowledge in Some Provinces of Medical Science" (1861), IX, 209-72.

²⁴ *Organic Chemistry in Its Applications to Agriculture and Physiology* (London: Taylor & Walton, 1840). On Liebig see the article devoted to him in *Encyclopedia Britannica,* 11th ed., XVI, 590-92; and Nordenskiold, *History of Biology* (New York: Tudor Publishing Co., 1935), pp. 448-49. Cf. Whitman, above, p. 112.
²⁵ *Animal Chemistry, or Organic Chemistry in Its Application to Physiology and Pathology* (Cambridge: J. Owen; New York: D. Appleton & Co., 1842).
²⁶ *Works,* II, 28.
²⁷ *Currents and Counter-Currents in Medical Science,* p. 288.
²⁸ "The Mechanism of Vital Actions," *op. cit.,* p. 52.
²⁹ *Ibid.,* p. 55.
³⁰ *Ibid.,* p. 54.
³¹ *Ibid.,* p. 63.
³² *Ibid.,* p. 56.
³³ *Ibid.,* p. 64.
³⁴ *Contributions to the Natural History of the United States* (Boston: Little, Brown & Co., 1857), I, 9.
³⁵ "Agassiz's Natural History," *Atlantic Monthly,* I (January, 1858), 320-33.
³⁶ *Ibid.,* p. 333.
³⁷ "The Mechanism of Vital Actions," *op. cit.,* p. 45.
³⁸ *Ibid.,* p. 45.
³⁹ *Ibid.*
⁴⁰ *Ibid.,* p. 46.
⁴¹ *Ibid.,* p. 47.
⁴² Nordenskiold, *op. cit.,* pp. 392-96.
⁴³ *Microscopical Researches into the Accordance in the Structure and Growth of Animals and Plants,* trans. Henry Smith (London: The Sydenham Society, 1847). Abridged reprint in *Classics of Modern Science,* ed. W. S. Knickerbocker (New York: Alfred A. Knopf, 1928), pp. 245-72.
⁴⁴ "Position and Prospects of the Medical Student," *op. cit.,* p. 286.
⁴⁵ *Ibid.,* pp. 286-87.
⁴⁶ Nordenskiold, *op. cit.,* p. 396.
⁴⁷ *Cellular Pathology* (New York: R. M. DeWitt, 1860), which is quoted in "Border Lines of Knowledge in Some Provinces of Medical Science," *Works,* IX, 234.
⁴⁸ *Ibid.,* pp. 233-34.
⁴⁹ J. T. Morse, Jr., *Life and Letters of Oliver Wendell Holmes* (Boston: Houghton, Mifflin & Co., 1896), I, 45.
⁵⁰ *Works,* III, 83.
⁵¹ *Ibid.,* II, 113-14.
⁵² *Ibid.,* III, 180-81.
⁵³ *Life and Letters,* II, 141.
⁵⁴ *Ibid.,* p. 142.
⁵⁵ *Works,* V, 318.
⁵⁶ An excellent account is that of Huxley, "Spontaneous Generation" (1870), *Lay Sermons* (New York: D. Appleton & Co., 1871), pp. 344-78.
⁵⁷ For evidence of the friendship and mutual understanding of these two men see Holmes' eulogy, "Professor Jeffries Wyman," *Atlantic Monthly,* XXXIV (November, 1874), 611 ff.
⁵⁸ "Experiments on Spontaneous Generation," *The American Journal of Science,* XCIV (1867), 152-69.

⁵⁹ *Works,* III, 179.
⁶⁰ *Ibid.,* pp. 177-79.
⁶¹ See above, p. 220.
⁶² *Works,* III, 179-80.
⁶³ "Mechanism in Thought and Morals," *Works,* VIII, 302. See also "Crime and Automatism," *ibid.,* pp. 358-60, and "Jonathan Edwards," *ibid.,* pp. 377-82.
⁶⁴ *The Poet at the Breakfast-Table* in *Works,* III, 268-69.
⁶⁵ *Oliver Wendell Holmes: Representative Selections* (New York: American Book Co., 1939), pp. lii-liii.
⁶⁶ *Works,* VIII, 263-64.
⁶⁷ *Ibid.,* p. 303.
⁶⁸ It should be noted that the science of Holmes' early years tended in general toward dualism rather than monism. Nordenskiold, for example (*op. cit.,* p. 393), writes as follows of views expressed by Schleiden in 1842: "In a purely philosophical connexion he maintains, with Kant, the contrast between subject and object, and consequently also between spiritual and material entities. . . . His 'free-thinking' brought him into dispute with the theologians; at that period the latter were monists, following Hegel, while dualism was upheld by their opponents among the biologists; in Haeckel's time, it will be remembered, just the contrary was the case. . . ." Cf. also Darwin's collaborator, Alfred Russell Wallace, who later departed from the fold in excepting the soul of man from the evolutionary process. See Wallace's *Darwinism* (London: Macmillan & Co., 1889), p. 295.
⁶⁹ *Works,* III, 304-5.
⁷⁰ *Ibid.,* IV, 255.
⁷¹ "Autobiographical Notes," *Life and Letters,* I, 38-39.
⁷² That is, "the higher criticism, which is only another phrase for *honest* criticism," *ibid.,* p. 47.
⁷³ Letter to Harriet Beecher Stowe, c. 1876, *ibid.,* II, 248.
⁷⁴ "Autobiographical Notes," *ibid.,* I, 46.
⁷⁵ B. G. Wilder, "A Sketch of Jeffries Wyman," *Popular Science Monthly,* VI (January, 1875), 358.

CHAPTER X

THE PERSISTENCE OF TELEOLOGY

¹ J. S. Clark, *Life and Letters of John Fiske* (Boston: Houghton Mifflin Co., 1917), II, 261-62.
² *Evolution in Its Relation to Religious Thought* (New York: D. Appleton & Co., 1889), p. 67.
³ *The Complete Writings of James Russell Lowell* (Cambridge: Printed at the Riverside Press, 1904), XVI, 172.
⁴ *The Heart of Burrough's Journals,* ed. Barrus (Boston: Houghton Mifflin Co., 1928), p. 98.
⁵ See above, p. 220.
⁶ *The Poems of Madison Cawein* (Boston: Small, Maynard & Co., 1908), V, 143.
⁷ See above, p. 134.
⁸ *Reason in Art* (New York: Charles Scribner's Sons, 1928), p. 100.
⁹ *Boston Monday Lectures: Biology* (Boston: James R. Osgood & Co., 1877), p. 32.
¹⁰ G. T. W. Patrick, *Introduction to Philosophy* (Boston: Houghton Miff-

lin Co., 1935), pp. 142-43.

[11] *History of Biological Theories* (London: H. Milford, Oxford University Press, 1930), p. 274.

[12] *The Origin of the Fittest,* 1887; quoted in Radl, *op. cit.,* p. 275.

[13] Alfred Weber and R. B. Perry, *History of Philosophy* (New York: Charles Scribner's Sons, 1925), p. 491.

[14] Quoted by Vergilius Ferm in *First Adventures in Philosophy* (New York: Charles Scribner's Sons, 1936), p. 169. Ferm also writes briefly on Trine and Mrs. Eddy on pp. 167-68.

[15] See below, p. 301.

[16] *Philosophy in America* (New York: D. Appleton-Century Co., 1939), p. 492.

[17] An excellent account of this development is to be found in J. H. Muirhead's *The Platonic Tradition in Anglo-Saxon Philosophy* (New York: The Macmillan Co., 1931), pp. 147-73, 307-23.

[18] Quoted by Walter G. Muelder and Laurence Sears in *The Development of American Philosophy* (Boston: Houghton Mifflin Co., 1940), p. 218.

[19] *New England: Indian Summer* (New York: E. P. Dutton & Co., 1940), p. 82n.

[20] "The Genteel Tradition in American Philosophy," *Winds of Doctrine* (New York: Charles Scribner's Sons, 1940), pp. 186-215.

[21] *Ibid.,* p. 189.

[22] *The Spirit of Modern Philosophy* (Boston: Houghton, Mifflin & Co., 1893), pp. 437-39.

[23] *Op. cit.,* p. 189.

[24] *Ibid.,* p. 193.

[25] *Ibid.,* p. 195. Italics supplied.

[26] *The Limits of Evolution and Other Essays* (2nd ed.; New York: The Macmillan Co., 1901).

[27] *Op. cit.,* p. 290.

[28] *Outlines of Cosmic Philosophy* (10th ed.; Boston: Houghton, Mifflin & Co., 1889), II, 402.

[29] *Ibid.,* II, 400.

[30] *Ibid.*

[31] *Ibid.,* I, 181.

[32] "I subsequently saw the need for making such preliminary explanation as is now given in Part I (The Unknowable) *simply for the purpose of guarding myself against the charges of atheism and materialism, which I foresaw would most likely be made in its absence."* (Letter to Fiske, February 2, 1870, quoted by Clark, *Life and Letters of John Fiske,* I, 368). See also Clark's discussion, pp. 370 ff.

[33] *The Destiny of Man Viewed in the Light of His Origin* (8th ed.; Boston: Houghton, Mifflin & Co., 1884), p. 25.

[34] *The Idea of God as Affected by Modern Knowledge* (Boston: Houghton, Mifflin & Co., 1885), pp. xxiii-xxiv.

[35] A possible solution of Fiske's difficulties, in interestingly similar language, is indicated by Santayana: "The entire history and destiny of the universe, if they could be surveyed . . . would make a total dramatic impression which imagination might regard as the moral *reason* (not the antecedent cause) of the whole reality. In the same way, imagination might regard particular parts of the process, such as human choices or human works of art, as *justified* (not produced) by the rightness or beauty or in-

tention discernible in them. Teleology would thus be a sympathetic moral method of appreciating mechanism, and not an alternative natural process." ("Apologia pro mente sua," *The Philosophy of George Santayana,* ed. P. A. Schilpp [Evanston: Northwestern University Press, 1940], p. 510). As long as Fiske continued to hypostatize his Purpose as a Power, however, as in his last sentence, this view was impossible for him; and to do otherwise would have rendered his later philosophical writings meaningless.

[36] *The Miscellaneous Writings of John Fiske* (Boston: Houghton, Mifflin & Co., 1902), I, cxxviii.

CHAPTER XI

SILL AND CERTAIN MINOR POETS

[1] See above, p. 148.

[2] *The Poetical Works of Edward Rowland Sill* (Household Edition; Boston: Houghton, Mifflin & Co., 1906), p. 52. The poem is grouped by the editor with others written between 1862 and 1867, but the lines on Lincoln and the references to California make it possible to narrow the range of probable dating, placing it between the assassination of Lincoln in April, 1865, and Sill's departure from California in the autumn of 1866.

[3] P. H. Boynton, "Theodore Dreiser," *Some Contemporary Americans* (Chicago: University of Chicago Press, 1924), p. 139.

[4] Quoted by W. B. Parker in *Edward Rowland Sill, His Life and Work* (Boston: Houghton Mifflin Co., 1915), p. 27.

[5] *Poetical Works,* pp. 3-4.

[6] *Ibid.,* pp. 1-2.

[7] "Midnight," *ibid.,* pp. 6-7. The same question and answer are repeated in "Evening," presumably written later, *ibid.,* pp. 125-26.

[8] July, 1862; Parker, *op. cit.,* pp. 55-56.

[9] *Ibid.,* p. 76.

[10] *Ibid.,* p. 77.

[11] *Ibid.,* p. 73.

[12] *Ibid.,* p. 88.

[13] *Ibid.,* p. 253.

[14] June 9, 1885. Sill wrote Aldrich asking that remarks in this tenor be stricken from an article, "The XIXth Century," which he had submitted to the *Atlantic Monthly* (*ibid.,* p. 254).

[15] Letter to Henry Holt, November 18, 1885. *Ibid.,* p. 256.

[16] *Ibid.,* p. 255.

[17] *Ibid.,* pp. 134-35. It should be noted that Sill experienced some discomfiture as a result of what was regarded as irreligion in his teaching (*ibid.,* pp. 177, 241).

[18] *Ibid.,* pp. 66-67.

[19] *Ibid.,* p. 71.

[20] *Ibid.,* p. 26.

[21] Others will be found in *ibid.,* pp. 192, 262-63, and 152-53.

[22] *Ibid.,* pp. 179-80.

[23] *The Prose of Edward Rowland Sill* (Boston: Houghton, Mifflin & Co., 1900), p. 201.

[24] "Herbert Spencer's Theory of Education," *Atlantic Monthly,* LI (February, 1883), 171, note 1.

[25] *Essays on Education and Kindred Subjects* (Everyman's Library edition; New York: E. P. Dutton & Co., 1911), pp. 6-7.

[26] See Parker, *op. cit.*, pp. 25, 32.
[27] *Poetical Works*, pp. 74-108.
[28] *Ibid.*, p. 133.
[29] *Atlantic Monthly*, LVI (November, 1885), 667.
[30] *Ibid.*, pp. 669-70.
[31] See *Principles of Psychology* (New York: D. Appleton & Co., 1910), Part IX, chap. ix.
[32] *Principles of Ethics* (New York: D. Appleton & Co., 1892-93), pp. 523-31. Though Part I, *The Data of Ethics*, appeared in 1879 and was much admired by Sill, the work was not completed until 1893, six years after Sill's death.
[33] *Essays on Education*, p. 32.
[34] "Herbert Spencer's Theory of Education," *op. cit.*, p. 175.
[35] To be strictly accurate, Spencer went beyond this, reasoning that survival is good because life is good and life is good because it is pleasant. Thus he was a hedonist, which many evolutionary ethical theorists were not. See R. B. Perry, *The Present Conflict of Ideals* (New York: Longmans, Green & Co., 1918), p. 124. But see also the statement from *The Data of Ethics* quoted at the end of this paragraph.
[36] *Op. cit.*, p. 220.
[37] *The Data of Ethics* (New York: D. Appleton & Co., 1894), p. 25.
[38] *Op. cit.*, p. 221.
[39] *Ibid.*, p. 202.
[40] See above, p. 254.
[41] "The Prose and Verse of Ralph Waldo Emerson," *The Overland Monthly*, IV, 2nd series (October, 1884), 439.
[42] *Ibid.*, p. 440.
[43] *Ibid.*, p. 439.
[44] *Ibid.*, p. 442.
[45] *Poetical Works*, pp. 362-63.
[46] "The Prose and Verse of Ralph Waldo Emerson," *op. cit.*, p. 439.
[47] *Poetical Works*, p. 225.
[48] *Op. cit.*, p. 440.
[49] See below, p. 340.
[50] Hence the title, "Man, the Spirit," and the words (*Poetical Works*, p. 54):

> it is still the man,
> The individual spirit, something far
> Beyond earth's chemistry. . . .

Hence also the discontinuity implied in his ethic and his definition of "humanics" (see above, p. 257). Cf. Woodberry, below, pp. 338-39.
[51] For the theological consequences of this principle, see "Blindfold" (*Poetical Works*, p. 383) and "Nature and Her Child" (*ibid.*, p. 242).
[52] See above, p. 174.
[53] See above, p. 244.
[54] *Atlantic Monthly*, XLI (February, 1878), 565-67. *Idyls of Norway and Other Poems* (New York: Charles Scribner's Sons, 1882), pp. 124-28. *Popular Science Monthly*, XXIII (June, 1883), 237-39.
[55] *Change: The Whisper of the Sphinx* (Philadelphia: J. B. Lippincott & Co., 1879). Revised as *The Whisperings of the Sphinx* (Chicago: R. R. Donnelly & Sons Co., 1906). Another poem by Leighton dealing with evolution is "The Birth of Beauty," *A Scrap-Book of Pictures and Fancies*

(Chicago: R. R. Donnelly & Sons Co., 1906), pp. 137-42.
[56] 1879, II, 13; 1906, II, 16.
[57] 1879, II, 14; 1906, II, 17.
[58] 1879, V, 45; 1906, V, 40.
[59] 1879, V, 46-47; 1906, V, 41.
[60] 1879, VIII, 62; 1906, VIII, 54-55.
[61] 1879, X, 80; 1906, X, 69.
[62] 1879, XII, 94; 1906, XII, 79. Titles were given to the sections only in the 1906 edition.
[63] 1879, XII, 94, 89; 1906, XIII, 82, 80.
[64] 1906, XI.
[65] 1906, X, 70.
[66] 1879, XVII, 138; 1906, XIX, 111.
[67] 1906, XIX, 112.
[68] 1879, XIII, 99; 1906, XVI, 91.
[69] 1879, XII, 93; 1906, XII, 78.
[70] 1879, XIII, 104; 1906, XVII, 96.
[71] *Ibid.*
[72] *Ibid.*
[73] 1879, XIII, 105; 1906, XVII, 97.
[74] 1879, XVIII, 142; 1906, XX, 115.
[75] *The Vision of Esther* (New York: D. Appleton & Co., 1882), p. viii.
[76] *The Vision of Nimrod* (New York: D. Appleton & Co., 1881), "The Tarn of Kaf," pp. 55-84.
[77] *Agnosticism and Other Essays* (New York: Belford, Clarke & Co., 1889).
[78] "Cameos VI. Herbert Spencer," *Fantasy and Passion* (Boston: Roberts Bros., 1878), p. 189.
[79] "Individuality," *ibid.*, p. 111.
[80] "Albert F. Webster, Jr. (Died at Sea, December 27, 1876)," *ibid.*, pp. 136-37.
[81] "Conception," *ibid.*, p. 114.
[82] "Memorial Verses: To Courtland Palmer," *Songs of Doubt and Dream* (New York: Funk and Wagnalls Co., 1891), pp. 48-50.
[83] *Ibid.*, pp. 309-11.
[84] *Ibid.*, pp. 240-41.
[85] *Ibid.*, p. 240.
[86] *Ibid.*
[87] *Ibid.*, pp. 240-41.
[88] *Ibid.*, p. 311.
[89] "The Republic," *Song and Story* (Boston: J. R. Osgood & Co., 1884), pp. 51-64.
[90] *Romance and Revery* (Boston: Ticknor & Co., 1886), p. 145.
[91] "The Dying Archangel," *ibid.*, pp. 62-66.
[92] *Ibid.*, p. 65.
[93] *Songs of Doubt and Dream*, pp. 51-60.
[94] *Ibid.*, p. 51.
[95] *Ibid.*, p. 54.
[96] *Ibid.*, p. 55.
[97] *Ibid.*, p. 52.
[98] *Monte Rosa: The Epic of an Alp* (Boston: Houghton, Mifflin & Co., 1883).
[99] *Ibid.*, pp. 9-10.

[100] *Ibid.*, Book II, chap. iii.
[101] *Ibid.*, p. 107.
[102] *Ibid.*, pp. 116-17.
[103] *Evolution: Popular Lectures and Discussions before the Brooklyn Ethical Association* (Boston: J. H. West, 1889), pp. 343-66.
[104] *The Breath of the World* (New York: G. P. Putnam's Sons, 1908), pp. 25-26.
[105] "Materialism," *ibid.*, p. 126.
[106] *Ibid.*, p. 37.
[107] "Evolution's Orchestra," *ibid.*, p. 37.
[108] *Ibid.*, p. 42.
[109] *Ibid.*, p. 43.
[110] "Brain," *ibid.*, p. 38.
[111] *Ibid.*, p. 42.
[112] *Ibid.*, p. 41.
[113] *Ibid.*
[114] "The Radical," *ibid.*, p. 39.
[115] "The Tale of Years," *ibid.*, p. 39.

CHAPTER XII

STEDMAN, GILDER, AND CAWEIN

[1] "Milton," *Critical and Historical Essays* (Everyman's Library edition; New York: E. P. Dutton & Co., 1907), I, 153.
[2] *The Nature and Elements of Poetry* (Boston: Houghton, Mifflin & Co., 1892), pp. 32-33.
[3] *Poets of America* (Boston: Houghton, Mifflin & Co., 1885), pp. 153-55. The same criticism is applicable to his praise of Poe (p. 262) and Whitman (p. 382) for their scientific "prescience." See also his criticism of Bryant (p. 69) for his "lack of scientific vision."
[4] *Victorian Poets* (Boston: Houghton, Mifflin & Co., n. d.), p. 17.
[5] *Nature and Elements of Poetry*, p. 37.
[6] *Ibid.*, p. 250. See also p. 296.
[7] See below, p. 280.
[8] "Victorian Poets," *Scribner's Monthly*, V (January, 1873), 364. Later incorporated in the first chapter of *Victorian Poets* (pp. 31-32), of which he said: "A chapter which I devoted to it [the relation of science and poetry] in 1874 was almost the first extended consideration that it received." (*Nature and Elements,* p. 33). Nearly fifty years before, however, Bryant had considered it at some length in his lecture "On Poetry in Its Relation to Our Age and Country," taking a position opposite to that which Macaulay was to take four months later.
[9] Laura Stedman and G. M. Gould, *Life and Letters of Edmund Clarence Stedman* (New York: Moffat, Yard & Co., 1910), II, 538.
[10] "Mater Coronata," *Poems of Edmund Clarence Stedman* (Boston: Houghton Mifflin Co., 1908), p. 146.
[11] *Nature and Elements*, p. 37.
[12] *Life and Letters,* II, 585-86.
[13] Pp. 256-57. Cf. James McCosh, *The Religious Aspect of Evolution* (New York: Charles Scribner's Sons, 1890), p. 8: "In the geological development I am privileged as it were to enter God's workshop and see his modes of operation, and the result reached so full of provisions in bones,

muscles, joints, for the good of the creature." Stedman corresponded with McCosh and in one case suggested a reservation to what will be said below. Apropos of his "Corda Concordia" he wrote: "Let me add that the poem read at Concord does not connect me with the down-East philosophy." (*Life and Letters,* II, 299). It must be added, however, that the reservation was extremely mild and in itself typically "transcendental": "But I am not a transcendentalist, so far as one man's transcendentalism is held to be a guide for others. I hold, with every true poet, that a man's 'inner light' is a guide for himself, but that any attempt to found a system upon it must fail." (*Ibid.*)

[14] *Poems,* pp. 456-57.
[15] *Nature and Elements,* p. 291.
[16] *Poems,* p. 457.
[17] *Ibid.,* p. 458. Italics supplied.
[18] *Life and Letters,* II, 579.
[19] *Ibid.,* II, 168.
[20] See, for example, "The Watchman on the Tower," *Poems of Richard Watson Gilder* (Boston: Houghton Mifflin Co., 1908), pp. 422-24.
[21] *Ibid.,* p. 47.
[22] *Ibid.,* p. 369.
[23] *Ibid.,* pp. 55-57.
[24] *The Riddle of the Universe* (New York: Harper & Bros., 1900), p. 224.
[25] "Mors Triumphalis," *Poems,* p. 47.
[26] "Non sine Dolore," *ibid.,* p. 183.
[27] "The Soul," *ibid.,* p. 61.
[28] *Ibid.,* pp. 368-69.
[29] *Ibid.,* pp. 174-75.
[30] *The Nature and Elements of Poetry,* p. 257.
[31] "A Midsummer Meditation," *Poems,* p. 175.
[32] "The Invisible," *ibid.,* p. 369.
[33] *Ibid.,* p. 48.
[34] See Royce, *The Spirit of Modern Philosophy* (Boston: Houghton, Mifflin & Co., 1892), pp. 448-54.
[35] *Ibid.,* p. 459.
[36] *Poems,* p. 48.
[37] "Non sine Dolore," *ibid.,* pp. 183-84. Italics supplied.
[38] *The Spirit of Modern Philosophy,* p. 470.
[39] *Poems,* p. 52.
[40] *Poems* (Boston: Small, Maynard & Co., 1908), V, 38-39.
[41] *Ibid.,* V, 3.
[42] See above, p. 45.
[43] "Intimations of the Beautiful," *Poems,* V, 42.
[44] *Ibid.,* V, 10.
[45] See above, p. 235.
[46] *Poems,* V, 11.
[47] "Fulfillment," *ibid.,* III, 237.
[48] *Ibid.,* V, 40.
[49] "Deity," *ibid.,* V, 142-43.
[50] *Ibid.,* V, 10-11.
[51] See above, pp. 9-10.
[52] See above, p. 50.

CHAPTER XIII

HOVEY, LODGE, AND MOODY

[1] "The 'Nature' Revival in Literature," *The Complete Edition of Frank Norris* (Garden City: Doubleday, Doran & Co., 1928), VII, 108.
[2] Quoted in Hartwick, *The Foreground of American Fiction* (New York: American Book Co., 1934), p. 45.
[3] *Songs from Vagabondia* (7th ed.; Boston: Small, Maynard & Co., 1903), p. 1.
[4] "The Call of the Bugles," *Along the Trail* (3rd ed.; Boston: Small, Maynard & Co., 1903), p. 15.
[5] "Peace," *Last Songs from Vagabondia* (3rd ed.; Boston: Small, Maynard & Co., 1903), p. 74.
[6] "America," *Along the Trail*, p. 17.
[7] "Accident in Art," *More Songs from Vagabondia* (5th ed.; Small, Maynard & Co., 1903), p. 71.
[8] "A View of Parnassus," *To the End of the Trail*, ed., with notes, by Mrs. Hovey (New York: Duffield & Co., 1908), p. 30.
[9] "America," *loc. cit.*
[10] *Along the Trail*, p. 17.
[11] *American Poetry* (New York: Charles Scribner's Sons, 1918), p. 689.
[12] *The Holy Graal and Other Fragments*, ed., with introduction and notes, by Mrs. Hovey (New York: Duffield & Co., 1907), p. 86.
[13] *The Spirit of Modern Philosophy* (Boston: Houghton, Mifflin & Co., 1892), p. 213. For Hegel's use of a term rendered by the same English word see *Philosophy of History*, trans. J. Sibree (New York: The Colonial Press, 1900), p. 23.
[14] *Op. cit.*, p. 214.
[15] See above, p. 289.
[16] *Along the Trail*, p. 99.
[17] *Op. cit.*, p. 23. See also p. 15.
[18] "Quatrains," *Last Songs from Vagabondia*, p. 78.
[19] Cf. Hegel, *op. cit.*, p. 457: "That the History of the World, with all the changing scenes which its annals present, is this process of development and the realization of the Spirit—this is the true *Theodicaea*, the justification of God in History. Only *this* insight can reconcile Spirit with the History of the World—viz., that what has happened, and is happening every day, is not only 'without God,' but is essentially His Work."
[20] *Along the Trail*, p. 100.
[21] *To the End of the Trail*, p. 15.
[22] See above, pp. 205 ff.
[23] "The Laurel," *op. cit.*, p. 11.
[24] See Odell Shepard, *Bliss Carman* (Toronto: McClelland & Stewart, 1923).
[25] Quoted by L. Brough, "Delsarte and Delsartism," *Encyclopedia and Dictionary of Education*, ed. Foster Watson, I, 445.
[26] Quoted in "Delsarte," *Cyclopedia of Education*, ed. Paul Monroe, II, 291.
[27] *The Making of Personality* (Boston: L. C. Page & Co., 1908), pp. v-vi. Cf. pp. 2-3: "Under the stress of divine evolutionary impulse, we wish to disentangle personality from the crushing monotony of mere circumstantial mechanical existence. Man is not willing to remain an automaton,

but must somehow achieve and vindicate an individual selfhood. We feel sure that it is to this end that we were created, and to this end surely all progress is seen to be tending. The seed of the gods, sown in the dust of the ground, exerts its infinitesimal but mighty force to break from the enveloping darkness and put forth at last the perfect-long-awaited flower of mankind."

[28] *The Holy Graal*, pp. 86-87.
[29] *Ibid.*, p. 23.
[30] *Ibid.*, pp. 127-28.
[31] *Ibid.*
[32] *The Quest of Merlin* (Boston: Small, Maynard & Co., 1898), p. 64.
[33] *Taliesin* (Boston: Small, Maynard & Co., 1907), p. 50.
[34] *Ibid.*, pp. 51-52.
[35] *Ibid.*, p. 57.
[36] *New England: Indian Summer* (New York: E. P. Dutton & Co., 1940), p. 433.
[37] *Ibid.*, p. 409.
[38] "A Song for Revolution," *The Poems and Dramas of George Cabot Lodge* (Boston: Houghton Mifflin Co., 1911), I, 137.
[39] "The Song of Man," *ibid.*, I, 225.
[40] "Egypt," *ibid.*, II, 23.
[41] *Poems 1899-1902*, 1902. In *Poems and Dramas*, I, 227.
[42] *Poems and Dramas*, I, 252.
[43] *Ibid.*, pp. 252-57.
[44] *Ibid.*, p. 338.
[45] *Poems and Dramas*, II, 407-13.
[46] "The Method of Nature," *Complete Works* (Centenary Edition; Boston: Houghton Mifflin Co., 1903-4), I, 198.
[47] That is, they are in long lines of triple meter with a decidedly Whitmanian swing. The influence of Whitman on the young Lodge seems to have been considerable. *Poems 1899-1902* is dedicated to him, and its initial poem is "To W. W." The following lines from "The Passage" in the same volume reveal the similarity better than any exposition could do:

    And the bonds of allegiance that fetter the spirit, the
        oaths of obedience sworn in the past,
    Shall be words of the lesson of life we inherit, embraced,
        understood, superseded at last.
    We are done with the Gods of our old adoration, we acknowledge
        they served in their turn and were fair,
    But we go, for behold! after long preparation what no man
        has dared to discover we dare!
        Till the Body and Soul and all time
            Shall be blended,
        Aspiration and virtue and crime
            Comprehended,
    We must fathom the sense and the spirit till we stand
        self-possessed of the whole,
    Onward ever and outward ever, over the uttermost verge of the
        soul!

[48] The chapters on Hegel and Schopenhauer had also appeared in the *Atlantic Monthly*. See the Preface to the work, p. xii.
[49] The doctrine of which is that "the universe is the Brahman but the Brahman is the Atman"—that is, that "the world is God and God is the

soul." Arthur Christy, *The Orient in American Transcendentalism* (New York: Columbia University Press, 1932), p. 20.

[50] *Poems and Dramas,* I, 63-65.
[51] *Ibid.,* II, 5.
[52] "The Soul's Inheritance," *ibid.,* II, 92.
[53] *Op. cit.,* p. 447.
[54] *Life of George Cabot Lodge* (Boston: Houghton Mifflin Co., 1911), p. 109.
[55] I do not mean to suggest that Adams believed he did. Adams continues: "Thus the sole tragic action of humanity is the Ego,—the Me,—always maddened by the necessity of self-sacrifice, the superhuman effort of lifting himself and the universe by sacrifice, and, of course, by destroying the attachments which are most vital, in order to attain. . . . All Saviors . . . were insane, because their problem was self-contradictory, and because, in order to raise the universe in oneself to its highest power, its negative powers must be paralyzed or destroyed. In reality, nothing was destroyed; only the Will—or what we now call Energy—was freed and perfected." This goes considerably beyond Schopenhauer.
[56] *Poems and Dramas,* p. 333.
[57] *Poems and Dramas,* II, 411.
[58] *The Spirit of Modern Philosophy,* pp. 262-64.
[59] *Poems and Dramas,* II, 407-8.
[60] *Ibid.,* II, 453-55.
[61] Royce, *op. cit.,* p. 215.
[62] See above, p. 308.
[63] *Poems and Dramas,* II, 159.
[64] *Ibid.,* I, 292.
[65] *Ibid.,* II, 91.
[66] *Ibid.,* I, 280.
[67] *Ibid.,* II, 413.
[68] "A Free Man's Worship," *Mysticism and Logic* (New York: W. W. Norton & Co., 1929), p. 47.
[69] *Some Letters of William Vaughn Moody,* ed. Daniel Gregory Mason (Boston: Houghton Mifflin Co., 1913), p. 131.
[70] *Poems and Plays of William Vaughn Moody,* ed. J. M. Manley (Boston: Houghton Mifflin Co., 1912), I, 355-56.
[71] *Ibid.,* pp. 281-82.
[72] "Road-Hymn for the Start," *ibid.,* p. 14.
[73] *Ibid.,* p. 366.
[74] Robert Morss Lovett in the Introduction to *Selected Poems of William Vaughn Moody* (Boston: Houghton Mifflin Co., 1931), p. lxxxii.
[75] "Second Coming," *Poems and Plays,* I, 119-20.
[76] *Ibid.,* p. 282.
[77] *Ibid.,* p. 279.
[78] *Ibid.,* p. 359.
[79] *Ibid.,* p. 390.
[80] *Enchiridion,* chap. xiii, in *Readings in Philosophy,* ed. A. E. Avey (New York: D. Appleton & Co., 1924), p. 205.
[81] *The Spirit of Modern Philosophy,* p. 211.
[82] *Poems and Plays,* I, 391.
[83] *Ibid.,* p. 359. For a suggestive use of the same image in *The Fire-Bringer,* see *ibid.,* p. 247.

[84] *The Present Conflict of Ideals* (New York: Longmans, Green & Co., 1918), p. 247.
[85] *Poems and Plays,* I, 292.
[86] *Ibid.,* pp. 188, 203.
[87] *Ibid.,* p. 198.
[88] *Ibid.,* p. 245.
[89] *University of Chicago Record,* July, 1927; quoted by D. D. Henry in *William Vaughn Moody, a Study* (Boston: B. Humphries, Inc., 1934), p. 92.
[90] *Poems and Plays,* I, 140.
[91] *Ibid.,* p. 283.
[92] *Ibid.,* p. 358.
[93] *Ibid.,* pp. 382-83.
[94] *Ibid.,* pp. 340-42.
[95] *Ibid.,* p. 258.
[96] *Ibid.,* p. 262.
[97] *Ibid.,* p. 279.
[98] *Ibid.,* p. 276.
[99] "I stood within the heart of God," *ibid.,* pp. 267-68.
[100] Arthur H. Quinn, *A History of the American Drama from the Civil War to the Present Day* (New York: Harper & Bros., 1927), II, 10.
[101] *Poems and Plays,* I, 359.
[102] *Some Letters,* p. 97. Italics supplied.
[103] *Letters to Harriet by William Vaughn Moody,* ed. Percy Mackaye (Boston: Houghton Mifflin Co., 1935), p. 352.
[104] *Poems and Plays,* II, 333.
[105] *Ibid.,* II, 165-66.
[106] For Moody's attitude toward the cruder sort of Darwinism, see Matthew's business after Martha leaves the stage early in Act I of *The Faith-Healer, ibid.,* II, 179.
[107] *Ibid.,* I, 65.
[108] *Ibid.,* pp. 65-66.
[109] *Ibid.,* pp. 66-67.
[110] *Ibid.,* p. 13.
[111] *Ibid.,* p. 5.
[112] *Ibid.,* p. 57.
[113] *Ibid.,* I, 58.
[114] *Ibid.,* p. 343.
[115] "Song-Flower and Poppy," *ibid.,* p. 90.

CHAPTER XIV

SOME NEW TURNS OF THOUGHT

[1] "The Torch-Bearers' Race," *Roan Stallion, Tamar, and Other Poems* (New York: The Modern Library, 1935), pp. 104-7.
[2] "The Tower Beyond Tragedy," *The Selected Poetry of Robinson Jeffers* (New York: Random House, n. d.), pp. 115-16.
[3] *The Bashful Earthquake* (New York: Charles Scribner's Sons, 1898), printed in frontispiece.
[4] "The Lesson for Today," *A Witness Tree* (New York: Henry Holt & Co., 1942), p. 51.
[5] *Poems Old and New* (Boston: Houghton, Mifflin & Co., 1894), pp. 49-56. See also "The Modern Odyssey," *ibid.,* pp. 28-35.

⁶ *The Works of Stephen Crane,* ed. Wilson Follett (New York: A. A. Knopf, 1926), VI, 56.
⁷ "The Open Boat," *ibid.,* XII, 56.
⁸ *The Collected Poems of Stephen Crane,* ed. Wilson Follett (New York: A. A. Knopf, 1930), pp. 129-30.
⁹ *Works,* VI, 131.
¹⁰ *The Education of Henry Adams* (Riverside Library Edition; Boston: Houghton Mifflin Co., n. d.), p. 289.
¹¹ "Apology for Bad Dreams," *Selected Poetry,* p. 177.
¹² "Roan Stallion," *ibid.,* p. 149.
¹³ Orestes: "I have fallen in love outward." In "The Tower Beyond Tragedy," *ibid.,* p. 139.
¹⁴ *Ibid.,* p. 140:
> But young or old, few years or many, signified
>   less than nothing
> To him who had climbed the tower beyond time, consciously,
>   and cast humanity, entered the earlier fountain.

¹⁵ "Hellenistics," *ibid.,* p. 603.
¹⁶ H. G. Wells, *Mind at the End of Its Tether* (New York: Didier, 1946). See especially p. 30: "The writer sees the world as a jaded world devoid of recuperative power. In the past he has liked to think that Man could pull out of his entanglements and start a new creative phase of human living. In the face of our universal inadequacy, that optimism has given place to a stoical cynicism. . . . Man must go steeply up or down and the odds seem to be all in favour of his going down and out. If he goes up, then so great is the adaptation demanded of him that he must cease to be a man. Ordinary man is at the end of his tether."
¹⁷ The position of Reinhold Niebuhr is particularly interesting here because he defines the philosophic idea of progress in the same sense as that employed in this study: "The guiding principle of the philosophy which underlies the idea of progress is that of an immanent *logos* which is no longer believed to transcend history as an eternal form, but is thought of as operating in history, bringing its chaos gradually under the dominion of reason." (*The Nature and Destiny of Man* [New York: Charles Scribner's Sons, 1943], II, 164). He rejects this philosophy, however: "It assumes that all development means the advancement of the good. It does not recognize that every heightened potency of human existence may also represent a possibility of evil. The symbol for this difference is that in Christian eschatology the *end* of history is both judgment and fulfillment. The modern conception sees the end as only fulfillment." (*Ibid.,* p. 166.)
¹⁸ See Max Eastman, *Marxism: Is It Science?* (New York: W. W. Norton & Co., 1940), p. 15 and *passim.*
¹⁹ "Demeter," *A Day at Castrogiovanni* (Boston: Printed for the Woodberry Society, 1912), p. 24.
²⁰ Spoken by Urania at the end of the second scene of "Agathon." *The North Shore Watch and Other Poems* (Boston: Houghton, Mifflin & Co., 1890), p. 68.
²¹ *The Roamer and Other Poems* (New York: Harcourt, Brace & Howe, 1920). The quotations that follow are from pp. 29-32. According to the Preface, the first two books were written "immediately after the publication of the author's first verse."
²² *Ibid.,* Book IV, p. 140.
²³ Quoted by John Erskine, in *George Edward Woodberry, 1855-1930*:

An Appreciation (New York: The New York Public Library, 1930), p. 3.

[24] "Demeter," *A Day at Castrogiovanni*, p. 26.

[25] *Ibid.*, p. 27.

[26] *Ideal Passion: Sonnets* (New York: Printed for the Woodberry Society, 1917), Sonnet XXIX, p. 37.

[27] See above, p. 31.

[28] *The American State University* (Chapel Hill: University of North Carolina Press, 1937), p. 216.

[29] See above, pp. 259-60.

[30] Quoted by Woodbridge Riley, *American Thought from Puritanism to Pragmatism and Beyond* (New York: Peter Smith, 1941), p. 320.

[31] "The Influence of Darwin on Philosophy," *The Influence of Darwin on Philosophy and Other Essays* (New York: Henry Holt & Co., 1910), pp. 13 f.

[32] *The Will to Believe and Other Essays* (New York: Longmans, Green & Co., 1909), p. 29.

[33] *Ibid.*

[34] *Ibid.*, p. 253.

[35] This is not to deny the influences and continuities running from transcendentalism to pragmatism pointed out by Frederick I. Carpenter and others (see Carpenter, "Points of Comparison between Emerson and William James," *New England Quarterly*, II [July, 1929], 458-74, and "William James and Emerson," *American Literature*, XI [March, 1939], 39-57). Emerson's subjectivist approach to knowledge invited a transition to some form of scepticism or pragmatism as soon as it was believed that the intuitions of the Over-Soul were simply the whisperings of the individual will. There are also important differences, however, as Carpenter carefully recognizes, and for the purposes of this study the differences are more important than the similarities. Justifiably or not, Emerson believed that the essential nature of what is can be known, while the pragmatist holds that our knowledge is never a "transcript of reality" (James, *Pragmatism* [New York: Longmans, Green & Co., 1925], p. 57), but a body of hypotheses that are acceptable or unacceptable according as they prove good or bad for the purposes of life.

[36] See above, p. 258.

[37] *John Jay Chapman and His Letters*, ed. M. A. DeWolfe Howe (Boston: Houghton Mifflin Co., 1937), p. 193.

[38] *Ibid.*, p. 136.

[39] Quoted by John Dewey in *Experience and Nature* (Chicago: Open Court Publishing Co., 1925), pp. 418-19.

[40] *Ibid.*, pp. 33-35. It is worth noting that Dewey denies the validity of the dilemma of Royce's which has played so important a part here (see above, pp. 28 ff.), and therefore rejects both the materialistic and idealistic resolutions of it: "The notion of causal explanation involved in both conceptions implies a breach in the continuity of historic process; the gulf created has then to be bridged by an emission or transfer of force. If one starts with the assumption that mind and matter are two separate things, while the evidence forces one to see that they are connected, one has no option save to attribute the power to make the connection, to carry from one to the other, to one or the other of the two things involved. . . . The eventual has somehow been there from the start, 'implicitly,' 'potentially,' but efficaciously enough to attend to its own realization by using material conditions at every stage. . . . When mind is said to be implicit, involved, latent,

or potential in matter, and subsequent change is asserted to be an affair of making it explicit, evolved, manifest, actual, what happens is that a natural history is first cut arbitrarily and unconsciously in two, and then the severance, is consciously and arbitrarily cancelled. It is simpler not to start by engaging in such manoeuvers." (*Ibid.*, pp. 273-76.)

[41] Santayana makes the point many times, but the most interesting for our purposes is a comment on metaphysical systems in *The Realm of Spirit*: "those pious philosophers do not altogether waste their time studying their fabulous universes: for they are but reversed images of the spiritual life, and the deeper the devotee penetrates into their magic economy the better he learns to know his own heart." (*Realms of Being* [New York: Charles Scribner's Sons, 1942], p. 776.)

[42] See "As Deceivers, Yet True," *Beyond Tragedy* (New York: Charles Scribner's Sons, 1937), pp. 2-24, and *An Interpretation of Christian Ethics* (New York: Harper & Bros., 1935), pp. 26 ff. For the paradoxes mentioned below see *The Nature and Destiny of Man*, I, 1-4.

[43] *Some Imagist Poems, An Anthology* (Boston: Houghton Mifflin Co., 1915), p. vii; quoted in J. W. Beach, *The Concept of Nature in Nineteenth-Century English Poetry* (New York: The Macmillan Co., 1935), p. 550.

[44] *Collected Poems* (New York: Henry Holt & Co., 1939), p. 347.

[45] "The Poet's Next of Kin in a College," talk given at Princeton University, October 26, 1937, printed in the Princeton *Biblia*, IX, No. 1 (February, 1938).

[46] "Education by Poetry: A Meditative Monologue," *Amherst Graduates' Quarterly*, XX (February, 1931), 81.

[47] *Ibid.*

[48] *Ibid.*, p. 78. See also "The Constant Symbol," *The Poems of Robert Frost* (New York: The Modern Library, 1946), p. xvi.

[49] "Education by Poetry," *op. cit.*, p. 81.

[50] *Ibid.*

[51] *Ibid.*, p. 78.

[52] *Ibid.*, pp. 80-81.

[53] Besides "The Bear," quoted above, and "A Star in a Stone-Boat," quoted below, see "Neither Out Far Nor In Deep," "The Secret Sits," "Boeotian," and "The Star-Splitter."

[54] "A Star in a Stone-Boat," *Collected Poems*, pp. 214-15.

[55] I do not mean to suggest any special sympathy for or indebtedness to Santayana. One would guess, in fact, that Frost has little more taste for Santayana than Robinson, who called Santayana "a sophisticated corpse."

[56] "Nature," *Works* (Centenary Edition; Boston: Houghton Mifflin Co., 1903-4), I, 27.

[57] *Ibid.*, pp. 32-34.

[58] "Education by Poetry," *op. cit.*, p. 79.

[59] See "A Line-Storm Song," "Wild Grapes," "Sitting by a Bush in Broad Sunlight," "Trespass," "The Literate Farmer and the Planet Venus," "To an Ancient," and "Etherealizing."

[60] *A Witness Tree* (New York: Henry Holt & Co., 1942), pp. 87-88.

[61] *Collected Poems*, pp. 327-30.

[62] Quoted by Lawrence Thompson in *Fire and Ice: The Art and Thought of Robert Frost* (New York: Henry Holt & Co., 1942), p. 198.

[63] *Ibid.*, p. 199.

[64] Thompson continues in his next sentence: "He speaks as one 'acquainted with the night,' and finds that the moon, as his favorite time-piece, 'pro-

claimed the time was neither wrong nor right.' "
⁶⁵ *Ibid.,* p. 199.
⁶⁶ Quoted by Thompson, p. 207. For other expressions of this pervasive theme see "At Woodward's Gardens," "An Empty Threat," "On a Tree Fallen Across the Road," "There Are Roughly Zones," and "Sand Dunes."
⁶⁷ Quoted by Thompson, *op. cit.,* pp. 188-89.

CHAPTER XV

SOME OF ROBINSON'S CONTEMPORARIES

¹ "Star of Achievement," *Far Quests,* 1912; *The Collected Poems and Plays of Cale Young Rice* (Garden City: Doubleday, Page & Co., 1915), I, 13.
² "Galileo," *Far Quests; Poems and Plays,* I, 127.
³ *At the World's Heart,* 1914; *Poems and Plays,* I, 424.
⁴ "Submarine Mountains," *At the World's Heart; Poems and Plays,* I, 327-28.
⁵ *Nirvana Days,* 1909; *Poems and Plays,* II, 250.
⁶ *Far Quests; Poems and Plays,* I, 58-59.
⁷ *Across Spoon River* (New York: Farrar and Rinehart, 1936), p. 318.
⁸ *Ibid.,* p. 110.
⁹ See, for example, Webster Ford, "Oh, Giant Fate," *Songs and Sonnets* (Chicago: The Rooks Press, 1910), pp. 61-63.
¹⁰ *Songs and Satires* (New York: The Macmillan Co., 1916), pp. 125-29.
¹¹ *Toward the Gulf* (New York: The Macmillan Co., 1918), p. 272.
¹² *Ibid.*
¹³ *Ibid.,* p. 274.
¹⁴ *Ibid.*
¹⁵ *Ibid.*
¹⁶ *Invisible Landscapes* (New York: The Macmillan Co., 1935), p. 52.
¹⁷ "Hymn to the Earth," *ibid.,* p. 11.
¹⁸ "Ultimate Selection," *ibid.,* p. 52.
¹⁹ "Hymn to the Earth," *ibid.,* p. 11.
²⁰ *Ibid.,* p. 12.
²¹ "Ultimate Selection," *ibid.,* p. 54.
²² *Ibid.,* p. 59.
²³ *Ibid.*
²⁴ Santayana, *Reason in Religion* (New York: Charles Scribner's Sons, 1933), p. 170.
²⁵ *The Open Sea* (New York: The Macmillan Co., 1921), p. 300.
²⁶ "Botanical Gardens," *Toward the Gulf,* pp. 287-88.
²⁷ "Hymn to Nature," *Invisible Landscapes,* pp. 46-47.
²⁸ *Realms of Being* (New York: Charles Scribner's Sons, 1942), pp. 355-56.
²⁹ This poem was sung at the Columbian Exposition in 1892 and published several times in that year and the next as well as in *The Difference and Other Poems* (Chicago: Covici-McGee Co., 1924) and *Chosen Poems* (New York: The Macmillan Co., 1935). Not only was its optimism based on local circumstances—national resources, democracy, science—rather than on any cosmic motivation, but it was repudiated by its author in "The Difference," which was printed alongside it in the 1924 volume for purposes of contrast. For comment on the relation of the two poems see the Introduction to *Chosen Poems,* pp. vii-viii.

³⁰ *You and I* (New York: The Macmillan Co., 1914), p. 191.
³¹ *Ibid.*, pp. 192-93.
³² *The New Poetry*, ed. Harriet Monroe and Alice Corbin Henderson (rev. ed.; New York: The Macmillan Co., 1937), p. 411.
³³ *Chosen Poems*, p. 33.
³⁴ *Ibid.*, pp. 201-3.
³⁵ *Ibid.*, p. 215.
³⁶ *A Poet's Life* (New York: The Macmillan Co., 1938), p. 449.
³⁷ *Ibid.*, p. 457. Italics supplied.
³⁸ *Ibid.*, p. 454.
³⁹ John Dewey, *Democracy and Education* (New York: The Macmillan Co., 1916); p. 60.
⁴⁰ Henri Bergson, *Creative Evolution,* trans. Mitchell (New York: Henry Holt & Co., 1911), p. 248.
⁴¹ "The Wonder of It," *You and I,* p. 57.
⁴² "Bergson and Romantic Evolutionism," *University of California Chronicle,* XV (October, 1913), 429-87.
⁴³ Though not fully developed as such at any time, this is a constantly recurring theme in Santayana's writings. See, for example, chap. ii, "The Protestant Heritage," in *Egotism in German Philosophy* (2nd ed.; New York: Charles Scribner's Sons, 1940); pp. 142 ff of "Goethe's *Faust"* in *Three Philosophical Poets* (Cambridge: Harvard University Press, 1944); and pp. 61-64 of his essay on Hamlet in *Obiter Dicta* (New York: Charles Scribner's Sons, 1936).
⁴⁴ See above, pp. 116 ff.
⁴⁵ *Op. cit.,* pp. 456-58. See also Lovejoy's quotation from Schelling in Chapter I above, p. 29.
⁴⁶ See above, pp. 111 ff., 121 ff.
⁴⁷ *The Caged Eagle and Other Poems* (San Francisco: A. M. Robertson, 1916), pp. 102-3.
⁴⁸ *Yosemite* (San Francisco: A. M. Robertson, 1916), pp. 15-16.
⁴⁹ *The Caged Eagle and Other Poems,* p. 93.
⁵⁰ *Ibid.,* p. 97.
⁵¹ *Ibid.,* p. 99.
⁵² *Selected Poems* (New York: Henry Holt & Co., 1923), p. 47.
⁵³ "The Last Monster," *Beyond the Breakers and Other Poems* (San Francisco: A. M. Robertson, 1914), p. 42.
⁵⁴ *The Caged Eagle and Other Poems,* pp. 91-92.
⁵⁵ "The Moth of Time," *The House of Orchids and Other Poems* (San Francisco: A. M. Robertson, 1914), p. 42.
⁵⁶ *The Testimony of the Suns and Other Poems* (San Francisco: W. E. Wood, 1903). The text used here is that of *Selected Poems.*
⁵⁷ *Selected Poems,* p. 195.
⁵⁸ *Ibid.,* p. 196.
⁵⁹ In contrast to his friend Jeffers, Sterling retained enough of the progressive view to hold that the human is genuinely the highest level in the evolutionary series. Rather curiously, he also ascribed the same judgment to Jeffers, writing as follows of the "humanity is the mould to break away from" passage in *Roan Stallion:* "True, perhaps. But that humanity, however imperfect and transcendible, is yet, in its 'still, small music,' alone of import to itself, the flower of those infinities that it apperceives and contemplates. Than Robinson Jeffers, there is no deeper voice in the choir that sings its glories and its shames. Let him not weary of the singing, for hu-

manity is life at its highest, blind in many ways, yet conscious of the suns that are to it but candles 'in houses of death and birth.'" (*Robinson Jeffers: The Man and the Artist* [New York: Boni & Liveright, 1926], p. 40). Note the following statement also, which is reminiscent of *The Testimony of the Suns:* "As to his philosophy of life, it seems to me that he may be classed with the Pantheists, for he identifies himself with all nature, as an atom in the infinite ferment of space. He believes, naturally, in the continued renewal of suns and their attendant planets, but not in individual immortality. . . . He accepts the fact of the tragedy of life, but thinks existence worth the while." (*Ibid.,* p. 14). If Sterling tended to lighten the philosophy of Jeffers, however, Jeffers emphasized the dark side of Sterling's: "His life was troubled and his philosophy involved hopelessness. . . . He lent me once a prose statement of his philosophy, some twenty pages, a condensed *De Natura Rerum,* but the thought, in the actualities of modern science, more grand and desolating than that of Lucretius. He said 'I shall never publish this, it would be bad for many people, it might bring someone to suicide.' He had written it especially for his friend Dreiser, tough old mastodon, who could digest strong medicines. . . ." (*The Carmel Cymbal,* November 24, 1926; reprinted by S. S. Alberts in *A Bibliography of the Works of Robinson Jeffers* [New York: Random House, 1933], pp. 135-36.)

[60] *Selected Poems,* pp. 197-98.
[61] *Ibid.,* p. 207.
[62] *Ibid.*

CHAPTER XVI
ROBINSON

[1] Louis V. Ledoux, "Psychologist of New England," *Saturday Review of Literature,* XII (October 19, 1935), 4.

[2] Letter to Hermann Hagedorn, December 1, 1913. *Selected Letters of Edwin Arlington Robinson,* ed. Ridgley Torrence (New York: The Macmillan Co., 1940), p. 81.

[3] Ledoux, *loc. cit.*

[4] See "Credo," *Collected Poems of Edwin Arlington Robinson* (New York: The Macmillan Co., 1940), p. 94.

[5] "The Altar," *ibid.,* p. 92.

[6] The poem will be found in early editions of Robinson and in H. H. Waggoner's "Edwin Arlington Robinson and the Cosmic Chill," *New England Quarterly,* XIII (March, 1940), 74-75. Since the ideas in the poem are repeated elsewhere, it seems likely that it was rejected for literary rather than philosophical reasons. This is made the more likely by the baldness of statement of the poem, which is foreign to both Robinson's idiom and his way of thinking.

[7] *Collected Poems,* p. 100.

[8] *Ibid.,* p. 102.

[9] *Ibid.,* p. 307.

[10] *Ibid.,* p. 101.

[11] *Op. cit.,* p. 74. The faith expressed in the poem seems to me rather a faith in immortality. See below, pp. 368-69.

[12] "The Optimism Behind Robinson's Tragedies," *American Literature,* X (March, 1938), 19-20.

[13] "In writing *Tristram* I was merely telling a story, using the merest

outline of the old legend. . . . There is no symbolic significance in it, although there is a certain amount in *Merlin* and *Lancelot,* which were suggested by the world war—Camelot representing in a way the going of a world that is now pretty much gone." *Selected Letters,* p. 160. See also *ibid.,* p. 112.

[14] *Op. cit.,* p. 21.
[15] *Collected Poems,* p. 917.
[16] "The Garden of the Nations (1923)," *ibid.,* p. 902.
[17] *Ibid.,* p. 85.
[18] *Selected Letters,* p. 164.
[19] Quoted from Waggoner, *op. cit.,* pp. 74-75.
[20] *Collected Poems,* p. 67.
[21] *Ibid.,* p. 1471.
[22] *Ibid.,* p. 1472.
[23] *Selected Letters,* p. 177.
[24] "Ben Jonson Entertains a Man from Stratford," *Collected Poems,* p. 28. Note the parallel between the image of the insect used by Jonson and that used by Robinson in "The Altar." See above, p. 365.
[25] *Collected Poems,* p. 64.
[26] *Ibid.,* p. 1142.
[27] *Ibid.,* p. 1127.
[28] *Ibid.,* p. 1107.
[29] *Selected Letters,* p. 165.
[30] *Ibid.,* p. 160.
[31] *Ibid.,* p. 164.
[32] Timberlake in *Matthias at the Door. In Collected Poems,* p. 1129.
[33] Laramie in *Cavender's House.* See *ibid.,* p. 972.
[34] "Octaves," *ibid.,* p. 106.
[35] *Ibid.,* p. 1151.
[36] *Selected Letters,* p. 165.
[37] Nancy Evans, "Edwin Arlington Robinson," *Bookman,* LXXV (November, 1932), 680.
[38] *Collected Poems,* p. 1136.
[39] Hermann Hagedorn, *Edwin Arlington Robinson: A Biography* (New York: The Macmillan Co., 1938), p. 94.

BIBLIOGRAPHY

THE complete poetical works of each poet discussed in this book have been examined to secure data for this study. Also, all available books and articles that throw light on each poet's views on evolution have been utilized. Because bibliographical data on works by or about individual poets may be found in the text, it has been deemed appropriate to refer the reader to the relevant chapters for such information. The following bibliography lists only works of general significance in this study.

ADAMS, HENRY. *The Education of Henry Adams: An Autobiography.* Riverside Library Edition. Boston: Houghton Mifflin Co., n. d.
———. *The Tendency of History.* New York: Book League of America, 1929.
AGASSIZ, LOUIS. *Contributions to the Natural History of the United States.* Boston: Little, Brown & Co., 1857.
———. "Evolution and Permanence of Type," *Atlantic Monthly,* XXXIII (January, 1874), 92-101.
———. *Louis Agassiz, His Life and Correspondents,* ed. Elizabeth Cary Agassiz. 2 vols. Boston: Houghton, Mifflin & Co., 1887.
ANDERSON, PAUL RUSSELL, and FISCH, MAX HAROLD, EDS. *Philosophy in America from the Puritans to James, with Representative Selections.* New York: D. Appleton-Century Co., 1939.
BALDWIN, J. M. *Darwin and the Humanities.* Baltimore: Review Publishing Co., 1909.
———. "Darwin and Logic: A Reply to Professor Creighton," *Psychological Review,* XVI (November, 1909), 431-36.
———. "The Influence of Darwin on Theory of Knowledge and Philosophy," *Psychological Review,* XVI (May, 1909), 207-18.
BARZUN, JACQUES. *Darwin, Marx, Wagner: Critique of a Heritage.* Boston: Little, Brown & Co., 1941.
BAVINK, BERNHARD. *The Natural Sciences: An Introduction to the Scientific Philosophy of Today.* New York: The Century Co., 1932.
BEACH, JOSEPH WARREN. *The Concept of Nature in Nineteenth-Century English Poetry.* New York: The Macmillan Co., 1936.
BEARD, CHARLES and MARY. *The Rise of American Civilization.* New York: The Macmillan Co., 1930.
BECKER, CARL L. *The Heavenly City of the Eighteenth-Century Philosophers.* New Haven: Yale University Press, 1932.
BERGSON, HENRI. *Creative Evolution,* tr. Arthur Mitchell. New York: Henry Holt & Co., 1911.
BOAS, GEORGE. "Romantic Philosophy in America." In *Romanticism in America: Papers Contributed to a Symposium Held at the Baltimore Museum of Art, May 13, 14, 15, 1940,* ed. George Boas. Baltimore: The Johns Hopkins University Press, 1940.
BOWEN, FRANCIS. *Modern Philosophy from Descartes to Schopenhauer and Hartmann.* New York: Charles Scribner's Sons, 1906.
BOWERS, DAVID F. "Hegel, Darwin, and the American Tradition." In *Foreign Influences in American Life: Essays and Critical Biographies,* ed. David F. Bowers. Princeton Studies in American Civilization. Princeton: Princeton University Press, 1944.
BOWNE, BORDEN P. *Personalism.* Boston and New York: Houghton Mifflin Co., 1908.
BUCKE, RICHARD MAURICE. *Cosmic Consciousness: A Study in the Evolution of the Human Mind.* New York: E. P. Dutton & Co., 1923.

BURROUGHS, JOHN. *Accepting the Universe.* Boston and New York: Houghton Mifflin Co., 1920.

———. *The Heart of Burroughs's Journals,* ed. Clara Barrus. Boston and New York: Houghton Mifflin Co., 1928.

BURTT, E. A. *The Metaphysical Foundations of Modern Physical Science.* 2nd ed. New York: Harcourt, Brace & Co., 1932.

BURY, J. B. *The Idea of Progress: An Inquiry into Its Origin and Growth.* Introduction by Charles A. Beard. New York: The Macmillan Co., 1932.

BUSHNELL, HORACE. *Nature and the Supernatural as Together Constituting the One System of God.* New York: Charles Scribner & Co., 1870.

CAIRD, EDWARD. *Hegel.* Philadelphia: J. B. Lippincott Co., 1896.

CALKINS, MARY W. *The Persistent Problems of Philosophy: An Introduction to Metaphysics through the Study of Modern Systems.* 5th ed. New York: The Macmillan Co., 1936.

CARGILL, OSCAR. *Intellectual America: Ideas on the March.* New York: The Macmillan Co., 1941.

[CHAMBERS, ROBERT]. *Vestiges of the Natural History of Creation: To Which Is Appended an Article from the North British Review.* 4th ed. from the 3rd London ed. New York: Wiley & Putnam, 1846.

CHRISTY, ARTHUR. *The Orient in American Transcendentalism.* New York: Columbia University Press, 1932.

CLARK, HARRY HAYDEN. *Major American Poets: Selected and Edited, with Chronologies, Bibliographies, and Notes.* New York: American Book Co., 1936.

CLARK, JOHN SPENCER. *The Life and Letters of John Fiske.* 2 vols. Boston and New York: Houghton Mifflin Co., 1917.

CLODD, EDWARD. *Pioneers of Evolution from Thales to Huxley, with an Intermediate Chapter on the Causes of the Arrest of the Movement.* London: Rationalist Press Association, 1896.

COHEN, MORRIS. "Later Philosophy." In *Cambridge History of American Literature,* III, 226-65. New York: The Macmillan Co., 1933.

COLERIDGE, SAMUEL TAYLOR. *The Complete Works, with an Introductory Essay upon His Philosophical and Theological Opinions,* ed. W. G. T. Shedd. 7 vols. New York: Harper & Bros., 1884.

CONGER, G. P. *New Views of Evolution.* New York: The Macmillan Co., 1929.

COOK, JOSEPH. *Boston Monday Lectures: Biology, with Preludes on Current Events.* Boston: James R. Osgood & Co., 1877.

COOKE, G. W. *Unitarianism in America.* Boston: American Unitarian Association, 1910.

COPE, EDWARD DRINKER. *The Origin of the Fittest: Essays on Evolution.* New York: D. Appleton & Co., 1887.

CREIGHTON, J. E. "Darwin and Logic," *Psychological Review,* XVI (May, 1909), 170-87.

CRUM, RALPH B. *Scientific Thought in Poetry.* New York: Columbia University Press, 1931.

CURTI, MERLE. "The Great Mr. Locke, America's Philosopher, 1783-1861," *Huntington Library Bulletin,* XI (1937), 107-51.

———. *The Growth of American Thought.* New York: Harper & Bros., 1943.

DAMPIER, SIR WILLIAM. *A History of Science and Its Relations with Philosophy and Religion.* New York: The Macmillan Co., 1932.

DARWIN, CHARLES. *Darwinism as Stated by Darwin Himself: Characteristic Passages from the Writings of Charles Darwin.* Selected and arranged by Nathan Sheppard. New York: D. Appleton & Co., 1890.

———. *The Descent of Man and Selection in Relation to Sex.* 2nd ed. New York: D. Appleton & Co., 1917.

———. *Life and Letters of Charles Darwin, Including an Autobio-*

BIBLIOGRAPHY 435

graphical Chapter, ed. Francis Darwin. 2 vols. New York: D. Appleton & Co., 1896.
──────. *The Living Thoughts of Darwin,* ed. Julian Huxley. Philadelphia: David McKay Co., 1939.
──────. *More Letters of Charles Darwin,* ed. Francis Darwin and A. C. Seward. 2 vols. New York: D. Appleton & Co., 1903.
──────. *The Origin of Species by Means of Natural Selection, or the Preservation of Favored Races in the Struggle for Life.* 6th ed. New York: P. F. Collier & Son, 1901.
DAWSON, SIR J. WILLIAM. *Modern Ideas of Evolution as Related to Revelation and Science.* 2nd ed. London: The Religious Tract Society, 1890.
DEWEY, JOHN. *Experience and Nature.* Chicago: Open Court Publishing Co., 1925.
──────. *The Influence of Darwin on Philosophy and Other Essays.* New York: Henry Holt & Co., 1910.
──────. *Reconstruction in Philosophy.* New York: Henry Holt & Co., 1920.
DRACHMAN, JULIAN M. *Studies in the Literature of Natural Science.* New York: The Macmillan Co., 1930.
DRAPER, JOHN WILLIAM. *History of the Conflict between Religion and Science.* New York: D. Appleton & Co., 1897.
DRIESCH, HANS. *History and Theory of Vitalism,* tr. C. K. Ogden. London: Macmillan & Co., 1914.
DRUMMOND, HENRY. *The Ascent of Man.* New York: James Pott & Co., 1894.
EKIRCH, ARTHUR A. *The Idea of Progress in America, 1815-60.* Columbia Studies in History, Economics and Public Law, No. 511. New York: Columbia University Press, 1943.
Evolution: Popular Lectures and Discussions before the Brooklyn Ethical Association. Boston: James H. West, 1889.
FAULKNER, HAROLD UNDERWOOD. *The Quest for Social Justice: 1898-1914.* Vol. XI in *A History of American Life,* ed. Dixon Ryan Fox and A. M. Schlesinger. New York: The Macmillan Co., 1931.
FERM, VERGILIUS. *First Adventures in Philosophy.* New York: Charles Scribner's Sons, 1936.
FISCH, MAX H. "Evolution in American Philosophy," *Philosophical Review,* LVI (July, 1947), 357-73.
FISKE, JOHN. *A Century of Science and Other Essays.* Boston and New York: Houghton, Mifflin & Co., 1900.
──────. *Darwinism and Other Essays.* Boston: Houghton, Mifflin & Co., 1884.
──────. *The Destiny of Man Viewed in the Light of His Origin.* 8th ed. Boston: Houghton, Mifflin & Co., 1885.
──────. *Edward L. Youmans: Interpreter of Science for the People.* Boston and New York: Houghton, Mifflin & Co., 1894.
──────. *The Idea of God as Affected by Modern Knowledge.* Boston and New York: Houghton, Mifflin & Co., 1885.
──────. *The Letters of John Fiske,* ed. Ethel F. Fisk. New York: The Macmillan Co., 1940.
──────. *Life Everlasting.* Boston and New York: Houghton, Mifflin & Co., 1901.
──────. *Outlines of Cosmic Philosophy: Based on the Doctrine of Evolution, with Criticisms on the Positive Philosophy.* 2 vols. 10th ed. Boston and New York: Houghton, Mifflin & Co., 1889.
──────. *Through Nature to God.* Boston and New York: Houghton, Mifflin & Co., 1899.
FOERSTER, NORMAN. *Nature in American Literature: Studies in the Modern View of Nature.* New York: The Macmillan Co., 1923.

FREDERICK, SISTER MARY. *Religion and Evolution since 1859.* Chicago: Loyola University Press, 1935.
FROTHINGHAM, O. B. *Transcendentalism in New England: A History.* Boston: American Unitarian Association, 1876.
FULLER, B. A. G. *A History of Philosophy.* New York: Henry Holt & Co., 1938.
GABRIEL, R. H. *The Course of American Democratic Thought: An Intellectual History since 1815.* New York: The Ronald Press Co., 1940.
GODDARD, H. C. "Transcendentalism." In *Cambridge History of American Literature,* I, 326-48. New York: The Macmillan Co., 1933.
GRAY, ASA. *Darwiniana: Essays and Reviews Pertaining to Darwinism.* New York: D. Appleton & Co., 1878.
―――. *Letters of Asa Gray,* ed. Jane Loring Gray. 2 vols. Boston and New York: Houghton, Mifflin & Co., 1893.
―――. *Natural Science and Religion.* New York: Charles Scribner's Sons, 1880.
GRUENBERG, BENJAMIN C. *The Story of Evolution.* Garden City: Garden City Publishing Co., n. d.
HADLEY, A. T. "The Influence of Charles Darwin on Historical and Political Thought," *Psychological Review,* XVI (May, 1909), 152-69.
HAECKEL, ERNST. *The Evolution of Man: A Popular Exposition of the Principal Points of Human Ontogeny and Phylogeny.* 2 vols. New York: D. Appleton & Co., 1897.
―――. *The Riddle of the Universe at the Close of the Nineteenth Century.* New York: Harper & Bros., 1900.
HALDANE, J. S. *The Philosophical Basis of Biology.* New York: Doubleday, Doran & Co., 1931.
HEGEL, G. W. F. *The Philosophy of History,* tr. J. Sibree. New York: Colonial Press, 1900.
―――. *Selections,* ed. J. Loewenberg. New York: Charles Scribner's Sons, 1929.
HENKIN, LEO J. *Darwinism in the English Novel, 1860-1910.* New York: Corporate Press, Inc., 1940.
HERSCHEL, J. F. W. *Preliminary Discourse on the Study of Natural Philosophy.* London: Longman, Rees, Orme, Brown, & Green, 1830.
―――. *A Treatise on Astronomy.* London: Longman, Rees, Orme, Brown, & Green, 1833.
HÖFFDING, HARALD. *A History of Modern Philosophy.* 2 vols. London: Macmillan & Co., 1935.
HOFSTADTER, RICHARD. *Social Darwinism in American Thought, 1860-1915.* Philadelphia: University of Pennsylvania Press, 1945.
HORTON, WALTER M. *Theism and the Scientific Spirit.* New York: Harper & Bros., 1935.
HOWISON, G. H. *The Limits of Evolution and Other Essays Illustrating the Metaphysical Theory of Personal Idealism.* Rev. ed. New York: The Macmillan Co., 1904.
HUNT, ROBERT. *The Poetry of Science, or Studies of the Physical Phenomena of Nature.* 1st American from the 2nd London ed. Boston: Gould, Kendall, & Lincoln, 1850.
HUXLEY, JULIAN. *Essays of a Biologist.* Harmondsworth, England: Penguin Books, Ltd., 1939.
HUXLEY, LEONARD. *The Life and Letters of Thomas H. Huxley.* 2 vols. New York: D. Appleton & Co., 1901.
HUXLEY, THOMAS H. *Collected Essays.* 9 vols. New York: D. Appleton & Co., 1893-94.
INGE, W. R. "The Idea of Progress." In *Outspoken Essays: Second Series.* New York: Longmans, Green & Co., 1922.
JAMES, WILLIAM. *Pragmatism: A New Name for Some Old Ways of Thinking.* New York: Longmans, Green & Co., 1907.

———. *The Will to Believe and Other Essays in Popular Philosophy.* New York: Longmans, Green & Co., 1909.
JOAD, C. E. M. *Guide to Philosophy.* New York: Random House, n. d.
JOHNSTON, G. A., ED. *Selections from the Scottish Philosophy of Common Sense.* Chicago: Open Court Publishing Co., 1915.
JOSEPHSON, AKSEL G. S. *A List of Books on the History of Science.* Chicago: John Crerar Library, 1911.
———. . . . *Supplement.* Chicago: John Crerar Library, 1917.
JUDD, JOHN W. *The Coming of Evolution: The Story of a Great Revolution in Science.* Cambridge: Cambridge University Press, 1911.
KRUTCH, JOSEPH WOOD. *The Modern Temper: A Study and a Confession.* New York: Harcourt, Brace & Co., 1929.
LAURIE, HENRY. *Scottish Philosophy in Its National Development.* Glasgow: Maclehose, 1902.
LE CONTE, JOSEPH. *Evolution and Its Relation to Religious Thought.* New York: D. Appleton & Co., 1889.
LOEWENBERG, B. J. "The Controversy over Evolution in New England, 1859-1873," *New England Quarterly,* VIII (March, 1935), 232-57.
———. "Darwinism Comes to America," *Mississippi Valley Historical Review,* XXVIII (December, 1941), 339-68.
———. "The Reaction of American Scientists to Darwinism," *American Historical Review,* XXXVIII (July, 1933), 687-701.
LOVEJOY, ARTHUR O. "The Argument for Evolution before 'The Origin of Species,'" *Popular Science Monthly,* LXXV (November, December, 1909), 499-514, 537-49.
———. "Bergson and Romantic Evolutionism," *University of California Chronicle,* XV (October, 1913), 429-87.
———. "Buffon and the Problem of Species," *Popular Science Monthly,* LXXIX (November, December, 1911), 464-73, 554-67.
———. "Eighteenth Century Evolutionists," *Popular Science Monthly,* LXV (July, August, 1904), 238-51, 323-40.
———. *The Great Chain of Being: A Study of the History of an Idea.* Cambridge: Harvard University Press, 1936.
———. "Metaphysician of the Life-Force," *Nation,* LXXIX (September 30, 1909), 298-301.
———. "Schopenhauer as an Evolutionist," *Monist,* XXI (April, 1911), 195-222.
LULL, RICHARD SWAN. *Organic Evolution.* Rev. ed. New York: The Macmillan Co., 1932.
LYELL, SIR CHARLES. *The Geological Evidences of the Antiquity of Man.* Everyman's Library edition. New York: E. P. Dutton & Co., n. d.
———. *Principles of Geology: Being an Inquiry How Far the Former Changes of the Earth's Surface Are Referable to Causes Now in Operation.* 4 vols. 3rd ed. London: John Murray, 1834.
MCCOSH, JAMES. *Realistic Philosophy, Defended in a Philosophic Series.* 2 vols. New York: Charles Scribner's Sons, 1887.
———. *The Religious Aspect of Evolution.* Rev. ed. New York: Charles Scribner's Sons, 1890.
———. *The Scottish Philosophy, Biographical, Expository, Critical, from Hutcheson to Hamilton.* New York: Robert Carter & Bros., 1875.
MCGIFFERT, A. C. *The Rise of Modern Religious Ideas.* New York: The Macmillan Co., 1915.
MATTHIESSEN, F. O. *American Renaissance: Art and Expression in the Age of Emerson and Whitman.* New York: Oxford University Press, 1941.
MEAD, G. H. *Movements of Thought in the Nineteenth Century,* ed. Merritt H. Moore. Chicago: University of Chicago Press, 1936.
———. "The Philosophies of Royce, James, and Dewey in Their Ameri-

can Setting," *International Journal of Ethics,* XL (January, 1930), 211-31.
MERRILL, G. P. *The First One Hundred Years of American Geology.* New Haven: Yale University Press, 1924.
MERZ, J. T. *The History of European Thought in the Nineteenth Century.* 4 vols. London: W. Blackwood & Sons, 1907-12.
MILLER, HUGH. *The Footprints of the Creator: or, the Asterolepis of Stromness.* Boston: Gould & Lincoln, 1870.
MILLER, PERRY. *The New England Mind: The Seventeenth Century.* New York: The Macmillan Co., 1939.
MOORE, E. C. *An Outline of the History of Christian Thought since Kant.* New York: Charles Scribner's Sons, 1912.
MORE, LOUIS TRENCHARD. *The Dogma of Evolution.* Princeton: Princeton University Press, 1925.
MORE, PAUL ELMER. "Evolution and the Other World." In *Shelburne Essays,* 11th series, pp. 141-66. Boston and New York: Houghton Mifflin Co., 1921.
―――. "Victorian Literature: The Philosophy of Change." In *Shelburne Essays,* 7th series, pp. 254-69. Boston and New York: Houghton Mifflin Co., 1910.
MORELL, J. D. *An Historical and Critical View of the Speculative Philosophy of Europe in the Nineteenth Century.* New York: Robert Carter & Bros., n. d. [c. 1850].
MORISON, S. E., and COMMAGER, H. S. *The Growth of the American Republic.* 2 vols. 3rd ed. New York: Oxford University Press, 1942.
MORSE, E. S. "American Zoologists and Evolution," *Popular Science Monthly,* X (November, December, 1876), 1-16, 181-98.
―――. "What American Zoologists Have Done for Evolution," *Popular Science Monthly,* XXXI (October, 1887), 804-13; XXXII (February, 1888), 494-502.
MUELDER, WALTER G., and SEARS, LAURENCE, EDS. *The Development of American Philosophy: A Book of Readings.* Boston and New York: Houghton Mifflin Co., 1940.
MUIRHEAD, J. H. "How Hegel Came to America," *Philosophical Review,* XXXVII (1928), 226-40.
―――. *The Platonic Tradition in Anglo-Saxon Philosophy: Studies in the History of Idealism in England and America.* New York: The Macmillan Co., 1931.
NEVINS, ALLAN. *The Emergence of Modern America, 1865-1878.* Vol. VIII of *A History of American Life,* ed. Dixon Ryan Fox and A. M. Schlesinger. New York: The Macmillan Co., 1927.
NICHOL, JOHN. *Architecture of the Heavens.* Library of Illustrated Standard Scientific Works, vol. IX. 9th ed. London: Hippolyte Bailliere, 1851.
―――. *Thoughts on Some Important Points Relating to the System of the World.* Boston and Cambridge: James Munroe & Co., 1848.
―――. *Views of the Architecture of the Heavens in a Series of Letters to a Lady.* New York: H. A. Chapin & Co., 1840.
NORDENSKIOLD, ERIK. *The History of Biology: A Survey,* tr. L. B. Eyre. New York: Tudor Publishing Co., 1935.
OERSTED, HANS CHRISTIAN. *The Soul in Nature, with Supplementary Contributions,* tr. Leonora and Joanna B. Horner. London: Henry G. Bohn, 1852.
OSBORN, HENRY FAIRFIELD. *From the Greeks to Darwin: The Development of the Evolution Idea through Twenty-four Centuries.* 2nd ed. New York: Charles Scribner's Sons, 1929.
PACKARD, A. S. "A Century's Progress in American Zoology," *American Naturalist,* X (October, 1876), 591-98.

———. "Evolution," *New International Encyclopedia,* VIII, 221-35. 2nd ed. New York: Dodd, Mead & Co., 1923.
PALEY, WILLIAM. *Natural Theology; or, Evidences of the Existence and Attributes of the Deity, Collected from the Appearances of Nature.* Boston: Lincoln & Edmands, 1829.
PARRINGTON, V. L. *Main Currents in American Thought.* 3 vols. New York: Harcourt, Brace & Co., 1927-30.
PATRICK, G. T. W. *Introduction to Philosophy.* Revised with the assistance of Frank Miller Chapman. Boston and New York: Houghton Mifflin Co., 1935.
PAULSEN, FRIEDRICH. *Introduction to Philosophy,* tr. Frank Thilly. New York: Henry Holt & Co., 1928.
PERRY, RALPH BARTON. *In the Spirit of William James.* New Haven: Yale University Press, 1938.
———. *The Present Conflict of Ideals: A Study of the Philosophical Background of the World War.* New York: Longmans, Green & Co., 1918.
———. *Present Philosophical Tendencies: A Critical Survey of Naturalism, Idealism, Pragmatism, and Realism Together with a Synopsis of the Philosophy of William James.* New York: Longmans, Green & Co., 1912.
———. *The Thought and Character of William James as Revealed in Unpublished Correspondence and Notes, Together with His Published Writings.* 2 vols. Boston: Little, Brown & Co., 1935.
POST, ALBERT. *Popular Freethought in America, 1825-1850.* Columbia Studies in History, Economics and Public Law, No. 497. New York: Columbia University Press, 1943.
POTTER, G. R. "Coleridge and the Idea of Evolution," *Publications of the Modern Language Association,* XL (June, 1925), 379-97.
———. "James Thomson and the Evolution of Spirits," *Englische Studien,* LXI (1926), 57-65.
———. "Mark Akenside, Prophet of Evolution," *Modern Philology,* XXIV (August, 1926), 55-64.
RADL, EMANUEL. *The History of Biological Theories,* tr. E. J. Hatfield. London: H. Milford, Oxford University Press, 1930.
RAND, BENJAMIN. "Philosophical Instruction in Harvard University from 1636 to 1906," *Harvard Graduates' Magazine,* XXXVII (1928-29), 29-47, 188-200, 296-311.
RANDALL, J. H., JR. *The Making of the Modern Mind.* Rev. ed. Boston and New York: Houghton Mifflin Co., 1940.
——— and BUCHLER, JUSTUS. *Philosophy: An Introduction.* New York: Barnes & Noble, Inc., 1942.
RILEY, WOODBRIDGE. *American Thought from Puritanism to Pragmatism and Beyond.* New York: Peter Smith, 1941.
ROGERS, A. K. *English and American Philosophy since 1800: A Critical Survey.* New York: The Macmillan Co., 1922.
ROYCE, JOSIAH. *Herbert Spencer: An Estimate and Review.* New York: Fox, Duffield & Co., 1904.
———. "Introduction." In *Outlines of Cosmic Philosophy* by John Fiske. Vol. I. Standard Library Edition of the *Miscellaneous Works of John Fiske.* Boston and New York: Houghton Mifflin Co., 1902.
———. JOSEPH LE CONTE; G. H. HOWISON; and SIDNEY EDWARD MEZES. *The Conception of God: A Philosophic Discussion Concerning the Nature of the Divine Idea as a Demonstrable Reality.* New York: The Macmillan Co., 1909.
———. *Lectures on Modern Idealism.* New Haven: Yale University Press, 1919.
———. "Relations between Philosophy and Science in the First Half

of the Nineteenth Century in Germany," *Science,* n. s. XXXVIII (October 24, 1913), 567-84.
————. *The Spirit of Modern Philosophy: An Essay in the Form of Lectures.* Boston and New York: Houghton, Mifflin & Co., 1893.
————. *The World and the Individual.* 2 vols. New York: The Macmillan Co., 1923, 1927.
RUNES, D. D., ED. *Dictionary of Philosophy.* New York: Philosophical Library, 1942.
RUSSELL, BERTRAND. *The Scientific Outlook.* New York: W. W. Norton & Co., Inc., 1931.
SANTAYANA, GEORGE. *Character and Opinion in the United States, with Reminiscences of William James and Josiah Royce and Academic Life in America.* New York: Charles Scribner's Sons, 1920.
————. *Egotism in German Philosophy.* 2nd ed. New York: Charles Scribner's Sons, 1940.
————. "The Genteel Tradition in American Philosophy." In *Winds of Doctrine: Studies in Contemporary Opinion,* pp. 186-215. New York: Charles Scribner's Sons, 1940.
————. *Interpretations of Poetry and Religion.* New York: Charles Scribner's Sons, 1900.
————. *The Life of Reason.* 5 vols. 2nd ed. New York: Charles Scribner's Sons, 1922.
————. *Realms of Being.* New York: Charles Scribner's Sons, 1942.
————. *Three Philosophical Poets: Lucretius, Dante, and Goethe.* Cambridge: Harvard University Press, 1935.
SARGENT, MRS. JOHN T. *Sketches and Reminiscences of the Radical Club of Chestnut Street, Boston.* Boston: J. R. Osgood & Co., 1880.
SCHLESINGER, ARTHUR M. "A Critical Period in American Religion, 1875-1900," *Proceedings of the Massachusetts Historical Society,* LXIV (1932), 525-27.
————. *The Rise of the City, 1878-1898.* Vol. X in *A History of American Life,* ed. Dixon Ryan Fox and Arthur M. Schlesinger. New York: The Macmillan Co., 1933.
SCHNEIDER, HERBERT W. "Evolution and Theology in America," *Journal of the History of Ideas,* VI (1945), 3-18.
————. *A History of American Philosophy.* New York: Columbia University Press, 1946.
SCHWEGLER, ALBERT. *A History of Philosophy in Epitome,* tr. J. H. Seelye. New York: D. Appleton & Co., 1908.
SCUDDER, VIDA D. "Science and the Modern Poets." In *The Life of the Spirit in the Modern English Poets,* pp. 5-56. Boston and New York: Houghton, Mifflin & Co., 1895.
SEDGWICK, W. T., and TYLER, H. W. *A Short History of Science.* Rev. ed. New York: The Macmillan Co., 1939.
SEWARD, A. C., ED. *Darwin and Modern Science: Essays in Commemoration of the Centenary of the Birth of Charles Darwin and of the Fiftieth Anniversary of the Publication of* THE ORIGIN OF SPECIES. New York: G. P. Putnam's Sons, 1909.
SHAW, GEORGE BERNARD. *Back to Methuselah: A Metabiological Pentateuch.* New York: Brentano's, 1922.
SOMERVELL, D. C., *English Thought in the Nineteenth Century.* 2nd ed. Methuen & Co., Ltd., 1929.
SPENCER, HERBERT. *The Data of Ethics.* New York: D. Appleton & Co., 1894.
————. *An Epitome of the Synthetic Philosophy,* compiled by F. Howard Collins. London: Williams & Norgate, 1889.
————. *Essays on Education and Kindred Subjects.* Everyman's Library edition. New York: E. P. Dutton & Co., 1911.

———. *First Principles of a New System of Philosophy.* 2nd ed. New York: D. Appleton & Co., 1875.
———. *The Principles of Ethics.* 2 vols. New York: D. Appleton & Co., 1892-93.
STACE, W. T. *The Philosophy of Hegel: A Systematic Exposition.* London: Macmillan & Co., 1924.
STALLO, J. B. *General Principles of the Philosophy of Nature.* Boston: Wm. Crosby & H. P. Nichols, 1848.
STEDMAN, E. C. *Poets of America.* Boston and New York: Houghton, Mifflin & Co., 1885.
———, ED. *An American Anthology, 1787-1900.* Boston and New York: Houghton, Mifflin & Co., 1900.
STEVENSON, LIONEL. *Darwin among the Poets.* Chicago: University of Chicago Press, 1932.
STRONG, AUGUSTUS H. *American Poets and Their Theology.* Philadelphia: The Griffith & Rowland Press, 1916.
SULLY, JAMES. "Evolution in Philosophy." *Encyclopedia Britannica,* VIII, 751-72. 9th ed. Chicago: The Werner Co., 1894.
TENNEMANN, W. G. *A Manual of the History of Philosophy,* tr. A. Johnson. London: Henry G. Bohn, 1852.
THORNDIKE, A. H. *Literature in a Changing Age.* New York: The Macmillan Co., 1920.
TODD, E. W. "Philosophical Ideas in Harvard College, 1817-1837," *New England Quarterly,* XVI (1943), 63-90.
TOWNSEND, H. G. *Philosophic Ideas in the United States.* New York: American Book Co., 1934.
TUFTS, JAMES H. "Darwin and Evolutionary Ethics," *Psychological Review,* XVI (May, 1909), 194-206.
TYLOR, EDWARD B. *Anthropology: An Introduction to the Study of Man and Civilization.* New York: D. Appleton & Co., 1897.
UEBERWEG, FRIEDRICH. *History of Philosophy from Thales to the Present Time,* tr. G. S. Morris, with additions by Noah Porter. 2 vols. New York: Charles Scribner's Sons, 1884.
VERNON, AMBROSE WHITE. "Later Theology." In *Cambridge History of American Literature,* III, 201-25. New York: The Macmillan Co., 1933.
WARREN, AUSTIN. "The Concord School of Philosophy," *New England Quarterly,* II (1929), 199-233.
WARREN, SIDNEY. *American Freethought, 1860-1914.* Columbia Studies in History, Economics and Public Law, No. 504. New York: Columbia University Press, 1943.
WATSON, JOHN. *Schelling's Transcendental Idealism: A Critical Exposition.* 2nd ed. Chicago: S. C. Griggs & Co., 1892.
WEBER, ALFRED. *History of Philosophy,* tr. Frank Thilly, with *Philosophy since 1860* by Ralph Barton Perry. New York: Charles Scribner's Sons, 1925.
WELLS, H. G. *Mind at the End of Its Tether and The Happy Turning, a Dream of Life.* New York: Didier, 1946.
———; HUXLEY, JULIAN; and WELLS, G. H. *The Science of Life.* New York: The Literary Guild, 1934.
WHITE, ANDREW D. *A History of the Warfare of Science with Theology in Christendom.* 2 vols. New York: D. Appleton & Co., 1920.
WHITEHEAD, ALFRED NORTH. *Science and the Modern World.* New York: The Macmillan Co., 1926.
WHITNEY, LOIS. *Primitivism and the Idea of Progress.* Baltimore: The Johns Hopkins University Press, 1934.
WOLFF, SAMUEL LEE. "Divines and Moralists, 1783-1860." In *Cambridge History of American Literature,* II, 196-223. New York: The Macmillan Co., 1933.
WOODROW, MARION W., ED. *Dr. James Woodrow as Seen by His Friends:*

Character Sketches by His Former Pupils, Colleagues, and Associates. Columbia, S. C.: R. L. Bryan Co., 1909.

WRIGHT, CONRAD. "The Religion of Geology," *New England Quarterly,* XIV (1941), 335-58.

WRIGHT, W. K. *History of Modern Philosophy.* New York: The Macmillan Co., 1941.

YOUNG, R. T. *Biology in America.* Boston: Richard G. Badger, 1922.

INDEX

Absolute, the, of Schelling, 13-14; Coleridge on, 18
Adams, Henry, 305, 309, 334, 363, 423
Agassiz, Louis, 18, 131-32, 133, 134, 173, 175, 214; difference with Emerson, Moncure Conway on, 58, Lowell's elegy on, 190; Holmes differs with, 219
Akenside, Mark, on chain of being, 9-10
Albee, John, "Evolution," 159
Alcott, Amos Bronson, 240; his emanational doctrine, 42, 291; as Emerson's Orphic poet, 42; and "personalism," 109
Aldrich, Thomas Bailey, "Metempsychosis," 161
Alexander, Samuel, 31
Analogy, Poe's doctrine of, 80-82; parallels in contemporary writers, 389-90
Anderson, Paul R., and Fisch, Max H., 239
Aristotle, 7; on relation of cause and effect, 29
Arnold, Matthew, 338
Attraction and repulsion, Stallo on, 16; matter exists only as, Poe on, 75; matter definable as, Schelling and Kant on, 392-93; derived by Schelling from nature of perception, 392-93; matter known only as, Holmes on, 412
Augustine, Saint, 319, 355

Bacon, Sir Francis, 272, 275
Barnum, P. T., 131
Bastian, H. C., and spontaneous generation, 225
Beach, Joseph Warren, 41, 43
Beck, Maximiliam, 125
Beecher, Henry Ward, on evolution and design, 135
Bell, Sir Charles, *The Hand*, 41
Bergson, Henri, 111, 121, 235, 237, 360; on relation of cause and effect, 32

Berkeley, George, 33, 100, 258, 341
Blavatsky, Madame, 239
Boker, George Henry, evolutionary references in *Calaynos*, 131; "The Ivory Carver," 155
Bosanquet, Bernard, 319
Boscovich, Roger Joseph, 75
Bowne, Borden P., his personalism, 109
Boyesen, H. H., "Evolution," 260-62
Boynton, Percy H., on Hovey, 297
Bradley, F. H., 63, 239, 319
Bradley, W. A., 172
Bridgewater Treatises, The, 79
Brokmeyer, H. C., 240
Brooks, Van Wyck, 240, 305, 309
Broussais, F. J. V., 217
Bryant, William Cullen, 138, 155, 165, 167-74, 235; inversion of Darwinism in Williams College address, 167-68; interest in the sciences, 168; antipathy to materialism and agnosticism, 168; poet of the flux, 169; on death as deliverer, 169-70; on progress, 170; cosmic optimism, 171-72; on immortality and the law of progress, 171; transcendence of his God, 172; creationism, 173; "After a Tempest," 170; "The Ages," 170, 171-72; "The Battle-Field," 170; "An Evening Revery," 171; "A Forest Hymn," 172, 173; "Hymn to Death," 169; "The Order of Nature," 172; "The Rivulet," 169
Büchner, Friedrich, 175
Bucke, Richard Maurice, *Cosmic Consciousness*, 65-66
Buffon, George Louis LeClerc de, 24
Burroughs, John, 235, 237
Burton, Richard, "To an Evolutionist," 159
Burtt, E. A., definition of mechanism, 88-89
Bushnell, Horace, 30, 167, 173; on Emerson, 137

Butler, Samuel, 237

Calvinism, 140, 148, 167, 355; Holmes and, 229, 230; Santayana on, 241; Moody and, 324
Carlyle, Thomas, 239, 256; influence on Sill, 252-53
Carman, Bliss, his unitrinianism, 301-2; "The Measure of Man," 301-2
Carruth, W. H., "Each in His Own Tongue," 150
Catastrophic theory in geology, 23
Cause, effect cannot "contain more" than, 28-33; Jacobi on, 29; Schelling on, 29; Aristotle on, 29; Descartes on, 29-30; Locke on, 30, 379; Joseph Cook on, 30-31; denied by emergent evolutionists, 31-32; Bergson on, 32; Maritain on, 32; Santayana on, 32-33, 379-80; McCosh on, 136; J. G. Holland on, 142; J. T. Trowbridge on, 142; C. P. Cranch on, 143; Lanier on, 202; William James on, 379; the Scholastic view, 379; Samuel Johnson on, 379; Thomas Cooper on, 379; in Melville's *Clarel*, 403; Dewey on, 426-27
Cavendish, Henry, 74
Cawein, Madison, 290-93; his emanationism, 290-91; adapted to theory of evolution, 291; the divine goal of evolution, 292-93; "Diety," 235, 291, 292; "Intimations of the Beautiful," 290, 291, 292, 293; "Fulfillment," 292
Chadwick, John White, 165; "The New Science," 163-64; "The Rise of Man," 152
Chain of Being, The Great, 6-10, 160-61; Lovejoy on, 6-9; not evolutionary, 8, 40; temporalizing of, 8-9; evolutionary interpretation of, 9; James Thomson and, 9-10; Mark Akenside and, 9-10; Coleridge on, 19-20; Emerson and, 39; in Longfellow's *Hyperion*, 175-76; in Taylor's *Prince Deukalion*, 198

Chambers, Robert, 34, 212, 214. See *Vestiges of Creation*.
Channing, W. E., 375
Chapman, John Jay, on the impossibility of philosophy, 341
Clark, Harry Hayden, 211, 380, 412
Coleridge, Samuel Taylor, 87, 41, 239; borrowing from Schelling, 18-20; on opposite forces, 19; dynamic chain of being, 19-20; G. R. Potter on his refusal to accept evolution, 57; possible source of Poe's attitude toward Kepler, 390
Comte, Auguste, 240, 274
Concord School of Philosophy, The, 109, 240
Cone, Helen Gray, "The Inheritance," 147
Conflict of opposites, 87; Stallo on, 16; Coleridge on, 19; matter definable as, Kant and Schelling on, 392-93. See also Dialectic.
Conger, G. P., 7; on concept of evolution, 3
Continuity, principle of, 7
Conway, Moncure D., story illustrating difference between Emerson and Agassiz, 58
Cook, Joseph, 30-31, 237
Coolbrith, Ina, "Atom," 164
Cooper, Thomas, 379
Cope, E. D., on mind in evolution, 238
Cosmic optimism, 150, 295; meaning of, 6, 92, 135, 245-46; Randall on, 35-36; Stedman on, 280; Hovey on, 304-5; Moody provides review of, 314-15; Rice on, 350-51; of the Puritans, Miller on, 375; Parker on, 375-76; Hegel on, 421; Niebuhr on, 425; its premise, 118; and the problem of evil, 125-26, 355-57; its paradox, 126, 376; sources of opposition to, 331; in evolutionary science, 331-36; in humanism, 336-39; in pragmatism, 339-43; its demise, 259; the twilight of, Crane and, 334-35; Jeffers and, 335; Frost and, 343-9; Dewey and, 340; and the new evolutionary optimism of Bergson and Dewey, 360

INDEX

Coulomb, Charles Augustin, 74
Cranch, Christopher Pearse, 147, 165; "The Human Flower," 162; "Ormuzd and Ahriman," 152, 156-69; that an effect cannot "contain more" than its cause, 143; *Satan: A Libretto,* 152, 156-59; "A Word to Philosophers," 143, 145-46
Crane, Stephen, and the twilight of cosmic optimism, 334-35; "I saw a man pursuing the horizon," 334; "A man said to the universe," 334; "The Open Boat," 334
Cuvier, Baron Georges, 22, 214; controversy with Geoffroy Saint-Hilaire, 25

Darwin, Charles, 23, 26, 150, 202, 207, 223, 266, 267, 272; Emerson on, 50; Whitman on, 95; on American reviews of *Origin of Species,* 132; American editions of *Origin of Species* and *Descent of Man,* 132, 400-401; reception of in America by scientists, 132-33; his criticism of Paley, 133, 401; view that his theories need to be supplemented, 142; did the work of a friend to theology, 149, 404; on progress, 151; on good and evil, 154; on immortality, 159; Lowell undertakes translation of his life into Spanish, 183; Taylor on, 192-93; Holmes and, 211; and Spencer, influence of, 247-74; and the Creator, 404; Lanier on, 410
Darwin, Erasmus, 20, 25; Paley on his evolutionism, 401-2
DeKay, Charles, 265-68; his Darwinism, 267-68; *The Vision of Esther,* 266; *The Vision of Nimrod,* 266-68
Delsarte, François, 239; his doctrines, 301
Descartes, René, 107; on cause and effect, 29-30
Design, argument from, Darwinian evolution and, 133-35

Dewey, John, 259; and the twilight of cosmic optimism, 340; on *the philosophic fallacy,* 342; his evolutionary optimism contrasted with cosmic optimism, 360; denies principle that effect cannot contain more than its cause, 426-27
Dialetic, 87, 302-3; and evolution, 12-13, 51; Hegelian, 297-98; Frost on, 348; biological analogy of, 383-84. *See also* Conflict of Opposites.
Dick, Thomas, 68, 79
Diderot, Dennis, 25
Dissolution, cosmic, Poe on, 83-84; Leighton on, 262-63; Fawcett on, 269; Gilder on, 281-82; and the twilight of cosmic optimism, 331-33; Sterling on, 363; Nichol on, 390; would be followed by renewal, Poe on, 84; Spencer on, 391, Nichol on, 391
Dreiser, Theodore, 248, 294
Driesch, Hans, 237
Drummond, Henry, 165

Eddy, Mary Baker, 239
Effect. *See* Cause.
Egoism, of Whitman, Emerson, and Poe, 107; of Lodge, 306-7, 423
Eimer, Theodor, 237
Eliot, George, Lanier on, 202
Emanationism, Emerson and, 41-42; Alcott and, 42; Cawein and, 290-91
Emergent evolution, 31-32, 338
Emerson, Ralph Waldo, 5, 8, 10, 86, 87, 90, 100, 104, 107, 108, 112, 122, 126, 154, 163, 165, 167, 174, 239, 240, 247, 253, 259, 260, 266, 272, 280, 286, 287, 293, 306-7, 314, 315, 319, 320, 321, 327, 336, 355, 359; on Schelling, 17-18; his idealism, 37-38; consequences of his idealism for his treatment of evolution, 38-40; attitude toward science, 38; and chain of being, 39; did not accept evolution at beginning of his career, 40-41; accepts geological account of past, 40; absence of idea of evolution

from 1836 *Nature;* emanationism in *Nature,* 41-42; hesitates between emanationism and evolutionism, 43; influence of sciences, 43-45; on geology, 24, 44; evolutionary drift of "The Method of Nature" and "Woodnotes," 45-47; extension of evolutionary drift in 1844 "Nature"; on *Vestiges of Creation,* 48; and Lamarck, 48-49, 54; evolution and transmigration, 49-50; on Darwin, 50; dialectical character of his evolutionism, 51-55; *natura naturans* and *natura naturata,* 47, 51-52; "fate involves the melioration," 52-53; evolutionism in his poetry, 55-57, 59; question whether his is a true evolutionism, 57-58; no gulf between natural and transcendent cause, 58; difference with Agassiz on evolution, 58; difference between his evolutionism and that of science, 58-59; his optimism, 59-60; and the problem of evil, 60-63, 320, 384-85; on evil as privative, 61; on evil as necessary, 62; and the idea of progress, 63-66; "arrested and progressive development," 64-65, 385-86; compared with R. M. Bucke, 65-66; and Poe, 67; on materialism, 90; and Whitman, 92, 105-6; a pre-Darwinian evolutionist, 131; on Tyndall, 133; Horace Bushnell on, 137; and later poets, 165-66; and Lanier, 203, 208; Sill on, 256-57; Stedman on, 276-77, 280; Cawein and, 291; Frost and, 345; his lines on spiral evolution antedate Stallo, 382; source in Lyell of his knowledge of Lamarck, 382-83; and pragmatism, 426

"Bacchus," 49; "Circles," 38; "Compensation," 39, 52; "Considerations by the Way," 62; "Cosmos," 55; Divinity School Address, 61; "Emancipation in the British West Indies," 61; *English Traits,* 17; "Ever the Rock of Ages melts," 59; "Fate," 50, 52, 53, 54, 58, 60, 62; "Immortality," 108; "Inspiration," 65; *Journals,* 18, 40, 41, 42, 43, 44, 45, 48, 49, 50; letters, 44, 48, 50, 60; "Life and Letters in New England," 24; "The Method of Nature," 38, 45; "The Natural History of Intellect," 38, 39, 65; *Nature* (1836), 37, 38, 39, 41, 42, 93, 342, 345; "Nature" (1844), 44, 47; "On the Relation of Man to the Globe," 40; "The Over-Soul," 52; "The Philosophy of History," 41; "The Poet," 53; "Poetry and Imagination," 59; "Self-Reliance," 39, 63; "Solution," 56; "Song of Nature," 56-57; "The Sovereignty of Ethics," 55, 62; "Speech at the Second Annual Meeting of the Free Religious Association," 61; "Swedenborg," 62; "Success," 62; "Wealth," 55; "Woodnotes," 46-47

Epigenesis, 22

Epistemology, Kant and Fichte, 12; of Romanticism, 394-95; Whitman on, 395

Evil, justification of, 8; Stallo on problem of, 17; Emerson on, 60-63; Whitman on, 124-26; cosmic optimism and, 125-26, 355; some minor poets on the good of, 154-59; Darwin on, 154; Spencer on, 154; Lanier on, 208-10; Holmes on, 231; Santayana on genteel tradition and, 241; Royce on, 241, 288, 289, 319; contrast of genteel tradition and mysticism in respect to, 287; genteel tradition and, 294-95; Hovey and, 303-5; Moody and, 316-20; Perry on idealistic attitude toward, 319; Santayana on, 355; evolutionary meliorism takes place of Fall in liberal theology, 375; Jorgenson on Emerson and, 384-85; Poe on, 392

Evolution, two streams of evolutionary thought, 3-36; definition of, 3-5; by Conger, 3; by Perry, 3; by Packard, 4; by Spencer,

21; and progress, 4-5, 10-11, 151-54; and Chain of Being, 8-9, 40; Royce on rise of the doctrine of, 11-12; and Romantic idealism, Mead on, 13; Schelling and, 14-15; Coleridge and, 19-20; development of scientific theories of, 20-27; and nebular hypothesis, 21; geology as preparation for, 22-24; emergent, 31-32, 338; criticism of, by Hegel and Stallo, 34; in Poe's *Eureka,* 75-78; controversy over, 133-34; and teleology, 133-35, 236; qualified acceptance of, 136, 140-41; and materialism, 141-42; and the reality of time, 144; not degrading to man, 152, 184, 192, 291; and immortality, 159-64; established doctrine in scientific world, 235; criticism of natural selection, 237-38; as a basis of idealism, 238, 242; as a metaphor, Frost on, 346; Santayana on Darwin and Aristotle, 379-80; Nichol on, 387, 388-89; fulfillment of selfhood its aim, Carman on, 421-22

Fawcett, Edgar, 268-70; on immortality, 268; on progress, 269-70; *Agnosticism and Other Essays,* 268; "Albert F. Webster, Jr.," 268; "Cameos," 268; "Conception," 268; "Courage!" 268, 269; "The Future," 269-70; "In the Year Ten Thousand," 270; "Individuality," 268; "Intermezzos," 268-69; "Memorial Verses: To Courtland Palmer," 268; "The Republic," 269
Fechner, Gustav, 102
Felton, Cornelius, 176
Fichte, Johann Gottlieb, 240, 320; his dialectical principle, 12-13, 51; Whitman on, 103-4; Longfellow on, 177
Fiske, John, 22, 28, 149, 165, 247, 260, 261, 262, 265, 370; on evolution and teleology, 135, 244-45; on evolution and immortality, 160; Lanier on his "Sociology and Hero-Worship," 202-3; on spiritualistic philosophy, 242-43; and Spencer on religious significance of Unknowable, 243-44; Royce on his incipient idealism, 245
Foerster, Norman, 338-39
Fontenelle, Bernard de, 10
Franklin, Benjamin, 296
Frost, Robert, and the twilight of cosmic optimism, 343-49; his attitude toward philosophy, 343-44; on the metaphorical character of thinking, 344; compared with Santayana and Emerson, 345; evolution as a metaphor, 346; evolution and "West-Running Brook," 346-48; sense in which he is an optimist; "The Bear," 343; "Education by Poetry," 344, 346; "The Lesson for Today," 332-33; "The Literate Farmer and the Planet Venus," 346; "The Poet's Next of Kin in a College," 344; "A Star in a Stone-Boat," 345; "West-Running Brook," 346-48; "Wild Grapes," 346

Genteel Tradition, The, 275-93; Santayana on, 241-42; the two senses of, 294; the paradox of, 294-328
Geology, prepares ground for evolution, 22-24; catastrophic theory, 23; uniformitarianism, 23; Emerson and, 24, 40, 44; Poe and, 75-76; Holmes on, 223-24
Gilder, Richard Watson, 240, 247, 280-90, 298, 332; interested in eternal good more than in progress, 281; on fate of solar system, 281-82; evolution and the soul, 282-83; and Royce's dilemma, 283-84; his transcendentalism, 285-86; on immortality, 285; an idealist, 286-87; the mystic's intuition of union, 287; the good of evil, 288-90; optimism contrasted with Stedman's, 288-89; God suffers also, 289-90; "Cost," 289-90; "Destiny," 281-82; "The Invisible," 284-85, 286, 287; "A Midsummer Meditation," 286,

287; "Mors Triumphalis," 281, 287, 288, 289, 298; "Non Sine Dolore," 284, "Recognition," 282-83, 284, 285, 286; "The Soul," 284

God, and the world, Poe on, 392; in Indian philosophy, 422-23; ontological argument for existence of, 383

Goethe, Johann Wolfgang von, 191, 193; on Cuvier-Saint-Hilaire controversy, 25

Gostwick, Joseph, 17, 103, 104, 106, 118; Whitman's indebtedness to, 395-96

Gradation, principle of, 7

Gray, Asa, 132, 134, 174; on reconciliation of evolution and religion, 35

Green, T. H., 239

Greenslet, Ferris, 305, 309

Guyot, Arnold, 24

Haeckel, Ernst, 223, 284, 287, 373

Hagedorn, Hermann, 374

Hale, Edward Everett, 62

Harbinger, The, 150

Harris, William Torrey, 106, 240, 297, 390

Harrison, Frederic, 165

Harte, Bret, "A Geological Madrigal," 139, 162; "The Society upon the Stanislaus," 139; "To the Pliocene Skull," 139

Harvey, William, 22

Hayne, Paul Hamilton, 199; "Pre-existence," 161

Hearn, Lafcadio, 161

Hegel, G. W. F., 15, 18, 103, 107, 124, 193, 240, 299, 348, 373, criticism of organic evolution, 34; conception of evil as necessary, Emerson and, 62; Whitman and, 104-5, 118, 396; attitude toward past, 120; Hovey and, 297-99; Royce on his "logic of passion," 297-98; Royce on *Phenomenology of Spirit,* 312; Lodge and, 311-14; biological analogy of his dialectic, 383-84; annihilation would follow elimination of gravitation, 390-91; on the true theodicy, 421

Helmholtz, Hermann von, on medical science at beginning of nineteenth century, 216

Henley, W. E., 161

Herbert, George, "Man," 48

Herder, Johann Gottfried, 11, 25; Taylor and, 193, 195

Herford, Oliver, "If this little world to-night," 332

Herschel, Sir John, 68; quoted in illustration of Poe's theory of electricity, 73-74

Higginson, Thomas Wentworth, qualified acceptance of evolution, 141

Hitchcock, Edward, 24

Hodge, Reverend Charles, on Darwinism and design, 134

Höffding, Harald, 102

Holland, Josiah G., effect cannot contain more than cause, 142

Holmes, Oliver Wendell, 28, 35, 135, 138, 211-31; and Darwin, 211, 229-30; pre-Darwinian evolutionary theory, 211-16; evolution of plant life, 212-13; of animal life, 213; rejection of "progressive development," 214; exclusion of soul of man from evolution, 214-15; his dualisms, 214-15, 414; reasonableness of a theory of creation, 215-16; state of medical science during his early career, 216-17; debt to Pierre Louis, 217; influence of organic chemistry, 217-19; immanent action of God, 219-20; difference with Agassiz, 219; debt to cell theory of Schleiden and Schwann, 220-22; summary of pre-Darwinian phase of his thinking, 222-23; acceptance of geological record, 223-24; experiments of Jeffries Wyman on spontaneous generation, 225; repeats spontaneous generation theory as late as 1872, 225-27; on freedom and determinism, 227-29, 412; evolution a reinforcement of optimism, 230; problem of evil, 231; matter known only as attraction and repulsion, 412

"Agassiz's Natural History," 219; "Autobiographical Notes," 223-24, 231; "Border Lines of Knowledge in Some Provinces of Medical Science," 222; "Crime and Automatism," 227; "De Sauty, an Electro-Chemical Eclogue," 217; *Elsie Venner,* 224, 227; letters, 224, 231; "Mechanism in Thought and Morals," 227, 229; "Mechanism of Vital Actions," 212-16 *passim,* 218-19, 220, 226, 228, 235; *Over the Teacups,* 230; *The Poet at the Breakfast Table,* 224, 225-26, 228, 229-30; "The Position and Prospects of the Medical Student," 217, 218, 221-22, 226; *The Professor at the Breakfast Table,* 224

Holmes, Oliver Wendell, Jr., on man's philosophic ignorance, 341

Hovey, Mrs. Richard, 301, 302, 303

Hovey, Richard, 295-305; reaction against convention, 295; God works through battle, 296-97; influence of Hegel, 297-99; strife the law of life and of God, 298; on immanence and transcendence, 299-300; and Lanier, 300; melioration, 300; unitrinianism, 301-2; problem of evil in Arthurian dramas, 303-5; cosmic optimism, 304-5; "Accident in Art," 296; "America," 296; "Angromainyus," 298; *Avalon,* 303; "The Call of the Bugles," 295, 297, 298; "Immanence," 299; "The Laurel," 300; *Merlin,* 303-4; "Peace," 295; "Quatrains," 299; *Taliesin,* 304-5; "Transcendence," 299-300; "Unmanifest Destiny," 296-97; "A View of Parnassus," 296

Howard, Leon, on Emerson and Whitman, 105

Howe, Julia Ward, "First Causes," 147; "Kosmos," 148, 247; "Without and Within," 147

Howison, George Holmes, 110, 239, 242; his personalism, 108-9; on immortality, 115, 398

Humboldt, Alexander von, Taylor and, 191, 409

Hume, David, 259

Hunter, John, and Emerson, 385-86

Huxley, Julian, 5

Huxley, Thomas H., 50, 133, 144, 151, 165, 167, 207, 223, 227, 242

Hyatt, Alpheus, 237

Idealism, Romantic, and evolution, Mead on, 13; Berkeleian, 33-34; post-Kantian, 33-34, 51; Emerson and, 37-40; absolute, Perry on, 38; Whitman not a phenomenalist, 97-98; not progressive, according to Perry, 126-27; derivation from evolution, 238; resurgence of at end of century, 239-40; Santayana on, 241-42; Fiske and, 242-43, 245; Gilder and, 285-86; Masters' approach to, 353; Jonathan Edwards, 395

Identity, Emerson's doctrine of, 39

Imagists, the, opposition to the cosmic poet, 343

Immanence, doctrine of, 27-28, 149, 404; Trowbridge on, 142; Cranch on, 143; Holmes on, 219-20; Stedman on, 278-80; transcendence and, 284, 291, 299-300; Rice on, 350; needed by science, according to Parker, 378

Immortality, Emerson on, 108; Whitman on, 108, 111-12; evolution and, some minor poets on, 159-64; Darwin on, 159; Le Conte on, 160; Fiske on, 160; Longfellow on, 177; Taylor on, 198-99; Leighton on, 263-64; Fawcet on, 268; Stedman on, 278; Gilder on, 285; Cawein on, 292-93; Sterling on, 361-62 Robinson on, 368-69. *See also* Transmigration.

Immutability of species. *See* Species.

Ingersoll, Robert, 268

Irving, Washington, pre-Darwinian evolution in *Knickerbocker History,* 25

Jacobi, F. H., on cause and effect, 29
James, Henry, 60, 183
James, William, 60, 102, 187, 259; philosophy of evolution a metaphysical creed, 340; on cause and effect, 379
Jeffers, Robinson, and the twilight of cosmic optimism, 332, 335; on Sterling, 429-30; "Apology for Bad Dreams," 335; "Hellenistics," 335; *Roan Stallion*, 335; "The Torch-Bearers' Race," 332; "The Tower Beyond Tragedy," 332, 335
Joad, C. E. M., 111, 383
Johnson, Samuel (1696-1772), on cause and effect, 379
Johnson, Samuel (1709-84), 100
Jones, H. M., and Hayakawa, S. I., 228
Jones, Rufus, 102
Jorgenson, C. E., on Emerson and evil, 60, 384-85

Kant, Immanuel, 12, 21, 33, 75, 175, 180, 201, 240; defines matter in terms of attraction and repulsion, 392-93
Kepler, Johann, Poe and, 81, 390
Kingsley, Charles, 249

Lamarck, Jean Baptiste, 22, 25, 34, 212, 268, 272, 273, 412; Emerson and, 44, 48-49, 54, 382-83; Neo-Lamarckism at end of the century, 237-38; Lyell's version of, 382-83
Lanier, Mary Day, 300
Lanier, Sidney, 84, 138, 165, 199-210; praise of Taylor's *Prince Deukalion*, 199; scientific interests, 199-201; limitations of science, 201-2; rejection of deterministic evolutionisms, 202-4; principle of autonomous selfhood in *The English Novel*, 202; on Emerson, 203; acceptance of evolution as statement of pattern of change, 204-5; etherealization, 205-8; illustrated in geology, 206-7; nature-love a culmination of the process, 207-8; evil a condition of good, 208-10; and Hovey, 300; on Darwin, 410; debt to James Woodrow, 410; difference between his cosmic optimism and Whitman's, 411-12; "Acknowledgment," 201; "Clover," 209-10; "The Crystal," 203; *The English Novel*, 200, 201, 202, 203, 205, 206, 207; "A Florida Sunday," 203; "Individuality," 203-4; letter to J. F. Kirk, 204; "The Mocking Bird," 201; *Music and Poetry*, 207; "Opposition," 209; "Psalm of the West," 210; "Retrospects and Prospects," 206; *Shakspere and His Forerunners*, 207; "The Symphony," 201-2; *Tiger-Lilies*, 200, 208; "To Bayard Taylor," 201
Laplace, Pierre Simon, 21, 68, 72, 78, 282
Le Conte, Joseph, 160, 235
Leibnitz, Gottfried Wilhelm, 125
Leighton, William, *Change: The Whisper of the Sphinx*, 262-65; on dissolution, 262-63; on progress, 263-64; on immortality, 263-64; theism, 264-65
Lessing, Gotthold Ephraim, 11, 193, 194
Lewes, G. H., 165, 258, 341
Liebig, Justus von, Whitman and, 112; Holmes and, 217
Locke, John, 64; on cause and effect, 30, 379
Lodge, George Cabot, 294, 295, 305-14; pessimism, 305; egoism, 306-7; influence of Schopenhauer, 307-9; departure from Schopenhauer, 309-11; Hegel and, 311-14; difference from Hegel in evolutionism, 313; influence of Whitman on, 422; *Cain*, 306, 309, 313, 314; "Egypt," 305; *Herakles*, 306, 309-10, 311, 312, 314; "Hourly to find perfection in all things," 313; "Pride, power and substance of created things," 308; "A Song for Revolution," 305; "The Song of Man," 305, 306; "The Soul's Inheritance," 308, 313; "The Will," 307-8

Loewenberg, B. J., 133
Longfellow, Henry Wadsworth, 138, 174-78; slight interest in speculative questions, 174-75; dallies with quasi-evolutionary speculations of German Romanticism, 175-78; distrust of transcendentalism, 176-77; on death as transition, 177; Sill and, 260; "By the Fireside," 177; "Excelsior," 178; *Hyperion,* 175-76; Journals, 174-75; "Keramos," 178; "Rain in Summer," 177; *Tales of a Wayside Inn,* 174, 176
Louis, Pierre, Holmes's debt to, 217
Lovejoy, Arthur O., 17, 29, 121, 360; on the Great Chain of Being, 6-9; on pre-Darwinian evolution, 26; on the two gods of Romantic pantheism, 111; definition of mechanism, 393
Lovett, Robert Morss, on Moody's natural paganism, 317
Lowell, James Russell, 138, 145, 147, 178-90, 235, 272, 338; his mixed temperament, 178-79; on the limits of knowledge, 180-82; tendency to historical relativism, 181-82; scientific allusions, 182-83; on Darwin, 183; evolution interpreted as a reinforcement of optimism, 184; reservations concerning evolution, 185; failure of science to solve problem of origins, 186; the man of faith, 187-90; on faith and doubt in letters to Leslie Stephen and others, 188-89; "Agassiz," 190; "The Cathedral," 179, 180, 185; "Credidimus Jovem Regnare," 184, 185, 186; "The Footpath," 187; "The Function of the Poet," 187; "Harvard Anniversary," 185; "How I Consulted the Oracle of the Goldfishes," 180-81, 182, 187-88; "In the Half-Way House," 187; "The Lesson," 181; letters, 179, 183, 188, 189, 190; "The Progress of the World," 183-84; unpublished German epigram, 186
Lyell, Sir Charles, 23, 54, 140; American printings of his books, 24; criticism of Lamarck, 25; Emerson's reading of, 44; on evolution and design, 134; source of Emerson's knowledge of Lamarck, 382-83

Macaulay, Thomas Babington, 80, 200, 275
McCosh, James, 30, 167, 278; qualified acceptance of evolution, 135-36; and E. C. Stedman, 419-20
McKnight, George, "Consummation," 151-52, 160
Manly, John Matthews, 317
Maritain, Jacques, on evolution and the soul of man, 32
Marxism, and the "escalator" theory of history, 336, 375
Masters, Edgar Lee, 351-57; his naturalism, 351; two strains in his poetry, 352; optimistic treatment of evolution, 352-54; his immaterialism, 353-54; qualification of his cosmic optimism, 355-56; *Across Spoon River,* 351; "Botanical Gardens," 356; "The Conversation," 352; "Hymn to Nature," 356; "Hymn to the Earth," 353-54; "Nature," 355-56; "Neanderthal," 352; "Ultimate Selection," 353, 354
Materialism, Poe and, 67, 78, 87-91; Whitman and, 92-94; apparent, of evolution, 141-42; Lowell on, 186
Matthiessen, F. O., 98
Maupertuis, Pierre de, 25
Mead, G. H., on Romantic idealism and evolution, 13; biological analogy of Hegelian dialectic, 383-84
Mechanism, nebular hypothesis and, 20-21; definition of, by Whitehead, 78; by Burtt, 88-89; by Lovejoy, 393; in Poe's *Eureka,* 78, 88-90; reaction against at end of nineteenth century, 237-42; and the twilight of cosmic optimism, 333-34
Melville, Hermann, *Clarel,* 140, 146-7, 403; "The New Ancient of Days," 139-40, 247

Mill, John Stuart, "On Liberty," 189
Miller, Hugh, 24
Miller, Perry, on cosmic optimism among the Puritans, 375. *See also* Preface.
Mims, Edwin, 200
Moleschott, Jacob, Lowell on his materialism, 186
Momerie, Dr., 297
Monboddo, Lord, 20, 25
Monroe, Harriet, 357-61; approach to cosmic optimism, 357-58; scepticism, 358-59; change good for its own sake, 360; "At the Prado," 358; "Columbian Ode," 357; "The Man of Science Speaks," 358; "Mother Earth," 357-58, 359; *A Poet's Life,* 359-60; "The Quest," 358; "Supernal Dialogue," 358, 359; "The Wonder of It," 360
Moody, Harriet Converse, on *The Death of Eve,* 324
Moody, William Vaughn, 294, 295, 314-28, 357, 359; provides review of pattern of cosmic optimism, 314-15; unity of Creator and created theme of his verse dramas, 215; God's motive in creation, 316-17; reflects Moody's own attitude toward life, 316-17; Raphael's justification of evil, 317-18; the Dionysus theme, 317; philosophical justification of evil in *Masque of Judgment,* 318-20; comparison with Hovey, Poe, and Emerson, 319-20; positive side of his optimism, 320-28; love as the goal, 323-25; speculation on the unfinished *Death of Eve,* 324-25; theme of "salvation by passion" in prose plays, 324-25; evolutionary relevance of this theme, 325-27; on progress, 327-28; attitude toward cruder sort of Darwinism, 424

"The Brute," 327-28; "The Death of Eve" (epic), 321; *The Death of Eve* (drama), 324; *The Faith-Healer,* 325; *The Fire-Bringer,* 320, 321, 324; "Gloucester Moors," 327; *The Great Divide,* 325; letters, 315, 325; *The Masque of Judgment,* 315, 317, 318, 319, 320, 322, 323, 324, 325, 328, 358; "The Menagerie," 325-27; "Road-Hymn for the Start," 316, 327; "Song-Flower and Poppy," 328
More, Paul Elmer, 60, 111
Morgan, C. Lloyd, 31
Morgan, T. H., 378
Morse, E. S., 132
Mutability of species. *See* Species.

Natura naturans, Emerson on, 47, 51-52
Nature-philosophy, Romantic, salient points in, 16-17
Nebular hypothesis, 20-21; Emerson and, 44; in Poe's *Eureka,* 68; 72-73
Nevins, Allan, on establishment of idea of evolution in America, 133
New American Cyclopedia, The, 103, 124
Newton, Sir Isaac, law of attraction, 68, 69, 70
Nichol, John Pringle, 68, 70, 80, 174; aim of evolution to develop all possible variety, 387; finitude of our firmament, 387; equability of diffusion of stars, 387; condensation within firmaments and among systems of firmaments, 388; future possibilities of evolution, 388-89; Sir William Herschel's use of analogy, 389-90; referred to in "Murders in the Rue Morgue," 389; dissolution of our system, 391; renewal following dissolution
Nichols, Starr Hoyt, 270-74; *Monte Rosa: The Epic of an Alp,* 271-72; "The Philosophy of Evolution," 272; sonnets in *The Breath of the World,* 272-74
Niebuhr, Reinhold, 342; definition and criticism of philosophic idea of progress, 425
Nietzsche, Friedrich, 294, 306
Nineteenth Century Club of New York, The, 133, 268

INDEX

Norris, Frank, 294
Norton, Andrews, 136
Norton, Charles Eliot, 189; on reception of *Origin of Species* in America, 132
Novalis (Friedrich von Hardenberg), 17, 206

Oersted, Hans Christian, 17
Oken, Lorenz, 15, 17, 18, 242
Ontological argument for existence of God, 383
Opposites, conflict of 205-6, 208; in Cranch's "Ormuzd and Ahriman," 157-58. *See also* Conflict of opposites and Dialectic.
Optimism. *See* Cosmic optimism.

Packard, A. S., 237; definition of evolution, 4; Darwin's influence on American zoology, 132
Paine, Thomas, 27
Paley, William, 27, 79, 133, 135, 149; on evolutionism of Erasmus Darwin, 401-2
Pantheism, Poe and, 77-78, 84-85, 392
Papini, Giovanni, 340
Parrington, Vernon L., 211
Parker, Theodore, 378; perfection of the universe a transcendent truth, 375-76
Parsons, T. W., "On Turning from Darwin to Thomas Aquinas," 147-48
Pasteur, Louis, 223, 225
Patrick, G. T. W., 237
Perry, Ralph Barton, 12, 108; definition of evolution, 3; critical statements on idealism, 38, 117-18, 126, 127, 319; on Howison's theory of immortality, 115, 398; on reconciliation of idealistic and materialistic monisms, 238; on Spencer as hedonist, 417
Personalism, of Howison and Bowne, 108-10; Whitman and, 109; Bliss Carman and, 421-22
Peterson, Henry, *The Modern Job*, 402
Peirce, Charles Sanders, 237

Pius IX, Pope, *Syllabus of Errors*, 140
Plato, 7, 8, 43, 107, 125, 272; Cawein and, 290-91
Plenitude, principle of, 7, 8; in Taylor's *Prince Deukalion*, 198
Plotinus, 43
Poe, Edgar Allan, 47, 67-91, 94, 107, 108, 131, 167, 263, 276, 282, 284, 306, 332, 342, 358; evolutionism compared with that of Emerson, 67; and materialism, 67, 78, 87-91; *Eureka* based on three areas of science, 67-68; sources of his scientific knowledge, 67-68, 79; from Newton's law of attraction to the principle of Oneness, 69; from the principle of Oneness to the process of irradiation, 69-70, 387; universal attraction the result of withdrawal of force of irradiation, 70-71; but irradiation probably deduced from gravitation, 71-72; nebular hypothesis and universal agglomeration, 72-73; theory of electricity in *Eureka*, 73-76; relation of electrical repulsion to spirit, 75-76; evolutionary theory, 75-78; lack of interest in biology and geology, 75-76; doubt cast by Poe on evolutionary implications, 77; summary of *Eureka*, 78; natural theology, 79-80; analogical reasoning, 80-81, 389-90; aboriginal unity of cosmos established on intuitive grounds, 82-83; annihilation and periodic recreation of the universe, 83-84; pantheism, 84-85, 392; parallels with transcendentalism, 86-87, 392; answers to objections to materialistic interpretation of *Eureka*, 88-90; degree in which *Eureka* is teleological, 89; Poe's apparent intention in *Eureka*; and Whitman, 92-93, 393; and Lanier, 208; and Moody, 320
"The Colloquy of Monos and Una," 81; *Eureka*, 67-91 *passim*; "The Fall of the House of Usher," 85; "The Island of the Fay," 85-86; letters, 67, 77; "Ligeia,"

85; "Mesmeric Revelations," 67, 85, 87; "The Poetic Principle," 81; "The Power of Words," 71; review of Drake's *Culprit Fay,* 79; review of R. H. Horne's *Orion,* 81; review of Macaulay's *Essays,* 80-81;

Poincaré, Henri, 237

Porter, Noah, 250

Potter, G. R., on Thomson and Akenside, 9-10; on Coleridge and evolution, 57

Pouchet, Félix, 225

Pragmatism, 182, 426; a source of opposition to cosmic optimism, 339-43; Darwinian contribution to, 339-40

Preformation, in embryology, 22

Proclus, 43

Progress, the idea of, evolution and, 4-5; historical background, 10-11, 193; Emerson on, 63-66; Whitman on, 117-23; absolute idealism not progressive, according to Perry, 127; some minor poets on, 151-53; Huxley, Darwin, and Spencer on, 151; Leighton on, 263-64; Fawcett on, 269-70; Stedman on, 275-77, 280; cosmic, Hovey on, 304-5; Moody on, 327-28; Masters on, 352-54; revision of view concerning, by H. G. Wells, 425; definition and criticism of, by Niebuhr, 425

Prometheus legend, versions of in the nineteenth century, 410

Puritans, the, their cosmic optimism, 375. *See also* Preface.

Quinn, Arthur H., on Moody's *Death of Eve,* 324

Radical Club of Chestnut Street, Boston, the, 133, 142, 165

Radl, Emanuel, on Neo-Lamarckism, 237-38

Rafinesque, Constantine, *The World; or Instability,* 382

Randall, J. H., Jr., *The Making of the Modern Mind,* 35-36, 63

Reed, H. B., 111

Rice, Cale Young, 357; last of the true cosmic optimists, 350-51; "The Atheist," 350; "Cosmism," 351; "Galileo," 350; "Star of Achievement," 350; "The Strong Man to His Sires," 350-51; "Submarine Mountains," 350

Riley, I. W., 35

Robinson, Edwin Arlington, 365-74; his limited cosmic optimism, 365-66; his limited transcendentalism, 366; reservations concerning evolutionary progress, 367-68; on the weakness of all evolutionary optimisms, 368; belief in immortality, 368-69; rejection of evolutionary mechanism, 370-71; negative character of his statements, 371-72; intuitive character of his optimism, 373-74; "The Altar," 365; "Amaryllis," 368; *Cavender's House,* 372; "Children of the Night," 366, 367, 369, 430; "Demos and Dionysus," 367; "The Garden of the Nations," 368; *King Jasper,* 369-70; letters, 365, 367, 368, 370, 371, 372, 373; "The Man Against the Sky," 369, 370, 371; *Matthias at the Door,* 372, 373; *Merlin,* 366, 430-31; "Octaves," 366, 367, 372

Roosevelt, Theodore, 294

Rousseau, Jean Jacques, 321

Roux, Wilhelm, 237

Romantic idealism and evolution, Mead on, 13; nature-philosophy, salient points in, 16-17; pantheism, its two gods, 111; Faust-spirit, Whitman and, 121; Santayana on, 399; epistemology, 394-95

Royce, Josiah, 15-16, 35, 63, 126, 239, 295, 307; on the rise of the doctrine of evolution, 11-12; the dilemma of evolution, 28, 91, 98, 136, 142, 283, 353; on the problem of evil, 241, 288, 319; on evolution as an evidence of idealism, 242; on Fiske's incipient idealism, 245; parallels with, in Gilder, 281; on suffering of God in Christ, 289; on Hegel's "logic

of passion," 297-98; on Schopenhauer, 310; on Hegel's *Phenomenology*, 312; John Jay Chapman on, 341
Russell, Bertrand, 314

Sandburg, Carl, 294
Saint-Hilaire, Geoffroy, 18, 25, 214
Santayana, George, 15, 117, 236, 281, 294, 342, 360; on materialistic explanation of life and consciouneess, 32-33; on the "genteel tradition in American philosophy," 241-42 (*see also* Preface); problem of evil, 241, 355; transcendentalism, 242; and Frost, 345; on confusion of matter and spirit, 356-57; on Locke, 379; on Darwin and Aristotle, 379-80; on Romantic Faust-spirit, 399; on teleology, 415-16; on the value of mythical philosophies, 427
Sargent, Epes, *The Woman Who Dared*, 161-62
Schelling, Friedrich Wilhelm von, 8, 51, 111, 124, 175, 193, 240, 242, 313, 360; influence in development of idea of evolution, 12-16; influence in America, 17-18; Emerson on, 17-18; Coleridge's borrowings, 18-20; on cause and effect, 29; Whitman on, 103-4; defines matter as attraction and repulsion, 392-93; and Lanier, 411
Schleiden, Matthias Jacob, his dualism, 414; and Theodor Schwann, Holmes's debt to their cell theory, 220-22
Schopenhauer, Arthur, Lodge and, 307-9
Schubert, Gotthilf Heinrich, a source for Longfellow's *Hyperion*, 175
Science, Emerson and, 38, 44, 58-59; Poe and, 67-68; Taylor and, 195-97; Lanier and, 199-202; Helmholtz on medical science at beginning of nineteenth century, 216; and poetry, Stedman on, 275-76; its need of an immanent God, Parker on, 378; tended toward dualism in Holmes's early years, 414
Scottish Philosophy, the, 240, 402
Shaw, George Bernard, 237
Shearer, Sextus, 249
Shenstone, William, 139
Shepard, Odell, on Alcott's emanationism, 42
Shinn, Millicent, 250
Shorey, Paul, on Moody's Eve, 321
Sill, Edward Rowland, 175, 247-60, 341; debt to Spencer, 247, 248; evolution not of primary interest to him, 248; quest for faith, 249-50; anti-Christian views, 250, 416; ethical idealism, 250; acquaintance with Spencer, 250-51; devotion to Spencer's ethic of "complete living," 252; influence of Carlyle, 252-53; aesthetic of "complete living," 253-54; criticism of Spencer's educational theories, 254-55; divergence from Spencer, 254-56; failure to recognize this divergence, 255-56; on Emerson, 256-57; positivism and the reason for his neglect of evolution, 257-60; and Longfellow, 260; "Five Lives," 257, 259; "Herbert Spencer's Theory of Education," 251; "The Hermitage," 252-53; "Infirmity," 257-58; letters, 249, 251; "Life," 253; "Man, the Spirit," 247-48, 416, 417; "Midnight," 249; "Morning," 249; "Opportunity," 257; "The Polar Sea," 249; "Principles of Criticism," 253-54, 256; "The Prose and Verse of Ralph Waldo Emerson," 257, 258; "What Do We Mean by 'Right' and 'Ought'?" 251, 255
Silliman, Benjamin, 24, 44
Silver, Mildred, on Emerson and the idea of progress, 63-64
Smith, Langdon, *Evolution, a Fantasy*, 162-63
Smith, William, 22
Smyth, A. H., *Bayard Taylor*, 198
Species, mutability of, 24-25
Spencer, Herbert, 5, 144, 150, 165, 167, 201, 202, 207, 208, 223,

240, 242, 261, 268, 273, 274; definition of evolution, 21; and Poe, 78, 391; American popularity and American editions, 132-33, 400-401; on progress, 151; on good and evil, 154; Lanier and, 205, 208; and Fiske, on religious significance of Unknowable, 243-44, 415; and Darwin, influence of, 247-74; and Sill, 247, 248, 250-52, 254-56, 258-59; on education, 252; his ethic 251-52, 417; and mechanism, 260; leaves opening for theism, 260; theory of dissolution, 262-63

Spiral pattern of evolution, 16-17, 184, 248, 382

Spirit, problem of its emergence in a material evolution, 28. *See also* Cause.

Spontaneous generation, 225-26

Stallo, J. B., *General Principles of the Philosophy of Nature*, 14-17, 34-35, 50, 87, 154

Stanley, Dean A. P., 240

Stedman, Edmund Clarence, 240, 247, 275-80, 285, 286, 292; on Taylor's *Masque of the Gods*, 194; on poetry as the herald of progress, 275-77; on poetry and science, 275-76, 419; aspects of his belief in progress, 277-78; on evolution and immortality, 278; doctrine of immanence, 278-80; belief in a divinely motivated progress, 280; and James McCosh, 419-20; "Fin de Siècle," 278-80, 285; letters, 277, 278, 280; "Mater Coronata," 277-78; *The Nature and Elements of Poetry*, 276, 278, 286; *Poets of America*, 419; *Victorian Poets*, 276, 277

Stephen, Leslie, Lowell and, 188-89

Sterling, George, 361-64; qualification of his optimism, 361-62; cosmic pessimism of "The Testimony of the Suns," 362-64; on Jeffers, 429-30; "The Builders," 361; "The Last Monster," 361; "The Midges," 361; "The Moth of Time," 361-62; "Ode on the Opening of the Panama-Pacific International Exposition," 361; "The Testimony of the Suns," 362-64; "Yosemite," 361

Stone, Jane Dransfield, "Evolution," 153

Stovall, Floyd, 81, 367-68

Street, Alfred B., "The Sympathy of Nature," 154-55; "Pre-existence," 161

Strong, Augustus H., 167

Sumner, Charles, "The Law of Human Progress," 64

Tabb, Father J. B., "Evolution," 159

Taine, H. A., 135, 191

Taylor, Bayard, 191-99; and science, 191-92; not primarily concerned with evolution of species, 192; not Darwinian, 192-93; influence of German literature, 193; *The Masque of the Gods*, 194-95; *Prince Deukalion*, 195-99; attitude toward sciences in *Prince Deukalion*, 196-97; love and wisdom the goals of progress, 197-98; "temporalized" principle of plentitude, 198; immortality, 198-99; "The Continents," 193; letters, 191, 194, 199; *The Masque of the Gods*, 192, 194-95; "Metempsychosis of the Pine," 193; *Prince Deukalion*, 161, 192, 195-99; *Studies in German Literature*, 195; "Studies of Animal Nature," 192-93

Teleology, immanent, 27-28; Paley and, 27-28, 45, 133, 135, 401-2; Emerson and, 45-46; Poe and, 79-80, 89; Whitman and, 96-97, 100; Darwin and, 133-35, 236, 238, 401; some minor poets on, 148-50; persistence of, 235-46; Fiske on, 135, 244-45; Leighton on, 265; Santayana on, 415-16

Tennyson, Alfred, Lord, 181, 191

Thayer, William Roscoe, "Disenchantment," 333-34

Theodicy, cosmic optimism a, 8, 295; Stallo on, 17; Hegel on, 421

INDEX 457

Thomas, Edith M., "Palingenesis," 164
Thompson, Lawrence, on the optimism of Frost, 348
Thomson, James, on the chain of being and transmigration, 9-10, 161, 293
Transcendentalism, Poe and, 67, 90; Longfellow and, 176; Santayana on, 242; Stedman and, 278-80, 419-20; contrasted with mysticism in respect to problem of evil, 287; Hovey and, 299-301; paradox of its evolutionism, 376, 385; relation to pragmatism, 426
Transmigration, and evolution, 9-10; Emerson and, 49-50; Whitman and, 112-15; some minor poets on, 159-64, 405-6; Cawein on, 292-93; Lodge and, 313
Trine, Ralph Waldo, 239
Trowbridge, J. T., 165, 332; that effect cannot contain more than its cause, 142; "Ancestors," 152-53, 155; "Hymn of the Air," 149; "Love," 148; "The Missing Leaf," 142, 145; "Under Moon and Stars," 149, 155; "The Winnower," 155-56
Twain, Mark, 139
Tyndall, John, 133, 142, 165, 168, 207

Uniformitarianism, 23
Upanishads, 307

Vaihinger, Hans, 359
Van Doren, Mark, Whitman's "erethism," 100
Venable, W. H., 165, "A Triune Creed," 150, 151
Very, Jones, "The Origin of Man," 143; "The Past," 144
Vestiges of the Natural History of Creation, 64; American editions of, 26; Chambers on discredit of, 26; Emerson and, 48, 385-86; its publication date, 382. *See also* Chambers, Robert.
Virchow, Rudolf, 222

Voltaire, 8, 175
von Baer, Karl Ernst, 16, 22

Waggoner, H. H., 367
Wallace, Alfred Russell, 414
Ward, Mrs. Humphry, 268
Wayland, Francis, and Poe, 389-90
Weber, Alfred, and Perry, R. B., *History of Philosophy,* 105, 134, 238
Weekes, W. H., production of living organisms by electricity, 220, 226, 388
Weismann, August, 237
Wells, H. G., *Mind at the End of Its Tether,* 336, 425
Wendell, Barrett, 305
Whitehead, Alfred North, 78, 91
Whitman, Walt, 8, 10, 86, 92-127, 137, 163, 167, 201, 247, 260, 261, 281, 295, 306, 307, 327, 332, 357, 360, 363, 372; compared with Emerson and Poe, 92-93, 105-6, 393; problem of his materialism, 92-94; not a phenomenalist, 93, 97-98, 100; and science, 95; reservations concerning Darwinian evolution, 95-96; teleology, 96-97; "vital materialism," 100-101; philosophical parallels of his view, 102-9; and German philosophy, 103-7, 117, 395-96; on Fichte and Schelling, 103-4; on Hegel, 104-5; egoism, 107; selfhood a fundamental category, 107-10; on immortality, 108, 111-12; "personalism," 109; theme of universal flux, 111-12; symbolism of leaves of grass, 112; evolution as transmigration, 112-15; evolution and his praise of death, 114; the universe a procession, 116-17; and progress, 117-23; attitude toward the past, 119-21; the goal of progress, 121-23; the poet as deliverer, 123-24; and the problem of evil, 124-26; equalitarianism in value, 125, 400; a pre-Darwinian evolutionist, 131; as metaphysician, 394; evolutionary confession of faith in *Democratic Vistas,* 398; difference from

Lanier in cosmic optimism, 411-12; influence on George Cabot Lodge, 422
"A Backward Glance O're Travel'd Roads," 97; "By Blue Ontario's Shore," 125; "Carlyle from American Points of View," 95, 106-7; *Collect,* 95; "Crossing Brooklyn Ferry," 109; "Darwinism," 96; *Democratic Vistas,* 93, 109, 121, 127, 398; "Good-Bye My Fancy," 116; "I Sing the Body Electric," 93, 97, 115, 116; " L. of G.'s Purport," 92; Notebooks (in *Complete Writings,* Vol. IX), 97, 98, 103, 104, 114, 118, 120; "The Oaks and I," 102; "O Me! O Life!" 125; "Passage to India," 92, 116, 120, 122, 123, 124; "Pioneers! O Pioneers!" 116; Preface to 1855 Edition, 120; Preface to 1876 Edition, 111-12, 115; "Roaming in Thought," 124; "A Song for Occupations," 93; "A Song of Joys," 114; "Song of Myself," 93, 94, 97, 100, 112, 113, 114, 115, 116, 120, 124-25; "Song of the Broad-Axe," 108; "Song of the Exposition," 120; "Song of the Open Road," 114, 116, 117, 118, 121, 125; "A Song of the Rolling Earth," 116; "Song of the Universal," 97, 119; "Starting from Paumonok," 93, 98, 116, 126; "Thou Mother with Thy Equal Brood," 92; "To Think of Time," 101; Traubel, *With Walt Whitman in Camden,* 93, 94, 95, 96, 99, 106, 108, 115, 117; *Uncollected Poetry and Prose* (ed. Holloway), 94, 98, 103, 112, 113, 121-22; *Walt Whitman's Workshop* (ed. Furness), 101, 103; "When the Full Grown Poet Came," 99; "When Lilacs Last in the Dooryard Bloom'd," 114; "Whispers of Heavenly Death," 115; "Yet, Yet, Ye Downcast Hours," 111

Whitney, Lois, 8, 9
Wilcox, Ella Wheeler, "Creation," 148-49; "Progress," 153; "The World Grows Better," 153
Wöhler, Friedrich, 217
Wolff, Caspar Friedrich, 22
Woodberry, George Edward, 305; and the humanists' abandonment of cosmic optimism, 336-39; acceptance of the worst science has to say, 336-37; but only in man do values exist, 337-38; "Agathon," 336; "Demeter," 336, 337-38; *Ideal Passion,* 338; "The Roamer," 337
Woodrow, James, influence on Lanier, 200
Wordsworth, William, 84, 160
Wyman, Jeffries, 186, 225, 231

Youmans, E. L., 132